TRAYECTOS

Volumen 1
Mi vida en la universidad

Gabriela C. Zapata

Publishing & License Information

This project was sponsored in part by the Center for European Studies at the University of Texas at Austin, which is a designated Dept. of Education National Resource Center for the grant period 2018-2022 under award number P229A180003.

Student Project Leader and Collaborator: Alessandra Ribota. Graduate Student Collaborators: Zaida Aguilar, Leanee Díaz Sardiñas, Amy King, Damián Robles, Julia Sainz, and Paloma Serrano

Undergraduate Student Collaborators: Marlenie Arzamendi, Sara Marie Berrett, Allison Beatty, Amy Beristain, Bailey Buchanan, Karina Cabrera, Carolina Cantú, Aimar Díaz, Efraín Hernández, Eileen Lynch, Dylan Manshack, Verónica Martínez, Rachael McBride, Jocelyn Rodríguez, Mariana Salazar, Paola Sparagana, and Faith Villarreal.

Práctica individual Author: Paloma Serrano

First Edition
ISBN: 978-1-937963-23-1 (Paperback - Lulu)
ISBN: 978-1-937963-25-5 (Paperback - Kindle Direct Publishing - Amazon)
Library of Congress number: 2022914701
Manufactured in the United States of America.

Front cover art by Nathalie Steinfeld Childre

Table of Contents

About the Project

Trayectos is an open curriculum for beginning second language (L2) learners of Spanish. The textbook offers the following features to L2 Spanish students and instructors:

- Learner-centered fresh, multimodal content, based on *Learning by Design*, a pedagogy inspired by the Multiliteracies movement (Kalantzis et al., 2005, 2016, 2019; Zapata, 2022). The four modules in Volume I connect the life worlds of learners with the life worlds of diverse Spanish speakers.

- Instruction incorporating the following features:

  1. Multimodal texts (e.g., readings, videos, posters) based on a variety of textual genres that contextualize topics about the lives of real university students;

  2. Communicative activities that bind language form to cultural meaning within real-life contexts, and offer students opportunities to discover how to use new Spanish vocabulary and grammar in diverse sociocultural situations;

  3. Critical thinking and language awareness tasks that showcase different varieties of Spanish, including those spoken in the United States, and help learners explore the Spanish-speaking world, including local Hispanic/Latinx communities; and

  4. Culminating tasks that oblige learners to synthesize their new linguistic and cultural knowledge into a personal, multimodal text.

- Supplementary digital resources that provide students with opportunities to practice the content learned through self-correcting activities (*Práctica individual*) and to use Spanish to broaden their knowledge of and critically analyze issues related to diversity, equity, and inclusion in the Spanish-speaking world (*Voces de nuestro mundo*; available at http://bit.ly/VocesMundo).

- An open copyright license (Creative Commons license) that gives all users the right to adapt the textbook and to share their new content with others, and digital how-to sections for instructors to answer their students' unique needs.

Program Features

Main Content

Trayectos consists of thematic modules. Each of them combines existing OER and novel materials. Each module consists of the following sections:

1. **Objetivos** (*Objectives*): Each module is introduced by an objectives section in which we give learners information about the instructional goals we have set for their learning in terms of language use (**Comunicación**), grammatical and vocabulary knowledge (**Lengua**), and culture (**Cultura**). We also ask students to record what they want accomplish in personal terms. We call it **Mis metas** (*My Goals*).

2. **Introducción comunicativa** (*Communicative Introduction*): In this section, we introduce, in context, the vocabulary and grammatical structures on which the module will focus. Here we draw learners' attention to the message that is conveyed and the language used in order to do so.

3. **Hablemos más** (*Let's talk a bit more*): In this section, we provide students with more vocabulary that they can use in their communication.

4. **Manos a la obra** (*Let's Do It*): These sections appear throughout each module, and they provide learners with multiple opportunities to actively use their new vocabulary and structures. The activities in **Manos a la obra** allow students to work collaboratively with their classmates, and to use Spanish to communicate in different modes--interpersonal (speaking); interpretive (reading/listening); and presentational (writing/oral presentations with multimodal elements).

5. **Trayectos hispanos:** The purpose of these sections is to highlight different aspects (e.g., people, places, art, activism, etc.) of the Hispanic/Latinx communities in the United States through thematic readings and/or videos and images and tasks that will allow students to know more about the unique ways in which members of these groups have contributed to the country.

6. **Hablemos de gramática** (*Let's Talk About Grammar*): In this section, we present the rules guiding the grammatical structures included in each module. Through contextualized examples, we guide students' learning by tying the forms presented to the meaning they convey.

7. **Hablemos de cultura** (*Let's Talk About Culture*): This section focuses on cultural aspects of different countries in the Spanish-speaking world. Culture is presented through thematic readings, videos, and images and critical thinking tasks that allow learners to reflect on the target culture and their own.

8. **Más comunicación** (*More Communication*): This section focuses on functional language—the structures and vocabulary that are used in specific social contexts (e.g., ordering a meal, buying a ticket to see a movie, etc.). Here we draw learners' attention to the message that is conveyed and the language used in order to do so.

9. **Conversemos** (*Let's Talk*): This section offers opportunities to use Spanish in conversation (interpersonal mode of communication).

10. **Cartelera** (*Billboard*): This section introduces students to short films developed in the Spanish-speaking world. Learners will watch the chosen productions, and they will work individually and collaboratively with a variety of comprehension and interpretation tasks.

11. **Lectura** (*Reading Comprehension*): This section offers learners the opportunity to read a variety of texts written by different authors in the Spanish-speaking world. Students will read the chosen texts, and they will work individually and collaboratively with a variety of comprehension and interpretation tasks.

12. **Proyecto digital** (*Digital Project*): The objective of the digital project is to provide students with the opportunity to apply the Spanish they have learned to create a personal profile in Spanish to introduce themselves and aspects of their life to Spanish speakers. In each module, learners will develop different parts of this project applying the specific vocabulary and structures they have learned in it.

13. **Antes de partir** (*Before We Go*): In this final section, we revisit the contents of each module, the goals we set for students at the beginning of the chapter, and the personal aims they wanted to accomplish. Our hope is that this section will offer learners the chance to reflect on their learning process and to set new objectives for the next step in their growth as Spanish speakers.

Supplementary Digital Resources

1. **Práctica individual** (*Individual Practice*): At the end of most sections in each module in Volume 1 of *Trayectos*, we provide links to activities that offer learners more opportunities to use the language learned. These exercises are self-correcting, and can be completed individually.

2. **Voces de nuestro mundo:** This section consists of self-standing units based on multimodal ensembles that connect learners to authentic texts through different semiotic modalities (e.g., audio, visual, textual, etc.). However, the language and themes are connected to those in *Trayectos*. The main objective of these units is to provide students with the opportunity to use Spanish to learn more about socially-relevant issues related to diversity, equity, and inclusion in the Spanish-speaking world. Even though the activities in **Voces de nuestro mundo** can be adapted to cater to a variety of proficiency levels, they have been developed for novice-high/intermediate-low students. The units or some of the tasks in them can also be used as summative assessment tools (e.g., project-based learning, portfolio-based assessment). This resource is available at http://bit.ly/VocesMundo.

3. **El mundo tejano** (*The Texan World*): The purpose of these sections is to highlight different aspects (e.g., people, places, art, etc.) of Hispanic Texas through thematic readings and/or videos and images and tasks that will allow students to know more about the unique ways in which members of Texas' Hispanic/Latinx communities have contributed to the state. We recommend this section for instructors teaching in Texas. This resource can be found at http://bit.ly/MundoTejano.

Theoretical and Pedagogical Framework

Learning by Design in Trayectos

I. Learning by Design: Principles and Knowledge Processes

Trayectos is grounded in the main tenets of the multiliteracies framework *Learning by Design* (Kalantzis et al. 2005, 2016, 2019; Zapata, 2022). In the next section, we will show you how these tenets are embedded in the textbook's components, but first, let's learn more about this pedagogy.

Principles: Belonging and Transformation

Important: Curricula that are based on relevant materials that connect closely to who the learners are—to their personal world, including the community to which they belong—by taking into account their diverse social and cultural backgrounds. This is what Kalantzis and her colleagues (2005) call *belonging*: Emphasis on the need for instructional environments to which learners can connect at a deep, personal level and to which they feel they "belong."

Also essential: Students' depth of involvement and engagement in their learning process. In order for learning to broaden learners' knowledge in effective and life-long ways, it needs to result in a process of transformation (Kalantzis et al., 2005). For this transformation to happen, instructors need to "take the learner into new and unfamiliar terrains. However, for learning to occur, the journey into the unfamiliar needs to stay within a zone of intelligibility and safety. At each step, it needs to travel just the right distance from the learner's lifeworld starting point" (Kalantzis et al., p. 51).

Knowledge Processes

In *Learning by Design*, learning is interpreted as an active, dynamic process involving four interwoven knowledge processes: **experiencing**, **conceptualizing**, **analyzing**, and **applying**. Their objective: To guide students' learning process in order for them to learn how meaning is conveyed through multimodal ensembles and to apply their new knowledge in similar/more creative tasks.

These four processes of discovery mirror those that are present in informal learning (students' personal experiences and learning outside the classroom), and, in formal learning (academic learning), they are embedded in instructional activities that allow learners to do the following:

- experience known and new meanings (departing from known concepts and experiences and moving forward to explore new situations and/or information);

- conceptualize meanings by naming (grouping into categories, classifying, defining) and with theory (formulating generalizations and establishing connections among concepts as well as developing theories);

- analyze meanings functionally (focusing on structure and function, establishing logical connections) and critically (evaluating different perspectives, interests, and motives); and

- apply meanings appropriately (engaging in real-life applications of knowledge) and creatively (applying new knowledge in innovative and creative ways) (Kalantzis & Cope, 2010, 2012).

Los procesos de conocimiento en español:

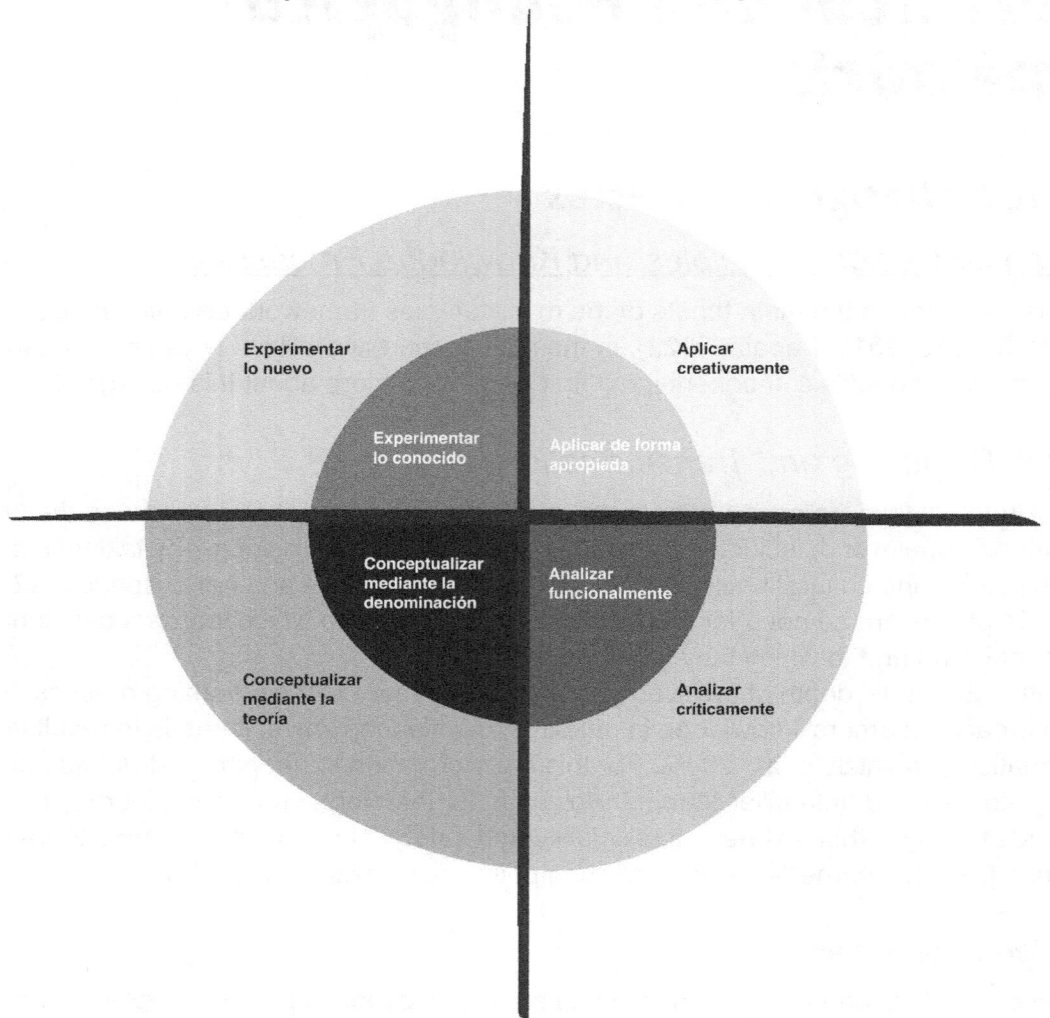

Link to a visual representation of the eight knowledge processes: http://bit.ly/KnowledgeProcesses. Kalantzis, Cope, & Zapata (2019, p. 64). Used with authors' permission.

If you want to learn more about *Learning by Design*, we recommend the following resources:

- Short videos (http://bit.ly/LbyDVideos) on different aspects of literacies by Dr. Mary Kalantzis and Dr. Bill Cope

- A video presentation on multiliteracies (http://bit.ly/LbyDPresentation) by Dr. Mary Kalantzis and Dr. Bill Cope

- A video presentation on *Learning by Design* and materials development (http://bit.ly/LbyDZapataPres) by Dr. Gabriela C. Zapata

- The Placemat Curriculum Planning Tool: http://bit.ly/LbyDPlacemat

References

Kalantzis, M., & Cope, B. (2010). The teacher as designer: Pedagogy in the new media age. E-learning and Digital Media, 7(3), 200-222. https://doi.org/10.2304/elea.2010.7.3.200

Kalantzis, M., & Cope, B. (2012). Literacies. Cambridge University Press. Kindle DX edition.

Kalantzis, M., Cope, B., & the Learning by Design Project Group. (2005). Learning by Design. Victorian Schools Innovation Commission and Common Ground Publishing.

Kalantzis, M., Cope, B., Chan, E., & Dalley-Trim, L. (2016). Literacies (2nd ed.). Cambridge University Press.

Kalantzis, M., Cope, B., & Zapata, G. C. (2019). Las alfabetizaciones múltiples: Teoría y práctica. Editorial Octaedro.

II. Trayectos

Belonging and Transformation in "Trayectos"

The contents of Trayectos (topics and activities) are tied to the personal experiences of university students in the state of Texas. The point of departure is always the learner. In all sections of our textbook, we have tried to integrate students' informal and formal learning through activities that incorporate resources that not only connect closely to who students are (i.e., to their lifeworld, including the community to which they belong), but also reflect their diverse, multidimensional social and cultural backgrounds. Also, when we introduce a new topic, we always do it within the realm of learners' knowledge and experience.

The Knowledge Processes in "Trayectos"

The following examples illustrate how Learning by Design's knowledge processes are embedded in Trayectos.

1. Experiencing

Módulo 1: Somos estudiantes universitarios

En este módulo, vamos a hablar (*talk*) de las clases, los estudiantes universitarios y la universidad.

Antes de comenzar: ¿Es tu universidad una institución importante? ¿Cómo son las clases? ¿Hay tradiciones? ¿Cuál es tu tradición favorita? You can answer these questions in English, but try to use some of the Spanish you already know! Remember **los cognados!**

Attribution: By Mariana Salazar, licensed under CC BY-SA 4.0.

Objetivos en este mó

c

Mi nepantla

Now you are going to take into account Anzaldúa's concept of **nepantla**, and you will create your own. Your work can be completed in different ways. It can be:

- A visual representation with or without text;
- A video with images and a narrative and/or text;
- A text-based representation (e.g., a word cloud);
- A conceptual map; or
- A bilingual poem (you can use some of the words you already know in Spanish)

If you want to know more about this concept, you can consult ⌐ this Wikipedia entry (⌐ http://bit.ly/NepantlaConcept).

Paso 1. Explore the following examples from Anzaldúa herself and university students like you.

- Gloria Anzaldúa's poem ⌐ *To Live in the Borderlands* (⌐ http://bit.ly/LiveBorderlands).

Ejemplos de estudiantes:

- **Ejemplo #1:**

Mi nepantla ⬛ ...ltad +

2. Conceptualizing

III. Los adjetivos descriptivos

Now that we know what structures and words we can use to refer to possessions, let's talk about the words we can use to describe them–**los adjetivos descriptivos** (*descriptive adjectives*). Let's go back to Dylan's blog. What do you notice about adjectives in these examples?

Modelo(s):	• ¡La familia de Mariana es muy amable!
	• Ellos son muy divertidos y graciosos.
	• La **familia lejana** de Mariana
	• Mi **familia mexicana**

Yes! You guessed! Descriptive adjectives in Spanish must agree with the gender and number of the noun they describe. This is different from English. Another difference is that adjectives are usually placed **after** the noun they describe (e.g., la familia **lejana**). You already know some descriptive adjectives (remember **los cognados** we learned in **Módulo introductorio y Módulo 1**?). And here we offer you more!

 Describimos la apariencia física

alto	tall
bajo	short (height)
pequeñ...	small

desk). ¡Y ya!

Carolina: ¡Gracias, amigas!

¿Comprendiste? Responde estas preguntas sobre la conversación.

1. Let's talk about verbs first. See if you can find an example of the following in the dialogue:

Un verbo en infinitivo (An infinitive verb that does not have a conjugation. E.g., to talk, to write):

Unos verbos conjugados:

- Verbs conjugated in second person singular (**tú** form):
- Verbs conjugated in second person plural (**ustedes** form):

What do these verb share? What do you already know about these verbs endings?

Now let's talk about the content of the dialogue (continue paying attention to the verb endings):

2. ¿Qué necesita Carolina en la biblioteca?
3. ¿Quiénes ayudan a Carolina?
4. Si tú necesitas un libro, ¿dónde buscas el libro?

All the conjugated verbs that appear in the dialogue are in the present tense (**el tiempo presente**). In this section, we will learn how to conjugate verbs with the **–ar** ending in the present tense. ¡Manos a la obra!

The present Tense of *–ar* Verbs

I. _____ions

_____ _____ _____ _____it _____ _____he word **to**. In

3. Analyzing

Y después... Uso, forma y cultura: El Día de la Madre

Las mamás

I. Antes de ver

As these photos show, moms come in all forms and sizes, but they all play an important role in our lives. In this section, we will watch a video made by the Mexican actor and director ⧉ Diego Luna for Mother's Day. What do you think the video is going to be like? What ideas will he include? Write three ideas. Use the photos to think of possible topics.

Attribution: By quinet, licensed under CC BY 2.0.

Attribution: Public domain

Attribution: Public domain

 **II. A ver**

Now watch the Día de la Madre video en ⛶ https://youtu.be/wDfI9iiXoy0, and check if your ideas coincide with the ones that appear in it.

III. Después de ver

Actividad 2-7. Are there any similarities/differences between your ideas and the ones shown in the video? Name two.

Actividad 2-8. Now watch the video again, and do the following exercises.

Actividad A. ¿Cómo son las mamás en el vídeo? Describe su personalidad.

Actividad B. En el vídeo, Diego Luna dice *(says)*: "Todas las mamás son unas mentirosas (mienten = no hablan con la verdad [*truth*])". "Mentir" is usually a negative verb. Is it negative in this video? These are some of instances in which Diego Luna says mothers don't the truth:

- "Cuando siempre [dice] que eres el mejor (*the best*)."
- "Esa cena (*dinner*) no [es] especial para astronautas."
- "[Dice] que [eres] el más guapo (*the most handsome*)."
- "También miente a sus necesidades. Miente cuando dice que no le importa levantarse más temprano (*she doesn't care about getting up early*)."
- "Miente porque no la tiene fácil (*life is not easy for her*)."
- "Cuando te dice que todo estará bien (*everything will be OK*)."

Is the use of the verb "mentir" really negative in this video? What is the message of the video? Using the information and images in the video, describe its main purpose. Who is the audience for this video? Justify your opinions.

Actividad C. The last phrase of the video is "Gracias, Jefas." What does the word "jefa" mean? Look it up, and think about why this word is used in the video. What does it say about the role of the mother in Hispanic families?

Act ... al features. ... ll th... ... izational feat... ...the clues in the video?

Actividad C. Los personajes en la segunda parte del film. Ahora hablamos de los personajes en la segunda parte del film. You can answer these questions using both Spanish and English.

1. ¿Quiénes son los personajes?
2. ¿Dónde viven?
3. ¿Tienen parientes?
4. ¿Qué actividades tienen en su día?
5. ¿Cómo están? Describe sus emociones.
6. ¿Qué necesitan estos niños?
7. ¿Qué problemas sociales hay en el país de estos niños?

Actividad D. Análisis. Contesta estas preguntas sobre el vídeo.

1. How do the filmmakers show the contrast between the first part of the film and the second part? Talk about different visual, auditory, and linguistic tools.
2. What message about the family does this film want to convey?
3. Do you think American audiences would enjoy this short film? Why? Why not?

Click ... ...ing button to c... ...ntent of this m...

4. Applying

Ahora leemos un aviso de una agencia de limpieza en un país hispano hablante. Mira el aviso y con un@ compañer@, responde estas preguntas.

Attribution: By Novalimpio, licensed under CC BY-SA 4.0

1. ¿Dónde está la agencia? Mira el vocabulario e hipotetiza en qué país está.
2. ¿Qué hay en las fotos? Describe las fotos.
3. ¿Por qué usa la empresa estas fotos? ¿Cuál es el objetivo?
4. ¿Qué lugares limpia?
5. Si contratas (*hire*) esta agencia, ¿qué tareas de la casa hacen? Usa el texto y las fotos para contestar la pregunta.

 Paso 2. Una agencia de limpieza para estudiantes.

Imagina que tú y tres/cuatro compañer@s tienen una agencia de limpieza. You want to offer your services to university students. What do students need? Create an ad for your agency. Include the following:

1. Nombre de la agencia;
2. Tres o cuatro fotos (remember to use 🔗 https://search.creativecommons.org/ to look for open resources);
3. Un eslogan (como en el texto: "Somos una empresa líder en servicio de limpieza");
4. Una lista de tareas domésticas. Usa la primera persona del plural (por ejemplo, "planchamos tu ropa).

Be creative!

Paso 3. El aviso más popular. The class will now choose the most creative ad. Share your ad with your classmates. Was your ad the most popular? 😊

 Actividad 3-8. Proyecto multimodal opcional.

Create a short commercial (15-30 seconds) to advertise the agency you created in **Paso 2** in **Actividad 3-7**. Include the same type of information, but, instead of photos, add music and short video recordings of you and your classmates doing three or four household chores. Make sure your commercial is effective. 😊

Instrucciones para hacer un aviso publicitario: 🔗 https://www.wikihow.com/Make-a-Commercial

 Actividad 3-23. Nuestro proyecto de casa. En esta actividad trabajas con 3 o 4 compañer@s.

Paso 1. Imagine that you and your classmates are working on a project in one of the towns affected by recent hurricanes along the Texas coast. You are designing a house for a *familia necesitada*. Taking into account that there are 5 family members (including 3 children and a dog), you will need to draw a blueprint and write a description of the house, including the furniture needed in each room. Write at least 100 words. Start your paragraph like this:

"En nuestra casa…"

Paso 2. Presenten su casa a otro grupo de estudiantes. Comparen sus proyectos. ¿Qué similitudes y diferencias tienen?

- **Ideas for implementation and design template (p. 54): https://bit.ly/LbyDinclass**

Module Components and Organization

I. Section Overview

The contents of each module in Trayectos are organized in three sections: **comunicación**, **lengua**, and **cultura**.

Comunicación focuses on functional language and vocabulary presented in contexts related to university students' experiences. The sections included within **Comunicación** are the following: **Introducción comunicativa; Hablemos más; Y después… Uso, forma y cultura**; **Más comunicación**; **Cartelera**; **Lectura**; **Proyecto digital**; and **Conversemos**. The activities that are part of these sections allow students to use Spanish actively in pair and group activities, and to be exposed to and produce multimodal ensembles (i.e., texts in which different semiotic modalities—e.g., linguistic [written and oral], visual, auditory—are combined).

In **Lengua** students are introduced to the rules that govern our use of the language (**Hablemos de gramática** sections). All structures are presented in a communicative context, accompanied by simple explanations based on the comparison between Spanish and English (i.e., we always depart from what the student knows). First, we guide learners through the discovery of how each structure works by providing them with questions to analyze the content presented, and then we introduce them to rules. <u>Grammar is always tied to use</u>. In addition, all **Hablemos de gramática** sections are followed by individual, pair, and group activities in which students can apply what they have learned both appropriately and creatively (see page XV).

Cultura focuses on both cultural aspects of the Hispanic/Latinx communities in the United States (**Trayectos hispanos**) and different countries in the Spanish-speaking world (**Hablemos de cultura**). Our main goal is to go beyond the usual, sanitized version of culture presented in commercial textbooks, and instead, to give voice to the unique contributions of Hispanic/Latinx communities to the United States and the world. Cultural content is presented through thematic readings, videos, images, and critical thinking tasks.

II. Pedagogical Guidance

1. How to Use "Hablemos más"

The section **Hablemos más** comes after the presentation of the main topic of each instructional module. This section offers learners vocabulary that they will have opportunities to actively use in the next, practice section **¡Manos a la obra!** The vocabulary is presented in written form, but students can also listen to the pronunciation of each word by clicking on the audio icon.

Hablemos más: La familia

Familias diversas

En el mundo de hoy hay diferentes tipos de familia. ¿Cómo es tu familia? ¿Es similar a las familias de las fotos? Use the vocabulary in this section and the verb **hay** to talk about your or someone else's family. You can also describe one of the families in the photos below.

Attribution: By Airman Grace Nichols   Air F...   ...ensed under CC

Attribution: By Emily Walker from Wellingto...   ...land, licensed under CC ...

Attribution: Public domain

Attribution: By City of Seattle, licensed under CC BY 2.0.

 EL NÚCLEO FAMILIAR

el padre	father
la	

This is the way we suggest this section should be used:

- When preparing your lesson plan, go over the ¡**Manos a la obra!** activities. Identify those that require students to work individually.
- Assign those activities for homework. Students will need to use the vocabulary words in the **Hablemos más** section in order to complete them. This will provide them with the opportunity to learn the new words through use.
- Next class: Check one or two of the assigned activities, and clarify any doubts students might have about the vocabulary.
- Then do the pair and group activities in ¡**Manos a la obra!** in class.
- Assign the exercises in **Práctica individual** for homework (more information on how to work with this section is provided on pages xxi-xxii).

2. How to Work with the Grammar Sections

In *Trayectos*, grammatical structures are always presented in terms of use from the very beginning of each module. For example, in all **Introducción comunicativa** sections, there are questions related to the structures presented (under the **Lengua** title). This is the first time students will be guided to think explicitly about the grammar they will learn in the instructional module, but in connection to use (i.e., the questions are based on the role that the structure plays in the communicative context of the section).

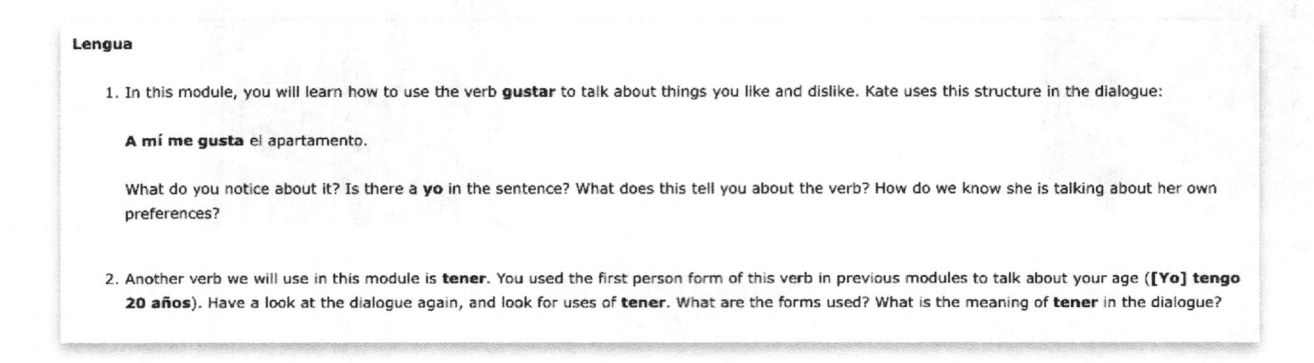

Lengua

1. In this module, you will learn how to use the verb **gustar** to talk about things you like and dislike. Kate uses this structure in the dialogue:

   A mí me gusta el apartamento.

   What do you notice about it? Is there a **yo** in the sentence? What does this tell you about the verb? How do we know she is talking about her own preferences?

2. Another verb we will use in this module is **tener**. You used the first person form of this verb in previous modules to talk about your age (**[Yo] tengo 20 años**). Have a look at the dialogue again, and look for uses of **tener**. What are the forms used? What is the meaning of **tener** in the dialogue?

The next time students will explicitly learn about grammar will be in the sections **Hablemos de gramática**, <u>where grammar is always tied to use</u>. All structures are presented in a communicative context, and we guide learners through the discovery of how each structure works by providing them with questions to analyze the content presented.

Hablemos de gramática: Estructura 1

El verbo gustar + *infinitive* **& gustar + noun: Uso y forma**

Kate es de una familia bicultural. Su papá es de los Estados Unidos y su mamá es española. Kate usa el español con su mamá. Es sábado y Kate hace las tareas de la casa. Escribe un texto a su mamá en Tejas. ¿Cómo está Kate? ¿Por qué?

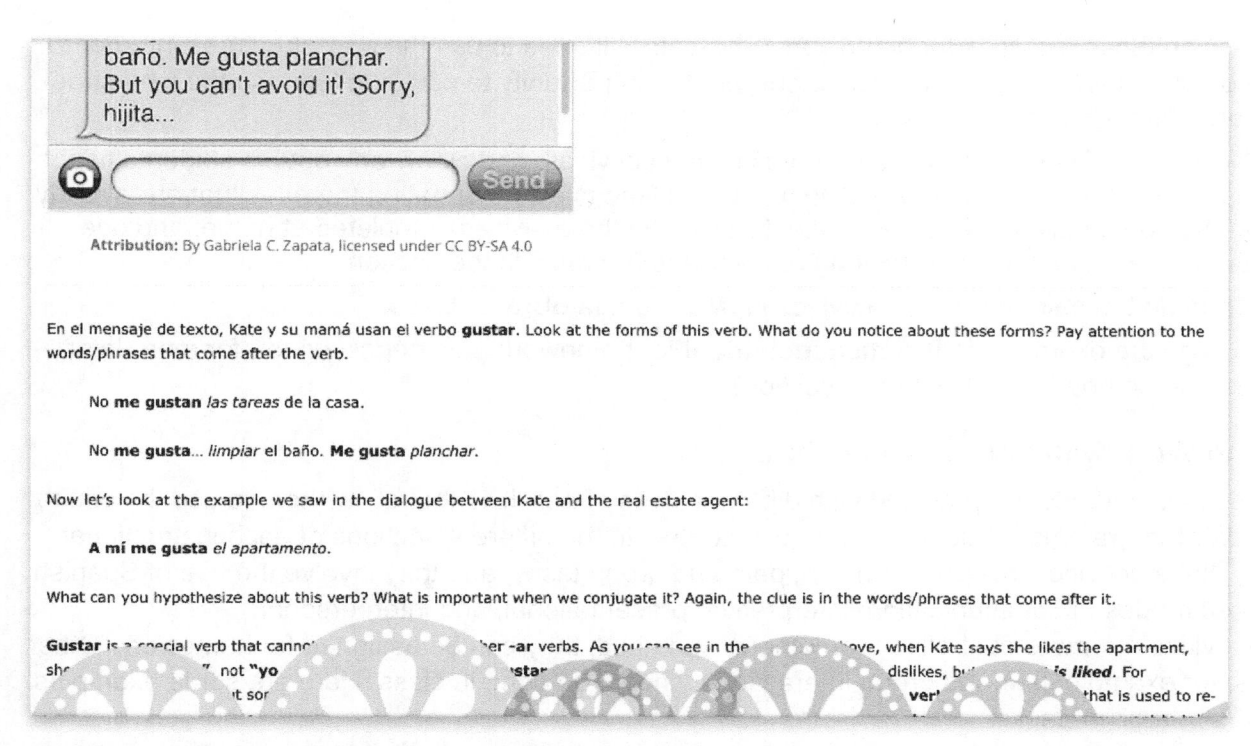

Attribution: By Gabriela C. Zapata, licensed under CC BY-SA 4.0

En el mensaje de texto, Kate y su mamá usan el verbo **gustar**. Look at the forms of this verb. What do you notice about these forms? Pay attention to the words/phrases that come after the verb.

No **me gustan** *las tareas* de la casa.

No **me gusta**... *limpiar* el baño. **Me gusta** *planchar*.

Now let's look at the example we saw in the dialogue between Kate and the real estate agent:

A mí me gusta *el apartamento*.

What can you hypothesize about this verb? What is important when we conjugate it? Again, the clue is in the words/phrases that come after it.

After this guided discovery, we provide students with simple rules and explanations based on the comparison between Spanish and English (i.e., we always depart from what the student knows).

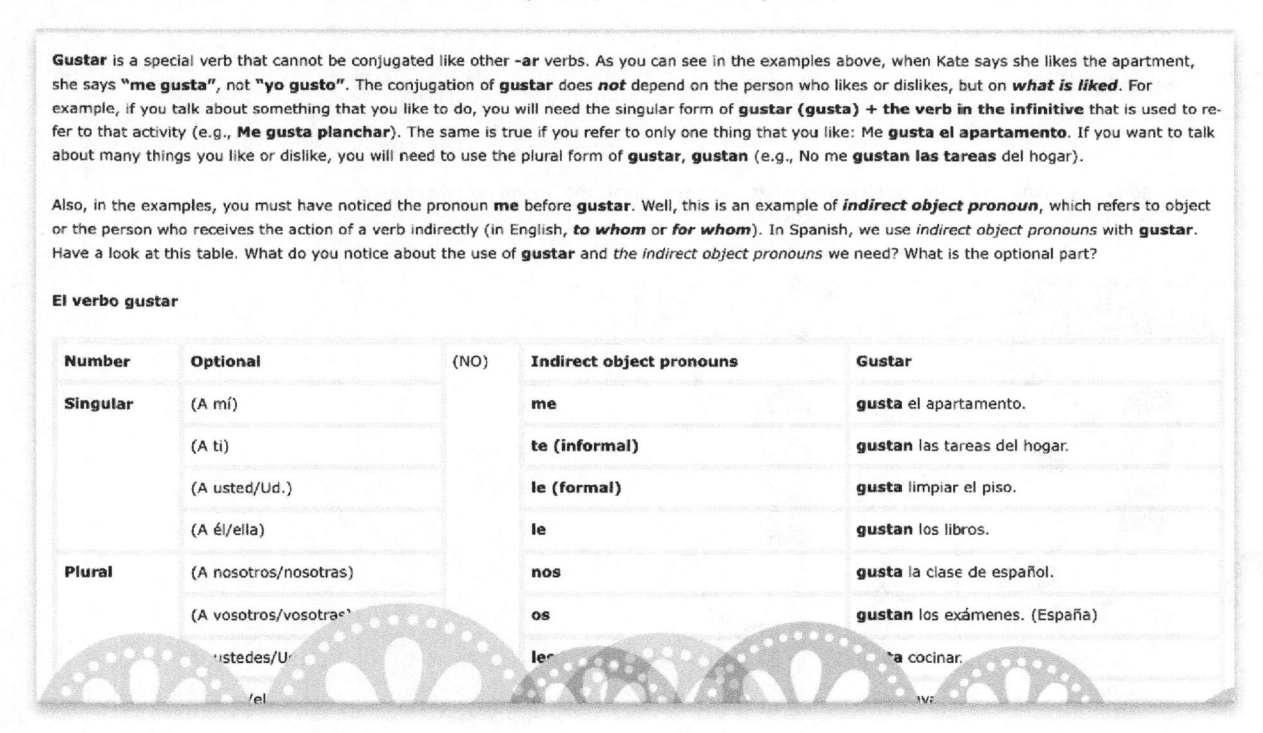

Gustar is a special verb that cannot be conjugated like other -ar verbs. As you can see in the examples above, when Kate says she likes the apartment, she says "**me gusta**", not "**yo gusto**". The conjugation of **gustar** does *not* depend on the person who likes or dislikes, but on *what is liked*. For example, if you talk about something that you like to do, you will need the singular form of **gustar (gusta)** + the verb in the infinitive that is used to refer to that activity (e.g., **Me gusta planchar**). The same is true if you refer to only one thing that you like: **Me gusta el apartamento**. If you want to talk about many things you like or dislike, you will need to use the plural form of **gustar, gustan** (e.g., No me **gustan las tareas** del hogar).

Also, in the examples, you must have noticed the pronoun **me** before **gustar**. Well, this is an example of *indirect object pronoun*, which refers to object or the person who receives the action of a verb indirectly (in English, *to whom* or *for whom*). In Spanish, we use *indirect object pronouns* with **gustar**. Have a look at this table. What do you notice about the use of **gustar** and *the indirect object pronouns* we need? What is the optional part?

El verbo gustar

Number	Optional	(NO)	Indirect object pronouns	Gustar
Singular	(A mí)		me	**gusta** el apartamento.
	(A ti)		te (informal)	**gustan** las tareas del hogar.
	(A usted/Ud.)		le (formal)	**gusta** limpiar el piso.
	(A él/ella)		le	**gustan** los libros.
Plural	(A nosotros/nosotras)		nos	**gusta** la clase de español.
	(A vosotros/vosotras)		os	**gustan** los exámenes. (España)
	...ustedes/U...		le...	...a cocinar.

The rules are followed by two practice sections: **¡Manos a la obra!** and **Práctica individual**.
This is the way we suggest **Hablemos de gramática** should be used:

- Do the first part of the section (i.e., the communicative context and the comprehension and lengua tasks that follow it) in class. You can put students in pairs to facilitate the task.

- When preparing your lesson plan, go over the **¡Manos a la obra!** activities that follow the rules and explanation part. Identify those that require students to work individually.

- Assign those activities for homework. Students will need to use the new structures in order to complete them. This will provide them with the opportunity to continue learning the new structures through use.
- Next class: Check one or two of the assigned activities, and clarify any doubts students might have about the new structures. Do not spend time in class repeating the rules that are already in the book. Instead, focus on students' errors in the activities completed at home, and use them to elicit their source, making reference to the rules in the section.
- Then do the pair and group activities in **¡Manos a la obra!** in class.
- Assign the exercises in **Práctica individual** for homework (see pages xxi-xxii for more information on how to work with this section).

3. How to Work with "¡Manos a la obra!"

In this section, students are provided with different kinds of activities that allow them to use the vocabulary and/or the grammar structures learned in context in the different sections of each instructional module. These activities include individual, pair, and group tasks, and they involve the use of Spanish in the three modes of communication—interpretive, presentational, and interpersonal.

Some activities are more controlled than others, and, thus, they can be assigned for homework. Other activities, for example, pair and group interactions, should be done in class. Here are some examples of **¡Manos a la obra!** tasks.

Example #1: *¿Qué le gusta a Verónica?* (this activity can be assigned for homework).

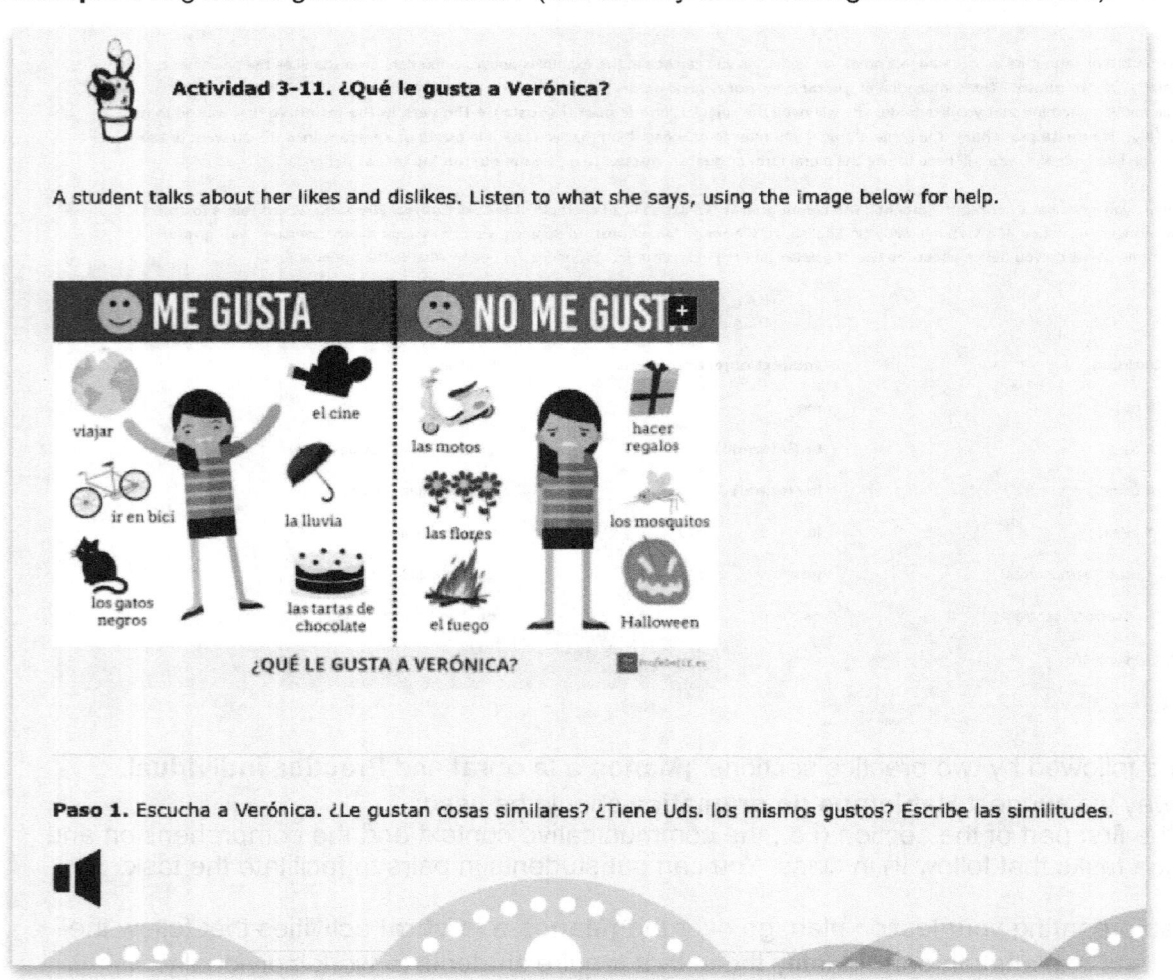

Actividad 3-11. ¿Qué le gusta a Verónica?

A student talks about her likes and dislikes. Listen to what she says, using the image below for help.

😊 ME GUSTA — viajar, el cine, ir en bici, la lluvia, los gatos negros, las tartas de chocolate

☹ NO ME GUSTA — las motos, hacer regalos, las flores, los mosquitos, el fuego, Halloween

¿QUÉ LE GUSTA A VERÓNICA?

Paso 1. Escucha a Verónica. ¿Le gustan cosas similares? ¿Tiene Uds. los mismos gustos? Escribe las similitudes.

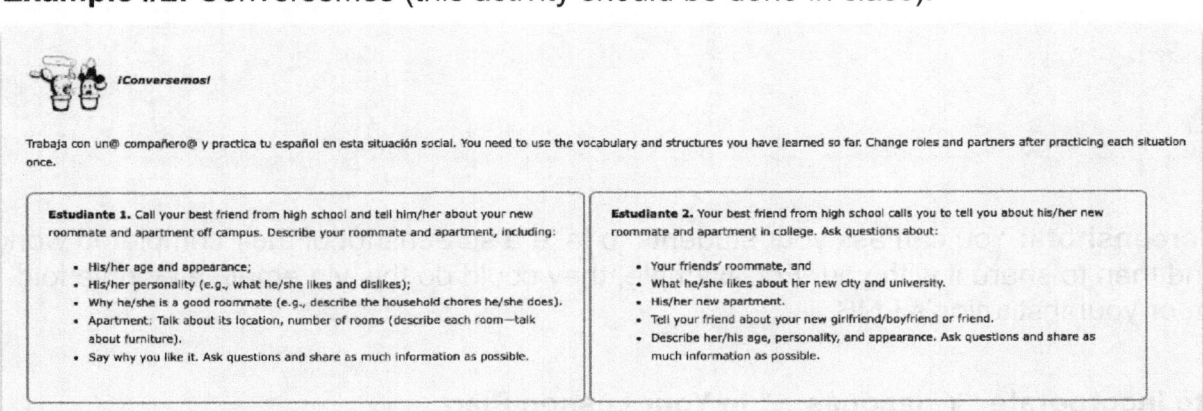

Paso 2.

Escucha a Verónica otra vez y decide si estas afirmaciones son Ciertas (C) o Falsas (F). Trabaja con un@ compañer@. Work with someone you haven't worked with before.

	C	F
1. Para Verónica, el mundo no es interesante.	C	F
2. Verónica vive en una ciudad.	C	F
3. A Verónica le gusta caminar a la universidad.	C	F
4. A Verónica le gustan los perros de color negro (*black*).	C	F
5. La celebración favorita de Verónica es Halloween.	C	F
6. A Verónica no le gustan los mosquitos.	C	F
7. A Verónica le gusta comprar regalos (*gifts*) para sus amigas.	C	F
8. A Verónica le gusta Netflix.	C	F

Example #2: Conversemos (this activity should be done in class).

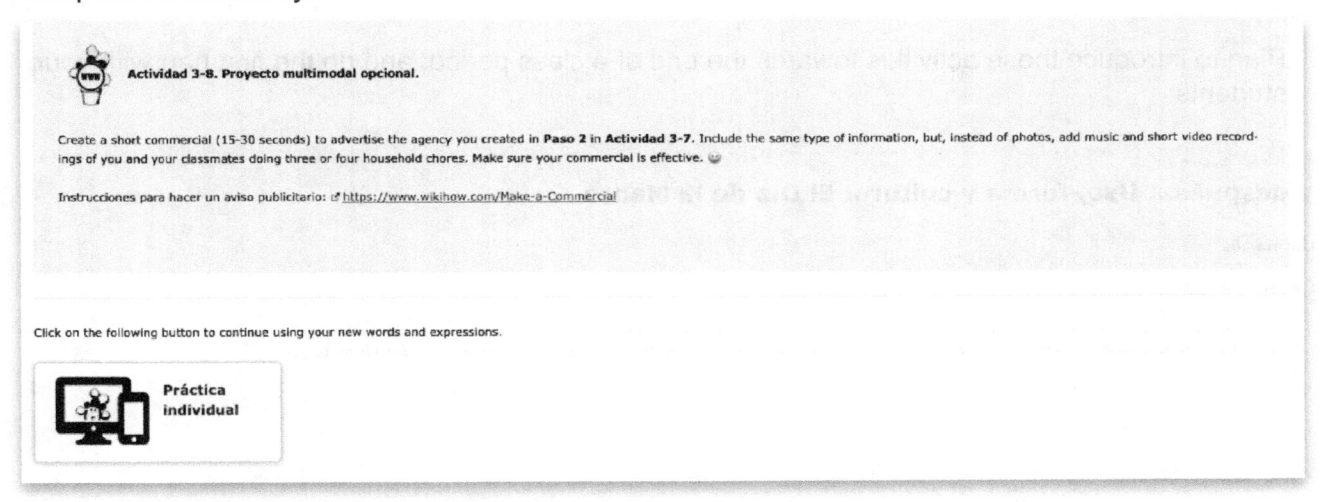

¡Conversemos!

Trabaja con un@ compañero@ y practica tu español en esta situación social. You need to use the vocabulary and structures you have learned so far. Change roles and partners after practicing each situation once.

Estudiante 1. Call your best friend from high school and tell him/her about your new roommate and apartment off campus. Describe your roommate and apartment, including:

- His/her age and appearance;
- His/her personality (e.g., what he/she likes and dislikes);
- Why he/she is a good roommate (e.g., describe the household chores he/she does).
- Apartment: Talk about its location, number of rooms (describe each room—talk about furniture).
- Say why you like it. Ask questions and share as much information as possible.

Estudiante 2. Your best friend from high school calls you to tell you about his/her new roommate and apartment in college. Ask questions about:

- Your friends' roommate, and
- What he/she likes about her new city and university.
- His/her new apartment.
- Tell your friend about your new girlfriend/boyfriend or friend.
- Describe her/his age, personality, and appearance. Ask questions and share as much information as possible.

3. How to Work with "Práctica individual"

At the bottom of most of the sections in each module, there are links to activities that provide learners with more opportunities to use the structures learned. These exercises are self-correcting, and can be completed individually.

Actividad 3-8. Proyecto multimodal opcional.

Create a short commercial (15-30 seconds) to advertise the agency you created in **Paso 2** in **Actividad 3-7**. Include the same type of information, but, instead of photos, add music and short video recordings of you and your classmates doing three or four household chores. Make sure your commercial is effective. 😊

Instrucciones para hacer un aviso publicitario: ☞ https://www.wikihow.com/Make-a-Commercial

Click on the following button to continue using your new words and expressions.

Práctica individual

This is the way we suggest Práctica individual should be used:
Assign these activities for homework. These are discrete-point exercises (http://bit.ly/DiscretePoint), and they should not be done in class. Class time should be used for students' active use of Spanish for communication. If you want to verify that students have completed the assigned homework, you have two possible options:

- **Email:** You can ask your students to email you their results using the button provided at the bottom of all the activities.

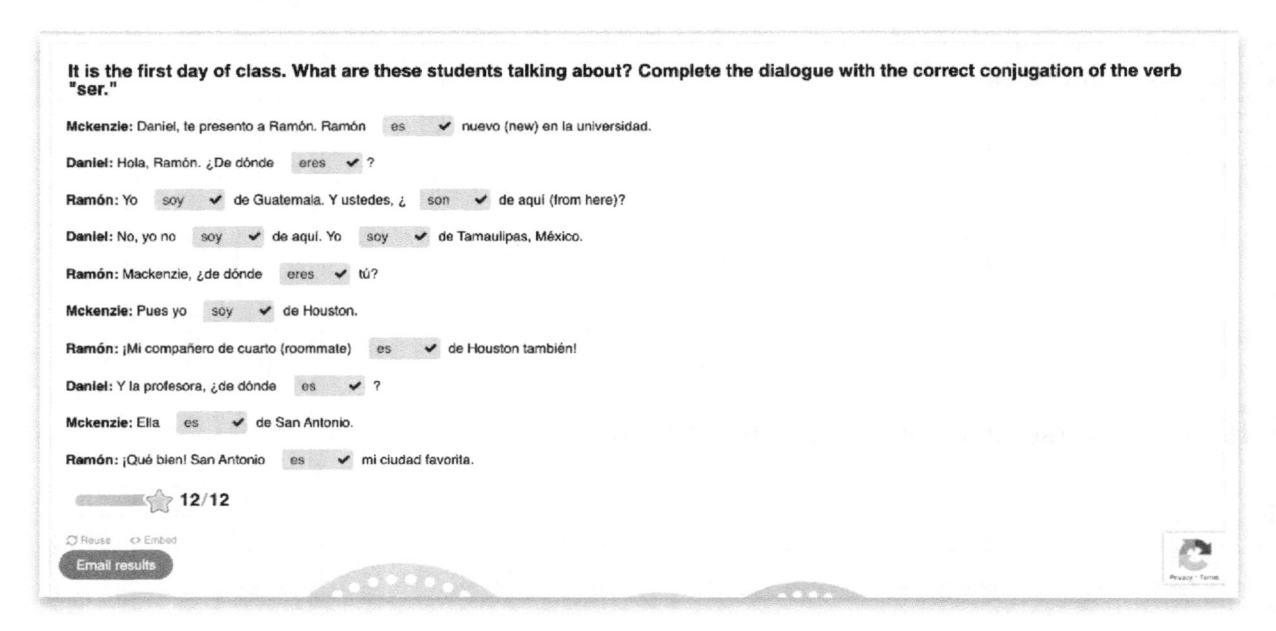

- **Screenshots:** You can ask your students to take a screenshot of their completed work, and then to share it with you. For example, they could do this via email, a Google folder, or your institution's LMS.

4. How to Incorporate "Y después…" in Your Lesson Plan

The section Y después... synthesizes use, form, and culture through students' use of the language to work with different kinds of texts, thus epitomizing Learning by Design's principles and knowledge processes (see pages ix-xv).

We suggest you work with these sections in this way:

1. Plan to introduce these activities towards the end of a class period, and do the first part with your students:

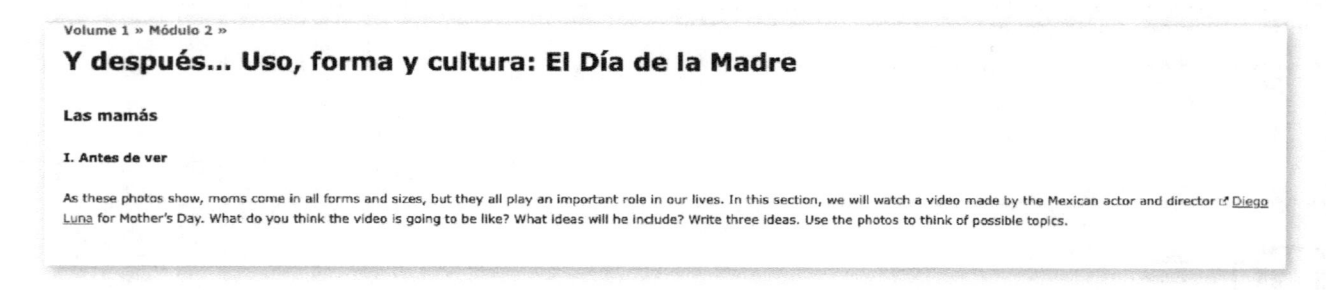

Attribution: By quinet, licensed under CC BY 2.0.

Attribution: Public domain

Attribution: Public domain

a, lic

2. Assign the activities that require reading or viewing for homework:

 II. A ver

Now watch the Día de la Madre video en 🔗 https://youtu.be/wDfI9iiXoy0, and check if your ideas coincide with the ones that appear in it.

III. Después de ver

Actividad 2-7. Are there any similarities/differences between your ideas and the ones shown in the video? Name two.

Actividad 2-8. Now watch the video again, and do the following exercises.

Actividad A. ¿Cómo son las mamás en el video? Describe su personalidad.

3. Next class: Check your students' work, and complete the rest of the activities in class. Organize students in pairs and/or groups to facilitate their task:

Actividad B. En el vídeo, Diego Luna dice *(says)*: "Todas las mamás son unas mentirosas (mienten = no hablan con la verdad [*truth*])". "Mentir" is usually a negative verb. Is it negative in this video? These are some of instances in which Diego Luna says mothers don't the truth:

- "Cuando siempre [dice] que eres el mejor *(the best)*."
- "Esa cena *(dinner)* no [es] especial para astronautas."
- "[Dice] que [eres] el más guapo *(the most handsome)*."
- "También miente a sus necesidades. Miente cuando dice que no le importa levantarse más temprano *(she doesn't care about getting up early)*."
- "Miente porque no la tiene fácil *(life is not easy for her)*."
- "Cuando te dice que todo estará bien *(everything will be OK)*."

Is the use of the verb "mentir" really negative in this video? What is the message of the video? Using the information and images in the video, describe its main purpose. Who is the audience for this video? Justify your opinions.

Actividad C. The last phrase of the video is "Gracias, Jefas." What does the word "jefa" mean? Look it up, and think about why this word is used in the video. What does it say about the role of the mother in Hispanic families?

Actividad D. Organizational features. How is the video organized? Choose all that apply and explain briefly why you selected each organizational feature—what were the clues in the video?

1. Chronological
2. Description
3. Cause and effect
4. Compare and Contrast
5. Informational

Justification from video

Actividad E. Do you think this commercial would work in the US? Why? Why not?

Actividad 2-9. Representaciones de la familia. Now we are going to analyze a painting by Colombian artist ⤴ Fernando Botero (we will learn about Colombia in this module). Mira la obra y describe:

1. Qué miembros de la familia están en la obra;

2. Cómo son, cómo están;

3. Qué roles tienen (de acuerdo a su posición y actitud en el cuadro).

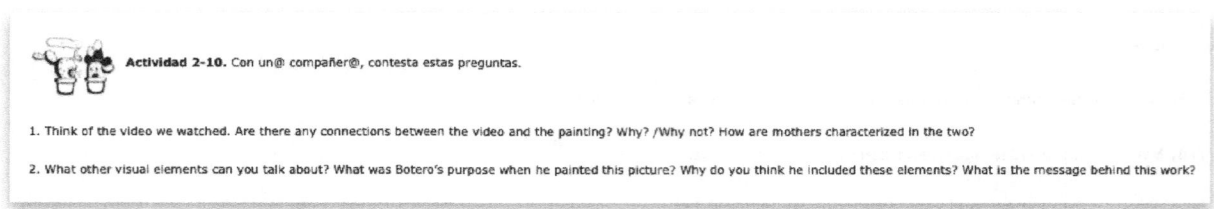

Actividad 2-10. Con un@ compañer@, contesta estas preguntas.

1. Think of the video we watched. Are there any connections between the video and the painting? Why? /Why not? How are mothers characterized in the two?

2. What other visual elements can you talk about? What was Botero's purpose when he painted this picture? Why do you think he included these elements? What is the message behind this work?

4. If the section incorporates work with other texts and/or research tasks, you can assign them for homework, and discuss your students' work the following class

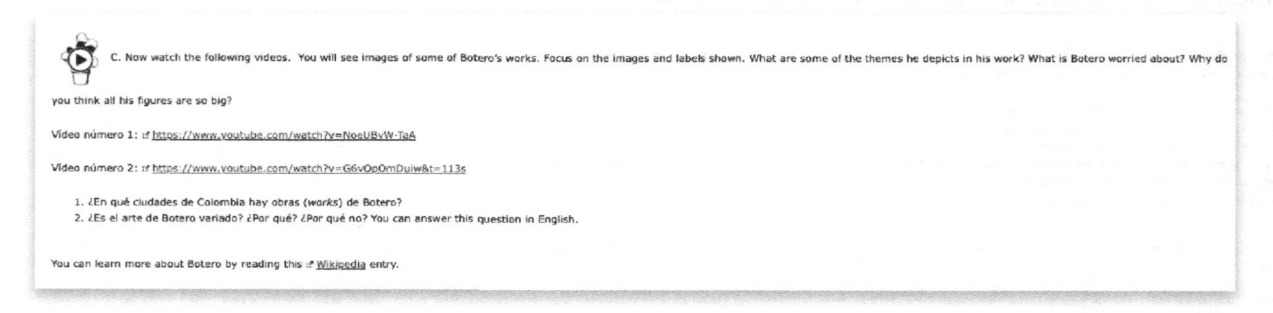

C. Now watch the following videos. You will see images of some of Botero's works. Focus on the images and labels shown. What are some of the themes he depicts in his work? What is Botero worried about? Why do you think all his figures are so big?

Vídeo número 1: ⤴ https://www.youtube.com/watch?v=NoeUByW-TqA

Vídeo número 2: ⤴ https://www.youtube.com/watch?v=G6vOpOmDuIw&t=113s

1. ¿En qué ciudades de Colombia hay obras (works) de Botero?
2. ¿Es el arte de Botero variado? ¿Por qué? ¿Por qué no? You can answer this question in English.

You can learn more about Botero by reading this ⤴ Wikipedia entry.

Important: These activities are based on authentic materials, so some of your students might complain about not understanding everything, and they might feel frustrated and stressed out. Therefore, it is crucial that you train your students to work with these kinds of resources. Emphasize the importance of understanding the main ideas of a text and not every single word, and to concentrate on the tasks they need to complete. Also, provide them with strategies, clear instructions, and modeling. Resort to pair and group work to facilitate your students' work. ¡Sí se puede!

4. How to Work with "Proyecto digital"

The objective of the digital project is to offer students the opportunity to apply the Spanish they have learned to create a personal profile in Spanish to introduce themselves and aspects of their life to Spanish speakers. In each module, learners will develop different parts of this project applying the specific vocabulary and structures they have learned in it. This project can be adapted depending on each teacher and their students' interests.

Here are links to sample documents (in Google doc format) that you can use and/or adapt to provide guidance to your students to complete their digital projects:

- Guía para los instructores (español): https://bit.ly/GuiaInstructor
- Rubric for evaluation of project (English): https://bit.ly/RubricProjectEvaluat
- Instructions for peer review work (English): https://bit.ly/PeerReviForm
- Instructions for formatting and classroom presentation of students' work (English): https://bit.ly/InstructFormat
- Instructions for student volunteers (publication of magazine) (English): https://bit.ly/InstrExtra-Cred
- Template for the development of each section of the project: https://bit.ly/TemplateProj

Icons

 Audio materials and/or listening comprehension and interpretation tasks.

 Reading comprehension and interpretation tasks.

 Video materials and/or taks that involve the comprehension and interpretation of short movies/videos.

 Pair work in activities in the three modes of communication (interpretive, interpersonal, and presentational).

 Group work in activities in the three modes of communication (interpretive, interpersonal, and presentational).

 Activities that involve students' work with digital resources, such as multimodal ensembles. Interpretive and presentational modes of communication.

 ¡Manos a la obra! Section: Tasks that offer students opportunities to use recently learned vocabulary and structures in the three modes of communication (interpretive, interpersonal, and presentational).

 This icon highlights important information or directs students to additional instructional resources.

 This icon introduces information about dialectal differences in the Spanish-speaking world.

 This icon introduces the section Trayectos hispanos, which provides information about sociocultural/sociohistorical aspects of Hispanic/Latinx communities in the United States.

 This icon introduces the section Hablemos de cultura, which offers information about Spanish-speaking regions outside the United States.

 This icon connects students to the self-correcting activities in Práctica individual, which can be assigned for homework or as extra practice outside the language classroom.

Credits

https://trayectos.coerll.utexas.edu/more/credits/

Introducción

The title of this book is *Trayectos*, which in Spanish means pathways. We have developed the material in this volume to guide your learning process and your pathway of discovery of the Spanish-speaking world with the objective of preparing you linguistically and culturally to use Spanish to communicate with speakers in this country and around the world.

Each instructional module in *Trayectos* will offer cultural and linguistic information, and ample opportunities to use Spanish in three modes of communication: Interpersonal (oral interactions with other speakers), interpretive (reading and listening comprehension), and presentational (writing/oral presentations). Also, we will help you make connections between grammatical forms and the social contexts in which you use them.

Are you ready to start your learning process? Entonces, ¡comencemos a descubrir! (So, let's start our discovery!)

Módulo introductorio: Interacciones

Attribution: Public domain

Objetivos en este módulo

Comunicación

In this instructional module, you will learn how to…
- Introduce yourself
- Greet friends and people you don't know very well
- Provide some personal information (e.g., your name, country/city of origin)
- Use numbers 0 - 30 to talk about quantities
- Ask simple questions
- Spell names and words in Spanish (the alphabet)
- Pronounce Spanish consonants and vowels
- Use classroom expressions in Spanish

Lengua
- Subject pronouns
- The present tense of the verb **ser**
- The present tense of the verb **haber** Question words

Cultura
- El español y sus protagonistas

Mis metas

In your Spanish notebook, describe what you want to accomplish in this instructional module in personal terms.

Introducción comunicativa: *A conocernos*

In this instructional module, we will learn how to greet friends and family members, and people we may not know very well. Think about how you greet people in English. Do you use different expressions depending on who the person is? What social cues (e.g., age) do you rely on? Do you think greetings in English differ from greetings in Spanish? Let's have a look… Pay attention to the following conversations and see if you can notice some social patterns.

Audio link: http://bit.ly/Audio01Trayectos

Situación 1. Rosy and her boyfriend Ramón are having lunch with Rosy's mother. Ramón and Rosy's mother are meeting for the first time.

Attribution: Public domain

Rosy:	¡**Hola**, mamá! **¿Cómo estás?**
Mamá de Rosy:	¡**Hola**, hijita! **Bastante bien, gracias. ¿Y tú?**
Rosy:	**Muy bien, gracias.** Mami, este es mi novio. [Rosy looks at her boyfriend.]
Mamá de Rosy:	**Buenos días**, joven. **¿Cuál es su nombre?**
Ramón:	**Buenos días**, Señora González. **Me llamo** Ramón. **Mucho gusto.**
Mamá de Rosy:	**El gusto es mío**, Ramón.

Situación 2. Mariana and Kareza are students at Texas A&M University and are very good friends. Mariana is with her new friend Jessica. On their way to class, they see Mariana's good friend Kareza. Kareza and Jessica meet for the first time.

Attribution: By Katiebordner, licensed under CC BY 2.0.

Kareza:	¡Mariana! **¿Qué tal** la clase de español con la Srta. Ribota?
Mariana:	**Hola**, Kareza. **Muy bien. La clase es interesante.**
Jessica:	¡Howdy! **Soy** Jessica. **¿Y tú? ¿Cómo te llamas?**
Kareza:	**Mi nombre es Kareza. Mucho gusto.**
Jessica:	**Encantada.** Y, **¿de dónde eres?**
Kareza:	**Soy de Houston.** ¿Y tú?
Jessica:	**Yo soy de Laredo.**
Mariana:	OK, chicas. ¡Vamos que llegamos tarde a clase! (*Come on! We'll be late for class*).

As the previous dialogues show, in the Spanish-speaking world, when you greet someone or you introduce yourself, there are two types of situations: **formal** and **informal**. In order to use socially-appropriate forms, it is important to know the difference between the expressions and structures you need in these two types of situations. Let's have a look…

- **Introductions in an informal situation:** When you meet someone who is your same age or younger than you, you can ask these questions:
    - To ask someone's name: *¿Cuál es tu nombre?* / *¿Cómo te llamas?*
    - To ask where someone is from: *¿De dónde eres?*

- **Introductions in a formal situation:** When you meet someone who is older than you or you are in a professional situation, you can ask these questions:
    - To ask someone's name: *¿Cuál es su nombre?* / *¿Cómo se llama?*
    - To ask where someone is from: *¿De dónde es usted?*

Situación 3. Dr. Suárez and Dr. Campos are new colleagues in the Department of Hispanic Studies. They are meeting for coffee to discuss a possible collaboration on a grant.

Dr. Suárez:	**Buenas tardes,** Doctora Campos. **¿Cómo está usted?**
Dra. Campos:	**Bien, gracias. ¿Y usted?**
Dr. Suárez:	**Bastante bien. ¿De dónde es usted?**
Dra. Campos:	Soy de Perú. ¿Y usted?
Dr. Suárez:	Yo soy de Puerto Rico.

Attribution: Public Domain

¿Comprendiste? The objective of this section is to check for your understanding of the dialogues/ texts presented in each of the modules. This section is intended to help you analyze critically and appropriately the multimodal text presented. You can use other resources such as the **Hablemos más** section below to get extra help to answer the questions posited.

1. Is **Situación 1** _formal_ or _informal_? How can you tell whether the conversation is _formal_ or _informal_? What expressions led you to this conclusion? Would you have changed the register in this situation? Why or why not?

2. **Situación 2:** Why is the conversation informal when Jessica and Kareza meet for the first time? What does this tell you about the use of _informal_ expressions in Spanish? What are the similarities and differences between this exchange and the one that you would have had in English?

3. Compare **Situación 2** and **Situación 3** and write a few ideas on the different use of greetings in _formal_ and _informal_ situations. Why did Dr. Suarez and Dr. Campos use a different register than Kareza and Jessica?

Based on your newly-gained knowledge, what are some ways you can tell a conversation will be formal or informal? What social cues are important?

 **Práctica individual:** To practice your new vocabulary and structures, go to http://bit.ly/PracticaIndividual01.

Hablemos más: _Saludamos_

Below you will find a variety of greetings you can use in Spanish. Think about some of the people in your life. What greetings would you use to greet tus amigos (_your friends_), tus profesores, tu mamá o tu papá? Choose different greetings, and practice them next time you see these people.

 **Audio link: http://bit.ly/Audio02Trayectos**

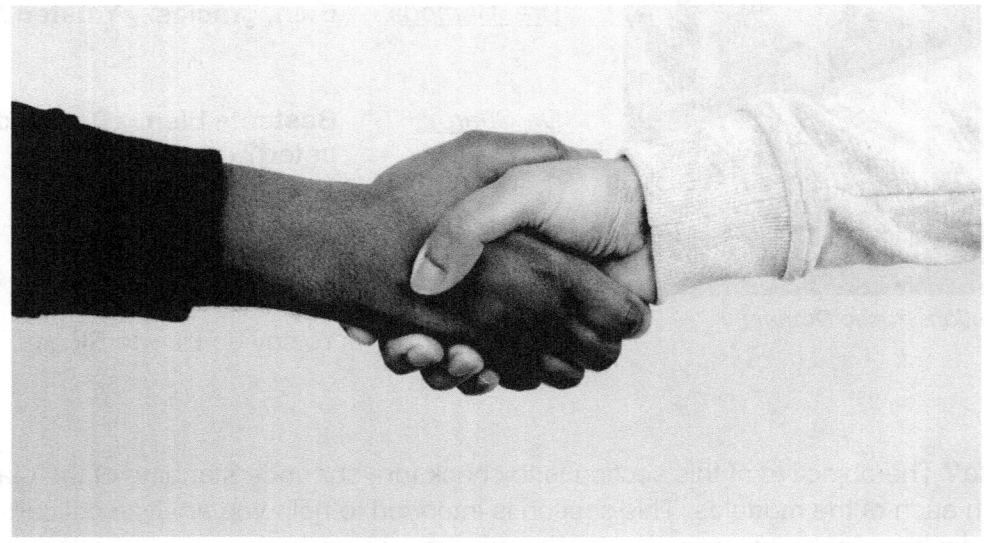

Attribution: Public Domain

Saludamos (*We greet people*)

Buenos días.	*Good morning.*
Buenas tardes.	*Good afternoon.*
Buenas noches.	*Good evening / night.*
¡Hola!	*Hi! / Hello! (informal)*
¿Qué tal?	*What's up? (informal)*
¿Qué hay?	*What's new? (informal)*
¿Cómo te va?	*How's it going?*
¿Cómo estás?	*How are you? (informal)*
¿Cómo está usted?	*How are you? (formal)*

Contestamos los saludos (*We answer people's greetings*)

(Muy) Bien, gracias.	*(Very) well, thanks.*
Bastante bien, gracias.	*Pretty well, thanks.*
Más o menos.	*So-so*
¿Y tú?	*And you? (informal)*
¿Y usted?	*And you? (formal)*

Nos despedimos (*We say goodbye*)

Chau.	*Bye! (informal)*
Adiós.	*Goodbye.*
Hasta luego.	*See you later.*
Hasta mañana.	*See you tomorrow.*
Hasta pronto.	*See you soon.*
Buenas noches.	*Good night.*
Nos vemos.	*See you later.*

Conocemos a la gente (We get to know people)

¿Cómo te llamas?	*What's your name? (informal)*
¿Cómo se llama usted?	*What's your name? (formal)*
¿Cuál es tu nombre?	*What's your name? (informal)*
¿De dónde eres?	*Where are you from? (informal)*
¿De dónde es usted?	*Where are you from? (formal)*

Nos presentamos (*We introduce ourselves*)

Me llamo _____. / My nombre es _____.	*My name is…*
(Yo) Soy…	*I am…*
(Yo) Soy de…	*I'm from*
Mucho gusto.	*Nice to meet you.*
El gusto es mío. / Igualmente.	*The pleasure is mine. / Likewise.*
Encantado/a.	*Nice to meet you.*

 El cactus viajero.

¿Qué onda? Yo soy el cactus viajero, and I am here to teach you interesting facts about the Spanish-speaking world. Before I start, in how many ways do you think we can say *What's up?* in Spanish? Definitely more than one! Let me show you some ways young Spanish-speakers say *What's up?* or *What's happening?*

- **¿Qué hay de nuevo?**
- **¿Qué pasa?**
- **¿Qué hubo?**
- **¿Cómo andas? / ¿Cómo andás?**
- **¿Cómo va?**
- **¿Qué onda?**
- **¿Qué hacés?**

Google these expressions and find out where they're used.

 **¡Manos a la obra!**

 **Actividad 0-1. Conversaciones**

Paso 1. Have a look at the following situations, and decide whether you would use a formal or informal register. Justify your answers. In some case, both registers would be appropriate. Explain why.

1. Two strangers holding a conversation on the bus.
2. A patient talking with their doctor.
3. You are being interviewed for a new job by your future boss.
4. A young boy is having a conversation with his grandfather.
5. A father is talking with his daughter/son.
6. Two neighbors are talking to each other.

Paso 2. With a classmate, create short dialogues for each of the situations in **Paso 1**. Use **Situations 1-3** (pgs. 2-4) and the information in **Hablemos más** (pgs. 5-6) as guidance (e.g., imagine that people are greeting each other and/or introducing themselves).

 **Actividad 0-2. Estudiantes**

Paso 1. Look at the image below and, with a classmate, create two different dialogues: Introductions and greetings. Use **Situations 1-3** (pgs. 2-4) and the information in **Hablemos más** (pgs. 5-6) as guidance.

By Informedmag, licensed under CC BY 2.0.

Paso 2. What register did you choose for your conversation? Why? Is this the same way you greet your friends? What other expressions can you use in Spanish? Are your classmates' dialogues similar to yours?

 *¡Conversemos!*
In this section, you will apply what you've learned to communicate with your peers.

Conversación 1. Imagine that you and your classmate meet on campus. Greet each other using the informal forms. Ask each other how you are doing. Conclude the conversation saying goodbye.

Conversación 2. You are meeting your instructor on the first day of class. **Estudiante 1** (*Student 1*) will play the role of the student and **Estudiante 2** (*Student 2*) will be the instructor. Greet each other using formal and/or informal forms, depending on your role. Make sure you:

1. ask the other person how they are doing;
2. introduce yourself;
3. say where you are from. Answer each other's questions.

 **Práctica individual:** To practice your new vocabulary and structures, go to http://bit.ly/PracticaIndividual02.

Hablemos de gramática: *Subject pronouns and the present tense of the verb "ser"*

 ¿Quién es Marlenie? (*Who is Marlenie?*)

Marlenie is a university student in Texas. Here she introduces herself and her favorite building on campus.

Video link: http://bit.ly/Video01_Trayectos.

Attribution: By Marlenie Arzamendi and Dylan Manshack, licensed under CC BY-SA 4.0.

¡Hola! **Yo soy** Marlenie. **Yo soy** tu guía (*your guide*). **Yo soy** tu compañera en la clase de español. Este **es** el edificio (*building*) académico.

In this introduction, Marlenie uses the verb **ser** in the first person to talk about herself. A **verb** is a word that describes an action (e.g., write, eat, etc.) or a state of being (e.g., feel, is, etc.). In Spanish, verbs have different forms, **conjugaciones** (conjugations), depending on who or what is doing an action, which are called the subjects of the verb. A subject can be expressed through a **noun** (a person, animal, or thing; e.g., Sean, Marlenie, the dog, the car, etc.) or a **pronoun** (e.g., I, he, they, etc.). The pronouns that indicate who is doing an action are called subject pronouns. Subject pronouns in Spanish are both similar to and different from English. For example, like in English, subject pronouns have singular and plural forms, but, unlike English, some of the pronouns have gender (feminine and masculine). Have a look at this table and compare subject pronouns in both languages. What other similarities/differences do you notice?

Number	Subject pronouns in Spanish	Subject pronouns in English
Singular	yo	*I*
	tú	*you* (informal)
	vos	*you* (informal). Used predominantly in Argentina and Uruguay, but also in other South and Central American countries. More information: http://bit.ly/PronombreVos.

	usted/Ud.	*you* (formal)
	él/ella	*he/she*
Plural	nosotros (masc.)/nosotras (fem.)	*we*
	vosotros (masc.)/vosotras (fem.)	*you* (plural; informal–only used in Spain)
	ustedes/Uds.	*you* (plural: Both informal and formal in Latin America; formal in Spain)
	ellos (masc.)/ellas (fem.)	*they*

One important difference between Spanish and English is that, while subject pronouns are obligatory in English, ***they are optional*** in Spanish unless there is ambiguity with respect to who is doing the action, or you want to emphasize the subject. Why do you think this is the case? Have a look at the next table. Pay attention to the different **conjugaciones** (conjugations) of **ser**. What do you notice?

Number	Subject Pronoun	Forms of "ser"	
Singular	yo	soy	*I am*
	tú	eres	*you are* (informal)
	vos	sos	*you are* (informal). Used predominantly in Argentina and Uruguay, but also in other South and Central American countries. More information: http://bit.ly/PronombreVos.
	usted/Ud.	es	*you are* (formal)
	él/ella	es	*he/she is*
Plural	nosotros (masc.)/nosotras (fem.)	somos	*we are*
	vosotros (masc.)/vosotras (fem.)	sois	*you are* (plural; informal--used only in Spain).
	ustedes/Uds.	son	*you are* (plural; Both informal and formal in Latin America; formal in Spain).
	ellos (masc.)/ellas (fem.)	son	*they are*

You can use these forms of the verb **ser** (*to be*) to introduce and describe yourself (what you are like, where you are from) and others, and also to describe things/animals/places. For example, when Marlenie talks about her friends, she says:

- Efraín **es** carismático y activo. **(Él) es** de Killeen, Tejas.
- **Ellas son** Bailey y Carolina. **(Ellas) son** responsables y estudiosas.

If you want to use **ser** in a negative sentence, it is super easy! Just place the word **no** before the conjugated verb:

- Efraín **no es** carismático y activo.
- Bailey y Carolina **no son** responsables.

Sugerencia: If you want to learn more about **ser** and **subject pronouns**, you can consult the following pages:

- **Subject Pronouns:** http://bit.ly/SubjectPron
- **Ser:** http://bit.ly/VerboSer

 **¡Manos a la obra!**

 **Actividad 0-3. ¡Hola!**

Can you introduce yourself? Can you describe yourself and your classmates? Well, you already know how the verb **ser** works. Let's now help you with some easy words you can use. These are forms that are very similar in English and Spanish. They are called **cognados** (*cognates*). You will encounter cognados throughout this textbook. These are your first tools for communication. Here are some examples:

inteligente	elegante	optimista
paciente	pesimista	admirable
interesante	responsable	independiente
importante	sentimental	materialista
flexible	liberal	arrogante
idealista	tolerante	rebelde
extravagante	informal	realista

Try to describe yourself like Marlenie did. Find a classmate that you haven't met yet. First, greet them, and introduce yourself (remember to also use the expressions you learned in **Hablemos más**, pgs. 5-6). Say what you, your instructor, and your classmates (**mis compañeros**) are like. Use different cognates for each description.

 ¡Ojo! (*Pay attention!*)

In Spanish, adjectives have number, so, if you are talking about your classmates in the plural, you need to add an "s" to the words above (e.g., pacientes).

Actividad 0-4. Más sobre mí... (*More about me...*)

Paso 1. This activity will allow you to talk about more aspects of your ideas, personality, and interests. You will first develop some ideas using the verb **ser** and **los cognados** we learned in **Actividad 0-3** and some others that we give you below. Prepare some ideas. Complete the sentences with the appropriate form of the verb **ser** and the words necessary to convey your meaning.

> **Modelo(s):**   Mis lugares (*places*) favoritos... *Mis lugares favoritos son Escocia y San Antonio.*
> Mi hombre (*man*)/mujer (*woman*) ideal... *Mi hombre/mujer ideal es inteligente.*

Más cognados: profesión, estudiante, actor, artista, atleta, extrovertido (masc.), extrovertida (fem.), honesto (masc.), honesta (fem.), generoso (masc.), generosa (fem.), serio (masc.), seria (fem.), profesor (masc.), profesora (fem.).

Otras expresiones útiles: Mis amigos (*my friends*) Mis padres (*my parents*) de Tejas (*from Texas*) de los Estados Unidos (*from the United States*)

1. Mi profesión ideal...
2. Los profesores ideales...
3. Mis padres y yo... / Mis profesores y yo...
4. El estudiante ideal...
5. Yo...
6. Mi (*my*) artista favorito...
7. Mis amigos y yo...
8. Los estudiantes ideales...

Paso 2. Now find a classmate that you haven't met yet. First, greet them, and introduce yourself (use the expressions you learned in **Hablemos más**, pgs. 5-6). Ask how they are doing. Then exchange the information you develop in **Paso 1**.

Paso 3. Now think of two simple yes/no questions to ask your partner using the verb ser and the words in **Paso 1** and **Actividad 0-3**. Follow the model, and ask questions to find out information you still do not know about your classmate. Answer your partner's questions too.

> **Modelo(s):**   **Estudiante 1:** *¿Eres de College Station?*
> **Estudiante 2:** *Sí, (yo) soy de College Station.* o   *No, no soy de College Station. Soy de Austin.*

Paso 4. Present some of the information you gathered about your partner to the rest of the class. Follow the model, and ask your instructor for help!

> **Modelo(s):**   *El nombre de mi compañero/a es... Él/Ella... de... Sus padres y él/ella... Su profesión ideal... etc.*

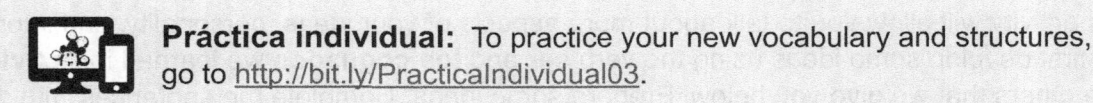

Práctica individual: To practice your new vocabulary and structures, go to http://bit.ly/PracticaIndividual03.

Y después... Uso, forma y cultura: *¡Hola! ¿Cómo estás?*

I. Antes de ver

Actividad 0-5. You are now going to listen to a song. Look at these images, and imagine what these two singers are like and what kind of songs they sing. Write three ideas.

Attribution: Screen capture of El Barrio's official Twitter feed, licensed under CC.

Attribution: Peret. Screen capture of Peret's Vimeo video "El muerto vivo", licensed under CC.

 **II. A ver**

Now watch the video on http://bit.ly/HolaComoEstasVideo, and check if your ideas coincide with the video.

Now watch the video once more, and do the activities that follow.

Actividad 0-6. Answer these questions about the song.

1. ¿Cómo se llama la canción *(song)*?
2. ¿Cómo se llaman los cantantes *(singers)*?

Now read the information about the singers that appears on these two websites and answer the questions that follow.

Cantante 1: http://bit.ly/Cantante1
Cantante 2: http://bit.ly/Cantante2

1. El verdadero (*real*) nombre de los cantantes es… y ….
2. ¿De dónde son? Mention country and city of origin.
3. ¿Cómo son? Use some of the images in the song and the information on the websites to describe each singer. Remember to use the verb ser and los cognados that you learned in previous sections.

 **Actividad 0-7**

Find three words other than the ones in the title that you recognize or you know. Tell your classmates what you think they mean.

 **Actividad 0-8. Tus opiniones**

Discuss the song with a classmate using the following questions. Do you have similar opinions?

1. What do you find appealing about this song? Do you like it? Why? / Why not?
2. This song combines two different musical genres: *flamenco* and *rumba catalana*. What do you know about them? Where do they come from? What are the cultural features that distinguish them? Work with a classmate to answer these questions. You can find information on these websites:
   ○ http://bit.ly/FlamencoInfo
   ○ http://bit.ly/CatalanRumba
3. Is there a particular musical genre in the US or Texas that shares characteristics with *flamenco* or *rumba catalana*? Justify your answer with examples (e.g., you can find music videos to show the similarities and differences).

Más comunicación: *"Hay" y los números del 0 al 30*

Tejas en números: Uso y forma

In this section, we will use Spanish to talk about numbers (**los números**). To introduce the topic, we will focus on sociocultural and geographical/historical aspects of our state, Texas. What aspects do you think are the most interesting about the state? What does the information in the poster tell you about Texas?

While you are looking at the data, also pay attention to the verb **hay**. What do you think it means and how do we use it?

Tejas en números

Hay dieciséis (16) períodos históricos desde la prehistoria hasta el siglo **veintiuno (21)**.

Attribution: Public domain.

Hay doce (12) ligas de deporte profesionales.

Attribution: Manu. By Zereshk, licensed under CC BY-SA 3.0.

Hay dos (2) prendas (*clothing items*) oficiales: las botas y el sombrero de cowboy.

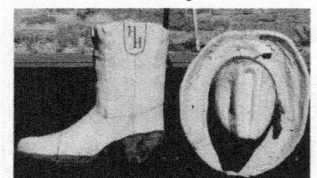

Attribution: Cowboy Essentials. By mikecogh, licensed under CC BY-SA 2.0.

Hay veinticinco (25) naciones indígenas principales. **Cinco** (5) de ellas son las naciones Tonkawa, Tawakoni, Hueco, Sana, Wichita y Coahuilteca.

Attribution: John Williams, Tonkawa. By BPL, licensed under CC BY 2.0., via Wikimedia Commons.

Hay siete (7) sistemas universitarios.

Attribution: Logo of Texas A&M Engineering Extension Service. Public domain.

Hay cuatro (4) plantas oficiales: la flor conejo (*bluebonnet*), el árbol de pacanas (*pecan tree*), el mirto de cresta (*crape myrtle*) y el nopal.

Attribution: Bluebonnet. By Gabriela C. Zapata, licensed under CC BY-SA 4.0.

Hay diez (10) animales oficiales. **Tres (3)** de ellos son la mariposa monarca, el sinsonte (*mockingbird*) y la vaca de cuernos largos (*longhorn*).

Attribution: Mockingbird. By Charles Patrick Ewing, licensed under CC BY 2.0.

Hay ocho (8) alimentos (*foods*) y platos (*dishes*) oficiales. Seis (6) de ellos son el chili, el pan de campo (*camp bread*), el jalapeño, el pastel de pacanas, los chips de tortilla y la salsa y el pastel de durazno (*peach cobbler*).

Attribution: Mmm... chili. By jeffreyw, licensed under CC BY 2.0

Attribution: By Gabriela C. Zapata, licensed under CC BY-SA 4.0.

Have you discovered what **hay** means and how we use it in Spanish? Yes, we use **hay** followed by a number to express the existence of people, animals, things, and places. It is equivalent to there is/ there are in English, but **hay** is used on its own: *It is not followed by any other verb* (as you can see in the examples we have just seen). Let's see how we ask questions using **hay**. It's very easy.

> **Modelo(s):** ¿**Hay** doce ligas profesionales de deportes en Tejas? Sí, **hay** doce ligas.
> ¿Cuántas plantas oficiales **hay** en Tejas? **Hay** cuatro.

If we want to use hay in a negative sentence, simply say **no hay** (e.g., **No hay** jirafas en Tejas.) Let's have a look at numbers:

Audio link: http://bit.ly/Audio03Trayectos

Los números del 0 al 30

0	cero				
1	uno	11	once	21	veintiuno
2	dos	12	doce	22	veintidós
3	tres	13	trece	23	veintitrés
4	cuatro	14	catorce	24	veinticuatro
5	cinco	15	quince	25	veinticinco
6	seis	16	dieciséis	26	veintiséis
7	siete	17	diecisiete	27	veintisiete
8	ocho	18	dieciocho	28	veintiocho
9	nueve	19	diecinueve	29	veintinueve
10	diez	20	veinte	30	treinta

The number one has several forms in Spanish. When we are counting, we use the form **uno** (e.g., **uno**, **dos**, **tres**…). The forms **una** and **un** are used before nouns (e.g., **una** profesora, **un** profesor). How do you know which form to use? It will depend on the gender of the noun (feminine or masculine). We will talk about this in more detail in **Módulo 1**.

Another interesting number is twenty-one. It works like the number one. When we are counting, we say **veintiuno**. But we use **veintiún** before masculine nouns (e.g., **veintiún** profesores) and **veintiuna** before feminine nouns (e.g., **veintiuna** profesoras).

¡Manos a la obra!

 ## Actividad 0-9. La clases, la universidad y los Estados Unidos

Paso 1. Imagine that a prospective international student from a Spanish-speaking country, Mariana, wants to know more about universities in the United State and the country itself. With a partner, answer the following questions about the typical university class, your university, and the United States. Take turns asking and answering questions.

1. ¿Cuántos (*How many*) estudiantes hay en una clase típica de la universidad? ¿Cuántos días (*days*) de clase hay? ¿Cuántos días de vacaciones hay en el semestre de otoño (*fall*)? ¿Y en el semestre de primavera (*spring*)?

2. En esta (*this*) universidad, hay muchos edificios (*many buildings*). Pero (*But*), ¿hay una cafetería? (Sí, hay... / No, no hay…) ¿Un teatro? ¿Un restaurante? ¿Una clínica? ¿Un hospital? ¿Un museo? ¿Una galería de arte? ¿Muchos estudiantes? ¿Muchos profesores?

3. ¿Cuántos estados hay en el sur/norte/este/oeste de los Estados Unidos? ¿Cuántos parques nacionales y/o provinciales hay en Tejas/en tu estado? ¿Cuántos feriados (*holidays*) hay en los Estados Unidos? ¿Cuántos bares buenos (*good bars*) hay en esta ciudad (*this city*)? ¿Y cuántas discotecas buenas?

Paso 2. Now imagine that your partner and you write to Mariana with the information you gathered in

Paso 1. You want to brag about the Spanish you know, so you decide to use this language to communicate with her. Draft the email you could send her. Include the following information:

1. Greet the student;

2. Introduce yourselves and say where you are from (use **yo** if you are from different places and **nosotros** if you are from the same place);

3. Mention the name of the institution where you are university students (use **nosotros**);

4. Describe the information you gathered.

Use the template below and the answers to the questions in **Paso 1**. Use the verb **ser** (don't forget to conjugate it depending on the subject!). Use subject pronouns (e.g., **yo**, **tú**, etc.) when appropriate. Also, connect your ideas with **y** (*and*), **o** (*or*), **también** (*also*), **además** (*also*), and **pero** (*but*).

> **Texto modelo:**
> Estimada Mariana:
> [Greeting]. Mi nombre [ser] [Nombre] y mi nombre [ser] [Nombre]… En nuestra universidad, hay… en una clase típica. Las clases [ser] [number] o [number] días por semana… etc.
> ¡Hasta luego!
> [Nombre] y [Nombre]

Paso 3. Listen to your classmates' emails. Do they have the same information as you and your partner? Does the class agree? Do you all know the university well?

 **Actividad 0-10. Nuestro estado/ciudad/región**

Paso 1. In this activity, you and three/four other students are going to create a digital, multimodal (text + images) poster similar to the one on Texas (**Tejas en números**). You can focus on your state, if you are not in Texas, or your city/region. You need to include **8 pieces of information** with **different numbers** and **a title**. You can focus on Native American nations, languages, history, foods, universities, national parks, musicians, artists, etc. Use the Texas poster as your model.

To develop your poster, you can use free templates in platforms such as Canva (https://www.canva.com/) or Visme (http://bit.ly/VismeTool). Your images need to be open (i.e., copyright free). You can find this type of images using the search engine offered by Creative Commons (https://search.creativecommons.org/). Also, you need to provide attributions for all of them. To learn more about Creative Commons licenses and how to cite the open materials you find, see https://creativecommons.org/licenses/ and http://bit.ly/CreativeCommonsAttr.

Paso 2. Each group presents their poster in class. Each group member introduces themselves in Spanish (name, where they are from), and the group explains their choices.
What are some of the aspects of your state/city/region you did not know? Based on the team's work, each team member will need to find an adjective in Spanish that describes the state/city/region on which you focused.

 **Práctica individual:** To practice your new vocabulary and structures, go to http://bit.ly/PracticaIndividual04.

Hablemos de gramática: *Question Words*

Carolina es una estudiante universitaria. She is talking to some of her fellow students. What is she asking? Pay attention to the answers to see if you can discover what each question word she uses means. What do you notice about question words in Spanish?

 ¡Los estudiantes preguntan (*ask questions*)!

Video link: http://bit.ly/Video02_Trayectos.

Carolina:	¡Los estudiantes preguntan! ¿**Quiénes** son?
Los estudiantes:	¡Somos estudiantes!
Carolina:	¿**Cuántas** personas hay en tu clase de español?

Attribution: By Trayectos Creative Team, licensed under CC BY-SA 4.0.

Estudiante 1:	Hay trece personas en mi clase de español.
Carolina:	¿**Cuántas** clases estás tomando?
Estudiante 2:	Estoy tomando cinco y tres son de español.
Carolina:	¿**Quién** es tu profesor de español?
Estudiante 3:	La Doctora Moyna. Es una de mis favoritas.
Carolina:	¿**Cómo** es tu clase de español?
Estudiante 4:	Mi clase de español es muy interesante y aprendemos mucho de la cultura española.
Carolina:	¡Muchas gracias!

Did you discover what each question word means? Question words in Spanish and English work in similar ways, but there are also differences. Have you noticed any differences? Let's see…

Question words that work in similar ways in both languages	Examples
¿**Cómo?** *How? / What (to be) like?*	¿**Cómo** estás? (*How are you?*) ¿**Cómo** es tu clase de español? (*What is your Spanish class like?*)
¿**Cuándo?** *When?*	¿**Cuándo** es tu clase de español? (*When is your Spanish class?*)
¿**De dónde?** *From where?*	¿**De dónde** eres? (*Where are you from?*)
¿**Dónde?** *Where?*	¿**Dónde** es la clase de español? (*Where is the Spanish class?*)
¿**Por qué?** *Why?*	¿**Por qué** es interesante la clase? (*Why is the class interesting?*)

As you can see, like in English, these words are always placed at the beginning of the question, and they never change, regardless of the noun or verb that follows them.

Question words that are different in Spanish	Examples
¿Cuánto? (masc.) / **¿Cuánta?** (fem.) *How much?*	**¿Cuánto** jug**o** hay? (*How much juice is there?*) **¿Cuánta** harin**a** hay? (*How much flour is there?*)
¿Cuántos? (masc.) / **¿Cuántas?** (fem.) *How many?*	**¿Cuántos** hombres hay en la clase? (*How many men are there in the class?*) **¿Cuántas** profesor**as** hay en el departamento? (*How many female professors are there in the department?*)
¿Quién? (sing.) *Who?*	**¿Quién es** tu instructor de español? (*Who is your Spanish instructor?*)
¿Quiénes? (plural) *Who?*	**¿Quiénes son** tus amigos? (*Who are your friends?*)
¿Cuál? (sing.) *Which?*	**¿Cuál** es tu clase favorita? (*Which is your favorite class?*)
¿Cuáles? (plural) *Which?*	**¿Cuáles** son tus clases favoritas? (*Which are your favorite classes?*)

As you can see, most of these question words change their ending depending on the gender and number of the noun that follows them.

 ¡Ojo! (*Pay attention!*)

1. **Quién** and **cuál**, which ***are always followed by a verb***, only change their ending for number. ***These two question words can never be followed by a noun***.
2. Notice that questions in Spanish always start with an obligatory inverted question mark [¿]. Also, ***all*** Spanish question words (when used in a question) ***always have accents***.

 **¡Manos a la obra!**

 **Actividad 0-11. Las preguntas de Mariana**

Remember Mariana, the international student you wrote to in **Actividad 0-9** (p. 16)? She has replied to your message, and she has some questions. What is she asking? Fill in the blanks with the appropriate question words depending on the context.

Hola, Chicos. ¡Muchas gracias por el mensaje! Su español es fenomenal. 1. ¿_____ están? Yo estoy muy bien.

Tengo (*I have*) unas preguntas para ustedes. 2. ¿_____ son los profesores en la universidad? ¿Son serios? ¿Son difíciles?

3. ¿_____ libros (*books*) hay para la clase de Biología 101? ¿Uno? ¿Dos?

Y 4. ¿_____ son los partidos (*matches*) de fútbol americano? ¿Son todos (*all*) en el estadio de la universidad?

5. ¿_____ son los exámenes finales? ¿En diciembre?

6. ¿_____ es una ciudad interesante en Tejas? ¿Austin? ¿Houston?

7. ¿_____ es José Antonio Navarro? ¿Es un profesor?

8. ¿_____ son la mayoría de los estudiantes de la universidad? ¿De Tejas?

¡Muchas gracias por la información! Saludos, Mariana

 **Actividad 0-12. Una invitación**

Your Spanish-speaking friend asks you some questions about an invitation to a wedding (**una boda**) you have received. What is she asking? Using the information in the following invitation and the answers provided, ask appropriate questions. Remember to use the conjugated forms of the verb **ser** (pp. 5-6) and the verb **hay** (p. 14).

Useful words:

- **la boda** (*the wedding*)
- **los novios** (*bride and groom*)
- **invitados** (*guests*)
- **iglesia** (*church*)

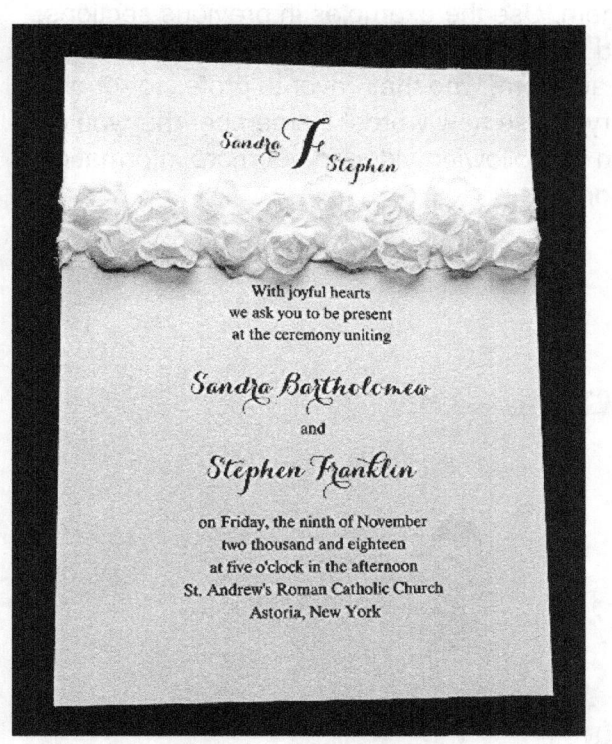

Attribution: By Michael LoCascio, licensed under CC BY-SA 4.0.

Amiga: 1. ¿_____ este sobre (*this envelope*)?

Tú: Es una invitación para una boda.

Amiga: 2. ¿ _____?

Tú: Los novios son mis amigos, Sandra y Stephen.

Amiga: 3. ¿Sandra y Stephen? ¿_____?

Tú: Son de New York

Amiga: Sí, ahora recuerdo… (*now I remember*) Tus amigos de la escuela secundaria (*high school*). 4. Y ¿_____?

Tú: La boda es el 9 de noviembre. Es una boda muy importante.

Amiga: 5. ¿_____?

Tú: Porque Sandra es mi mejor amiga (*my best friend*) de la escuela secundaria.

Amiga: Ah! 6. Y ¿_____?

Tú: La boda es en una iglesia en Astoria.

Amiga: 7. ¿_____?

Tú: La iglesia es St. Andrew's Roman Catholic Church.

Amiga: 8. ¿_____?

Tú: Hay 30 invitados en la boda. Es una boda íntima.

 **Actividad 0-13. Seguimos conociendo a nuestros compañeros de clase (*We continue getting to know our classmates*)**

Through this activity, you will continue to get to know your classmates. You need to work with two classmates you still do not know very well.

Paso 1. Think of six different questions you can ask them. Use the examples in previous sections, and the questions we have already practiced. You need to use the verbs **ser** and **hay**. For example, you can ask what their name is, of course; where they are from; who their favorite professor or class is; etc. But you can always be more adventurous and try to use new words! Remember that you can always ask your instructor for help! Also, you can watch the following video to get more information about ways in which you can get to know another person.

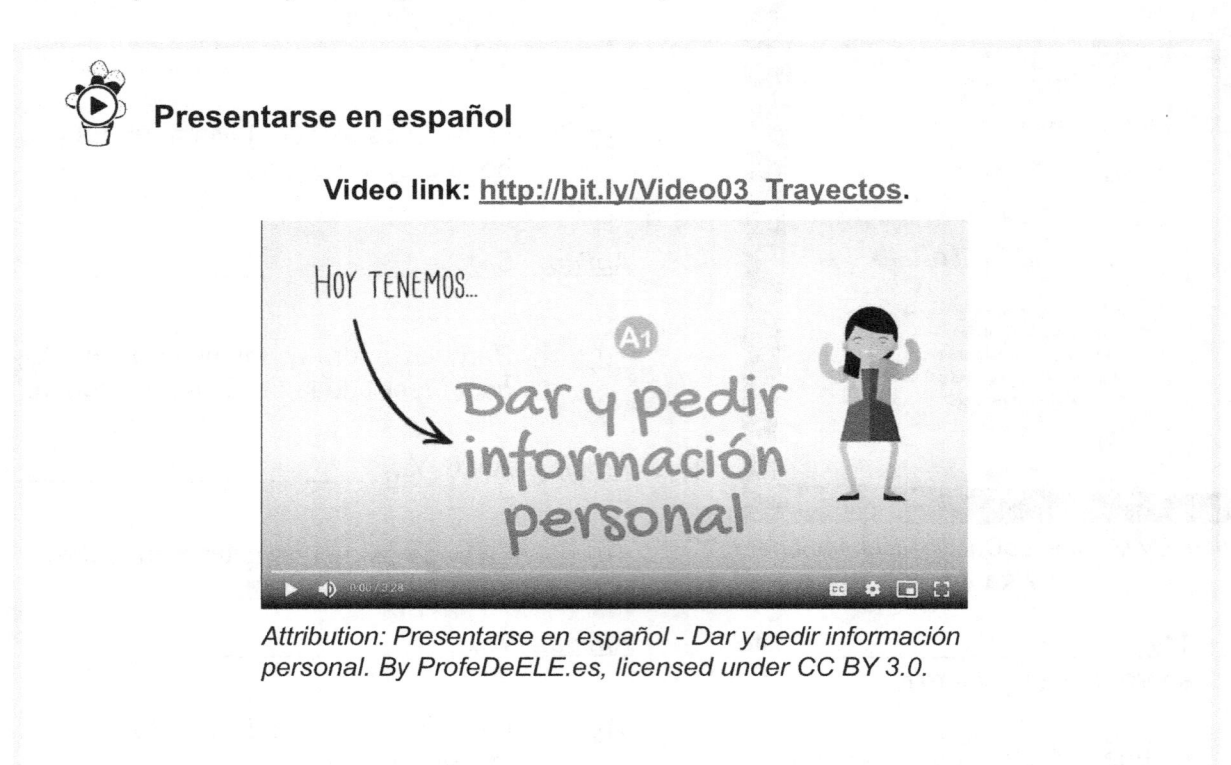

Presentarse en español

Video link: http://bit.ly/Video03_Trayectos.

Attribution: Presentarse en español - Dar y pedir información personal. By ProfeDeELE.es, licensed under CC BY 3.0.

Paso 2. Now interact with your two classmates and get to know them better! Take turns asking and answering one another's questions. Are you guys similar or different?

Práctica individual: To continue using question words, go to http://bit.ly/PracticaIndividual05.

El alfabeto español

In Spanish, there are twenty-seven letters in the alphabet (**el alfabeto** or **el abecedario**)—one more than in the English alphabet. The additional letter is **ñ**, which comes after **n** in alphabetized lists in Spanish. The letters **k** and **w** appear only in words borrowed from other languages. When you talk about letters in Spanish, you need to use the feminine gender (e.g., **la letra a, la b, la ele**, etc.).

 Have a look at the table below (you can listen to the audio files attached to each letter at http://bit.ly/Audio04Trayectos). For example, what difference do you notice in the pronunciation of the letter u? What do you notice about the pronunciation of the other vowels?

Letters	Names of Letters	Examples		
a	a	armadillo	Álamo	San Antonio
b	be, be larga	bota	burro	bailar
c	ce	caballo	cactus	casería
d	de	Dallas	Río Grande	disparo
e	e	extenso	explorar	Eldorado
f	efe	fábrica	flor	familia
g	ge	generoso	gente	General Santa Ana
h	hache	heno	huerto	cohete
i	i	iguana	independencia	Irene
j	jota	jaripeo	jinete	jornalero
k	ca (ka)	bikini	Karina	kilo
l	ele	Libélula	Laredo	libreta
m	eme	margarita	campesino	maestro
n	ene	Nevada	Natalia	Navarro
ñ	eñe	niño	ñandú	español
o	o	Odesa	petróleo	rodeo
p	pe	El Paso	pescador	patriota
q	cu	queso	Raquel	Quemado
r	erre	barril	becerro	corral
s	ese	Sarita	Salado	San Benito
t	te	Tejas	taco	tornado
u	u	Uvalde	único	universidad
v	uve, ve, *or* ve corta	vaca	vaquero	venado
w	uve doble, doble ve, *or* ve doble	Wildorado	Weslaco	kiwi
x	equis	anexar	xilofón	Extremadura
y	i griega *or* ye	yegua	Yucatán	yacaré
z	zeta	zoológico	zacate	corazón

More information on the pronunciation of Spanish letters

Most letters in Spanish have only one pronunciation, and thus, spelling can be said to be easier in Spanish than in English. However, there are some exceptions:

- When **c** appears before **a**, **o**, **u** and the consonants **l** and **r**, it sounds like /k/ (e.g., **carismáti-co**, **Costa Rica**, **cultura**, **clima**, **crema**). When **c** is followed by **e** or **i**, it sounds like /s/ (e.g., **centro**, **emocional**) in Latin America, but like /th/ in some parts of Spain. When **c** is followed by **h**, it is pronounced like the **ch** in *cheese* (e.g., **China**).

- When **g** appears before **a**, **o**, **u** and the consonants **l** and **r**, it sounds like an English hard /g/ (e.g., **arrogante**, **amigo**, **gusto**, **globo**, **gracias**). When **g** is followed by **e** or **i**, it sounds like the English /h/ (e.g., **generoso**, **ágil**). However, if a **u** is between **g** and **e** or **i**, **g** is pronounced like a hard /g/, and the **u** is NOT pronounced (e.g., **guía**, **espagueti**). Sometimes, in the combinations **gue** and **gui**, the **u** is pronounced if it is marked with a **diéresis** (the two dots above the **ü**). In these cases, the **g** in combination with the **u** is pronounced /w/. Examples: **bilingüe**, **lingüística**.

- Double **l** (**ll**) is pronounced like English /y/ in *yes*. In some parts of Argentina and Uruguay, this sound is pronounced like /sh/ (e.g., me **llamo**).

- **Q** can only be found in the combinations **que** and **qui**. In these cases, the **u** is silent, and the **q** is pronounced /k/ (e.g., ¿**qué**?, **quinto** [*fifth*]). **Q** *cannot* be followed by **a**, **o**, or **u** (unless **u** is followed by **e** or **i**).

- When **r** is at the beginning or in the middle of a word and appears as a double **r** (**rr**), it is pronounced like a rolling **r** (e.g., **Río Grande, Rosa, guitarra**).

 **¡Manos a la obra!**

 **Actividad 0-14. La reserva (*The reservation*)**

One of the most common situations when spelling comes in handy is when we make a reservation by phone (e.g., a restaurant, a room, etc.), and we have to spell our name. Imagine that you are in this situation with a Spanish-speaking employee (**empleado**). The employee is asking you to spell your full name. Can you do it? Interact with a classmate, and exchange roles.

Modelo(s):	**E1 (empleado):** Perfecto. Para continuar la reserva, necesito (*I need*) su nombre. ¿Cómo se llama?
	E2 (estudiante): Me llamo / Mi nombre es Sam Heughan.
	E1 (empleado): ¿Cómo se escribe? (*How do you spell/write it?*)
	E2 (estudiante): Ese-a-eme [espacio (*space*)] hache-e-u-ge-hache-a-ene

 **Actividad 0-15. La Tejas hispana**

Paso 1. One of the unique aspects of Texas is its Hispanic present and past. Many different places have Spanish names, and have played a role in the history of the state. The same can be said about the Hispanic community. Have a look at the following names. Do you know where they are/who they are? What is their connection to the state's past and present? Spell these names aloud in Spanish, and google them to answer these questions. Work with two classmates. Your instructor can help you!

1. San Antonio de Valero
2. Misión San José
3. Rancho de las Cabras
4. José María de León Hernández ("Little Joe")
5. Antonio Gil Ibarvo
6. El Camino Real
7. El Paseo de Santa Ángela
8. Casa Navarro
9. Misión del Espíritu Santo
10. Segundo Barrio

Paso 2. What other names do you guys know? Find five more Spanish names that are important in Texas or your state's past/present. Spell the names and be ready to tell the class more about the names you've found.

 **Práctica individual:** To continue applying what you learned about the alphabet, go to http://bit.ly/PracticaIndividual06.

Hablemos de cultura: *El español y sus protagonistas*

 **The Spanish-Speaking World: Unity in Diversity**

The beauty of Spanish lies in both its human and linguistic diversity. The Spanish-speaking world is made up of people belonging to different races and ethnicities, who share cultural, linguistic, and historical ties. Our world would not be the same without the rich contributions of our many diverse and unique flavors: our colors, our dialects, our cultures. Also, our language is in contact with other languages, which have left their indelible mark in our world. So who are we? Let's see…

Attribution: By Administración Nacional de la Seguridad Social, Argentina, licensed under CC BY-SA 2.0.

 ## Hispanic, Latin American, Latina/o, Latino@, Latinx...[1]

Latin America has a rich and diverse history of indigenous cultures, European colonization, African slavery, and global immigration that makes it complex and difficult to describe its people with a single ethnic category or identifier (https://bit.ly/Video04_Trayectos). People in the US who have origins in a Latin American country occasionally self-identify or are referred to as Latin American, but many prefer the term Latino/a (for Latino, masculine, or Latina, feminine). However, some people (including us!) prefer to use the more gender-inclusive term **Latinx.**

What's the difference between Hispanic and Latino/a/Latinx? Primarily, the reference to Spain. Hispanic refers to *linguistic* origins from a Spanish-speaking country, in particular Spain. **Latino/a/Latinx** refers to people living in the USA who have *ethnic* and *cultural* origins from a country in Latin America.

Hispanic, Latin American, Latino/a, and Latinx are not considered racial terms or descriptors of race; these terms are used only to describe ethnic and cultural origins. For example, these umbrella terms encompass **indigenous Latinx**, **Afro-Hispanics** (or **Afro-descendants**), **Asian Latin Americans**, and **white Latinx**.

Some individuals, however, choose not to self-identify by any of these terms and prefer to use other descriptors that more appropriately represent their personal identity. For some, the terms **Tejano/a** (Latinx or Hispanic from Texas), **Boricua** (of Puerto Rican descent), **Chicanx** (of Mexican Descent), **Bicho/a** (of Salvadoran descent), **Blaxican** (of Black and Mexican descent), or **Afro-Latinx** (of Black descent) better describe who they are.

---

1 *Attribution: Text adapted from An Overview of Latino and Latin American Identity. By Emma Turner-Trujillo, Marisa del Toro, and April Ramos, licensed under CC BY 4.0. Original text available at https://blogs.getty.edu/iris/an-overview-of-latino-and-latin-american-identity/.*

Tu turno (*your turn*)

1. Focus on your university community. Interview classmates or friends of Hispanic or Latin American heritage. Ask them how they identify themselves, and why they have chosen to do so. Get to know more about their families' experiences.

2. Find examples of cultural contributions (e.g., art, music, etc.) from Latinx artists in this country. How do these artists identify themselves? How is their identity reflected in their work?

 **African Diasporas in Latin America**

The African diaspora in Brazil and throughout the Americas is one of the "five great African diasporas" connected to the transatlantic slave trade. From the fifteenth to the nineteenth centuries, Africans—primarily from the central and western parts of Africa—were captured, traded, and sold into slavery and brought to the New World as forced labor for the Portuguese, the British, the French, the Spanish, and the Dutch trading nations.

There is and was a broad diversity of black experience in the Americas. According to data by the Pew Research Center, about 130 million people of African descent live in Latin America. Currently, Brazil has the largest African diasporic community in Latin America, and the world. Numerous other countries and communities throughout Latin America have deep African roots, including Bolivia, Peru, Colombia, Venezuela, Panama, Dominican Republic, Cuba, and Mexico. We will explore some of these communities in *Trayectos*.

Attribution: By geya garcia, licensed under CC BY 2.0.

The presence of African heritage in Latin American culture is visible in the arts and music of many regions. For instance, *reggaetón* was invented by black Panamanians in the 1980s, inspired by black Jamaican dancehall music by way of Puerto Rico. However, Afro-Latin-American and Afro-Latinx identity has not always been visible or respected in mainstream Latin American and US culture.

Only in 2015, for example, did Mexico begin to count individuals of African descent in their own separate category, as black or Afro-Mexican, for their general census. This 2015 census showed that 1,381,853 individuals identify as being of African descent, representing
1.2% of Mexico's population. Currently, there is a movement of individuals creating communities, festivals, and literature to address their Afro-Latinx identity and culture.

 Tu turno

We invite you to discover the wonderful piece "Poem for My Grifa-Rican Sistah Or Broken Ends Broken Promises" (https://bit.ly/MariposaPoem) by Afro-Latina **Mariposa (María Teresa Fernandez; http://bit.ly/MariposaPoeta)**. What is the topic of the poem? What feelings is Mariposa expressing? How are they related to her Afro-Latina identity? Do you identify with them? You can also watch the poet in the following video:

Video link: http://bit.ly/Video05_Trayectos
Attribution: By afrolatin@ forum, licensed under CC BY-SA.

 **East Asian Diasporas in Latin America**

There are 6,000 Chinese restaurants (called **chifas**) in Peru. Havana is home to one of the oldest Chinatowns in Latin America. Almost 1% of the population of Latin America, over four million people, is of Asian descent. Yet the history of this East Asian diaspora is not well known outside of Latin America.

The so-called "abolition" of the transatlantic African slave trade in 1807 created a vacuum in the free labor force, leading the Portuguese, Spanish, and British Empires to seek new low-wage laborers in East and South Asia. Citizens of these nations were kidnapped, deceived, or sold into indentured servitude, which was equal to slavery in all regards except in name. Laborers from East and South Asia were dispersed throughout Latin America. Laborers of East Asian descent were primarily sent to the Caribbean and Latin America to work on sugar cane, cotton, and coffee plantations, alongside an existing population of African slaves. In Peru, Chinese laborers were integral to the construction of the Andean railroad and worked in the silver mines.

In the early twentieth century, Havana had one of the largest and most vibrant Chinese communities in Latin America. Chinese indentured laborers were brought to work in the sugar and tobacco fields alongside the existing population of African indentured laborers. Chinese laborers fought in Cuba's Ten Years' War (1868–78) and were essential in the battle for independence from Spanish rule. Today there are fewer than 150 native Chinese people still living in Cuba, but their traditions still live on. Traditional Chinese opera is still performed, and a reed instrument originating from China, called the **corneta china** in Cuba, remains a staple of Cuban music.

Many of the diasporic populations of both African and Asian descent in Latin America have embraced their dual heritages. Despite the persistence of racism, systemic discrimination, and forced assimilation, many of the Afro and Asian Latinx communities within and outside Latin America continue to celebrate and discover their multilayered heritages.

 Tu turno

One of the most important figures in the Asian-Latinx community is Dr. Franklin Chang-Diaz. Who is he? Google his name, and find information about his work. In what area was he a pioneer?

We hope this overview has given you a better idea of the immense diversity of the Spanish-speaking world. There's much more to learn, and we'll do so throughout our **trayecto**.

Más comunicación: *Las expresiones de la clase*

One of the keys to succeed as a language learner is to actively use the language you are learning as much as you can. A good beginning are classroom expressions. Let's learn some common classroom phrases that will help you understand and speak Spanish.

 **Audio link: http://bit.ly/Audio05Trayectos**

1. Abran los libros en la página 8, por favor (please).

2. Levanten la mano, por favor.

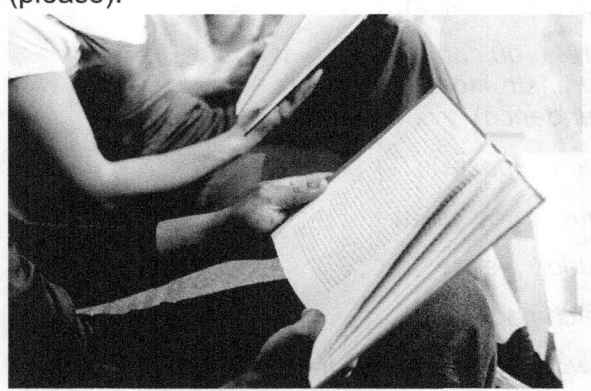

Attribution: Public domain

Attribution: By HBS1908, licensed under CC BY-SA 3.0.

3. Escuchen, por favor.

Attribution: By Tulane Public Relations (Student in Class; Uploaded by AlbertHerring), licensed under CC BY 2.0

4. Escriban, por favor.

Attribution: Public domain

Más expresiones de la clase: El instructor / La instructor	
Cierren los libros.	*Please close your books.*
Repitan, por favor.	*Please repeat.*
Lean, por favor.	*Please read.*
¿Comprenden?	*Do you guys understand?*
Contesta, por favor	*Please answer.*
¿Tienen preguntas?	*Do you guys have questions?*
De tarea…	*For homework…*

Más expresiones de la clase: Los estudiantes	
Sí, comprendo. / No, no comprendo. No entiendo.	*Yes, I understand. / No, I don't understand. I don't understand.*
Tengo una pregunta…	*I have a question…*
Presente	*Here! (you can say this when your instructor is checking attendance)*
Otra vez, por favor.	*Again, please.*
Más despacio, por favor.	*More slowly, please.*
Más alto, por favor.	*Louder, please.*
¿Qué página?	*Which page?*
¿Cómo se dice "pen" en español?	*How do you say "pen" in Spanish?*
¿Cómo se escribe "libro"?	*How do you spell "libro"?*
Lo siento, no sé.	*I'm sorry, but I don't know.*

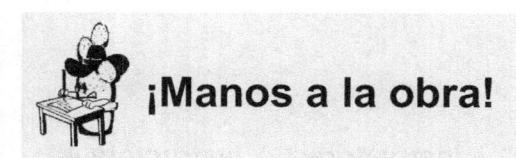

¡Manos a la obra!

 **Actividad 0-16. En la clase de español**

Paso 1. Practica estas expresiones con un compañero/compañera. What could you or your instructor say in the following situations? Choose one or more appropriate expressions.

1. You cannot understand what your instructor is saying because she's speaking Spanish too fast.
2. Your instructor wants the class to listen to her.
3. The class has just started, and your instructor is checking who is in class. She calls your name.
4. Your instructor has just played an audio, and it's hard for you to understand the speakers.
5. You don't know how to spell "carismático."
6. You didn't hear on what page an activity in the book is.
7. You can't hear what your classmate is saying.
8. Your classmate has asked you a question, but you don't know the answer.
9. Your instructor wants the class to read something.
10. The class is almost over, and your instructor is assigning homework.
11. You would like to know how to say "dorm" in Spanish.
12. You have a question.

Paso 2. Are there any other expressions you and your classmate would like to know? Write two or three expressions and ask your instructor how to say them. Remember to use the Spanish question we just learned to do it!

 **Práctica individual:** To continue practicing your new classroom expressions, go to http://bit.ly/PracticaIndividual07.

Para terminar... ¡A escuchar!

Los hispanos hablan

One of the most interesting aspects of Spanish is its variety of dialects and accents. Even though the language is the same, people from, for example, Argentina sound very different from people from Mexico, or Spain, or the Spanish speakers in Texas. Throughout the textbook, we will include audio and video clips featuring speakers with different accents. This is your first exposure to four different varieties. Let's see how much you can understand. Don't worry: The speakers will be using the same words and structures you have learned in this module. These four speakers are Spanish instructors at a university in Texas. Listen to what they say, and fill in the table below with information you hear.

 **Audio link:** http://bit.ly/Audio06Trayectos

Instructor/Instructora	*Instructora* 1	Instructor 2	Instructora 3	Instructora 4
¿Cómo se llama?				
¿De dónde es?				
¿Cuál es su lugar favorito en el campus?				
¿Cuántos días tiene (*has*) clases?				
¿Cuántas clases tiene (*has*)?				
¿Cuántos estudiantes hay en su clase?				

Para terminar... *Lectura*

I. Antes de leer (*Before you read*)

How do people greet each other in the US? Are there different ways of greeting people? Do people ever kiss when they greet? Write a couple of ideas.

II. A leer (*Let's read*)

This is your first reading in Spanish. Don't be afraid: The text talks about different kinds of greetings, and it is short! Rely on cognates and the images provided to read it. Have a look at the information presented. ¿Son los saludos en América Latina similares a los Estados Unidos? ¿Son los saludos similares en América Latina y en España?

 **Los saludos en el mundo (*world*)[2]**

El saludo es una forma de comunicación, de introducir a una persona con otra (*another*).

---

2 *Attribution: Text modified from https://www.protocolo.org/social/presentar-saludar/el-saludo-en-los-distintos-paises-del-mundo-besos-abrazos-dar-la-mano-.html, licensed under CC BY-SA 4.0. Attribution for photos: [1] Licensed under public domain. [2] By Lowndes [Public domain], from Wikimedia Commons. [3] By Steven Depolo, licensed under CC BY 2.0.*

El saludo más común en todo el mundo es el **apretón de manos**.  [1].

Saludar y dar la mano es mundialmente aceptado. En los Estados Unidos y Canadá, el saludo más usado es el **apretón de manos**, a nivel social y laboral.

A nivel familiar, se puede (*can*) usar **el beso**  [2] como forma de saludo, para su pareja (*your partner*) o cónyuge (*spouse*) y la familia.

Entre amigos (*friends*) es común **el abrazo** . [3]

En América del Sur, predomina el carácter latino y social del saludo, y **los besos** en una mejilla (*on one cheek*) son los saludos más comunes, incluso entre (*even among*) los hombres (*men*), entre amigos y familia.

En los contextos formales, es común **el apretón de manos**. En España, **los besos** son muy habituales en los saludos, no solo (*only*) en el contexto social o familiar, sino que también (*but also*) en el laboral. Por ejemplo, no es difícil ver (*to see*) a la Reina (*queen*) de España dando (*giving*) dos besos a una persona que ha obtenido una medalla (*has been awarded a medal*). **Los dos besos** (un beso en cada [*each*] mejilla) son la norma.

III. Después de leer (*After you have read*)

Actividad A. ¿Son los saludos en América Latina similares a los Estados Unidos? ¿Son los saludos similares en América Latina y España? ¿Cuáles son las similitudes y diferencias entre los Estados Unidos y el mundo hispano? You can answer these questions in English.

Actividad B. What is the main idea of this text? What kind of information is the author conveying? Why is it important to know this information?

Actividad C. Why do you think the writer decided to include the example of the Queen of Spain? What idea are they trying to convey?

Actividad D. Read the text again and find five cognates. What new words have you learned?

Para terminar... ¡Conversemos!

Attribution: By Mosborne01, licensed under CC BY-SA 2.0.

Paso 1. Now think about everything you have learned about greetings and introductions in this module and through this text. With one or two classmates, summarize the information you could give someone who is interested in knowing what to do in formal and informal situations in a Spanish-speaking country. Use the following table.

	América Latina		España	
	Situación formal	**Situación informal**	**Situación formal**	**Situación informal**
Saludo verbal	*Buenos días,…*			
Saludo no verbal	*Apretón de manos*			
Pronombre de sujeto (singular y plural)				
Presentaciones (*Introductions*)				

Paso 2. Create a formal or informal situation with your partners. Use the verbal and non verbal forms of communication you included in your table in **Paso 1**. You will present your skit to the rest of the class. Include the following:

1. Greeting
2. Introductions
3. One or two questions to get to know the other person.

Antes de partir...

¡Misión cumplida!

We have reached the end of Módulo introductorio. Go back to the first page of this module, and review what you have accomplished. Check the outcomes you have achieved. What are you proud of? What aspects of your Spanish would you like to improve? ¡Buen trabajo!

Summary of Contents

Comunicación

- Introducción comunicativa (pg. 2)
- Hablemos más (pg. 4)
- Los números del 0-30 (pg. 14)
- El alfabeto español (pg. 23)
- Las expresiones de la clase (pg. 30)

Otras palabras útiles (Other useful words)

- **sí/no**   *yes/no*
- **hoy/mañana**   *today/tomorrow*
- **y/o**   *and/or*
- **de**   *of; from*
- **en**   *in; on; at*
- **pero**   *but*
- **también**   *also*
- **además**   *also*
- **la palabra**   *word*
- **los días**   *days (of the week)*
- **los cognados**   *cognates*

Lengua

- Los verbos

  - **Ser**   *to be*
  - **Hay**   *there is/there are*
  - **No hay**   *there isn't/there aren't*

- Los pronombres personales (pg. 9)

- Las palabras interrogativas
  - **¿Cómo?** *How?*
  - **¿Dónde?** *Where?*
  - **¿De dónde?** *Where from?*
  - **¿Cuándo?** *When?*
  - **¿Por qué?** *Why?*
  - **¿Qué?** *What?*
  - **¿Cuál(es)?** *Which?*
  - **¿Quién(es)?** *Who?*
  - **¿Cuánto(a)?** *How much?*
  - **¿Cuántos(as)?** *How many?*

Cultura
- El español y sus protagonistas (pg. 26)

Mis palabras

In your Spanish notebook, write down other words and phrases you learned in this module.

Módulo 1: Somos estudiantes universitarios

En este módulo, vamos a hablar (*talk*) de las clases, los estudiantes universitarios y la universidad.

Antes de comenzar: ¿Es tu universidad una institución importante? ¿Cómo son las clases? ¿Hay tradiciones? ¿Cuál es tu tradición favorita? You can answer these questions in English, but try to use some of the Spanish you already know! Remember los cognados!

Attribution: By Mariana Salazar, licensed under CC BY-SA 4.0.

Objetivos en este módulo

Comunicación

In this instructional module, you will learn how to…

- Talk about your life as a university student: Classes, activities, people in your life
- Tell time
- Talk about when your classes and other activities take place (time and days)

Lengua

- Indefinite and definite articles
- Nouns: Gender and number
- The present tense of regular *-ar* verbs

Cultura

- México: San Miguel de Allende
Trayectos hispanos: Educadores

Mis metas

In your Spanish notebook, describe what you want to accomplish in this instructional module in personal terms.

Introducción comunicativa: *Compañeras de cuarto*

Carolina es una estudiante de México. Es su primer (*first*) semestre en una universidad de Tejas. Bailey, su nueva compañera de cuarto, la espera (*is waiting for her*) en el aeropuerto. Escucha (*listen to*) el diálogo y responde estas preguntas: ¿qué estudian Carolina y Bailey en la universidad? Usa el vocabulario en **Hablemos más** (pg. 40) para ayudarte (*help you*).

Audio link: http://bit.ly/Audio1-1Trayectos

Attribution: Public domain

Bailey: ¡Hola! Soy Bailey, tu nueva compañera de cuarto… ¡Bienvenida a Tejas! ¿Cómo estás?

Carolina: ¡Hola, Bailey! Mucho gusto. Encantada de conocerte. (*She shakes hands with Bailey.*)

Bailey: Igualmente, Carolina… Yo soy de San Antonio. Y tú, ¿de dónde eres?

Carolina: Soy de Coahuila, México. ¿Qué estudi**as** aquí?

Bailey: Estudi**o geografía, literatura, historia** y **lingüística**. ¿Y tú?

Carolina: Dese**o** (*I want to*) estudiar **sicología, teatro, lingüística** y **literatura inglesa**.

Bailey: ¡Guau! Tú necesit**as** (*You need*) la **biblioteca** para estudiar mucho.

Carolina: ¡Sí! También yo necesit**o** ir a la **librería** de la universidad para comprar (*to buy*) mis (*my*) **libros, cuadernos**, un **diccionario** y cuatro **bolígrafos**.

Bailey: ¡Vamos! (*Let's go!*) Te llevo (*I'll take you to*) a la **librería** y también puedo mostrarte (*I can show you*) el campus y tu **salón de clase**. ¿Quién es tu **profesor** de **lingüística**?

Carolina: La doctora Moyna. ¿Tienes (*do you have*) clases con la doctora Moyna, también?

Bailey: ¡Sí! Sus clases me encantan (*I love her clases*). Para la clase de lingüística, nosotras necesit**amos** el libro "El español en los Estados Unidos".

Carolina: Perfecto. Bailey, ¿dónde está (*is*) la **cafetería**? ¡Tengo hambre! (*I'm hungry!*)

¿Comprendiste? Contesta (*answer*) las siguientes preguntas de comprensión.

1. ¿De dónde es Carolina?
2. ¿Las dos chicas tom**an** una clase juntas (*together*)? ¿Qué clase es? ¿Quién es la profesora?
3. ¿Qué útiles escolares (*school supplies*) necesit**a** Carolina?
4. ¿Qué lugar busc**a** Carolina?

Lengua

1. Look at the verb forms in the dialogue. Pay attention to the verbs **estudiar, desear, tomar,** and **necesitar**. Write down the different forms on the verb in the dialogue. Can you guess how we conjugate verbs that end in **-ar** in Spanish?
2. What subject pronouns (e.g., **yo**) do Carolina and Bailey use in this dialogue? Would you say this is an informal or formal conversation? Justify your answer.
3. Have a look at the title of the book Carolina and Bailey need for their linguistics class ("El español en los Estados Unidos"). What do you notice about the way titles are written in Spanish?

 **Práctica individual:** To practice your new vocabulary and expressions, go to http://bit.ly/PracticaIndividual1-1.

Hablemos más: *Las clases en la universidad*

¿Cómo son las diversas clases en la universidad? ¿Qué hay en las clases? Look at these photographs, and discover how many of these words you already know. Again, **los cognados** will help you! Click on the following link to listen to the words.

 **Audio link:** http://bit.ly/Audio1-2Trayectos

En el aula: La clase de español

Attribution: By Lead Beyond, licensed under CC BY 2.0.

En el salón de clase: La clase de sociología

Attribution: Public domain.

Los objetos de la clase

la pizarra/el pizarrón	*the blackboard*
el borrador	*the eraser (for the blacboard)*
la tiza	*chalk*
la tableta	*the tablet*
el libro (de texto)	*the book / the textbook*
el lápiz /los lápices	*the pencil / pencils*
la pluma	*the ink pen*
el reloj	*the clock*
la mochila	*the backpack*
la cola (de pegar)	*Elmer glue*
el pegamento	*the glue stick*

Las personas en la universidad

el bibliotecario	*the (male) librarian*
la bibliotecaria	*the (female) librarian*
el compañero (de clase)	*the (male) classmate*
la compañera (de clase)	*the (female) classmate*
el compañero de cuarto	*the (male) roommate*
la compañera de cuarto	*the (female) roommate*

el consejero	*the (male) advisor*
la consejera	*the (female) advisor*
el hombre	*the man*
la mujer	*the woman*
el novio	*boyfriend*
la novia	*girlfriend*

Los lugares (*places*) en la universidad

el salón de clase/ el aula	*the classroom*
la biblioteca	*the library*
el edificio	*the building*
la librería	*the bookstore*
la papelería	*A place where only school and office supplies are sold.*
la residencia	*the dormitory*
el baño	*the bathroom*
mi cuarto	*my room/ my bedroom*

Los cognados

These words are very similar in Spanish and English. What do they mean? Write the meaning in the right column.

En la clase	
la calculadora	
el marcador	
el examen	
la lección	
la actividad	
el ejercicio	
el diccionario	
el calendario	
el mapa	

Los lugares en la universidad

la cafetería	
el centro estudiantil	
el estadio	
el gimnasio	
el laboratorio	
la oficina	

Las clases y las especializaciones: Las lenguas extranjeras

el chino	
el francés	
el inglés	
el griego	
el italiano	
el portugués	
el ruso	

Otras clases y especializaciones

la antropología	
la arquitectura	
el arte	
la biología	
las ciencias biomédicas	
la ciencias políticas	
la comunicación	
la estadística	
la educación bilingüe	
la geografía	
la historia	

la ingeniería

la lingüística

la literatura

**las relaciones internac-
ionales**

la música

la sicología

el teatro

 ¡Ojo!

Words for classes or majors (e.g., **la sociología**, **la historia**, etc.) are not capitalized in Spanish.

 **¡Manos a la obra!**

 **Actividad 1-1. Las clases de verano (*summer*)**

En las universidades en los Estados Unidos, hay clases de verano. The same happens at universities in the Spanish-speaking world. But are the same classes offered? Watch the video on http://bit.ly/CursosTrayectos and answer the following questions.

1. ¿Cómo se llama la universidad?
2. ¿De dónde es la universidad?
3. ¿Cuándo son las clases? ¿En mayo, junio o julio?
4. ¿Dónde son? Nombra (*Name*) dos lugares.
5. ¿Qué clases hay en la universidad? Nombra dos clases.
6. ¿Cuántas clases de verano hay en la universidad?
7. ¿Son las clases similares a las clases en tu universidad?
8. ¿Cuáles son tus clases de verano?

 **Actividad 1-2. Las clases este semestre**

¿Y este semestre? ¿Qué clases hay? Visit the schedule of classes for this semester, and find examples of the following courses. Fill in the blanks with the information required in the table provided. Are any classes similar to the ones offered by the university we have just talked about? ¿Tomas alguna de (*any of*) las clases? ¿Cuál?

Clase	Nombre de la clase	Instructor/a	¿Cuántos estudiantes hay?	Edificio
Antropología				
Arte				
Comunicación				
Historia				
Relaciones internacionales				
Sicología				

 *Conversemos.* **Soy un/una estudiante nuevo/nueva (*new*)**

Paso 1. To do this activity, you will need a map of your campus (we recommend you use the one online). Prepare it before you start the activity.

Paso 2. With a classmate, prepare a conversation. You will need to use the verbs **ser** (p. 8) and **hay** (p. 14), and the vocabulary and structures you learned in **Módulo introductorio** and in this module. Include the following information:

Estudiante 1. You are a new student at the university, and you do not know where some of the buildings are located. You talk to a fellow student.

- Introduce yourself, and ask your classmate's name.
- Say where you are from, and that you are a new student (**un/una estudiante nuevo/a**).
- Ask where the following buildings are:
  - La biblioteca
  - La cafetería
  - El edificio de sicología
- (When your classmate gives you the information, react appropriately [e.g., say "thank you" or "oh, ok".)
- Answer your classmate's question, and ask where their (**tus**) classes are.
- Answer your classmate's question, and ask what their phone number (**tu número de teléfono**) is.
- Say thanks and goodbye.

Estudiante 2. You meet a new student on campus.

- Answer your classmate's question, and say where you are from. Ask your classmate where they are from.
- Answer your classmate's questions. On the digital map, show your classmate where the buildings they are asking about are.
- Ask your classmate what their (**tus**) classes are.
- Answer your classmate's question, and ask what their phone number (**tu número de teléfono**) is.

Answer your classmate's question, and say goodbye.

 **Práctica individual:** To practice your new vocabulary and expressions, go to http://bit.ly/PracticaIndividual1-2.

Hablemos de gramática: *Gender, Number, and Definite and Indefinite Articles*

Identifying People, Places, Things, and Ideas: La lista de Carolina

Carolina, the student we met in the first section of this module (p. 36), has made a list of the school supplies she needs some of her classes this semester. What does she need? Have a look at her list. ¿Es tu lista similar a la lista de Carolina?

En el **Módulo introductorio**, we learned the words for *one* or *a* (**un** or **una**). Have a look at Carolina's list. What do **el** and **la** mean? What is the difference between **un** and **el** and **una** and **la**?

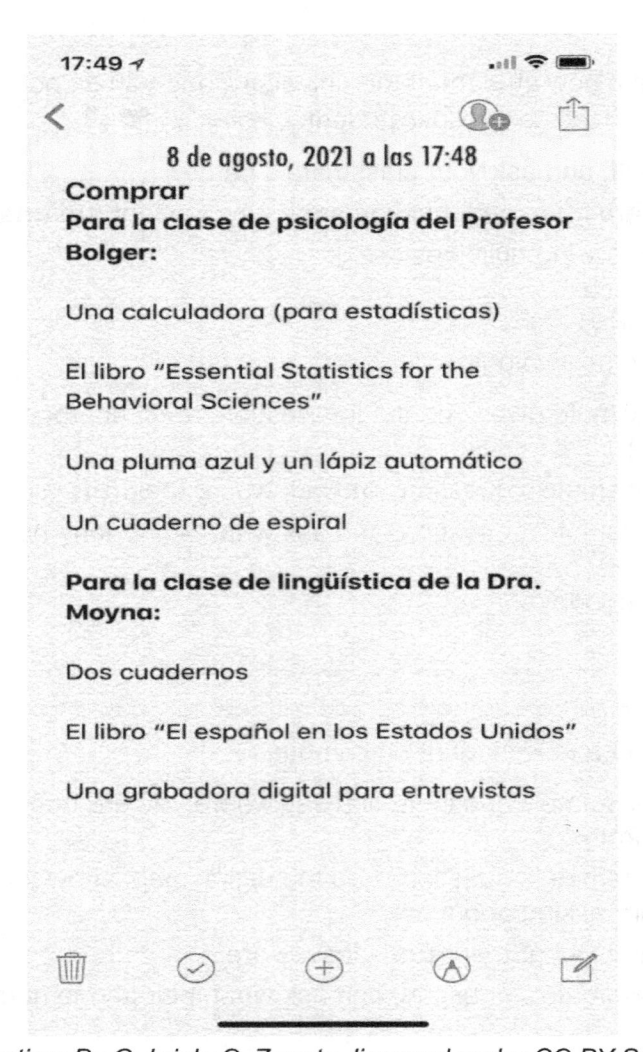

Attribution: By Gabriela C. Zapata, licensed under CC BY-SA 4.0.

¿Comprendiste? Responde las preguntas a continuación sobre la lista de Carolina.

1. ¿Es tu lista similar o diferente? ¿Por qué? ¿Qué útiles escolares hay en tu lista? Usa **un/una** and **el/la** to talk about your list.
2. ¿Quién es el profesor de la clase de sicología?
3. ¿Qué necesita Carolina para el curso de la Dra. Moyna?
4. ¿Qué compra (*buys*) Carolina para las entrevistas?
5. ¿Hay un libro en la clase de sicología? ¿Cuál es el nombre?

In **Módulo introductorio**, we saw that we use nouns (**los sustantivos**) to talk about people, animals, places, things, and ideas, and we learned that **los sustantivos** have gender (**género--femenino o masculino**). Of course, this does not mean that Spanish speakers believe that all things have gender. In Spanish, gender is a grammatical feature. Sometimes, the ending in a noun can tell you if it has feminine or masculine gender. For example, most nouns ending in **-a** are feminine, and most nouns ending in **-o** are masculine. When a noun is accompanied by an indefinite article (**un** *o* **una**) or by a definite article (**el** *o* **la**), the article will match the gender of the noun. Have a look at these examples.

	Masculine Nouns		**Feminine Nouns**	
Definite Articles	**el niño**	the boy	**la niña**	the girl
	el escritorio	the desk	**la puerta**	the door
Indefinite Articles	**un niño**	a (one) boy	**una niña**	a (one) girl
	un escritorio	a (one) desk	**una puerta**	a (one) door

Unfortunately, with some endings, it is difficult to determine gender (e.g., those that end in a consonant, such as **lápiz**, which is masculine, or in other vowels, such as **clase**, which is feminine). Therefore, we recommend that when you learn a new word, you also learn the definite article that accompanies it. That way, you will remember the gender of the noun, and it will also be easy to figure out what the indefinite articles is when you need it. Here are other rules that might help you determine the gender of some nouns.

1. Nouns that that end in **-ión, -tad,** and **-dad**, or end in other consonants and refer to beings with female attributes are *feminine* in gender.

> **Modelo(s):** la mujer, la canción (*the song*), la amistad (*friendship*), la ciudad (*the city*).

2. Many nouns that end in **-ta** or **-ma** are masculine.

> **Modelo(s):** el cometa, el planeta, el tema (*the theme, the topic*), el poema.

3. Some nouns that refer to people have a single form; therefore, they can be both masculine and feminine, and gender is indicated by the article chosen to refer to them. You already know one of these nouns, **estudiante** (**el/la estudiante**).

> **Modelo(s):** el/la paciente (*the patient*), el/la dentista, el/la periodista.
> (*the journalist/reporter*)

 ¡Ojo!

There are some words that do not follow the rules discussed above, and thus, you need to follow our recommendation: **Learn the word and the article to remember their gender**. Some of the words in this category are: **La mente** (*the mind*), **la gente** (*[the] people*), **la clase**, **el mapa**, **el día**, **la mano** (*the hand*), **el agua** (*water*). The following video summarizes the information discussed in this section.

Attribution: Género masculino y femenino en español.
By ProfeDeELE.es, licensed under CC BY 3.0.

Video link: http://bit.ly/Video1-1Trayectos

¿Y el plural? What happens if we need to talk about people, things, places, etc. in the *plural*? Well, it is quite easy.

1. If we need an article to refer to them, we need to transform the singular form of the indefinite **(un --> unos; una --> unas)** or the definite **(el --> los; la --> las)** articles into the plural.

2. We need to use the plural form of the noun. As in English, when a noun ends in a vowel, to make the plural form, you only need to add **-s** to the singular noun (e.g., **un/el libro --> unos/ los libros**). If a noun ends in a consonant, you need to add **-es** (e.g., **una/la universidad --> unas/las universidades**).

 Nota importante: Inclusive Spanish

In recent years, there has been a movement to make Spanish more inclusive in terms of gender. To learn more about this important issue, we recommend the following resources:
- *A Language for All*: Article in the Washington Post (https://wapo.st/3dNLqlg)
- *A New Effort In Argentina Seeks To Make Spanish Nouns Gender Neutral*: Report on NPR (https://n.pr/3EX6sjJ).
- En español y en inglés: Información sobre el lenguaje inclusivo (https://spark.adobe.com/page/uFztHGXOMt2tL/#page-content-lenguaje-inclusivo-inclusive-language)

En español:
- *Una guía para entender cómo el lenguaje inclusivo evolucionó alrededor del mundo*: Artículo del diario argentino "La Nación" (http://bit.ly/LenguajeInclusivoEsp)
- Video sobre el tema: http://bit.ly/LenguajeInclusivoVideo

¡Manos a la obra!

 **Actividad 1-3. Snapchat en universidad**

¡La vida (*life*) en la universidad es muy interesante! ¿O no?

Paso 1. With three or four classmates, look at the Snap photos below, and describe what you see in them in as much detail as possible. Usa el vocabulario de este módulo y los artículos indefinidos (**un**, **una**, **unos**, **unas**) y definidos (**el**, **la**, **los**, **las**). Let's see which of the class groups gets the highest number of details. Here's an example:

Attribution: Staff Favorites - University of Washington bookstore. By brewbooks, licensed under CC BY-SA 2.0.

Hay *unos* libros en *la* librería. *Los* libros son de temas de ficción, historia y biología y son *los* libros favoritos del personal de *la* librería. Hay *unos* autores internacionales como Slavoj Zizek y *unas* autoras nacionales como Sally Jenkins.

Escena 1

Attribution: By Airman 1st Class Curt Beach by U.S. Air Force, licensed under CC 2.0.

Escena 2

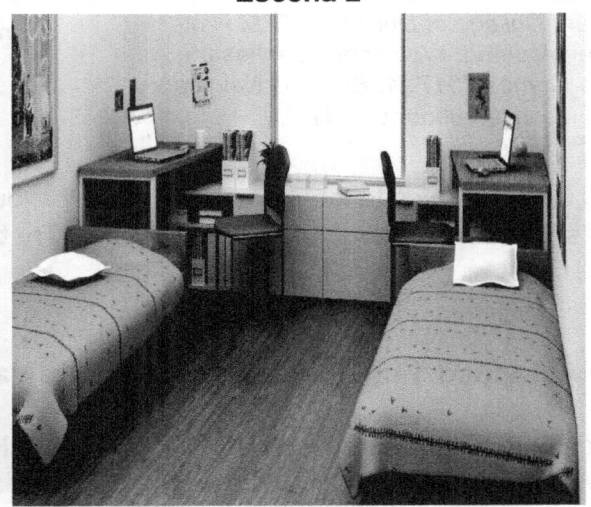

Attribution: College dorm room. By Footprint, licensed under CC 2.0.

Escena 3

Attribution: By Mariana Salazar, licensed under CC BY-SA 4.0.

Escena 4

Attribution: Public domain.

Escena 5

Attribution: College of DuPage STEM Professional Development Workshop Teaches the Art of Escape Games 2017 11. By COD Newsroom, licensed under CC BY 2.0.

Escena 6

Attribution: R Glow. By roanokecollege, licensed under CC BY 2.0.

Paso 2. ¿Con qué fotos te identificas? ¿Por qué? Would you post photos like these? What would you upload to show your life as a university student? Try to use as much Spanish as possible to answer these questions!

 **Actividad 1-4. Mariana en la universidad**

Remember Mariana, the international student we met in **Módulo introductorio**? She is finally on campus, and she wants to know more about the university. What information are you going to give her? With two or three classmates, take turns using the cues to give Mariana information about the university. Usa el vocabulario y los artículos definidos e indefinidos en este módulo. Which class group knows the university the most?

> **Modelo(s):** librería → *En la universidad hay una librería. Se llama MSC*
> presidente → *En la universidad el Doctor Young es el presidente.*

En la universidad…

1. biblioteca principal
2. profesor(a) de _____ (subject--you can ask your instructor!)
3. edificio de _____ (subject--you can ask your instructor!)
4. biblioteca
5. restaurante (*masc.*)
6. edificio de clases

 ### Actividad 1-5. Otra (*Another*) universidad

Do you think campuses in other parts of the world are similar to campuses in the US? Look at the following map of a university in Colombia (for a bigger version, go to http://bit.ly/MapaTrayectos) and compare it in terms of what your university offer to students (e.g., **cafeterías**, **librerías**, etc.). With a classmate, make sentences using the definite and indefinite articles and the verb **hay**. Before you begin your work, look at the map below, and find out:

1. ¿De dónde es la universidad?
2. ¿En qué continente está (*is*)?
3. ¿Cómo se llama la universidad?
4. ¿Es este campus similar o diferente a tu campus?

> **Modelo(s):** *En mi universidad hay un estadio de fútbol americano y en la universidad hay…*

Attribution: By Medios Digitales, licensed under CC BY-SA 4.0.

 ## Actividad 1-6. Nuestra (*Our*) universidad ideal

Now you and three or four classmates need to create your ideal university. Do the following:

1. Describe the buildings and places you want in your university. Use the verbs **hay** and **ser**, the words learned in this module and the previous one, and the indefinite and definite articles.

2. Develop a map like the one in activity 1-5. Draw the map and write a reference section.

3. Create a logo for your university and give it a name. Be creative! And remember, you can always ask your instructor for help!

4. Each member of the group will be responsible for presenting parts of the activity to the rest of the classmates.

 **Práctica individual:** To continue using your new structures, go to http://bit.ly/PracticaIndividual1-3.

Y después... Uso, forma y cultura: *Los materiales de estudio/Los útiles escolares*

Attribution: El Rastro una tarde de entre semana. By manuel m. v., licensed under CC BY 2.0.

I. Antes de ver

In Spanish, name three items you always needed to have when you were a student in elementary school.

 **II. A ver**

Now watch the video at http://bit.ly/Video1-2Trayectos about school items for elementary school children in Latin America, and see if there are any similarities/differences with the school items you used to have.

III. Después de ver

Actividad 1-7. Are there any similarities/differences between your school items and the ones shown in the video? Name two.

Actividad 1-8. Now watch the video again, and do the following exercises.

Actividad A. What is the main idea of this video? What kind of information is this video providing?

Actividad B. Responde las preguntas or choose the best option.

1. The reporter mentions the month of "marzo" as the beginning of the academic year. What is the English work for "marzo"? What does this tell you about the location where this video takes place? ¿Es el hemisferio norte o el hemisferio sur?

2. ¿Dónde está Lima (city where the video takes place)?
   i. México
   ii. Perú
   iii. Ecuador

3. ¿Cuál es la moneda (currency) en el video?
   i. Dólares
   ii. Pesos
   iii. Soles

4. ¿Cuál es el precio de los lápices de colores?
   i. Siete
   ii. Cinco
   iii. Seis

5. ¿Cuál es el precio de un cuaderno?
   i. $2.50
   ii. $4.50
   iii. $3.50

6. A lady is interviewed as part of the report. ¿Cuántas hijas (*daughters*) tiene (*does she have*)?
   i. Dos
   ii. Una
   iii. Tres

7. Which of these items are not discussed/do not appear in the video?
   a. silla
   b. escritorio
   c. marcadores
   d. tableta
   e. libro
   f. mochilas
   g. bolígrafo

Actividad C. What kind of information do you think is given in the video? How is the information supported (e.g., talk about images, evidence, etc.)?

Actividad D. What are the cultural similarities and differences that you can think of when it comes to buying school supplies in the city featured in the video and the store in the photo on p. 49 and in your city/town? What are some of the social/cultural aspects that you think might contribute to the differences?

Hablemos de cultura: *México*

 **San Miguel de Allende**

Hoy vamos a San Miguel de Allende. ¿Dónde está esta ciudad pequeña? Busca en este mapa interactivo: http://bit.ly/MapaSanMiguelA. Why do we want you to know more about this town? Well, it is one of the most beautiful places in the world, and it is also a place where you can broaden your knowledge of Mexico and its culture. Why do you think this is the case? Let's read!

Attribution: By Jiuguang Wang, licensed under CC BY-SA 2.0.

 **¡Ojo!**

Remember los cognados? You will not know all the words in the text, so you can rely on cognados to understand the main ideas of the text. Also, always look at the context around a particular word. Usually, the context surrounding a word can help you figure out what it means. Trust us: Language learning is our business!

 **A leer: *San Miguel de Allende***

San Miguel de Allende es una ciudad pequeña del estado mexicano de Guanajato. Está localizada a una altitud de 1910 (mil novecientos diez) metros y a 274 (doscientos setenta y cuatro) kilómetros de la Ciudad de México. En 2008 (dos mil ocho) la ciudad se transforma en Patrimonio Cultural de la Humanidad de la UNESCO por su cultura y arquitectura tradicional de estilo colonial y barroco. En 2017 (dos mil diecisiete) San Miguel de Allende recibe el título de mejor (*best*) ciudad del mundo (*world*) por la publicación *Travel + Leisure* por la calidad de su servicio turístico, su gastronomía, la belleza (*beauty*) de sus calles tradicionales y sus lugares de diversión (*fun*)

Attribution: The Streets of San Miguel de Allende.
By cezzie901, licensed under CC BY 2.0.

San Miguel de Allende es además famoso por su clima templado y sus aguas termales. Por eso (*That's why*), hay una gran comunidad de residentes extranjeros (*foreign*) (especialmente de los Estados Unidos) en la ciudad. Hay también iglesias católicas de arquitectura barroca como la Parroquia San Miguel Arcángel, construida en el siglo XVIII (*18th century*). Este edificio es símbolo de la ciudad y un modelo de la gran riqueza (*richness*) arquitectónica de México.

Attribution: Una novia entra a la Parroquia de San Miguel Arcángel.
By Silvia Ruth Perez Salas, licensed under CC BY-SA 4.0.

San Miguel de Allende y la región de Guanajuato en general son famosos por su industria vinícola (*wine industry*). Hay una fiesta muy popular todos los años (*every year*). La fiesta se llama "Fiesta de la vendimia" y es en agosto. Una de las actividades populares es pi-sar las uvas. ¿Cómo es la actividad de pisar las uvas? Mira (*Look at*) la foto a continuación.

Attribution: Viñedos San Miguel Vendimia 2016.
By Eugenio Gonzalez, licensed under CC BY 2.0.

San Miguel de Allende y Guanajuato.

¿Qué otras (*other*) actividades y cosas hay en San Miguel de Allende y Guanajuato? Mira este (*this*) video de unos estudiantes y responde las preguntas.

Video link: <u>http://bit.ly/Video1-3Trayectos</u>

Attribution: By Studyinqueretaro,
licensed under CC BY 3.0.

Actividad 1-9. Mi opinión

¿Qué opinas (*what do you think*) de San Miguel de Allende y Guanajuato? Responde las preguntas.

1. Now that you know more about San Miguel de Allende, would you like to study there? What places of the ones you read about and you saw in the video would you like to visit? What would you like to do there?

2. What aspects of Mexican culture and Mexico have you discovered in this section? Are there any areas in the United States that are similar to the region in Mexico we have talked about? Explain your answer with examples. Compare what you learned about Mexico with the US.

 **Práctica individual:** To check how much you remember about the cultural information you just learned, go to <u>http://bit.ly/PracticaIndividu-al1-4</u>.

Hablemos de gramática: *Los verbos en presente (present tense of regular "-ar" verbs)*

Carolina en la biblioteca

Carolina, the new student we met in this module, is still learning how to do things at the university. Today Eileen and Amy are helping her at the library. ¿Qué necesita Carolina? Listen to their conversation and look at the transcript below. Pay attention to the verbs. What do you notice about the endings?

Audio link: http://bit.ly/Audio1-3Trayectos

Attribution: By U.S. Air Force photo/2nd Lt. Mark Habermeye; Public domain.

Carolina:	¡Hola, compañeras! Necesi**to** un libro para mi clase de lingüística. ¿Me ayud**an** (*help*) a busc**ar** (*to look for*) el libro?
Eileen:	¡Sí, claro!
Amy:	Es fácil. Lo busc**as** en la computadora.
Eileen:	Aquí busc**as** el título.
Carolina:	¡Oh! ¡Aquí está!
Eileen:	Y ahora reserv**as** el libro.
Amy:	Luego us**as** tu tarjeta de estudiante (*student card*) y busc**as** el libro en el escritorio principal (*front desk*). ¡Y ya!
Carolina:	¡Gracias, amigas!

¿Comprendiste? Responde estas preguntas sobre la conversación.

Let's talk about verbs first. See if you can find an example of the following in the dialogue:

Un verbo en infinitivo (An infinitive verb that does not have a conjugation. E.g., to talk, to write)**:**

Unos verbos conjugados:

- Verbs conjugated in second person singular (**tú** form):
- Verbs conjugated in second person plural (**ustedes** form):

What do these verbs share? What do you already know about these verbs endings?

Now let's talk about the content of the dialogue (continue paying attention to the verb endings):

1. ¿Qué necesi**ta** Carolina en la biblioteca?
2. ¿Quiénes ayud**an** a Carolina?
3. Si tú necesi**tas** un libro, ¿dónde busc**as** el libro?

All the conjugated verbs that appear in the dialogue are in the present tense (**el tiempo presente**). In this section, we will learn how to conjugate verbs with the **-ar** ending in the present tense. ¡Manos a la obra!

The present Tense of *–ar* Verbs

I. Infinities and Conjugations

When you study verbs, you will need to know the difference between the *infinitive* form of the verb and the *conjugated* forms. In English, infinitives are verbs preceded by the word **to**. In Spanish, infinitives end in **-ar**, **-er**, or **-ir**.

> **Modelo(s):** **tomar** (*to drink, to take classes*); **comer** (*to eat*); **vivir** (*to live*)

These verbs are called ***infinitives*** because, like the concept of infinity, they are not bound by time. From the infinitive, we derive the conjugated forms of the verb. Of the three verb groups (**-ar**, **-er**, **-ir**), **–ar** verbs are the most numerous. To conjugate, drop the **–ar** from the infinitive. Next, add endings to the stem. The ending will depend on who is doing the action (remember *the subject*, discussed on page 9 in **Módulo introductorio**). Have a look at this example.

Ayudar (*to help*)		
yo	ayud**o**	*I help*
tú	ayud**as**	*you* (informal) *help*
vos	ayud**ás**	*you* (informal) *help* (mostly Argentina and Uruguay)
usted, Ud., él, ella	ayud**a**	*you* (formal) *help, he/she helps*
nosotros(as)	ayud**amos**	*we help*
vosotros(as)	ayud**áis**	*y'all* (informal: Spain) *help*
ustedes, Uds., ellos/ellas	ayud**an**	*y'all help, they help*

II. Usos del tiempo presente

As in English, in Spanish we use the present tense to talk about what people do every day or in a general sense.

> **Modelo(s):** Efraín **estudia** en la biblioteca todos los días (*every day*).
> Bailey **toma** la clase de lingüística de la Dra. Moyna.

Unlike English, the present tense in Spanish can be used to talk about actions that are happening right now or that will happen in the future. Compare the two languages:

> **Modelo(s):** Amy y Eileen **ayudan** a Carolina. (*Amy and Eileen are helping Carolina.*).
> Carolina **trabaja** mañana en la biblioteca. (*Carolina will work in the library tomorrow.*)

III. Ejemplos de verbos en -ar en las actividades de la universidad

bailar	*to dance*	**llamar**	*to call; to phone*
buscar	*to look for*	**mirar**	*to watch, to look at*
caminar	*to walk*	**necesitar**	*to need*
cantar	*to sing*	**pagar**	*to pay for*
comprar	*to buy*	**pasar tiempo**	*to spend time with*
contestar	*to answer*	**practicar**	*to practice*
desear	*to want*	**preguntar**	*to ask a question*
dibujar	*to dance*	**reservar**	*to reserve*
diseñar	*to design*	**terminar**	*to finish*
enseñar	*to teach*	**tocar**	*to touch; to play an instrument*
entrar	*to enter*	**usar**	*to use*
esperar	*to hope; to wait for; to expect*	**viajar**	*to travel*
hablar	*to talk; to speak*	**visitar**	*to visit*

IV. Frases útiles para hablar de actividades de la universidad

hablar por teléfono	*to talk on the phone; to call*	**Efraín habla por teléfono con su mamá todos los fines de semana (*every weekend*).**
descansar por unos minutos/por una hora	*to rest for a couple of minutes/for an hour*	**Los profesores descansan por unos minutos entre (*between*) sus clases.**
escuchar música	*to listen to music*	**Carolina y Amy escuchan música en el gimnasio.**

esperar el autobús	*to wait for the bus*	**¿Dónde esperás (vos) el autobús?**
estudiar en la biblioteca	*to study in the library*	**Mis compañeros de clase y yo estudiamos para el examen en la biblioteca.**
llegar a la clase/a la universidad	*to arrive at class/at the university*	**(Yo) llego a la universidad a las 8:00 de la mañana.**
mandar un correo electrónico/un texto	*to send an email/a text message*	**Dra. Moyna, ¿usted manda textos a sus estudiantes?**
regresar a casa	*to return home*	**¿(Tú) regresas a casa en autobús?**
tomar clases/un examen/ el autobús	*to take classes/exams/ the bus*	**¿Vosotros tomáis el examen de antropología mañana?**
trabajar por la mañana/ por la tarde/por la noche	*to work in the morning/ in the afternoon/at night*	**Las estudiantes trabajan por la tarde en el Starbucks en el centro estudiantil.**

 ¡Ojo!

1. As you can see in the examples above, in Spanish the meaning of the English word *for* is included in the verbs **buscar** (*to look for*), **esperar** (*to wait for*), and **pagar** (*to pay for*). Also, *to* is included in the verb **escuchar** (*to listen to*).

2. As in English, when you use two Spanish verbs together with the same subject, the second verb is usually in the infinitive. This is common with the verbs **desear**, **esperar**, and **necesitar**.

Modelo(s):   Carolina y Efraín **desean estudiar** en el edificio Académico.
Yo **espero trabajar** en la biblioteca.
Bailey **necesita llamar** a su familia.

Remember that when you want to use a conjugated verb in the negative form, the word **no** is placed before the conjugated verb. It's easy!

> **Modelo(s):**   Mi compañera de cuarto **no habla** español.
>
> No, chicos, ustedes **no necesitan comprar** un libro de texto para la clase.
>
> Carolina **no baila** en la discoteca.

 **¡Manos a la obra!**

Actividad 1-10. La fiesta de Bailey y Carolina

Paso 1. Bailey and Carolina decide to organize a party to celebrate the beginning of the semester. Carolina writes about it in her blog. What is she saying? First read the paragraph to get a general sense of its content. Then fill in the blanks with the correct present tense conjugation of the numbered infinitives. ¿Son tus fiestas similares o diferentes?

El blog de Carolina

Attribution: By Carolina Cantú, licensed under CC BY-SA 4.0.

¡Hola, amigos! Esta noche hay una fiesta en mi apartamento. Mi amiga Bailey y yo 1. (desear) _____ celebrar el comienzo del semestre. Nuestros (*Our*) amigos Efraín y Amy 2. (bailar) _____ y 3. (cantar) _____ mientras (*while*) Marlenie 4. (tocar) _____ la guitarra y otros estudiantes 5. (escuchar) _____ la música. Verónica 6. (llamar) _____ a su novio por teléfono y Mauro y yo 7. (tomar) _____ unas Coca Colas. Claro (*of course*), todos nosotros 8. (mirar) _____ nuestros teléfonos y 9. (mandar) _____ textos. La fiesta es fenomenal. Mis amigos 10. (descansar) _____ de las clases y la rutina de la universidad. Es importante el relax. OK. Yo 11. (terminar) _____ mi blog. Es hora de bailar. ¿Tú 12. (pasar) _____ tiempo con tus amigos también? ¿Tú 13. (esperar) _____ descansar este fin de semana (*this weekend*)? ¿Ustedes 14. (visitar) _____ a sus amigos este fin de semana? Deja (*Leave*) tus comentarios. ¡Nos vemos! Chau.

 **Paso 2.**

¿Son tus fiestas similares? Con un@ compañer@, describe tu fiesta. Write a blog similar to the one written by Carolina. Describe what happens at your party. Use at least 10 different verbs. You guys will need to present your party to the class! And, if you have photos, you can show them too!

Actividad 1-11. Las actividades de los estudiantes en el mundo hispano
In this activity, you will learn about an international student studying Spanish in Barcelona. Before you do the activities, let's learn more about the place.

 **Paso 1. Antes de ver**

Contesta las preguntas a continuación.
¿Dónde está Barcelona? Busca esta ciudad en un mapa

1. ¿Cómo es Barcelona? Consulta el sitio de web en http://bit.ly/BarcelonaFotos, y mira las fotos. ¿Qué lugares hay? Escribe dos.
2. ¿Qué son los "búnkers del Carmel"? Busca esta información en http://bit.ly/BunkerCarmel.
3. ¿Qué actividades hay en Barcelona para un estudiante? Escribe 3. Usa los verbos that you learned in the previous section.

 Paso 2. A ver

Ahora mira este video sobre una estudiante en Barcelona. Check if the activities that you mentioned appear in the video. Mira el vídeo en https://bit.ly/Video1-4Trayectos y contesta esta pregunta: ¿Las actividades de Caroline son similares o diferentes a tus actividades?

 **Paso 3. Después de ver**
Ahora mira el vídeo otra vez y completa las siguientes actividades. Trabaja con un@ compañer@.

Actividad A. Main idea
Using the information and images in the video, describe its main purpose. Who is the audience the filmmakers had in mind? Why? What meaning-making resources (e.g., images, music, etc.) have the filmmakers used to attract the attention of their intended audience?

Actividad B. Supporting details
Circle the number of each detail that is mentioned/shown in the video (not all are included!).

1. Caroline no estudia español en una clase.
2. Caroline estudia una maestría.
3. La familia de Caroline es de España.
4. Las personas caminan en Barcelona.
5. Caroline es estudiante en la Facultad de Ciencias de la Comunicación de la Universidad Autónoma de Barcelona.
6. Hay treinta estudiantes en cada clase en la facultad.

7. Caroline camina a la biblioteca.

8. Caroline estudia para sus clases en la biblioteca.

9. Caroline pasa tiempo en el "tandem" por la noche.

10. En el "tandem" los estudiantes hablan diferentes idiomas.

11. Los estudiantes bailan en el "tandem".

12. Caroline mira la ciudad de Barcelona desde los búnkers del Carmel.

Actividad C. More details

Now read the following sentences, and choose the option that appears in the video.

1. Caroline tiene (this refers to her age)
   a. 20 años.
   b. 22 años.
   c. 21 años.

2. Caroline es de
   a. Belize.
   b. Bélgica.
   c. Boston.

3. Carolina estudia en la biblioteca porque
   a. hay estudiantes.
   b. hay libros buenos.
   c. hay una cafetería.

4. Para llegar al "tandem", Carolina
   a. toma el metro.
   b. toma el autobús.
   c. camina.

5. Carolina lee (*reads*) en
   a. la residencia.
   b. el búnker.
   c. el laboratorio.

Actividad D. Análisis

Contesta estas preguntas sobre el vídeo. Use as much Spanish as you can.

1. What are the aspects of Barcelona that Caroline seems to enjoy the most?

2. Are her activities typical of those of a university student?

3. Why do you think the filmmakers have focused on Caroline? What kind of message do they want to convey?

4. What are the similarities/differences between studying in Barcelona and at your university? You can focus on buildings, activities, cultural aspects, etc.

5. Would you like to study in Barcelona? Why? / Why not?

 **Paso 4.**

Ahora con tres o cuatro compañer@s, create a table comparing your activities and Caroline's. Talk about at least 3 different activities **en la mañana, en la tarde** y **en la noche**. Talk about yourselves individually (**yo** forms), two of you (**ellos/ellas**), one of you in third person (**él/ella**), and you all (**nosotros**).

 **Actividad 1-12. Caroline y yo**

Imagine that you are on vacation in Barcelona, and you go to a party. You see Caroline, and you start a conversation with her. Work with a partner. One of you is going to be Caroline, and is going to use the information in the video to do this activity. Greet each other and get to know each other better:

1. First introduce yourselves. Provide names and talk about where you are from.
2. Ask and answer questions about your studies (what your especialización is, the classes that you take, where you study, etc.).
3. Talk about your routine and your activities during the weekend (e.g., En la mañana, yo…; Los fines de semana, mis amigos y yo…).

You need to use the vocabulary and questions in the previous sections and exercises in this module and in **Módulo introductorio**. You will share your conversation with other classmates.

 **Práctica individual:** To continue using your new verbs, go to http:// bit.ly/PracticaIndividual1-5.

Más comunicación: *¿Cuándo? La hora y los días de la semana*
El horario de Carolina
Before organizing their party, Bailey and Carolina had to agree on a day. Bailey asked Carolina about her schedule. Listen to their dialogue and read the transcript below. Pay attention to the way in which they talk about dates and times in Spanish. What do you notice?

 **Audio link:** http://bit.ly/Audio1-4Trayectos

AGOSTO

DOMINGO	LUNES	MARTES	MIÉRCOLES	JUEVES	VIERNES	SÁBADO
21 Mudanza al campus	22	23	24	25	26	27
28	29 Comienzo de clases 8:00-8:50 Teatro 10:20-11:00 Estadística 11:30-12:30 Practicar yoga con Bailey (gimnasio)	30 9:35-10:50 Lingüística 11:10-12:20 Literatura 13:00-17:00 Trabajar en la biblioteca	31 8:00-8:50 Teatro 10:20-11:00 Estadística 11:30-12:30 Practicar yoga con Bailey (gimnasio)	1 9:35-10:50 Lingüística 11:10-12:20 Literatura 13:00-17:00 Trabajar en la biblioteca	2 8:00-8:50 Teatro 10:20-11:00 Estadística 11:30-12:30 Practicar yoga con Bailey (gimnasio)	3 21:00 Fiesta: Comienzo del semestre (en casa)
4 10:00-14:00 Estudiar (biblioteca) 16:00-18:00 Fútbol (estadio)	5 Día del trabajo: ¡No hay clases!!! 😊	6 9:35-10:50 Lingüística 11:10-12:20 Literatura 13:00-17:00 Trabajar en la biblioteca	7 8:00-8:50 Teatro 10:20-11:00 Estadística 11:30-12:30 Practicar yoga con Bailey (gimnasio)	8 9:35-10:50 Lingüística 11:10-12:20 Literatura 13:00-17:00 Trabajar en la biblioteca	9 8:00-8:50 Teatro 10:20-11:00 Estadística 11:30-12:30 Practicar yoga con Bailey (gimnasio)	10 Visitar a mi familia (Corpus Christi) 🖤

Attribution: By Gabriela C. Zapata, licensed under CC BY-SA 4.0.

Bailey: Hey, Caro, ¿cuándo es tu clase de teatro?

Carolina: Hm… Dejame ver mi calendario (*let me look at my schedule*). La clase de teatro es los **lunes**, **miércoles** y **viernes**.

Bailey: **¿Y a qué hora es?**

Carolina: **Es a las ocho de la mañana.**

Bailey: Hm… So you need to get up early **los viernes**…

Carolina: Sí. ¿Por qué?

Bailey: I want to have a party para celebrar el semestre. I had thought of Thursday…

Carolina: Oh… No, el **sábado** es el mejor (*best*) día. **Por la noche. Alrededor (*Around*) de las nueve de la noche.** El **domingo** estudio en la biblioteca con Amy y hay un partido de fútbol **a las seis de la tarde** en Ellis Field.

Bailey: Cool. La fiesta es el **sábado**. By the way, **¿qué hora es?**

Carolina: **Son las nueve y cuarto.** ¡Uy! La clase de lingüística de la Dra. Moyna **es a las nueve y treinta y cinco**. ¡Vamos (*let's go*), chica!

¿Comprendiste?

1. First, we're going to discover what you do in Spanish to express days and times.

   a. Have a look at the photo of Carolina's schedule. What do you notice about the way in which she expresses time?

   b. What article do you use to express time? ¿**El**, **la**, **los**, or **las**?

   c. What word do we use to express *at a certain time*? Do you need that word when you just ask what time it is?

   d. How do you write days in Spanish? Is it the same as in English?

2. Now answer these questions taking both the photo and dialogue into account.

   a. ¿Qué días toma Carolina su clase de literatura?

   b. ¿Quién enseña la clase de lingüística?

   c. ¿A qué hora es la clase de estadística?

   d. ¿Cuándo viaja Carolina a Corpus Christi?

   e. ¿Cuándo estudia Carolina en la biblioteca? ¿Con quién estudia?

   f. ¿Qué hora es en el diálogo?

I. Los días de la semana

To ask for the date in Spanish, you can use ¿**Cuál es la fecha?** or ¿**Qué día es hoy?** (meaning *What is the date?* or *What day is today?*). To answer this question, you can say **Hoy es** day of the week and date of the month.

> **Modelo(s):** **Hoy es jueves diecisiete (de agosto).**

 ¡Ojo!

1. The days of the week are NOT capitalized in Spanish.

2. The masculine forms of the definite article (**el lunes, los lunes**) are used to refer to specific days. Notice that there is not a plural form for most days of the week. Exceptions: Saturday (**el sábado, los sábados**) and Sunday (**el domingo, los domingos**).

Los días de la semana	
el lunes	*Monday*
el martes	*Tuesday*
el miércoles	*Wednesday*
el jueves	*Thursday*
el viernes	*Friday*
el sábado	*Saturday*
el domingo	*Sunday*

II. ¿Qué hora es?

1. You use this question to ask for the time. As you saw in Carolina's schedule, in the Spanish-speaking world (except for the United States), the 24-hour system is the most common. However, in informal settings (for example, with family or friends), the 12-hour system is preferred, and you use the expressions **de la mañana** (a.m.), **de la tarde** (early p.m.) y **de la noche** (late p.m.) to clarify what time of the day you are referring to. Have a look at these examples.

> **Modelo(s):**   La recepción para los estudiantes nuevos es **el jueves 23 a las diecinueve treinta horas (19:30).** (Formal)
>
> La recepción para los estudiantes es **el jueves 23 a las siete y treinta / a las siete y media de la noche.** (Informal)

2. To talk about time, you always use the verb **ser**. For all times of the day, you use **son** (**Son las once de la noche.**). Exceptions: You use **es** when:

   1. You ask for the time (**¿Qué hora es?**), and
   2. You express any time between 1:00 and 1:59 (e.g., **Es la una y veinte.**)

3. As you have seen, there are different ways to express on the quarter or half hour:

9:15   **Son las nueve y cuarto.**   9:45   **Son las diez menos cuarto.**
        Son las nueve y quince.   **Son las nueve cuarenta y cinco.**

9:30   **Son las nueve y media.**
        Son las nueve y treinta.

These examples also show you that when you refer to minutes after the hour, you need the word **y** (e.g., **Es la una _y_ veinte [1:20]**), and when you talk about minutes before the hour, you need the word **menos** (e.g., **Son las dos _menos_ veinte [1:40]**).

III. ¿A qué hora es?

You use this question to ask at what time something takes place. As we saw in the dialogue, you need the word **a** to introduce the time phrase.

> **Modelo(s):**   **¿A qué hora es la clase de la Dra. Moyna? Es a las nueve y treinta y cinco de la mañana. / Es a las diez menos veinticinco de mañana.**

IV. Algunas expresiones importantes

Las expresiones de tiempo		
en punto	*on the dot*	**La Profesora Dexter enseña su clase a las ocho en punto de la mañana.**
a tiempo	*on time*	**Carolina y Bailey llegan a la clase de lingüística a tiempo.**

la medianoche	*midnight*	**Efraín estudia hasta (*until*) la medianoche.**
el mediodía	*noon*	**Yo regreso a casa al mediodía.**
todos los días	*every day*	**¿Tú tomas clases todos los días?**
mañana	*tomorrow*	**¿Usted viaja a San Antonio mañana?**

 The following video summarizes the information discussed in this section:

Video link: http://bit.ly/Video1-5Trayectos.

Attribution: La hora en español. By ProfeDeELE.es, licensed under CC BY 3.0.

 **¡Manos a la obra!**

 **Actividad 1-13. Tomamos el autobús**

Remember Caroline, the student studying in Barcelona? She, a group of friends, and you, decide to visit the area of Toledo, Spain (google Toledo to find out where it is).

Paso 1. You want to visit at least five different cities. Have a look at the following schedule, and choose five different towns to visit. Answer the following questions about each of them. En esta actividad, trabajas con tres o cuatro compañer@s.

HORARIO DE AUTOBUSES

MÉNTRIDA – TOLEDO

	De lunes a viernes					Sábados
	-	6:30	7:15	-	14:45	7:15
La Torre de Esteban Hambrán	-	6:40	7:25	-	14:55	7:25
Quismondo	6:45	-	-	-	-	-
Santa Cruz de Retamar	6:50	6:50	7:30	10:00	15:00	7:30
Novés	-	-	7:35	10:05	15:05	-
Portillo de Toledo	6:55	6:55	7:40	10:10	15:10	7:40
Fuensalida	7:00	7:00	7:45	10:15	15:15	7:45
Huecas	7:05	7:05	7:50	10:25	15:25	7:50
Villamiel de Toledo	7:15	7:15	8:00	10:35	15:35	8:00
Toledo	7:35	7:35	8:20	10:55	15:55	8:20

TOLEDO – MÉNTRIDA

	De lunes a viernes				Sábados
Toledo	12:00	13:00	15:00	18:45	13:30
Villamiel de Toledo	12:20	13:20	15:20	19:05	13:50
Huecas	12:30	13:30	15:30	19:15	14:00
Fuensalida	12:35	13:35	15:35	19:20	14:05
Portillo de Toledo	12:40	13:40	15:40	19:25	14:10
Novés	12:45	-	-	19:30	-
Santa Cruz de Retamar	12:50	13:50	15:50	19:35	14:20
Quismondo	-	13:55	-	-	-
La Torre de Esteban Hambrán	12:55	-	15:55	19:40	14:25
Méntrida	13:05	-	16:05	19:50	14:35

INFORMACIÓN: 91 539 31 32

CEVESA - CEVESA - CEVESA - CEVESA - CEVESA - CEVESA - CEVESA

Attribution: El horario de autobuses. By Huecanito, licensed under CC BY-SA 3.0.

1. ¿A dónde viajan?
2. ¿A qué hora toman el autobús?
3. ¿A qué hora sale (*leaves*) el autobús de lunes a viernes?
4. ¿A qué hora sale el autobús los sábados y domingos?

 Paso 2.

Busca fotos de las cuatro ciudades que tus compañer@s y tú visitan. ¿Dónde están estas ciudades? Busca un mapa de España, and be ready to show the rest of your classmates the result of your search. ¿Cómo son las ciudades? Describe las ciudades. Habla de dos o tres características.

 **Actividad 1.14. Nuestros horarios.**

En esta actividad, trabajas con tres o cuatro compañer@s.

Paso 1. Taking Carolina's schedule as an example, create your own. List the classes that you are taking in the same way she did, and include two extracurricular activities (e.g., a part time job, plans to study, etc.) during the week and on the weekend. Draw your calendar, and prepare to share it with your classmates.

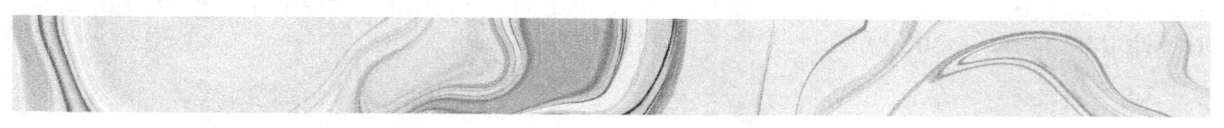

A G O S T O

DOMINGO	LUNES	MARTES	MIÉRCOLES	JUEVES	VIERNES	SÁBADO
21 *Mudanza al campus*	22	23	24	25	26	27
28	29 *Comienzo de clases* *8:00-8:50 Teatro* *10:20-11:00 Estadística* *11:30-12:30 Practicar yoga con Bailey (gimnasio)*	30 *9:35-10:50 Lingüística* *11:10-12:20 Literatura* *13:00-17:00 Trabajar en la biblioteca*	31 *8:00-8:50 Teatro* *10:20-11:00 Estadística* *11:30-12:30 Practicar yoga con Bailey (gimnasio)*	1 *9:35-10:50 Lingüística* *11:10-12:20 Literatura* *13:00-17:00 Trabajar en la biblioteca*	2 *8:00-8:50 Teatro* *10:20-11:00 Estadística* *11:30-12:30 Practicar yoga con Bailey (gimnasio)*	3 *21:00 Fiesta: Comienzo del semestre (en casa)*
4 *10:00-14:00 Estudiar (biblioteca)* *16:00-18:00 Fútbol (estadio)*	5 *Día del trabajo: ¡No hay clases!!!* 😄	6 *9:35-10:50 Lingüística* *11:10-12:20 Literatura* *13:00-17:00 Trabajar en la biblioteca*	7 *8:00-8:50 Teatro* *10:20-11:00 Estadística* *11:30-12:30 Practicar yoga con Bailey (gimnasio)*	8 *9:35-10:50 Lingüística* *11:10-12:20 Literatura* *13:00-17:00 Trabajar en la biblioteca*	9 *8:00-8:50 Teatro* *10:20-11:00 Estadística* *11:30-12:30 Practicar yoga con Bailey (gimnasio)*	10 *Visitar a mi familia (Corpus Christi)* 🖤

Attribution: El horario de Carolina. Attribution: By Gabriela C. Zapata, licensed under CC BY-SA 4.0.

Paso 2. Ahora con tres o cuatro compañer@s, compare your classes and activities. Find similaries. Talk about yourselves individually (**yo** forms), two of you (**ellos/ellas**), one of you in third person (**él/ella**), and you all (**nosotros**). Create a summary of your discussion to present to your classmates.

 **¡Conversemos!**

Paso 1. With a classmate, prepare a conversation. You will need to use the vocabulary and structures you learned in **Módulo introductorio** and in this module. Include the following information.

> **Estudiante 1.** You are conducting a survey about classes and buildings on campus. Interview a volunteer about the classes that they take (What are they? What time and what days do they take place? What are they like? Etc.). Also, ask them about some of the buildings where they spend more time (**pasar más tiempo**) while on campus (Where are the buildings? What do they have inside? Etc.).

> **Estudiante 2.** You are being interviewed about the classes that you are taking this semester and some of the buildings around campus. Answer the questions providing as much information as possible.

Paso 2. When you are done, work with another classmate. Reverse your roles.

Actividad 1-15. Mis clases

It has been a week since classes started. You are going to write an email to your high school Spanish teacher/university instructor telling them about the classes that you are taking. Tell them about your schedule (talk about times and days of the week), how many people are in each class, where you take them, and what the professors who teach them are like. Don't forget to start and finish the email with a proper salutation and goodbye.

> **New Message**
>
> To
>
> Subject
>
> Estimado/a Prof. García:
> ¿Cómo está? Yo…
>
> SEND

 **Práctica individual:** To continue using your new vocabulary and expressions, go to http://bit.ly/PracticaIndividual1-6.

Trayectos hispanos: *Educadores*

 Introducción: Gente, arte, historias, lugares

In these sections of *Trayectos*, we will learn more about people, artistic manifestations, stories, and places connected to this country's Hispanic/Latinx heritage. In this module, our focus is on our studies (classes, places, activities, etc.). Therefore, we will start with some notable teachers…

Attribution: Public domain

Gloria Anzaldúa[3]

Attribution:
Gloria Anzaldúa. By K. Kendall,
licensed under CC BY 2.0.

Gloria Evangelina Anzaldúa (1942 –2004) es una profesora, escritora (*writer*) y académica de Harlingen, Texas. Sus estudios se enfocan en la teoría cultural chicana y las teorías feminista y *queer*. Su libro más conocido (*well-known*), *Borderlands/La Frontera: The New Mestiza*, está basado en parte en su vida (*life*) en la frontera entre México y Texas. En sus escritos (*written works*), Anzaldúa explora sus emociones sobre la marginación social y cultural. Esta escritora también (*also*) desarrolló (*developed*) teorías sobre las culturas marginales e híbridas de las fronteras.

After obtaining a Bachelor of Arts in English from the then Pan American University (now University of Texas Rio Grande Valley), Anzaldúa worked as a preschool and special education teacher. In 1977, she moved to California, where she supported herself through her writing, lectures, and occasional teaching stints about feminism, Chicano studies, and creative writing at San Francisco State University, the University of California, Santa Cruz, Florida Atlantic University, Florida Atlantic University, and other universities. She authored many fictional and poetic works.

Anzaldúa died on May 15, 2004, at her home in Santa Cruz, California, from complications due to diabetes. At the time of her death, she was working toward the completion of her dissertation to receive her doctorate in Literature from the University of California, Santa Cruz. It was awarded posthumously in 2005. Several institutions now offer awards in memory of Anzaldúa.

Nepantla

Un concepto importante en los escritos de Anzaldúa es el de **nepantla**. **Nepantla** es una palabra náhuatl y significa (*means*) "tierra de en medio" (*land in-between*). Anzaldúa habla sobre (*talks about*) este concepto:

"Bridges are thresholds to other realities, archetypal, primal symbols of shifting consciousness. They are passageways, conduits, and connectors that connote transitioning, crossing borders, and changing perspectives. Bridges span liminal (threshold) spaces between worlds, spaces I call *nepantla*, a Nahuatl word meaning *tierra entre medio*. Transformations occur in this in-between space, an unstable, unpredictable, precarious, always-in-transition space lacking clear boundaries. *Nepantla* es tierra desconocida [*unknown land*], and living in this liminal zone means being in a constant state of displacement--an uncomfortable, even alarming feeling. Most of us dwell in nepantla so much of the time it's become a sort of 'home.' Though this state links us to other ideas, people, and worlds, we feel threatened by these new connections and the change they engender."[4]

---

3 *Text adapted from the original: Gloria E. Anzaldúa. By Wikipedia, licensed under CC BY-SA 3.0.*

4 *Attribution: "(Un)natural Bridges, (Un)safe Spaces" from This Bridge We Call Home: Radical Visions for Transformation (2002), p. 1. By Wikiquotes, licensed under CC BY-SA 3.0.*

Mi nepantla

Now you are going to take into account Anzaldúa's concept of **nepantla**, and you will create your own. Your work can be completed in different ways. It can be:

- A visual representation with or without text;
- A video with images and a narrative and/or text;
- A text-based representation (e.g., a word cloud);
- A conceptual map; or
- A bilingual poem (you can use some of the words you already know in Spanish)

If you want to know more about this concept, you can consult this Wikipedia entry: http://bit.ly/NepantlaConcept.

Paso 1. Explore the following examples from Anzaldúa herself and university students like you.
- Gloria Anzaldúa's poem *To Live in the Borderlands* (http://bit.ly/LiveBorderlands).

Ejemplos de estudiantes:

Ejemplo #1:

Attribution: Mi nepantla. By J.R., licensed under CC BY-SA 4.0.

Ejemplo #2:

Attribution: Mi nepantla. By G.H., licensed under CC BY-SA 4.0.

Paso 2. Develop your **nepantla**. Express any contradictory emotions you might be feeling or any transitions that are happening in your life. You can also use this project to give voice to your different social identities, focusing on those that place you in **nepantla** (e.g., bicultural/biracial/bilingual identities). Try to use as much Spanish as you can.

Paso 3. Get ready to present your work to your class. You can be as personal as you want. What do you and your classmates have in common? Do you share some of the feelings expressed by Anzaldúa and las nepantlas de los estudiantes?

Francisco Jiménez[5]

Attribution: Prof. Francisco Jiménez during a lecture at Stanford University in 2018. By Effeietsanders, licensed under CC BY-SA 4.0.

Otro profesor importante es el Dr. Francisco Jiménez (1943). El Dr. Jiménez es originariamente de México y por muchos años enseñó (*taught*) en la Universidad de Santa Clara en California. También (*Also*) es un escritor muy importante. Sus libros son autobiográficos y su historia de vida es muy interesante:

Up until he was four years old, Dr. Jiménez lived in a town in the state of Jalisco, Mexico. His family then immigrated without documents to California to work as migrant farm workers. When he was six years old, he had already started working in the fields with his family. Growing up, his family would move with the seasons of crops, causing him to miss months of school every year.

When Dr. Jiménez was in eighth grade, his family was deported back to Mexico. A few months later, they returned and settled down in a migrant labor camp in Santa Maria, California, called Bonetti Ranch. His father could not work anymore because of severe back problems, so they would no longer move from place to place.

Throughout high school, Dr. Jiménez and his older brother, Roberto, worked as janitors to support their family.

After high school, Dr. Jiménez went on to attend Santa Clara University, getting a B.A. in Spanish in 1966. He became a US citizen during his junior year at Santa Clara. Then, he went to Columbia University to get his Master's and Ph.D. in Latin American Literature.

In 1997, Dr. Jiménez published his first autobiographical novel, *The Circuit: Stories from the Life of a Migrant Child* [http://bit.ly/JimenezCircuit] (*Cajas de cartón* in the Spanish version). This book documents his early life, from crossing the border as a child to attending elementary school and working in the fields. There are three sequels to this book, which continue documenting his life through its next few stages. *Breaking Through* (*Senderos fronterizos*) is about his time in high school, *Reaching Out* (*Más allá de mí*) is about his time attending Santa Clara University, and *Taking Hold: From Migrant Childhood to Columbia University* documents his years in graduate school.

Jiménez has also written some autobiographical picture books, including *La mariposa* (1998) and *The Christmas Gift/El regalo de Navidad* (2000). In *La mariposa*, Jiménez writes about the challenges of not speaking English during his year in first grade.

 Now watch this video (http://bit.ly/JimenezCircuitVideo) of Dr. Jiménez talking about his first book, *The Circuit*, and the play that was written based on it.

- Why is this play important?
- What topics did it bring to the forefront?

5 *Text adapted from the original: Francisco Jiménez. By Wikipedia, licensed under CC BY-SA 3.0.*

- Why was Dr. Jiménez's writing so important in his life? What role did it play?
- How can Gloria Anzaldúa's and Francisco Jiménez's work contribute to our understanding of some of the issues that affect the Hispanic/Latinx communities in the United States?

 **Investigación (*Research*)**

Now you will do some research on other important teachers that belong to the Hispanic/Latinx communities in the United States.

Paso 1. You and the classmates in your group will gather information on the following for each of the people in the list. You can distribute the research tasks among the members of the group.

Información	Personas
1. Year of birth and place of origin	**--Gloria Anzaldúa** Página de Wikipedia: http://bit.ly/GAnzaldua Vídeo con información: http://bit.ly/GAnzalduaVideo
2. Information about family/childhood (e.g., if they were migrant workers)	**--Francisco Jiménez** Página de Wikipedia: http://bit.ly/FJimenezWiki *Living and Writing a Migrant's Life* (vídeo): http://bit.ly/FJimenezVideo
3. Education	
4. Contributions to the United States	**--Tomás Rivera** Página de Wikipedia: http://bit.ly/TRiveraWiki *Tomás Rivera: Social Mobility Through Education* (vídeo): http://bit.ly/TRiveraVideo
5. Activism (what topics they brought to the forefront in connection to their community)	**--Carmen Tafolla** Página de Wikipedia: http://bit.ly/CTafollaWiki *Carmen Tafolla - A Life in Letters Documentary* (vídeo): http://bit.ly/CTafollaVideo

Paso 2. Now, with the information you have gathered, create a conceptual map (http://bit.ly/Concept-MapWiki) that highlights the similarities among these educators.

- What do they have in common?
- What aspects of their lives are emphasized in their personal stories?
- With whom do you identify the most? Why?

 **Experiencias similares**

In this section, you will listen to and view two children's books on the childhood experiences of Dr. Francisco Jiménez and Dr. Tomás Rivera. What did Francisco and Tomás have in common? Bear this question in mind when you watch the videos.

Libro #1: *La mariposa* (http://bit.ly/JimenezMariposa) (Autor: Francisco Jiménez). ¿Qué significa **mariposa**? Why do you think Jiménez chose this title for his book?

Libro #2: *Tomás and the Library Lady* (http://bit.ly/TomasRLibraryLady) (Autora: Pat Mora; http://bit.ly/PatMoraSite)

Now fill out the following table and compare the two stories.

- What did Francisco and Tomás have in common?
- Why do you think the authors decided to write these stories?
- What message did they want to convey to children?

	La mariposa	*Tomás and the Library Lady*
Personajes (*characters*)		
Escenarios donde toman lugar las historias (*Places where the stories take place*)		
Eventos (eventos principales de la historia) (*Main events in the stories*)		
Temas (*topics*) importantes		
Spanish words that you learned		

 Explora más (*more*) los temas

In this lesson, we learned how these Hispanic/Latinx teachers have used their words to highlight issues that affect migrant workers and their children, and people with bicultural/bilingual/diverse identities. If you want to learn more about these topics, we recommend you explore the following resources:

Nepantla:

Artist Santa Barraza (http://bit.ly/SBarrazaWiki) has created her own representation of this concept in her work *Nepantla* (http://bit.ly/SBarrazaNepantla). Explore this work, and listen to the artist talk about it (http://bit.ly/SBarrazaVideo). What aspects of Anzaldúa's concept are present in this work? How does this work connect to her identities?

Now visit the artist's website (https://www.santabarraza.com/). What topics does she focus on in her works? How is her art related to her identities? Write examples of elements that represent who she is. Do you identify with any of her works? Which one? Why?

Books:

- Treviño Hart, E. (1999). *Barefoot heart: Stories of a migrant child*. Tempe, AZ: Bilingual Press. ISBN: 978-0927534819
- Olivares, J. (2008). (Editor). *Tomás Rivera: The complete works*. Houston: Arte Público Press.

Children's Books:
- Medina, J. (1999). *My name is Jorge: On both sides of the river.* Honesdale, PA: Wordsong/ Boyds Mills Press.
- Herrera, J. P., & Simmons, E. (1995). *Calling the doves/El canto de las palomas* (http://bit.ly/ CantoPalomas). New York: Children's Book Press. (The webpage linked to the title contains articles and videos on the topics discussed in this lesson).

Poem:
Conflict: A poem for America's migrant workers. http://bit.ly/PoemMigrantW

Para terminar... *Cartelera*

 Mighty Boy (España)

This section introduces you to short films developed in the Spanish-speaking world. You will watch the chosen productions, and you will work individually and collaboratively with a variety of comprehension and interpretation tasks. In this module we will watch the short film *Mighty Boy*, directed by the Spanish director Javier Yañez.

I. Antes de ver

El nombre de este cortometraje (*short film*) es *Mighty Boy* y el slogan del fim es "Un auténtico héroe no necesita superpoderes". What do you think the film is about? Write two or three ideas.

Attribution: By Thibault, licensed under CC BY-SA 3.0

II. A ver

Ahora mira el film. Chequea si tus ideas sobre el film son correctas. Mira el vídeo en http://bit.ly/Video1-6Trayectos.
¿Son tus ideas correctas? ¿Cuál es el tema del film? You can answer these questions in English.

 **III. Después de ver**

Ahora mira el cortometraje otra vez y completa las siguientes actividades. Trabaja con un@ compañer@.

Actividad A. Main idea
Using the information and images in the video, describe its main purpose. Who is the audience the filmmaker had in mind? Why? ¿Qué tipo de film es? ¿Cuál es el género?

Actividad B. Los personajes (*the characters*)

Describe cómo son los personaje e imagina una rutina diaria para cada uno (en la mañana, en la tarde, en la noche). ¿Cuál es tu personaje favorito? ¿Por qué? (You can answer this question in English). Usa los cognados. Also, ask your instructor for help!

Personajes	Profesión presente y pasada	¿Cómo es?	Rutina (en la mañana, en la tarde, en la noche)
Jaime			
Lucía, la novia de Jaime			
Aleska, la amiga de Jaime			

Actividad C. Análisis

Contesta estas preguntas sobre el vídeo.

1. ¿Cómo es el profesor de la universidad? Why do you think he is depicted in that way?

2. Do you identify with any of the characters? When you were a child, did you ever dream of being a superhero? Who was your favorite superhero? Why?

3. What kind of message do the filmmakers want to convey? Do you think they just want to entertain or is there something more to this movie?

4. What cultural aspects in the movie surprised you? Explain your answer.

5. Do you think American audiences would enjoy this short film? Why? Why not?

 ## Actividad D. Nuestras rutinas

Ahora con tres o cuatro compañer@s, create a table comparing your routine and Jaime's or Lucia's or Aleska's. Talk about at least 3 different activities en la mañana, en la tarde y en la noche. Talk about yourselves individually (**yo** forms), two of you (**ellos/ellas**), one of you in third person (**él/ella**), and you all (**nosotros**).

> **Modelo(s):** *Jaime trabaja en la mañana, pero nosotros tomamos clases en la universidad.*

 ## Actividad E. Cognados y lengua

Paso 1. Working on your own, busca tres cognados y tres verbos/palabras that you already know that appear in the film (the words **sí**, **que**, and **no** do not count!).

Paso 2. Share your words with your partner. What new **cognados** have you guys learned?

 **Práctica individual:** To continue using your new vocabulary and expressions , go to http://bit.ly/PracticaIndividual1-7.

Para terminar... *Lectura*

 **Cursos de español**

I. Antes de leer

In this module, we have talked about different kinds of classes at your university and the Spanish-speaking world. In this section, we will read a short, digital text for immigrants who want to learn Spanish. What characteristics should a course for different kinds of immigrants have? Think of one or two ideas, and then read the text to see what such a course offers in Spain.

II. A leer[6]

CURSOS GRATUITOS ONLINE PARA CIUDADANOS EXTRANJEROS

Los cursos tienen una duración de 6 meses y hay 600 lugares disponibles.

BENEFICIOS
--Entrar al sistema las 24 h al día, 7 días de la semana
--Estudiar desde PC, teléfonos celulares y tabletas
--El curso se adapta al nivel del estudiante. No es posible trabajar off-line.
--Un tutorial en vídeo enseña el sistema en varias lenguas (inglés, francés, alemán, italiano y español)
--Asistencia técnica en español, inglés y francés

REQUISITOS
--Ser ciudadano (*citizen*) extranjero en la provincia de Alicante.
--Una computadora con conexión de Internet y micrófono

Para estudiar en este curso, enviar (*send*) un email de interés a ciudadadanosextranjeros@diputacionalicante.es

---

6   Text modified from *600 plazas. Cursos gratuitos de español online para ciudadanos extranjeros* by Marca Empleo, licensed under CC BY 4.0. Modified by Gabriela C. Zapata. Public domain.

III. Después de leer

 Completa las siguientes actividades con un@ compañer@.

Actividad A. ¿Cierto (C) o falso (F)?
Decide si las siguientes oraciones son C (*true*) o F (*false*) teniendo en cuenta (*taking into account*) el contenido del texto.

1. Este curso es solamente (*only*) para estudiantes universitarios.	C	F
2. La gente toma el curso por un semestre.	C	F
3. El curso es en la universidad de Alicante	C	F
4. Las clases en el curso son en la mañana.	C	F
5. El curso es de lunes a domingo.	C	F
6. Los materiales para el curso son digitales.	C	F
7. Los estudiantes miran un video para saber (*to know*) cómo usar el sistema.	C	F
8. Los estudiantes de Madrid toman este curso.	C	F
9. En el curso, los estudiantes hablan.	C	F
10. La gente manda un mensaje de texto para tomar el curso.	C	F

Actividad B. Análisis
Contesta estas preguntas.

1. What characteristics make this course ideal for an immigrant? Why? Do you believe this is a good alternative for newly-arrived immigrants? Why? Why not? What might be the problems an immigrant may encounter when enrolling in this course?

2. Does this state offer similar English courses for immigrants? Do some research online to find out.

Actividad C. Lengua
Busca tres cognados. Did these words help you understand the text? What other strategies did you use to read it?

 **Actividad D. Curso de inglés para inmigrantes**

Ahora con tres o cuatro compañer@s, create an ad similar to the one we read to advertise an English course for immigrants from Spanish-speaking countries. You can add information on different types of classes (e.g., **conversación**, **cultura**, **historia**, etc.), and have a mixture of online (**en línea**) and face-to-face (**en persona**) classes. You need to have all the sections that appear in the original text. You can also add a logo to your course.

 **Práctica individual:** To continue working with the content of this text, go to http://bit.ly/PracticaIndividual1-8.

Para terminar... ¡Conversemos!

Attribution: Public domain.

Trabaja con un@ compañer@ y practica tu español en estas situaciones sociales. You need to use the vocabulary and structures you learned in **Módulo introductorio** (e.g., **saludos**, **el verbo *ser***, **el verbo *hay***, **question words**) and in **this module** (e.g., ***-ar* verbs**, **la hora y los días de la semana**).

Conversación 1

> **Estudiante 1.** Besides studying, your new roommate has a job at the university. You come back from your first day of classes, and you start a conversation with them.
> Greet your roommate. Ask:
>
> - Where they work.
> - The days of the week and the hours they work.
> - What classes they are taking this semester.
>
> Answer your roommate's questions.

Estudiante 1. Your new roommate has come back from their first day of classes. They start a conversation with you. Greet your roommate, answer their questions, and also ask:

- What classes they are taking this semester.
- The days of the week and the times when they take classes.
- What their favorite class is.
- What they need for their classes.

Conversación 2

Estudiante 1. You have just met your new roommate. You ask questions to find out what they are like:

- Greet your roommate.
- Ask their name.
- Say where you are from, and how old you are (Tengo… años).
- Answer your roommate's questions. Ask them similar questions.

Estudiante 2. You have just met your new roommate. You ask questions to find out what they are like:

- Greet your roommate. Answer your roommate's question, and ask a related question.
- Say where you are from, and how old you are (Tengo… años).
- Tell what you are studying at the university and, specifically, the classes you are taking.
- Ask your roommate what they study, and what classes they are taking this semester.
- Answer your roommate's question, and ask a related question.

Conversación 3

Estudiante 1. Imagine that this is your first semester studying at the Universidad de Málaga in Spain. You meet with a **consejero/a** (*academic advisor*) to talk about your classes, routine at the university, etc. Since this is a formal meeting, remember to use the "usted" forms in your conversation:

- Introduce yourself.
- Answer the consejero/a's question, and say how old you are (**Tengo… años**).
- Ask questions about what classes you need to take, at what time they are, when they are (days of the week, etc.).
- Also, ask who the instructors of the courses are and what they are like.
- Answer your advisor's questions.

Estudiante 2. Imagine that you are a **consejero/a** (*academic advisor*) at the Universidad de Málaga in Spain. You meet with a new student. Get as much information as possible about this person. Since this is a formal meeting, remember to use the "usted" forms in your conversation:

- Introduce yourself, and say where you are from.
- Find out where the student is from.
- Ask about routines and major (e.g., if they work, where, what their major [su especialización] is, etc.).
- Tell the student which classes they need to take, and answer the student's questions.

Conversación 4

Estudiante 1. You and your roommate are discussing your classes. You need to add a history class. Your roommate is in a class that looks promising. Ask:

- Who the professor is.
- Ask them what the professor is like (use the appropriate gender form based on your roommate's answer).
- Where the class is.
- If there is a lot of homework.
- When and at what time the class meets.
- How many exams there are in the class.

Estudiante 2. You and your roommate are discussing your classes. You want to know more about your roommate's schedule, and they have questions for you too. Answer their questions and ask:

- How many classes they are taking.
- On what days they take classes.
- Where they are working this semester.
- Where they study.
- What time they study.

Para terminar... *Proyecto digital*

 **Introducción al proyecto**

The objective of this assignment is for you and your classmates to develop a magazine that introduces the members of the class (e.g., who they are; where they are from; what they're like; their likes, activities, hobbies, etc.) to Spanish speakers in this country and abroad. Each student will work on their personal profile throughout the instructional modules of this volume. The work will be divided into three different parts.

The instructions offered in these sections will be complemented with those provided by your instructor.

Primera parte: Mi vida académica.

In this module you will express who you are as a student in Spanish.

Attribution: Public domain

I. Antes de escribir

Use the questions that follow to organize your ideas. Your instructor can help you with words or constructions that are unfamiliar to you.

1. ¿Cuál es tu nombre?

2. ¿De dónde eres? (mention city/state)

3. ¿Cómo se llama tu universidad?

4. ¿Cuál es tu especialización (*major*)?

5. ¿Qué clases tomas este semestre?

6. ¿Qué días y a qué hora son tus clases?

7. ¿Dónde estudias generalmente? ¿Por qué? (Your instructor can help you answer this question)

8. ¿Cuál es tu lugar favorito en la universidad? ¿Por qué? (Your instructor can help you answer this question)

II. A escribir

Now write your paragraph and…

- Remember to use the vocabulary from this module and **Módulo introductorio**.

- Pay attention to gender and number when you use articles and nouns (e.g., **la** profesor**a**), and to the correct verb conjugations (e.g., yo estudi**o**, mis amigos y yo trabaj**amos**).

- Use connectors and conjunctions to connect your ideas. For example, use **y**, **también** (*also*), **además** (*also*), **pero** (*but*). Your instructor can help you to use these words correctly.

Complement your paragraph with:

- At least one photo that shows you in an academic activity (e.g., taking classes, studying at the library)

- Additional photos (a maximum of two) of: 1. Your favorite part of campus; 2. Anything about your university that you like

- If you use photos that you have not taken, please do not forget to cite the source. We recommend that you use open images (i.e., copyright free). You can find this type of images using the search engine offered by Creative Commons (https://search.creativecommons.org/). Also, you need to provide attributions for all of them. To learn more about Creative Commons licenses and how to cite the open materials you find, see https://creativecommons.org/licenses/ and http://bit.ly/CreativeCommonsAttr.

III. Después de escribir

Now read your paragraph, and focus on the following:

- **Content:** Have you included all the information required? Are your photos big and clear enough to convey your message?

- **Grammar:**
  - Articles and nouns: Do they agree in gender and number?
  - **-ar** verbs: Have you conjugated your **-ar** verbs correctly?

- **Cohesion:** Have you connected your ideas with the suggested connectors and conjunctions?

Go over your text, improve it, and write a new, polished version.

Antes de partir...

¡Misión cumplida!

We have reached the end of **Módulo 1**. Go back to the first part of the module (p. 35) , and review what you have accomplished. Check the outcomes you have achieved. What are you proud of? What aspects of your Spanish would you like to improve? ¡Buen trabajo!

Summary of Contents

Comunicación

- En el aula: La clase de español

  - **la estudiante/la chica**   *the (female) student/the young woman*

  - **el estudiante/el chico**   *the (male) student/the young man*

☐	**el bolígrafo**	*the pen*
☐	**el cuaderno**	*the notebook/the composition book*
☐	**los papeles**	*the sheets of paper*
☐	**la mesa**	*the table*
☐	**la ventana**	*the window*

- En el salón de clase: La clase de sociología

☐	**el profesor/la profesora**	*the (male) instructor/the (female) instructor*
☐	**la computadora portátil**	*the laptop*
☐	**el escritorio**	*the desk*
☐	**la luz/las luces**	*the light/the lights*
☐	**la pantalla**	*the projection screen*
☐	**la pared**	*the wall*
☐	**la puerta**	*the door*
☐	**las sillas**	*the chairs*

- Los objetos de la clase

☐	**la pizarra/el pizarrón**	*the blackboard*
☐	**el borrador**	*the eraser (for the blacboard)*
☐	**la tiza**	*chalk*
☐	**la tableta**	*the tablet*
☐	**el libro (de texto)**	*the book / the textbook*
☐	**el lápiz /los lápices**	*the pencil / pencils*
☐	**la pluma**	*the ink pen*
☐	**el reloj**	*the clock*
☐	**la mochila**	*the backpack*
☐	**la cola (de pegar)**	*Elmer glue*
☐	**el pegamento**	*the glue stick*

- Las personas en la universidad

☐	**el bibliotecario**	*the (male) librarian*
☐	**la bibliotecaria**	*the (female) librarian*
☐	**el compañero (de clase)**	*the (male) classmate*
☐	**la compañera (de clase)**	*the (female) classmate*
☐	**el compañero de cuarto**	*the (male) roommate*

☐ **la compañera de cuarto**   *the (female) roommate*

☐ **el consejero**   *the (male) advisor*

☐ **la consejera**   *the (female) advisor*

☐ **el hombre**   *the man*

☐ **la mujer**   *the woman*

☐ **el novio**   *boyfriend*

☐ **la novia**   *girlfriend*

● Los lugares (*places*) en la universidad

☐ **el salón de clase/ el aula**   *the classroom*

☐ **la biblioteca**   *the library*

☐ **el edificio**   *the building*

☐ **la librería**   *the bookstore*

☐ **la papelería**   *A place where only school and office supplies are sold.*

☐ **la residencia**   *the dormitory*

☐ **el baño**   *the bathroom*

☐ **mi cuarto**   *my room/ my bedroom*

● Los cognados (pgs. 42-44)

● Frases útiles para hablar de actividades de la universidad

☐ **hablar por teléfono**   *to talk on the phone; to call*

☐ **descansar por unos minutos/por una hora**   *to rest for a couple of minutes/for an hour*

☐ **escuchar música**   *to listen to music*

☐ **esperar el autobús**   *to wait for the bus*

☐ **estudiar en la biblioteca**   *to study in the library*

☐ **llegar a la clase/a la universidad**   *to arrive at class/at the university*

☐ **mandar un correo electrónico/un texto**   *to send an email/a text message*

☐ **regresar a casa**   *to return home*

☐ **tomar clases/un examen/el autobús**   *to take classes/exams/the bus*

☐ **trabajar por la mañana/por la tarde/por la noche**   *to work in the morning/in the afternoon/at night*

- Los días de la semana

  - ☐ **el lunes**   *Monday*
  - ☐ **el martes**   *Tuesday*
  - ☐ **el miércoles**   *Wednesday*
  - ☐ **el jueves**   *Thursday*
  - ☐ **el viernes**   *Friday*
  - ☐ **el sábado**   *Saturday*
  - ☐ **el domingo**   *Sunday*

- Las expresiones de tiempo

  - ☐ **en punto**   *on the dot*
  - ☐ **a tiempo**   *on time*
  - ☐ **la medianoche**   *midnight*
  - ☐ **el mediodía**   *noon*
  - ☐ **todos los días** *every day*
  - ☐ **mañana**   *tomorrow*

Lengua
- Gender, Number, and Definite and Indefinite Articles (pg. 46)
- Los verbos en presente (present tense of regular "-ar" verbs) (pg. 58)

Cultura
- México: San Miguel de Allende (pg. 55)
- Trayectos hispanos: *Educadores* (pg. 73)

Mis palabras
In your Spanish notebook, write down other words and phrases you learned in this module.

Módulo 2: Mi vida fuera de la universidad: Mi familia

En este módulo, hablamos de tu vida (*life*) más allá (*beyond*) de las clases. Hablamos de tu vida familiar.

Antes de comenzar: ¿Cómo es tu familia? ¿Cuántas personas hay en tu familia?

Attribution: By Mariana Salazar, licensed under CC BY-SA 4.0.

Objetivos en este módulo

Comunicación

In this instructional module, you will learn how to…

- Describe your family
- Ask questions about someone else's family
- Answer questions about your own family
- Talk about activities you do with friends and family
- Use numbers between 30 and 100

Lengua
- Possessive and descriptive adjectives
- Nationalities
- Present tense of *-er* and *-ir* verbs
- Los números del 30 al 100

Cultura
- Colombia
- Trayectos hispanos: Visiones artísticas de la familia

Mis metas

In your Spanish notebook, describe what you want to accomplish in this instructional module in personal terms.

Introducción comunicativa: *La familia de Mariana*

In this instructional module, we will learn how to describe our families as well as learn about other people's families. Think about your family and how you would describe it in English. Now, pay attention to the following conversation about Mariana's family.

Dylan es un estudiante de intercambio en Oaxaca, Mexico. Él estudia español en la Universidad de Oaxaca. Mariana's family is hosting Dylan during his stay. In the following conversation, Dylan asks Mariana about his new host family. To understand the dialogue, focus on los cognados and use the information in **Hablemos más** (pp. 88-89).

 **Audio link:** http://bit.ly/Audio2-1Trayectos

Attribution: By Mariana Salazar and Dylan Manshack, licensed under CC BY-SA 4.0.

Dylan:	¡Hola, Mariana! ¿Qué tal?
Mariana:	¡Hola, Dylan! Muy bien. ¡Bienvenido a México!
Dylan:	Muchas gracias. ¿Cómo es **tu familia**?
Mariana:	**Mi** familia es muy **grande** (*big*). Somos ocho en **mi** familia. Tengo (*I have*) cinco **hermanos**. **Mi padre** se llama Ramón y **mi madre** se llama Margarita.
Dylan:	¡Tienes (*you have*) una familia muy **grande**! ¿Quién es **tu hermano** favorito?
Mariana:	**Mi** hermano favorito es **mi** hermano **menor**. **Su** nombre es Santiago, pero lo llamo Santi.
Dylan:	¿Cuántos años tiene Santi? ¿Por qué es **tu** favorito?
Mariana:	Santi tiene dos años. Él es **mi** favorito porque es **cómico**, **dramático** y **gordo** (*chubby*).

El Blog de Dylan

Dylan is blogging about his experiences in Mexico. The following is a blog post in which he describes Mariana's family.

Attribution: By Mariana Salazar, licensed under CC BY-SA 4.0.

Mi familia mexicana

¡La familia de Mariana es muy **amable**! Me siento como parte de **su** familia al instante. Todos son muy **divertidos** y **graciosos**. Toman muchas fotos, como **mi** familia. Como **ves** en la foto, **la familia de Mariana es enorme**. Hoy vamos a comer a la casa **de sus primos**. La familia **lejana** (*extended*) de Mariana incluye sus **tíos**, **abuelos**, **primos**, **sobrinos** y **amigos**. Mariana y **su** familia **mexicana** siempre **comen** juntos (*eat together*). ¡Tenemos mucha hambre! (*We're very hungry!*) Para comer, **su** tío cocina chilaquiles. ¡Son muy **deliciosos**!

¿Comprendiste? Decide si las oraciones a continuación son Ciertas (C) o Falsas (F) de acuerdo al contexto en el diálogo y el blog.

1. Dylan estudia arquitectura en México.	C	F
2. Mariana es hija única.	C	F
3. En la familia de Mariana hay muchas personas.	C	F
4. Santi es el compañero de cuarto de Dylan.	C	F
5. La familia de Dylan es similar a la familia de Mariana.	C	F
6. Una actividad favorita de la familia de Mariana es comer juntos (*together*).	C	F

Lengua

In the dialogue and blog, what two verbs are used to describe Mariana's family (e.g., what the family is like and how old her favorite brother is)? As we saw in **Módulo introductorio**, in Spanish, the verb **ser** is used with adjectives to describe people, places, things, etc. What are some of the adjectives (e.g., **grande**) used in the dialogue and blog? What adjectives could you use to describe your own family? Remember los cognados.

Hablemos más: *La familia*

En el mundo de hoy hay diferentes tipos de familia. ¿Cómo es tu familia? ¿Es similar a las familias de las fotos? Use the vocabulary in this section and the verb **hay** to talk about your or someone else's family. You can also describe one of the families in the photos below.

 **Audio link:** http://bit.ly/Audio2-2Trayectos

Attribution: By Airman Grace Nichols, U.S. Air Force photo, licensed under CC BY 4.0.

Attribution: By Emily Walker from Wellington, New Zealand, licensed under CC BY-SA 2.0.

Attribution: By Catherine Scott, licensed under CC BY-SA 2.0.

Attribution: By joseloya, licensed under CC BY 2.0.

Attribution: Public domain.

Attribution: By City of Seattle, licensed under CC BY 2.0.

El núcleo familiar

el padre	*father*
la madre	*mother*
el hermano	*brother*
la hermana	*sister*
el esposo	*husband*
la esposa	*wife*
la pareja	*partner*
el hijo	*son*
la hija	*daughter*
el padrastro	*stepfather*
la madrastra	*stepmother*
el hermanastro	*stepbrother*
la hermanastra	*stepdaughter*
el medio hermano	*half-brother*
la media hermana	*half-sister*
la mascota	*pet*

Los parientes (Relatives)

el tío	*uncle*
la tía	*aunt*
el sobrino	*nephew*
la sobrina	*niece*
el primo	*cousin m.*
la prima	*cousin f.*
el abuelo	*grandfather*
la abuela	*grandmother*
el suegro	*father-in-law*
la suegra	*mother-in-law*
el yerno	*son-in-law*
la nuera	*daughter-in-law*
el bisabuelo	*great grandfather*
la bisabuela	*great grandmother*

el hijo único	*only child/son*
la hija única	*only daughter*
(el/la) menor	*(youngest) younger*
(el/la) mayor	*(eldest) older*
los ancestros/	*ancestors*
los antepasados	

¡Manos a la obra!

Actividad 2-1. La familia de Mariana

Paso 1. The following is Mariana's family tree. Describe each person's relationship to Mariana. Follow the example provided.

> **Modelo(s):**   Carlos → *Carlos es el abuelo de Mariana.*

El árbol familiar de Mariana

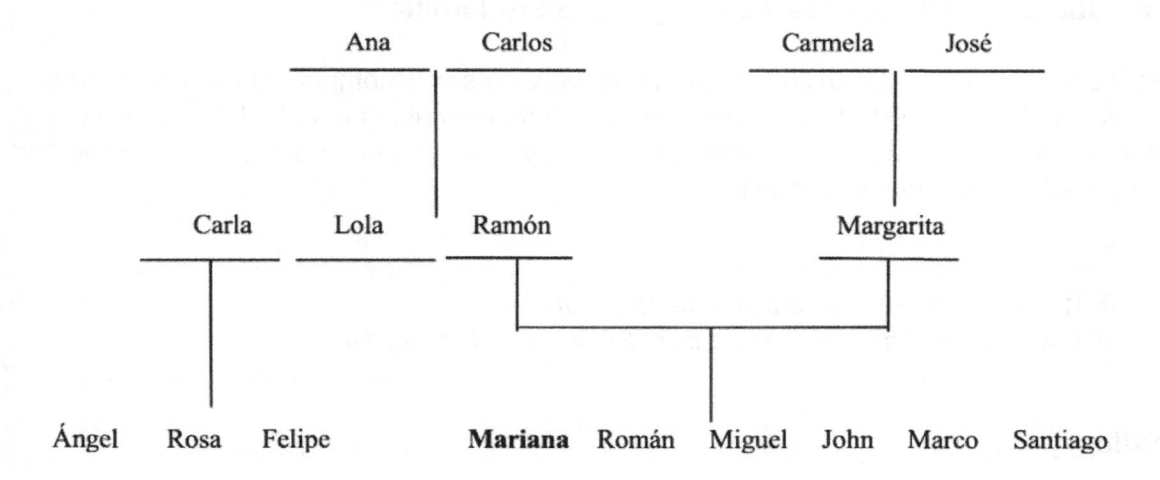

Paso 2. Ahora observa el árbol familiar de Mariana y decide si las oraciones a continuación son Ciertas (C) o Falsas (F). **If the statements are false, explain why**.

1. Los hijos de Carla son los primos de Mariana.	C	F
2. Carmela y José son los tíos de Marco.	C	F
3. Ana es la suegra de Margarita.	C	F

4. Lola es la tía de Felipe.	C F
5. José es un pariente de Rosa.	C F
6. Santiago es el menor de los hijos de Carla.	C F
7. John tiene seis hermanos y dos hermanas.	C F
8. Ramón es el yerno de José y Carmela.	C F
9. Margarita es la hija única de sus padres.	C F
10. Margarita es la tía de Ángel, Rosa y Felipe.	C F

 **Actividad 2-2. Tu árbol genealógico**

Paso 1. Work with a classmate to construct each other's family trees (real or imagined). Each partner creates the other's tree based on the information provided by the partner. Make sure to include names and each person's relation to your partner. While working together, try to use as much Spanish as possible.

> **Modelo(s):** Emily → *Emily es mi hermana.*

Paso 2. How does your partner's family tree compare to Mariana's? How does it compare to your family tree? Are there any similarities? Are there any differences? If so, explain. Be ready to present your work to the rest of the class.

 **Actividad 2-3. ¿Hay una persona _____ en tu familia?**

When we describe our families in Spanish, we often use the verb **ser** accompanied by one or more adjectives. Below you will find a list of adjectives appropriate for describing people. Use this list to ask your partner if these adjectives describe anyone in their family. Use as much Spanish as possible and take turns asking each other about your families.

> **Modelo(s):** **E1:** *¿Hay una persona **simpática** en tu familia?*
> **E2:** *Sí, mis primos son **simpáticos**. Se llaman Alfredo y Gloria.*

Cognados útiles

admirable	arrogante	extravagante
elegante	flexible	idealista
importante	independiente	informal
inteligente	interesante	liberal
materialista	optimista	paciente
pesimista	realista	rebelde
responsable	sentimental	tolerante

Hablemos de gramática: *Expressing Possession and Using Adjectives*

Let's revisit Dylan's blog on Mariana's family. Read the blog once more, and focus on the way Dylan tells us that he is talking about his new Mexican family, Mariana's family. Also look at the adjectives (those words that give us information about the characteristics of a person, place, or thing). What do you notice about the placement of adjectives and their endings?

Attribution: By Mariana Salazar, licensed under CC BY-SA 4.0.

Mi familia mexicana

¡**La familia de Mariana** es muy **amable**! Me siento como parte de **su** familia al instante. Ellos son muy **divertidos** y **graciosos**. Toman muchas fotos, como **mi** familia. Como **ves** en la foto, **la familia de Mariana** es **enorme**. Hoy vamos a comer a la casa **de sus primos**. La familia **lejana** (*extended*) **de Mariana** incluye sus **tíos**, **abuelos**, **primos**, **sobrinos** y **amigos**. Mariana y **su** familia **mexicana** siempre **comen** juntos (*eat together*). ¡Tenemos mucha hambre! (*We're very hungry!*) Para comer, **su** tío cocina chilaquiles. ¡Son muy **deliciosos**!

I. Possession with *de*

In English, we express possession by using an apostrophe (') + the letter "s" (e.g., *Dylan's blog*). But what happens in Spanish? Have a look at these examples from Dylan's blog:

- La familia **de Mariana**
- La familia lejana **de Mariana**

As you can see in these examples, in Spanish we show possession by using the preposition **de + the name of the person or thing to whom/which something belongs**. Also notice that there is a change in word order. In English, the person whose possessions we are talking about comes first, followed by the object they possess (e.g., *Dylan's family*). This is reversed in Spanish: The object comes first, and it is followed by **de**, and the person or thing whose possessions we are talking about (e.g., **la familia de Mariana**).

 **¡Ojo!**

In the examples above we used people's names, but if we have the article **el** before the person/thing whose possessions we are talking about, we must combine **de** and **el** to form *del*.

| **Modelo(s):** | El libro **del** [de + el] estudiante |
| | La computadora **del** profesor |

Note that the articles **la**, **las**, and **los** are not combined with **de**.

Modelo(s):	El libro **de la** profesora
	Las computadoras **de las** niñas
	La clase **de los** estudiantes

II. Using adjectives to express possession

In Dylan's blog, we can also notice possession can be expressed with possessive adjectives. What are these words? Have a look at these examples:

| **Modelo(s):** | **Mi** familia mexicana |
| | **Su** tío. |

Yes, words like **mi** (*my*) and **su** (*her*) are possessive adjectives. We have them in English too, but in Spanish they work in a slightly different way. First, let's have a look at them. What do you notice that is different from English?

mi(s)	*my*
tu(s)	*your*
su(s)	*his/her / your (formal)*
nuestro/a(s)	*our*
vuestro/a(s)	*your (plural; Spain)*
su(s)	*their / your (plural)*

As you can see, possessive adjectives in Spanish have plural and singular forms. This is different from English. Why is this the case? Well, in Spanish, all possessive adjectives agree in number (singular or plural) **with the object being possessed** (**NOT** with the person whose possession we are talking about). Also notice that **nuestro/a(s)** and **vuestro/a(s)** have gender, which means that their form will agree in **both gender and number** with the noun they're referring to. Have a look at these examples:

> **Modelo(s):** Carlos busca **su libro/sus libros**.
> **Mis profesoras** son muy amables.
> **Nuestra aula** es muy cómoda. vs. **Nuestras aulas** son muy cómodas.
> **Los hijos** de Carmen estudian en Tejas. **Sus hijos** son muy inteligentes.
> Gabriela, ¿tú hablas por teléfono con **tu madre/tus padres** todos los días?

III. Los adjetivos descriptivos

Now that we know what structures and words we can use to refer to possessions, let's talk about the words we can use to describe them--**los adjetivos descriptivos** (*descriptive adjectives*). Let's go back to Dylan's blog. What do you notice about adjectives in these examples?

> **Modelo(s):** ¡La familia de Mariana es muy amable!
> Ellos son muy divertidos y graciosos.
> La **familia lejana** de Mariana
> Mi **familia mexicana**

Yes! You guessed! Descriptive adjectives in Spanish must agree with the gender and number! of the noun they describe. This is different from English. Another difference is that adjectives are usually placed **after** the noun they describe (e.g., la familia **lejana**). You already know some descriptive adjectives (remember **los cognados** we learned in **Módulo introductorio** y **Módulo 1**?). And here we offer you more!

 **Audio link:** http://bit.ly/Audio2-3Trayectos

Describimos la apariencia física	
alto	*tall*
bajo	*short (height)*
pequeño	*small*
grande	*big*
delgado/flaco	*thin*
moreno	*with dark hair/dark-skinned*
güero/rubio	*blonde or light-skinned*

Describibimos la personalidad	
abierto/a	*open-minded/open*
aburrido/a	*boring*
amable	*nice*
antipático/a	*unfriendly*
cómico/agracioso/a	*funny/witty*
divertido/a	*fun*
grosero/a	*rude*
perezoso/a	*lazy*
simpático/a	*friendly*
tímido/a	*shy*
trabajador/a	*hard-working*

Los cognados: These words are very similar in Spanish and English. What do they mean? Write the meaning next to the word in Spanish.

Los cognados	
ansioso/a	
complicado/a	
difícil	
energético/a	
extrovertido/a	
introvertido/a	
liberal	
conservador/a	
moderno/a	
nervioso/a	
optimista	
pesimista	
perfeccionista	
sociable	

 **El cactus viajero.**

- In Mexico, the word **güero** can be used interchangeably with **rubio** (*blonde*).
- In Argentina and Spain, the word **vago** is used in place of **perezoso**. In Mexico, **flojo** is preferred.

 **¡Manos a la obra!**

Actividad 2-4. La reunión familiar de Mariana

Mariana is writing an entry in Dylan's blog. She is describing a road trip with her family. La familia viaja para visitar unos parientes en Oaxaca, Mexico. How is Mariana using her possessive adjectives? Complete the following paragraph with the appropriate possessive adjective.

1. _____ (My) padres, 2. _____ (my) hermanos, 3. _____ (their) gato y yo vivimos (*live*) en Houston, pero 4. _____ (our) parientes son de Oaxaca, México. Nosotros viajamos en el auto de 5. _____ (my) padre desde Houston a Oaxaca. 6. _____ (His) auto es muy viejo y entonces (*so*) 7. _____ (our) viaje dura cinco días! Primero, pasamos la frontera (*border*). Después, viajamos a San Luis Potosí. Allí está la casa de 8. _____ (my) tíos, Carla y Fernando. 9. ¡_____ (Their) perros ladran (*bark*) mucho! Finalmente, llegamos a Oaxaca y pasamos mucho tiempo con 10. _____ (our) abuela y otros parientes. ¿Tú visitas a 11. _____ (your) familia seguido (*often*)? ¿De dónde son 12. _____ (your) padres? Deja (*leave*) un comentario.

 **Actividad 2-5. Una familia**

Paso 1. Con un@ compañer@, mira la ilustración y habla sobre las posesiones: **¿De quién son las cosas en la lista?** Follow the model and use your creativity. Take turns asking and answering questions.

> **Modelo(s):** **E1:** ¿De quién son los barcos (*the boats*)?
> **E2:** Son de los turistas.

1. La casa

2. Las plantas

3. El libro

4. Los gatos

5. Los autos

6. La soga de saltar (*jump rope*)

Attribution: Public domain.

Paso 2. ¿Quién es esta familia?

Ahora con tu compañer@, describe a la familia en la ilustración. Use the following questions to come up with ideas. Remember that you can ask your instructor for help if you want to use a word you haven't learned yet! And, of course, there's always Google! Be creative!

1. ¿Quiénes son los miembros de esta familia? ¿Cómo se llaman? ¿Cuántos años tienen?

2. ¿Qué son (profesión)?

3. ¿Cómo son los miembros de esta familia? Usando las palabras en **Hablemos de gramática** (pgs. 98-99), describe la apariencia física y la personalidad de cada (*each*) miembro de esta familia.

4. ¿De dónde son?

5. ¿Dónde están ahora (*now*)? ¿De quién es la casa? ¿Dónde está la casa? ¿Cómo es la casa?

 ¡Ojo!

In **Módulo introductorio**, we introduced the question **¿Cuántos años tienes?** to ask about someone's age. You can learn the forms of the verb **tener** to talk about people's age. The forms are presented below. Also, pay attention to the example.

Modelo(s): **(Yo) tengo** veinte años.

Formas: **Tú tienes/vos tenés; él/ella/usted tiene; nosotros/nosotras tenemos; vosotros/vosotras tenéis; ellos/ellas/ustedes tienen.**

Paso 3. Now use the ideas you guys discussed, and write a short composition describing the family in the painting. Be prepared to share your work with your other classmates.

 **Actividad 2-6. Una entrevista a Cintia**

Cintia is the president of the Mexican Student Association at a university in Texas. In the following interview, she talks about her family from the state of Guanajuato, Mexico. Remember the city of San Miguel de Allende? We learned about it in **Módulo 1**. San Miguel de Allende is in Guanajuato. Ahora mira el video y contesta las siguientes preguntas.

 ¡Los estudiantes preguntan (*ask questions*)!

Video link: https://bit.ly/Video21Trayectos

Attribution: By Marlenie Arzamendi and Dylan Manshack, licensed under CC BY-SA 4.0.

1. ¿A qué hora es la entrevista?
2. ¿De dónde es Cintia?
3. ¿Qué ciudad de Tejas es la ciudad de Cintia?
4. ¿Cuántos años tiene Cintia? ¿Cómo es? (Describe a Cintia usando las imágenes.)
5. ¿Quién es el ídolo de Cintia? ¿Cómo es esta persona?
6. ¿De qué otros parientes habla Cintia? ¿Cómo son?
7. ¿Es Cintia hija única?

 **¡*Conversemos!*￼**

Today in your Spanish class you are learning about families. Your Spanish professor asks you to work with a classmate to find out about each other's family. Talk about the members of your immediate family and your relatives. Talk about their personality and physical appearance and age (remember to use the verb **tener**; see **Actividad 2-5**); where they are from; what they do for a living. Also give information about their routines (e.g., activities during the week and weekend, etc.). Use the vocabulary and structures we learned in **Módulo introductorio** y **Módulo 1**.

 **Práctica individual:** To practice your new vocabulary and structures, go to http://bit.ly/PracticaIndividual2-2.

Y después... Uso, forma y cultura: *El Día de la Madre*

I. Antes de ver

As these photos show, moms come in all forms and sizes, but they all play an important role in our lives. In this section, we will watch a video made by the Mexican actor and director Diego Luna (http://bit.ly/DiegoLunaInfo) for Mother's Day. What do you think the video is going to be like? What ideas will he include? Write three ideas. Use the photos to think of possible topics.

Attribution: Public domain

Attribution: Public domain.

Attribution: By Gabriela C. Zapata, licensed under CC BY-SA 4.0.

Attribution: Public domain.

 II. A ver

Now watch the Día de la Madre video en http://bit.ly/Video2-2Trayectos, and check if your ideas coincide with the ones that appear in it.

III. Después de ver

Actividad 2-7. Are there any similarities/differences between your ideas and the ones shown in the video? Name two.

 **Actividad 2-8.** Now watch the video again, and do the following exercises con un@ compañer@.

Actividad A. ¿Cómo son las mamás en el vídeo? Describe su personalidad.

Actividad B. En el vídeo, Diego Luna dice *(says)*: "Todas las mamás son unas mentirosas (mienten = no hablan con la verdad [*truth*])". "Mentir" is usually a negative verb. Is it negative in this video? These are some of instances in which Diego Luna says mothers don't tell the truth:

- "Cuando siempre [dice] que eres el mejor (*the best*)."
- "Esa cena (*dinner*) no [es] especial para astronautas."
- "[Dice] que [eres] el más guapo (*the most handsome*)."
- "También miente a sus necesidades. Miente cuando dice que no le importa levantarse más temprano (*she doesn't care about getting up early*)."
- "Miente porque no la tiene fácil (*life is not easy for her*)."
- "Cuando te dice que todo estará bien (*everything will be OK*)."

Is the use of the verb "mentir" really negative in this video? What is the message of the video? Using the information and images, describe its main purpose. Who is the audience for this video? Justify your opinions.

Actividad C. The last phrase of the video is "Gracias, Jefas." What does the word "jefa" mean? Look it up, and think about why this word is used in the video. What does it say about the role of the mother in Hispanic families?

Actividad D. Organizational features. How is the video organized? Choose all that apply and explain briefly why you selected each organizational feature—what were the clues in the video?

1. Chronological
2. Description
3. Cause and effect
4. Compare and contrast
5. Informational justification from video

Actividad E. Do you think this commercial would work in the US? Why? Why not?

Actividad 2-9. Representaciones de la familia
Now we are going to analyze a painting by Colombian artist Fernando Botero (we will learn about Colombia in this module).

Mira la obra y describe:

1. Qué miembros de la familia están en la obra;

2. Cómo son, cómo están;

3. Qué roles tienen (de acuerdo a su posición y actitud en el cuadro).

 **Actividad 2-10.** Con tres o cuatro compañer@s, contesta estas preguntas.

1. Think of the video we watched. Are there any connections between the video and the painting? Why? /Why not? How are mothers characterized in the two?

2. What other visual elements can you talk about? What was Botero's purpose when he painted this picture? Why do you think he included these elements? What is the message behind this work?

3. Now watch the following videos. You will see images of some of Botero's works. Focus on the images and labels shown. What are some of the themes he depicts in his work? What is Botero worried about? Why do you think all his figures are so big?

   - Vídeo número 1: http://bit.ly/Video2-3Trayectos
   - Vídeo número 2: http://bit.ly/Video2-4Trayectos

     A. ¿En qué ciudades de Colombia hay obras (*works*) de Botero?
     B. ¿Es el arte de Botero variado? ¿Por qué? ¿Por qué no? You can answer this question in English.

You can learn more about Botero by reading this Wikipedia entry: http://bit.ly/BoteroInfo.

Más comunicación: *Las nacionalidades*

¿De dónde son los estudiantes?

Remember Carolina, the new student we met in **Módulo 1**? She is interviewing fellow students to ask where they are from. Mira el video. ¿De dónde son los estudiantes? ¿Hay estudiantes en tu clase de estos tres países?

 ¿De dónde son los estudiantes?

Video link: https://bit.ly/Video25Trayectos

Attribution: By Dylan Manshack and Carolina Cantú, licensed under CC BY-SA 4.0

In the video, the students mention three different countries. Take a look at the table below to learn more about nationalities in Spanish. Keep in mind nationalities are descriptive adjectives, and, thus, **they must agree in gender and number with the person that they describe**.

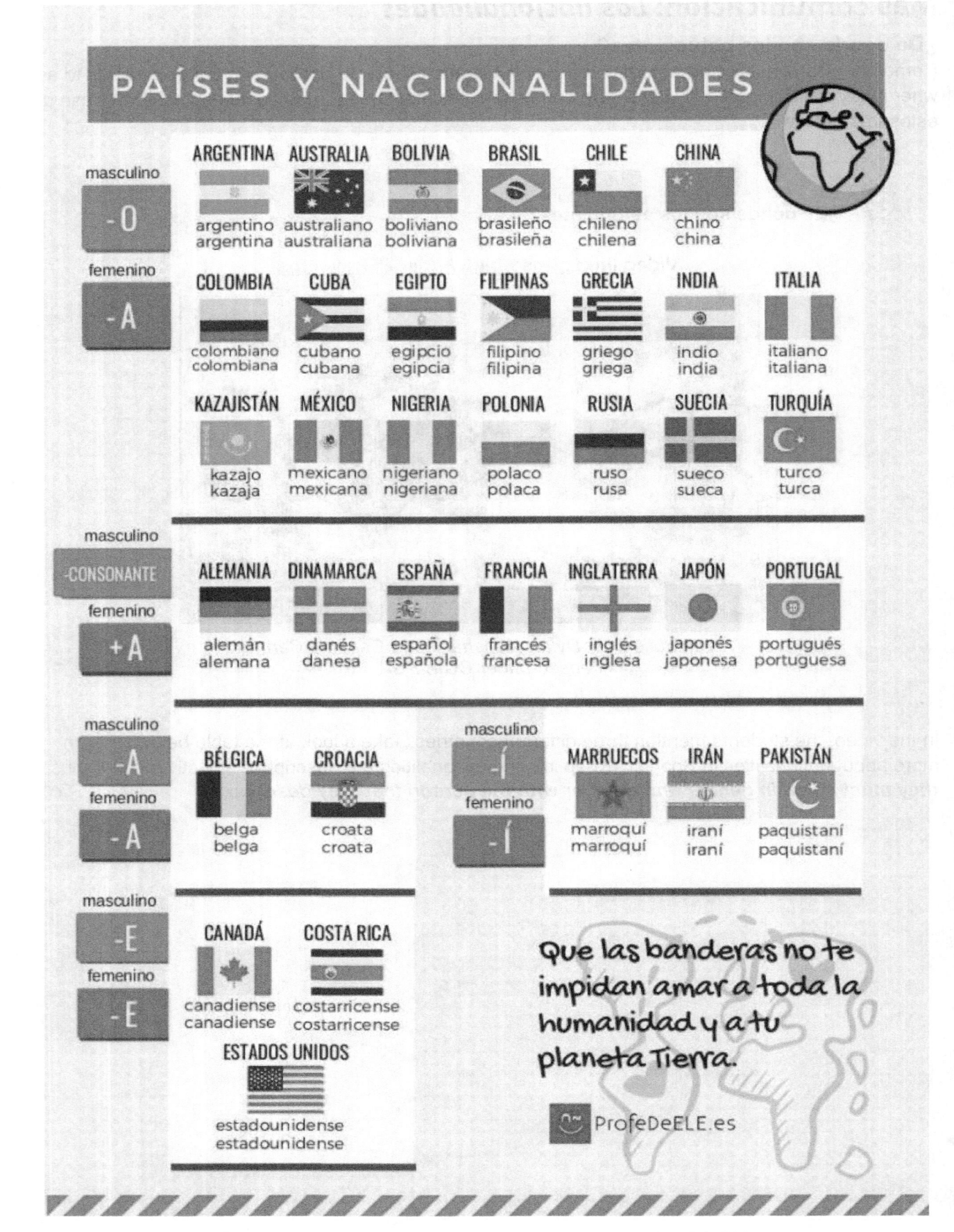

PAÍSES Y NACIONALIDADES

Ahora mira este video. You will find more comprehensive information on countries and nationalities, and how to use adjectives to describe them.

 Más sobre las nacionalidades

Video link: https://bit.ly/Video26Trayectos

Attribution: By Daniel Hernández Ruiz, licensed under CC BY 4.0.

 ¡Ojo!

English and Spanish do not have the same rules for capitalization when we use **gentilicios** (adjectives to describe nationalities). In Spanish nationalities are never capitalized (e.g., **mexicano**, **estadounidense**); however, the names of countries and continents are.

 **¡Manos a la obra!**

Actividad 2-11. ¿Cuánto sabes (*do you know*) del mundo?

¿De dónde son? Name the nationality/place of origin of these people and things. If you don't know what they are, google them!

Modelo(s): Los vaqueros (cowboys) → *Los vaqueros son tejanos.*

1. Las tortillas de maíz	6. El tango
2. La Nutella	7. Los koalas
3. Las baguettes	8. Los camellos (*camels*)
4. Las empanadas	9. El regatón
5. El flamenco	10. El son
	11. Los mariachis.

Actividad 2-12. Más nacionalidades

Write the nationality that corresponds to the flags shown in the illustration in the sentences provided. Pay attention to gender and number. When gender is not specified, write both forms (e.g., italiano/italiana).

BANDERAS DEL MUNDO

NACIONALIDADES DEL MUNDO

1. ¿Vos sos **italiano/italiana** (de Italia)?
2. Nosotros somos _____.
3. Ellos son _____.
4. Vosotras sois _____.
5. Tú eres _____.
6. Él es _____.
7. Yo soy _____.
8. Tú eres _____.
9. Nosotros somos _____.
10. Él es _____.
11. Tú eres _____.
12. Ellos son _____.
13. Vosotros sois _____.
14. Ellas son _____.
15. Yo soy _____.
16. Él es _____.
17. Ellas son _____.
18. Vosotras sois _____.
19. Ella es _____.
20. Vos sos _____.
21. Vosotras sois _____.
22. Nosotros somos _____.
23. Yo soy _____.
24. Usted es _____.

Attribution: By Daniel Hernández Ruiz, licensed under CC BY 4.0

Actividad 2-13. El mundo hispano

Go to this website (http://bit.ly/ActividadNacionalidades), and do **Actividad 2: El mundo hispano**. Take down notes to discuss your work in class.

Actividad 2-14. Nacionalidades escondidas (hidden)

Con tres o cuatros compañer@s, busca las 14 nacionalidades hidden in this box. The group that finishes first wins!

L	K	J	V	C	U	B	A	N	O	H	H	O	M
G	C	E	B	H	W	L	D	L	O	G	X	X	O
C	U	S	E	I	A	T	P	S	L	Y	J	J	Y
K	E	K	L	L	W	V	C	U	H	C	R	V	V
B	A	W	G	E	J	A	P	O	N	É	S	U	G
V	H	D	A	N	E	S	A	L	E	M	Á	N	R
N	Z	D	N	O	J	U	Q	R	F	T	B	Z	I
L	O	E	N	U	Y	S	U	E	C	O	F	D	E
U	F	B	O	L	I	V	I	A	N	O	S	P	G
Q	U	G	Y	L	H	E	S	P	A	Ñ	O	L	A
H	B	G	L	Z	P	Z	T	C	W	X	T	O	A
Q	I	N	G	L	E	S	A	X	F	O	M	W	T
C	A	N	A	D	I	E	N	S	E	X	L	C	I
M	A	R	R	O	Q	U	Í	T	I	U	U	P	Y

1. _____
2. _____
3. _____
4. _____
5. _____
6. _____
7. _____
8. _____
9. _____
10. _____
11. _____
12. _____
13. _____
14. _____

Attribution: By Daniel Hernández Ruiz, licensed under CC BY 4.0.

 **Práctica individual:** To practice your new vocabulary, go to http://bit.ly/PracticaIndividual2-3.

Hablemos de gramática: *Present tense of "-er" and "-ir" verbs*

Las actividades de Carolina

Do you remember Carolina? Today she is writing an email to a member of her family in México.

¿Cuáles son las actividades de Carolina? Read the email below, paying attention to the verbs in bold. What do you notice about the endings?

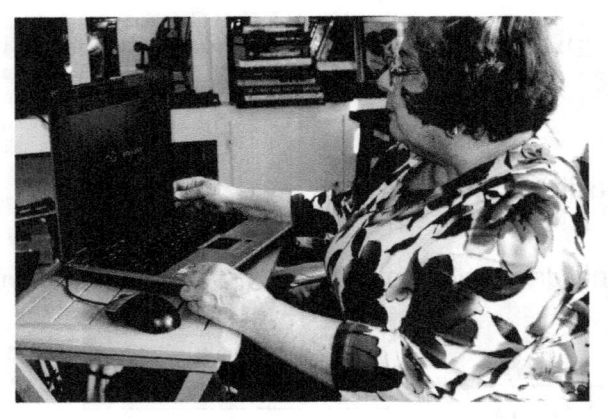

Hola, abuelita. ¿Cómo estás? ¡Espero que muy bien! La universidad es difícil, pero muy interesante. En general, los estudiantes **asisten** (*attend*) a clase todos los días. En mis clases, **leo** muchos libros y **escribo** muchos ejercicios y ensayos (*essays*). Bailey y yo **aprendemos** mucho sobre el español en los Estados Unidos en la clase de la Dra. Moyna. Extraño (*I miss*) mucho tus chilaquiles. Siempre **como** comida rápida. También **corro** 3 millas en el parque tres veces por semana…

La abuelita de Carolina lee el email
Attribution: Public domain.

¿Comprendiste? Responde estas preguntas sobre el email.

1. Let's talk about verbs first. See if you can find an example of the following in the email:

   Unos verbos conjugados:

   - Verbs conjugated in first person singular (**yo** form):
   - Verbs conjugated in first person plural (**nosotros** form):
   - Verbs conjugated in third person plural (**ellos** form):

   What do these verbs share? What do you already know about these verb endings?

2. Now let's talk about the content of the email (continue paying attention to the verb endings):

   1. ¿A quién escrib**e** Carolina?
   2. ¿Cuándo asist**en** a clase los estudiantes? Y tú, ¿cuándo asist**es** a clase?
   3. ¿Qué escrib**e** Carolina en sus clases?
   4. ¿Qué comida com**e** Carolina?
   5. ¿Cuántas millas corr**e** Carolina? Y tú, ¿corr**es**?

All the conjugated verbs that appear in the dialogue are in the present tense (**el tiempo presente**). In this section, we will learn how to conjugate verbs with the **-er** and **-ir** endings in the present tense.

 **¡Manos a la obra!**

The Present Tense of –er and -ir Verbs
I. Infinitives and Conjugations

-er verbs: To conjugate, drop the **–er** from the infinitive. Next, add endings to the stem. The ending will depend on who is doing the action (remember *the subject*, discussed in **Módulo introductorio** [p. 9]). Have a look at this example:

Comer *(to eat)*		
yo	**como**	*I eat*
tú	**comes**	*you (informal) eat*
vos	**comés**	*you (informal) eat; mostly Argentina & Uruguay*
usted, Ud., él, ella	**come**	*you (formal) eat, he/she eats*
nosotros(as)	**comemos**	*we eat*
vosotros(as)	**coméis**	*y'all (informal: Spain) eat*
ustedes, Uds., ellos/ellas	**comen**	*y'all eat, they eat*

-ir verbs: To conjugate, drop the **–ir** from the infinitive. Next, add endings to the stem. The ending will depend on who is doing the action (remember *the subject*, discussed in **Módulo introductorio** [p. 9]). Have a look at this example.

Vivir *(to live)*		
yo	**vivo**	*I live*
tú	**vives**	*you* (informal) *live*
vos	**vivís**	*you (informal) eat; mostly Argentina & Uruguay*
usted, Ud., él, ella	**vive**	*you* (formal) *live, he/she lives*
nosotros(as)	**vivimos**	*we live*
vosotros(as)	**vivís**	*y'all* (informal: Spain) *live*
ustedes, Uds., ellos/ellas	**viven**	*y'all live, they live*

II. Ejemplos de verbos en *-er* e *-ir* en las actividades de la universidad y con la familia.

 **Audio link: http://bit.ly/Audio2-4Trayectos**

asistir	*to learn*
beber	*to attend*
compartir	*to drink*
correr	*to share*
escribir	*to run*
imprimir	*to write*
leer	*to print*
ver	*to read*
vender	*to see/watch*
vivir	*to sell*
	to live

The following video summarizes the information discussed in this section, and it reviews what we already know about **-ar** verbs.

 Presente regular en español

Video link: https://bit.ly/Video27Trayectos

Attribution: Presente regular en español - Spanish Regular Verbs in Present Tense. By ProfeDeELE.es, licensed under CC BY 3.0.

 **¡Manos a la obra!**

Actividad 2-15. Go to this website (http://bit.ly/ActividadPresente), and do **Actividad 4: Completar**. Take down notes to discuss your work in class.

Actividad 2-16. Un correo electrónico

Remember Dylan? He is writing an email to introduce himself to his future host family in Guanajuato, Mexico. He needs some help! Complete the following paragraph with the appropriate forms of the verbs in parenthesis.

New Message

To _____

Subject _____

Estimada Sra. Salazar:

Me llamo Dylan. Soy estudiante universitario en Tejas. Yo 1. _____ **(aprender)** mucho español este semestre y 2. _____ **(leer)** muchos artículos sobre la cultura mexicana. Mis amigos y yo 3. _____ **(asistir)** a clases todos los días a excepción de los sábados y domingos. También mi mejor amigo, Francisco, y yo 4. _____ **(trabajar)** para una organización de ayuda (*help*) a inmigrantes hispanos. Los dos somos activistas y 5. _____ **(compartir)** muchas ideas!

Los fines de semana, yo 6. _____ **(visitar)** a mi familia en Corpus Christi. Ellos 7. _____ **(vivir)** en una casa cerca del monumento *El Mirador de la Flor*. ¿Ustedes 8. _____ **(escuchar)** música de Selena? Mi canción favorita es *Bidi Bidi Bom Bom*. Los domingos, mi novio, Matt, y Mariana 9. _____ **(beber)** café en Starbucks y 10. _____ **(comer)** *bagels* allí también. Ellos son muy buenos amigos. :-)

¿Qué actividades 11. _____ **(compartir)** usted con su familia? Pronto yo 12. _____ **(escribir)** otro email.

¡Hasta pronto!

Dylan

SEND

 **Actividad 2-17. ¿Dónde?**

Find a Google map of your city. Con un@ compañer@, habla de tus lugares favoritos to do the following activities. Take turns asking and answering questions. Don't forget to point out the locations on the map.

> **Modelo(s):** **E1:** ¿Dónde **beben** tú y tus amigos?
> **E2: Bebemos** en Harry's
> **E1:** ¿Dónde **comes/comés** los fines de semana?
> **E2: Como** en Napa Flats.

1. aprender
2. bailar
3. comprar
4. correr
5. escribir
6. estudiar
7. imprimir
8. trabajar
9. vivir
10. ver películas *(movies)*

 **Actividad 2-18. Las familias de la clase**

Con tres o cuatros compañer@s, you will need to create a summary of the main characteristics that can be used to describe **la familia tejana** as represented by students' families.

Paso 1. You will need to ask and answer questions in Spanish (use the vocabulary and structures you have learned so far) to find out the following information:

> **Modelo(s):** **E1:** ¿De dónde son tus padres?
> **E2:** Son de Austin. ¿Y tus padres?
> **E1:** Son de Lubbock

1. Place where the family lives
2. Number of family members and names
3. Professions (your instructor can help you with vocabulary)
4. Common activities among the members of the family (include at least three different verbs; your instructor can help you with vocabulary)

Paso 2. Write a summary of your results to present to the rest of the class. ¿Cuáles son las similitudes?

 **Práctica individual:** To continue using your new verbs, go to http://bit.ly/PracticaIndividual2-4.

Hablemos de cultura: *Colombia*

 Una estudiante colombiana

Erika es una estudiante de Colombia. Mira el siguiente video y completa el cuadro a continuación. ¿De qué habla?

Video link: https://bit.ly/Video28Trayectos

Erika estudia en…

Erika es de…

Su lugar favorito es…

Su familia vive en…

Su familia: Erika habla de…

Attribution: By Dylan Manshack, licensed under CC BY-SA 4.0.

Antes de leer el texto, busca información sobre la comida de Erika y la música de Colombia. Presenta a tus compañeros tu información. Ahora lee el texto.

 **Cartagena de Indias[7]**

En el vídeo, Erika habla de la ciudad de Cartagena (de Indias). ¿Dónde está en Cartagena? Busca en un mapa. Luego lee la información del texto.

La ciudad de Cartagena está en el norte de Colombia en las costas del mar Caribe y es considerada como una de las ciudades más fascinantes y mágicas del mundo. La ciudad fue fundada (*was founded*) por los españoles en el siglo XVI (dieciséis) como un puerto de comercio entre los continentes. Hay una gran diversidad racial y miles (*thousands*) de turistas visitan la ciudad cada año.

Cartagena está dividida en dos secciones, la primera es la parte colonial o tradicional de la ciudad. Aquí hay restaurantes de primera categoría, clubes, bares y hoteles coloniales pequeños. En esta parte de la ciudad también está el centro histórico, con muchas casas coloniales restauradas, parques y muchas calles coloridas. La parte moderna de la ciudad se llama Bocagrande y allí hay grandes hoteles frente del mar y playas (*beaches*) con muchos turistas. En las fotos a continuación, vemos las dos partes de la ciudad de Cartagena.

---

7   Text modified from: "Cartagena de Indias" by Wikiviajes, licensed under CC BY-SA 3.0.

Attribution: Public domain   *Attribution: Public domain.*

Actividades en Cartagena

En Cartagena hay actividades para toda la familia. Una actividad favorita de los turistas es caminar por la parte colonial de la ciudad y apreciar la historia y arquitectura del lugar. También es posible explorar puntos de interés como la Entrada o Torre del Reloj (http://bit.ly/TorreRelojCartagena), el Castillo de San Felipe y sus murallas (*walls*) (http://bit.ly/CastilloSanFelipeCart) y las iglesias de estilo barroco (http://bit.ly/IglesiasCartagena). Otra opción es visitar los museos de la ciudad como el Museo Histórico y Palacio de la Inquisición (http://bit.ly/MuseoInCartagena) y otros museos interesantes (http://bit.ly/MuseosRutaCartagena).

El Castillo de San Felipe.
Attribution: Public domain.

Pasar tiempo en la playa también es posible. Cartagena ofrece alternativas magníficas como la Isla Tierrabomba (https://bit.ly/IslaTierrabomba) y Playa Blanca (http://bit.ly/PlayaBlancaCol). Allí hay complejos turísticos con una variedad de actividades acuáticas para toda la familia. En esta área también es posible visitar el acuario y nadar con los delfines. De noche, hay en Cartagena lugares para bailar, escuchar conciertos de música, comer comida típica o internacional y mucho más.

Attribution: Public domain

Attribution: Plaza Santo Domingo, Night Scenes, Cartagena, Colombia, By Joe Ross, licensed under CC BY-SA 2.0.

 Más sobre Cartagena.

Ahora vemos un video que habla sobre las actividades nocturnas en Cartagena. Mira el vídeo en este enlace: http://bit.ly/Video2-9Trayectos

Actividad 2-19. ¿Comprendiste?
Lee las oraciones a continuación y based on the video, decide if they are **Ciertas (C)** o **Falsas (F)**.

1. La Plaza de Santo Domingo es un parque donde hay mucha diversión *(fun)*.	C	F
2. En el centro histórico compramos copias de las esculturas de Botero.	C	F
3. En Cartagena, no hay muchas actividades para las familias.	C	F
4. Los bailes tradicionales colombianos incluyen mucho cardio.	C	F
5. Los bailarines *(dancers)* enseñan a los turistas sobre la variedad de música colombiana.	C	F
6. Los turistas únicamente visitan el centro histórico en carreta *(carriage)*.	C	F
7. En las discotecas de Cartagena solo hay música tradicional.	C	F

Actividad 2-20. Más sobre el video.
1. ¿Qué lugares hay cerca de la plaza Santo Domingo?
2. ¿Qué actividades nocturnas hay para los turistas? Usa los verbos de los **Módulos introductorio, 1 y 2**.
3. ¿Cómo son las artesanías *(crafts)* de Cartagena? Describe algunas. Usa los adjetivos de los **Módulos introductorio, 1 y 2**.

Actividad 2-21. Tu opinión

A. Do you think Erika's description of Cartagena matches the information and images in the text and video? What information or perceptions do they have in common?
B. What activities would you do in Cartagena? You can watch this video to gather more info about the place: http://bit.ly/Video2-10Trayectos. Try to use the verbs you already know.
C. Use three adjectives in Spanish to describe Cartagena based on the text and videos.
D. What are some of the similarities and differences between the "vida nocturna" in Cartagena, Colombia and the city where you live? Which one do you think is more interesting?

 **Práctica individual:** To check how much you remember about the information you just learned, go to http://bit.ly/PracticalIndividual2-5.

Más comunicación: *Los números 30 a 100*

Colombia en números

En la sección anterior, **Hablemos de cultura**, vemos a la gente de Colombia y visitamos virtualmente la ciudad de Cartagena. ¿Es Colombia un país diverso? ¿Cuál es el grupo étnico con más personas? En este cuadro, hay algunos números del país. Lee la información a continuación:

Números importantes

--Población: 49 millones

--Número de provincias: 32

--37,5% tierra de agricultura

--54,4% bosque

--79% de la población son católicos

--60% de la población vive en los llanos del sur y este

84,5% Mestizos y blancos
10,4% Afrocolombianos
3,4% Amerindios

Attribution: Datos de Colombia. By Gabriela C. Zapata, licensed under CC BY-SA 4.0.

121

¿Comprendiste?

Usa la tabla a continuación y la información sobre Colombia para contestar estas preguntas.

1. ¿Cuántos estados (por ejemplo, Iowa, Tejas, etc.) hay en los Estados Unidos?
2. ¿Cómo se llaman los estados en Colombia? ¿Cuántos hay?
3. ¿Cuántos habitantes hay en Colombia?
4. ¿Cuál es la religión mayoritaria del país?
5. ¿Qué etnias hay en Colombia? ¿Qué porcentaje de afrocolombianos hay? Para aprender más sobre los afrodescendientes en América Latina, te recomendamos este recurso: http://bit.ly/AfrodesBancoMundial.

Ahora veamos cómo expresamos los números del 30 al 100.

Audio link: http://bit.ly/Audio2-5Trayectos

Los números del 30 al 100

30	treinta	40	cuarenta
31	treinta y uno	50	cincuenta
32	treinta y dos	60	sesenta
33	treinta y tres	70	setenta
34	treinta y cuatro	80	ochenta
35	treinta y cinco	90	noventa
36	treinta y seis	100	cien
37	treinta y siete		
38	treinta y ocho		
39	treinta y nueve		

 **¡Ojo!**

In Spanish, decimals are usually expressed with a comma (e.g., 10,4%). However, in recent years, both, a dot (**un punto**) and a comma, are accepted (http://bit.ly/DecimalesRAE).

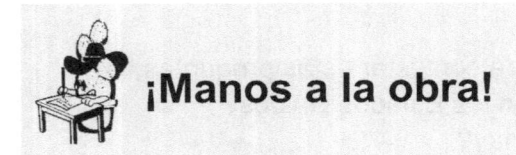 **¡Manos a la obra!**

 Actividad 2-22. Más sobre Botero

Mira el siguiente vídeo y elige (*choose*) una opción según la información presentada.

Video link: https://bit.ly/Video211Trayectos

Attribution: "Fernando Botero presenta su obra en Roma,
By NotimexTV, licensed under CC BY 4.0.

1. Botero tiene
   1. ochenta años.
   2. ochenta y cinco años.
   3. ochenta y siete años.

2. Botero trabaja por
   1. cincuenta años.
   2. setenta años.
   3. sesenta años.

3. En la exhibición de Botero, hay más (*more than*) de
   1. treinta obras.
   2. cuarenta obras.
   3. cincuenta obras.

4. La exhibición de las obras de Botero está en
   1. Roma.
   2. Bogotá.
   3. Cartagena.

5. En la exhibición, las obras de Botero están divididas en
   1. siete secciones.
   2. ocho secciones.
   3. nueve secciones.

6. Vemos las obras de Botero hasta *(until)* el día
    1. veintisiete de agosto.
    2. veintiocho de agosto.
    3. veintinueve de agosto.

Actividad 2-23. Dylan va al mercado

Dylan is helping his host mother organized a family dinner. Complete the following paragraph with the numbers in parenthesis.

Dylan tiene 1. _____ (99) pesos para comprar la comida para la cena familiar con los parientes de Mariana en Oaxaca. Primero, compra 2. _____ (27) limones para el agua fresca (http://bit.ly/AguaFrescaInfo), 3. _____ (33) aguacates *(avocados)* para la salsa, 4. _____ (40) kilos de pollo *(chicken)* y 5. _____ (77) duraznos (peaches) para el postre *(dessert)*.

El costo de la comida es 6. _____ (84) pesos. Dylan quiere *(wants)* tomar un taxi, pero necesita 7. _____ (21) pesos.

¿Cuánto dinero extra necesita Dylan para el taxi? 8. _____.

 **Actividad 2-24. Los números locales**

Con un compañer@, busca la siguiente información sobre tu universidad/ciudad/estado.

1. Número de estudiantes en la banda de música de la universidad
2. Número de profesores en
    a. La facultad de humanidades
    b. La facultad de ciencias
    c. La facultad de educación
    d. La facultad de negocios
3. Número de habitantes en tu estado y ciudad (usa el número + millones o mil *(thousand)*; (e.g., cuarenta millones; treinta y tres mil)
4. Número de museos en tu estado y ciudad
5. Número de restaurantes en tu ciudad
6. Otros números interesantes

Práctica individual: To continue using your new numbers, go to http://bit.ly/PracticalIndividual2-6.

Trayectos hispanos: *Visiones artísticas de la familia*

 En esta sección, aprendemos sobre artistas y escritores hispanos y su visión de la familia.

Attribution: Una familia feliz con Noel y Nelly Valencia.
By Noel Valencia, licensed under CC BY-SA 4.0.

A continuación, hay una foto de la obra *The Washington Family* (1789-1796) del artista Edward Savage (http://bit.ly/EdwardSavage). ¿Qué otros artistas en los Estados Unidos representan la familia a través de la historia? Escribe ejemplos. ¿Cómo son sus representaciones?

Attribution: The Washington Family (1789-1796). Public domain.

 Ahora leemos sobre los artistas/escritores hispanos/latinx.

Carmen Lomas Garza[8]

Attribution: Carmen Lomas Garza. By Texas State Library and Archives Commission from Austin, TX, United States, licensed under CC BY 2.0.

Carmen Lomas Garza (1948) es una artista e ilustradora de Kingsville, Texas. Sus trabajos están inspirados en su herencia mexicoamericana y es parte permanente de las colecciones de estos museos: the Smithsonian American Art Museum, the Hirshhorn Museum and Sculpture Garden, the National Museum of Mexican Art, the San Jose Museum of Art, the Mexican Museum, the Pennsylvania Academy of the Fine Arts y the Oakland Museum of California. Sus obras muestran (*show*) escenas de las actividades de su familia y su comunidad en Kingsville.

Lomas Garza también combina su arte con escritos (*written pieces*) y escribe varios libros para niños sobre su vida familiar. En su arte, hay símbolos y elementos culturales. En estos libros, hay escenas con colores vívidos y texto bilingüe, en español e inglés.

The initial roots of Lomas Garza's artwork lay in her family, to whom she is close, and in the Chicano Movement (http://bit.ly/ChicanoMov). She believes that the Chicano Movement nourished her goal of becoming an artist and gave her back her voice. She says that her artistic creations helped her "heal the wounds inflicted by discrimination and racism." She also feels that by creating positive images of Mexican-American families, her work can help combat racism.

 Exploración

En este video, Carmen Lomas Garza habla de su arte e inspiración.

Video link: http://bit.ly/CarmenWork

Attribution: Papel picado. By timlewisnm, licensed under CC BY-SA 2.0.

---

8 Text adapted from the original: Carmen Lomas Garza. By Wikipedia, licensed under CC BY-SA 3.0.

Trabajas con 4 o 5 compañer@s y exploran una obra de Carmen Lomas Garza. En esta obra, hay elementos culturales. Mira la obra y completa estas actividades:

Paso 1. Mira la obra *Lotería-Tabla Llena* (https://bit.ly/TablaLlena), one of Lomas Garza's first works. ¿Qué miembros de la familia de Carmen están en la obra? Escribe una lista. Usa el vocabulario de este módulo.

 Paso 2.

En esta obra hay elementos culturales. Investiga qué son y qué significan en la cultura mexicana/mexicoamericana. Usa los enlaces. Each group will explore one element. Be prepared to share the information you gather with other groups.

- **Grupo 1: Lomas Garza's family is playing lotería. ¿Cómo es el juego de la lotería?**
  - ○ Consider the information and examples on this webpage: https://bit.ly/loteriasite. Is *lotería* just a game? What is its significance for the Mexican-American communities in this country? How have artists used *lotería*?

- **Grupo 2:** In Lomas Garza's work, we see *papel picado*. ¿Qué es *el papel picado*?
  - ○ Consider the information and examples presented on this webpage: http://bit.ly/PaPicado. What is the history of *papel picado*? What is its significance for the Mexican-American communities in this country? Watch this video (http://bit.ly/CarmenPicado) of Carmen Lomas Garza showing how to create *papel picado* ¿Es fácil?

- On this page (http://bit.ly/MagicWindows), you can also see examples of Lomas Garza's use of *papel picado* in her book *Magic Windows/Ventanas mágicas*. What aspects of her heritage and family did she choose to portray? Why do you think she chose them?

- **Grupo 3:** In Lomas Garza's work, we see *la Virgen de Guadalupe* on the table (on the right-hand side). ¿Quién es la Virgen de Guadalupe y cuál es su significado para la comunidad mexicoamericana?
  - ○ Consider the information on this webpage: http://bit.ly/VirgenG. ¿Quién es Juan Diego (http://bit.ly/JuDiego)? How is the Virgen de Guadalupe connected to both the Indigenous and Spanish aspects of Mexican culture? Based on the information you have gathered, why do you think Lomas Garza chose to include the Virgin in her painting? What is the symbolism?

Paso 3. Now go back to the first work we saw *The Washington Family* and compare it with la obra *Lotería-Tabla Llena* (https://bit.ly/TablaLlena). Con tus compañer@s, compara las dos obras, teniendo en cuenta (*taking into account*):

- Miembros de la familia
- Lugar—¿dónde están?
- Cosas (*things*) en la escena
- Uso de colores

Based on this information: What are the similarities and differences between the two works? Explain them in terms of artists' objective, time when the works were created, and social identities (artists and people in the paintings).

Gary Soto[9]

Gary Soto (1952) es un escritor mexicoamericano de Fresno, California. Como [Like] Francisco Jiménez y Tomás Rivera (pgs. 77-78), Soto trabajó (*worked*) en los campos del valle de San Joaquín. Escribe una variedad de escritos (por ejemplo, poemas, cuentos cortos [*short stories*], novelas). Los escritores favoritos de Soto son Ernest Hemingway, John Steinbeck, Jules Verne, Robert Frost y Thornton Wilder. Soto estudió (*studied*) en Fresno City College y California State University, Fresno. En 1976, obtiene un M.F.A. en la Universidad de California, Irvine.

Attribution: Author and poet Gary Soto speaks at the 2001 National Book Festival in Washington, D. C. Public domain

¿Sobre qué tipo de temas (*topics*) escribe Soto? ¿Quién es su audiencia principal? Responde estas preguntas con la información en su sitio de web (https://garysoto.com/books/) y el vídeo a continuación.

Video link: https://bit.ly/GarySotVideo

En el libro *Baseball in April and Other Stories*, Gary Soto escribe sobre la relación entre una madre y su hija. Lee la historia en https://bit.ly/SotoMothDaugh y completa las actividades a continuación.

Paso 1. Taking into account what Soto talks about in the video you just saw, explain why he might have chosen to write this story. What are the main themes of the story?

Paso 2. ¿Cómo es la relación entre la madre y la hija? Do you identify with the interactions between the mother and daughter?

Paso 3. ¿Cómo es Yollie y cómo es su mamá? Llena (*Fill*) los siguientes mapas araña (http://bit.ly/SpiderMap) con las características de cada personaje (*character*). How are their social identities related to their behavior and the events in the story?

---

9   Text adapted from the original: Gary Soto. By Wikipedia, licensed under CC BY-SA 3.0.

Yollie:

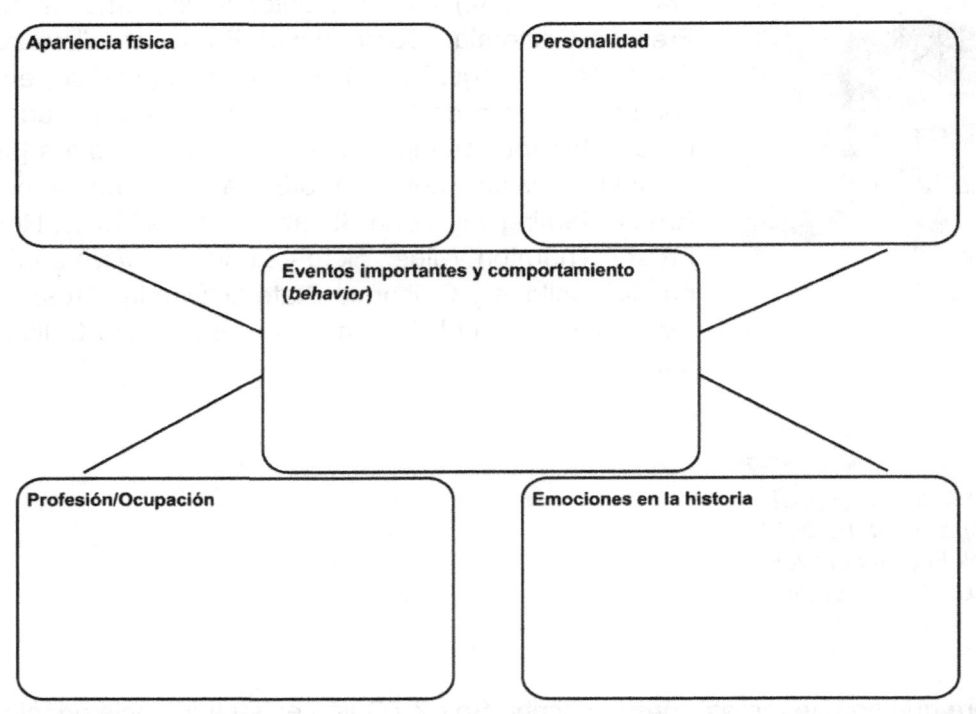

Attribution: Spider Map Mother and Daughter. By Gabriela C. Zapata, licensed under CC BY 4.0.

La Sra. Moreno (su mamá):

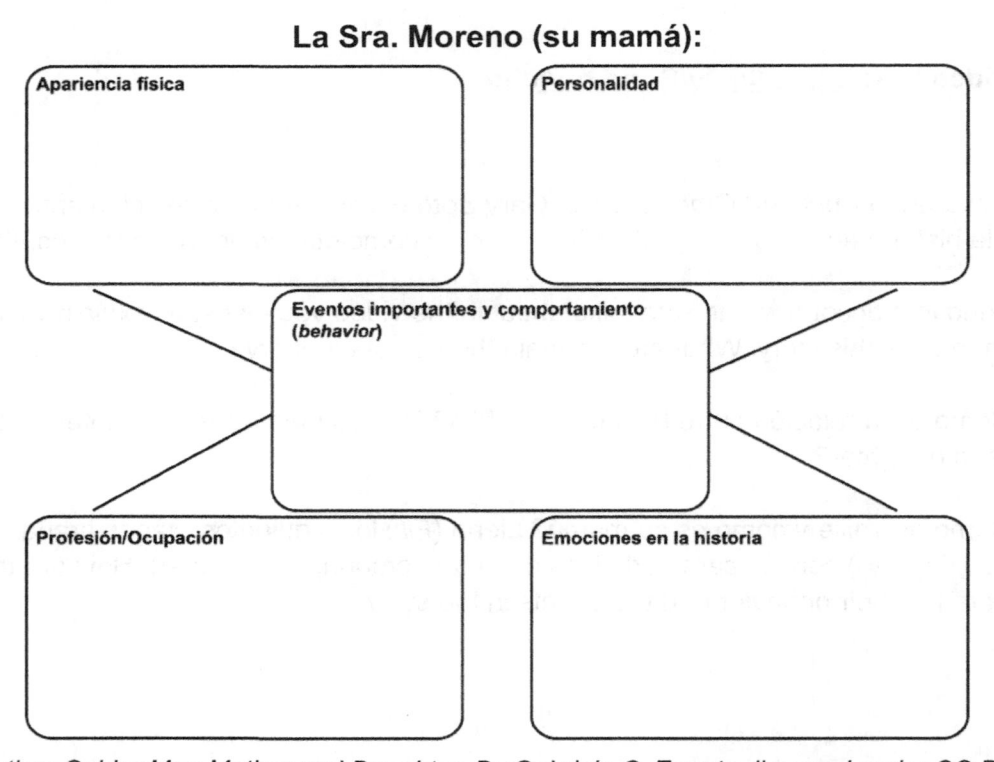

Attribution: Spider Map Mother and Daughter. By Gabriela C. Zapata, licensed under CC BY 4.0.

 **Investigación**

Hay otros escritores y artistas hispanos/latinx con obras sobre la familia. Learn more about their work. Compare them with the Lomas Garza and Gary Soto. Escribe similitudes (*similarities*) y diferencias. You can write your ideas in both Spanish and English. Trabaja con dos o tres compañer@s.

Yuyi Morales

Visita las páginas web y mira los vídeos a continuación. Completa el cuadro (*table*) con la información sobre Yuyi Morales. Pay attention to the topics she addresses in her story *Dreamers*.

- What aspects of the Hispanic/Latinx experience does she highlight?
- What kind of family is presented in the story?
- Reflect on the use of color and Spanish text in the illustrations and their connection to the themes addressed.

Attribution: Illustrator and Author Yuyi Morales visits Biblioteca. By San José Public Library, licensed under CC BY-SA 2.0.

 **Páginas de web:**

1. http://bit.ly/YuyiMorales
2. http://yuyimorales.com/

 Video links: 1. http://bit.ly/YMoralesVideo
2. *Dreamers:* http://bit.ly/YuyiDreamers

Información de la investigación:
Lugar y año de nacimiento (*birth*)
Profesiones
Audiencia principal

Información de la investigación:

Títulos de sus libros

Premios (*awards*)

**Temas (*topics*) y personas
de la familia en sus libros**

Matt de la Peña

Visita las páginas web a continuación y mira los vídeos. Completa el cuadro (*table*) con la información sobre Matt de la Peña. Pay attention to the issues that affect the Hispanic/Latinx communities in the US that are embedded in de la Peña's book *Carmela Full of Wishes*. Why has the author decided to focus on them?

Attribution: Matt de la Peña and Christian Robinson, author and illustrator of Carmela Full of Wishes. By Bank Square Books, licensed under CC BY 2.0.

 Páginas de web:

1. http://bit.ly/MPenaSite
2. http://bit.ly/MPenaWiki

 **Videos y página de web:**

1. *Carmela Full of Wishes*: **http://bit.ly/CarmelaMP**

2. **http://bit.ly/CarmelaMP1**

3. **http://bit.ly/CarmelaCuento**
   (This webpage contains articles and videos on the topics discussed in the story *Carmela Full of Wishes* [en español, *Los deseos de Carmela*] and in this lesson).

Información de la investigación:
Lugar y año de nacimiento (*birth*)
Profesiones
Audiencia principal
Títulos de sus libros
Premios (*awards*)
Temas (*topics*) **y personas de la familia en sus libros**

Reflexión final

- What are the cultural elements that the works you have seen/read in this lesson have in common? What about representation? What different social identities are present in these works?
- What kinds of families are presented in the stories/art? Why are these representations important?
- All of the authors/illustrators focus on children and teenagers. Why? Why do you think they have chosen this audience?
- If you were to write stories for children, what current topics would you include? What would you want children to know/understand/reflect on?

Para terminar... *Cartelera*

 La familia perfecta (México)

 In this module, we will watch the short film *La familia perfecta*, produced by a group of young students in Mexico, *Miembros Film* (http://bit.ly/MiembrosFilm).

I. Antes de ver

El nombre de este cortometraje es *La familia perfecta*. En tu opinión, ¿cómo es una familia perfecta? Escribe dos o tres ideas.

II. A ver

Ahora mira el film. Chequea si tus ideas sobre el film son correctas. Mira el vídeo en <u>http://bit.</u> <u>ly/Video2-12Trayectos</u>.

III. Después de ver

¿Son tus ideas correctas? ¿Cuál es el tema real del film? You can answer these questions in both Spanish and English.

 Ahora mira el cortometraje otra vez y completa las siguientes actividades. Trabaja con un@ compañer@

Actividad A. Main idea

Using the information and images in the video, describe its main purpose. Who is the audience the filmmakers had in mind? Why? What are they trying to accomplish? ¿Qué tipo de film es?

Actividad B. Los personajes en la primera parte del film

Paso 1. Contesta estas preguntas sobre la primera parte del film.

1. ¿Quiénes son los personajes?

2. ¿Dónde viven?

3. ¿Es la familia en la primera parte una familia típica? ¿Por qué?

Describe cómo son los personajes en la primera parte del film. Habla de su rutina (en la mañana, en la tarde, en la noche) también. Usa los cognados y los verbos en los **Módulos introductorio**, **1** y **2**. Also, ask your instructor for help!

Personajes	Profesión	¿Cómo es?	Rutina (en la mañana, en la tarde, en la noche)
El niño mayor			
El hermanito			
La mamá			
El papá			

Actividad C. Los personajes en la segunda parte del film

Ahora hablamos de los personajes en la segunda parte del film. You can answer these questions using both Spanish and English.

1. ¿Quiénes son los personajes?

2. ¿Dónde viven?

3. ¿Tienen parientes?

4. ¿Cuáles son sus actividades durante el día?

5. ¿Cómo están? Describe sus emociones.

6. ¿Qué necesitan estos niños?

7. ¿Qué problemas sociales hay en el país de estos niños?

Actividad D. Análisis
Contesta estas preguntas sobre el vídeo.

1. How do the filmmakers show the contrast between the first part of the film and the second part? Talk about different visual, auditory, and linguistic tools.

2. What message about the family does this film want to convey?

3. Do you think American audiences would enjoy this short film? Why? Why not?

 **Práctica individual:** To continue working with the content of this movie, go to http://bit.ly/PracticaIndividual2-7.

Para terminar... *Lectura*

 **Ser indígena, ser mujer**

I. Antes de leer

In this module, we have talked about our families, and we have learned more about different aspects of the Spanish-speaking world. Now we will read a text about indigenous women from the Wichí tribe in Argentina, otro país sudamericano como Colombia. ¿Dónde vive el grupo amerindio wichí? Mira el mapa de Argentina y busca esta información.

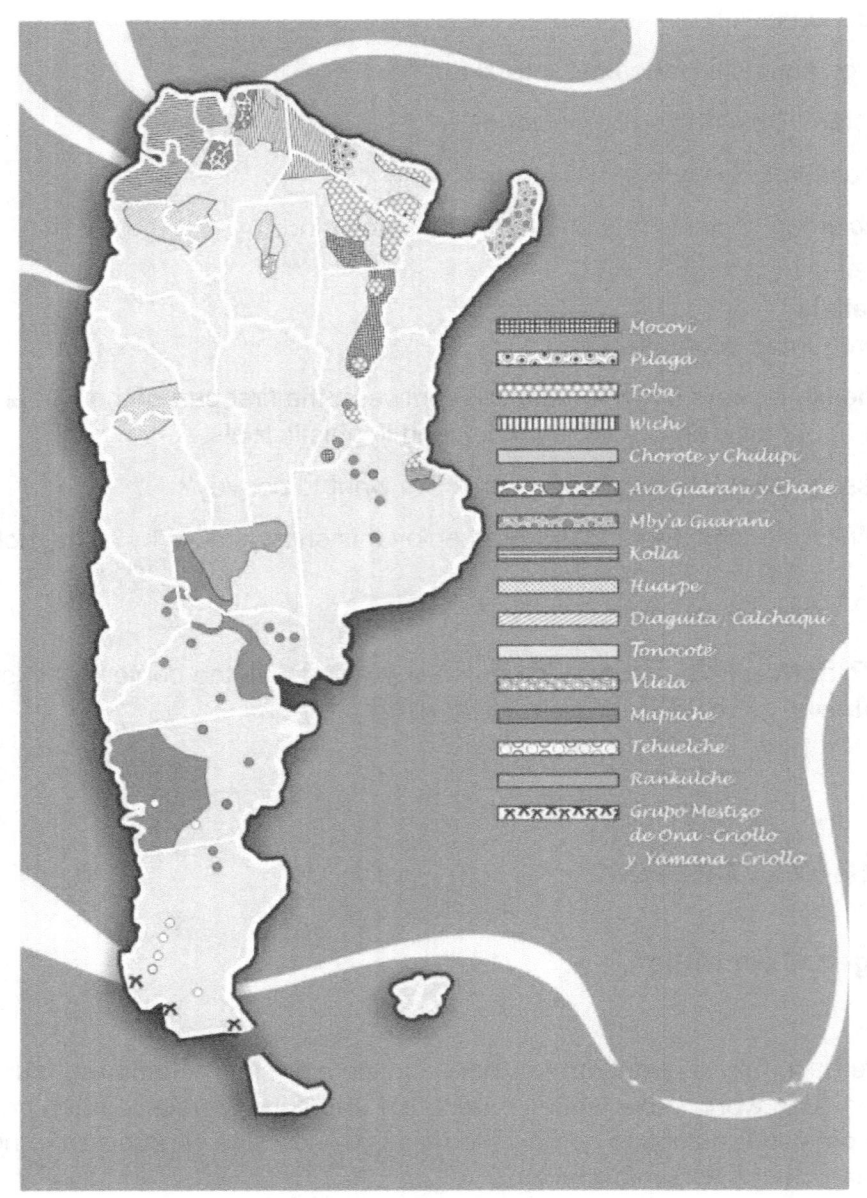

Attribution: Public domain

II. A leer

Ahora leemos el siguiente texto sobre la mujer wichí y contestamos esta pregunta. ¿Cuál es el rol de la mujer wichí en su comunidad?

Ser indígena, ser mujer[10]

La mujer wichí tiene tareas muy importantes en su comunidad: es la responsable de la seguridad y bienestar (*well-being*) de cada uno de los niños y niñas. Además, la mujer tiene una tarea muy importante: transmitir la cultura. La mujer wichí es la artesana (*artisan*), la doctora, la madre, la profesora, la religiosa. Las mujeres enseñan a los niños la lengua wichí de origen de la familia lingüística mataco-guaycurú.

---

10   Modified from *Ser indígena, ser mujer* by Esteban Ruffa (ANRed), licensed under CC BY 4.0. Photos in text are part of the original text, by Esteban Ruffa (ANRed), licensed under CC BY 4.0.

Desde muy pequeñas, las niñas wichí aprenden a tejer (*to knit*), una actividad que es netamente femenina en la comunidad. Las mujeres caminan por el monte (*bushes*) argentino en grupos reducidos y buscan las plantas de chaguar (http://bit.ly/ChaguarInfo). Luego usan esta planta para producir el hilo (*thread*) para sus tejidos. La planta de chaguar es ideal para los tejidos por su tamaño (*size*) y calidad (*quality*).

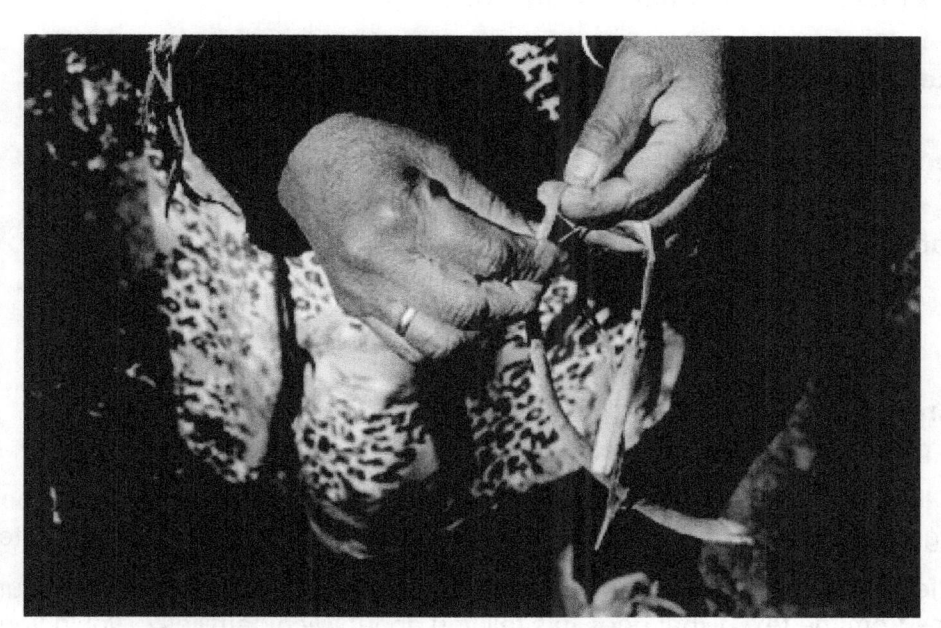

Las mujeres wichí trabajan en sus tejidos durante la noche porque durante el día están a cargo (*in charge*) de las casas, los animales y los niños de la comunidad

Con el chaguar, las mujeres producen ropa (*clothing*), canastos (*baskets*) y bolsas o redes de pesca (*fishing bags or nets*) que usan los hombres para buscar comida para la comunidad. También las mujeres viajan a ciudades de la provincia de Salta y venden sus productos a la gente de la ciudad. Sin embargo (*Nevertheless*), vender los productos no es fácil: "Sufrimos abusos de todo tipo. Vivimos discriminadas. Muchas veces llega la policía y tenemos que volver (*we have to return*) a la comunidad. No nos permiten vender", denuncian las mujeres. Desafortunadamente, la discriminación en muy común hacia la gente de las comunidades wichí.

A pesar (*Despite*) de las dificultades, la mujer wichí es una mujer del conocimiento (*knowledge*), experta en la cultura y madre de la lucha (*fight*) de su pueblo indígena.

III. Después de leer

Completa las siguientes actividades con un@ compañer@.

Actividad A. ¿Cuál es el rol de la mujer wichí? ¿Es un rol activo o pasivo? Explica tu respuesta.

Actividad B. Completa el siguiente cuadro con la información del texto.

¿Dónde viven las mujeres wichí?	
¿Qué dos lenguas probablemente hablan?	
Recursos (resources) naturales en su vida	
Actividades durante el día y en la noche	
¿Qué venden en la ciudad?	
¿Trabajan las mujeres en forma individual o en colaboración?	

Actividad C. Análisis
Contesta estas preguntas.

1. What is the main idea of this text? What does the author want to emphasize about Wichí women in Argentina? Who is the audience? Why do you think the author wrote this text?

2. Do you feel Wichí women have a more active role than Wichí men? Explain your answer with examples from the text. What does this tell you about Wichí families? Would you say they're similar to your or/and your classmates' families? Justify your answer.

3. What can you infer about the social situation of indigenous populations like the Wichí in Argentina? How similar/different is their situation to that of Native Americans in the United States?

4. Taking into account Diego Luna's video for Día de la Madre and this text, how would you characterize women in Latin America? Usa tres adjetivos en tu descripción.

Actividad D. Lengua

Busca tres cognados. Did these words help you understand the text? What other strategies did you use to read it?

 **Práctica individual:** To continue working with the content of this text, go to http://bit.ly/PracticaIndividual2-8.

Para terminar... *¡Conversemos!*

Attribution: Edificio de Bellas Artes - Universidad Nacional de Colombia, Sede Bogotá. By nicolasgalindo, licensed under CC BY 2.0.

 **Estudiar en español en Colombia**

Trabaja con un@ compañero@ y practica tu español en estas situaciones sociales. You need to use the vocabulary and structures you have learned so far. Change roles and partners after practicing each situation once.

Conversación 1

Estudiante 1. You're studying Spanish in Colombia, and you meet another student at a party.

- Greet your classmate.
- Tell your classmate your name, where you are from, and that you are a student. Ask what their name is and where they are from.
- Answer your classmate's question.
- Tell your classmate about your life at the university. Include information about classes, activities at the university, and weekend activities.
- Listen as your classmate tells you about their activities.

Ask questions and share as much information as possible.

Estudiante 2. You're studying Spanish in Colombia, and you meet another student at a party.

- Greet your classmate.
- Answer your classmate's questions.
- Ask where they study.
- Tell your classmate about your life at the university. Include information about classes, activities at the university, and weekend activities.
- Listen as your classmate tells you about their activities.

Ask questions and share as much information as possible.

Conversación 2

You are studying in Colombia. Your partner and you have to prepare a report about your families for your Spanish class. Talk about the members of each family:

- Talk about their personality, personal appearance, and age.
- Say where they are from.
- Mention where they live.
- Describe what they like to do (favorite activities, hobbies, etc.).
- Ask what they do for a living.

Compare your information, and say if your families are similar and explain why/why not.

Para terminar... *Proyecto digital*

 Segunda parte: Mi familia

En este módulo, escribes sobre tu familia.

Attribution: Familia Wayuu en Colombia. By Gustavo La Rotta Amaya, licensed under CC BY 2.0.
To learn more about the Wayuu people in Colombia, go to http://bit.ly/WayuuPeople.

I. Antes de escribir

Answer the following questions about your family or an American TV family (e.g., family in *Modern Family*) in Spanish. Write the answers in paragraph form. Write a paragraph between **90-110 words.**

1. ¿Cómo es tu familia (pequeña o grande)?/¿Cómo es la familia de la televisión? ¿Cuántos miembros hay en tu familia/la familia?

2. ¿Dónde vive tu familia/la familia?

3. ¿Quiénes son los miembros de tu familia/la familia? Escribe el primer nombre de cada miembro y su rol en la familia.

4. ¿Cómo es cada miembro? Describe su edad, aspecto físico y personalidad.

5. ¿En qué trabajan los miembros de tu familia/la familia? Habla de sus profesiones/trabajos.

6. ¿Cuáles son las actividades típicas de tu familia/la familia (tus actividades con la familia)?

7. ¿Quién es tu persona favorita en tu familia/la familia? ¿Por qué?
   (Your instructor can help you answer this question)

II. A escribir

Now write your paragraph and…

- Remember to use the vocabulary from the three modules we have seen.

- Pay attention to gender and number when you use articles, nouns, and adjectives (e.g., **l**a madr**e** simpátic**a**), and to the correct verb conjugations (e.g., yo estudi**o**, mis amigos y yo cor**remos**).

- Use connectors and conjunctions to connect your ideas. For example, use **y**, **también** *(also)*, **sin embargo** *(nevertheless)*, **además** *(also)*, **pero** *(but)*. Your instructor can help you to use these words correctly.

Complement your paragraph with:
- At least one photo that shows you with your family (or the American TV family you have chosen).

- If you use photos that you have not taken, please do not forget to cite the source. We recommend that you use open images (i.e., copyright free). You can find this type of images using the search engine offered by Creative Commons (https://search.creativecommons.org/). Also, you need to provide attributions for all of them. To learn more about Creative Commons licenses and how to cite the open materials you find, see https://creativecommons.org/licenses/ and http://bit.ly/CreativeCommonsAttr.

III. Después de escribir

Now read your paragraph, and focus on the following:

- **Content:** Have you included all the information required? Are your photos big and clear enough to convey your message?

- **Grammar:**
  - Articles and nouns: Do they agree in gender and number?
  - **-ar**, **-er**, and **-ir** verbs: Have you conjugated your verbs correctly?
  - Descriptive adjectives: Are your adjectives in the correct position? Do they agree in gender and number with the noun they describe?
  - Possessive adjectives: Do they agree in number (and gender in case of **nuestro/a**) with the noun they modify?

- **Cohesion:** Have you connected your ideas with the suggested connectors and conjunctions?

Go over your text, improve it, and write a new, polished version.

Antes de partir...

¡Misión cumplida!

We have reached the end of **Módulo 2**. Go back to the first part of the module (p. 85), and review what you have accomplished. Check the outcomes you have achieved. What are you proud of? What aspects of your Spanish would you like to improve? ¡Buen trabajo!

Summary of Contents

Comunicación

- El núcleo familiar

  - ☐ **el padre** — *father*
  - ☐ **la madre** — *mother*
  - ☐ **el hermano** — *brother*
  - ☐ **la hermana** — *sister*
  - ☐ **el esposo** — *husband*
  - ☐ **la esposa** — *wife*
  - ☐ **la pareja** — *partner*
  - ☐ **el hijo** — *son*
  - ☐ **la hija** — *daughter*
  - ☐ **el padrastro** — *stepfather*
  - ☐ **la madrastra** — *stepmother*
  - ☐ **el hermanastro** — *stepbrother*
  - ☐ **la hermanastra** — *stepdaughter*
  - ☐ **el medio hermano** — *half-brother*
  - ☐ **la media hermana** — *half-sister*
  - ☐ **la mascota** — *pet*

- Los parientes (*Relatives*) [La familia lejana]

  - ☐ **el tío** — *uncle*
  - ☐ **la tía** — *aunt*
  - ☐ **el sobrino** — *nephew*
  - ☐ **la sobrina** — *niece*
  - ☐ **el primo** — *cousin m.*

☐	**la prima**	*cousin f.*
☐	**el abuelo**	*grandfather*
☐	**la abuela**	*grandmother*
☐	**el suegro**	*father-in-law*
☐	**la suegra**	*mother-in-law*
☐	**el yerno**	*son-in-law*
☐	**la nuera**	*daughter-in-law*
☐	**el bisabuelo**	*great grandfather*
☐	**la bisabuela**	*great grandmother*

- Más palabras para describir la familia

☐	**el hijo único**	*only child/son*
☐	**la hija única**	*only daughter*
☐	**(el/la) menor**	*(youngest) younger*
☐	**(el/la) mayor**	*(eldest) older*
☐	**los ancestros/los ante-pasados**	*ancestors*

- Describimos la apariencia física

☐	**alto**	*tall*
☐	**bajo**	*short (height)*
☐	**pequeño**	*small*
☐	**grande**	*big*
☐	**delgado/flaco**	*thin*
☐	**moreno**	*with dark hair/dark-skinned*
☐	**güero/ rubio**	*blonde or light-skinned*

- Describimos la personalidad

☐	**abierto/a**	*open-minded/open*
☐	**aburrido/a**	*boring*
☐	**amable**	*nice*
☐	**antipático/a**	*unfriendly*

☐ **cómico/a**	*funny/witty*	
☐ **gracioso/a**		
☐ **divertido/a**	*fun*	
☐ **grosero/a**	*rude*	
☐ **perezoso/a**	*lazy*	
☐ **simpático/a**	*friendly*	
☐ **tímido/a**	*shy*	
☐ **trabajador/a**	*hard-working*	

- Los cognados (pg. 101)
- Las nacionalidades (pg. 108)
- Los números del 30 al 100 (pg. 122)

Lengua

- Los adjetivos posesivos (pg. 99)
- Ejemplos de verbos en **-er** e **-ir** (pg. 114)

Cultura

- Colombia: Cartagena de Indias (pg. 118)
- Trayectos hispanos: Visiones artísticas de la familia (pg. 125)

Mis palabras

In your Spanish notebook, write down other words and phrases you learned in this module.

Módulo 3: Mi vida fuera de la universidad: Mi hogar

En este módulo, continuamos hablando de tu vida más allá de las clases. Hablamos de tu cuarto, apartamento o casa (*house*). ¿Cómo son las casas en tu ciudad/estado? ¿Hay casas históricas? ¿Qué estilos tienen? **Antes de comenzar:** Miramos estas fotos. ¿Dónde están las casas? ¿Cómo es la arquitectura en estas casas?

Casa número 1
Attribution: Dietz-Castilla House, by Billy Hathorn, licensed under CC BY-SA 3.0.

Casa número 2
Attribution: Reeves-Womack House, by Billy Hathorn, licensed under CC BY-SA 3.0.

Casa número 3
Attribution: Casa de adobe. Public domain

Casa número 4
Attribution: Steel House. Public domain..

Objetivos en este módulo

Comunicación

In this instructional module, you will learn how to…

- Describe household rooms and furniture
- Talk about chores in and outside the house and activities you like or don't like
- Talk about emotions and temporary states
- Use numbers 100 to 1.000.000

Lengua
- **Gustar** + infinitive & **gustar** + noun
- Irregular verbs in the *yo* form
- El verbo **tener**

Cultura
- España
- Trayectos hispanos: El activismo en los espacios urbanos

Mis metas

In your Spanish notebook, describe what you want to accomplish in this instructional module in personal terms.

Introducción comunicativa: *Busco un apartamento*

In this instructional module, we will learn how to talk about our rooms, apartments, or houses. Think about your room and the place where you live. ¿Cómo es una típica casa de estudiante? Now, read the following conversation and see if you can find similarities between the place where you live and the one that is mentioned in the dialogue.

Kate es una estudiante universitaria de Tejas. Ahora estudia español en Madrid y busca un apartamento nuevo con su amiga Lauren. Kate llama a la agencia inmobiliaria (*real estate agency*) para preguntar por el apartamento en el anuncio (*ad*). Puedes usar el vocabulario en **Hablemos más** (pg. 147) para leer el diálogo.

Piso en alquiler

Piso en el barrio Casa de Campo – Moncloa en la calle Santa Fe. 2 habitaciones, amplio salón-comedor de 22m, baño completo con ducha, cocina. Calefacción individual y ascensor.

Para más información llamar al 912 234 567.

Attribution: Public domain.

Agente:	Dígame
Kate:	Buenos días. Necesito información sobre un **apartamento** en Casa de Campo-Moncloa.
Agente:	Ah, sí. **Tenemos** un **piso** allí.
Kate:	¿Cuál es la dirección?
Agente:	Está en la calle Santa Fe 15. Es un **piso** en la **segunda planta.**
Kate:	¿Cuánto es la **renta** al mes?
Agente:	El **alquiler** es de **€950 (novecientos cincuenta euros) al mes**.

Kate:	¿Hay **muebles** en el apartamento? Por ejemplo, **¿un sofá?**
Agente:	En las **habitaciones**, hay una **cama** y dos **mesitas de noche**. En el **salón-comedor** no hay **muebles**. En la **cocina** hay un **lavaplatos,** una **refrigeradora, una** estufa y un **horno de microondas.**
Kate	¿**Tiene lavadora** el **apartamento**?
Agente	Sí, hay una **lavadora** pequeña en la **cocina**
Kate	Otra pregunta. ¿Quién **limpia** (*cleans*) el **apartamento**?
Agente	El **inquilino (*the person who rents the apartment*).** Usted y su compañera **hacen** las tareas domésticas: **pasan la aspiradora**, **limpian el baño, sacan la basura, lavan las ventanas** y **sacuden los muebles**
Kate:	Muy bien. Gracias por la información. **A mí me gusta** (*I like*) el **apartamento**

¿Comprendiste?

Ahora contesta estas preguntas sobre el diálogo. ¿Es tu apartamento similar al apartamento del diálogo?

1. ¿Dónde está el apartamento?
2. Kate habla del apartamento. ¿Qué otra palabra usa la agente para hablar del apartamento?
3. ¿Para cuántas personas es el apartamento?
4. ¿Cuál es el precio del apartamento por mes? ¿Qué dos palabras usan Kate y la agente para hablar del precio?
5. ¿Hay muebles en el apartamento? ¿Cuáles son?
6. ¿Qué hacen (*do*) Kate y Lauren si (*if*) viven en el apartamento?

Lengua

1. In this module, you will learn how to use the verb **gustar** to talk about things you like and dislike. Kate uses this structure in the dialogue:

   A mí me gusta el apartamento.

   What do you notice about it? Is there a **yo** in the sentence? What does this tell you about the verb? How do we know she is talking about her own preferences?

2. Another verb we will use in this module is **tener.** You used the first person form of this verb in previous modules to talk about your age (**[Yo] tengo 20 años**). Have a look at the dialogue again, and look for uses of **tener.** What are the forms used? What is the meaning of **tener** in the dialogue?

Práctica individual: To continue using your new words, go to http://bit.ly/PracticaIndividual3-1.

Hablemos más: *Las casas*

 **La casa de Kate en los Estados Unidos**

¿Y cómo es la casa de la familia de Kate en los Estados Unidos? ¿Es similar al piso de España? Con un@ compañer@, mira los planos (*blueprints*) y las fotos a continuación y escribe una lista de similitudes y diferencias. ¿Y tu casa? ¿Es similar?

Modelo(s):   **Similitud:** *En la sala hay un sofá.*

   Diferencia: *Hay dos dormitorios en el piso y hay cuatro en la casa.*

 **Audio link:** http://bit.ly/Audio3-1Trayectos

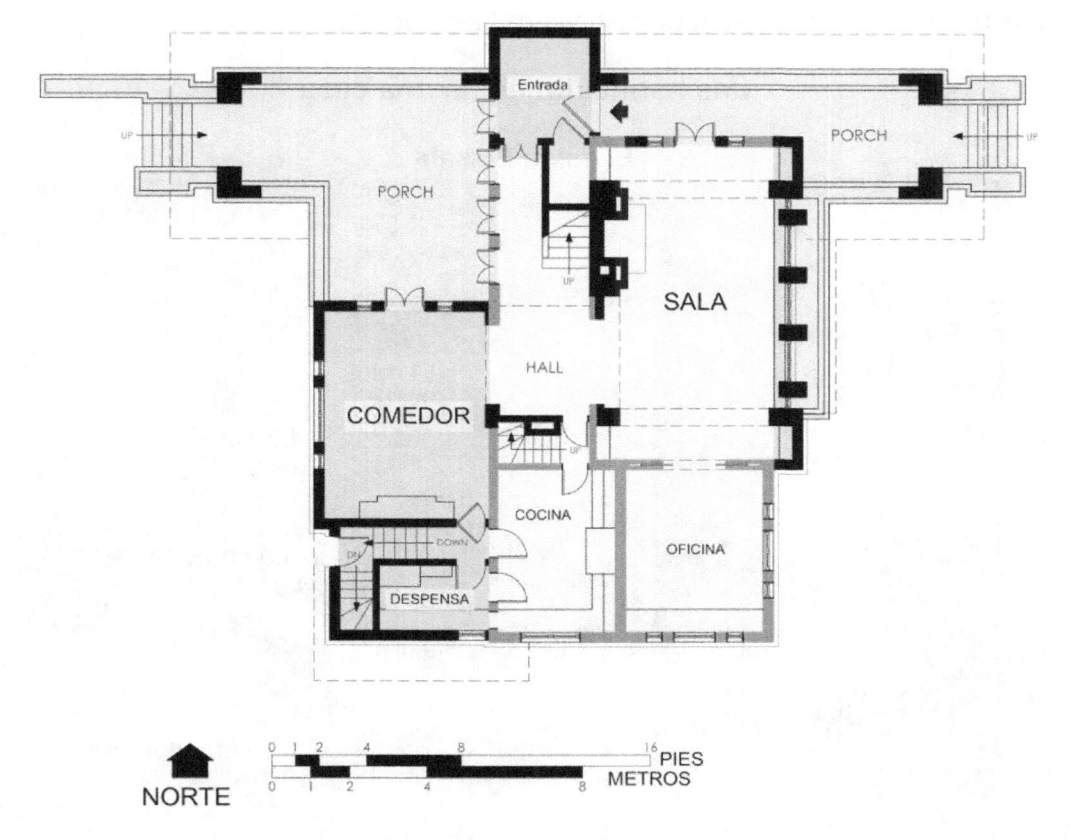

Attribution: Planta baja. By Fox69, licensed under BY-SA 3.0.

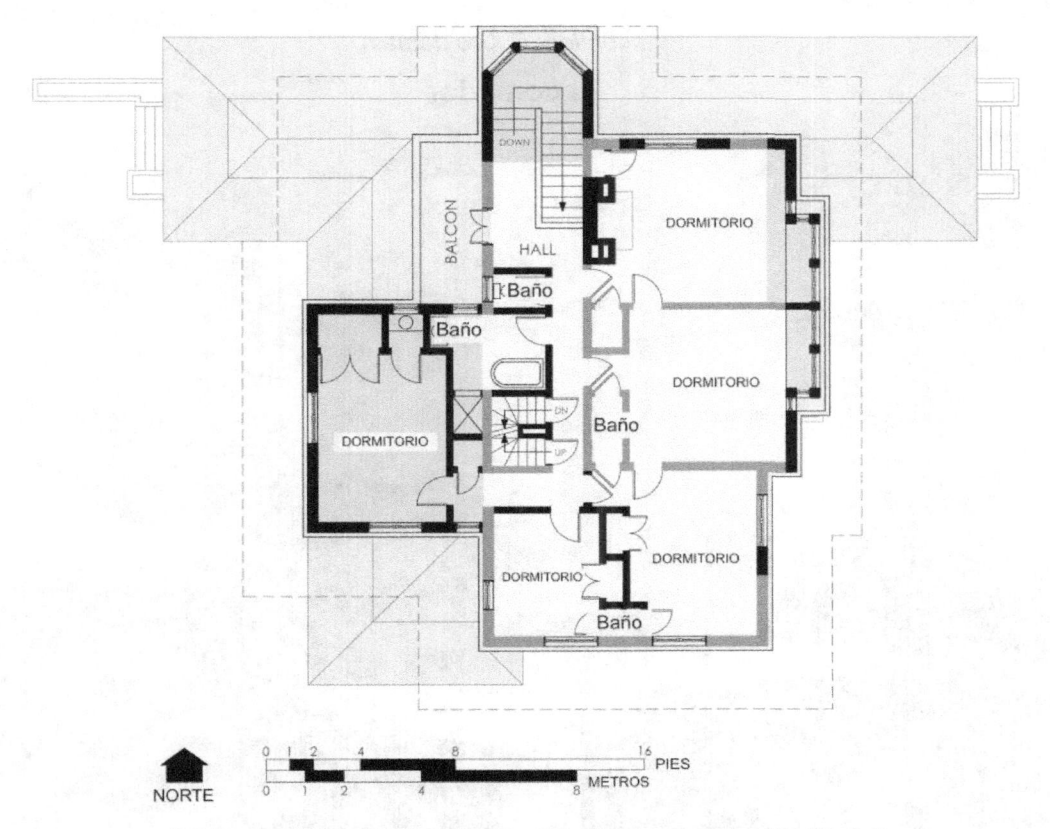

Attribution: Primer piso. By Fox69, licensed under BY-SA 3.0

In Spanish, the ground floor of a house or building (the *first floor* in English) is called **planta baja. El primer piso** is used to refer to what in English we call *second floor.*

Las habitaciones de una casa

El salón/La sala

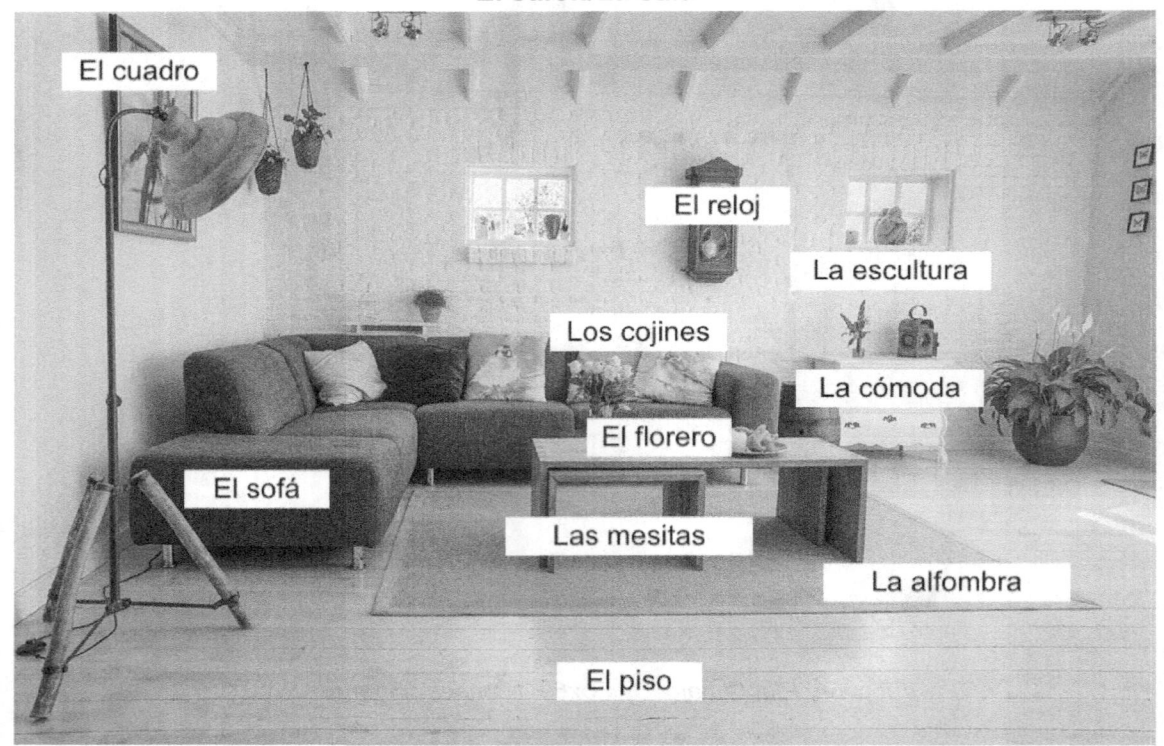

Attribution: Public domain

El comedor

Attribution: Public domain

La cocina

Attribution: Public domain

Los electrodomésticos (*appliances*)

Electrodomésticos

¿Qué aparatos hay en la cocina
y casa de Kate?

*Attribution: On picture
CC BY-SA 3.0*

El dormitorio/La habitación

Attribution: By Tim Collins, licensed under CC BY-SA 3.0.

El baño

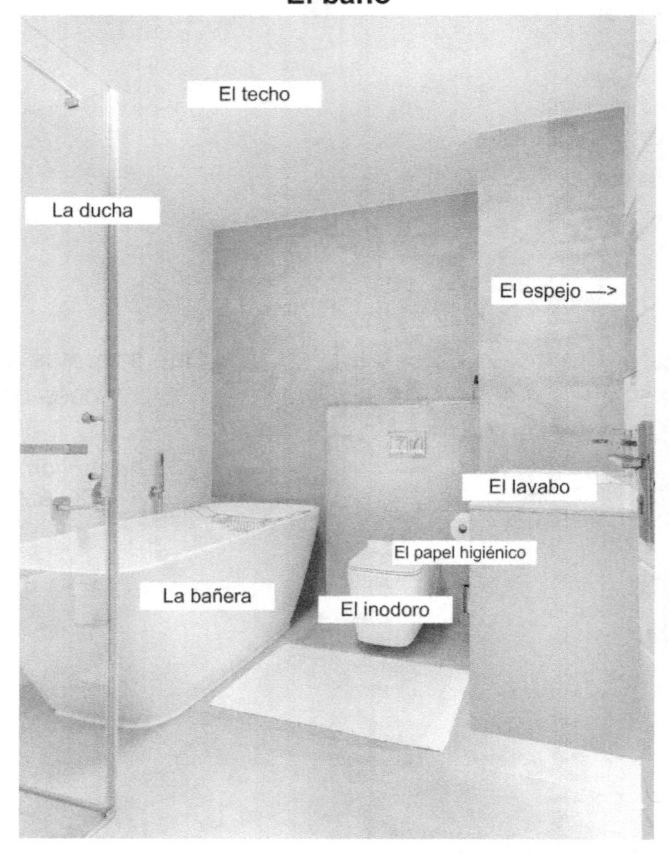

El jardín

Los árboles

La sombrilla

La parrilla

La reposera

Las flores

El césped

 ## El cactus viajero.

As we have seen in the previous modules, there are many varieties of Spanish in the Spanish-speaking world. In this module, we have already seen that there are at least two words for the word "apartment," **apartamento** (used in most of the Spanish-speaking world) and **piso** (used in Spain). And guess what? There's one more word, **departamento** (used in South America).

What happens with the other words we have seen? What different words are used to talk about rooms, furniture, and appliances? Let's find out.

Paso 1. Get together with 4 or 5 classmates, and choose one of the photos in the **Hablemos más** section. Print or download the picture to your phone.

Paso 2. Create a table like the following one with all the words in your picture.

Palabra	*Partici-pante 1 Nombre, país y palabra*	*Partici-pante 2 Nombre, país y palabra*	*Partici-pante 3 Nombre, país y palabra*	*Partici-pante 4 Nombre, país y palabra*	*Partici-pante 5 Nombre, país y palabra*
el apartamento					

Paso 3. Interview at least 5 native speakers of Spanish (e.g., students in your other classes, instructors, neighbors, etc.). Show them the picture and ask them to give you the words that they use to refer to the things shown in the image. Write down their words as well as their first name and country of origin. Follow the example below.

Palabra	Partici-pante 1 Nombre, país y palabra	Partici-pante 2 Nombre, país y palabra	Partici-pante 3 Nombre, país y palabra	Partici-pante 4 Nombre, país y palabra	Partici-pante 5 Nombre, país y palabra
	Gabriela Argentina	Irene Uruguay	Alessandra México	Mariana Estados Unidos	Paloma España
el apartamento	el departa-mento	el departa-mento	el aparta-mento	el aparta-mento	el piso

Paso 4. Choose the words that show the greatest variety and run simple statistics (e.g., percentages--you can also create a graph). What are the most popular words in your sample? Where are they used? Be ready to present your results to the rest of the class.

Paso 5. When your classmates are presenting their results, add the new words you hear to your glossary for this module.

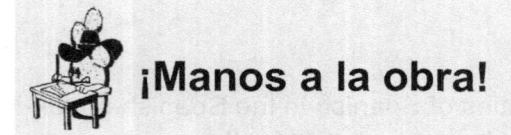 **¡Manos a la obra!**

Actividad 3-1. Más sobre los muebles
Visita la página en http://bit.ly/ActividadMuebles.

Paso 1. Using the first picture in the page, review and learn more words to describe furniture. ¿Dónde están estos (*these*) muebles?

Paso 2. En la misma página (http://bit.ly/ActividadMuebles), completa las actividades 1, 2, 3 y 4. Be ready to discuss your results with other classmates.

Paso 3. Add the new words to your glossary for this module.

Actividad 3-2. Casa en venta

 **Paso 1**

Imagina que tú y tu compañer@ son agentes inmobiliarios. You have been hired by Kate's family to sell their house. Write an ad for it, including information about rooms, furniture, and appliances. Use the blueprints, photos, and vocabulary in **Hablemos más** (pp. 140-144). Include some of the new words you learned in your interaction with native speakers and **Actividad 3-1**. We have included an example to help you:

Piso en venta. Piso en Málaga, Camino de la Térmica, 28-30, segundo piso. Se vende estupendo piso de 114 (ciento catorce) m² (metros cuadrados). 3 habitaciones; 2 baños (con espejos); salón independiente; cocina con isla y armarios y equipada con horno microondas, estufa a gas y lavadora. Aire acondicionado en toda la casa. Armarios en todas las habitaciones y entrada. A tan solo 100 metros de la playa (*beach*), 5 minutos del aeropuerto y centro de Málaga en coche, con 3 líneas de autobuses y a 50 metros del Hospital de Salud. Cámaras de seguridad en áreas comunes. Parque para niños y piscina (*swimming pool*) comunitaria. Estado: totalmente nuevo. Teléfono de contacto: 600-456-789. Sr. Carlos Tapia.

 **Paso 2**

Share your ad with another pair of classmates. Compare your work. What are some of the similarities and differences between your ads? Are real estate ads in the US similar to those in Spain? Discuss these questions and be ready to share the answers with your classmates.

 **Actividad 3-3. La casa de Cristina**

Cristina es una amiga de Kate en España. En este segmento, Cristina habla de su casa. ¿Cómo es la casa?

Paso 1. Escucha a Cristina (http://bit.ly/Audio3-2Trayectos) (by Orlando R. Kelm, licensed under CC BY 3.0) y decide si estas afirmaciones son **Ciertas (C)** (*true*) o **Falsas (F)**. ¿Es la casa de Cristina similar a la casa de Kate?

1. Cristina vive en Madrid.	C	F
2. En la casa de Cristina hay un jardín.	C	F
3. La familia de Cristina probablemente mira programas de televisión.	C	F
4. En la familia de Cristina hay cuatro hermanos.	C	F
5. En la casa de Cristina hay cuatro dormitorios.	C	F
6. La cocina es pequeña.	C	F
7. El papá de Cristina limpia la casa.	C	F

Paso 2. In the audio, Cristina describes her house as "una casa típica andaluza". She is referring to an architectural style in Spain. What is it like? Read the information on this link (http://bit.ly/Andalusia-Casas), and write a list of features that characterize the style. Find photos of houses built in this style to share with your classmates. Remember to use the Creative Commons search page to find your photos (https://search.creativecommons.org/). ¿Dónde está la región de Andalucía en España?

 **Práctica individual:** To continue using your new words, go to http://bit.ly/PracticaIndividual3-2.

Y después... Uso, forma y cultura: *Las casas ecológicas*

 La casa Teo

I. Antes de leer

In the previous section, we saw that un aspecto interesante de España es su arquitectura. Cristina, por ejemplo, vive en una casa andaluza. En el presente, para los españoles son importantes las casas ecológicas. ¿Qué es una casa ecológica? Escribe una definición y dos características.

II. A leer

Ahora lee el siguiente texto sobre una casa ecológica en España y chequea si tiene las características que escribes en la sección I. ¿Dónde está la casa?

La arquitectura ecológica tiene sus ejemplos[11]

Casa Teo

Según sus constructores, Natureback (https://natureback.com/), la Casa Teo es un ejemplo de ecointeligencia en materiales, propiedades y ciclo de vida (*life*). La casa está en Madrid.

Como vemos, esta casa es una vivienda sostenible y forma parte del paisaje (*landscape*). La casa está hecha (*made*) de materiales reciclables desmontables (*removable*). Además, la vivienda incorpora un sistema domótico (*home automation*) avanzado.

Debido a (*Due to*) estos materiales y sistemas, la casa es desmontable: Con sus partes, podemos (*we can*) construir otra casa. El material principal es la madera (*wood*). También la casa usa energías renovables. Por ejemplo, la casa usa energía solar y materiales locales de la región. Otro aspecto positivo es su construcción fácil. Podemos vivir en este tipo de casa en unas semanas.

---

11 Text adapted from original on https://www.ecointeligencia.com/2013/03/arquitectura-ecologica-ejemplos-5/.

La domótica en la Casa Teo es eficiente y fácil de usar para controlar la calefacción (*heating*), las luces internas, los sistemas de ventilación, la seguridad del interior de la casa y la activación de los electro-domésticos.

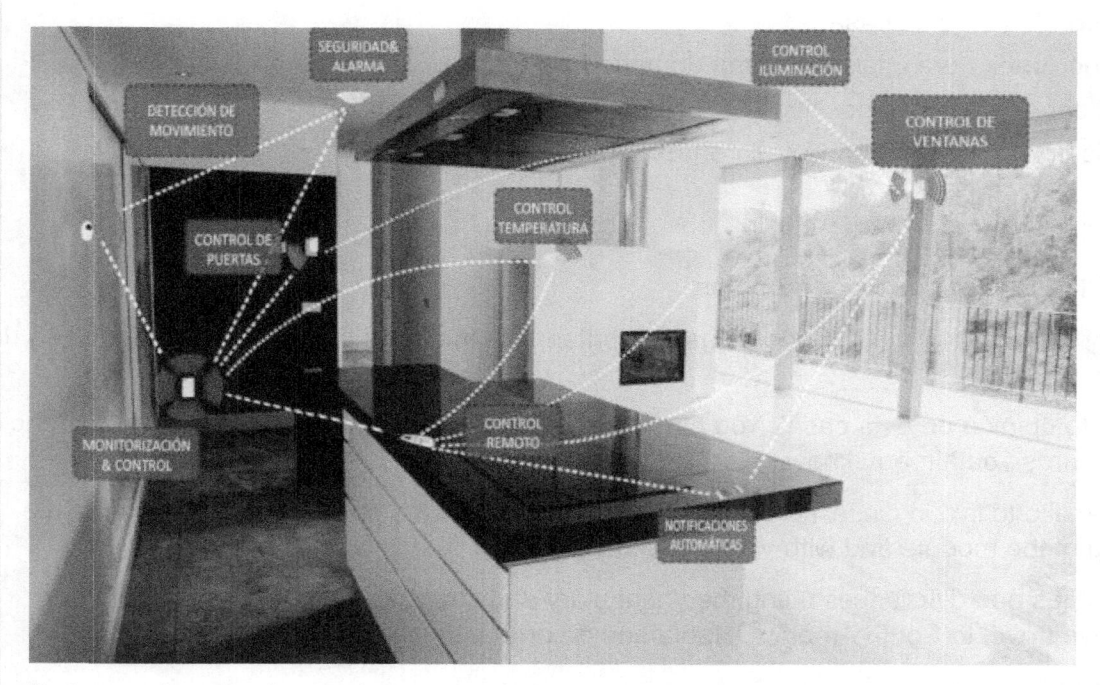

En la casa hay dos dormitorios, una cocina, una sala-comedor y dos baños. Esta casa ecointeligente es así confortable y un ejemplo de la posibilidad de vivir bien sin dañar (*hurt, damage*) nuestro planeta. ¡Te la recomendamos! Para ver los planos de la casa y fotos adicionales, visita el sitio http://bit.ly/CasaTeo.

Attribution for text and all photos: By RES, licensed under CC BY-SA 4.0.

III. Después de leer

Actividad A. ¿Coincide tu definición con la casa ecológica del artículo?

Actividad B. Using the information in the text, describe its main purpose. Justify your opinions with information from the text. ¿Cuál es el objetivo del autor?

Actividad C. Supporting details
For each of the following,

- Circle the number of each detail that is mentioned in the text (not all are included!)
8. Write the number of that idea next to where it appears in the text.

1. La casa tiene varias características de una casa ecológica.
2. La casa está en una ciudad española.
3. La casa es para familias con niños pequeños.
4. La casa se mimetiza (*camouflages*) con su localización.
5. La casa tiene planta baja y primer piso.
6. Es posible hacer otras casas con los materiales de la Casa Teo.
7. La casa es automática.
8. El origen de la energía de la casa es el sol (*sun*).
9. No es difícil construir esta casa.
10. La casa controla las luces.
11. Hay dos cuartos en esta casa.
12. Hay instrucciones para usar el sistema domótico de la casa.
13. La casa tiene un mensaje positivo.
14. Es posible comprar este tipo de casa en España.

 **Actividad D. Opiniones personales**

Trabaja con un@ compañer@ y responde estas preguntas. Compara tus opiniones y las opiniones de tu compañer@.

1. ¿Cuál es tu opinión de esta casa? You can express your opinion in English, but try to use the Spanish words you already know.

2. Would you like to live in Casa Teo? Compare Casa Teo with the houses we discussed at the beginning of the module and with your house/apartment.

Talk about similarities and differences using the vocabulary and structures you already know.
And from Spain we travel to South America. Hablamos de otra casa ecológica famosa…

 Casa Terracota

I. Antes de ver el vídeo
En la sección anterior, hablamos de Casa Teo, una vivienda ecointeligente. ¿Qué otros tipos de casas ecológicas hay en el mundo? Escribe dos. Pregunta a tu instructor/a si necesitas una palabra nueva.

II. A ver
Ahora mira el vídeo en http://bit.ly/Video3-1Trayectos. ¿Qué tipo de vivienda ecológica presenta el vídeo?

III. Después de ver

Actividad A. ¿De qué tipo de vivienda ecológica habla el vídeo? ¿Adivinaste? *(Did you guess?)*

Actividad B. ¿Cuál es la idea principal del vídeo? ¿Qué objetivo tiene? You can answer these questions in both Spanish and English.

Actividad C. Ahora mira el vídeo otra vez y contesta estas preguntas.

1. ¿Dónde está Casa Terracota?
2. ¿Cómo son sus muebles?
3. ¿Cómo es el baño?
4. ¿Qué energía usa?
5. ¿Qué diferencias y similitudes tiene con la Casa Teo? (Piensa en las partes de la casa, energía, materiales, etc.).

 **Actividad D. Opiniones personales**

Trabaja con un@ compañer@ y responde estas preguntas. Compara tus opiniones y las opiniones de tu compañer@.

1. Why do you think Casa Terracota's architect, Octavio Mendoza Morales, built this house? What is the message he wants to convey?
2. What are the possible advantages and disadvantages of an adobe house such as Casa Terracota?
3. Do you think it is expensive? Why? / Why not?
4. Would Casa Terracota be popular in the United States? Why? / Why not?

 Actividad 3-4. Una casa ecológica en venta

 **Paso 1**

Imagina que tú y tu compañer@ son agentes inmobiliarios. You have been hired to sell Casa Teo o Casa Terracota. First, choose what house you want to focus on. Then, think of your favorite celebrity. Write them an email stating why Casa Teo/Casa Terracota is ideal for them. Describe the house you have chosen in detail using the ideas in the text on Casa Teo or in the video on Casa Terracota. Describe each room in detail, resorting to the vocabulary/structures we have seen in this module and in previous ones (e.g., verbs **hay**, **está**, **es**, etc.) Put a dollar price for the house. **Write at least 100 words.**

- Fotos adicionales de Casa Teo: https://bit.ly/CasaTeo
- Fotos adicionales de Casa Terracota: http://bit.ly/CasaTerracotaCol

 **Paso 2**

Share your email with another pair of classmates. Compare your work. What are some of the similarities and differences between your messages?

Más comunicación: *Las tareas de la casa*

¿Quién hace qué?

Paso 1. Kate y Lauren rentan el piso de la calle Santa Fe en Madrid. Las dos amigas limpian el apartamento. ¿Qué hace cada una? Mira el calendario.

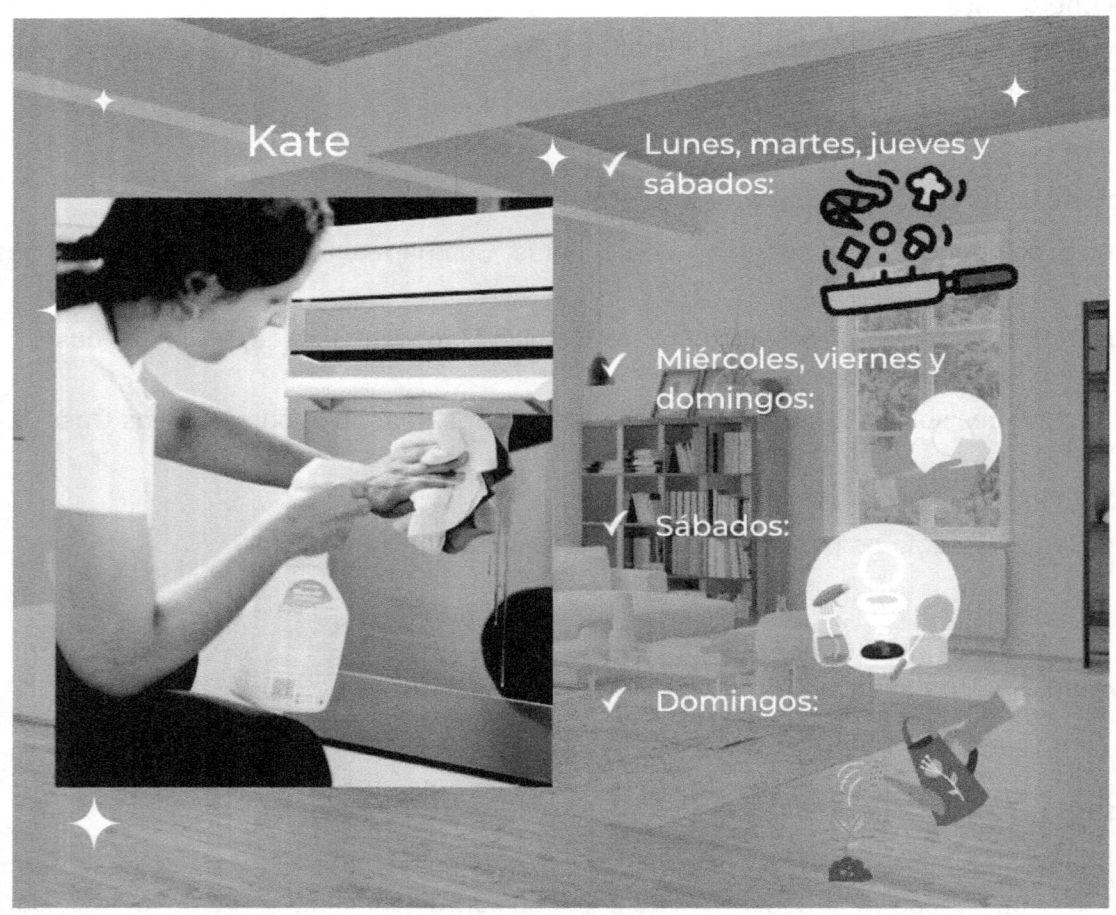

Attribution: By Gabriela C. Zapata, licensed under CC BY-SA 4.0.

Attribution: By Gabriela C. Zapata, licensed under CC BY-SA 4.0.

 **Paso 2**

Ahora, con un@ compañer@, describe the chores that Kate and Lauren do every week and when they do them. You need to use the list of chores below. To conjugate the verbs, remember the rules for the conjugation of **-ar**, **-er**, and **-ir** verbs that you learned in the previous modules.

> **Modelo(s):**   Kate pone agua a las plantas los domingos.

 **Audio link: http://bit.ly/Audio3-3Trayectos**

Las tareas domésticas / Los quehaceres de la casa	
barrer (el piso)	*to sweep (the floor)*
cocinar / hacer la comida	*to cook*
cortar el césped	*to mow the lawn*
limpiar (el piso)	*to clean (the floor)*
lavar los platos	*to wash the dishes*

hacer la cama	*to make the bed*
lavar la ropa / poner la lavadora	*to do laundry*
limpiar el baño	*to clean the bathroom*
limpiar los cristales/los vidrios	*to clean the windows*
pasar la aspiradora	*to vacuum*
planchar	*to iron*
poner agua a las plantas	*to water the plants*
poner la mesa / recoger la mesa	*to set the table/to clear the table*
quitar el polvo	*to dust the furniture*
tirar/sacar la basura	*to take out the trash*

 **Paso**

Con tu compañer@, go back to the **Hablemos más** section (p. 139). Divide the photos among the two of you, and describe the chores that Kate and her family need to take care of to keep their house clean. Try to include as many activities as possible. Habla de las actividades de Kate, sus dos hermanos (Tim y Samantha), su mamá y su papá.

> **Modelo(s):**   Parte de la casa: Sala
> *Kate y su hermano Tim barren el piso.*

 **¡Manos a la obra!**

Actividad 3-5. Más sobre las tareas domésticas
Visita la página en http://bit.ly/TareasCasaActividad y completa las actividades 1 y 2. Be ready to discuss your results with other classmates. ¿Tienes unas frases nuevas? Add the new phrases you have learned to your glossary for this module.

 **Actividad 3-6. Las tareas de los Simpson**

En esta actividad trabajas con un@ compañer@. Imagine that you work at an agency that creates scripts (audio captions) for videos for the visually-impaired. You need to do that for a Spanish audience for an excerpt of the show The Simpsons.

Mira este video (http://bit.ly/Video3-2Trayectos).

Describe what happens in the video (how people feel, what they do), including the chores that you see. You need to use the vocabulary and structures in this module and previous ones. ¿Cómo son las voces de los Simpson en español? ¿Son similares o diferentes a las voces en inglés?
Palabras y expresiones útiles:

1. bajar las escaleras (*go down the stairs*)
2. pisar (*step on*)
3. un/unos calzoncillo(s) (*men's underwear*)
4. una bola de bolos (*bowling ball*)

Actividad 3-7. Una agencia de limpieza

El trabajo de una empresa de limpieza es limpiar casas, apartamentos u oficinas. ¿Hay agencias de limpieza en tu ciudad? ¿Cómo se llaman? ¿Usas tú alguna agencia? ¿Cuál? ¿Cuál es el precio por hora?

 **Paso 1**

Ahora leemos un aviso de una agencia de limpieza en un país hispanohablante. Mira el aviso y con un@ compañer@, responde estas preguntas.

Attribution: By Novalimpio, licensed under CC BY-SA 4.0.

1. ¿Dónde está la agencia? Mira el vocabulario.
2. ¿Qué hay en las fotos? Describe las fotos.
3. ¿Por qué usa la empresa estas fotos? ¿Cuál es el objetivo?
4. ¿Qué lugares limpia?
5. Si contratas (*hire*) esta agencia, ¿qué tareas de la casa hacen? Usa el texto y las fotos para contestar la pregunta.

Paso 2. Una agencia de limpieza para estudiantes

Imagina que tú y tres/cuatro compañer@s tienen una agencia de limpieza. You want to offer your services to university students. What do students need? Create an ad for your agency. Include the following:

1. Nombre de la agencia;
2. Tres o cuatro fotos (remember to use https://search.creativecommons.org/ to look for open resources);
3. Un eslogan (como en el texto: "Somos una empresa líder en servicio de limpieza");
4. Una lista de tareas domésticas. Usa la primera persona del plural (por ejemplo, "planchamos tu ropa"). Be creative!

Paso 3. El aviso más popular

The class will now choose the most creative ad. Share your ad with your classmates. Was your ad the most popular?

 Actividad 3-8. Proyecto multimodal opcional

Create a short commercial (15-30 seconds) to advertise the agency you created in **Paso 2** in **Actividad 3-7**. Include the same type of information, but, instead of photos, add music and short video recordings of you and your classmates doing three or four household chores. Make sure your commercial is effective. Instrucciones para hacer un aviso publicitario: http://bit.ly/WikiCommercial.

 **Práctica individual:** To continue using your new words and expressions, go to http://bit.ly/PracticaIndividual3-3.

Hablemos de gramática: *El verbo "gustar" + infinitive & "gustar" + noun*

Sábado de limpieza

Kate es de una familia bicultural. Su papá es de los Estados Unidos y su mamá es española. Kate usa el español con su mamá. Es sábado y Kate hace las tareas de la casa. Escribe un texto a su mamá en Tejas. ¿Cómo está Kate? ¿Por qué?

Attribution: By Gabriela C. Zapata, licensed under CC BY-SA.

En el mensaje de texto, Kate y su mamá usan el verbo **gustar**. Look at the forms of this verb. What do you notice about these forms? Pay attention to the words/phrases that come after the verb.

- No **me gustan** *las tareas* de la casa.
- No **me gusta**… *limpiar* el baño. **Me gusta** *planchar*.

Now let's look at the example we saw in the dialogue between Kate and the real estate agent:

- **A mí me gusta** *el apartamento*.

What can you hypothesize about this verb? What is important when we conjugate it? Again, the clue is in the words/phrases that come after it.

Gustar is a special verb that cannot be conjugated like other **-ar** verbs. As you can see in the examples above, when Kate says she likes the apartment, she says **"me gusta"**, not **"yo gusto"**. The conjugation of **gustar** does *not* depend on the person who likes or dislikes, but on *what is liked*. For example, if you talk about something that you like to do, you will need the singular form of **gustar (gusta) + the verb in the infinitive** that is used to refer to that activity (e.g., **Me gusta planchar**). The same is true if you refer to only one thing that you like: Me **gusta el apartamento**. If you want to talk about many things you like or dislike, you will need to use the plural form of **gustar**, **gustan** (e.g., No me **gustan las tareas** del hogar).

Also, in the examples, you must have noticed the pronoun **me** before **gustar**. Well, this is an example of *indirect object pronoun*, which refers to object or the person who receives the action of a verb indirectly (in English, *to whom* or *for whom*). In Spanish, we use *indirect object pronouns* with **gustar**. Have a look at this table. What do you notice about the use of **gustar** and *the indirect object pronouns we need*? What is the optional part?

El verbo gustar

Number	Optional (NO)	Indirect object pronouns	Gustar	
Singular	(A mí)	me	gusta	el apartamento
	(A ti/A vos)	te (informal)	gustan	las tareas del hogar.
	(A usted/Ud.)	le (formal)	gusta	limpiar el piso.
	(A él/ella)	le	gustan	los libros.
Plural	(A nosotros/nosotras)	nos	gusta	la clase de español.
	(A vosotros/vosotras)	os	gustan	los exámenes. (España)
	(A ustedes/Uds.)	les	gusta	cocinar.
	(A ellos/ellas)	les	gusta	lavar los vidrios.

Ahora mira este video. It offers a summary of the way in which we use **gustar**, and it introduces other likes-dislikes verbs that behave in a similar way as **gustar**.

 **Me gusta y no me gusta**

Video link: https://bit.ly/Video33Trayectos

Attribution: By Daniel Hernández Ruiz, licensed under CC BY 4.0.

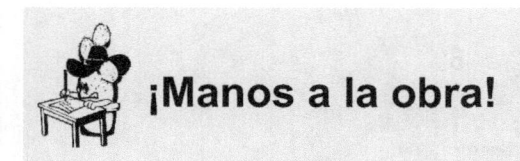 **¡Manos a la obra!**

Actividad 3-9. Más sobre gustos

Visita la página en http://bit.ly/ActividadGustar y completa las actividades 1, 2 y 3. Be ready to discuss your results with other classmates. ¿Tienes unas palabras nuevas? Add the new words you have learned to your glossary for this module.

 ### Actividad 3-10. ¿Qué te gusta hacer?

Paso 1. Trabaja con un@ compañer@. Usa el gráfico a continuación y compara tus gustos y los gustos de tu compañer@. You can also talk about other likes and dislikes. Remember to ask your instructor for help! Discuss 5 or 6 likes and dislikes.

Modelo(s):	**E1:** *¿Qué te gusta hacer?*
	E2: *Me gusta twittear. ¿Y a ti/ a vos?*
	E1: *No me gusta twittear. Me gusta Instagram.*

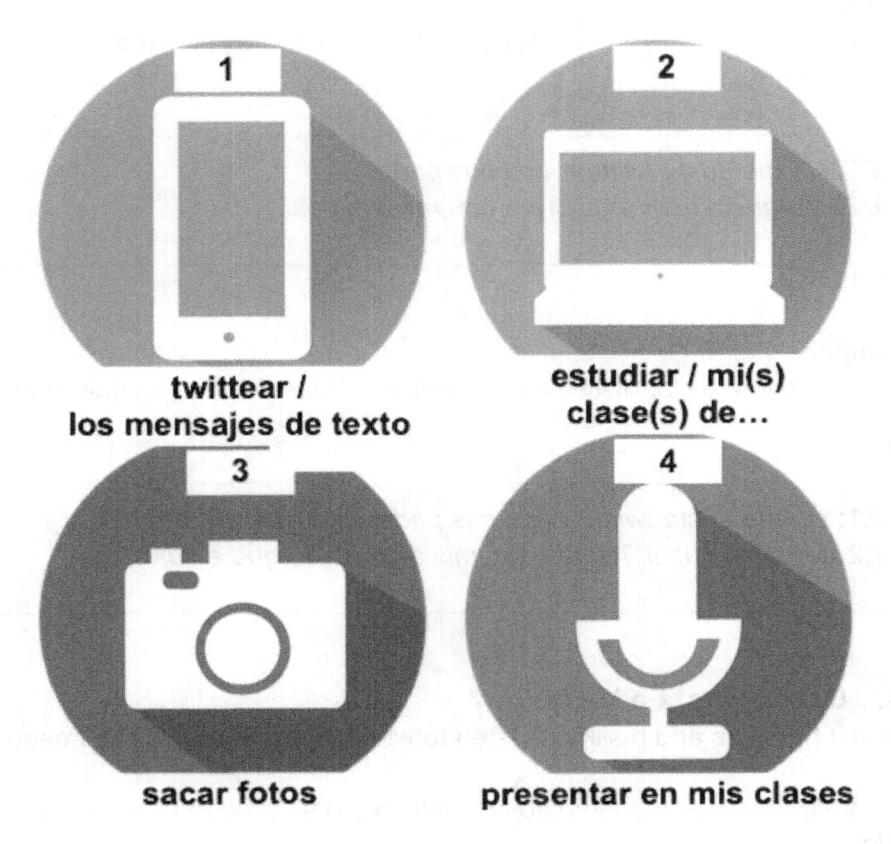

Attribution: Public domain.

leer / los libros

jugar videojuegos /el videojuego [nombre]

escuchar música / la música [nombre]

mirar shows / el show [nombre]

Attribution: Public domain.

Paso 2. ¿Con quién?

Now write the persons with whom you like/dislike to do the activities in **Paso 1**. Use **con** *(with)* to help you formulate your responses.

> **Modelo(s):** **E1:** *No me gusta twittear con mis padres.*
> **E2:** *Me gusta usar Instagram con mis amigos.*

Paso 3. ¿Por qué?

Now write a reason why you like or dislike the activities in **Paso 1**. Use **porque** to expand your sentences.

> **Modelo(s):** **E1:** *No me gusta twittear con mis padres porque son aburridos.*
> **E2:** *Me gusta usar Tik Tok con mis amigos porque es divertido.*

Actividad 3-11. ¿Qué le gusta a Verónica?

A student talks about her likes and dislikes. Listen to what she says, using the image below for help.

Paso 1. Escucha a Verónica. ¿Le gustan cosas similares a ti? ¿Tiene Uds. los mismos gustos? Escribe las similitudes.

 **Me gusta y no me gusta**

Audio link: http://bit.ly/Audio3-4Trayectos
(To listen to the audio, go first to Actividad 3-11, and click on the audio icon.)

Attribution: By Daniel Hernández Ruiz,
licensed under CC BY 4.0.

 **Paso 2**

Escucha a Verónica otra vez y decide si estas afirmaciones son **Ciertas (C)** o **Falsas (F)**. Trabaja con un@ compañer@. Work with someone you haven't worked with before.

1. Para Verónica, el mundo no es interesante.	C	F
2. Verónica vive en una ciudad.	C	F
3. A Verónica le gusta caminar a la universidad.	C	F
4. A Verónica le gustan los perros de color negro (*black*).	C	F
5. La celebración favorita de Verónica es Halloween.	C	F
6. A Verónica no le gustan los mosquitos.	C	F
7. A Verónica le gusta comprar regalos (*gifts*) para sus amigas.	C	F
8. A Verónica le gusta Netflix.	C	F

Paso 3. Now compare your likes and dislikes with Verónica's. ¿Son ustedes similares a Verónica? To discuss your preferences, use **gustar**, of course! Also, try to ask more questions to get to know your classmate.

¡Conversemos!

Trabaja con un@ compañero@ y practica tu español en esta situación social. You need to use the vocabulary and structures you have learned so far. Change roles and partners after practicing each situation once.

Conversación 1

> **Estudiante 1.** Call your best friend from high school and tell them about your new roommate and apartment off campus. Describe your roommate and apartment, including:
>
> - Their age and appearance;
> - Their personality (e.g., what they like and dislike);
> - Why they are a good roommate (e.g., describe the household chores they do).
> - Apartment: Talk about its location, number of rooms (describe each room—talk about furniture).
> - Say why you like it. Ask questions and share as much information as possible.

> **Estudiante 2.** Your best friend from high school calls you to tell you about their new roommate and apartment in college. Ask questions about:
>
> - Your friend's roommate, and
> - What they like about their new city and university.
> - Their new apartment.
> - Tell your friend about your new girlfriend/boyfriend or friend.
> - Describe their age, personality, and appearance. Ask questions and share as much information as possible.

Práctica individual: To continue using your new structures, go to http://bit.ly/PracticaIndividual3-4.

Trayectos hispanos: *El activismo en los espacios urbanos*

En esta sección, aprendemos sobre la importancia de los espacios urbanos para el activismo. Nos enfocamos en dos artistas hispanas/latinx y analizamos cómo usan el arte de los murales para "hablar" sobre temas importantes para sus comunidades. ¿Hay murales en las calles (*streets*) de tu ciudad (*city/town*)? ¿Qué temas presentan las representaciones en los murales?
Ahora mira los dos murales a continuación. Estos murales están en las ciudades de El Paso y Los Ángeles.

- ¿Qué aspectos de las comunidades hispanas/latinx representan?
- ¿Qué mensaje transmiten los artistas?
- ¿Qué personas de la historia mexicoamericana hay en los murales? ¿Por qué?

Attribution: El paso. Mural downtown. By Kamahele, licensed under CC BY-SA 4.0.

Attribution: Across the street from La Esrtrella taco shop. By Camiloarenivar, licensed under CC BY-SA 4.0.

These two murals address what some people might consider "controversial" issues, such as the grape strike in California and the Zapatista movement in Mexico. Murals are important in that they bring art into the public sphere. Also, they can be a relatively effective tool of social emancipation and activism. Often, their visual effects are an enticement to attract public attention to social issues. Murals can have a dramatic impact whether consciously or subconsciously on the attitudes of passers-by when they are added to areas where people live and work.[12]

Sometimes muralists are censored. This was the case of two contemporary Chicana artists. Now, we will learn more about them and their activism, and why their work was not considered appropriate to be shown in public spaces.

Barbara Carrasco[13]

Attribution: Artist Barbara Carrasco in front of her mural L.A. History: A Mexican Perspective with a commendation from Los Angeles County presented by County Supervisor Hilda Solis at the opening of the temporary exhibition Sin Censura: A Mural Remembers LA at the Natural History Museum of Los Angeles County, which was on view from March 9, 2018 through August 11, 2019.

Barbara Carrasco y la censura de su trabajo: *L.A. History: A Mexican Perspective*

---

12 Text adapted from the original: *Mural.* By Wikipedia, licensed under CC BY-SA 3.0.
13 Text adapted from the original: Barbara Carrasco. By Wikipedia, licensed under CC BY-SA 3.0.

Bárbara Carrasco (1955) es una artista y activista chicana de El Paso, Texas. Sus trabajos expresan críticas a los estereotipos culturales que se basan en diferencias socioeconómicas, de raza, género y sexualidad y son mensajes (*messages*) sociales sobre los problemas de las comunidades hispanas/latinx y la sociedad en general. Carrasco crea obras de gran escala, como murales y también obras más pequeñas. Su trabajo más famoso es el mural en la foto, *L.A. History: A Mexican Perspective*. Sus obras se exhiben en museos nacionales e internacionales. Actualmente (*At present*), Carrasco vive en Los Ángeles y está muy involucrada (*involved*) en la comunidad.

Carrasco has been publicly acknowledged for her role in making the Chicano art movement (http://bit.ly/ChicanoArtM) aware of sexist attitudes. She was also an activist working closely with César Chávez (http://bit.ly/CChavezWiki) and the United Farm Workers (http://bit.ly/UFWWiki) between 1976 and 1991. For example, she created flyers and banners for conventions, rallies, and supermarket demonstrations. The last work she did for the organization was Cesar Chavez's funeral banner. By protesting within her artwork, Carrasco has educated people about systemic racism and sexism towards people of color. One of her famous works connected to her involvement with the United Farm Workers is *Dolores* (https://s.si.edu/3sHBQ2t), which pays homage to Dolores Huerta, the co-founder of the organization. You will learn more about this activist in Volume 2 of *Trayectos*.
En este vídeo (https://vimeo.com/38243236), Carrasco habla de inspiración, César Chávez y el objetivo de su trabajo. ¿Cómo es su experiencia con Chávez? ¿Qué desea Carrasco lograr (*achieve*) con su arte?

Paso 1. ¿Qué significa la palabra **censura**? ¿A quiénes afecta? Lee el título de la obra de Carrasco. Why do you think it might have been censored? Lee el texto a continuación e indica las razones principales de la censura.

Carrasco pinta el mural *L.A. History: A Mexican Perspective* para el grupo Community Redevelopment Agency (CRA) en Los Ángeles en 1981. El objetivo de Carrasco es presentar a la audiencia una perspectiva de la historia de la ciudad desde el punto de vista de los grupos marginalizados. La ciudad de Los Ángeles primero (*first*) aprueba (*approves*) los dibujos (*sketches*) de Carrasco, pero (*but*) cuando ella pinta, CRA se opone al uso de 14 imágenes. Estas imágenes representan la esclavitud, los campos de concentración (*internment camps*) de los ciudadanos japoneses durante la Segunda Guerra Mundial (*World War II*) y los ataques a los jóvenes mexicano-americanos durante el incidente *zoot suit riots* (http://bit.ly/ZootSuitR).

Carrasco refused to comply with CRA's request, and the project was canceled. The mural was then put in a storage room for nearly a decade. There were fifty-one separate events related to discrimination and racism depicted in the mural. In 2019, the mural came back to life in the temporary exhibition *Sin Censura: A Mural Remembers LA* at the Natural History Museum of Los Angeles County. This work was also featured in the exhibit *Murales Rebeldes* in Los Angeles (we will learn more about this event shortly). The mural will be permanently exhibited in the new building of the Natural History Museum, the NHM Commons, when its construction is finalized.

Paso 2. Ahora, mira las fotos del mural en estas páginas y vídeo.

- Página: http://bit.ly/SinCensuraBC
- Vídeo: http://bit.ly/SinCensuraBCVideo

    1. ¿Qué personas/eventos/problemas sociales puedes (*can you*) descubrir en la obra?
    2. ¿Por qué las representaciones son históricamente correctas (*historically correct*)?

3. Why do you think CRA was so opposed to the mural?

4. Do you think the artist would have faced the same attitudes/censorship today? Explain.

Yreina Cervantez[14]

Attribution: La Ofrenda. By Thomas Tracy, licensed under CC BY 2.0.

Yreina Cervantez (1952) es amiga de Barbara Carrasco y también una artista y activista chicana muy importante. Es originariamente de Garden City, Kansas. Como Carrasco, está muy involucrada en su comunidad y es una de las fundadoras del grupo colectivo de artistas de Los Ángeles *Self Help Graphics* (http://bit.ly/SelfHelpArtWiki). Sus trabajos reflejan aspectos culturales y sociales importantes de la comunidad hispana/latinx y combinan diferentes modalidades (*modes*) como texto e imágenes y elementos del arte precolombino y el paisaje (*landscape*) urbano. Su trabajo más famoso es el mural en la foto, *La Ofrenda*. Sus obras se exhiben en museos nacionales e internacionales. Actualmente (*At present*), Cervantez vive en Los Ángeles y es profesora de estudios chicanos en California State University, Northridge.

En 2016, el programa de la ciudad de Los Ángeles, *CityWide Mural Program*, trabaja con Cervantez para restaurar (*restore*) el mural *La Ofrenda*.

Mira el vídeo "Restauración de *La Ofrenda*" en http://bit.ly/LaOfrendaVideo y la foto arriba.

1. ¿Qué mensaje comunica Cervantez en su mural?
2. ¿Qué temas representa el mural?
3. ¿Quién es la figura más prominente? ¿Por qué?
4. Tie some of the opinions featured in the video, as well as the artist's, to the social purpose of murals we discussed at the beginning of this lesson.

Como Bárbara Carrasco, some of Cervantez's works have been censored. To learn more about censorship and Hispanic/Latinx art, we invite you to explore the exhibit *Murales rebeldes*:

- Página: https://muralesrebeldes.org/exhibition/
- Vídeo: http://bit.ly/MuralesRebeldesVideo

Los murales en nuestra sociedad y tu comunidad

---

14 *Text adapted from the original: Yreina Cervantez. By Wikipedia, licensed under CC BY-SA 3.0.*

Paso 1. Trabajas con 4 o 5 compañer@s.
Mira los siguientes murales contemporáneos. ¿Qué temas sociales representan? ¿Qué mensajes comunican los artistas? ¿Cómo lo hacen (por ejemplo, colores, imágenes específicas, etc.)? Explica.

Mural #1

Attribution: Mural: Trayvon Martin. By Franco Folini, licensed under CC BY-SA 2.0.

Mural #2

Attribution: Fighting Pollution. By cogdogblog, licensed under CC BY 2.0.

Mural #3

Attribution: Amazing feminist mural in San Francisco. By skyfaller is licensed under CC BY-SA 2.0.

Paso 2.

Opción #1. Investigación

Paso 1. En esta actividad, tú y tus compañer@s investigan los murales de su comunidad. Cada miembro del grupo busca un mural y prepara un póster virtual sobre el mural. En tu trabajo, tienes esta información:

- Una o varias fotos del mural
- Dónde está el mural (por ejemplo, nombre de la(s) calle(s). You can include a picture or link to the Google map location.)
- Autor@ (if it is known who created the mural)
- Información breve sobre autor@
- Temas
- Significado social/cultural

Usa inglés y español. Para hacer el póster, te recomendamos una plataforma como *Canva* (https://www.canva.com/).

Paso 2. Cada persona en el grupo presenta su póster en inglés y español.

Paso 3. El grupo resume (*summarizes*) los temas sociales/culturales de los murales comunitarios. ¿Cuál es el tema más importante? How are these themes connected to the community?

Opción #2: Diseño de un mural

Paso 1. En esta actividad, tú y tus compañer@s crean las ideas para hacer un mural. Ustedes tienen que decidir:

- Los temas del mural. Estos temas deben estar relacionados con aspectos sociales/culturales importantes en tu comunidad.
- Lugar para el mural. Explican por qué eligen (*choose*) ese lugar.
- Imágenes y texto a incluir. Usan ejemplos de imágenes (find open images in *Unsplash* [https://unsplash.com/] o *Creative Commons Search* [https://search.creativecommons.org/], and don't forget to include the attribution).
- Explican por qué eligen (*choose*) los colores.
- Mensaje a comunicar.

Usan inglés y español.

Paso 2. Cada grupo presenta su idea a los otros grupos de la clase. ¿Qué temas sociales/ culturales comunica la clase?

Más comunicación: *Los números de 100 a 1.000.000*

Los números en la ciudad de El Paso
En la sección anterior, hablamos de unos murales en la ciudad texana de El Paso. Esta ciudad tiene una herencia hispana muy importante. También, la artista Barbara Carrasco es de El Paso. Ahora aprendemos algunos números sobre esta ciudad. ¿Cómo decimos estos números?

Have a look at the following numbers, and write down what you notice about them. For example, how do we say 1,000? How do we form numbers in the hundreds? Do we use "and" in numbers such as a hundred and two? Do we use a comma, like in English? Let's see…

Attribution: #WIP by VisitElPaso, licensed under CC BY 2.0.

El Paso tiene aproximadamente **302 (trescientos dos)** días de sol anualmente por su clima desértico. En el verano, la temperatura es de más de **100°F [cien grados farenheit])**. En esta ciudad, viven **683.577 [seiscientos ochenta y tres mil quinientos setenta y siete personas]**. **El Camino Real de Tierra Adentro** (http://bit.ly/CaminoRealTierra) fue (*was*) una ruta de comercio entre la Ciudad de México y San Juan Pueblo en Nuevo México entre los años **1598 (mil quinientos noventa y ocho)** y **1882 (mil ochocientos ochenta y dos)**.

As you can see in this short text on the city of El Paso, numbers in Spanish are similar to and different from English. What have you noticed? What are the similarities? What are the differences? Here we offer you some rules that can help you use complex numbers in Spanish:

- Unlike English, there is not an "y" directly after the number one hundred (**ciento** in combination with other numbers). Ejemplos: 101 (**ciento uno**), 133 (**ciento treinta y tres**).

- **Ciento** is used in combination with numbers from 1 to 99: **ciento uno**, **ciento dos**, **ciento ochenta**, and so on. **Cien** is used when counting and before numbers greater than 100: **cien mil (100.000), cien millones (100.000.000).**

- Like we saw in **Módulo introductorio**, numbers agree in gender and number with the noun they modify: doscien**tos** cuadern**os,** trescien**tas** computador**as.**

- The word **mil** does not have a plural form in counting. However, the word **millón** has the plural form **millones**. When followed directly by a noun, **millón** (**dos millones**, and so on) must be followed by **de**.

> **Modelo(s):** $3000 --> *tres mil dólares.*
> $20.000.000 --> *veinte millones de habitantes*

- When expressing dates, years are never written with a period or a comma. Also, the numbers 200-900 will be masculine and plural to agree with the implied or stated masculine plural noun **años.** Years must be spelled out (**1992: mil novecientos noventa y dos)** rather than broken into two-digit groups (nineteen ninety-two)

> **Modelo(s):** 2019 --> *dos mil diecinueve*
> 1876 --> *mil ochocientos setenta y seis*

Los números de cien al millón

Audio link: http://bit.ly/Audio3-5Trayectos

100	**cien**		700	**setecientos(as)**
	(ciento + número)			
200	**doscientos(as)**		800	**ochocientos(as)**
300	**trescientos(as)**		900	**novecientos(as)**
400	**cuatrocientos(as)**		1.000	**mil**
500	**quinientos(as)**		1.000.000	**un millón**
600	**seiscientos(as)**		2.000.000	**dos millones**

 **El cactus viajero.**

In many parts of the Spanish-speaking world, a period is used when English uses a comma, and a comma is used to indicate the decimal: **$1.600; $1.000.000; 5,4%.**

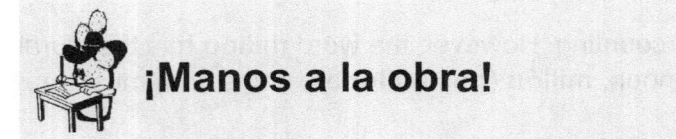 **¡Manos a la obra!**

Actividad 3-12. ¿Cuánto cuesta ser estudiante?

Remember Mariana? We met her in **Módulo introductorio**. She has decided to attend your university, and she needs help preparing her budget. You want to give her an idea of the prices of things in your town.

Paso 1. Tell Mariana how much the following things cost. Prepara los número en español para su presupuesto (*budget*).

1. Alquilar un apartamento por un mes.
2. Alquilar un coche por dos semanas.
3. El costo de un galón de gasolina.
4. El costo de 5 galones de gasolina a usar durante una semana.
5. La matrícula de un curso de cuatro créditos.
6. Una computadora portátil de una buena marca (*brand*).
7. La factura (*bill*) mensual del gas y de la electricidad.
8. El costo total de la cuenta (*bill*) semanal del supermercado para dos personas.
9. Una cena en tu restaurante favorito.
10. El libro de una de tus clases (por ejemplo, historia, estadística, etc.)

Paso 2. Compara tus números con un@ compañer@.
¿Tienen números similares? ¿Quién de ustedes tiene un presupuesto más barato (*cheaper*)?

Actividad 3-13. Subasta (*Auction*) de pinturas de Manuel Gregorio Acosta

En esta actividad trabajas con cuatro compañer@s. Otro artista importante de El Paso es Manuel Gregorio Acosta (http://bit.ly/ManuelGregAcosta). And in this activity, you and your classmates will create a brochure in Spanish to advertise an auction of some of Acosta's paintings.

Paso 1. Watch this video (http://bit.ly/Video3-4Trayectos) about an auction of Acosta's paintings. Each member of the group will be responsible for one painting. Watch the video and fill out the following table.

Pintura	Número 1	Número 2	Número 3	Número 4
Nombre				
Dimensiones (en pulgadas [*inches*])				
Valor				
Oferta [*bid*] inicial				

Paso 2. You want to attract Spanish speakers in Texas to the auction. Create a script for a video for this audience similar to the one you saw in English. Your group will present the script to the rest of the class. Include the following:

- Greeting
- Brief information about Manuel Acosta (http://bit.ly/ManuelGregAcosta).
- Date and place for the auction (**subasta**)
- Information about each painting (**pintura**): Include the information you wrote in **Paso 1**.

> **Modelo(s):** ¡Bienvenidos, amigos de El Paso! Los invitamos a una subasta de las pinturas del artista mexicoamericano Manuel Gregorio Acosta. Este artista…

Actividad 3-14. Investigación: ¿Es caro estudiar en tu estado?

En esta actividad trabajas con cuatro compañer@s. You are going to find out how much it costs for a university student to study in your state. You and your partners will choose four different universities in the state. One of them should be your own institution.

Paso 1. Choose the institutions on which you want to focus. Distribute them among the members of the group.

Paso 2. Visit the universities' pages, and fill out the following table. Write the cost of each of the categories given. Each person should be responsible for one institution.

Universidades	Universidad 1	Universidad 2	Universidad 3	Universidad 4
Matrícula (*Tuition and fees*)				

Libros y otros materiales				
Habitación y comidas				
Gastos personales				
Viajes (*Traveling*)				
Total				

Paso 3. Share the results of your research with your partners. ¡Usa el español! ¿Cuánto necesita un@ estudiante en cada universidad? ¿Qué universidad es la más barata (*cheapest*)? ¿Es tu universidad? ¿Cuál es la más cara?

Actividad 3-15. Los afrodescendientes

Como vimos (*we saw*) en el **Módulo introductorio**, uno de los grupos importantes del mundo hispanohablante son **los afrodescendientes**. En esta actividad, usas tus nuevos números para aprender más sobre estas personas. Trabajas con tres compañer@s. Para buscar información, necesitas visitar estas páginas:

- http://bit.ly/AfrolatinxInfo
- http://bit.ly/AfrolatinosInfo

Paso 1. ¿Quiénes son los afrodescendientes? ¿Qué otros nombres reciben? ¿Cuál es la población total?

Paso 2. You and your group will focus on four countries. Each member will choose one of the four Spanish-speaking countries in the table assigned to your group, and will gather information about the AfroLatinx population. Each person will fill out the table with the information for which they are responsible.

Grupo 1:

Países	Colombia	Honduras	Cuba	México
Localización del país (continente y fronteras)				
Población total del país				
Número de afrodescendientes				
Datos históricos/ culturales importantes				
Nombres en el país				

Grupo 2:

Países	Venezuela	Guatemala	República Dominicana	Estados Unidos
Localización del país (continente y fronteras)				
Población total del país				
Número de afrodescendientes				
Datos históricos/ culturales importantes				
Nombres en el país				

Grupo 3:

Países	Perú	Nicaragua	Puerto Ricoa	México
Localización del país (continente y fronteras)				
Población total del país				
Número de afrodescendientes				
Datos históricos/ culturales importantes				
Nombres en el país				

Grupo 4:

Países	Uruguay	Costa Rica	Panamá	Estados Unidos
Localización del país (continente y fronteras)				
Población total del país				
Número de afrodescendientes				
Datos históricos/ culturales importantes				
Nombres en el país				

Paso 3. Share the results of your research with your partners. ¡Usa el español! ¿Qué similitudes y diferencias hay entre los países? What surprised you about these groups?

 **Práctica individual:** To continue using your new numbers, go to http://bit.ly/PracticaIndividual3-5.

Hablemos de cultura: *España*

 Una estudiante española

Begoña es una estudiante de España. Mira el siguiente video y responde las preguntas a continuación.

Video link: https://bit.ly/Video35Trayectos

1. ¿De dónde es Begoña en España?

2. ¿De dónde son sus padres?

3. ¿Cuántos años tiene Begoña?

Attribution: By Efrain Hernandez, licensed under CC BY-SA 4.0.

En esta sección, aprendemos más sobre la ciudad y el país de Begoña. Lee los textos a continuación y compara las similitudes y diferencias entre España y los Estados Unidos.

Attribution: Vista aérea de Madrid, Palacio Real, By Tim Adams, licensed under CC BY 3.0.

Datos generales sobre España

CAPITAL:	Madrid (6.507.184 de habitantes)
POBLACIÓN DEL PAIS:	46.698.569 de habitantes
IDIOMAS OFICIALES:	El español o castellano, el catalán (catalá, se habla en Cataluña, las Islas Baleares, Andorra y el País Valenciano [valenciano]), el gallego (*galego,* se habla en Galicia) y vasco (*euskera,* se habla en el País Vasco o Euskadi).
CIUDADES PRINCIPALES:	Barcelona, Valencia, Sevilla, Zaragoza, Málaga y Murcia.
MONEDA:	El euro

 ## Un paseo por España

La historia de España

España tiene una historia muy rica. Muchos grupos diferentes habitan el país a través de los siglos. Los primeros habitantes son los celtas y los íberos. Luego llegan los fenicios, los cartagineses, los griegos y los romanos. Durante la época romana, España se llama la Hispania Romana. Los romanos ocupan Hispania entre los años 200 a.C. (*B.C.*) y 419 d.C. (*A.D.*). Los romanos dejaron (*left*) numerosas estructuras arquitectónicas, como acueductos, teatros, anfiteatros, templos y puentes (*bridges*). Estas fotografías son de lugares famosos romanos en España.

Attribution: El acueducto de Segovia. By Josemanuel, licensed under CC BY-SA 2.5.

Attribution: Anfiteatro romano en Málaga. By Gabriela C. Zapata, licensed under CC BY-SA 4.0.

Los árabes llegan a la Península en el año 711 d.C. y tienen una influencia muy importante en todas las áreas de la vida: la agricultura, la arquitectura, las ciencias, la lengua, el comercio, etc. Algunas palabras de procedencia árabe en el español son almohada (*pillow*), alfombra (*carpet*), café, alcohol. Do you find this information surprising? Do you know more words of Arabic origin in Spanish? You can do a quick Google search and add more to the previous list.

 Un estilo muy tradicional de arte y arquitectura con influencia árabe en España es el mudéjar. ¿Cómo es este estilo? Lee este artículo: http://bit.ly/ArteMudejar. What does the content of this article tell you about Spain's history and heritage?

Hay muchas construcciones con estilos típicamente árabe en España. Algunos de estos lugares son muy famosos. ¿Cómo se llaman? ¿Dónde están? Mira el vídeo a continuación y contesta estas preguntas. Escribe algunas características del estilo árabe. You can use English to talk about the characteristics you notice, but try to use as much Spanish as you can.

Video link: https://bit.ly/Video36Trayectos

Attribution: By i geotv, licensed under CC BY-SA 4.0.

Ahora mira estas fotos de la arquitectura árabe y mudéjar en España. ¿Te gusta?

Attribution: La Alhambra de Granada. By Paloma Serrano Viñuelas, licensed under CC BY-SA 4.0.

Attribution: Detalle de la decoración de la Alhambra. By Paloma Serrano Viñuelas, licensed under CC BY-SA 4.0.

La música tradicional

En el **Módulo introductorio**, aprendemos sobre dos estilos de música en España. ¿Cómo se llaman estos estilos? ¿A qué cantantes escuchamos en ese módulo? Consulta las páginas 12-13.

Además de los dos estilos de música que aparecen en el **Módulo introductorio**, en España hay otros. Cada región del país tiene su estilo de música folclórica, bailes e instrumentos típicos. Por ejemplo, en el norte, en el País Vasco, son típicos la pandereta (*tambourine*) y el acordeón. Mira el vídeo de **Kepa Junkera** (http://bit.ly/KepaJunkeraVideo); ¿cantan en español? ¿En qué lengua cantan?

En la región de Cataluña, dos instrumentos comunes son el flabiol (*tabor-pipe*) y el tamboril (*small drum*). Mira el vídeo de **Sardana** en Barcelona (http://bit.ly/SardanaBarce); ¿dónde está la gente? ¿Quién baila?.

En la música de Andalucía, hay guitarras y el cajón (*box shaped percussion instrument from Peru*) y el **cante jondo** (*style of singing flamenco music*). Esta música es una fusión de tradiciones gitanas (*Gypsy*) y árabes. Mira los vídeos de **Sara Baras** (http://bit.ly/FlamencoDanza) y de **Camarón** y **Paco de Lucía** (http://bit.ly/CamaronPaco).

 **Investigación**

¿Y la música contemporánea? ¿Conoces (*Do you know*) bandas o cantantes españoles que hacen rap, hip hop u otro estilo? Con un@ compañer@, usa Google y busca un ejemplo de un@ cantante o banda contemporánea español@.

 Nota

La pintura de Picasso **Mujeres de Argel** es la obra más cara (*most expensive*) del mundo. Su precio en una subasta de 2015 es de $160.000.000.

Attribution: Women of Algiers, after Delacroix (1955). By NichoDesign, licensed under CC BY-SA 2.0.

Otro artista importante es **Salvador Dalí** (1904-1989). Este artista es uno de los más versátiles y prolíficos del siglo XX. Su estilo artístico es el surrealismo.

Attribution: Salvador Dalí en 1965 con su mascota. Public domain.

 En los Estados Unidos, hay muchas obras de Salvador Dalí en St. Petersburg, Florida. Explora el museo virtualmente en https://thedali.org/.

 Un dato interesante: En 1946, Dalí colabora con Walt Disney en un film. El título es **Destino**. Mira el film (http://bit.ly/Video3-7Trayectos). ¿Cuál es el tema? ¿Por qué es el título **Destino**? ¿Qué características tiene? ¿Te gusta?

La gastronomía española[15]

La gastronomía española es un ejemplo de la famosa dieta mediterránea. En la cocina española es característico el uso del aceite (*oil*) de oliva. Es posible encontrar una gran variedad de ingredientes de origen animal y vegetal. La comida se sirve por lo general con pan (*bread*) y un poco de vino (*wine*).

Las tapas españolas

Las populares tapas (llamadas también *pintxos* en el norte de España) consisten en pequeños platos de comida o aperitivos (*appetizers/snacks*). Las tapas son muy variadas. Mira estas fotos con ejemplos de tapas. What do you see? Habla de los ingredientes y otras características. You can answer in English, but try to use as much Spanish as possible.

Attribution: Tapas españolas. By Juan Fernández, licensed under CC BY-SA 2.0.

Attribution: Tapas españolas. By Elemaki, licensed under CC BY 3.0.

---

15 Adapted from original text in https://es.wikivoyage.org/wiki/Espa%C3%B1a, by Wikiviajes, licensed under CC BY-SA 3.0.

¡Manos a la obra!

 **Fechas importantes de España**

Before we leave Spain, let's have a look at some of its important historical events. Con un@ compañer@, google the following events and say in what year they happened.

> **Modelo(s):** **Sevilla celebra la Exposición Universal.**
>
> *Sevilla celebra la Exposición Universal en mil novecientos noventa y dos.*

1. Los árabes llegan a la península ibérica.
2. Cristóbal Colón llega a América.
3. Los españoles llegan a los Estados Unidos.
4. Miguel de Cervantes publica la primera parte del libro *Don Quijote de la Mancha*.
5. La Guerra Civil Española.
6. Penélope Cruz es la primera actriz española en ganar un Óscar.
7. España gana el Mundial de Fútbol.
8. España adopta el euro como moneda (*currency*).

 **Práctica individual:** check how much you remember about the cultural information you just learned, go to http://bit.ly/PracticaIndividual3-6.

Hablemos de gramática: *Irregular verbs in the "yo" form*

Una fiesta en el apartamento de Kate

Kate, Lauren y su amiga mexicoamericana, Karina, organizan una fiesta en el apartamento de las chicas. ¿Qué hace cada una de ellas? Lee su conversación. Pay attention to the forms that they use in the first person (**yo**). Also, look at the **tener** forms. Use the list of verbs below to make sure you understand the content of the dialogue.

Attribution: Public domain.

Lauren: OK, chicas. Entonces, ¿**tenemos** una fiesta este fin de semana?

Kate: Uy, la fiesta… Me había olvidado (*I had forgotten!*). Sí, claro. Necesitamos limpiar y hacer varias cosas. Yo **hago** la comida, **pongo** la ropa en la lavadora y limpio el baño. **Tengo** unas recetas (*recipes*) para tapas de mi mamá.

Lauren Great! Yo paso la aspiradora y compro la comida en el supermercado. **Salgo** temprano de mis clases mañana y **traigo** los ingredientes. ¿Me **das** una lista, Kate?

Kate Sí, te **doy** la lista en un minuto…

Karina Perfecto, chicas. Yo **traigo** unas Coca-Colas y les **digo** a los chicos de la fiesta. ¿A quién invitamos?

Did you discover the differences in the conjugations of the bolded verbs in the **yo** form? These verbs have a different conjugation pattern in the first person singular than the verbs we've seen so far. They're *irregular verbs*. Have a look at the following tables. What do you notice about the verbs **tener** and **decir**? What happens in other persons?

	Poner	Hacer *(to do)* *(to make)*	Traer *(to bring)*	Salir *(to get out)* *(to go out)*	Dar *(to give)*
yo	pon**go**	ha**go**	trai**go**	sal**go**	do**y**
tú	pones	haces	traes	sales	das
vos	ponés	hacés	traés	salís	das
usted, Ud., él, ella	pone	hace	trae	sale	da
nosotros(as)	ponemos	hacemos	traemos	salimos	damos
vosotros(as)	ponéis	hacéis	traéis	salís	dais
ustedes, Uds, ellos/ellas	ponen	hacen	traen	salen	dan

There are some verbs that are irregular in other persons. This verb has a stem-change of **e** --> **i**. What do you notice about its conjugation? Which persons have conjugation irregularities?

Decir *(to tell, to say)*	
yo	di**go**
tú	di**c**es
vos	decís
usted, Ud., él, ella	di**c**e
nosotros(as)	decimos
vosotros(as)	decís
ustedes, Uds., ellos/ellas	di**c**en

These verbs have a stem-change of **e** --> **ie**. What do you notice about their conjugation? Which persons have conjugation irregularities?

	Tener *(to have)*	Venir *(to come)*
yo	ten**go**	ven**go**
tú	**tie**nes	**vie**nes
vos	tenés	venís
usted, Ud., él, ella	**tie**ne	**vie**ne
nosotros(as)	tenemos	venimos
vosotros(as)	tenéis	venís
ustedes, Uds., ellos/ellas	**tie**nen	**vie**nen

Ahora mira este video. It offers a summary of the ways in which we conjugate these verbs, and others that behave in a similar way.

 **Las formas irregulares en el presente**

Video link: https://bit.ly/Video38Trayectos

HOY TENEMOS...

2ª PARTE

PRESENTE

FORMAS IRREGULARES

Attribution: By Daniel Hernández Ruiz, licensed under CC BY 4.0.

 **¡Manos a la obra!**

Actividad 3-16. Más verbos interesantes

Visita la página en http://bit.ly/ActividadVerbos y completa todas las actividades en línea. Be ready to discuss your results with other classmates. ¿Tienes unos verbos nuevos? Add the new words you have learned to your glossary for this module.

 **Actividad 3-17. Una fiesta en casa**

Trabaja con un@ compañer@. Ustedes son compañer@s de apartamento y tienen una fiesta en su apartamento. Hablan y organizan la fiesta. Usan estos verbos: **tener**, **poner**, **traer**, **salir**, **hacer**, **venir**, **decir**, **dar** y el vocabulario de este módulo y los módulos anteriores. Usan el diálogo entre Kate y sus amigas como ejemplo. You need to decide when the party is going to be, what time, and who you're going to invite. ¿Qué música ponen en la fiesta?

> **Modelo(s):** **E1:** Yo hago la comida.
> **E2:** Muy bien. ¿Qué haces?
> **E1:** Hago hamburguesas. Y tú, ¿qué haces?

Actividad 3-18. Un email a mamá

Remember Karina, Kate and Lauren's friend? En Madrid, Karina comparte (*shares*) un piso con su hermano Ricardo. Karina no está contenta con su hermano y decide escribir un email a su mamá en Laredo. También ella le manda (*send*) a su mamá estas fotos.

Paso 1. Complete los espacios en el email de Karina con la conjugación de los verbos en paréntesis.

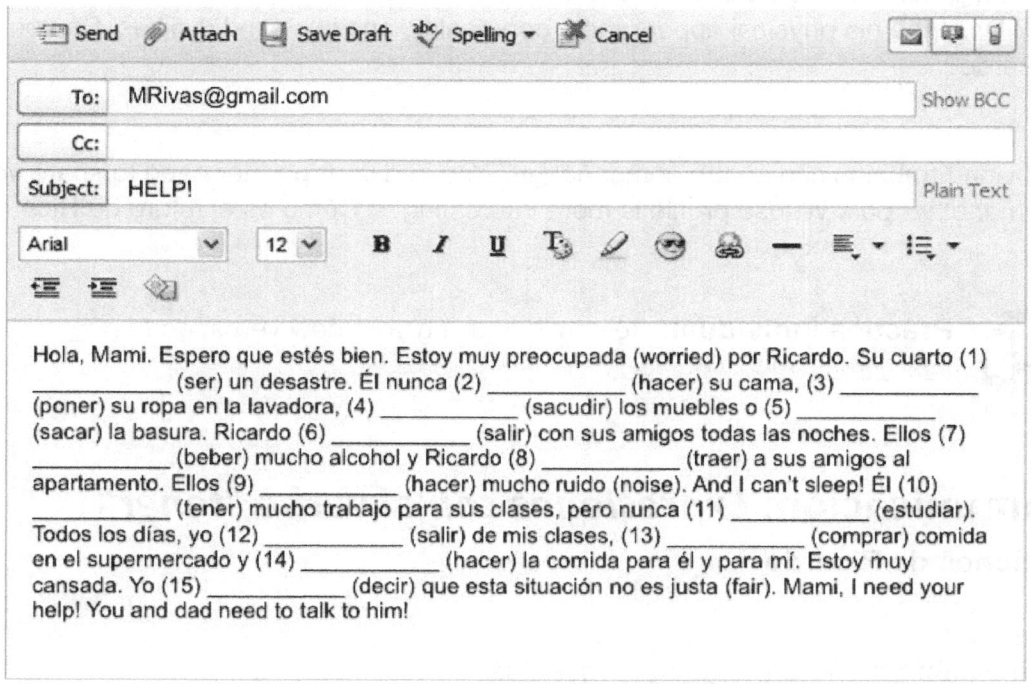

Send · Attach · Save Draft · Spelling ▾ · Cancel

To: MRivas@gmail.com · Show BCC
Cc:
Subject: HELP! · Plain Text

Arial · 12 · **B** *I* U T ✎ 😎 — ☰▾ ☰▾

Hola, Mami. Espero que estés bien. Estoy muy preocupada (worried) por Ricardo. Su cuarto (1) _____ (ser) un desastre. Él nunca (2) _____ (hacer) su cama, (3) _____ (poner) su ropa en la lavadora, (4) _____ (sacudir) los muebles o (5) _____ (sacar) la basura. Ricardo (6) _____ (salir) con sus amigos todas las noches. Ellos (7) _____ (beber) mucho alcohol y Ricardo (8) _____ (traer) a sus amigos al apartamento. Ellos (9) _____ (hacer) mucho ruido (noise). And I can't sleep! Él (10) _____ (tener) mucho trabajo para sus clases, pero nunca (11) _____ (estudiar). Todos los días, yo (12) _____ (salir) de mis clases, (13) _____ (comprar) comida en el supermercado y (14) _____ (hacer) la comida para él y para mí. Estoy muy cansada. Yo (15) _____ (decir) que esta situación no es justa (fair). Mami, I need your help! You and dad need to talk to him!

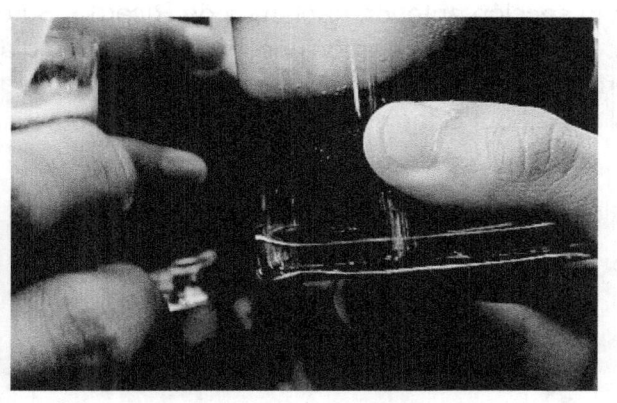

Paso 2

Trabaja con un@ compañer@. Based on the three photos above, create a profile of Ricardo. ¿Cómo es Ricardo? Describe his physical appearance, personality, and likes and dislikes. Do you know anyone like Ricardo?

Paso 3

En esta actividad trabajas con cuatro compañer@s. You and your partner need to share your profile of Ricardo with another pair. Whose profile is more interesting? ¿Cómo es el futuro de Ricardo?

 **Práctica individual:** To continue using your new verbs, go to http://bit.ly/PracticaIndividual3-7.

Más comunicación: *Expresiones con el verbo "tener"*

Las emociones de Ricardo

 **Audio link: http://bit.ly/Audio3-6Trayectos**

En la sección anterior, hablamos de Ricardo. Su estilo de vida en España no es muy bueno. ¿Cómo son sus emociones y necesidades diarias? Pay attention to how we use the verb **tener** to talk about them. How are these ideas expressed in English? What does this tell you about Spanish and English? Let's see…

Ricardo **tiene** 23 años. Ahora vive en Madrid con su hermana Karina. Los hermanos son de Laredo. Ricardo hace una maestría en negocios, pero no es muy responsable. **Tiene** un estilo de vida muy caótico.

Por ejemplo, todas las noches bebe alcohol y en la mañana **tiene mucha sed**.

Se acuesta (*goes to bed*) muy tarde y no come en el desayuno (*breakfast*). Entonces siempre **tiene hambre**.

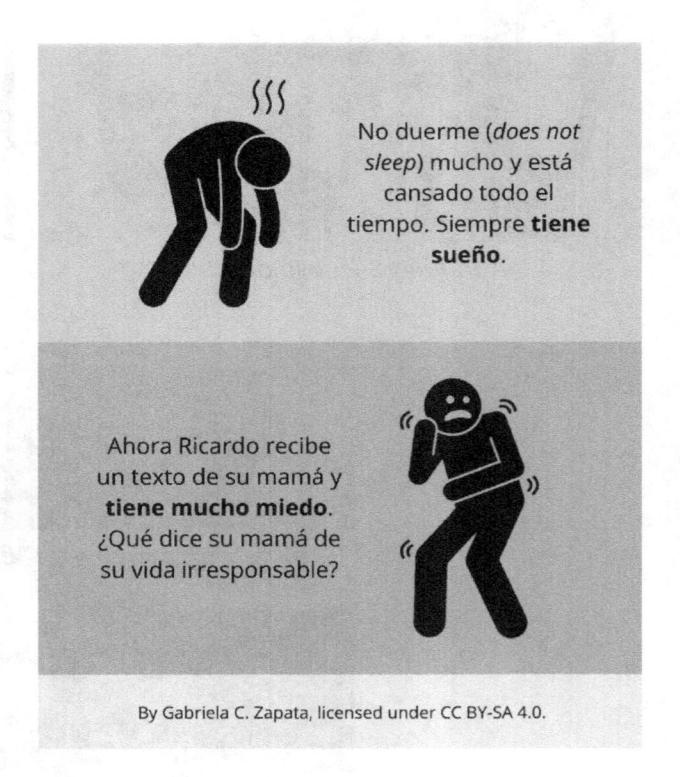

No duerme (*does not sleep*) mucho y está cansado todo el tiempo. Siempre **tiene sueño**.

Ahora Ricardo recibe un texto de su mamá y **tiene mucho miedo**. ¿Qué dice su mamá de su vida irresponsable?

By Gabriela C. Zapata, licensed under CC BY-SA 4.0.

Las expresiones con *tener*

As you can see in the statements about Ricardo's life, in Spanish, the verb **tener** is used to describe emotions and states that, in English, we express with the verb *to be* (e.g., to be thirsty, to be hungry, to be a certain age, etc.). Here are some expressions that work in this way:

tener	
tener calor	*to be hot*
tener frío	*to be cold*
tener hambre	*to be hungry*
tener miedo	*to be afraid*
tener prisa	*to be in a hurry*
tener razón	*to be right*
tener sueño	*to be sleepy/tired*

Y tú, ¿cuándo sientes estas emociones? ¿Por qué? Describe los momentos cuando experimentas estas emociones o estados.

> **Modelo(s):** *Tengo razón cuando tengo evidencia legítima sobre un tema.*

 **¡Manos a la obra!**

Actividad 3-19. Estudiantes en el mundo
Es lunes y los estudiantes hacen sus actividades en el mundo.

 **Paso 1**

Mira las fotos a continuación y con un@ compañer@ describe qué ocurre en cada una. Describe cada fotografía respondiendo estas preguntas.

- ¿Qué hora es?
- ¿Dónde están los estudiantes?
- ¿Qué hacen?
- ¿Qué tienen? Usa las expresiones con el verbo **tener**.
- ¿Qué les gusta?

Foto número 1

Attribution: By Enoch Leung, licensed under CC BY-SA 2.0.

Foto número 2

Attribution: By Andre' Askew, Air Education and Training Command,
Air Force, Mississippi, Official United States Air Force Website. Public domain.

Foto número 3

Attribution: By Sesse, licensed under CC BY 3.0.

 **Paso 2**

Compara tus descripciones con otro par. ¿Tienen descripciones similares?

 **Práctica individual:** To continue using your new vocabulary and expressions, go to http://bit.ly/PracticaIndividual3-8.

Para terminar... *Cartelera*

 Una tesis como una casa (Argentina)

In this module, we will watch the short feature on a project by young students like yourself.

I. Antes de ver

Actividad A. Mira esta foto. What do you see? Are you familiar with this organization? What does this organization do for the community? Responde estas preguntas. Usando la foto, también escribe 2 ideas sobre esta organización.

Attribution: By Savannah River Site, licensed under CC BY 2.0.

Are there any similar organizations at your university? Do you know of any similar organizations in Latin America?

 **Actividad B**

El título de este mini documental es *Una tesis como una casa*. What do you think the video is going to be about? Habla con tu compañer@, ¿cuál es el tema este vídeo?

II. A ver
Ahora mira el vídeo en http://bit.ly/Video3-9Trayectos (Attribution: By AJ+ en español. Used with permission from the producers). Chequea si tus ideas en **Actividad B** son correctas.

III. Después de ver

 **Actividad 3-20. Preguntas de comprensión**

Trabaja con un@ compañer@. Usa las preguntas a continuación para analizar el contenido del vídeo.

    a. ¿De dónde es el vídeo?

    b. ¿Para quién es la casa?

    c. ¿Cómo es la familia en este vídeo?

d. ¿Quién hace la casa?

e. ¿De qué universidad es este proyecto?

f. Keyword Recognition: Find in the video the Spanish word/phrase that best expresses the meaning of the following words in English:

    1. family in need _____

    2. thesis _____

    3. dirty _____

    4. self-sustainable _____

    5. solar panels _____

    6. social networks _____

g. ¿Cómo es la casa? Describe la casa.

 **Actividad 3-21. Opiniones personales**

Trabaja con un@ compañer@. Usa las preguntas a continuación para analizar el objetivo y las características de este vídeo.

a. What is the purpose of the video? Who is the audience?

b. Why did the students choose to build the house that way?

c. Why does the video emphasize the names of the family members? Why does the video focus on the children?

d. In the video, some words are in yellow. Why?

e. La casa es el proyecto final de los estudiantes universitarios. If you had the opportunity, would you like to participate in a similar project/service organization? Explica.

f. Reflexión: This video was posted on Facebook. With a partner, discuss if social media is a useful tool for promoting social projects. What other social networks could be used for promoting a cause? What are the pros & cons?

 **Actividad 3-22. Nuestro proyecto de casa**

En esta actividad trabajas con 3 o 4 compañer@s.

Paso 1. Imagine that you and your classmates are working on a project in one of the towns affected by recent hurricanes, fires, tornados, or other natural disasters. You are designing a house for a ***familia necesitada***. Taking into account that there are 5 family members (including 3 children and a dog), you will need to draw a blueprint and write a description of the house, including the furniture needed in each room. Write at least 100 words. Start your paragraph like this:
"En nuestra casa…"

Paso 2. Presenten su casa a otro grupo de estudiantes. Comparen sus proyectos. ¿Qué similitudes y diferencias tienen?

Para terminar... *¡Conversemos!*

 **Busco apartamento**

Trabaja con un@ compañero@ y practica tu español en estas situaciones sociales. You need to use the vocabulary and structures you have learned so far. Change roles and partners after practicing each situation once.

Attribution: By Tulane Public Relations, licensed under CC BY 2.0.

Conversación 1

(You can use the conversation between Kate and the real estate agent as example; pp. 187-188)

Estudiante 1. You want to rent out your apartment during the summer. Now you are having a phone conversation with someone that is interested in renting it. Make sure you provide as much information as you can about your apartment.

- Ask what the person does and when they want to rent the apartment;
- Ask if they have pets (**mascotas**);
- Describe the apartment and give information about rooms;
- Tell the person about the neighborhood (**barrio**), neighbors (**vecinos**), and rent (how much it is per month).

Estudiante 2. You're going to take classes during the summer, and you need a find an apartment to rent. Now you are having a phone conversation with someone that wants to rent out their apartment.

- Say that you are interested in the apartment (use the phrase tener interés por [don't forget to conjugate the verb!]);
- Answer the person's questions;
- Ask questions about the apartment and the rooms/furniture in it;
- Inquire about the neighborhood (**barrio**) and neighbors (**vecinos**);

Make a decision based on what the owner of the apartment tells you.

Conversación 2

Propiedad 3. Barrio: Cielo Vista (http://bit.ly/CieloVistaInfo)

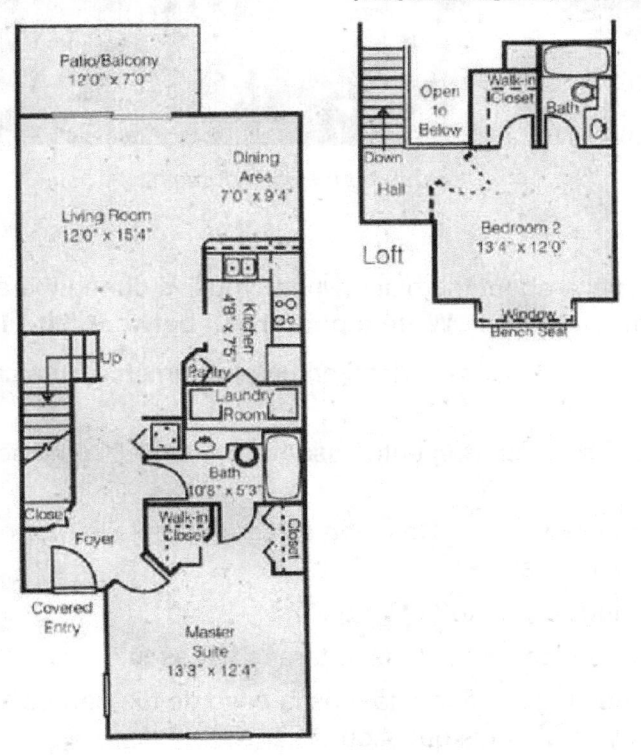

Attribution: Orchid Townhome Floor Plan. By Addison Place at Boca Raton, licensed under CC BY 2.0.

Estudiante 2. You are a Spanish speaker in El Paso. You want to buy your first property. You would prefer a two-bedroom place. Call a real estate agent. Tell this person about yourself and what kind of house you want (e.g., number of bedrooms, bathrooms, etc.). Find out what the houses they offer you are like. Ask questions about rooms, amenities, neighborhood (**barrio**), prices, etc.

Para terminar... *Proyecto digital*

 Tercera parte: Mi hogar (*home*) en la universidad

En este módulo, escribes sobre tu casa/apartamento/cuarto en la universidad.

Attribution: Public domain.

I. Antes de escribir
Answer the following questions about the place where you live during the academic year. Write the answers in paragraph form in Spanish. **Write a paragraph between 90-110 words**.

1. En qué lugar de la ciudad vives? ¿Vives en un apartamento, una casa o una residencia en el campus?

2. ¿Tienes compañer@s de apartamento/casa/habitación? ¿Cómo son? Describe a tus compañer@s.

3. ¿Cómo es el lugar donde vives? Describe el lugar en detalle (por ejemplo, muebles, número de habitaciones, colores, etc.).

4. ¿Cuál es tu cuarto/lugar favorito? ¿Por qué?

5. ¿Quién hace las tareas del hogar? ¿Qué tareas haces tú?

6. ¿Te gusta vivir en ese lugar o te gusta más la casa de tus padres? Explica tu respuesta. (Your instructor can help you with this question).

II. A escribir
Now write your paragraph and…

- Remember to use the vocabulary from the four modules we have seen.

- Pay attention to gender and number when you use articles, nouns, and adjectives (e.g., **la sala es pequeña**), and to the correct verb conjugations (e.g., yo viv**o**, mis amigos y yo viv**imos**). Be careful with the use of the verb **gustar!**

- Use connectors and conjunctions to connect your ideas. For example, use **y**, **también** (*also*), **sin embargo** (*nevertheless*), **además** (*also*), **pero** (*but*). Your instructor can help you to use these words correctly.

- Complement your paragraph with:
  - At least two photos that show where you live at the university (e.g., neighborhood, outside view of your apartment/photo of your room, etc.).
  - If you use photos that you have not taken, please do not forget to cite the source. We recommend that you use open images (i.e., copyright free). You can find this type of images using the search engine offered by Creative Commons (https://search.creativecommons.org/). Also, you need to provide attributions for all of them. To learn more about Creative Commons licenses and how to cite the open materials you find, see https://creativecommons.org/licenses/ and http://bit.ly/CreativeCommonsAttr.

III. Después de escribir

Now read your paragraph, and focus on the following:
- **Content:** Have you included all the information required? Are your photos big and clear enough to convey your message?
- **Grammar:**
  - **Articles and nouns:** Do they agree in gender and number?
  - **Gustar, -ar, -er**, and **-ir**, and irregular verbs: Have you conjugated your verbs correctly?
  - **Descriptive adjectives:** Are your adjectives in the correct position? Do they agree in gender and number with the noun they describe?
  - **Possessive adjectives:** Do they agree in number (and gender in case of **nuestro/a**) with the noun they modify?
- **Cohesion:** Have you connected your ideas with the suggested connectors and conjunctions?

Go over your text, improve it, and write a new, polished version.

IV. Trabajo final
Compile all the parts of your project, and publish the final documents (with all the parts you wrote in **Modules 1**, **2**, and **3**) digitally. Your instructor will provide you with information on how to do this.

Antes de partir...

¡Misión cumplida!
We have reached the end of **Módulo 3**. Go back to the first part of the module (p. 137), and review what you have accomplished. Check the outcomes you have achieved. What are you proud of? What aspects of your Spanish would you like to improve? ¡Buen trabajo!

Summary of Contents

Comunicación
- Las casas y los muebles (pg. 147)
- Las tareas de la casa (pg. 159)
- Los números de 100 a 1.000.000 (pg. 175)
- Expresiones con el verbo *tener* (pg. 191)

Lengua
- El verbo *gustar* (pg. 163)
- Irregular verbs in the *yo* form (pg. 186)

Cultura
- España (pg. 182)
- Trayectos hispanos: *El activismo en los espacios urbanos* (pg. 170)

Mis palabras
In your Spanish notebook, write down other words and phrases you learned in this module.

Golf Course Architects:
Perry Maxwell, 1926
Ed Seay, 1982

LOCAL RULES
- USGA Rules of golf and etiquette govern play.
- Yardages are measured to center of green.
- Repair ball marks and rake bunkers.
- Please keep pace with the group in front of you.

HILLCREST COUNTRY CLUB
Bartlesville, Oklahoma
EST. 1926

P.G.A. Professional:
Jerry Cozby

G.C.S.A.A. Superintendent:
Ed Brookshire

Date: _____

Scorer: _____

Attest: _____

BARTLESVILLE MEANS BUSINESS

Hillcrest Country Club & Civic Culture

BY

GALE MORGAN KANE

ISBN
978-1-885596-78-2

Library of Congress Control Number
2009923859

Printed by Baker Group, LLC
405.503.3207

Designed by Kris Vculek

CONTENTS

ACKNOWLEDGMENTS

This book has been inordinately long in preparation and along the way I have become indebted to a number of people. Don Johnson, 4 club managers ago, was the person who mused in 2001 that the club was 75 years old and there ought to be a good history. Once the idea captured me, like most authors, I can't fail to thank my long-suffering family who have endured my chronic preoccupation with people who are long dead and ideas and things that are long past. My mother-in-law, Mary Kane, died in 2005, but she was a wonderful resource. My father-in-law, Dick Kane, even remembers old Oak Hill Club. Jerry Cozby and Eddie Brookshire have been a great help and encouragement. Marie Freiberger helped identify many old photos.

It would be impossible to recount all of the individuals who have offered different kinds of information, among them, Art Gorman, John Hughes, and Mike May have been associated with civic life in Bartlesville all of their lives, and they are also among those gifted bards who can clearly recall long ago people and events. They are responsible for many a contact, and for telling many a memory. The History Room staff at Bartlesville Public Library was so helpful, literally for years. I especially thank Ann Cleary and Carol Gougler. It would not have been possible to produce this book without the help of the Bartlesville Area History Museum. Several on the staff at the museum have been exceptionally helpful. Thanks to Jo Crabtree for finally shouldering the photographs project, to Kay Little for her many helps, and to Debbie Neece whose work made some photos useable.

*There is only one way
to play
Hillcrest Country Club:*

*Play Old Man Par
and try not to attack.*

COURSE RECORD:
1926 to 1982 — 65
1982 to 2008 — 64

INTRODUCTION

In 2001, Bartlesville's Hillcrest Country Club was 75 years old. That year, some of the members realized that there ought to be a club history, and I said I would write it. Initially, I thought of a pamphlet of about 30 to 50 pages with the club champs and presidents, and some of the old parties. It didn't take long to discover that over the years Hillcrest retained no old records at all. Even worse, when members had given some of the past managers old pictures or other memorabilia, they had simply thrown the stuff out. There was nothing at Hillcrest to begin the research. I knew that there had been an antecedent club west of town, but no one knew quite when it began or much about it. So, I was driven to the newspaper microfilm for basic information. It turned out to be serendipitous. As I began to scan the ancient pages, it put the country club(s) into context within the entire community. I quickly realized that Bartlesville's country club was not simply an exclusive social organization – it is a broad-based civic organization, a voluntary association, as the sociologists call them. Our civic leaders had consciously used the country club as an instru-

ment to build Bartlesville, not just in the beginning, but consistently, through many years; and that the club was an integral part of the growth and fascinating history of the city. It was one of the key means of building social capital, which in turn, as Robert Putnam points out, generated business.

A few names are familiar to us: Frank Phillips, H.V. Foster, Boots Adams, even Perry Maxwell, Edward Beuhler Delk, and J. C. Nichols. Other historic Oklahomans are well noted such as H.R. Straight, Aramais Artunoff, Hal Price, L. E. Phillip; and national figures, from Ben Hogan to Alf Landon, are part of the story. This tale is also chocked full of contributions by middle class Bartlesville, the ordinary people with stories, local heroes of once upon a time, antiheroes, even villains. Milestone events in the city usually involved the country club. A well-developed theory of community building was uncovered, involving the club. It is an uncommon story of the civic culture and memorable leadership of the city, intertwined with an interesting narrative of the history of the country club(s).

We are like dwarfs on the shoulders of giants...

—BERNARD OF CHARTRES

HOLE NUMBER ONE • 376 YARDS • PAR 4
Straight away tree lined par 4 with small landing area
when hitting driver.
Smart player will use fairway wood or driving iron with
125 yard shot into 5,000 square feet.

CHAPTER ONE

The Flight of the Phoenix: THE ANTECEDENT CLUBS

Several rocking chairs were pulled up on the veranda, catching a soft breeze in the shade, where some of the Don Tyler family whiled an easy afternoon with cousins who were visiting from Kansas for the week. It was the summer of 1921. Just west of Bartlesville, at the very edge of the Osage Hills, locusts droned in the blackjack trees surrounding Oak Hill Club. The veranda on the east side of the frame clubhouse enjoyed precious shade from the hot afternoon sun. Burdette Blue and H. R. Straight strolled past the clubhouse, followed by a couple of caddies who were lugging their leather golf bags. As they came in from the links and headed for the locker room, the men were intently discussing Harry Sinclair's big new lease at Teapot Dome, and also the potential new tariff on Mexican oil.

The swimming pool just a little distance to the south of the clubhouse, was un-tiled concrete, though without a filtering system. By topping it off with fresh water every day it was kept cool and refreshing, a relaxing refuge from the steamy town. Nearby, Louise Kane and her lanky thirteen-year-old son, John, sat in two lawn chairs, visiting about the golf round that John had just played, and making small talk with passing friends while keeping an eye on little Dickie in the shallow of the swimming pool. A new man whom Mr. Brodnax, the club superintendent, had recently hired, approached with a tray carrying two lemonades in tall frosty glasses, ice tinkling as he set them on small linen napkins on the table between them. John eagerly grasped his glass and began to drink thirstily. He was wearing the prescribed summer golf dress, light-colored flannel knickers and a starched white shirt with a tie.

There was a small smudge of brown at one knee and one of his knee socks, where he had kneeled down to check the lie of his ball on the sand greens, as Mr. Dudley had instructed him to do. His cap lay under his chair, near his mother's bag and white cotton gloves. Louise was a slim, average sized woman with the ramrod straight posture, legs crossed properly at the ankles, of a true finishing school lady. Her hair swept up softly and pinned, off her neck, she had a twinkle in her light blue eyes and a gentle, inviting smile as she spoke. Her meticulously pressed navy and white silk dress was in the summer fashion of the year. It had a slightly dropped waist with a broad sash, the skirt at mid-calf length. She wore a Milan straw picture hat, pulled down low, silk stockings, and white pumps with straps across the instep.

Little Dickie bounced up and down, up and down, delighted with his buoyancy in the pool. Suddenly, he bounced off onto the slope into the deep water, dunking under and floundering. John and Louise fixed their gazes on his distress for only a moment. John yanked off his shoes, cast them aside, and leaped fully clothed into the pool. There was no difficulty fishing his sputtering little brother from the water, but some discomfiture over John's ruined clothes and wristwatch.

The site of this little tale was at the old Oak Hill Club, just west of where the Bartlesville airport is today. It was Hillcrest's immediate antecedent. The dunking incident is true, though the scene is largely imaginary. It is an enigma of the era of this early club in Bartlesville that sufficient time has passed that we are largely left with the memories of children from the time to shed light on the tale. There's almost nobody left who remembers much about the club champs, the tennis tournaments, the important civic events, or

fancy parties and dances that took place. Things have changed immensely, along with the dress, since circa 1921, when this little dunking took place. It is only a snapshot from the fabric of the early years of Bartlesville's country club. Still, it is interesting to know that the club's history fits into a much bigger picture.

The longer history of American country clubs begins with several threads from the more remote past. In England during the eighteenth century groups of gentlemen often had regularly scheduled meetings at designated coffeehouses or taverns. As the popularity of the practice grew, they outgrew the tavern meeting sites and began building clubhouses. By early in the nineteenth century gentlemen's city clubs were permanent institutions. They served a valuable social function. Besides the pleasure of camaraderie, the social connections that were formed enabled members to exhibit social status, and they fostered business relationships. [1]

While this was developing, in the years following the Great Awakening, an important religious revival in eighteenth century England and the American colonies, an initiative known as the Sunday School Movement arose. In those days children of impoverished families were often sent to heavy work in mines or factories, at ages as young as six or seven, without any education at all. For them the only days available to learn to read and write were Sundays. So, church ladies organized schools on Sunday, with a little bite of lunch as a lure. The effort was so successful that people in the new, rising middle class quickly learned to organize themselves for all sorts of ends. This behavior was so marked in the young United States that when Alexis de Tocqueville visited this country in the 1830s he wrote extensively on the effectiveness of voluntary associations as an essential instrument of self-government and social mobility.

Harvard political scientist, Robert D. Putnam, calls this essential process "building social capital."[2]

The usefulness of the English city club was not missed by American businessmen. It was not long before they began to organize themselves in emulation of the British clubs. The first of these was the Temple Club in Boston in 1826. The Union Club, the first in New York City, was organized in 1836. Nearly a hundred years later, it was one of the clubs that was frequented by Bartlesville's Frank Phillips when in New York on business.

In the years after the Civil War the populations of American cities exploded, deluged with immigrants and industrial growth. It was a time of booming economic expansion and wrenching philosophical and cultural change. Wealthy families in the North took a cue from earlier Southern practices and began to take extended summer holidays at elegant resorts, away from the heat and hubbub of urban summers. The restful elbowroom of these resorts stimulated a new interest in country estates at the perimeters of the cities, an early move toward suburbanization. Within a short time, husbands were commuting to the city during their work week on trains and trolleys, and continuing to utilize their city clubs as part of their business life. At about the same time, many wealthy families began to maintain country estates for weekends and holidays besides their city houses and clubs. These estates and country homes often formed whole new suburban villages or moved into an already organized older rural community. These neighborhoods gave the urbanites a sense of ideal community and order in a time of social change.[3]

The history of ideas sheds a little light on how those people understood the world they lived in. Nineteenth century Americans ardently believed in the Kantian (Immanuel Kant, 1724-1804) idea

of progress, as mid-century they embraced work and family as the pre-eminent moral values. This is called the Victorian consensus. At the same time there was also a holdover of Romantic enthusiasm for nature, which was part of the attraction that drew urban people to the suburbs. But, after the Civil War, disillusionment set in and the consensus began to break down as late nineteenth century men turned to glimpse the emerging Modern Era. Men became convinced that science and planning would hold all the new answers. As always happens, these things began to play themselves out in the general culture, and the development of country clubs is, in part, a manifestation of the combination of these several impulses.[4]

Actual country clubs began to appear on the East Coast near the country homes and resort areas that were being built by wealthy families. These clubs usually formed around equestrian sports such as racing, polo, steeplechase, fox hunting, and coaching. Various other outdoor sports were very important. Cricket, lawn tennis, croquet, and baseball, even archery and shooting were some sports pursued at the early clubs. Tennis became increasingly popular, partly because it was a good game for women. For the first time, clubs included facilities for women and children, becoming truly family clubs.

The first golf course was built in this country in 1885, but the first country club to build a golf course was St. Andrews Golf Club at Yonkers, New York in 1888. Enthusiasm for the game spread like wildfire. In the spring of 1895 there were forty golf courses in the United States, but three months later there were one hundred. There were one thousand golf courses in 1900. By the turn of the century growth of country clubs had broken out beyond the very elite enclaves on the East Coast and moved to aspiring cities and communities all over the United States. In the years right after the turn of the century, the country club movement throughout America could no longer be described as a pale for Eastern social Brahmans, but a vehicle of community building and upward mobility in middle class America. Two important magazine articles were written in 1909 and 1912, both titled "Country Clubs for Everyone." One historian summarizes the author of the earlier article:

> [*Country Life* magazine] *contends that country clubs, which were once the sole possession of the upper classes, are now available to everyone. He puts the claim into a community context, presenting the club as an asset to the whole community.* [5]

Some writers of the time also mention the role of country clubs in fostering emancipation of the lives of women, which was seen by them as a benefit. Though it was usually the husband who was the club member, the clubs became an alternative social focus for women, away from the home and traditional ladies circles. Golf and tennis were new athletic outlets for women in a previously limited repertoire.

When Wichita Country Club was organized in 1900, a small group of men in town agreed to associate in a golf club, inspired by the enthusiasm of the Episcopal rector in town who had played the game with parishioners at his previous rectorate in St. Louis, and by another man who had worked in Washington, D. C. None of the other men at the organizational meeting had ever played golf, though they were all aware of the golf craze that was sweeping the country. Only one of them had "several fine golf sticks," evidently the only golf clubs in town. There was no place in town to buy equipment. No clubs, no balls. So that everything had to be improvised. The place to play was no less a problem. Property owners were reluctant to give them permission to play on their land, and neighbors were wary. Soon enough

they settled on a field near Fairmont College. They began with only six holes. The greens, fairways, and rough were all virgin buffalo grass. The holes were tin cans.

> *Golf for some time was played by many Wichitans, particularly younger ones, with only one club. For some years there were separate divisions in tournaments for players using only one club for all purposes, from putting to driving!* [6]

At about the same time that these early golf clubs were popping up in places like Wichita, around groups of erstwhile enthusiasts for the sport, city planners were already learning to use country clubs as a feature for urban development. One of the pioneers in this field was J. C. Nichols of Kansas City, a man who was very influential to the development of Bartlesville, because of his local ties. Nichols was the brother-in-law of Bartlesville attorney John H. Kane, and he became a close friend of Frank Phillips, the founder of Phillips Petroleum Company. As a young entrepreneur, Nichols seized on the theories of one of his economics professors at Harvard to launch on a spectacular career as a real estate developer. Nichols' early efforts in Kansas City during the first decade of the twentieth century were so innovative that they set a course that made him one of the most influential men in city planning in the United States. In his early residential developments, Nichols used the already existing Kansas City Country Club as a protective barrier to undesirable development. He quickly realized that as families moved into the neighborhoods near a club, it would create a demand for memberships. Soon he was simultaneously planning residential developments and country clubs. [7]

It is interesting to note how revolutionary these moves were. In the past, when wealthy families built new urban homes, the houses lost value even as they were being built. This was because it was assumed that the neighborhood would soon begin to fill with small businesses and ordinary homes that would bring down property values. Banks would only loan a fraction of the building costs because of this. When developers like Nichols began to build attractive, protected neighborhoods, values held, and even increased. Of course, this was a great inducement to this kind of city planning and to the development of neighborhood covenants and zoning laws.

The Bartlesville Country Club

The 1907 statehood census for Oklahoma shows that Bartlesville had a population of 4,215. Only three years later, the 1910 census found 6,181 people in Bartlesville, a nice sprightly increase for such a short time. Most of the growth had come with the three zinc smelters west of town. They were located in Bartlesville after the discovery of natural gas in the Bartlesville area. Because the gas was very cheap, it was quite economical to ship the zinc ore

to Bartlesville by rail for smelting from mines in the region. There were also active stockyards, and Dewey had the new Portland Cement plant. The streets of Bartlesville were not paved and the oil derricks had only recently been removed from the backyards of the city. But the little town was exceedingly prosperous. The city directory for 1907/08 listed 121 oil and gas producers in Bartlesville. Harve W. Pemberton, Frank and L. E. Phillips platted Pemberton Heights addition in 1907, then Johnstone Heights in 1908. [8] It was planned that the developments would have paved streets, sidewalks, and electric lights. [9] The two additions moved the city south of the original town plat, from 7th Street to around 11th Street and between Osage and Shawnee. This is the new residential area where the Phillipses built their big houses. In the spring of 1908, the Bartlesville Interurban Railroad Company completed its tracks to Dewey. Interurban streetcars eventually ran between Bartlesville and the zinc smelters on 4th Street, and between Bartlesville and Dewey via Tuxedo Park.

In 1906 Bartlesville was a maze of dusty streets, modest homes, and a nucleus of small businesses downtown, amidst a forest of oil derricks. *Courtesy Bartlesville Area History Museum.*

Amidst all the growth, on 11 December 1908, the front page of the newspaper carried the following story:

COUNTRY CLUB INCORPORATED OFFICERS HAVE BEEN ELECTED FOR YEAR

New Organization Starts Off Auspiciously – Golf Links Will Be Ready Jan 1

The Bartlesville Country Club has been organized, officers elected, and the club incorporated under the laws of Oklahoma, and by the first of the year it is expected that grounds will have been secured, a golf links laid out, and a handsome building be under construction. A committee having in charge the securing of subscriptions from charter members sold $3,000 worth of stock yesterday afternoon and are confident that by this evening the amount will reach $15,000. Shares are sold at $100, one-half cash and the balance payable in monthly installments of ten dollars each.

No definite arrangement has yet been made for securing grounds for the new club but there are several sites under consideration and a choice will be made in a few days. It is probable that it will be somewhere along the Interurban railway, although a site to the south of the city is being seriously considered.

These officers were elected: Robert D. Rood, president; J. H. McMorrow, secretary; Frank Bucher, treasurer; George C. Priestly and J. J. Curl, governors for three years; J. J. Shea and Frank Phillips, governors for two years and William Johnstone and W. H. Aspinwall, governors for one year.

As soon as the club gets under way applications will be received for those wishing to join who have not signed as charter members and their names will be presented to the governors and executive officers for approval. [10]

Bartlesville had become one of those ambitious little towns, all over the United States, that was establishing a country club. From the description, it sounds as if the new golf club was conceived on a mixed model similar both to the Wichita Country Club and to the Kansas City developments. *The Story of Golf in Oklahoma* cites Spalding's *Athletic Library Official Golf Guide* for 1925, which claimed the country club in Bartlesville served as a social club early in the century. More likely, the person who gave Spalding the information about the club was referring to the 1908 organization which accordingly might have functioned as an informal social club for two or three years, though there is no other indication that this is what happened. [11]

The Bartlesville Country Club was incorporated 13 February 1908, so it is likely that plans had been in the offing since before statehood in November 1907. [12] Though we don't have a list of the 1908 charter members, the published officers are an impressive list of the most influential men in town. It is no surprise that Frank Phillips was one of the governors, but most of the names are no longer familiar. Though most of them had multiple business interests beyond their primary occupation listed in the city directory, it is interesting to see who they were in 1907/08:

William H. Aspinwall (and Mabel)
501 Choctaw • oil producer

Frank Bucher (and Birdie)
900 Johnstone • cashier, First National Bank

Joseph J. Curl (and Viola)
616 Cherokee • vice president, First National Bank

John H. McMorrow (bachelor)
Almeda Hotel • secretary and treasurer, Colgen Mining Co. • pipeline contractor

George C. Priestley (and Lulu)
1111 Johnstone • president, Lumberman's Oil Co. • secretary-treasurer, Ft. Pitt Oil Co.

The grand Frank Phillips mansion was finished in 1909 in the new upscale neighborhood south of 7th Street, developed by Harve Pemberton, Frank Phillips, and L. E. Phillips, and called Pemberton Heights. It was designed by Walton Everman, who would also designed Belle Meade, the Lanom mansion; The Bartlesville Country Club clubhouse; and eventually the Burlingame mansion across from Hillcrest Country Club. *Courtesy Bartlesville Area History Museum.*

Dr. Robert D. Rood (and Ethel)
1117 Johnstone • manager, Stevens Point Oil Co.

John J. Shea (and Agnes)
820 Johnstone • attorney

William Johnstone (and Stella)
Cherokee and 9th • president, Bartlesville National Bank • Johnstone & Johnstone Oil Producers

Frank Phillips (and Jane)
1001 Johnstone • president, Citizen's Bank & Trust • president, Phillips & Co. [13]

The articles of incorporation for the country club contain the names of a few additional men, not mentioned by the newspaper, who were involved in the organization of the club during the previous February.

Hal C. Moore (and Zoe)
1119 Dewey • general insurance and surety bonds

Homer M. Preston (bachelor)
517 Delaware • vice president and treasurer, The Warren Co. • treasurer, Vinita Gas Co.

John O Taylor (bachelor)
Almeda Hotel • real estate [14]

Though Joseph Curl gave his principle occupation for the city directory as vice president at First National Bank, he also owned Almeda Oil Company, was the president of the Bartlesville Interurban Railroad, president of the company which published the Bartlesville Weekly Examiner newspaper, and the same day as the country club announcement he left for St. Louis to buy equipment that made him also the principle owner of the local electric company. [15] Running as a Democrat, by a healthy margin he won the election to represent the 57th District for the State Constitutional Convention in 1906 where he served as quite an active member. It was his proposal that the name of the county should be changed from "Bartlesville County" to Washington County. [16] He was a respected and popular person in town. There is little doubt that Curl, Frank Phillips, Dr. Rood, J. H. McMorrow, Frank Bucher, William Johnstone, and John Shea were the prime movers in the organization of the country club. [17] So, we see that there were some vested interests involved. The newspaper, published by Curl, emphasized that the new club would be near the Interurban route, another Curl interest. As an aside, the article mentions that a site south of town, doubtless immediately south of Johnstone Heights and Pemberton Heights (Phillips interests), was being considered. [18]

Since there are no surviving club records there is no way of knowing for sure why the golf club did not gel at that time. The articles of incorporation filed by John J. Shea at the Secretary of State's office in Guthrie gave the following statement of purpose:

> *That this corporation is formed for the following purposes, namely, the promotion of legitimate recreation, including out-door sports, such as golf, tennis, rowing, sailing and the like, and to promote education in music and other arts, and to own a Club House, grounds and appurtenances to be used in accomplishing the objects above set forth, to acquire, own and hold, in the vicinity of Bartlesville, Oklahoma, such grounds as may be necessary for the use of the corporation for the purposes set forth herein.* [19]

The Teague history of Washington County says that The Bartlesville Country Club was at the same site as the old Oak Hill Club. [20] A check of Washington County deeds did not find any record of property ever owned or leased by The Bartlesville Country Club in the county. As expected, the deeds in the Osage County Clerk's office show that on 14 April 1911 The Bartlesville Country Club leased 40 acres in section 4-26-12 for $200 and taxes. [21] A month later they bought 20 acres in the same section. [22] This is the parcel of land, just west of today's airport and at the very edge of the Osage Hills that eventually contained the clubhouse.

Why the lapse of time between 1908 incorporation and 1911 start-up? Part of the explanation was probably the interim economic climate. Early in 1910, Bartlesville businessmen suddenly grew dissatisfied with the poor growth in the last couple of years and organized a booster group they called "25,000 in 1912." [23] The cause of the slow-down may have owed to the Crash of 1907 which led to high national unemployment rates in 1908, along with low, flat commodity prices that must have made oil men who were prospective country club members feel a little more

By 1910 the Bartlesville Commercial Club knew no bounds to its ambition for the growth of the city. Here Bartlesville businessmen prepare to board a passenger car on a Booster tour to tell neighboring cities about Bartlesville. *Courtesy Bartlesville Area History Museum.*

conservative about their finances for a time. Early in 1910, a group of real estate investors bought Johnstone Heights that "still had ninety of the choicest lots left." The original developers were probably anxious to turn the slow-moving property by then. The new interest was a sign that the local economic doldrums of the interim period since 1907 were beginning to pick up. [24] By the summer of 1910, the 25,000 organization had resolved to push through a comprehensive plan of community improvement, including paving the city streets, laying sidewalks, planting maple trees, and adding parks. These expensive improvements were very controversial and took many months to enact. Meanwhile, the boosters vigorously set about a program to bring new business to town.

It appears that another dynamic may have been operative to delay progress in starting up the new club. One can only surmise that at the time there was an impasse between Frank Phillips and his partners, who wanted the club adjacent to their development south of town, and Joseph Curl, who wanted development along his Interurban route. There has been a great deal of research on Frank Phillips and we know it was characteristic of his *modus operandi* to avoid public controversy because it might adversely impact business, instead he preferred dealing with problems quietly. This sort of thing may be part of what slowed down choosing a club site. Whatever the case, the organizers probably were not immediately able to sell enough memberships to start the project, since they had only $3,000 on hand in December 1908, eight months after incorporation. Curl divested himself of most of his local business holdings by 1912, and moved to Ohio in 1914.

Judge Shea, Dr. Rood, Harve Pemberton, and George Priestly were very active in instigating the community revitalization activity that started in 1910,

and the country club pointedly became part of their plan to promote Bartlesville. The newspaper reported:

Before leaving for Pawhuska yesterday morning, Judge Shea made arrangement for a meeting of the country club members at his office next Saturday morning. This club matter has been allowed to drag for a time, but the time has come to boost that as well as everything else. A large stock subscription has been secured and it is now hoped that an immediate move may be made... [25]

This is a clear statement of the understanding of the country club organizers, that the club would serve as a vehicle of community formation and upward mobility, not only for the members of the club who would benefit directly, but also for the entire city. They plainly viewed the country club as a civic organization.

Unmentioned amidst the organizational hubbub is H. V. Foster. Yet, in later years he clearly viewed this club with personal interest, serving a president for several years right up to the time of its closure. It is a hunch that he was actually the prime mover, the hidden hand in this seminal civic initiative.

Why was the country club established west of Bartlesville, in Osage County? There is no sure answer to that question either. The newspaper revealed:

It was desired to have the club sufficiently near the city to be easily accessible and at the same time

> *This club matter has been allowed to drag for a time, but the time has come to boost that as well as everything else.*
> (Judge John J. Shea, 31 March 1910.)

sufficiently remote to insure privacy. The country was scoured. Enthusiastic members returned from scouting parties with stories of wonderful locations. But in each instance some fatal flaw developed. They were either too near or too far, too badly scarred by the mutilating hand of man or yet pertained too much of the untouched wilderness. [26]

The site they chose could be described as on the very edge of the Wild West. Only a mile to its southwest was "Hold-up Hollow" where the Martin gang, one of the storied Osage outlaw gangs, plied their trade. [27] All the while the club was established on a very attractive site. In those days the veranda on the east side of the clubhouse had a lovely view of the Caney River Valley toward the city, the Mound [28], and a stretch of beautiful wheat land. One additional suggested explanation for the choice of that site comes from the perusal of the old Bartlesville newspapers. Reports of

frequent raids of local "hotels," drug stores, pool halls, known traffickers, and incoming trains make it clear that circa 1910 and 1911 draconian liquor restrictions in the laws of the new state were widely ignored in boomtown Bartlesville, drawing sporadic, but very vigorous efforts of enforcement in Washington County. It is presumed that at least some of the club members were tipplers, and that the founders wished to avoid scrutiny.

Once the club property was secured, things began to develop rapidly. The Examiner article says an architect was consulted and contracts let immediately. No one remembers who the architect was, but it is likely he was Walton Everman, the designer of the Frank Phillips home. [29] That must have been the late spring of 1911. By summer, construction must have been fully underway. The Enterprise carried a helpful story on 6 October 1911:

The very first photograph of The Bartlesville Country Club's new clubhouse was published in *The Morning Examiner* 30 November 1911. The trees are still in leaf, so the picture must have been taken earlier in the fall. *Courtesy Hillcrest Country Club.*

A professional golf player and caretaker for the greens has been employed by the country club. His name is Thomas Chisholm and he comes from Tulsa here. He is formerly of England and had a reputation there as a player and teacher of the game. [30]

Since the club had hired a pro who was a club maker, greens keeper, and teacher, it can probably be assumed the course was nearing completion by this time. Spalding's Athletic Library Official Golf Guide says golf wasn't played in Bartlesville until 1912, which is only partly true. Chisholm's tenure in Bartlesville was very short – and probably disappointing. He played only one round on the little golf course, late in October in which he scored 34 strokes. Par on the original holes were 3,4,4,4,4,3,4,4,4 for a par 34. The inclement weather of that dreadful winter shut the golf course to all but one round on 29 January 1912 for an L. E. Phillips party. By then, Chisholm had already completed his temporary engagement and moved on. [31]

Near the end of November 1911, the society page suddenly became alive with excited expectation of the opening of the new country club. The big gala was planned for Monday, 27 November 1911. A ladies golf tournament was to be the opening event, a men's contest for the afternoon, then a dinner and concert by the Oklah Orchestra, followed by a ball. From the society column, we have a record of the results of the very first golf tournament played in Bartlesville:

In the contest on the links yesterday morning, Mrs. Frank M. Breene led for high score, having made the course in seventy-two, and was awarded the silver loving cup. For second place Mrs. A. D. Morton and Miss Elizabeth Shea finished with a tie. The prize for second place was a set of golf sticks and bag. Mrs. Clyde Fowler won third place

and prize, a set of golf balls.

Among the other contestants were: Mrs. Huntington B. Henry, Miss Hazel Larkin, Mrs. E. C. Boggs, Miss Jeanne Kirwan, Miss Jeanne Shea, Miss Hazel Priestley, Mrs. Willis Priestley, Mrs. Keeler, and Mrs. W. A. Smith. [32]

No sooner had the ladies tournament been decided, than a cold northerner swooped down. It must have been quite a weather system, for the men's tournament and evening festivities were postponed to Wednesday. Nevertheless, a number of the club ladies spent the afternoon decorating the clubhouse.

On Wednesday the men's tournament resumed. Jack Shaw won the silver loving cup with a score of 33. Judge Shea came in second with 35, earning a set of balls, and Dr. Rood got third with 38 to win a half dozen balls. [33]

The clubhouse was dedicated in the evening. We have a glowing description of the new facilities:

It is a model club house. There are lounging rooms and reading rooms, a banquet hall and a ball room, living rooms and card rooms… [34]

A banquet followed the dedication. The great hall was decorated with Japanese lanterns, mistletoe, holly, and chrysanthemums. Dinner music was furnished by the Durnell Orchestra (Durnell was the high school band teacher). Judge Shea, who had finally pushed the club to completion since his 1910 initiative, was the toastmaster. The speakers were John Brennan, H. V. Foster, George Priestley, Huntington B. Henry, Frank Breene, Frank Bucher, and H. C. Moore. Senator Fancher of New York (probably a friend of H. V. Foster) was the special guest speaker. After the dinner, the tables were cleared and removed from the dance floor for the ball to begin. All agreed it was the most brilliant social function ever seen in Bartlesville. "Bartlesville women are known for their beauty and charm, but they never showed a better advantage than last evening." Imagine the elegant ladies dressed in the finery of the era. Ethel Rood wore "a delicate Dresden panne velvet and net gown, trimmed with white jet and touches of pink and blue chiffon." Agnes Shea "wore a beautiful Parisian creation of black chiffon over Kings blue messaline trimmed with real lace and embroidered black jet." [35]

In the next month social events at the country club shed some light on the pattern of utilization of the clubhouse that was established at that early date. For a few days during the Thanksgiving weekend, while guests were still in town, there were several social events. Mr. And Mrs. Frank Stillwell gave a Thanksgiving afternoon dinner for several friends: the John H. Kanes, H. V. Fosters, Frank Breenes, Fred Graybills, John Hayes, Jesse Leachs, F. R. Suttons, R. E. Pryors, R. L. Gordons, J. J. Sheas, L. A. Rowlands, and significantly, out of town guests Mr. And Mrs. J.

C. Nichols. That weekend Frank and Harry Breene gave a stag party for forty men. During December, three notable dinner parties made the newspaper. The weekend before New Years, Ethel Rood and Louise Bucher were hostesses of an afternoon dance for seventy-five of the young people. Early in January, Jeanne Shea was hostess of a dinner at her home for several out-of-town guests, then they all motored to the club, to be joined by Bartlesville guests for a dance. The ballroom was decorated with holly, roses, and carnations. "Unique dance programs were soon filled and music was furnished by Durnell's orchestra." [36]

The officers of The Bartlesville Country Club in 1911 were: R. D. Rood, president; J. J. Curl, vice president; Frank Bucher, treasurer; H. C. Moore, secretary. The governors were H. V. Foster, J. J. Shea, J. S. Leach, George C. Priestley, John A. Bell, and L. E. Phillips. The house committee was Judge Shea, H. V. Foster, and Huntington B. Henry; and the grounds

Because of the dirt road in the background, we know that this photo of the golf course at The Bartlesville Country Club was taken in December 1911. The club member, holding a golf club is not identified, but the pro giving him instruction is Thomas Chisholm. He was the first (possibly the second) pro in Bartlesville. The Mound, a view of the city, and the smelters are in the background. *Courtesy Bartlesville Area History Museum.*

committee was Dr. Rood and Frank Breene. [37]

My mid-January club utilization had slowed to a trickle. Heavy precipitation that winter effectively closed the new dirt road to the clubhouse. In March an announcement was made that the road had been dragged to make it passable to carriages and automobiles, but the grounds were only in fair condition. They would not be ready to serve meals for a week, so it must be concluded that the club essentially had been closed for two months. [38] They tried to open the season with a young people's party, but then spring flooding started and the club remained essentially closed until May. [39] The problem was the roads. The governors took control of the situation promptly and proposed another $20,000 in improvements to their $25,000 investment in the clubhouse and grounds. They already had a garage and stables built, and a total of 80 acres of owned and leased land. They proposed that the road should to be graveled and the tennis courts built. They had consulted landscape architects to make new plantings and improve the golf course. This resulted in a 3,140 yards, par 36 course. [40] They also wanted to add a caretaker's house, locker rooms with showers and needle baths, a complete water system, and rock walls and hedges, more landscaping, and an arched entrance gate. A lot of these suggestions sound like the fruit of J. C. Nichols' visit during the grand opening. It is documented that Nichols gave similar suggestions to Frank Phillips at a visit shortly after opening Woolaroc in 1925. To kick-off this drive, the club officers held a spring party, consisting of a golf tournament, buffet luncheon, and dance. They asked club members to bring furnishings for the clubhouse. [41]

Over the next three months all news about the club completely disappeared from the newspaper. Early in June the temperatures soared, and the wives and children of prosperous Bartlesville families made an early departure for Colorado and the northland. The nation was preoccupied with the presidential election. The Democrats nominated Woodrow Wilson, and the Republicans split wide open, re-nominating Taft but turning Teddy Roosevelt into the Bull Moose Party. At the first of September, the newspaper reported that there had been only 1.36 inches of rain in the summer of 1912. Though there had not been a single society column printed in three steamy, hot months, right after school started, the social season began. All the "summertime bachelors" had been working diligently in the interim, supervising construction of all the new improvements to the club. The property boasted two new clay tennis courts on the east and croquet courts northwest of the clubhouse, the grounds were improved, and the drive had been rocked. Best of all, there were more than one hundred members. [42]

The vacationers are all home and the beautiful country club and grounds offer one of the most attractive resorts in the city for the members. The restaurant is now open and those who desire meals should order in advance as it has been the custom of some to make of it a sort of short order place, which is not possible. Four new members were taken in last week and the membership is about full. [43]

The men had been honing their golf games under the tutelage of the new golf professional, named William Brown. Brown had been on the job at least from early summer, since he was listed as the Bartlesville pro at the state open tournament in June. [44] The season opened with an eighteen-hole medal play tournament under full handicap. The prizes were a golf club for first place, two golf balls for second place, and one ball for third place. [45] Only seven of the seventeen participants turned in their scorecards that day, Kirol Holm won hands down with a score of 79. T. C.

The published membership roster one year after the grande opening had grown slightly to 102 members and 13 associate members, with possibly 1 lady member.

Frank Adams
George W. Akin
Dan Almen
J. P. Anderson
R. L. Beattie
John A. Bell
  (Pittsburgh, Pa)
John A. Bell, Jr.
  (Pittsburgh, Pa.)
W. T. Berentz
Burdette Blue
E. O. Boggs
James Brann
C. A. Brannon
Frank M. Breene
Harry H. Breene
John H. Brennan
Frank Bucher
C. E. Burlingame
E. M. Carrothers
  (Dewey)
G. C. Clark
Gerald S. Coburn
E. L. Connolly
Joseph J. Curl
Paul Dahlgren
T. C. Davis
W. N. Davis
John DeHart
H. G. Durnel
B. Elkan
  (New York)

A. T. Faucher
  (Salamanca, N.Y.)
H. V. Foster
J. Clyde Fowler
Benton Golden
Robert L. Gordon
Lou Gorham
J. P. Govreau
A. B. Henry
Huntington B. Henry
Harry Hewitt
J. H. Holm
J. S. Irwin
Ernest O. Jacobson
  (New York City)
Paul J. Johnson
Roswell H. Johnson
William H. Johnson
John Johnstone
William Johnstone
Archibald Jones
John H. Kane
C. E. Kayser
George G.. Keeler
Robert S. King
Robert Kraeer
John J. Larkin
J. J. Larkin
Jesse S. Leach
W. A. Letson
  (Dewey)

C. M. Loeb
  (New York City)
E. J. Maire
  (Lima, Oh.)
J. H. Markham
George S. Marshal
D. B. Mason
J. W. Masters
H. H. McClintock
B. Henry McGregor
Charles McMahon
John H. McMorrow
J. E. Meloy
Wayne Mendell
M. E. Michaelson
Clint Moore
Hal C. Moore
Asa D. Morton
J. H. Mullen
J. P. O'Meara
J. L. Overlees
Harve W. Pemberton
Frank Phillips
L. E. Phillips
Waite Phillips
T. C. Pike
L. C. Pollock
Homer M. Preston
George C. Priestley
Willis Priestley
M. R. Puckett
F. B. Reynolds
  (Nowata)

Otto Rissman
Harry S. Roll
  (Dewey)
Robert D. Rood
W. S. Sharpe
Jack Shaw
John J. Shea
J. A. Sivalis
W. A. Smith
F. J. Spies, Jr.
M. F. Stillwell
F. R. Sutton
J. O. Taylor
Fr. John Van Den Hende
J. A. Veasey
Howard Weber
L. W. Young

Associate members were:

D. A. Beatty
  (Parkersburg, W. V.)
Ralph R. Cain
  (Ochelata)
Frank Franz
M. P. Hanlin
R. M. Harley
G. V. Kerr
M. E. Michaelson
Mrs. Ellen Miller
F. H. Rollins
Byron H. Smith
O. S. Somerville
R. J. Wallace
William G. Wilson.

Davis was second (86) and Dr. Rood was third (87). The same day there was a ladies golf tournament and tennis play. [46] The fall season saw a series of matches between area clubs in which the participants met the out-of-town champions at the railroad station and motored out to the club for breakfast. Morning and afternoon golf rounds, a "dainty" luncheon, and tennis contests filled the day. Bartlesville soundly thrashed Independence Country Club on 5 October. A couple of weeks later the Bartlesville champs journeyed to the Tulsa Country Club for a similar exciting day. Fred Spies, B. L. Gordon, and J. E. Kiser were the tennis team; the Bartlesville golfers were Holm, Moore, Fowler, Shea, Davis, Taylor, Marshall, Durnell, Wilson, and Coburn. Once again, Bartlesville reigned supreme, beating the Tulsa golfers 17 to 2. The hard fought tennis matches ended in a draw. Two weeks later, Tulsa visited Bartlesville for a rematch. This time Tulsa won 22 to 11. [47] By December the competition for the first club golf championship was underway, and a handicap tournament was running. K. R. Holm became the champ for 1912. [48]

A few days after the Tulsa match, the country club fielded some sensational local publicity. It seems that Mrs. H. O. Dixon was learning to drive and took her car out to the country club. Nearing the clubhouse, she lost control of her automobile. H. G. Durnell was just approaching the east door with some friends when Mrs. Dixon's car pinned him to a tree. Durnell was fairly seriously injured. He was hurried to town in someone's car and taken to his home where he was attended by his physician. [49]

K. R. Holm was the first club golf champion at The Bartlesville Country Club, in 1912.

By the summer of 1912 Bartlesville's golf pro, William Brown, had assessed the men's golfing skills so that handicaps were assigned. They are interesting to know:

F. M. Breene 5	R. S. King 5
D. A. Beatty 5	W. A. Letson 20
E. O. Boggs 12	J. S. Leach 12
J. H. Brennan 25	H. C. Moore 5
Frank Bucher 25	G. S. Marshal 7
H. H. Breene 20	M. E. Michaelson 8
G. S. Coburn 12	J. H. Mullen 25
Harry Durnell 8	H. M. McClintock 10
T. C. Davis 7	L. E. Phillips 10
J. C. Fowler 7	Waite Phillips 20
H. V. Foster 12	Frank Phillips 25
Harry Hewitt 20	R. D. Rood 25
Kiral Holm 5	J. J. Shea 8
Paul Johnson 15	M. F. Stillwell 20
Leo Johnstone 15	J. O. Taylor 8
J. H. Kane 20	W. G. Wilson 7
C. E. Kayser 25	

The social schedule for the year closely followed the tournaments. Hardly an afternoon went by when there was not some event at the clubhouse, where Mrs. Elizabeth McCowan was employed as the "cateress." A lively schedule of bridge, luncheons, tennis, and dances filled the season. Several of the women took up "the mysterious fascination of the grand old game," lured from their old devotion to "a friendly rubber." The club officers at the end of 1912 were: R. D. Rood, president; J. O. Taylor, vice president; J. C. Davis, secretary-treasurer; J. J. Shea, chairman of the Board of Governors, and governors L. E. Phillips, H.

Bartlesville built a hospital in 1906, located at 12th and Keeler, but available treatment made it more of a last resort.

The Foster Cup was The Bartlesville Country Club, then Oak Hill Club's, club championship trophy. The sterling silver trophy was given to The Bartlesville Country Club by H. V. Foster in 1913. *Courtesy Bartlesville Area History Museum.*

V. Foster, J. S. Leach, George G. Priestley, and Frank M. Breene. The grounds committee was Breene, Rood, and Taylor; the house committee was L. E. Phillips, Foster, and Shea. [50]

The year 1912 ended with a New Years Eve costume party for the "kids." The adult hosts got right into the event. W. A. Smith and H. V. Foster went dressed as Buster Brown. Mrs. Smith was a Paris doll and Dr. Rood was a football hero. The Durnell's orchestra gave the music and they had a midnight luncheon. Miss Jeanne Kirwan was one of the hostesses of this party, strengthening the suspicion that she was the first "lady" member of the club. [51] Three weeks

Mrs. Elizabeth McCowan, employed as "cateress," was in effect the first club manager, and chef, at The Bartlesville Country Club.

later, during the cold weather doldrums of the winter, William Brown, the golf professional, gave a Scotch dinner on Robert Burns' birthday for some of the men who were his close friends. [52] Del Lemon says that in his research for The Story of Golf in Oklahoma he was told that virtually all the golf pros in America at this date were Scots, and it would seem that this dinner is an indication that Brown was too. [53]

In April, the social schedule for the month was postponed until the weather settled. A pattern in the social structure emerges at this point. In April,

May, and June a hostess committee was responsible for planning the activities at the club. The committee seems to have been composed of twelve women, with the chairwoman, rotating on a monthly schedule. The club began to be used in important civic events such as a dance given by the ladies committee for the Oklahoma Press Association convention in May. But, the ladies probably did not plan the functions surrounding the annual meeting in April. The men had a golf tournament in the afternoon, with K. R. Holm (45) emerging the scratch winner. Jesse Leach was first (38), J. T. Shipman was second (44), and E. O. Boggs was third (45) in the handicap. Nineteen men participated. At the election of officers that evening, Dr. Rood became president, John Taylor, vice president, H. J. Holm, secretary-treasurer, M. F. Stilwell and G. S. Coburn were directors. The governors were Stilwell, Coburn, L. E. Phillips, F. M. Breene, H. V. Foster, and Judge Shea. Phillps, Coburn and Foster were the house committee, and Breene, Taylor, and Shea were the grounds committee. After the election they had a dinner and smoker. That is, they passed the cigar box after dinner (and probably settled in for a few rounds of poker). [54]

Recently Tom Vogt found a stock certificate from The Bartlesville Country Club in an old file at National Zinc. It is the only surviving document from that first club. The certificate, issued 15 November 1912 to C. E. Kayser, was for a $100 membership. J. O. Taylor signed as president (though he was actually vice president) and T. C. Davis attested the certificate. [55] Carl E. Kayser was the General Manager of the Smelter Gas Company and in 1913 he was a bachelor

living at the country club. [56] It is interesting that the club evidently had boarding facilities at the time, but that was not an unusual practice at country clubs during the era. The Smelter Gas Company was formed to receive natural gas from ITIO and deliver it to the smelters. It was later acquired by National Zinc. Remarkably, Brooks Spies has a wonderful family story to relate from this period. Brooks' father, Fred Spies, was a close friend of Hal Price. The story is of Fred and Gladys Spies' first date. Gladys came to Bartlesville from Worcester, Massachusetts in 1912, to be a piano teacher. On the occasion of the first

The earliest surviving artifact of The Bartlesville Country Club is a stock certificate, issued to C. E. Kayser, the president of National Zinc, 15 November 1912. *Courtesy Hillcrest Country Club.*

date, possibly in the summer of 1913, they all rode out to the country club to play tennis. On the way out, Hal's car ran out of gas and Fred quickly jumped out to hike on up to the club for help, along the hot, dusty road. After a while, Hal remembered that he had some extra gas stashed somewhere and got the car running again, picking up Fred along the way. Gladys was quite impressed with the gallant spirit of her date, but it didn't prevent her from beating the young man, who was the club champ, at the tennis game - even though she was wearing one of those "hobble" skirts that were in fashion then. For his part, Fred was an inveterate tennis player and charmed by Gladys' skill and pluckiness. Brooks says his mother loved playing tennis, and his father was fanatical about the game. Unfortunately, in 1929, Fred Spies was in a terrible car wreck and received a bad concussion. After that, the doctors said he shouldn't play tennis. [57]

The story of the Spies' date gives us some other valuable information about the character of the club in those first years. We already know that some community leaders who were Cherokee and Delaware were founding members of the club. In the context of the time, it is also notable that several charter members were first and second generation Irish immigrants, and that Father John Van Den Hende, the Belgian-born priest at St. John Catholic Church, was a charter member. The information that Hal Price was a member of the club shortly after moving to town confirms that some members of Bartlesville's first country club were Jewish. [58] Though Price was not a religious man, two practicing Jewish Bartlesville families were also early members. Mike May knows that his father was a member of Oak Hill Club and has some wonderful old photographs. The Zofness family also joined and began to appear in the golf tournaments about 1921. Two or three of the charter

members who resided in New York City may have been Jewish. This was quite an unusual attitude in the cultural environment of the time. Bartlesville country clubs were conceived on an unusually broad base of inclusiveness that probably is a reflection of the culture of the oil patch. It was a complex world where the dirty drudgery of drilling and wildcatting came into direct contact with big business deals, finance, government policy, and the high technology of the day. The men who were building the American oil industry did not care much about foolish exclusionary prejudices; what mattered was if a man could do the job. The stated object was, "and now it is time to build Bartlesville."

The winter of 1913 was a cold one. Again the club utilization dwindled and club ladies played a lot of bridge in their homes. People began to get bored, holed up for the winter. Around town, the police arrested two men and three women for lewdness and drunkenness; one of the men in the quintet had a hop pipe (for opium). A little time later, a couple was arrested for dancing the tango in public. By spring, there was a new anti-tango city ordinance against "making love" in public. Federal agents swooped down on Bartlesville in July. The newspaper enjoyed the double-entendre, "Bartlesville is a Sahara desert right now," as the temperatures soared to 108°. "Even the clubs where was wont to journey the thirsty who by the magic word could unloosen the fountains and gain admittance into the inner circle, have ceased to flow." [59] After all of that, it is amusing that as the fall social season opened at the club, tango teas were all the rage. Bartlesville got a new dance instructor and by spring 1914, the society events were tango dances.

Right after the Fourth of July Bartlesville families began to head out for vacation in droves. The ticket agent at the station said it was the heaviest travel in years. While the wives and families were gone, Bartlesville businessmen were awed with the grand opening of the $125,000 Hotel Maire (now the city offices and History Museum). One hundred twenty-five people were invited to the summer formal opening. (An even bigger fall opening was planned so the vacationers could attend.) Webbers band played, while dinner was served with snow-white linen, sparkling crystal and gleaming silver. Trained waiters came from Kansas City for the affair. For 75¢ the buffet included – lobster cocktail, cream of tomato soup, broiled Lake Superior whitefish, sweetbreads under glass, country fried chicken, roast prime rib, cucumber and tomato salad, green beans, creamed peas, corn on the cob, apple pie, chocolate ice cream, assorted cakes, and lots of fancy garnishes along the way. By fall the businessman's lunches, and the Sunday dinner at the Maire, with music by the Webber orchestra, were immensely popular. Mrs. McCowan's advance-notice fare at the country club must have been pale competition.

BELOW: The Hotel Maire in the foreground was opened on the Southwest corner of 5th and Johnstone in the summer of 1912. This 1920 photo shows the view down Johnstone, the most sophisticated street in town, with First National Bank, then Zofness Brothers men's clothing next door. The hotel offered very comfortable accommodations for the time and a big city-style elegant dining room. RIGHT: It was by far Bartlesville's very best hotel until the era of the Phillips Apartment Hotel. It was also the site of weekly Rotary meetings and numberless other civic meetings and parties. *Courtesy Bartlesville Area History Museum.*

Meanwhile, the country club season started a little slow, finally getting off a Halloween dance, and fall golf. But by then, many, many ladies luncheons and bridge parties were being held at the Maire. [60]

By the spring of 1914, social events at the club had utterly disappeared from the society pages of the newspaper. The weather was fairly mild in comparison to the previous years, so that it surely didn't totally preclude utilization of the club as it had the first two winters, even though bad weather still meant impassible roads. Another possibility is that either the newspaper or the club fathers decided not to put every little social occasion in the paper. Whatever the case, as a consequence, the only event in the spring of 1914, was a very big one, indeed. The Bartlesville Country Club hosted the Oklahoma State Golf Association tournament the second week in June. One hundred professional and amateur championship golfers came from Oklahoma City, Tulsa, Muskogee, McAlester, Shawnee, and El Reno. Contestants began to arrive on Friday, to get a feel for the golf course before the tournament. William Nichols, the Muskogee pro, won the professional contest, with Bartlesville's William Brown coming in fifth on Sunday. The final round was played in a downpour of rain. Judge Furry of Muskogee emerged the state champion. A gala dinner and dance was planned at the club after the contest, but the rain forced them to move it to the Elks Club downtown. [61] This little detail is very revealing of the persistent problem posed by dirt roads and unpaved streets for simple access to the country club. It was, quite plainly, a dry weather country club.

In mid-October, the Foster Cup was played in competition for the eighteen-hole handicap trophy. The last year's champion was Frank Rollins. There were twenty-five entrants in the 1914 match. T.C. Davis and Dr. F. N. Buck tied so that there was to be a play-off on Thursday (which was never reported). There were high expectations for a series of club matches during the fall season. [62]

The national economy was beginning to show the effects of Progressive fiscal policy. The Sixteenth Amendment, allowing income taxes, and the Federal Reserve Act, giving control of the money supply to a central bank, were already effecting the economy. Predictably, Congress enthusiastically implemented a progressive income tax, with a top marginal rate of 6%, soon there was a 10% surtax called a "war tax," then a 13% surtax in 1916. In Oklahoma, the great success of drilling had created an oil glut. As output increased, prices plummeted and taxes dug into what was left. This began to show up in the Bartlesville economy early in 1914. In September, the Chamber of Commerce voted to send a telegram to Mr. Hanshaw of the Oklahoma State Corporation Commission,

All lines of business completely stagnated and commercial interests in jeopardy pending immediate re-establishment of permanent oil market. Quick action necessary to preserve the interests of our people. [63]

Compounding the local distress, the county assessor doubled the assessment on the finest homes in Bartlesville by doubling their evaluation. A group of homeowners went through the protest process, and finally sued. Signs of the pinch were going-out-of-business sales downtown, and residential lot auctions. People were leaving town.

On 22 October, there was a receivers sale of the Hotel Maire. The hotel was reorganized afterward

On 12 June 1914, The Bartlesville Country Club hosted the 1914 Oklahoma Open golf tournament. Judge Furry of Muskogee became the state Champion.

and was a vital part of the city for many years. It was too late for the country club. The combination of bad roads, a bad oil economy, and the damage done by the Hotel Maire competition had also done in the country club. Dr. Rood called a meeting of the stockholders to advise them of the extreme financial condition of the club. The club was $9,000 in debt to Union National Bank and Bartlesville National Bank and both principle and interest were long overdue. The membership was 106, the assets were valued at $15,000, and the annual receipts were $3,000. That was deemed enough to operate the club, but not to make the debt service. In a letter to stockholders, Dr. Rood wrote:

It is very surprising that the club had been oper-
ated for so long under such disadvantages. This,
perhaps, would have been impossible were it not
for the interest given to the management and the
personal expenditures by several members of the
club. The notes in the bank, on the one hand, and
the personal burdens assumed by several individual
members from time to time should not be toler-
ated by the club, and the stockholders should come
to the rescue and save the institution for the ben-
efit of the people of Bartlesville. [64]

Both the club leadership and the newspaper considered the prospect of losing the country club a blow to Bartlesville's honor. They clearly understood the country club was an important part of community formation and an adjunct to business. The next night the stockholders agreed to raise the necessary funds. They appointed Judge J. J. Shea, H. V. Foster, and Herbert Straight to act with the board of governors in disposing of the bond issue. Dr. Rood vaguely hinted to the newspaper that a part of the scheme that was afoot to revitalize the country club had something to do with the Interurban. [65]

The Bartlesville business community was going

through a slow period. The streetcar line had gone through two new owners in the years since Joseph Curl first started it up. Most recently, an Eastern investor, the Doherty Group, had bought in and the newest plans were to build an amusement park and fair grounds between Bartlesville and Dewey in order to increase ridership. The governors even toyed with the idea of moving the country club to a site near the fair grounds. [66]

10 December 1915, the Chamber of Commerce disintegrated and the president resigned. Even while the Chamber was in disarray, for many months the Bartlesville business community had hopes that first, the Doherty group, then the Katy Railroad would build a line between Bartlesville and Pawhuska. The country club's problems would, indeed, have been relieved by such a venture, but that was the least of the problem. Without paved roads anywhere in Oklahoma, commerce was severely hampered. Everybody had always just made do, but with the economy sludging along for the second year, the community leaders began to cast about desperately for ways to help themselves. At the time it seemed that the interurban system would be the solution in the state. In the end, the local Interurban was never profitable. The amusement park was built, but failed, and the Interurban, by then entirely owned by Bartlesville investors, failed in 1920.

Meanwhile, the country club struggled to stay afloat:

The country club has awakened from its inactivity
of the past six months and a renewed interest is
showing itself among its members. At a recent
meeting, plans for its reorganization were enacted,
pending the fulfillment of which the reorganiza-
tion committee has done everything in its power
to make everything as attractive as possible, to
induce members to exercise their privileges. The

golf course is, with the exception of the greens, in
excellent shape as both the fore ways and long
grass have been cut. The tennis courts are in bet-
ter shape than ever, while the locker rooms and
club house have been put in excellent condition.
Beginning Sunday, Mrs. Quackenbush, the new
stewardess, will open the restaurant and meals will
be served to all giving at least eighteen hours no-
tice. As the roads on the grounds have been re-
paired a large attendance is expected on Sunday. [67]

As the months dragged on, conditions improved some from better oil prices, and the resolution
of the Osage lease question, but the local economy remained slow. There was one last hurrah at The Bartlesville Country Club, reported in the first newspaper of
1916, "an informal dance for the younger set of the
country club." All the most eligible young people in
town were there. Judging from the guest list, it must
have been a whale of a party. [68]

William Brown played in the Oklahoma
State Golf Association tournament as the pro from
Muskogee in the summers of 1915 and 1916, and
there was no pro playing from Bartlesville. [69] The last
telltale signs that the club was totally non-function-
ing came late in the summer of 1916 when Hal Price
and Fred Spies organized a city tennis championship
tournament for the Bartlesville Tennis Association. A
majority of the entrants were members of the country club. The matches were played on the new clay
courts in Johnstone Park and on Cherokee Avenue.
Of course, there was no use or mention of the country
club in the weeks of tournament play. Fred Spies was
lauded as "the father of tennis in Bartlesville." For
what it's worth Price and Spies were contended for
the championship, with Spies emerging the champ in
an exciting match. [70]

The fact that a forgotten stock certificate for
The Bartlesville Country Club could be discovered in
the file of National Zinc eighty-five years later is also
clear evidence that the club failed financially. In fact,
a report by the Bartlesville Engineers Club in 1925,
plainly stated that Bartlesville Country Club was
"forced to dispose of its holdings due to financial difficulties." [71] Keyser's stock certificate was signed over to
the Smelter Gas Company on 15 November 1916. It
is also an indication that the reorganization effort was
indefinite but still active at that date. The dirt roads
made the club totally inaccessible whenever there was
wet weather, and the Maire Hotel siphoned off a big
portion of Bartlesville social activity. These factors
clearly cut into the viability of the club. The arrival
of the same economic forces that had persuaded the
Phillips brothers to move to sell their local oil holdings and plan to open a chain of banks in Kansas City
in that identical time frame, also were the forces that
caused the financially struggling infant club finally
to fail. At any rate, Frank and L. E. Phillips struck a
gusher at Number 8 in March of 1917 and the boom
was back on. [72]

Oak Hill Club

The first sign that there was stirring of interest in the country club problem came when articles
of incorporation were filed for Oak Hill Club on 27
April 1916, several months before Carl Kayser signed
over his stock certificate. [73] Osage County deeds
show that it was not until the spring of 1917, that
The Bartlesville Country Club sold its property to
Otto C. Massey, then Oak Hill Club bought the same
property from Massey. [74] It is notable that the articles
of incorporation for the Oak Hill Club were identical
to those of The Bartlesville Country Club, except that
they included a significant new phrase in the statement of purpose: "…to acquire, own, and hold stock

in transportation companies operating in Bartlesville and vicinity…"[75] The club may have purchased stock in the Interurban corporation in 1916, in hopes of influencing the development of the line to Pawhuska.

Along with the land, the Massey deed transferred the "clubhouse, men's bath house, barns, and other buildings and personal property" to Oak Hill Club. Of course, we already know from early newspaper accounts, there were also locker rooms, two clay tennis courts, and a superintendent's house. So, we have a rough idea of what was out there at the time. The two-story frame clubhouse had a dining room and large sandstone, screened-in veranda on the east, overlooking the golf course and toward the Mound and the town.

Bartlesville's second country club was organized by men whose names are more familiar to us than were those of the 1908 founders. In 1916 they were:

Gerald S. Coburn (bachelor)

314 ½ Johnstone • secretary Skelton-Moore Oil Co.

H. V. Foster (and Marie)

821 Johnstone • president ITIO.

C. E. Kayser (and Mildred J.)

712 Delaware • general manager Smelter Gas Co.

Frank Phillips (and Jane)

1107 Cherokee • president Bartlesville National Bank

Ray C. Russum (and Martha)

806 Osage • Quapaw Gas Co.

John H. McMorrow (and Mary)

415 Cherokee • cordage and wire lines.

Paul F. Dahlgren (and Mary)

613 Johnstone • Osage Producers Gas Co. [76]

The attorneys who handled the reorganization were Brennan, Kane & McCoy. John H. Brennan had worked with H. V. Foster since his early business days in Wisconsin. He was later general counsel for ITIO

and one of Foster's closest early associates. John H. Kane had been representing ITIO in some tax matters before the state supreme court in recent months. The reorganization committee, appointed at the emergency stockholders meeting in 1915, was Judge Shea, H. R. Straight, and H. V. Foster. In the interim, Judge Shea had moved to Tulsa, leaving the committee in the hands of Foster and Straight, the leaders of companies that were involved in the Doherty group of companies. Henry L. Doherty, who also controlled the Interurban, was a New York investor who had put together a large national conglomerate in utilities, including Quapaw Gas, and part of ITIO in Bartlesville. These companies came together, at the time, as Wichita Natural Gas, soon to be Empire Gas Company that was, in turn, part of Cities Service, all Doherty's interests. So, it appears that at this time Empire Gas and H. V. Foster's businesses were taking a keen interest in the effective reorganization of the club.

The $20,000 worth of stock in the new club was sold for $1.00 per share. The shareholders were:

H. V. Foster	$750
Indian Territory Illuminating Oil Company	$750
Smelter Gas Company	$750
Frank Phillips	$750
R. D. Rood	$750
Wichita Natural Gas Company	$16,250 [77]

At the time, it was common for small country clubs to be owned by companies for the benefit of their employees, so that the practice was available as a model to the re-organizers. Strong new measures were taken to insure the clubs' viability:

A committee of Quapaw representatives is planning to call on the citizens of Bartlesville to secure members for the country club for the purpose of reviving interest in that institution.

The son of a Pennsylvania oilman, H. R. Straight came to Oklahoma in 1911 to work for T. N. Barnsdall. After the Doherty Group purchased Barnsdall's interests, Straight was hired by Henry Doherty to run his new gas interests which soon became Empire Gas Company. After the reorganization of the country club in 1915, it became Oak Hill Club, and was largely controlled by Empire Gas for its employees. *Courtesy Bartlesville Area History Museum.*

Messers Russum, Straight, Williams, and Merritt will be active members of the committee and they hope to secure the cooperation of at least 150 new Members in making the club a success. The Quapaw company has recently expended $7,000 in equipping the establishment and putting the grounds, the tennis courts and golf links in first class condition and in building a swimming pool 60X120 feet, which is now nearly completed.

The corporation did this work primarily for the purpose of affording recreation for its employees, of which 240 have already joined, but they desire to make the club a thoroly (sic) representative institution. Anticipating the objection that some may make concerning the difficulty of getting out to the grounds from the end of the car line, it is proposed that if sufficient number of members can be secured to purchase a motor truck for use in transporting the members to the grounds. A truck suitable for this purpose can be purchased and fitted up for not to exceed $800, which would mean only a small payment by each new member. A truck for the use of the Quapaw members is already in operation, but the additional truck would be for the exclusive use of the city members.

The members of the committee plan to secure the services of a first class chef so that any member may order a luncheon or a dinner for any number of guests and have the advantage of superior service. With an enrollment of 300 to 400 members it is believed that the club can be made an attractive social center and a place where out of town guests may be fittingly entertained. [78]

The popular Willie Brown had already been hired back, for he played in the Oklahoma Golf Association tournament, listed as the pro from Bartlesville in June. [79] Brown probably organized the "two-bit" golf tournament that was played to benefit the Red Cross that weekend. [80] The swimming pool, which was concrete without tile or a filtering system, was not yet finished when another club tournament was played the last day of July. [81]

About that time, the newspaper reported that the committee had been busy with some other pressing business and would now finally begin to attend to the membership drive. By then, most of the Bartles-ville families had probably gone to Colorado for the summer season and only seventeen city members had been signed up to date. [82] Over the summer, Doherty Dancing Club was organized to hold a dance at the clubhouse each Saturday night. Partygoers were met at the end of the streetcar line by cars to take them to the country club. Usually the Webbers Orchestra played. The Foster Cup golf competition was played in September. D. D. Allison defeated Dr. Buck and G. E. Nash. [83] But, by the end of summer, the new club was pretty well established in minds around town as an Empire company organization.

Russell Davis said that there was not much social interaction between the employees of the bigger oil companies in town before the middle '20s. [84] Sure enough, for the next year virtually all social activity at the club was some variety of Doherty Auxiliary activity. In addition, the auxiliary was holding all of its regular, approximately semi-monthly, meetings at the clubhouse. One dinner dance is notable during this period, principally because of the Christmas season decorations that evening. In honor of Miss Lucille Robinson of Tampa, Florida, the "club rooms were uniquely decorated with black and yellow serpen-tine crepe paper rattlesnakes, pumpkins, carnations, and roses." [85] Meanwhile, the city was increasingly pre-occupied by the events of World War I. The newspapers regularly published long lists of young men being called up by the draft, and lists of men who

The club can be made an attractive social center and a place where out of town guests can be fittingly entertined. (Reorganization committee for Oak Hill Club, 1917.)

Henry Doherty also purchased the Bartlesville Interurban streetcar line that ran from the smelters, through town, and north to Dewey. Empire employees rode the streetcar from downtown to the end of the line, then a company truck met them to take them on out to the country club. The crowd in this 1917 photograph is men waiting for World War I draft reports in front of the newspaper office. *Courtesy Bartlesville Area History Museum.*

were labeled "shirkers." Increasingly, the only ladies activities in town surrounded some sort of Red Cross service. The bridge devotees of a year previous were now attending knitting parties and bandage-rolling teas. During August of 1918, a new dance floor was installed at the club. In that same month the newspapers first reported on the Spanish influenza epidemic.

Willie Brown had returned again to Muskogee Town and Country Club during the summer of 1917, and Oak Hill hired a new pro, William C. Garree, formerly from Shawnee Club in Kansas City. John H. McMorrow was the chairman of the golf committee and W. F. Brodnax was the club superintendent at the time. Mr. and Mrs. F. C. Logan were the full-time chefs promised by the re-organizational committee the year before. [86]

Garree was very actively planning a fall golf season of 1918. He was organizing a women's golf class and tournament – probably a prudent idea in an environment where most of the young men were being sent off to war. The first golf tournament of the season was already underway the last week in September, with the Foster Cup planned to start on 12 October, and the new McMorrow Cup, planned for Thanksgiving Day, along with competitions with several other cities. [87] It was all to come to naught. A week later the schools were closed because of the influenza epidemic. In only days, the city found it necessary to set up makeshift hospitals at the Elks Club, First Presbyterian Church, and First Baptist Church, and an emergency canteen at First Methodist Church.

The epidemic waned by Thanksgiving in Bartlesville, though illnesses lingered. Social life was slow to resume and winter weather hampered club utilization even with the Empire trucks providing transportation. This became apparent when Doherty Auxiliary meetings had to be moved to the Masonic

Building during March storms. Notwithstanding, one avant-garde young people's party that was held at the clubhouse in March featured dance music furnished by the victrola (an early type of phonograph) and the player piano.

> *The club performed its essential function of providing an "attractive social center where out of town guests could be fittingly entertained." (Judge Shea, 1910)*

The club did perform its essential function of providing an "attractive social center where out of town guests could be fittingly entertained." In April, Henry L. Doherty paid his first ever visit to Bartlesville. He was treated to the highlights of the Empire Gas empire. The final event was a dinner at the country club, given by the engineering research department, the company's most prestigious. [88] In the fall, the Mid-Continent Section of the American Mechanical Engineers planned to honor visiting delegates at a dinner at the country club, but the bad condition of the road forced them to move to the Maire. [89]

Again and again the road was the limiting factor to reliable club utilization. All remediation measures fell short. It is hard to really understand the problem. We have a tendency to visualize a dirt road such as some of the poorer ones we know of today. This is not the situation they were dealing with. In 1921, Bert Gaddis, the Ford dealer, ran for county commissioner. Doubtless he had a burr under his saddle about the roads because it directly impacted his business, but he was also a close friend of Frank Phillips who was very interested in improved roads too.

On the last weekend of the campaign, Gaddis took out a full page ad in the *Examiner* with several photographs of the county roads and bridges. To help us visualize, the pictures were more similar to an oil lease road through the river bottoms today, after a good mudding expedition by our high school 4-wheel enthusiasts, than any county roads we have ever seen. In this light it is understandable that most Bartlesville families simply decided club membership was socially problematic and not a very cost effective use of recreation dollars.

Meanwhile, the extent to which the club had come under Empire supervision becomes evident in a column that ran only once, "Empire Company Personal Items," which mentioned that R. E. Logan, the janitor at Oak Hill Club, was an Empire employee. [90]

In April the club made another of its expansion efforts, but outreach into the community was only half-hearted. They were providing a second truck for bus service to the club, they proposed expanding another two tennis courts to be situated on the site of the croquet grounds on the northwest of the clubhouse, and were considering additional dressing room and locker room space for the women. Amidst the spring facelift, they had signed up 100 new members, evidently from within the company, because they were again trying to figure out how to attract the citizens of Bartlesville to membership. N. B. Smiley was the new secretary-treasurer and he planned to begin to post delinquent accounts, and put restrictions of guest utilization. [91]

Chef Logan (listed as janitor on Empire payrolls) promised two-course dinners for only 75¢ if members would phone 224 to advise him early in the day. He boasted that all kinds of sandwiches and drinks were available at lunch. The management added, "the food and service were more than worth the cost." [92] It must have been futile, for the new cateress, Mrs. Henry (Edith) Thompson, came from Guthrie in October. [93]

Russell Davis gave a little description of the food available at the club by the early Twenties. He said lunch was usually sandwiches, as described above. Several kinds were available and they were served with some lettuce and tomato (in season), and olives. Potato chips could be requested, but French fries weren't on the menu. Soup was often available, usually served as a first course. Drinks were mostly limited to coffee and iced tea. Dessert was generally cake, ice cream, or sherbet and much more commonly than it is today, it was an expected part of the meal. Dinners had to be arranged in advance right up to the time that Oak Hill was closed. The dinner repertoire was also limited. Russell says all kinds of steaks were imported from Kansas City. Oyster stew was popular in the winter. He also mentioned fried chicken, fried fish, eggs benedict, and chicken a la king. Lettuce salad was available in season, and in the winter, Waldorf salad was considered very elegant, indeed.

Liquor and the bootlegger is also part of the story. Russell remembers that there was a man named Mose Cunningham, across the 7th Street Bridge, and a woman north of Dewey. There were others. If a man wanted to purchase some liquor, he would not call ahead, but would just go to the bootlegger. The choice of goods was limited to what the bootlegger happened to have in stock. Men that had business in the big cities, and also nearer places like Joplin, came home with valises packed with their favorite brands of good liquor. In the convention of the time, ladies did not buy liquor, or order from the bar. Many did not drink at all, and those who did were careful to nurse a single drink. Women who indulged more freely were either daringly avant-garde or of loose morals. The club kept a discrete bar and served drinks from their stock. It is clear that many parties became pretty rollicking. Enforcement seems to have become less rigorous after prohibition was federalized. There were certainly fewer raids reported in the newspaper.

The saga of the swimming pool throws another light on the problems of club maintenance. In the spring of 1919 the club announced:

On account of the scarcity of water for the swimming pool we have decided to clean and purify the water that is now in the pool and clean out the dirt that has settled in the bottom. [94]

This was April – they were reusing the water that had been in the pool throughout the winter! In that world before a filtration system was used and before the advent of modern, tight pool covers, by spring the pool must have been full of stagnant, swampy water, dirt and leaves, and various life forms. Some of the members must have been alarmed too, for there was further comment a few weeks later:

The chief chemist of the Empire Gas and Fuel company made a report a few days ago regarding the swimming pool at the country club. At the time when the gate to the pool was closed last year an analysis was made. It was found that the water contained in the cement reservoir had less bacteria germs in it [than] much of the drinking water being used in the city. Altho (sic) some are of the opinion that the water in the pool this year is very bad, an analysis made Thursday revealed but very few bacteria. The chemicals used to purify the water are harmless. The water is being changed all the time, the water coming into the pool through a quartz sand filter. [95]

It appears the membership was not to be placated, for the next spring the club announced they would be bringing a water line from the city, and would be changing the swimming pool water and refilling regularly with city water. [96] Russell Davis said this was never completely implemented.

By the end of World War I Bartlesville neared its 1910 dream of 25,000. The population of the bustling little city was 19,874. It boasted miles of paved streets, two railroads, Interurban, four banks, three zinc smelters, two wholesale grocery houses, telephone system, commission form of government, two city parks, two telegraph lines, four bakeries, bottling works, six savings and loans, express company, two ice cream factories, one ice cream cone factory, seven hotels, sixteen rooming houses, two foundries, two newspapers, twelve oil well supply companies, business college, fifteen restaurants, four theaters, two high schools, five ward schools, wholesale cigar house, the largest office building in the state.

It is important to understand the prominence of Empire Gas in Bartlesville in the nineteen-teens. Its position is fully analogous to Phillips Petroleum's importance in Bartlesville today. During the oil bust of 1914, Doherty bought up many of the local independent oil and gas producers, and many others had failed or moved elsewhere. The business landscape of Bartlesville had totally changed at the end of World War I. [97] Phillips Petroleum Company was only incorporated in 1917, and though growing like Topsy, was just a healthy upstart independent in comparison to Empire Gas in the city then. Empire was so big that in 1919, it could boast that its eight-story office building downtown was the largest in Oklahoma.

In some sense Empire held the social hegemony entirely in its hands, but was finding that it was not a healthy position. Richard D. Moss of Colby College points out that American country clubs have functioned as the social center of the surrounding area. He cites a study of country clubs by historian Benjamin Radar that says, "It not only fosters, it regulates and governs the social life of the place."[98] Maybe Empire sensed the undesirability of the image of the club belonging to the company; or maybe Empire felt it was more efficient to use their new skyscraper for company functions. If the goal of the country club in Bartlesville was community building, as was so often reiterated over the years, then splitting the social arbiters of the town diminished social cohesion and dispersed efforts to build up the business of Bartlesville. Whichever the cause, early in 1919, the Doherty Auxiliary ceased to meet at the country club, and they also largely ceased to have social functions, like dances, at the clubhouse. These were all moved to the social rooms at the Empire Building downtown. Meanwhile almost all other entertaining around town

was in homes, unless it was something very big indeed, so that it is difficult to assess how the clubhouse was actually being utilized. A few details showed up for no particular reason, for instance, a Halloween party in 1920, had a six-piece orchestra that featured a xylophone. The most exciting episode that year was in February, when H. V. Foster entertained former President Taft on a visit to Bartlesville. One of the principle events that day was a luncheon at the country club. H. V. was a camera buff, and so took lots of good photographs and also movies at the luncheon. [99]

During this period the Doherty dance club dissolved. Hal Price, recently back from heroic service in World War I, and a very eligible bachelor in town, was instrumental in organizing the Beau Monde dance club, which had a city wide membership, and very actively held dances at several places around town. At the same time, the YMCA had taken over

Former President Taft was a guest of H. V. Foster in Bartlesville 27 February 1920. Bartlesville leaders pose with Taft in front of the H. V. Foster home on Johnstone. (left to right, Fr. John Van Der Hende, number 1, H. V. Foster, number 4, President Taft, number 6, Paul Walgreen, 7, Burdette Blue, 8, Jess Leach, 9, Frank Finney, 11) Foster hosted a banquet at Oak Hill that evening, and even took movies of the event. *Courtesy of the Bartlesville Area History Museum.*

the tennis tournament that Price and Fred Spies organized before the war. It was a highly successful city wide annual event. The newspaper did report that Spies lost to Beal in the semi-finals of the tennis tournament at Oak Hill in October, but no champion was reported. In 1919, the city built concrete tennis courts, and the club probably did too, because the 1925 photo of the club shows concrete courts. It probably can be assumed the club had regular, though unreported, tennis tournaments organized by Price and Spies. In August the Oak Hill baseball team beat the Empires, 2 to 1. That is the only report of a country club baseball team.

It was only the golfing activities at Oak Hill that give a reliable indicator of the vital life of the club during the post war years. In the summer and fall season each year tournament competition for the Foster Cup, and the newer McMorrow Cup, gives us a somewhat incomplete record of the new arrival and ebb of each successive pro. George Marshal was the McMorrow Cup champion in 1918, Dr. F. N. Buck in 1919, M. E. Michaelson in 1920 and 1921. The Rotary golf team and the Kiwanis golf team played a thrilling tournament at Oak Hill in 1920, the first of many. Of course, all the participants were club members. Rotary won. There may not have been a golf pro at the club in 1920, for the newspapers never refer to a Bartlesville pro, and instead kept mentioning the superintendant, Mr. Brodnax, when reporting on golf activities. In the summer of 1921, Oak Hill Club joined the Southeastern Kansas Golf Association and ceased to participate in the Oklahoma Golf Association activities, though it appears they did continue membership in OGA. The simple, flat nine-hole and sand greens golf course, with no traps or hazards or trees, had fallen behind the facilities of some of the big clubs in the state and Bartlesville was a long ways north. It is possible that

some of the clubs didn't want to come up to play in Bartlesville. Certainly, it was closer to the southeastern Kansas clubs and very competitive with them. The Oak Hill golf team participated in a series of tournaments here and at several clubs in Kansas, emerging the area champs. [100] Marshal Hockensmith and L. B. Messner were the first and second place champions. The team trophies were proudly displayed at A. S. Eby jewelry store.

That year was the first in Bartlesville for golf pro Ed Dudley. Dudley is the first professional about whom we have extensive information. He was born in Brunswick, Georgia in 1901. He spent two years at Belmont College in North Carolina, and then turned professional. It happened that the year he left college, Bartlesville was in need of a pro and he took the job here. How that came about is a mystery. He was 6'4" tall and was later called "handsome Ed" in the professional golf world. He had all the energy of youth and was a gifted teacher. At Oak Hill, Ed met, and in 1923, married Ruth Johnson, daughter of William F. "Buick" Johnson, the local Buick dealer. During the club's tough financial time in early 1923, Dudley went to Pawhuska as pro, and soon after that went to Joplin, where he was pro in 1925. Shortly, he became pro at Oklahoma City Golf and Country Club. The next year he got an offer he couldn't refuse, and Oklahoma City couldn't match, moving on to Hollywood with a salary of $15,000. By 1929, he was in Wilmington, Delaware, and the Broadmoor, then in 1934, he became the pro at Augusta National. He was Bobby Jones' first choice for that post. Jones said his swing was "the most graceful I've ever seen." Jones was impressed with his gentlemanly demeanor and with his gifts and patience as an instructor. In the 1930s and 40s, Dudley was consistently one of the top ten professionals. He was president of the PGA for

Handsome Ed Dudley was Oak Hill's golf pro from 1920 to 1923, his first job out of college. He married a Bartlesville girl, Ruth Johnson. By the 1930s, he was one of the top 10 pros on the golf circuit. He later served as president of the PGA. He was probably influential in the choice of Jimmy Gullane for Hillcrest's first pro. *Courtesy Ruth Bateman*

seven years. He was Dwight Eisenhower's golf coach. He is also well remembered among some of Bartlesville people who knew him when he was still regularly visiting relatives here up until his sudden death in 1963; quite a remarkable man to have begun his career in Bartlesville. [101]

Meanwhile, in 1921, the structure of the country club organization was undergoing assertive change. A couple of articles early in 1921 shed light on this question. After the annual stockholders meeting, first vice president Fergesen protested, "there has been too much of an impression that the country club is an Empire and not a Bartlesville institution." This was in anticipation of another spring membership drive. Fortunately, the article published an extensive listing of the club leadership.

The different stockholders in the club met last Thursday afternoon in the executive room on the eighth floor of the Masonic-Empire building and appointed the following board of directors: H. V. Foster, R. D. Rood, Frank Phillips, R. C. Russum, J. H. McMorrow, C. E. Kayser and L. D. Messner.

The following officers were elected: H. V. Foster, president; E. J. Fergesen, first vice president;

Harold C. Price, second vice president; Mrs. W. A. Stoller, secretary and treasurer.

The following executive committee is composed of one member from each of the firms of the city holding stock in the club: Barnsdall Oil company, F. A. Rooney; general public, J. S. Leach; Rood Oil corporation, J. H. McMorrow; Smelter Gas Company, Harold C. Price; Phillips Petroleum company, O. K. Wing; Bartlesville Gas and Electric Company, A. V. Wynns; Meridian Petroleum corporation, M. E. Michaelson; Indian Territory Illuminating Oil company, C. H. Caldwell; First National Bank, Fred L. Dunn, Union National Bank, Marshal Hockensmith; Empire Gas and Fuel company, E. J. Fergesen. [102]

This oligarchy of local industries, now expanded from the 1916 list, was still the infrastructure of Oak Hill Club. A guess is that Empire Gas and some of H. V. Foster's interests, along with Frank Phillips and Dr. Rood had originally organized the club, as it appeared at the time, essentially a company club that was also open for general membership. "The club was operated under contracts entered into by the above mentioned stockholders, whereby they shared in the operating expense and all improvements in like proportion to their stock holdings." [103] Though the quality of amenities and services was excellent this way, it was not satisfactory socially. But, repeated invitation for community members did not get good response.

Probably in 1919, they resorted to the broader-based corporate support structure that we see in the above article. Since the total amount of stock was still 20,000 shares, the new stockholding companies must have purchased their interests from Empire, which was trying to reduce its presence. In the summer of 1919, Phillips Petroleum Company held a stag party at Oak Hill for H. E. Koopman who was getting married. Frank and L. E. Phillips, and John Kane, who are known to have been long time members, were not at this party. But most of the other Phillips executives were there to take advantage of the [new] company membership. This may be an example of a social event that points to the attempted reform. [104] We know that Smelter Gas Company held 750 shares of Oak Hill Club stock in 1929. [105] It's safe to assume that all of the represented companies held similar large blocks of stock. Shortly after the 3 February annual stockholders meeting in 1921, the corporation filed amendments to their articles of incorporation. Principally, these allowed them to increase of their capitalization from $20,000 to $75,000. Each share of stock was valued at one dollar. The attorney who filed the documents was Beryle R. Johnson, an Empire employee. [106] In November, Jack Warlick, who was chairman of the Oak Hill executive committee, met with the Chamber of Commerce executive committee, a new wrinkle in the struggle to restructure the club. He "presented the reorganization plan of that Club for consideration and stated that it was the desire of this committee that E. L. George should act as Secretary of the Country Club." [107] The engineer's club report describes this plan: "for the past two years the club had been operating on a strictly business basis." Despite this yeoman push, this time involving the Chamber of Commerce, in order to extricate themselves from the Empire image, Oak Hill was not able to get the increase in capitalization done. [108] However, in 1921, general memberships did finally significantly increase. They had an arrangement that is not altogether clear:

> ... a plan which enables membership to be held at a nominal cost and is unique in that no membership fees are required. [109]

They had a $20 initiation fee, and $40 annual dues (by 1925 the dues were $60). Non-resident's fees were one half the resident membership fees, as were the fees for single lady members. The club cleaning fee was $12, and locker rent was $3. [110] A guess is that these members did not hold stock, something like our present social membership, but with golf and tennis privileges, and evidently, also the right to serve on the board and committees.

The Bartlesville Country Club corporation was officially cancelled 10 June 1919, though for some reason the corporation may have continued electing officers with an annual meeting in March for several years. [111] In 1920, Oak Hill Club bought 20 acres from Paul B. Mason for $1.00. It was part of the land that had been leased in 1911. [112] They now owned a

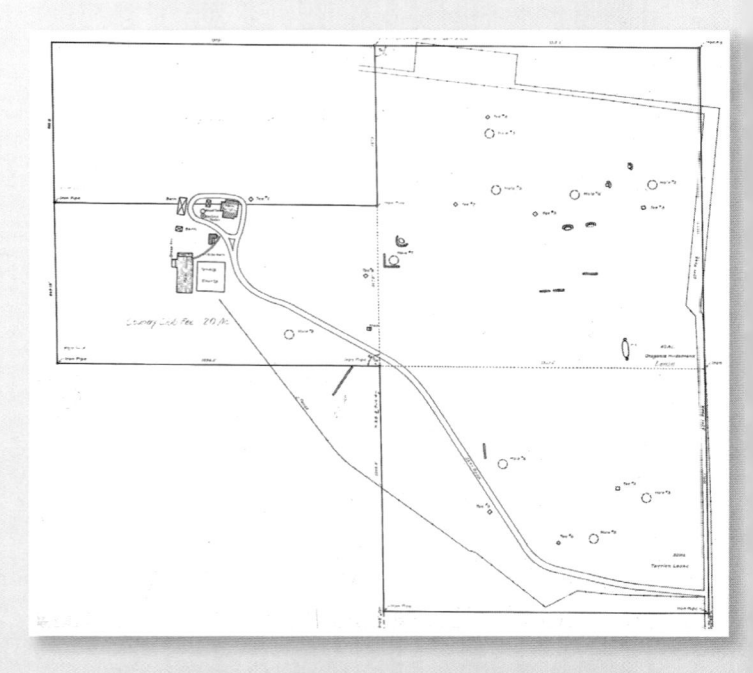

A plat map of Oak Hill Club, dated 14 August 1919 shows the 40 acre layout of the old country club. The road angles in from the southeast corner, leading to the clubhouse circle drive, 2 barns, water tank, coaling tank, locker room houses, swimming pool with dressing room, tennis courts, number one tee nearby, and 8 more tees in the golf course. *Courtesy Bartlesville Area History Museum.*

total of 40 acres. The golf course was almost entirely on leased land. Forty acres was leased from Mrs. Oragonia Hildebrand for $12 per acre (that lease expired 1 March 1926). They also leased 30 acres from Mary Tayrien for $250 per year. It came up for extension 1 January 1925, but could be canceled. [113]

In actual fact, the thing that probably was the most help in opening up the club for general membership at the time was what appeared to be a resolution to the ancient nemesis – the road problem. Late in 1920, the county let a contract for 3,000 feet of concrete road, extending from the city limit at Rogers Avenue out to Mound Avenue, to Phillips Street, south on Phillips Street to Second Street, and west on Second to the county line. "This road will give access to the Oak Hill Country Club grounds which lie a short distance beyond the county line." [114] Immediately, the country club applied to the Chamber of Commerce to help them with the road in Osage County. The Chamber did vote to give them $100 for the road, but another brainstorm was afoot. There was a serious movement that dragged on for a couple of years to persuade the State to allow Washington County to annex a portion of Osage County. That would have given Washington County jurisdiction over the country club road, and also some of the Barnsdall Road that Phillips was trying to get completed. [115] With the Washington County piece of the country club road paved early in 1921, for the first time ever, country club ladies believed they could reliably count on driving their automobiles out to the club for an afternoon of bridge. For the next year or two the social schedule at the club reflected the improved conditions and improved general membership. In 1925, the engineer's report mentioned that they believed their 200 club members were probably the maximum number possible for Bartlesville. The year that little Dickie

Kane got his dunking in the swimming pool was a watershed year for Oak Hill Club.

For the first time in years the club seemed to be effectively utilized both socially, as well as for civic and business events. Some Bartlesville people entertained the chief consul for the Santa Fe Railroad and an appraiser from Washington at the club during a stopover luncheon in October. A first for the country club was a golf contest and dinner for the dental association, hosted by Dr. Van Duzer. It was the club's first such event for a professional association. The car dealers also had a dinner-dance. Kiwanis had a huge Christmas banquet and dance. The biggest event of the fall season was the annual Thanksgiving tournament at which they celebrated their big golf season. J. S. Leach won a turkey for his best score at the tournament. [116] Mrs. T. K. Stout won the women's tournament. John McMorrow, who was head of the program, echoed the ancient vision of the club. "The country club will be active in the future. We want to take a part in all civic moments…" [117] The 1921 club reorganization finally had effectively reached out to the business community and brought in many new community members. The committee was A. V. Wynne, house; O. K. Wing, greens; J. H. McMorrow, competition; M. E. Michaelson, entertainment; Fred Dunn, finance; membership was C. H. Caldwell and L. D. Messner; Marshal Hockensmith, tennis; F. N. Buck, swimming; Jesse Leach, publicity; and the lease was M. E. Michaelson. That winter season saw the heaviest utilization of the clubhouse since 1911/12.

"The country club will be active in the future. We want to take part in all civic moments." (John H. McMorrow, 1921.)

The 1922 club year was very active, both socially and at golf, reflecting the improved social climate. A new kind of lady party was a morning golf game, followed by a luncheon and an afternoon of bridge. The Daughters of the American Revolution had two big events in the spring. The golf tournament season teed off on 7 May at a Chanute tournament. There were a number of dances, principally for the younger set. Russell Davis, who was a teenager on some of the published party lists, recalls that Bartlesville society was very stratified by age in those days. Small children fit into the "children should be seen and not heard" paradigm, but high schoolers enjoyed the beginnings of a real social life. Children in that age group were not old enough to date or drive, so parents drove them to the club for the parties. The big touring cars with jump seats could carry several kids out. The girls wore party dresses, but the boys mostly did not yet own suits. The music was played on the victrola, but jazz was not for children. The boys especially looked forward to the refreshments. Sometimes it was cookies, but usually it was layer cake and some kind of punch. The girls watched their figures, but the boys dove in when the treats were served. The party was over in time to get everybody home by the usual curfew of 11:00.

One of the biggest events in Bartlesville that summer was also one of the oddest. At the time the Ku Klux Klan was very active and very powerful in state and national politics, even sponsoring a slate of Klan candidates for the fall elections. They had first appeared in Washington County a couple of years earlier, and had a moderate-sized, though noisy membership. Bartlesville society largely disapproved of Klan activities, though some society gentlemen seem to have been involved to some degree. It should be pointed out, at the time the Klan, designated by

historians "the second Klan," was not the Neo-Nazi radicals we think of today. The movement of the 1920s seems to have sprung up as a sort of populist reaction to the social change of the times, a yearning for good old-time 19th century Romanticism. They were especially opposed to immigrants (Catholics and Jews especially), Socialism, and to moral degeneration, but under the mask of secrecy they had an endemic tendency to bully Black people and to become violent. So, when the Klan planned a big ceremony on the Fourth of July, it became a major local curiosity. The ceremony took place on the evening of the Fourth, west of town on property immediately north of the country club. About 300 local and state Klansmen participated in the affair, while it was estimated that 10,000 local people journeyed out from town to gawk at the torch-lit ceremony. The Twentieth Century bridge club ladies had a discreet picnic that evening on the Oak Hill Club grounds, affording prime seats (at a respectable distance) to observe the spectacle. [118]

The competition in the Southeastern Kansas Golf Association resumed for another year, with Bartlesville golfers dominating the links almost all summer. In addition, late in May there was an enthusiastic tournament in which Oak Hill beat the Pawhuska club soundly. The next week for a club tournament, Ed Dudley had his men, 60 contestants, arranged into two flights, the "All Stars" and the "Top Notchers." There was an exciting Scotch foursome, played in the rain on the first of July, and a flag tournament the next weekend. All in all, Ed Dudley kept his golf club very active. The summer seems to have been relatively cool and wet, and the club remained socially active long after the women usually had fled to the mountains. The Oak Hill tennis team even got into the act, but was badly beaten by Independence on 6 August. Ed Dudley, himself, made the biggest news of the summer, driving 360 yards off the first tee in a practice round, the longest drive on record at the club. [119] But, summer went out with a bang: a flood early in August, followed by a typhoid epidemic, and an 110° heat wave for Labor Day. Through it all, the Oak Hill golf team managed to dominate the Southeastern Kansas Golf Association competition. Myron Messner, who was also the winner of the state American Legion golf trophy, was the champion of the Kansas competition.

The McMorrow trophy competition and the Foster Cup were announced in September. Myron Messner won the McMorrow trophy for 1922, defeating Adam Johnstone in October. [120] Messner was having a banner year. Meanwhile, Bartlesville lucked into another golf coup. Mrs. W. S. Sickles moved from Independence to Bartlesville, giving Oak Hill another golf champ to crow about. Immediately, Ed Dudley got busy getting his ladies organized into a women's golf association. Golfer's Magazine offered trophies for the men's and women's competitions. While elimination rounds continued for the Foster Cup, Myron Messner set the club record low score of 18 holes in 73, with 36 and 37 in each round. [121] J. E. Sanderson became the winner of the men's *Golfers Magazine* trophy and Mrs. Paul Dahlgren was the women's winner on 25 October. Messner finished the season as winner of the Foster Cup at Thanksgiving.

Years later, cost estimates for the proposed new Hillcrest Country Club give an indication of Oak Hill Club salaries in the early 1920s. The golf pro's salary was estimated at $100, the greens keeper at $200, the club manager at $50. Russell Davis thought Mrs. Thompson employed 3 men in the clubhouse, but we have no idea how many men helped the greens keeper. [122]

The Purple Cats, a club for career girls, gave a rousing Halloween dance. The club was decorated with fall foliage and flowers and spooky cats, witches, and tombstones. The guests arrived in costume and danced to the music of the Dewey Davis jazz orchestra. At 10:00 the couples unmasked in time for refreshments. [123] The Huite Chevuax club had a New Years dance with forty-eight hosts to finish out the year. [124] Another group that frequently got together at Oak Hill was the Halcyon Club. John and Mildred Phillips, Dana Reynolds, Hal Price, and Jake May were among the young socialites that organized this Roaring Twenties crowd.

While there was definitely a flair for elegance associated with the Halcyons of Bartlesville, there was not especially anything calming or tranquil about any of them. The Halcyons' parties were memorable. They'd throw costume balls, stage elaborate dinners, and hire orchestras at the drop of a hat. At one impromptu bash, Halcyons were invited to come dressed the way they felt at that exact moment. One young man, already enjoying a crippling hangover, arrived prone on a hospital stretcher. Another guest wore his dress shirt, tie, coat, but no trousers. John Phillips said he felt stylish that day, but his feet were killing him, so he wore his tuxedo and went barefoot. [125]

Russell Davis added that these parties sometimes lasted for days. Armais Artunoff even told him that after one party, one man crawled home in his tuxedo.

Meanwhile, his diary notes that Frank Phillips went to H. V. Foster's office on 4 December 1922, for the annual stockholders meeting. [126] It appeared that the club seemed to be up and running at last, for the balance sheets for 1923 and 1924 were in the black, but surely the directors were already planning the next move.

Shortly after the first of the New Year, social activities at the club disappeared, corresponding with

The Halcyon Club was a Roaring Twenties social club, the whiskey and trombones crowd. The club was organized by John and Mildred Phillips, Jake May, Dana Reynolds, and Hal Price and held many parties at Oak Hill and Hillcrest. Some of the people identified at this costume party (left to right) back row: Paul? (flat hat), Vera?, Leo Johnstone, woman?, man in derby?. O.K. Wing, Dana Reynolds (white hat), Stewart Dewer (top hat), Johnny Holm, ?, John G. Phillips (hugging a girl), Sherman? Seated: ? woman, Esther Rood, ? woman, Mildred Phillips (plaid dress), Opal Wing, Vera Reynolds (white hat), Rowena Dewer (big hat). On floor: ? woman, ? woman, Hal Price in box, Katie Hood Wight behind Price. *Courtesy Bartlesville Area History Museum.*

the beginning of a terrible winter. Very heavy snows and low temperatures for the next several weeks must have once again closed the last section of unimproved road from the county line to the club. Ed Dudley was reduced to giving golf lessons indoors at the Rex Bowling Alley. [127] It was just the last straw! On 30 January Chamber of Commerce president, Fred Dunn, lead a discussion on the condition of the country club.

> *He made a statement setting forth the financial condition in which the club finds it's self (sic) at this time and advocated the co-operation of the Chamber of Commerce in an attempt to place the club on a firm financial basis. H. O. Caster stated that in his opinion the Country Club could not be maintained under existing conditions he also stated that in his opinion the club as now operating was of no particular value to the Empire Company or the other companies employing a large number of people in our city. It is his opinion that the country Club can be maintained by the citizens of Bartlesville as a community enterprise in which the larger companies do not have the controlling interest.* [128]

A committee was appointed to investigate. Shortly, a meeting notice appeared in the paper:

Members of the Oak Hill Country club have been requested to meet at the Chamber of Commerce rooms Friday night at 7:30 o'clock to consider ways and means to keep the club open during the next year.

The estimate of expenditures will be prepared it is planned, and the election of representatives to conduct the affairs of the organization will be held. [129]

Bartlesville wasn't the only small club with chronic troubles. After the Southeastern Kansas Golf Association competition, the newspaper reported that the Independence club was $10,000 in debt. Back in October they crowed, "the Bartlesville club may have assets to spare." [130] Evidently things had changed.

At the Chamber of Commerce on Friday night, fifty of the members met. Once again a committee was appointed. This time Burdette Blue was chairman, and Fred Dunn and James Sivalls were his committee members. It was taken for granted that a new club for Bartlesville must be constructed. The particulars, including whether to remain at the present site, were left to the committee. But, some details surfaced. A finance committee was also appointed, H. E. Hulen, Carl Wood, and A. C. Leike. They proposed raising $50,000 to $75,000 from 200 members at $250 each, and that dues must be raised from $40 to $50. One dedicated member volunteered to match funds by 25%. Someone even pointed out that Hominy, Oklahoma had recently raised $250 each from 100 businessmen for a country club there in only a period of three hours. [131] Afterwards members opined that a whole new site would be their best choice.

The heavy snows of winter gave way to constant rain in the spring and through the summer. The Arkansas and Canadian Rivers flooded seriously twice, in the spring and summer, and Bartlesville had repeated lowland flooding throughout the spring

and summer. In June, Ed Dudley took the Pawhuska Country Club golf team to the Oklahoma Golf Association tournament. The Bartlesville team reported its first tournament play in Independence 28 June. There don't seem to have been any golf association contests in Bartlesville during the entire summer. An eye-opener article in August revealed the extent to which the club was in some sort of suspended animation:

Golf aspirants of Bartlesville have been given the privilege of being tutored by a professional golfer from Pawhuska, according to an announcement made Tuesday night.

Ed Dudley is the new teacher for lovers of the golf game and he will visit the country club links every Monday and Tuesday. [132]

Oak Hill did participate in the Southeastern Kansas Golf Association Championship tournament in September in Independence. Meanwhile the Kiwanis and Rotary clubs planned another tournament in October at the Club. Kiwanis won. But, overall there was the impression of inactivity that comes from having no golf professional on staff, and by then the superintendent, Mr. Brodnax, was also gone.

There were some social functions at the clubhouse, giving the further impression of change in that quarter too, for Edith Thompson, who came as the cook in 1919, was now in charge at the clubhouse. Many social occasions had to be cancelled because of the weather. Dances were immensely popular during the era, and Mike May says that Paul Earley, who worked at the club in those days, told him that they often had "sunrise dances" at which they danced till dawn. Russell Davis said, yes, the sunrise dances were considered very dashing and elegant. Just like New York. The first sunrise dance that was reported in the society pages was a big one for college kids on 1 July 1923, though Russell Davis said they were popular between about 1919 and 1929. [133] Otherwise, though the clubhouse appeared to be open, at least through the early summer, there was not much happening. It appears that the committee appointed to work on relocating the club raised sufficient funds among the stockholders for a stopgap measure, renovating the existing clubhouse and maybe doing a little work on the golf course. During the slack social season of the late summer and fall months the work kept the club largely inactive. Finally, the newspaper announced that the club would be opened after its renovations for a housewarming party and informal dance. The party was to benefit a new victrola for the clubhouse. [134] They had enlarged the downstairs for a larger dance floor and porch area with all new flooring. Probably they had done some tinkering on the golf course to enlarge it from par 36 to par 38. [135]

Brooks Spies remembers that Hal Price took him out to the club when he was about five or six years old, probably about 1923 or 1924, to teach him a little golf. This would have been during the time when there was no pro at Oak Hill. Brooks has no memory of a pro then. Russell Davis confirmed that there was, indeed, no pro after Ed Dudley left. Hal Price may have taken on the task of introducing the lad to that social skill, since Fred Spies didn't play golf. Brooks became an accomplished and inveterate golfer, thanks to this early introduction to the game. He described the Oak Hill course in similar terms to the others that remember the old links there, especially the sand greens (called browns) and the a sandboxes next to the tees so that golfers could form a pinch of sand to tee up their balls. The greens were actually smelter tailings that had been oiled. He says they teed off down hill, then the rest of the course was very simple, up one side and back on the other, in the flat land near the air field, with the sand greens that everyone mentions, and ending up the ninth hole back at the

bottom of the hill. There were no traps or hazards. It was 3,180 yards for a par 38 course. [136] There was never water for greens, let alone fairways so that grass was always just native. Art Gorman remembers playing on the golf course in the 1940s, which was then public. He says the course was just west of where the runway now is at the Bartlesville airport, as the land begins to rise into the hills. At that time it was unimproved prairie grasses, with the holes laid out simply. The number one fairway was evidently changed when the property was partitioned. Martha May Beard said she and Sis Gray (Kane) played the course once in the 1930s, but there were so many snakes, they never returned.

During this time without a club golf professional, Henry Thompson, who was by then superintendent at the club, was in charge of keeping body and soul together on the golf course. In 1924, the club dropped its membership in the Southeastern Kansas Golf Association. In July 1924, Thompson's wife, Edith, formerly the cook, but by then the hostess in the clubhouse, helped him organize a little golf tournament and dinner for the club caddies. George Huffman won a shirt for first prize, and Henry Thompson, Jr. won golf sox (sic) for second prize. [137] In 1925, Joe Bowden was a twelve-year-old caddie at Oak Hill. He especially remembers caddying for H. V. Foster, John H. Kane, and Stewart Dewer. Joe says the bags were plenty heavy and you had to really keep an eye on that ball, because "if you lost a ball they were crankier than hell." It's no wonder – a ball cost $1.00. That is about $10 in today's money. He earned 50¢ for caddying a nine-hole round at Oak Hill, and later at Hillcrest he got $1.50 for eighteen holes, so they were paying about our present minimum wage for the work. Not bad for a twelve-year-old in a world where an unskilled man sometimes made $1.00 a day and the club manager was earning $50 per month. [138]

The Frank Phillips appointment diaries that we still have only begin in 1920. The Oak Hill Club was

Picking up a little work as a caddie had been a lucrative job for Bartlesville boys for several years. When club manager, Henry Thompson, organized a thank you party for the boys in 1924, for the first time we learn their names and how many there were.

Chrysie Locke (Crazy), Arthur Moore (Art), John Weber (Good Looking), Vergiol Torrey (Goose Eye), Neal Ford (Lincoln Pup), Wayne Ford (Little Lizzie), Clayton Kroh (Clay), Bill Ladd (Bailing Wire Bill), Rookie Smith (Mamma), Marbry Harmon (Bacon), Leo Huffman (Square Toe), Paul Locke (Padlock), Ralph Axsom (Buster), Charles Moore (Chuck), Vollie Carter (Decart), Loddie Matusek (Patootles), Louis Tiliot (Skinney), John Mills (Peanut Boy), Avery Weaver (Weinuies) George Huffman (Crazy Lula), Rodney Williams (Rod), Deroy Williams (De), Cyril Graham (Pugnose), Ray Weaver (Buzz), Thurman Hinkle (Hink), Calvin Cataway (Bull), Engelbert Matusek (Mat), Henry Thompson (Hank).

mentioned occasionally when Frank was in town. Several golf games there were mentioned, apparently in connection with his thinking about a better golf course. On 31 December 1923, Frank's secretary mentioned that Frank and Jane went to the "Winter Club Dance," and Frank didn't get up the next day until noon. [139] This, and another "Winter Dance" later on, were the only Oak Hill parties mentioned in the diaries. These Winter Dances were a very active series of events, approximately twice a month in 1923/24, designed to enliven club life in the newly expanded

clubhouse during the stopgap period before the plan for the new club could be launched. The first was the opening party that took place on 25 November 1923. This one was the house warming that provided a new victrola. The second dance took place on 1 December and was the opening event of the winter social season. It was followed by a series of dances and banquets for several organizations during the Christmas season. The big one was the winter dance that kept Frank Phillips up all night. It came on the heels of a Phillips Petroleum Company announcement that they had signed a new five-year lease, assuring the city of their permanency. No wonder everyone was in the mood for a stem-winder gala. The evening was preceded with several dinner parties all around town. One hundred couples attended the Winter Dance, including several out-of-town guests. The clubhouse was decorated with favors of horns, trumpets, confetti, and serpentines. Tall red candles graced the stone mantle, and Rice's orchestra played the dance music. [140]

The H. V. Foster biography contains a description of a New Years party, the same "Winter Dance" that only started at Oak Hill. It affords to us another glimpse of the character of the social life in Bartlesville in those days.

The parties did not consist of wine and cello music; this was whiskey and trombone town. J. Frank Rice, leader of the Melody Mixers band, particularly remembered one New Years Eve dance that summed up the town. Rice's band had played at one of the clubs in Bartlesville. When the dance was over, Frank Phillips took the band to his house where they played some more. Then they moved to the Foster house at 821 Johnstone Street. After the band played there for a while, the crowd thinned out somewhat, and the band was packing up to leave. At that point, Vernon came downstairs to ask, "Mr. Rice, where are you going?"

"Going home. The dance is over."

"No," Foster told him. "It's just started." And so they played until dawn. Vernon and Marie phoned their friends to wish them Happy New Year. The band played "Last Night On The Back Porch," a new song, and Marie invited the entire band for breakfast. [141]

Frank Phillips went to H. V. Foster's office on 31 December 1923, to attend the annual stockholders meeting of the club. Because there are no extant club records, there is scant memory of the business life of the club. Fortunately, two annual reports, one for 1923 and one for 1924 have come to light. That year's meeting had an encouraging report, made public by the chairman of the executive committee, O. P. Warlick, a month later. The club closed the year with a net profit of $211.18. They had charged off $1262.70 in bad debts and allowances, finishing with $1438.87 in cash. Their regular expenses had been $8,808.53 and the renovations had cost $4,123.60. [142]

The Winter Dances continued through the season, a total of seven. The one on 17 February was another very big event, the other dance noted in the Frank Phillips diaries, and there was a big masquerade ball to end the season on 15 March. Alternate Winter Dances were "informal," that is the evening's entertainment was dinner, dancing, and cards – not black tie. It is well that they were pushing so hard socially, for the winter had a lengthy period of bitter cold that might have shut down club activity in other years. It was so bad that the Salvation Army put out a call for help for the city's poor. Yet, they were heady times with Phillips and Empire purchasing half the leases at the Osage Sale. No season would be normal at Oak Hill without the weather causing cancellations, and sure enough the Business and Professional Women's monthly meeting had to be moved to the Maire twice. [143]

In May, Phillips Petroleum Company gave a dinner for the Oak Hill golfers. The golfers elected Forest Plank chairman of the golf committee, and organized an entertainment committee for a series of prospective matches with area clubs. They said, "The plan of the entertainment committee is to promote better inter-city relations by means of warm reception to visiting players." To that end, teams were chosen between all the golfing members in order to establish handicaps in a tournament on Decoration Day (Memorial Day). The tournament was concluded a week later when the 32-man team captained by V. T. Broaddus defeated the J. H. Collins team. The losers treated the champions to a dinner at the clubhouse. There was also a flag tournament at the club the same week. They were already planning reinstitution of the McMorrow Cup competition. [144] Meanwhile, J. H. Collins entered the Oklahoma Pro-Am championship that was played at Tulsa Country Club, and young Adam Johnstone made it to the final rounds. Ed Dudley, who was the pro at Joplin by then, won the professional title. The Bartlesville Tennis Association even resumed its tournament play at the country club courts in July. [145] Shortly afterward the club finally got the swimming pool opened up for the season. Phillips Petroleum Company donated a tower for some kind of circulating and cleaning system, their first filtration system. It is evident that there was a conscious effort to keep golf and tennis actively involved in the club during the waning months at the old site.

Around the first of July in 1925, the business environment coalesced to the point of critical need of a new club. "A group of men whose interests are permanent in Bartlesville…met Tuesday night for serious discussion of the future of the Bartlesville Country Club." Thought and research had obviously already gone into the project. They believed the cost of a new club would be from $100,000 to $125,000, and annual maintenance would be in the range of $18,000 to $20,000. The purchase of more land at the Oak Hill site would be $43,000, but an entirely new site would cost about $17,000. The outcome of the meeting was:

> *...to move to get engineering estimates of the cost of various features of a new club on the Bartlesville Tulsa road, get chemical analysis of water sources, and get men with money permanently invested here enthused with the idea that the present club is crowded, running under many handicaps, is paying exorbitant rents, and lacks adequate water supply and acreage for expansion.* [146]

Dana Reynolds, who was a broker and partner in R. T. Houghton Co., an insurance agency, and also the across the street neighbor and best friend of John G. Phillips, was charged with inquiring with the Bartlesville Engineer's Club to make the necessary surveys and figure the costs of impounding water in a lake, finding clean water for showers, and a source of potable drinking water.

Meanwhile, social life at Oak Hill continued apace right through the summer. Around the Fourth of July, C. E. Burlingame gave a very big, though informal, dinner party, and the same weekend Pawhuska guests were treated to a sunrise dance at the club. The occasion of the social festivities was the annual Dewey Roundup on that weekend.

The *Examiner* ran an informative story in August about the number of golfers at Oak Hill, which ended up being a sort of analysis of the condition of membership in the last year of the old country club. The membership was right at 200, having increased about 30 new members over the last year. Of these, about 140 men played golf, and about 20 women also played. They had given up their membership in the Southeastern Kansas Golf Association the year before. Two-thirds of the members were employees of either

Empire Gas or Phillips Petroleum Company: not a surprising statistic. They were proud of the clubhouse expansion of last year, and of the new circulating system at the swimming pool. The social activity at the clubhouse was organized among the women, with a different hostess each week. H. V. Foster was the club president. Jack Warlick was the chairman of the executive committee, Paul McBride was secretary, Henry Thompson was manager and Edith Thompson was hostess and cateress. [147]

The Dinner Dance season began again in mid-September, but inclement weather postponed at least one fall dance. The first big Winter Dance was planned for 22 November, followed the next day by a Thanksgiving dinner for club members. The social routine followed the pattern of the previous year with the series of Winter Dances, interspersed with the usual dinner parties and dances, Rotary banquets, special occasions for out-of-town dignitaries, club meetings, and civic affairs. [148]

Dick Kane recalls another tiny episode from his memories of Oak Hill. He was not there, but his parents came home talking about how engaging Vernon Foster had been on that evening. It is logical that it occurred in the socially active years of 1924 or 1925, after the renovation of the clubhouse. Everyone had been eating dinner on the veranda and something had gotten H. V. telling stories. He held forth for quite a long time, telling tales and pacing back and forth to the high entertainment of the whole crowd.

While normal social life transpired around town, in the summer of 1925, and while Woolaroc was actually in the construction stages, Frank Phillips was giving serious consideration to selling Phillips Petroleum Company. Through the late summer and all fall Frank was in tight negotiations with Blair & Company, who had bought Waite Phillips out earlier in the year. Waite later said that Frank was determined to sell, but suddenly had backed away from the deal, and Waite never knew why. The newspapers reported that the bankers who would finance the deal were not able to agree on terms. Whatever the case, the rumor surfaced late in October and Frank denied the deal soon after. Immediately all systems were go on the country club deal. J. C. Nichols was already in town, giving advice on the grand plan or community development, and by 16 November the new club was assured. The club fathers planned that Oak Hill would continue to be used until the new club was opened. [149]

The Morning Examiner reported that New Years 1926 was fairly quiet around town, and that there were only a few arrests. The Feds didn't show up to perform any raids (that rumor must have put the damper on all the celebrations). Many attended a vaudeville show at The Liberty. The Elks Club and Oak Hill Club had the only big parties in town. The old Oak Hill clubhouse was festooned with its very best showing for that last New Years celebration there. Miniature houses nestled amidst artificial snow decorated the mantle, while frosty icicles and silvery webs were suspended from the ceiling. The light fixtures were New Years bells. Palms, poinsettias, and spruce decorated the hall, and the dance floor was sprinkled with artificial snow. Everyone greeted the New Year with horns and streamers. [150]

As promised, normal social activity continued at Oak Hill throughout 1926, amidst sporadic excited reports about progress in the construction at Hillcrest. The tennis crowd, always marching to their own drummer, chose the summer of 1926 to hold the first "handicap" (whatever that is) tennis tournament in Oklahoma at Oak Hill's courts. [151]

For the last months that Oak Hill was open, the old war horse continued to do its civic duty less and less frequently, so that it can be said that "old soldiers never die; they just fade away." Notice was

published that the golf course would be closed 1 October, but that members could continue to store their gear there until the new clubhouse was opened. The last social function in the clubhouse was the regular monthly dinner and business meeting of the Lafayette Club on Monday night, 4 October. [152] The doors were closed, the pool was drained, the sheds were shut up, the gate was padlocked, the 40 acres were offered for sale by the trustee, O. P. Warlick, and Bartlesville moved on. Don Wilkie opened a nine-hole public golf course north of the Mound a few months later, on property that would eventually become Sunset Country Club. The course was a par 36 of 2,460 yards, with reconditioned sand greens. For two weeks play was free, after that the greens fee was $1.00. The country club property, now silent after the years of happy activity, soon overlooked the new airfield.

Early in the spring of 1929, it became suspicious that something was afoot, with a flurry of business activity at Hillcrest. Suddenly, there was a rattling of bones at the old Oak Hill links, and it was announced that the old soldier would be reopened as a privately owned competing golf club. R. W. Buzan and L. H. Overlees were the organizers. They planned to limit the membership to 150 men, and already had half subscribed. Of course, wives would have full privileges. By the end of March the membership goal had been reached and there was a waiting list, but the old nemesis, spring rains, put off the 1 April opening date. A month later the (old) Oak Hill Club corporation filed the lease of their land to O. P. Warlick. [154]

The original Oak Hill Club made its final appearance in Bartlesville history in 1930 when the sale to O. P. Warlick of their 40 acres was recorded. It was a transaction was the finalization of their 1929 agreement. [155] Two letters, found in National Zinc files by Tom Vogt, explain the terminal transaction. In March 1929, O. P. Warlick, general auditor of the

Empire Companies, who was trustee of Oak Hill Club, wrote James Surdoval, who had replaced Carl Kayser as general manager of Smelter Gas Company, that Ray Buzan had an option to purchase the stock of Oak Hill Club by 1 April. They chose to deal with the sale in this way because there was some problem with the title. [156] He wrote again a few weeks later, on 23 April:

> *Enclosed herewith please find Check No. 2 dated April 1, 1929 for $225.00, same being distributed at thirty cents per share on 750 shares of Oak Hill Club Stock standing in your name.*
>
> *You have been previously advised that an option was given January 28, 1929 to Mr. Raymond W. Buzan to purchase the entire outstanding Capital Stock, namely 20,000 Shares, of Oak Hill Club for the sum of $6,000.00, he to assume all indebtedness of the Club then outstanding. This option expired April 1, 1929 and Mr. Buzan has elected to and has completed payment. This check, therefore, represents final payment to you.*
>
> *In view of the very bad state of repair of the property, I feel that we have effected a reasonably good deal for the same.* [157]

The new Oak Hill Club had a membership that seems to have been entirely different from the original country club membership, now at Hillcrest. We have no idea of the structure of the operation, but it appears there was a sizeable reservoir of upwardly mobile families in Bartlesville who wanted to be members of a country club, but for many possible reasons could not or did not join Hillcrest. In the fall they had a stag party and smoker to plan activities. R. W. Buzon was president and L. H. Overlees was secretary-treasurer. The only members mentioned were Sandy Sanderson, and Art Hill. In November they hired Jess Pappin, recently a successful amateur,

for their pro. They began a program of improvements to the golf course and grounds during the winter. They were most proud of their new grass tees and lengthening of the golf course. This resurrected club was quite active in golf and some aspects of social life over the next couple of years. Their principle civic patron seemed to be the Lions Club. The Depression finally put an end to the chronically undercapitalized club west of town. Warlick sold the property to Mrs. C. A. Means early in 1932. The Means family lived in the clubhouse and operated a public golf course on the old links into the 1940s. [158]

Many old time Bartians are aware of the Oak Hill Club site still, though almost nobody remembers the existence of the even earlier The Bartlesville Country Club, and the businessmen and their wives who worked so diligently and thoughtfully to build their community in the years right after the turn of the century. Bartlesville's country club was clearly understood at the time as a vehicle for community building and upward mobility – an agent of middle class formation, functioning like those associations observed by De Tocqueville a century earlier. Despite the early struggles, the antecedent clubs evolved a vibrant nucleus of activity and membership for development of an effective country club. Much of the original club membership and leadership was still involved fifteen years after the opening of The Bartlesville Country Club, when Hillcrest Country Club finally opened. They had learned many lessons on the trials and errors of the years and they wisely applied them to the new organization. None can tell and few would guess the service to business and community that the little club west of town generated in those halcyon days. The lay of the land was about to change again during the 1920s, and the country club played no small part in that transformation.

2

HOLE NUMBER TWO • 405 YARDS • PAR 4

One of the most demanding holes in the front nine.
This dogleg right requires a perfect tee shot either with a fade, or long hitters
can gamble by cutting the dogleg lined with oak trees.
Second shot must be on line from 5,500 square foot narrow,
split level green with three bunkers.

3

HOLE NUMBER THREE • 396 YARDS • PAR 4
This is a 45° dogleg left at 240 yards off the tee.
Tee shot should stay down the right side and short of the hazard
255 yards from the tee.
Smart shot is fairway wood or driving iron leaving a 155-yard shot
into a 6,000 square foot elevated green.

CHAPTER TWO

The Most Enjoyable Decade in American History:
ORGANIZING *Hillcrest*

*T*he headlines in the evening *Enterprise* screamed:
OSAGE LEASE SALE POOREST IN YEARS. [159]

It was probably no surprise that the sale had been slow. The national economy slumped into a depression in 1921 and oil prices had been soft for months. But Frank Phillips had resolved many months before to find the financing he knew would be needed for Phillips Petroleum Company to prevail at this sale. Frank had a vision of spectacular growth of empire that few other men shared. Since he first scented it at the 1917 gusher in Lot 185, he had worked relentlessly. He spent half of his time in New York, establishing an office for his company with a foothold on Wall Street. He had phenomenal success attracting investors and securing the loans needed for the growth he envisioned, a remarkable feat in a world where a small, new oil company in the boonies of Oklahoma was usually much too risky a gamble for the likes of New York bankers.

For years he had brought potential Eastern investors on excursions with him to Oklahoma. "He conducted them on tours of Phillips operations, often arranging for the visitors to see a gusher, a sight which seldom failed to impress." [160] Still, it remained difficult to contrive the sophisticated sort of entertainment that would help him wow — and woo - his guests. More recently, he had begun to cast about in New York for a suitable country estate that would serve that purpose in the East. Meanwhile, he had memberships in several venerable city clubs, and through his directors, access to some of the most prestigious estates and country clubs in the nation.

By 1920, Frank Phillips was already making regular trips to New York, visiting city clubs, and exploiting years of business contacts in order to raise capital for the growth of Phillips Petroleum Company. In the 1920s, he began a grand plan for the development of the City of Bartlesville in order to develop a local infrastructure to support is increasing needs to promote capital investment. *Courtesy Bartlesville Area History Museum.*

On the chilly morning of 2 March 1922, the crowd that gathered in the Constantine Theater auditorium, just down the street from the budding boughs of Pawhuska's famous Million Dollar Elm, was sparse. Bidding was monotonous, as Col. Ellsworth E. Walters, the famous auctioneer hired by the Osage Tribe worked through the leases on the eastern side of the county, one by one. C. B. Peters did pay $48,000 for lot 198, but the morning auction only garnered a total of $55,000 on 57 tracts before it was adjourned for a luncheon. "At the opening of the sale Superintendent George Wright had announced that a minimum bid of $300 instead of the usual $500 would be accepted.

Col. Walters, the auctioneer, also stated that he would accept a $50 raise instead of the usual $100 minimum raise." [161]

After lunch, the bidding was scarcely more exciting. Finally, around 4:00, the representatives of the big oil companies began to filter into the sale. When Col. Walters finally arrived at the tracts on the west side of the county, he announced that the minimum bid was again $500. Bidding became lively on several initial tracts, the final tallies of a few of the leases in the hundreds of thousands of dollars.

And then came number 23 which with 24, was to be the star attraction. Nobody wanted to start it. Colonel Walters threatened, jocularly, very jocularly, to pass it. Friedman offered to pay him $100,000 for it if he would pass it – and throw in a cigar for Walters personally. Then Raney for Roxana bid $200,000 and the battle was on. The Sinclair and Phillips-Skelly delegations went to the mat. While Walters was seeking a bid of $450,000, one of the Roxana-Marland crowd tried to bid $500,000, but Phillips and McMahon for Sinclair were tilting along very rapidly at $5,000 and $10,000 a crack. Gypsy stepped in at $830,000 – a very sizeable amount and a record total – and soon it went up to perilously close to the million mark. Then McClintock for Gypsy bid the million.

Phillips went right on with it, and so did Mc Clintock. Finally McClintock baulked (sic) with the bid of $1,335,000, at which price it was sold to Phillips for the Phillips-Skelley (sic) companies... [162]

The bidding for Lot 24 was similarly spirited, with a final bid of $1,160,000. That day, Phillips and his partner, Skelly, spent just short of $2,500,000. Despite the lackluster general interest, they had set a new record, the highest price ever paid to lease a quarter section in the Osage Nation. Yes, Phillips Petroleum Company was really on its way, and Frank was already toying with the idea of a resort for his friends at the properties he was negotiating to buy from A. G. and Ruby Williams at Rock Creek near Lot 185. He was becoming increasingly certain that it would be possible to polish up Bartlesville. It was a concept that had elements from the villages around the great country clubs he frequented in the East. Maybe it was even better, on the lines of the upscale planned neighborhoods that his friend J. C. Nichols was so successfully developing in Kansas City.

In a political speech in May, L. E. Phillips alluded to the momentous decisions that had taken place in the previous few months.

"I don't mind telling you," said L. E. Phillips at the campaign workers' conference yesterday, "that there was a time a short while ago, and Mr. Straight is familiar with the circumstances, when the Phillips Petroleum company seriously considered the question of removal from Bartlesville…" [163]

Nevertheless, already the civic-improvement ball was rolling. As construction began on the long-discussed new "convention center," and L. E. Phillips tackled big improvements on his showy new farm south of town, Phillips Petroleum Company announced its largest-ever quarterly earnings. Both Phillips and Cities Service stocks lurched higher as oil prices finally seemed to bottom out in August.

Bartlesville indulged in another period of boosterism, the publicity from which leaves us a self-description of the city at the threshold of the Roaring Twenties. 1922 ended with the highest number of new building permits in the city's history. Meanwhile, a puff-piece in the paper crowed that few places in the state have higher moral or community spirit. "The new residential areas rival in beauty and magnificence

the famous Mission Hills district of Kansas City," might have been a bit of hyperbole, but was a comment that exposes the buzz around town and the city's amazing ambition. The article went on to tout the parks, homes, churches, schools, up-to-date business district, and thriving industries of the town, but some quick arithmetic calculates the remaining shortcomings.

The city has sixteen and a half miles of paving, forty-five miles of sewer mains, and many miles of water mains that furnish the people of the city with water from the Caney River at a short distance from the city. There has always been ample water supply at all times. [164]

It appears that some of the city streets were still being paved, and some parts of the community may not have had sewer service. Above all, the truth is that Bartlesville's water supply was such a chronic problem, it may even be one of the reasons the city, early on, lost the race with Tulsa for oil capitol. A 1908 reference gives a picture of the early problem: "the Indian Springs water wagon is stuck in the mud northwest of the city and there is a shortage of drinking water in the city as a result."

The Caney River water was heavily polluted and salty from careless oil production methods and just plain oil seepage upstream. The river flooded regularly, causing serious bacterial contamination of city water. There was no reservoir, so in drought years the water quality worsened as the river slowed to a trickle. There seemed to be sufficient water for ordinary needs, but there was serious concern about having enough pressure for good fire protection.

At the time, the city was struggling to find a source of better quality water in sufficient quantity to supply the growing town. A new engineering survey of water sources recommended using Butler Creek (which nowadays feeds Lake Hudson). A lot of worry and handwringing went into this expensive proposal, but it was not tried at the time. Instead, Mayor Buck recommended that those lovely homes being built in those fancy new residential areas ought to construct cisterns to augment their good water. Many people bought bottled water for drinking. There was an Ozarka plant just west of the tracks on First Street (Hensley), and families had regular home deliveries of five gallon bottles. As the years went by, many measures were taken to relieve the situation, but problems remained chronic even after Hulah Dam was constructed in 1951. [165]

The earliest sign that there was something rolling around in Frank Phillips' imagination was a note in his diary that he went to the country club to play golf with Murray Doan, L. E. Phillips, Bert Clark, J. A. Johnston of St. Louis, and John Kane on 4 June 1921. (Frank was a poor golfer, and no diary entries mentioned the game prior to this. Likewise, once the country club question was settled, the game was never mentioned again in his diaries.) Probably this specific game was a simple business golf game, coming only days before the Osage Sale, but it shows that Frank was also thinking about the Oak Hill course. Significantly, on 29 June, Frank played at Apawamis Club in Rye, New York, with Phillips' board member, R. H. Higgins, and with John Phillips. [166]

What a comparison! Apawamis Club is one of the oldest country clubs in the nation, right next door to Westchester Country Club, around the picturesque rural village of Rye, New York. Back in 1898, the club lost the lease on its old club site, and acquired a new 125 acre tract of land. The chairman of their golf committee, Maturin Ballou, consulted with the famous professional, Willie Dunn, to construct a new eighteen-hole golf course on the 125 acres, adjacent

to a new shingle style clubhouse. The result was so well done that there have been few changes to the golf course to this day.

The village of Rye pre-existed the organization of Apawamis Club, but by the time of the new construction, there had been marked changes. Many new and attractive homes had been built, and the Boston Post Road had become a splendid highway, flanked by palatial estates. "To the west the old farms had given way to delightful country homes, done in the grand manner. The older families were the ruling element and the tone of life was in a distinctly higher social plane." [167]

The club exercised a strong influence on the social life as well as government of the village. The clubhouse partially burned in 1907, and was significantly expanded when it was rebuilt at that time. It was not a pretentious building, but took its elegance from pride in a traditionally simple atmosphere. By the years that Frank played there, Apawamis was a model of restrained dignity and grace. Frank was used to rubbing elbows with the great capitalists of the time, but playing at Apawamis surely must have given the Oklahoma oilman a sense of having arrived. Returning to Bartlesville in early August, Frank played an evening round of golf with John Phillips on the 2nd, and with his new vice president and old friend, W. N. Davis, on the 15th. A month later, back in New York, R. H. Higgins took Frank to play 27 holes at Blind Brook Country Club. Possibly Frank wanted to know if there was any real benefit in building a golf course that was bigger than 18 holes. Two weeks after that Frank and John Kane played at Rockaway Club. [168]

On a whirlwind return to Bartlesville in late October, Frank had a series of meetings that appear to have concerned country club and/or city matters. On

28 October, R. D. Rood, one of the original Oak Hill stockholders, spent some time in the office. Then, on 1 November, Frank played at Oak Hill with John Kane and John Phillips, and the next day Murray Doar and F. E. Rice, chief engineer for the company, (and some others) were in a conference. He played with his son on the 3rd. Then, on the 5th, he played what appears to be a real business game with F. H. Wicketts. A guess is that these meetings were all to assess the feasibility of suitable renovations at the Oak Hill site. [169]

Frank returned to New York in mid-November and remained until shortly before Christmas. On his return, the meetings and golf games resumed with local men, outside of Phillips Petroleum Company, who would have an interest in the country club and the city, all before the annual meeting of the Oak Hill directors at H. V. Foster's office on 30 December. After the first of the year the meeting pace quickened for a while, including some dinners at H. V. Foster's house. [170] The club was enjoying the success of its 1921 reorganization, but the national economic downturn threatened to eat away at members' financial confidence.

The Depression of 1920-21 was quite severe, but also very brief. In a single year the U.S. prices declined 40%. When appointed Secretary of Commerce in March 1921, Herbert Hoover immediately began pushing for a presidential conference on unemployment. But, by the time the conference could meet and reports issued at the end of 1921, the economy had begun its recovery. Things did not turn around quite so fast in the oil patch. Huge recent discoveries in Venezuela and the Middle East added on to discovery of the Los Angeles Basin fields and new field upon huge new field in Oklahoma and Texas. There was an oil glut, complicated by a failure of demand during the short-lived depression. The situation took a while to work out and prices in the 1920s wobbled up and

down. Bartlesville oilmen were producing a whole lot of oil and selling it cheap. For them, the Twenties didn't really start Roaring until 1925.

It was no time to pitch a big new commitment for the country club, but community leaders were beginning to put out feelers ahead of the coming initiative. [171] Frank was in a fix 'em up mood, stalling until he could see a timeline for his plans, as the various pieces of the puzzle began to coalesce. Jane Phillips did a big redecoration at the Bartlesville home. About the time L. E. was making his revelation to that election committee, some furniture men from Kansas City were at the Phillips' mansion. Mr. Boghasair, a rug dealer from Wichita, took orders for new carpets, and Fred Beecroft had his painting crew at the house all of June. [172] The decision was not unlike the stopgap redecoration at Oak Hill in the summer of 1923.

Meanwhile, Frank's golf games at Oak Hill and visits to exclusive Eastern country clubs continued through 1922 and 1923. Among all the places he visited once, he played at Apawamis Club three times. There must have been something there that caught his fancy. Possibly it was the influence on, and integration of, the club and the village; possibly it was the dignity and understated elegance at the clubhouse and on the golf course.

During this time Frank was still toying with the idea of an Eastern estate. Frank and Jane spent many weekends at the magnificent country estates of their directors, on the yachts of their friends, and at exclusive resorts. In Bartlesville, on 15 February 1923, Clarence Burlingame came over to talk to Frank after dinner about a downtown Bartlesville property that he owned with Ed Maire where the company would eventually build the Phillips Building in 1925. [173] Only days before, the country club's emergency membership meeting had finally publicly voiced the rumors that had been rolling around for months – it was time for a new club. [174] Two weeks later the Phillips executive committee met with an architect and with Tulsa landscape architect, Philip Thomas. Finally, Frank seemed to have decided to make his move. In a single day in April he met with Police Chief Gaston (who sold him some fine riding horses), went over to talk to Grif Graham (who would become his Woolaroc foreman in 1925), then had meetings with Fred Dunn and Dana Reynolds (who were the point men for the polish-up-Bartlesville project). [175]

Way back in 1906, L. E. Phillips was already president of the Commercial Club, the forerunner of the Bartlesville Chamber of Commerce. The Phillips brothers knew the power of the Chamber. Chamber records show that by 1920, the organization was interested in pushing the bond for the new convention center, and a road bond election. They had been deeply involved in country club interests for quite a while. But, like everyone else, the Chamber was suffering from the bad economy, so that late in the year they found it necessary to reorganize. [176] It took a few months, but the new directors were a list of heavyweights: Judge H. O. Caster (Chief Council for Empire), Bert Gaddis, J. H. Hamilton, H. E. Hulen, J. H. Leonard, L. C. Pollock, and L. A. Rowland. Fred Dunn, the president of (Frank and L. E.'s) First National Bank, was elected Chamber president. It appears that Frank was focusing his attention on his still-seminal plans at Woolaroc. He had delegated the things that needed to happen in Bartlesville to Fred Dunn, and the Chamber of Commerce was out in front. Bartlesville needed to complete the civic center, she needed a paved highway to Tulsa, continued progress paving the city streets, improvements at the city water plant, a more up-to-date high school, some sort of higher education, some fancy new residential development, attention to city parks, a general facelift, and the

pièce de resistance – a new country club.

When the Chamber of Commerce finished its reorganization and took the reins early in 1923, they were already involved in the new convention center. Soon, the Good Roads Committee became one of the most active committees. It had been a standing committee of the Chamber since 1906, the successor to a 1904 roads and bridges committee. In fact, it was part of a statewide movement in those early days when often roads were little better than trails. For many years it simply involved conscientious local maintenance of county dirt and gravel roads. At one meeting in 1913,

President Sauer spoke of the need of improving the roads leading to Bartlesville and suggested the plan of setting aside one day to be known as Good Roads Day at which time everybody was to get out and work. [177]

Throughout American history, that is the way it had always been done. In that context, the story of getting the road to Tulsa paved is one of the astounding accomplishments of the period.

In the spring of 1921, Bert Gaddis ran a very aggressive, well-financed campaign for county commissioner. His campaign issue was good roads, and he published some dramatic photographs of the existing bad roads in the county. Commissioner-elect Gaddis was present at the Good Roads Committee meeting of the Chamber of Commerce on 20 June 1921, when the Washington County Good Roads Association was organized. T. J. Ellis was elected president, and Bert Gaddis was elected vice president of the organization at a meeting attended by community representatives of every town from Independence, Kansas to Muskogee, Oklahoma. Only two months later the Chamber was organizing an election campaign to support a $700,000 road bond ($8,591,135 in year 2007 dollars) in early October.

As is often the case, when the bond passed, lawsuits ensued. Finally, the Supreme Court of the State of Oklahoma handed down a decision validating the road bonds early in 1923. Meanwhile, the committee fulfilled its promise to the community by sending teams to investigate various types of hard surface construction around the United States. They learned, to their disappointment, that no federal aid would be awarded to any road that used concrete. In the end, aid or no aid, Dewey Portland Cement supplied the concrete that was used to build the Old Tulsa Road. It was one of the first paved highways in Oklahoma, an amazing feat of community determination and probably political clout. It was an early lifeline from rural isolation and a demonstration that Bartlesville was up to date. [178]

Paving the new highway to Tulsa was one of the most impressive civic initiatives in Bartlesville history. Bonds for the Old Tulsa Road were voted in 1923. Winding from town to town, it was a Roman road built to the specifications envisioned by of Don Tyler, a route out of rural isolation. *Courtesy Bartlesville Area History Museum.*

An adjunct to the Tulsa Road success was the construction of a suitably grand bridge over the Caney River, the entrance to Bartlesville from the highway. The idea of planting elm trees as a World War I veteran's memorial was being promoted by Mrs. Ellen Howard Miller in 1922. That was the year of the American Legion Convention in Bartlesville. In a maneuver that was classic Frank Phillips, betraying his personal interest in the highway, he asked Mrs. Miller if he could help with a more fitting memorial. Next, the Bartlesville legionnaires enthusiastically took up the cause, and the new bridge was a shoe-in. The Chamber studied types of construction and recommended the Bates concrete type. The project smacks of the sort of nice touch that would be suggested by J. C. Nichols. The bridge was completed in 1925. Mrs. Miller was given plenty of publicity credit for her wonderful idea, and Frank Phillips gave the bronze plaques, dedicated to the veterans. [179]

Early in 1921, the Chamber of Commerce took up promotion of the community convention hall that had long been discussed in Bartlesville, supporting a $300,000 bond. The city voted the bond on 6 April 1921. The project languished for months, wrangling over choice of a site and over the mounting expense, until the Kiwanis Club took up the initiative to push for the choice of the Johnstone site. As soon as the bond passed, a committee of women, appointed by the Chamber and headed by Mrs. H. R. Straight insisted on an opera-house style structure. The Chamber also proposed moving the city offices to the new building. Construction of the old civic center was fraught with problems, some of the city commission resigning along the way because of a bribery scandal in connection with the plans. As a consequence, the iron-reinforced balcony was safety-tested by loading it with 1800 sacks of cement to reassure the public. [180]

The Seventh Street Memorial Bridge, dedicated 24 May 1925, became to grand entrance to Bartlesville for traffic arriving on the Old Tulsa Road. Looking east in this photograph, traffic is using the bridge in the weeks before the dedication ceremony when the bronze World War I memorial plaques were installed at an opening ceremony. *Courtesy Bartlesville Area History Museum.*

A colorized photograph of the Bartlesville Civic Center, taken shortly after its grand opening in 1923. It was the fruit of a carefully crafted civic initiative to provide convention center for the cultural events of the city. Over the years it served functions from the arts and education, to revivals, to politics, and even a disaster relief shelter. *Courtesy Bartlesville Area History Museum.*

LEFT: After the deadly Spanish influenza epidemic of 1918, the community realized the need of a fully modern hospital. The Washington County Memorial Hospital was located in the gracious neighborhood just east of the downtown area on park-like grounds that gave a restful, upscale impression. It opened in 1922. *Courtesy Bartlesville Area History Museum.*

By the end of 1923, the newly constructed convention hall, dubbed the Civic Center, was the pride of Bartlesville. It was soon housing civic functions, dinners, concerts, plays, religious revivals, and public school events, meeting a sore community need. By the end of the decade the Civic Center was proudly expanded to house the public library and city offices.

Though not a conceptual part of the 1920s polish-up-Bartlesville group of initiatives, the Washington County Memorial Hospital needs to be mentioned. The pressing need of a modern hospital was realized after the crisis of the influenza epidemic. At the end of the war, local leaders began pushing for a new hospital, as a memorial to World War I veterans. Bonds were voted in 1920 and the hospital was dedicated in March 1922. If the hospital hadn't preceded the other polish-up civic initiatives, it would have had to be one of them.

Bartlesville's High School was finished in 1910, an elaborate-looking four story building with a clock tower, between 10th and 11th Streets, Dewey and Osage (where the Ritz Apartments are today). It was built with an eye to the future, designed for a maximum of 200 students. In 1915, the Bartlesville School Board purchased part of the land for Central Junior High School for $500, and the remaining lot was donated by William Johnstone, who moved his house from that site to 912 Cherokee. When it was completed in 1917, Central was one of the first junior high schools in the state, built to accommodate 450 students. By 1926, the old high school was bursting at the seams with 373 students and the junior high housed 653. The need was manifest. Fred Dunn was chairman of the 1924 school board that shouldered the public need. Once again Frank's point man was the force that pushed through a plan to modern-

Central Junior High School was one of the first in the state, built in 1917. As local population boomed and the need for modernization pressed, addition was made to the building, moving the high school, and even 2 years of junior college to the building which became Bartlesville High School in 1926. Shown from the backside on the east, the 1926 addition can be seen here. *Courtesy Bartlesville Area History Museum.*

ize Bartlesville schools. The $360,000 bond was to essentially double the size of Central, making it a combination junior high/high school. No sooner was the building completed in 1926, than rumors began about the possibility of a junior college on the campus. By the fall semester of 1927, junior college classes began at the High School building. The junior college was still operating successfully as the Depression years began, and College High opened in 1940, including the two junior college years. [181] Then, as now, Bartlesville businessmen viewed a good educational system as a fundamental for community building.

Another contentious initiative was the proposal to change the form of city government. Bartlesville had a mayor and city council. The city manager form of government was a darling of the Progressive Era, and Bartlesville could hardly have been modern if it didn't follow suit. In 1920, the idea was first floated in Bartlesville, with very little opposition at the time.

Again, the idea languished. Finally, in the 1925 polish-up, Frank Phillips put John Phillips' father-in-law, R. L. Beattie, the president of Union National Bank, out front, the Chamber sponsored the proposal, and the American Legion shouldered the campaign. By then, significant resistance had developed to the idea. The rumor mill got going, injunctions and protests were filed. In response, there were many public forums. Frank brought in the big boys from Kansas City, Harvey Walker of the University of Kansas, adding the testimony of a real academic expert in two speeches at the American Legion and the Civic Center just before the April voting. It all added to building the image of Bartlesville as a progressive city. [182]

Bartlesville had a park of sorts from a very early date, on property donated by Jake Bartles. In 1916, the city purchased the property for Johnstone Park from Nellie Johnstone Cannon. The park that was established there became the center of many

Johnstone Park was a work in progress for several years after the property was purchased from Jake Bartles in 1916. By the 1920s a quality park system became a part of the plan to improve Bartlesville. A photo from the era shows the Garden Center and the beautiful landscaping that was the city's pride in Johnstone Park. *Courtesy Bartlesville Area History Museum.*

summertime civic activities for many years. There was also a Westside Park at an early date. Development of both parks was minimal until the time of the polish-up Bartlesville push. The Westside Park soon had playground equipment and a bandstand. Frank Phillips donated the funds to build a wading pool there in 1922. Johnstone Park became a beautifully landscaped showpiece, flanked by the concrete tennis courts (1919), and Memorial Stadium (1926). In addition, Bartlesville had other small parks, maintained by Kiwanis, and Daughters of the American Revolution, and even a tourist court. [183] One would think this was only a routine development in the city, except for a speech given by J. C. Nichols to the Kiwanis in 1925, on a visit in Bartlesville during intensive country club consultation with Frank Phillips. Nichols specifically mentioned the importance of a good park system, doubtless, something he had already pointed out to Frank. [184]

One by one, the Chamber took up many of the community improvements in a period of only four years. They were completed or in the works by 1925; only the water plant remained as a persistent annoyance. [185] Significantly, when all was accomplished, the Chamber agendas returned to more routine daily fare. During this time, the south edge of town was at about 14th Street. The section line that corresponds roughly to today's Hillcrest Drive passed through bottom land south of the city that was dotted with over 100 oil wells, pumped by Bessemer engines in central powerhouses and connected to the wells by shackle rods. On summer nights south Bartlesville families listened to the soft lullaby, "putt-putt-putt skree-clank," from the oil field. Much of the land had been clear cut, some of it under cultivation and other parts in second-growth junk trees, most of it owned or leased by companies such as Cudahy, Central Petroleum, Prairie Oil, and

Wolverine Petroleum Company. Wolverine operated a gasoline plant on 80 acres near today's 16th and Shawnee. It was a perfect place for boys to plink squirrels or hunt rabbits around the pumps. Around 14th Street and Cherokee, there was a rock pit pond where those boys enjoyed hunting frogs. The Y in the river, where Sand Creek joins the Caney produced frequent lowland flooding so that the road through that area was one of those really bad ones that had Bert Gaddis so upset. In the early days there was an old ford, called the Delaware Avenue Ford that was used by cattle drives, but the banks were too steep for vehicles. In 1905 William Johnstone petitioned the court to operate a toll bridge in the Katy Day allotment, which was along the river, north of the present Hillcrest Heights development. The old piering for that bridge can still be seen along the banks of the river, near the present bridge. It was abandoned when the grant ran out in 1925. [186]

In 1923, William and Maggie Easley filed a plat for a new addition at the south edge of Bartlesville on Maggie's allotment land. The plat was a simple extension of Delaware Street straight south beyond 14th Street, with simple rectangular lots on either side of the street, and extra acreage reserved on the west for further development. [187] Richard Kane has personal knowledge that Frank Phillips, in consultation with J. C. Nichols, wanted new development in south Bartlesville to be along the lines of new neighborhoods growing up in Kansas City's Mission Hills. To accomplish this John H. Kane and Clarence Burlingame (one of the local independent oilmen and a contractor and real estate man) formed a partnership called Bartlesville Development Company. In June 1925, John H. Kane bought the Maggie Easley Tract and Addition and the mineral rights; the next month, it was all transferred to the Bartlesville Development

Company. A year later the Maggie Easley Addition plat was vacated and the plat for the Cherokee Hills Addition was filed. The prospective development had very restrictive neighborhood covenants, a typical Nichols method used to insure the attractiveness of the development. The partners had employed Wood and Witten, Consulting Engineers of Tulsa, to draw up the plans. The plat began just south of 13th Street, showing the Y at 14th Street, and the curves in Delaware, Valley Road, and Denver Road, ending just north of 16th Street, and extending to Shawnee on the east and a row of lots west of Hillcrest Drive. Richard Kane says that the curve of Valley Road was specifically a J. C. Nichols suggestion. Hare & Hare, landscape architects of Kansas City conferred with Clarence Burlingame and Fred Dunn on their plans. This addition remained the south edge of town for several years. [188]

The polish up Bartlesville era during the 1920s produced several remarkable civic and private initiatives. They were the result of a grand plan by civic leaders, and principally the vision of Frank Phillips: Memorial Hospital, L. E. Phillips Ranch (later Philson Farms), Civic Center, new water plant, Phillips Building, Woolaroc, paving the road to Tulsa, expansion of Central Junior High School into Bartlesville High School and the addition of a junior college, city park improvement, Memorial Bridge, move to city manager system, neighborhood covenants and zoning ordinances, Memorial Stadium, Cherokee Hills Addition, Hillcrest Country Club, ending with the country club road and the Hillcrest Bridge over the Caney in 1932.

Frank Phillips had been taking mental notes on country clubs in the East since 1921. In the weeks after the Winter Club Dance on New Years Eve 1923, (the all-nighter that went to Frank's house, and ended up at H. V. Foster's house) and before the Osage Sale, Frank remained in Bartlesville, but on returning to the East he resumed his weekend investigations of estates and country clubs. Finally, on 7 and 8 June 1924, there were lengthy private meetings in his rooms at the Ambassador Hotel in New York with J. C. Nichols, John Kane, and Obie Wing (the rising young head of accounting at Phillips and the coach of the Phillips basketball team). It was almost certainly the beginning of Frank's move on the country club development, because two years later Wing and John Phillips met with the executive committee in a meeting that Frank's diary specifically said concerned the country club.

A few days later, in Bartlesville, he conferred with L. E., John Phillips, and Dana Reynolds. [189] The Frank Phillips diaries record another series of meetings that probably concerned city and country club matters. On 12 November 1924, and again on 5 December, H. V. Foster came to Frank Phillips' office for a meeting, a very unusual occurrence. That evening Frank went to a party at Foster's in honor of Henry L. Doherty and other Empire officials who were in town from New York. H. V. and Frank probably had several interests to talk with Doherty about, and one of them would have been to pitch the new country club. Doherty, and hence, substantial Empire support was vital to success of the new country club. Another little series of meetings with H. V. Foster and some other city leaders, including Dana Reynolds, in Frank's office occurred in March 1925. Soon, Dana Reynolds was actively visiting with landowners, gathering up options to the land for Hillcrest Country

Club. Meanwhile, the Chamber of Commerce recommended some sort of action to support the club, and appointed a committee to help secure support. [190]

With the research in hand for land costs and the probability of being able to purchase the property, the Bartlesville Engineer's Club was enlisted to assess the old club and the proposed new site to see which would be most advantageous. The Chamber of Commerce golf committee chairman, Fred Dunn, called a series of meetings with his committee and about 15 other city leaders at First National Bank to weigh the propositions. By 18 June the engineers had some preliminary recommendations. They believed the Oak Hill site could not be made a satisfactory one and the new site was much more attractive and more reasonably priced. They recommended bringing in E. H. Tillinghast or Walter J. Travis, nationally known golf course architects, for consultation. [191] The committee asked the engineers to do further research in water availability and a few other things. By the end of the month enough information had been generated to provide some cost estimates and the engineers were asked to do genuine surveys. [192]

While this activity was going on, Frank Phillips returned to Bartlesville to announce the new seven-story office building and give the go-ahead for starting the work at Woolaroc and an addition on his house. [193] Unbeknownst to the town, he soon began the negotiations with Blair & Co. that nearly resulted in his selling out in the fall of 1925.

On 10 July, E. L. George, of the Engineer's Club golf committee, wrote A. H. Riney, president of the club, with a report concerning the assigned questions. The committee consulted with golf course architect Perry Maxwell concerning the Oak Hill golf course and on the potential of a golf course on the site south of town. In addition, E. L. George looked into

improvements and R. T. Wells checked the water situation at both sites. Before the end of the month, Don Tyler, the Engineer's Club golf committee chairman, filed an undated final report. It was determined that Oak Hill was an unsuitable site for an eighteen-hole golf course. The topography in the immediate area was not suited, the soil was poor, and it was treeless. Cost of adding to the existing nine-hole course would be less, but the resulting course would be unsatisfactory. The site was poorly accessible. Water could only be made adequate at considerable expense. Buildings were in need of extensive maintenance, and adjoining landholders wanted exorbitant prices. The committee recommended moving the club.

A national oil company needed a national office building. The Frank Phillips Building national offices of Phillips Petroleum Company were built in 1925. Only a few years later, the tower that still remains was added. *Courtesy Bartlesville Area History Museum.*

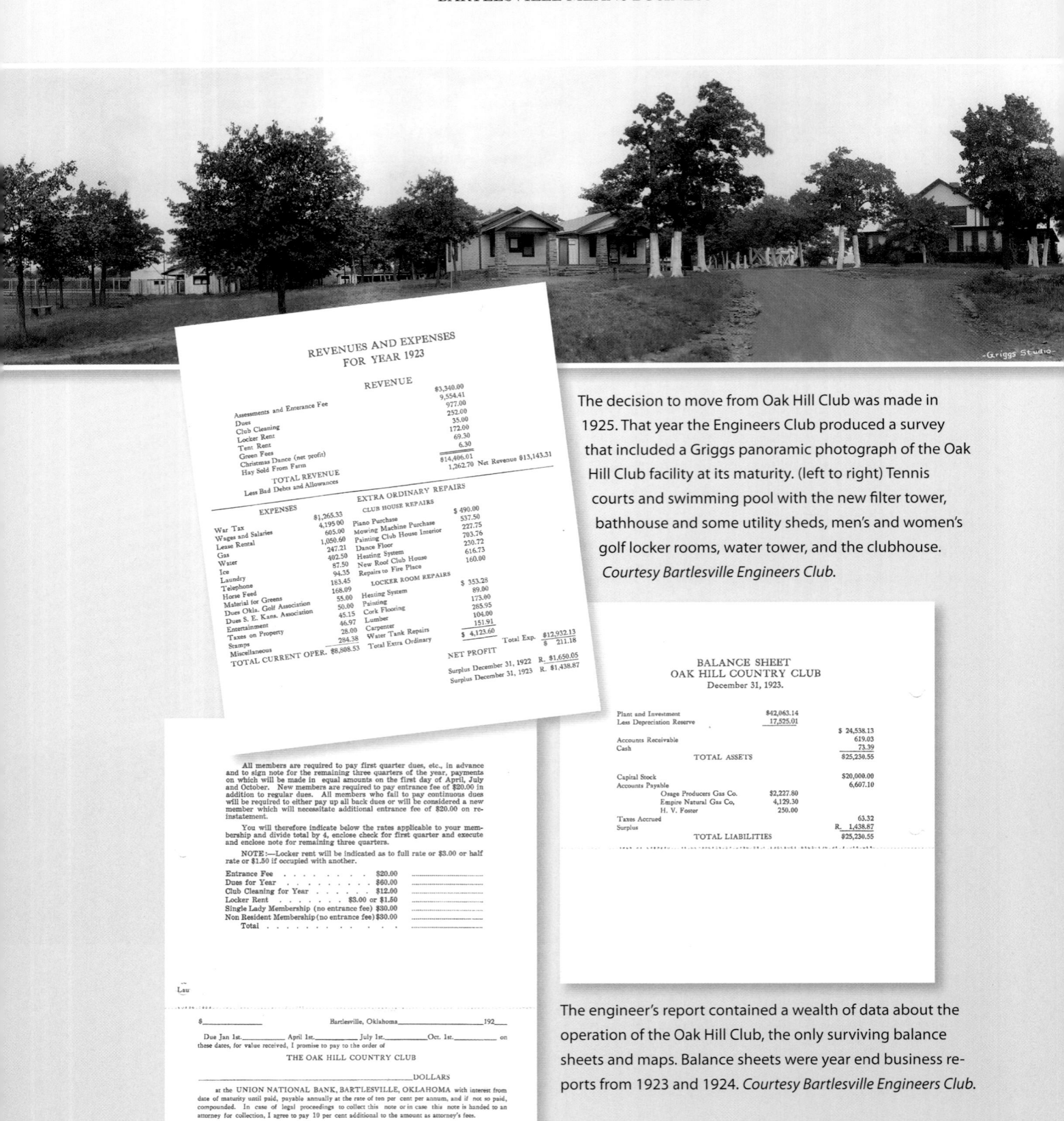

REVENUES AND EXPENSES
FOR YEAR 1923

REVENUE

Assessments and Enterance Fee	$3,340.00
Dues	9,554.41
Club Cleaning	977.00
Locker Rent	252.00
Tent Rent	35.00
Green Fees	172.00
Christmas Dance (net profit)	69.30
Hay Sold From Farm	6.30
	$14,406.01
TOTAL REVENUE	1,262.70 Net Revenue $13,143.31
Less Bad Debts and Allowances	

EXPENSES / **EXTRA ORDINARY REPAIRS**

EXPENSES		CLUB HOUSE REPAIRS	
War Tax	$1,265.33	Piano Purchase	$ 490.00
Wages and Salaries	4,195.00	Mowing Machine Purchase	537.50
Lease Rental	605.00	Painting Club House Interior	227.75
Gas	1,050.60	Dance Floor	703.76
Water	247.21	Heating System	230.72
Ice	402.50	New Roof Club House	616.73
Laundry	87.50	Repairs to Fire Place	160.00
Telephone	94.35		
Horse Feed	183.45	LOCKER ROOM REPAIRS	
Material for Greens	168.09	Heating System	$ 353.28
Dues Okla. Golf Association	55.00	Painting	89.80
Dues S. E. Kans. Association	50.00	Cork Flooring	173.00
Entertainment	45.15	Lumber	285.95
Taxes on Property	46.97	Carpenter	104.00
Stamps	28.00	Water Tank Repairs	151.91
Miscellaneous	284.38		$ 4,123.60
TOTAL CURRENT OPER. $8,808.53		Total Extra Ordinary	$ 211.18

Total Exp. $12,932.13

NET PROFIT

Surplus December 31, 1922 R. $1,650.05
Surplus December 31, 1923 R. $1,438.87

The decision to move from Oak Hill Club was made in 1925. That year the Engineers Club produced a survey that included a Griggs panoramic photograph of the Oak Hill Club facility at its maturity. (left to right) Tennis courts and swimming pool with the new filter tower, bathhouse and some utility sheds, men's and women's golf locker rooms, water tower, and the clubhouse. *Courtesy Bartlesville Engineers Club.*

BALANCE SHEET
OAK HILL COUNTRY CLUB
December 31, 1923.

Plant and Investment	$42,063.14	
Less Depreciation Reserve	17,525.01	
		$ 24,538.13
Accounts Receivable		619.03
Cash		73.39
TOTAL ASSETS		$25,230.55
Capital Stock		$20,000.00
Accounts Payable		6,607.10
Osage Producers Gas Co.	$2,227.80	
Empire Natural Gas Co.	4,129.30	
H. V. Foster	250.00	
Taxes Accrued		63.32
Surplus		R. 1,438.87
TOTAL LIABILITIES		$25,230.55

All members are required to pay first quarter dues, etc., in advance and to sign note for the remaining three quarters of the year, payments on which will be made in equal amounts on the first day of April, July and October. New members are required to pay entrance fee of $20.00 in addition to regular dues. All members who fail to pay continuous dues will be required to either pay up all back dues or will be considered a new member which will necessitate additional entrance fee of $20.00 on re-instatement.

You will therefore indicate below the rates applicable to your membership and divide total by 4, enclose check for first quarter and execute and enclose note for remaining three quarters.

NOTE:—Locker rent will be indicated as to full rate or $3.00 or half rate or $1.50 if occupied with another.

Entrance Fee	$20.00
Dues for Year	$60.00
Club Cleaning for Year	$12.00
Locker Rent	$3.00 or $1.50
Single Lady Membership (no entrance fee)	$30.00
Non Resident Membership (no entrance fee)	$30.00
Total	

Lau

$_____ Bartlesville, Oklahoma_____ 192__

Due Jan 1st._____ April 1st._____ July 1st._____ Oct. 1st._____ on these dates, for value received, I promise to pay to the order of

THE OAK HILL COUNTRY CLUB

_____DOLLARS

at the UNION NATIONAL BANK, BARTLESVILLE, OKLAHOMA with interest from date of maturity until paid, payable annually at the rate of ten per cent per annum, and if not so paid, compounded. In case of legal proceedings to collect this note or in case this note is handed to an attorney for collection, I agree to pay 10 per cent additional to the amount as attorney's fees.

The engineer's report contained a wealth of data about the operation of the Oak Hill Club, the only surviving balance sheets and maps. Balance sheets were year end business reports from 1923 and 1924. *Courtesy Bartlesville Engineers Club.*

They then took Maxwell to other sites, but all preferred the site 2 1/2 miles south of town. The topography was very good, there were many hazards and trees to make a sporty course, and it had a spectacular view of the Caney River Valley, Circle Mountain, and downtown Bartlesville. Water was available in suitable quantity. It was readily accessible and the land could be purchased reasonably. Costs were estimated at $125,000, assuming sand greens and a more modest clubhouse than was eventually built. They were especially interested in irrigating the golf course and maintenance of the swimming pool. Silver Lake and Sand Creek were tested as potential sources of drinking water, and found unsatisfactory, but there was certainly plenty of water for all other purposes. Don Tyler used the opportunity of the report as a bully pulpit to estimate operating expenses and to council budgetary conservatism. As a result, the report is a gold mine of information on costs and income at the time. [194]

Despite Maxwell's consultation on the new site, the club fathers were still thinking of Tillinghast or Travis as the potential architect for the new golf course at the time of the report to the Chamber of Commerce committee meeting on 18 July. That day Frank Phillips called in from his summer vacation at the Broadmoor to offer a matching grant of $50,000 for the new club. It is evident that Frank had big ideas and was willing to ante-up. He knew $125,000 wasn't going to do the job. H. R. Straight indicated that he was willing to underwrite the survey and consultation expense. It was realized that the new club would need to be financed at a hefty stock membership of at least $300. It is interesting to note that the entire site research and planning for the proposed new club was being routed through a committee of the Chamber of Commerce, chaired by Fred Dunn. He had a tiger

by the tail with many of the club activists who were certainly excited about a better golf course and more accessible site, but predictably skinflints about each new-fangled luxury and unnecessary expense. It was agreed that, "the new club is to become a community center." They wanted to be sure the clubhouse and dining room would be a magnet to membership. [195]

> "the new club is to become a community center."
> (*The Morning Examiner*, 18 July 1925.)

While the Chamber of Commerce was making the case for moving the country club south of town, Dana Reynolds was moving on getting the property purchased. On 17 June 1925, W. D. Reynolds bought 60 acres in Section 30 from James M. Thompson of Jackson County, Missouri. On 29 July 1925, Reynolds bought one-half interest in 77 acres, excluding the Delaware Cemetery, from J. B. McDonald. There is no telling if the Thompsons had any idea why Reynolds was purchasing their land. Mr. McDonald, on the other hand, owned a grocery store on 7th Street (now Adams Boulevard). He was the sort of careful man who would have fully known why Dana Reynolds wanted his acreage so badly. [196] McDonald did reserve the mineral rights to his land. On 19 August, Reynolds bought 10 acres from Nellie Knipe, a Cherokee living in Osage County. Not until 24 October did John G. Phillips succeed in buying the other half interest in the McDonald property from Anna McDonald. [197]

The wavering over the correct site choice continued. On 19 October, Frank Phillips stopped by Mission Hills Country Club in Kansas City, probably to look at Tom Bendelow's golf course, and by Kansas

City Country Club to see the new clubhouse designed by Edward Buehler Delk. [198]

Fred Dunn soon brought Bendelow to Bartlesville. Tom Bendelow was a Chicago landscape architect with a big firm, American Park Builders, Landscape Architects and Planners. The committee planned to take him to all the possible sites, claiming to not show preference to any one. Everyone was tantalized by Frank Phillips' big matching funds offer. Everyone understood the agenda. The newspaper referred to him as "a liberal member who is interested in beautifying and bettering the town." The committee of fifteen, including H. V. Foster, H. R. Straight, D. W. Harris, Paul McIntyre, N. D. Welty, Clarence Burlingame, Jesse Leach, Burdette Blue, Bert Gaddis, J. B. Sands, R. H. Hudson, Stewart Dewer, H. E. Hulen, H. H. McClintock, and Fred Dunn met that evening to hear Bendelow's report. He said he found nothing to recommend Oak Hill except the site of the clubhouse. On the other hand, he affirmed the committee's enthusiasm for the new site. [199]

Meanwhile, Cherokee Hills Addition was already attracting new homes. Over the next few years homes were built by:

Stewart Dewer, L. E. Phillips for his daughter, Martha Jane, Paul McIntyre, and Donald Knowlton were Phillips executives who built homes in the addition. Other early homes were built by Clay Smoot, president of First National Bank, C. E. Burlingame for his daughter, Ruth, and John M. Kane. [200]

Clyde Alexander (superintendent of production for Phillips) began plans for the beautiful home he built on the northeast corner of Cherokee Hills Addition, the corner of 14th Street and Shawnee, and as if on cue, the whole town seems to have begun a building and remodeling frenzy.

"Bartlesville is laying aside her pioneer clothes," began the lengthy newspaper article, describing the activity. "New rooms are being added, basements are being put in, the plumbers, and painters, and decorators are rushed." There was new construction everywhere from North Chickasaw and on Maple, to South Jennings, Keeler, Johnstone, Dewey, and Osage. "Many of the older houses in Bartlesville are being re-roofed, while the decorators and painters are being interviewed by owners who mean to keep progressive and give the city a new front." [201] How on earth did the polish-up leaders bring that off! They were determined that Bartlesville would never again be a dowdy little oil boomtown – and it never was.

The Examiner and several other businesses downtown put a map on display, showing the site of the new country club, two miles south of the Hicks Corners store on the paved highway to Tulsa. Tom Bendelow recommended the site to the Engineer's Club partly because of the adaptability of the locality for country homes. The newspaper enthusiastically reported that many country homes were to follow the new country club – reminiscent of the villages and grand homes around the Eastern clubs. A few people already had property near the club site. The Cherokee Hills Addition was considered close and the map on display showed the plan for a curving Hillcrest Drive extension through the lowlands and a bridge over the Caney River to make access to the country club only three-fourths of a mile from town. [202]

Finally, on 29 October, Dana Reynolds got the go ahead from the committee to begin fund-raising for the new club. He spoke to Kiwanis about the new club the very next week. They brought out the big guns the same day. John Kane entertained his brother-in-law, J. C. Nichols, in town from Kansas City, who had been persuaded to pitch the vision to Bartlesville

The new Cherokee Hills Addition was the showplace neighborhood in south Bartlesville with large fashionable homes on curving and landscaped streets. This photograph, taken from the curve where 14th Street joins Hillcrest and Cherokee Drives, shows the Burlingame home, Dewer home, and John Knox home. A quarry and oil fields are to the right. *Courtesy Bartlesville Area History Museum.*

leaders at a big dinner at Oak Hill. Nichols sold the vision at speeches for two other men's groups the next day, before weekending at Woolaroc. [203] The day after that, Dana Reynolds announced that they already had 193 prospective members, and would be closing the membership at 200. He was still pitching the new club.

> *The committee handling the country club securities will sell the shares for the benefit of the entire community. Each share will be sold to directly benefit the holder, for it will represent an equity in a $125,000 proposition in which the entire stock issued is being offered for a total of $50,000.*
>
> *Individual gifts to the club – for all the community – make up the balance.* [204]

The final date for the campaign was set for 20 November. The newspapers excitedly reported in regular articles as new memberships rolled in. They held up the drive so that Burdette Blue of ITIO and A. B. Collins of Empire could return from out-of-town business to finalize sales of memberships in their companies. The excitement heightened when Arthur Gorman submitted his plans for the clubhouse. They were also expecting plans from a Kansas City architect (Delk) and from Tom Bendelow's company.

By 16 November, they had 160 actual memberships in hand, with the final meeting only days out. It must not have been as easy as it sounded in the newspaper. Brooks Spies said "they made" Fred Spies buy two memberships. The job got done right on schedule. On 18 November, they announced there were 177 memberships sold, with 23 reserved for people who were out of town and planned to join. In actual fact there were 144 members, and 33 memberships held for some of the larger contributors who had purchased multiple memberships. When the books closed on the 20th, Burdette Blue was still holding two member

The engineers report had a map of the site of the proposed new Hillcrest Country Club. The map was on display at the Morning Examiner office and at several other downtown businesses. *Courtesy Bartlesville Engineers Club.*

ships for ITIO men, and H. E. Koopman was holding 10 memberships for Phillips personnel, including Frank Phillips and L. E. Phillips. [205]

The new stockholders' first meeting was held in the Civic Center on 4 December with 60 in attendance and 44 proxies in hand. The membership gap had closed and there was already a waiting list of three. The first directors, elected that night, were H. R. Straight, John H. Kane, H. V. Foster, E. F. Walsh, John Phillips, F. L. Dunn, H. E. Hulen, D. M. Tyler, and M. E. Michaelson. They were ready to get to work, with only $5,000 of the additional $75,000 still to be donated.

The new directors wasted no time in electing officers and appointing the committees. Fred

Dunn was the first president, H. R. Straight was the vice president, and W. D. Reynolds was secretary-treasurer. H. J. Holm was selected chairman of the general committee that had responsibility for building the clubhouse and golf course. Holm's committeemen were Burdette Blue (ITIO), Clay Briggs (chief engineer Empire), C. E. Burlingame, Clyde Alexander (operations for Phillips), A. H. Riney (chief engineer Phillips), and John Phillips. They had topographical maps ready in time for the committee meeting to choose an architect for the clubhouse the first week in January. [206]

The new by-laws were accepted. The object had changed from that of Oak Hill and The Bartlesville Country Club.

The object of this corporation shall be to foster and promote athletic sports, games, contests, tournaments, and wholesome and healthful outdoor sports for its members, and to provide opportunities for their social fellowship and enjoyment. [207]

There were three classes of members: active, non-resident, and women. Active members were to be American White male citizens over 21 years of age, living within a 15-mile radius of Bartlesville. They weren't overly rigorous with this standard. For instance, Don Tyler demanded that his wife own his second membership, and several men were tribal members. Active members had voting privileges. It is notable in the context of the 1920s, that the Hillcrest membership was quite inclusive. In a world that ignored non-whites, Mediterranian and Eastern European immigrants, women, Catholics, and Jews, most were represented in the Bartlesville business and professional community, and subsequently as members of the country club. Unmarried women could become Women Members. Non-resident Members and Women Members were not stockholders, but had full club privileges. Annual dues were $2.00 per month for non-resident members, and $3.00 per month for women members. An amendment was added 25 May 1926, providing for Associate Members, who by paying a subscription of $250 could become eligible for Active Membership as vacancies occurred.

By the time the general construction committee officially met, it was clear that the fix was in. Arthur Gorman had already submitted plans for a clubhouse back in November, while A. J. Love of Tulsa also presented plans reminiscent of his design for the Indian Hills clubhouse. The Bartlesville newspapers favored the hometown boy and waxed eloquent over Gorman's plans.

Notwithstanding, Edward Beuhler Delk was chosen that night by the committee. Delk was at the meeting with a résumé, but no plans. [208] It didn't matter. Frank Phillips already had Gorman fully employed on his Woolaroc project, and kept him occupied out there for twenty years. Richard Kane says that his father is the one who originally suggested to Frank Phillips to look at Delk's work for J. C. Nichols

in Kansas City. The committee selection was only a formality. Meanwhile, a work crew was already busy, clearing and preparing the site.

Edward Beuhler Delk was the son of an old aristocratic upstate New York Dutch family, born in Schoharie, New York 21 September 1885. Historic old Schoharie County was once the western edge of the frontier, the land of *The Deerslayer*, of Tory treachery, and of old Dutch and immigrant German settlers, heroes of the American Revolution. During Delk's youth, nearby Sharon Springs was a fashionable resort spa where Southern planters and city capitalists spent summer vacations. It must have been a place of prosperity and tradition for a youngster to grow up. Delk went off to preparatory school at Mercersberg Academy in Pennsylvania, a former Reformed Church seminary with a spectacular Gothic chapel. He attended the University of Pennsylvania, graduating with a degree in architecture in 1907. Afterward, he continued art studies and was part of a studio of the Beaux-Arts Society of New York. In 1909, the Society awarded him the Wallace Prize, with which he toured Italy and Greece to study architecture. Returned to Philadelphia, Delk began work as a draftsman, and by 1913, opened his own practice in architecture. He served in the U. S. Army Air Corps in Europe during World War I, and remained abroad to study city planning at the University of London after the war.

Delk's credentials were those of exactly the sort of man J. C. Nichols must have been searching for. He was the perfect mating of gracious tradition into

Edward Beuhler Delk was the architect of the Plaza in Kansas City, and of many notable buildings and homes, including some of the finest homes in Bartlesville and Tulsa, and of the Hillcrest Country Club clubhouse. *Courtesy Western Historical Manuscript Collection – Kansas City.*

a modern context. His aesthetic senses were impeccable and he was a perfectionist. It was John Taylor of the J. C. Nichols Company who discovered Delk and persuaded him to go to Kansas City in 1920. Ned Delk traveled to Spain with Nichols and to Latin America with Nichols' design team from Hare & Hare Company and George E. Kessler, in preparation for his plan for the Country Club Plaza in Kansas City, the very first shopping center in the United States, finished in 1922. Nichols envisioned it to appeal to the automobile age. Delk worked closely with Nichols' projects in Kansas City, and also planned a number of fine Kansas City residences, businesses, and public buildings. Through Bartlesville's connection to Nichols, Delk planned the original Hillcrest Country Club clubhouse, the 1930 addition to the Frank Phillips mansion, the John H. Kane home, H. V. Foster's La Quinta, the Dahlgren house, and collaborated on Foster's ranch house; he also built Philbrook and Philmont for Waite Phillips, and collaborated on the Philtower in Tulsa.

It is not surprising that a man, steeped in historical tradition, became a disseminator of gracious tradition in architecture. He worked in classic styles, including American Colonial, Tudor, Georgian, Italian Renaissance, Spanish, and Spanish Mission. But he was also very capable in modern styles. He served as local associate for two Frank Lloyd Wright projects in Kansas City. He also did the modern Memorial Campanile Carillon at the University of Kansas, which incorporated Gothic elements, as did the Philtower.

Delk was a good-looking, neatly dressed man of about medium size, with a pleasant, cultivated and gentlemanly bearing. He was very serious about his work. At the time of his death in 1956, a friend described him, "He could be firm, very firm with clients. One reminded him, that he, the client, had a very large investment at stake. 'And I,' said Delk, 'have invested my integrity as an architect." [209]

While Ned Delk returned to Kansas City to produce preliminary drawings for the new clubhouse, the construction committee took up the selection of a golf course architect. As with the selection of Delk, the fix was probably already in. Tillinghast and Travis had disappeared from discussion back in November, and the only candidates who seem to have interviewed for the job appear to have been Maxwell and Bendelow. At the meeting of the golf course construction committee on 11 January, Chairman H. J. Holm announced the selection of Perry Maxwell to do the job. Actually, in some sense, Maxwell had been the one who selected the Hillcrest property in the summer when he surveyed the various sites with the engineers. He said that he would not have been willing to do the project if they had selected a prairie site (Oak Hill). It is interesting to note that Maxwell was recommending sand greens. Maxwell opined that Bartlesville is too far south for blue grass, and too far north for Bermuda. He pointed out that the Bermuda greens at Tulsa and Oklahoma City had been killed out by sleet the previous winter. [210]

Perry Duke Maxwell was born in Princeton, Kentucky in 1879, where his father was a surgeon. Young Maxwell was at the head of his high school class, with gifts in mathematics, a special love for the classics, and impressive powers of persuasion in speech. He entered the University of Kentucky and was embarked on a stellar academic career. Unfortunately, while there he contracted tuberculosis. He tried transferring to Stetson University in the sunnier climes of Florida, but finally was unable to continue school. On doctor's advice, he tried traveling in the South and Southwest, finally settling in Ardmore,

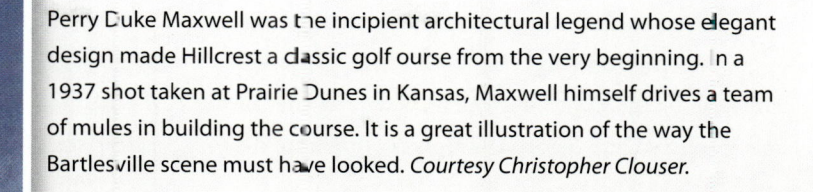

Indian Territory in 1904. There he found a job with Ardmore National Bank, where in time, he became vice president, winning the esteem, honor, and confidence of his associates. During this time, he married his high school sweetheart, Ray Woods, in 1902, and they had four children. Though not a university graduate, Maxwell had a true love of the arts, literature, and philosophy. He was an intellectual by temperment. Dean Monnet of the University of Oklahoma once commented, "Do you know that the more I am associated with him, the more thoroughly I am convinced that he is one of the most learned men I have met." He was also a man of traditional Presbyterian faith, which he lived out in an enthusiastic life of work and family. [211]

It was his wife who first showed Maxwell a Scribner's magazine article in 1909, and encouraged him toward an interest in golf. He took up the game with some enthusiasm, traveling to see Charles Blair MacDonald's National Golf Links in New York. In 1913, he enlisted the aid of his family to begin building a golf course on his own property in Ardmore, dubbing the place Dornick Hills. He read the only book on golf architecture that was published at the time, and traveled to Boston, Chicago, Cleveland, Detroit, Philadelphia, and Pittsburgh to see golf courses. The nine-hole golf course in Ardmore – his very first effort – betrayed his natural genius. [212]

To help himself take his mind off of the sudden death of his wife in 1919, Maxwell decided to travel to St. Andrews in Scotland. There he met the foremost golf course architect of the time, Alister MacKenzie. Back in Oklahoma, in 1921, Maxwell completed Shawnee Country Club, and Rollingwood Hills Country Club in Catoosa. He added the second nine holes at Dornick Hills in 1923, he designed Muskogee Town and Country Club in 1924. He did Twin Hills in Oklahoma City the same year as Hillcrest. [213]

In the next few years, Perry Maxwell completed more golf courses in Oklahoma. After Bartlesville's Hillcrest, he did Ponca City, and Oklahoma City Golf and Country Club before 1929, giving him a solid reputation as a regional architect. In 1931, Alister MacKenzie and Bobby Jones toured Ardmore and Oklahoma City with Maxwell, and afterwards MacKenzie invited him to become an associate.

> *…MacKenzie saw virtually all the characteristics he prized in a course: esthetics, minimal disturbance to the land, and the proper blend of hole lengths and tee sites so as to be equally challenging and interesting for handicap and expert players. Both men preferred that whenever possible , the lie of the land, not the requirements of a mule team or a dump wagon, should determine the location of green sites. Fairways and bunkers were positioned to direct traffic. Perhaps most significant, each believed that par was best protected nearer the hole, testing the short game of handicap players and experts alike. They generally favored broad fairways, shallow bunkers, bounce-and-run aprons, and undulating greens.* [214]

"P. D." put it more succinctly, "It is my theory that nature must precede the architect." He was adamant that no amount of earth moving could redeem a bad choice of site. Perhaps he was thinking of Oak Hill when he said, "The site of a golf course should be there, not brought there. A featureless site could not possibly be economically redeemed." [215]

As the Depression closed in, it is needless to say that country clubs curtailed golf course projects. The great golf course architects of the 1920s soon found themselves in desperate straits. However, after MacKenzie's death in 1934, Maxwell continued to have sufficient work, so that he became the pre-eminent golf course architect of the 1930s. His courses had some hallmarks. For instance, his bunkers all had faces; and he designed the tee box at an angle from the fairway in order to disorient the golfer. The "Perry Maxwell roll" of his greens contributes subtle tests of a golfer's steadiness. [216]

How did Perry Maxwell come to the attention of the Hillcrest selection committee in 1925? For one thing, surely both Frank Phillips and L. E. Phillips knew Maxwell through their old banking contacts, going back to the time when all three men were bankers. His business reputation must have stood him good stead. By then, the word must have been out that Bartlesville was about to build a new country club. Floyd Farley, an architect friend of Maxwell's said, "Perry would smell a golf course coming, hear someone talking about it, and he'd just go there and camp out and sell himself and get the job. He didn't need a set of plans, He'd just go out there and plot it in, by waving his arms and hands." [217] That sounds like an apt description of what seems to have happened in the summer of 1925, when Maxwell did the survey with the Engineers Club.

That's fine, but how did they know that Maxwell was just about to become one of the best? It is significant to us to remember that Willie Brown, who had been the pro in Bartlesville back in the days of The Bartlesville Country Club, and early Oak Hill, was still the pro at Muskogee Town and Country Club, where Perry Maxwell had just built a new golf course. Hillcrest pro, Jerry Cozby, confirms that a usual way of locating an architect candidate would be to talk to golf pros that you respect and trust. Why did Frank Phillips and the Hillcrest leaders choose the then local Maxwell over the other leading architects they were considering? Maxwell himself said, "The minimum of expense is actually my first consideration in designing a course." [218] Eureka! That must be the answer – and how really fortunate Hillcrest has been in that choice.

Maxwell collaborated with MacKenzie on golf courses at the University of Michigan, Ohio State Universtiy, Iowa State University, Crystal Downs. He did remodeling at Pine Valley in Clementon, N.J., work at Augusta National, Vencker Memorial, designed Southern Hills in Tulsa, Prairie Dunes, Ohio State, remodeling at Merion Golf Club in Ardmore, Pa., and Colonial Country Club in Ft. Worth. In all he built 70 golf courses and redesigned 40.

Ned Delk arrived in Bartlesville in a great flurry, with several preliminary drawings under his arm, to meet with the construction committee and talk with club members on 30 January. Delk planned to return the next week with a larger floor plan to go with the preliminary outside elevations that the committee selected. Delk promised final plans by the first of March, but significant details were already known: that the new clubhouse would be two-story Spanish Mission style of light stucco, the dimensions of many of the rooms were set, and even that the kitchen was to be designed by Albert Piele of Chicago. Already Maxwell's crew of twenty golf course construction specialists had arrived to begin clearing. They had been blessed with a mild season, and hoped to get trees cleared and roots grubbed, fairways staked, and grounds and greens started before any winter weather might disrupt their work. [219]

The contract for the new clubhouse was finally let near the end of May. A. E. Todd and Son Construction Company of Independence, Kansas got the job. Todd was a firm that took big jobs. They had built the Shrine Temple in Pittsburg, Kansas, the Memo-rial Hall and Booth Hall in Independence, Kansas, and at the time were building a tourist village at St. Lucia, Florida. Sell-Orr Heating of Bartlesville won the plumbing and heating contract, and Bartlesville Gas and Electric won the wiring contract. They hoped to have the clubhouse built in four months. [220]

By mid-September the club was planning a grand opening for Thanksgiving. Paul McIntyre was chairman of the entertainment committee, planning a big dance. Obie Wing, James Anderson and J. H. Collins, the greens committee, were making optimistic plans for a big grand opening. The handicap committee was Forest Plank, chairman, Newton Holman, and C. B. Fowler. The Tennis committee was no surprise, Fred Spies, chairman, Marshall Hockensmith, and H. C. Price. Stewart Dewer became chairman of the house committee with Fred Haskell and E. F. Walsh, Jr. also serving. Paul McIntyre was chairman of the entertainment committee, with Louise Kane, Floyd Brown Hal Price, and Harry Hewitt as his committee. W. D. Reynolds was chairman of the budget committee, O. P. Warlick and Glen Skinner serving with him. The executive committee was D. W. Harris, chairman, M. E. Michaelson, and W. C. Smoot. [221]

It was a perfect growing season, so that the golfers were already anxious to get on the links for the 10 October opening, and visitors to the nearly finished clubhouse exclaimed at the view from the west veranda and the dining room. The committee was in contact with Bobby Cruickshank and Wild Bill Mehlhorn, and their own homegrown professional, Ed Dudley, to play for the opening. One of the most exciting announcements was that Jimmy Gullane had been hired in Colorado as the new Hillcrest golf professional. [222]

James Gullane was born at North Berwick, Scotland 6 December 1892. The villages of North Berwick, Gullane, and Muirfield, within only a few

Jimmy Gullane, born at North Berwick in Scotland, came to the United States in 1912 to work at Merion Golf Club in Pennsylvania. After World War I, he worked at the Broadmoor in Colorado Springs where he was hired by Hillcrest in 1926 to be the first pro. *Courtesy Bartlesville Area History Museum.*

miles of each other, are the sites of some of Scotland's greatest old courses. It was there that Jimmy began as a caddy and learned the ancient game while working at those venerable old Scottish clubs. He was apprenticed to Ken Sayers who was a celebrated designer of the old hand made clubs.

Shortly before 1912, an American amateur named Hugh Wilson went on a fact-finding trip to the great courses of the British Isles before returning to his club at Ardmore, Pennsylvania to build the East Course at Merion Golf Club. [223] James Gullane, Jr. says his father told him that a Merion member (Wilson) who was visiting in North Berwick talked him into coming to the United States. The new holes at Merion were completed in 1912, the year that Gullane came to the United States, one of that early fraternity of Scotsmen who carried the love of golf to American country clubs.

After coming to the United States, Jimmy worked as an assistant pro and club maker in Merion Golf Club at Ardmore, Pennsylvania until late in the war. Since he was not an American citizen, he was not draftable, but a federal judge in Pennsylvania bargained that if he was willing to serve in the military, he would give Gullane immediate citizenship. Jimmy accepted the offer and subsequently served in the United States Army during the last few months of World War I. He did not serve overseas. [224]

After his discharge in 1918, Jimmy played for a short while on the pro circuit, but was soon hired as assistant golf professional to Jim Barnes and club maker at the Broadmoor in Colorado Springs. When Barnes resigned in 1919, Gullane was advanced to the head pro position. He married Hilda Eleanor Whitley Cooze in Colorado Springs, in 1920. [225]

The oft-told story is that in the summer of 1926, Frank Phillips just walked into the pro shop at the Broadmoor and hired Jimmy Gullane, who by then had been head pro for several years. That is doubtless a true story as far as it goes, but insufficient to explain Gullane's long tenure and the nearly reverent love of the people who remember him. Hiring Gullane was a well-considered move, and Frank Phillips was hardly qualified to make the judgment of his professional abilities.

There is no record in existence to answer how Frank Phillips came to select Jimmy Gullane. There is an insightful guess. Jimmy Gullane was a friend of Ed Dudley, who was becoming well-known in pro circles. Odds are that Frank had asked Ed Dudley to keep his eyes peeled for a man who would be the right fit for the new Bartlesville club. In 1926, Frank even played a round of golf at Ardmore, Pennsylvania, maybe to check references. [226] The Phillipses vacationed most summers at the Broadmoor, so that Frank, and probably other Bartlesville men, would have had opportunity to observe his prospect, and possibly take a lesson or two. In 1945, at an anniversary dinner given for Jimmy, Stewert Dewer claimed that he was the last of a committee sent to hire the pro. The process was probably a mixture of the above factors. You can bet that Gullane was hired only after the most thoughtful consideration.

He was a short, stocky man. Everyone who remembers him says he had such a heavy brogue that he was often hard to understand. He was a kind and gentle man, soft-spoken, and very affable. Art (P.) Gorman chuckled, remembering him always carrying his golf bag with only four clubs, no strap, and slung over his shoulder like a gun. (Often he didn't even carry a bag, just clubs in that manner.) Jimmy, Jr. recalls that he said you don't need all those clubs - but he carried a full bag at tournaments. He was a wonderful character. Several men, who were boys then, remem-

ber him as a patient and watchful teacher. He made a point of interacting with the high school golf team when they were practicing at the club, giving pointers and encouragement.

He was a very fine golfer. While he was the pro at the Broadmoor, he held the world record for the longest drive, 470 yards on 25 April 1925. Always self-effacing, he told his son that the drive was downhill, and besides, the air was thin at that altitude. Nevertheless, fellow pro from the time, Floyd Farley, remembers that Jimmy was noted for his long drives. In 1932, he won the Oklahoma Open with a score for the 72 holes of 304; in 1933, he won with a score of 296. Jerry Cozby remembers a comment made to him by Ben Hogan. Hogan explained that in 1933, he played the Open at Hillcrest with Jimmy Gullane. He made a 7 on the 18th hole, but Gullane beat him by one shot. Hogan fixed Cozby with his steely eyes, and said, "Hell of a hole, isn't it?" [227]

Gullane never shed his Scottish deference to club members. Frederick Drummond remembers asking him, one time, to just call him Frederick. Gullane's response was, in his thick brogue, "mi mother always said to say 'yes, mi'lord' and 'no, mi'lord' and then I won't get into trouble." He did not feel especially comfortable socializing at the club. He did attend Calcuttas and other golf tournament social events as part of his job. In the years after World War II, there was a social shift toward more egalitarian attitudes, but Jimmy never made that adaptation. It is probably just as well. Jimmy, Jr. says that he attended some of the open tournaments around the state with his dad, and the partying was pretty heavy among the gallery attendees. The pro also enjoyed taking young Jimmy to the Tulsa Airport on his day off, just to watch the airplanes come and go.

Gullane's pro shop was always old school – the

sort of place where you made your own clubs. It had a single counter on a concrete floor. In the corner stood his display, a Hot-z leather bag holding a set of Kroydon clubs. In the old days, that was the way all golf shops were, but as time went by, up-to-date country clubs had complete merchandizing lines of golf equipment and clothing. In 1953, Hillcrest built a new big pro shop next to the bathhouse at the swimming pool, which they wanted stocked like a modern shop. Gullane was not up to that task and they replaced him. He became director at the driving range that Don Wilkie started at Sunset Golf Course especially for him. He was there for a few years, then went to Pawhuska as pro until he retired in 1973. Art Gorman says that after he retired, he was a devoted walker who would get up early in the morning to get in a good hike to start the day. After his wife died, son, Jimmy, says he became quite a lady's man, stopping on those walks to help out some of the widows in town with their yards or around the house, and striking up acquaintances. About his only hobby outside of golf was that he enjoyed bird hunting. He died in Bartlesville in 1986. [228]

The Oak Hill golf course was to be closed on the first of October 1926, in anticipation of the Hillcrest opening on the tenth. Balmy Indian summer promised a glorious grand opening of the new golf course, after a perfect growing season. On 25 September, a massive Canadian cold front roared through like a freight train. Snows flew in the northern states, and the Mid-West had torrential rains and flooding. Bartlesville suffered an exceptionally early killing frost. Behind the weather front, the rains started, with flooding in several parts of the state. It was bad enough by the 29th that mail service was hampered in the entire region. Rainfall in Bartlesville since the frontal passage was a little over 5 inches by 1 October. That night it began raining – heavily – amounting to 7 inches on Friday, and it kept falling. By the next day, the Caney was out of its banks. The rise of the river in the night, without warning, was devastating to people in low-lying areas in the north part of the county. People had to be rescued from trees, and cars were marooned on the highway. The murky waters swirled through Johnstone Park and north Bartlesville, carrying trees, and livestock, and the flotsam of people's lives along with it.

The Flood of '26 was the worst flood in Bartlesville's history. It delayed the grand opening of the country club, as the city became an island. Bartlesville civic leaders rallied their resources in a notable flood relief program that was a remarkable and effective use of years of accrued social capital. *Courtesy Bartlesville Area History Museum.*

The flood of 1926 was the worst flood in Bartlesville history until the flood of 1986, but with far fewer public relief services. The city was an island, water in homes and businesses in low-lying parts of town. Refugees were housed in private homes and more than 100 were sheltered in the Civic Center, with more rains for days, keeping the river levels high. Routed out of bed in the middle of Saturday night, E. L. George, secretary of the Chamber of Commerce, manned the organization of emergency management. The carpenters union was called in and those men built the boats that were required to rescue dozens of families, supplies simply being donated on the spot by the local lumberyards. Police Chief Turner gave orders to shoot anyone seen looting, and the American Legion veterans took up the jobs of patrolling and a lot of rescue work.

The very first day, with the water still rising, community leaders organized an emergency flood relief to help the displaced families. George P. Gentry, chairman, with F. A. Bisel and H. E. Hulen headed the relief committee that was formed immediately. Within a day the committee took an organized structure. John H. Kane was head of ways and means, George Gentry was head of relief work, Mrs. R. D. (Ethel) Rood was chairman of health and sanitation, W. K. Blachky was secretary, and Howard Cannon was treasurer. The committee was working with the city/county government emergency chairman Keith Clevenger. "The immediate emergency will pass in a few days… a systematic check-up of sanitary, health, food, clothing, housing, and financial conditions in the flooded areas of Washington County will be necessary." [229] E. L. George, L. A. Rowland, and Howard Cannon took the message to the various men's civic groups in town, and the women's organizations shouldered their share toward the $30,000 goal.

The Salvation Army had immediately taken up organizing meals, clothing, and bedding. The new Memorial hospital was headquarters for public health measures, including a vaccination program. In the schools, teachers were instructed to be vigilant for signs of illness. The measures successfully headed off a typhoid epidemic that had previously been the hallmark of local floods. As the waters began to recede by Tuesday, there was left an army of big black hungry fleas. Finally after ten days, refugee families began to return to their ravaged homes. Almost as if symbolizing the end of an era, on 12 November, the Lannom home, Belle Meade, the old gracious mansion southwest of town, burned. It had become neglected with the diminuition of family fortunes in the passage of years, now nothing remained but a lifeless shell.

The Opening

There was certainly no gala opening of the Hillcrest golf course on the tenth. It was probably just as well. The flooding had delayed work on the clubhouse and the opening was now pushed well beyond the Thanksgiving deadline. The first photographs of Hillcrest Country Club appeared in the Enterprise on 20 November 1926. The just completed clubhouse was finally ready for Faber Studio of Tulsa and their decorator's ministrations. The golfers lockers were at last installed and keys were mailed out.

All was nearly completed and awaiting the grand opening, and the newspaper breathlessly reported on their tour of the clubhouse 4 December. The Thompsons moved into the manager's apartments in the second floor of the clubhouse that same weekend. Edith Thompson continued in her position as cateress, preparing to take reservations for the big party in a few days. [230]

Bartlesville residents journeyed out south of the city over the summer months of 1926 to inspect the progress of the beautiful new country club. Frank Griggs took a series of photographic portraits of the finished clubhouse shortly before the grand opening. These file photos appeared in the newspaper articles about Hillcrest for the next few years. This quartering shot was taken from the front, giving a view of the terrace colonnade on the south side. *Courtesy Hillcrest Country Club.*

"The purpose of the Club was for community betterment." (H. V. Foster, *The Morning Examiner*.)

Just before the grand opening, the finance committee made its report. The golf course had come in just under budget of $23,000. So far they had spent $130,000, and they were in line for a final budget of $165,500. Equipment for the clubhouse was budgeted at $22,000 and was funded by Empire, Phillips, ITIO, and a few individuals. Land and leases cost $14,524, water, telephones, and electricity cost $10,730. The tennis courts were not built yet, but budgeted at $1,369. [231] They still wanted to build stables, a swimming pool, and Turkish baths. Their objectives would not be reached until the road and bridge were built from the south of town to the club. [232]

On Friday night, before the grand opening, the men who got it done had a celebratory banquet. It was, indeed, a convocation of Bartlesville's oil barons, there to congratulate themselves. "Kings of oildom [vie] with working committeemen in passing the credit for the new Hillcrest country club," began the article that listed the men who shouldered the financ-

ing of the new club. They were proud to turn the club over to the members, debt free. It's no wonder, Frank Phillips, H. V. Foster, L. E. Phillips, Herbert R. Straight, John H. Kane, Clarence Burlingame, Burdette Blue, and Clyde Alexander contributed more than $90,000 to the project. Frank Phillips said, "the inspection of the club house was an inspiration to him and he had nothing but pride in it, and gratitude toward those who put the job over. He said it compared with the best of New York City's country clubs and was a credit to any city." The men at the dinner are a listing of the arm-twisters, plotters, and planners, the backbone of that golden age. Rounds of speeches arrived at the consensus that the purpose of the club was community betterment that it would bring happiness and prosperity to Bartlesville. Frank Phillips noted that it was the biggest tangible asset in Bartlesville. [233]

"the biggest tangible asset in Bartlesville…it will bring happiness and prosperity to the city." (Frank Phillips, *The Morning Examiner*.)

It is a monument to ideals and hopes made possible by a group of representative men who typify the spirit of Bartlesville from the day it started its growth from a struggling village on the banks of the Caney to the most modern city of its size anywhere. [234]

The biggest social event in several years drew guests from far and wide. Most of the out-of-town members came, as did many old members from Oak Hill and earlier who had moved away. Bartians made sure to be home for the party; for instance, Mrs. O. K. Wing came in from New York in the nick of time. More than a hundred members and their guests arrived for dinner in the sparkling new dining room. "Bartlesville strutted its stuff, evincing an entirely justifiable pride in its citizens." There are no descriptions of the ladie's gowns worn at the opening of The Bartlesville Country Club, but the newspaper admired the "display of feminine finery…gowns of unusually attractive design and costly materials made their debut at the dinner hour and on the dance floor."

It must have been very fine. Joanne Bennett says she still has the dress her mother, Mrs. A. H. (Margaret) Riney, wore to the gala opening dance at the country club. Margaret was a tiny young woman of only 27 then, with flaming copper hair and startling blue eyes, married to a rising young Phillips executive. Her dress was a fashionably short copper-colored silk shift with short sleeves and a round neckline, entirely beaded with copper-colored beads in a random design. She wore matching-dyed silk pumps and carried a beaded copper-colored bag. It was a dress to be saved for the generations. The Campbell Serenaders played into the night, the new clubhouse festooned in holiday trappings, for the most elegant event that Bartlesville could conceive. [236]

The ballroom was "carpeted with a handsome blue chenille seamless rug thirty feet by forty feet. About the hall and placed near the walls and in front of the many Spanish doors are a number of davenports covered with the bright hued Spanish stripes which are repeated in the draperies to the doors. High windows of colored glass add warmth to the spacious room. Just over the large mantle place on the west side of the hall is hung a priest's cape fashioned of red plush and just below it on the mantle is a Spanish ship model between two statues which further the decorative effect." *Photo from the 1931 Oklahoma Amateur Golf Tournament catalog, Courtesy Mike May.*

On 5 December, *The Morning Examiner* article announcing the opening of the new clubhouse wrote an excited description of the extravagant décor:

NEW COUNTRY CLUB IS OPEN TODAY

Public Invited To Club House Opening Next Sunday Afternoon

The Hillcrest Country Club which is receiving its final touches in decorating and fixtures will be officially open Saturday night for the club members. The public is invited to the club house opening from the hours of 12 to 1 o'clock Sunday, December 12.

Bartlesville visitors to the new country club this week express both astonishment and delight with the elaborateness of the club house which is said to surpass in beauty any country club in the state. It stands far back from the Tulsa-Bartlesville highway just south of the city, and is surrounded by shrubs newly set out, greens, and natural scenery. Spanish style of architecture is used throughout the club home in the detail of design and interior decorating which was done by the Faber Studios in Tulsa, expressing the popular mode for Spanish design.

There is a richness in coloring, material and arrangement used in the reception rooms. Importations from Spain and Italy create an effect of beauty.

Black Marble Floor

Upon entering the club through the large, heavy oak carved doors one steps onto the gray and black marble floor. Spanish wrought-iron gates close the entrance hall from the interior hall and reception room. Two handsome tapestries cover the wall facing the entrance door. Tall wrought-iron stands and Spanish lanterns which are importations, stand at either side of the entrance. Chairs, davenports, tables, and benches are strictly Spanish in design. Low tables of wrought-iron frame have decorative Italian tops of baked tile. These are placed in the ladies lounge and in the large dance hall at the ends of the davenports covered with brightly colored striped cloth which is typical of Spanish homes.

To the right of the entrance hall is the ladies' lounge with its soft coloring in rose and green glazed chintz overdrapes which created an effect of restfulness as well as beauty.

The main part of the country club is the large dance hall which is carpeted with a handsome blue chenille seamless rug thirty feet by forty feet. About the hall and placed near the walls and in front of the many Spanish doors are a number of davenports covered with the bright hued Spanish stripes which are repeated in the draperies to the doors. High windows of colored glass add warmth to the spacious room. Just over the large mantle place on the west side of the hall is hung a priest's cape fashioned of red plush and just below it on the mantle is a Spanish ship model between two statues which further the decorative effect. On the opposite wall from the mantle place is an Indian print hanging, and just below the mezzanine floor are two large Spanish banners used for decorative purposes in Spanish homes.

Beautiful Lighting Effects

The hall is lighted by four beautifully decorated lantern lights down the center of the ceiling. The covering for the lights is a heavy cloth similar to the material used in the draperies, but is hand painted with figures of toreadors and Spanish motifs. Through the center of the lantern shades a sunburst effect is created by the blending of the many colors. Wall lights are of hand painted parchment. Two large clay oil jars of natural colors are at each side of the fireplace and are filled with oak leaves whose dull autumn colors add a distinct note of comfortable hospitality to the hall. The fire place is five by six feet and two heavy rustic irons stand in front of the opening.

Floors throughout the club with the exception of the entrance hall are of hardwood while the dance hall is hard marble [this is an error, the dance floor was wood]. The walls are of stucco, distinctly Spanish.

Wrought-iron benches built low and covered with red plush are placed about the club house while tall iron stands with imported Spanish iron lanterns over the lights are used. Emblems and coat-of-arms in wall plaques add a note of distinction to the reception hall.

Large Dining Room

The dining room is equipped to accommodate three hundred and fifty guests. Furnishings are in black and red. Two iron stands with candles stand at the Spanish gates which divide the reception and dance hall from the dining room. Several candelabra are placed down the length of the room which [illegible] long open doors leading off to the portico on the west. At the north end of the dining room is a large drop Spanish lantern light with hand painted design.

The mezzanine floor overlooks the dance hall. In visiting the country club our attention is immediately attracted to the path which is entered from the dining room and reception hall. Tall jars, fountain and statue are placed about the court around the stone path.

Smoking Room For Men

The men's smoking room in the basement of the club house just below the ladies lounge in the east end of the house is brightened with wide Spanish awning stripes which cover the ceiling over the stairway and the ceiling of the room where the furnishing is in similar but of less elaborate style than used in the first floor.

The kitchen and locker rooms are completely furnished for convenience of the users. Mr. and Mrs. Henry Thompson have their apartments on the second floor of the club. Mrs. Thompson will continue to have charge of the catering for the club members just as she did at the Oak Hill country club. [235]

Hole 1. "FORE" A good starter. Drive should have a slight hook, second a spade or mashie to a medium sized green guarded by three traps and several trees. *Courtesy Mike May, 1930 HCC Tournament Catalog.*

Hole 2. "TESTER" A well named hole. Tee shot must be as unerring as the freeway is very narrow and closely guarded by trees. A creek to catch topped balls. The green is small, well trapped and elevated behind. Owing to wind can be played with anything from 3 iron to spoon. A well earned par. *Courtesy Mike May, 1930 HCC Tournament Catalog.*

Hole 3. "BOTTLE NECK" Tee shot must be true out of wooded bottle neck to a left sloping fairway. Second shot either long iron or spoon to an elevated green. Deep trap front left. Long shallow trap paralleling the right. *Courtesy Mike May, 1930 HCC Tournament Catalog.*

Hole 4. "LITTLE JOE" Drive is usually into a head wind down a narrow tree-lined fairway, where a hook or slice costs strokes. Green is very small and severely trapped with approximately an eight yard opening. *Courtesy Mike May, 1930 HCC Tournament Catalog.*

Hole 5. "EREEZY" A good one-shotter. Green must be carried as there is creek in front for topped balls. Trees to right and left. Five yawning sand traps. Prevailing cross winds make this a very sporty hole. *Courtesy Mike May, 1930 HCC Tournament Catalog.*

Hole 6. "RELAXATION" A fairly easy par. A good tee shot leaves a pitch to a large green surrounded by three traps and some trees. *Courtesy Mike May, 1930 HCC Tournament*

Hole 7. "LAKE" A blind left dog leg hole. Tee shot must be well placed, tall rough for the hook, trees and rough for the slice. Second about a 3 or 4 iron over lake to a very tricky green. Two traps to right, trees to left. *Courtesy Mike May, 1930 HCC Tournament Catalog.*

Hole 8. "GAMBLER" Hillcrest's shortest and most dangerous par 4. Very narrow and left sloping fairway. Out of bounds for any slice. Woods and creek for the hook. Best played with a long iron and high pitch over water hazard to a small well-trapped green. *Courtesy Mike May, 1930 HCC Tournament Catalog.*

Hole 9. "SUNSET" A long drive, to a left sloping fairway leaves a blind second with a spoon or long iron to a large open green. Traps to right and left for balls off line. A well earned par. *Courtesy Mike May, 1930 HCC Tournament Catalog.*

Hole 10. "WESTWARD HO" Dog leg to right. Slice tee shot is in orchard or tall rough. Second, a long brassie, if hooked is a dense woods. Then a pitch to a well-banked green Three traps to catch wandering balls. *Courtesy Mike May, 1930 HCC Tournament Catalog.*

Hole 11. "SCENIC" Hillcrest's most beautiful hole. Tee shot must be accurate. Second a spade to a 4 iron. Green is very small, well banked and severely trapped. Any bad shots will result in penalty. *Courtesy Mike May, 1930 HCC Tournament Catalog.*

Hole 12. "GRAVE YARD" A long iron or spoon, all carry to a green much higher than the tee. Fairway slopes severely to right. Out of bounds and trees to left. Deep traps and trees to right. Trees behind. A well earned three. *Courtesy Mike May, 1930 HCC Tournament Catalog.*

Hole 13. "LUCKY" Slight dog leg to left, requiring a long well placed tee shot. Wood paralleling entire left side of fairway. Out of bounds to right. Second, either 3 or 4 iron shot, over a very deceiving fairway to a large undulating green. *Courtesy Mike May, 1930 HCC Tournament Catalog.*

Hole 14. "CLIMBER" A long straight drive to a left rolling fairway. Trees and bunkers for a slice shot. Water hazards for hooked or topped balls. Second, a long iron to a small green, trapped right and left and scattered trees. Up hill all the way. *Courtesy Mike May, 1930 HCC Tournament Catalog.*

Hole 15. "WOODLAND" Dog leg fairway cut out of dense timber. Drive must be straight and long. Second, a long iron or spoon as you are usually bucking a head wind. Green is small and well guarded. The elusive ball will cost strokes on this hole. *Courtesy Mike May, 1930 HCC Tournament Catalog.*

16

Hole 16. "MIDGET" While this is Hillcrest's shortest hole, by no means is it the easiest to par. An exacting mashie to mashie niblic shot over a lake to a small narrow green completely surrounded by trouble. *Courtesy Mike May, 1930 HCC Tournament Catalog.*

17

Hole 17. "DOG LEG" Hillcrest's most extreme dog leg hole. A well placed drive with a slight left bend leaves a mashie or spade to a well banked green. Two yawning traps to the right. Woods to left and behind. *Courtesy Mike May, 1930 HCC Tournament Catalog.*

18

Hole Eighteen.jpg: Hole 18. "HIGH BALL" Hillcrest's classic. A drive must be high and straight, down a long ribbon-like fairway. Tall rough and out of bounds for a hook. Trees for a slice. Second, a long exacting brassie, should be played on left side of fairway. Third, a long pitch. Water hazard paralleling right side of fairway and in front of green which is guarded by two traps. *Courtesy Mike May, 1930 HCC Tournament Catalog.*

In the next weeks, the bridge clubs settled right in. Bartlesville partiers lost no time either. The Halcyon Club had the clubhouse the very next weekend for a dinner and huge bash. Harriett and Lois Straight gave a Christmas dance for the younger set. The Foster girls were hostesses for many girlfriends before the holiday dance on Monday night, then John M. Kane hosted a dance and buffet for high school and college friends on Tuesday. Ruth Burlingame was hostess of a dance for the same set on Wednesday night. The dances resumed right after Christmas. Martha Jane and Lee Phillips had Tommy Johnson's orchestra from the University of Kansas play at a pre-New Year's Eve dance and supper. The next day the adults took over when the two Rood families hosted a gala holiday dance and buffet supper. The Campbell Serenaders played, and the buffet table was bedecked with the most beautiful flowers. Of course, the New Years dance and midnight supper at the club was the season's finale. There were a number of dinner parties at the clubhouse before the dance. The dining room was arranged with long tables, decorated with red poinsettias and red taper candles. An orchestra from the University of Kansas played the very latest tunes for 350 party-goers. [237]

1927

The news was good all the way around. Cities Service decided to move its financial offices to Bartlesville. A new company bought the city water facilities from the George Priestly family, and there were promising plans to upgrade the plant. [238] Bartlesville had a new zoning board, another sign of the progressiveness of the city. The national economy lurched into high gear, heated up by the Federal Reserve's easy credit policy, pumping new money into the economy. Bartlesville business was booming. E. L.

George, secretary of the Chamber of Commerce, told the newspaper, "I want to say right now that things never looked brighter in the city's history and never before has Bartlesville entered the New Year with such continued expansion and prosperity eminent… Bartlesville is solid from within and from without." Amidst the euphoria, Frank Phillips topped off the season with a company office party for 600 from 4:00 to 12:00 on 16 January. In the early evening a California orchestra played, then after a buffet supper, Campbell's Serenaders finished the evening. [239]

In an interesting episode after the March board meeting, the directors offered the Boy Scouts use of approximately 15 acres of land west of the golf course, next to the river, with a "splendid swimmin' hole." [240] Nothing seems to have come of the offer. The golf season opened with a bang, starting with a Nassau tournament on 19 March. V. T. Broaddus' team was in the lead the next week, but heavy rains slowed down the play. It was W. J. Neumann's team that enjoyed the dinner put on by the losers on 5 April. The fun continued through May with a series of exhibition games. The team of Jimmy Gullane and V. T. Broaddus lost to the Tulsa Country Club team on 8 May; our pro, Gullane, lost to Phil Hessler, the pro at Oakhurst Club in Tulsa, but the Hillcrest team won on 24 May; and Gullane scored 163 in the state open, well back from the 152 winning score. There was a flag tournament for Memorial Day. [241]

Meanwhile, the Izaak Walton League had its convention in Bartlesville the first week in May. The feature entertainment on the weekend was trapshooting at the Bartlesville Gun Club and a barbecue at Woolaroc. On Thursday afternoon, Dr. and Mrs. Rood entertained the visiting ladies for tea, with governor Henry S. Johnston their honored guest. Afterwards, they took the governor and his entourage out to see

V. T. Broaddus was Hillcrest's golfing hero of the era. He was the owner of Bartlesville Stationary. Broaddus takes a practice swing, watched by 3 other unidentified men. *Courtesy Bartlesville Area History Museum.*

the new country club. Governor Johnston was so impressed with the club that he insisted on inspecting the entire building; the whole time his aide was begging him to "make it snappy." He ended up being late to his next engagement in Tulsa. [242]

It was the summer that aviation finally came of age. On 22 May, Bartlesville families got up to the news that Lindbergh had safely landed in Paris after his historic intercontinental flight. Lindbergh instantly became a national hero. Phillips' development of their Nu-Aviation fuel was incredibly timely. The company took a long-term lease on the flying field owned by Bert Gaddis west of town, opening up Bartlesville's airport. A Tulsa-Kansas City airmail delivery route, via Bartlesville, was soon opened. The Woolaroc, sponsored by Phillips, won the Dole Race to Honolulu on 17 August, setting off a series of celebrations and Phillips publicity campaigns back in Bartlesville. It is fascinating to read of new feats of daring, as week after week, new advances were made

and records were set, all reported to a wonderstruck and breathless American public.

Both Kiwanis and Rotary celebrated ladies' nights with dinners at Hillcrest in June. DAR had its annual Flag Day luncheon at the club. On the Fourth of July, Bartlesville crowds flocked to the new Sani-pool on North Seneca, as 2500 attended the picnic at the West Side Park, given by the Spanish-American War Veterans, and a medal golf tournament was played at Wilkies (now Sunset Golf Course). That evening C. E. Burlingame gave a big dinner-dance at Hillcrest to honor F. L. Maire. ITIO was declared the largest producer in the state that same week. On the first of August, Empire was reorganized into one major company, with three operating subsidiaries, significantly increasing Bartlesville's position in the company.

The golf season continued unabated. Qualifying rounds for the men's club championship started in June. The club team visited Oakhurst again, and this time won the match. In mid-July, Adam Johnstone

Another of the civic improvements was the Sanipool, opened in 1927. The name may have been an illusion to the unfiltered pool at Oak Hill that caused so much consternation, the only pool in town at the time. Previously, in hot weather people swam in the Caney River, or some of the local creeks and ponds. *Courtesy Bartlesville Area History Museum.*

emerged the new club champion. The state qualifying rounds for the national professional golf tournament were held at Hillcrest during August. "Bartlesville golfers are telling everyone to watch their own Jimmy Gullane…Gullane recently negotiated the course in 65 for a new record, going out in 31 and returning in 34." Shortly all of their braggadocio came true. Hillcrest's Jimmy Gullane and member Bill Feist won the handicap tourney on Saturday with a 66 even though it had been raining. Then, on Sunday, "Gullane unsheathed his lethal putter, his deadly driver, a screaming brassie, to say nothing of a miracle working set of irons," his winning score 34-38-72. [243] Bartlesville could be proud of the prowess in Oklahoma golf that Gullane had brought to their country club. They were also enjoying the respect for their community, afforded by the networking of a first class country club among the other big players in the region.

Leo Johnstone (Sr.) emerged as a new contender in the handicap tournament early in September. This created new excitement about the keen competition for the Foster Cup competition that began the next week. Meanwhile, V. T. Broaddus made the semi-final round for the International Petroleum Exposition tournament in Tulsa. It was an unusually exciting convention, with Art Goebel and Charles Lindbergh as honored guests at the IPE festivities that year. Kiwanis and Rotary played their annual golf match at Hillcrest on 2 October, followed by a dinner. Warren Stone and C. H. Caldwell were the semi-

final contestants for the Foster Cup, but the winner was not reported. Ed Dudley came through town, on the way to the national meet in Dallas. Gullane and Dudley were matched in that contest at Cedar Crest Country Club a few days later, with Dudley defeating Gullane 8 and 7. Jimmy Gullane brought Joe Kirkwood, noted for his trick shots, to Hillcrest for an exhibition round, with Phil Hessler of Oakhurst, Gullane, and Clarence Clark of McFarland Country Club in Tulsa. "I had heard about you having a fine club," exclaimed the impressed Kirkwood, "But I was astounded when I saw how pretty it really is." Kirkwood had only one misgiving, "I don't understand why such a wonderful course is without grass greens." [244]

Hillcrest women golfers scheduled their championship early in September, but the qualifying rounds were delayed by rain into October. Mrs. Carl Wood won the F. L. Dunn trophy, defeating Mrs. F. B. Plank. Right away qualifying rounds started for the women's handicap tournament. Mrs. A. C. Leike won from a field of sixteen competitors. It was as exciting as the men's play of the summer. "A play-off in a golf tournament is nothing unusual, but seldom are two necessary, and three extra matches are almost unheard of." [245]

The first annual tennis tournament was started on 8 October. The upper bracket pitted Fred Spies against Jake May, J. C. Duffendack with R. L. Gordon, and V. T. Broaddus with Obie Wing; the lower bracket was Hal Price, F. E. Rice, Carl Kayser, Paul

Dahlgren, J. M. Hockensmith, M. E. Michaelson, Warren Stone, and Don Tyler. The final round pitted Hockensmith against Fred Spies, but as seems to have repeatedly happened with tennis reporting, the results weren't published. [246]

There were big changes in the clubhouse management in the fall of 1927. Albert (Tom) Moore came as the new manager from Chicago. Moore brought along H. Y. Bostick, who had previously worked at golf clubs in New York and Chicago, as superintendent of service, and Frederick Thompson, who had 15 years experience in big city clubs, as the new chef. [247]

The social season opened with a banquet given by the Rotary club for the city's schoolteachers. A buffet dinner was punctuated with speeches. The highlight was school board president L. A. Rowland's talk which derided "iconoclastic and cynical literature of the day and made a strong plea for practical idealism." There was a comical one-act play, a Rotary songfest, and it all concluded with dancing to Campbell's Serenaders. The McClintocks entertained a newly-wed English couple with a party for 300 guests in October. The highlight of the party came when Woolaroc manager Grif Graham crashed the dance with a troupe of square dancers, dressed in bright silk shirts and big cowboy hats, and put on a Western dance exhibition to fiddle music. The American Legion gave an Armistice Day dinner-dance. The clubhouse was decorated with American and French flags, and artillery shells. The menu was a parody of Army chow such as peas Argonne, whizbangs, salad Pershing, potatoes à la Mause, and victory ice cream. Empire entertained newspapermen to brag about their new reorganization, and a pipeline they were building from Amarillo to Wichita. Amidst it all, there was the usual routine of bridge parties and luncheons. [248]

The first Winter Dance was on Thanksgiving weekend. The society editor for the newspaper mused about the busy social calendar for the holiday season. With the college kids due home soon, the social schedule was already filling right up. "Elaborate plans are being carried out by the hostesses and the season is anticipated to be an unusually gay and festive one after a long period of rest society has indulged in for the past season." The college set planned several parties in their homes, but big December social events included the Kiwanis banquet, a dance given by the H. R. Straights, a dance given by the Burlingames, a dinner-dance given by the L. E. Phillipses and the John Kanes, and a large party given by the Munchmeyers. [249]

As had come to be expected, the country club New Years party was the place to be in Bartlesville at year's end. More than 100 couples had dinner reservations at the club and several large dinner parties were given around town before the dance began. Frank Phillips was entertaining his Oklahoma City friends at Woolaroc and they attended a large dinner party at the Phillips home before they came to the Hillcrest party. Among them were Attorney General Dabney, corporation commissioner Fred Capshaw, Supreme Court justices Fletcher Reilly and Charles W. Mason, and Walter Harris, editor of the *Daily Oklahoman*. Bitter cold gripped the city so that the newspaper reported 1 pistol shots and the whistle at the smelter as the only signs of revelry around town. The cabaret party at Hillcrest was another matter. The clubhouse was bedecked to fit the season: holiday greenery and festive balloons, with floodlights in the mezzanine strafing the dance floor. Members of the club, posing as characters who might be at Tex Guyman's New York cabaret, mingled in the crowd. Obie Wing was Tex Guyman, Ralph Morton was Al Smith, Keith

Clevenger was Will Rogers, J. E. Holm was movie star Marilyn Miller. Tommy Johnson and his Serenaders from Lawrence, Kansas were the dance band. [250] At the end of its first year, Hillcrest was fulfilling its function in the community. It was a focal point for important civic and business events and a social arbiter in the city, while it was at the forefront of Bartlesville boosterism at golf tournaments around the state and for important visitors to Bartlesville.

1928

The winter social season in 1928 continued with some notably interesting activity. A Saturday night dinner in February was turned into a Dinty Moore supper with an Irish menu. The Phillips University coach and his assistant were guests at a stag dinner before the big basketball game in February. Another Saturday dinner had special music. Vocal solos, a quartet, a sing along, piano selections, and a violin ensemble were the program. Some popular Saturday dinners also featured Southern barbecue, and Chinese night. On Chinese night they also featured an "official government war picture made by Eastman Kodak company," and several reels of comedy. In May a group of Wichita boosters were in town, and of course, they were entertained at a banquet at the club. [251]

Beginning in 1927, women's golf activities in Bartlesville began to pick up steam. By 1928, women's golf had become exceedingly active. Bartlesville women were organizers of the new Northeastern Oklahoma Women's District Golf Association. Meanwhile, Hillcrest women began to have golf luncheons each Wednesday. On 4 May 1928, they had a whopper. Two hundred ladies from northeastern Oklahoma country clubs attended the luncheon in connection with the golf meet here. Hillcrest women competed actively in tournaments all over the state and consis-

tently had good success. The northeastern Oklahoma championship was played at Hillcrest in October with Mrs. Carl Wood emerging as the victor of a hard-fought series. Mrs. Wood also retained the club championship that month. [252]

Men's golf followed the long-established patterns. J. H. Collins made a good showing at the state pro-am at Lakeside Country Club in Oklahoma City in June. The Foster Cup handicap tournament was played in the summer with W. J. Neumann the surprise winner. The several trophies for men's and women's play were all displayed at Home Savings and Loan. During the second round of play for the club championship in September, J. H. Collins set the amateur course record with a 68. The next week, he broke his own record with a 67. There is no justice – V. T. Broaddus beat Collins in the final round for club championship. Jimmy Gullane had a good year, winning the Oklahoma pro golf championship at Indian Hills, for the second year. A few days later, Ed Dudley and V. T. Broaddus played Gullane and Jimmy Collins in an exhibition game at Hillcrest. Gullane and Collins won. [253]

The first match of the club championship tennis tournament was reported, but nothing more appeared. It is clear that the tennis players were active, as they had been for many years. It can only be concluded that they had no one in charge of publicity for tennis events, and maybe they didn't especially want the publicity.

1928 was a presidential election year and there was unusual local interest. Senator Charles Curtis of Kansas emerged as part of the pack early in the year. Curtis was half Kaw and had strong ties in Oklahoma. But really there was no contest. Herbert Hoover had been preparing for the run for a long time. Mrs. Rood was a delegate to the Republican convention, support-

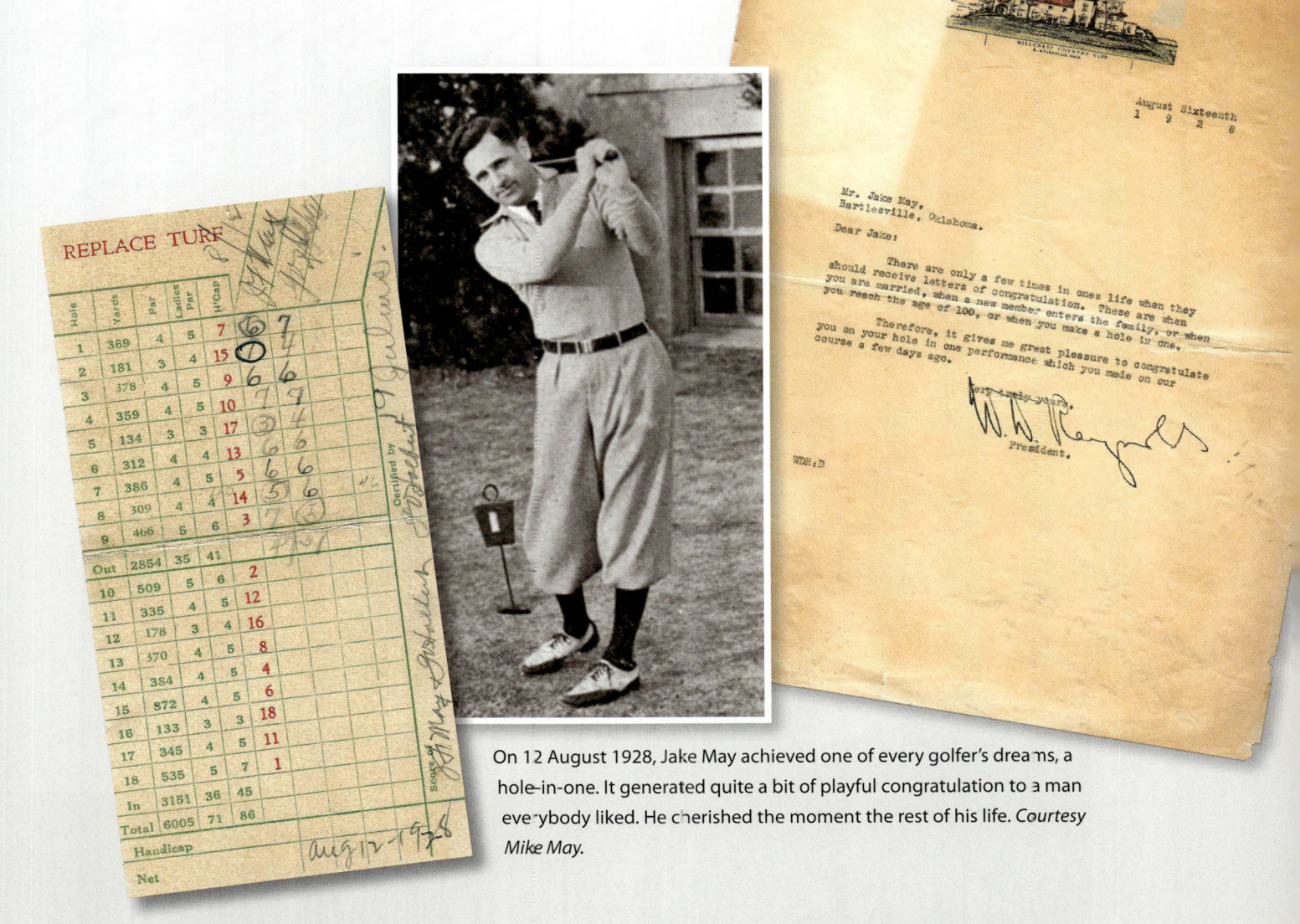

On 12 August 1928, Jake May achieved one of every golfer's dreams, a hole-in-one. It generated quite a bit of playful congratulation to a man everybody liked. He cherished the moment the rest of his life. *Courtesy Mike May.*

ing Curtis. As soon as it became evident that Curtis was a lost cause, Bartlesville Republicans threw in their lot with Hoover, even if Coolidge did somewhat acidly refer to him as the "wonder boy." After all, the Democrats nominated Al Smith, a man with close ties to New York machine politics. In the end, Curtis became Hoover's vice president and Bartlesville oil men had a heady period of some clout in Washington. While the political primary season raged, another battle swept the state. After the Flood of '26 and the terrible flooding in the Mississippi Basin the next spring, there had been several serious floods in the Bartlesville area and two very wet summers. A malaria epidemic followed on the heels of the swarms of

mosquitoes, hatched in the whole central watershed. It was worst in Southeastern Oklahoma, but Bartlesville residents fought the battle with quinine and by watching for standing water. General Electric announced the development of television. It all sounded just too fantastic, like going to the moon. [254]

There was a normal routine of civic functions over the next few years. Kiwanis had a regional meet at the club. A highlight of the summer of 1928 was the Empire company picnic for 1000 at Hillcrest the first week in June. In September, they hosted the Quarter Million Club, 161 crack Doherty salesmen from the securities division. A Hillcrest breakfast was a feature of the whirlwind awards that day. Empire

Gas company social requirements were fast taking the character of a company headquarters since the reorganization. The U. S. Bureau of Mines entertained H. H. Hill, their chief petroleum engineer from Washington, at a large Hillcrest dinner-dance. The reporter made a point that punch was served, so the local men may have decided not to let Washington know just how wide-open things were out here. Rotary again entertained the local schoolteachers. The state convention of Federated Women's Clubs met in Bartlesville and DAR, UDC, and PEO were hostesses of a tea at Hillcrest for them. The American Legion had another successful Armistice Day dance. VFW furnished transportation to Civil War veterans who wished to attend the observances. Rotary had an inter-city dinner-dance at Hillcrest. [255]

Thanksgiving was the formal opener for the social season with the first winter dance. It wasn't long before the social schedule for the holiday season was stacked up. A new kind of event was an "all day" party. The H. V. Fosters gave an "all day" party on 27 December, and the Dahlgrens gave one on the 28th. Of course, the New Year's party was the season highlight. Evidently the cabaret party of the previous year was a big success, so they did a variation on that theme. This time they had Russian and Hawaiian dancers, a silhouette cutter, and star-gazers. It was a cold night in Bartlesville, and the newspaper said, "the New Year got a warm welcome from everyone but the weatherman." [256]

The Empire Company had a picnic for 1,000 employees at the Hillcrest picnic grounds on 7 June 1928. *Courtesy Bartlesville Area History Museum.*

1929

Since the organization of Hillcrest, there had been no public reporting of the election of officers or business at the club. On 10 January 1929, there was an announcement of the annual meeting where there would be election of new directors, and a proposal to increase capital stock from $50,000 to $62,500. We already know that there was a waiting list for membership; perhaps they wanted to relieve some of that pressure. A month later the membership met for a stag dinner before the meeting. H. V. Foster was elected to fill L. M. Tidd's unexpired term as director, and Paul Dahlgren, M. E. Michaelson, and G. A. Thompson were elected to regular three-year terms.

The capital increase was routinely approved. The directors elected Dana Reynolds the new president, F. C. Brown was vice president (to replace L. M. Tidd who had moved), and W. C. Feist was secretary-treasurer and became chairman of the entertainment committee. The committee of Hillcrest Country Club women, Mrs. Harry Carpenter, chairman, Mrs. C. H. Caldwell, Mrs. Paul McIntyre, and Mrs. E. F. Walsh presently announced spectacular arrangements for the next winter dance and a series of bridge parties for the spring. Meanwhile the Northeast Oklahoma Women's

On the cold, crisp New Years Eve, 31 December 1928, the club had a costume party featuring Hawaiian dancers and Russian dancers. The group photo with men in hula skirts on the right show it was a whale of a party. L. E. Phillips was one of the Russians dancers, shown on the left of the group of four. *Courtesy Bartlesville Area History Museum.*

Golf Association met for at a luncheon at Hillcrest to plan for the season. Something was afoot. This was a lot of activity for that time of year. [257]

On the same day that the club ladies announced their bridge parties, R. W. Buzon took a lease on 40 acres adjacent to the Oak Hill Club property. The next day, Buzon and L. H. Overlees announced the re-opening of Oak Hill Club with a proposed membership of 150. Now the race was wide open and the keen competition was on. The very first event that the Hillcrest ladies scheduled was a corker. The St. Patrick's Day dance had been on the books for a long time. Now they added feature entertainment. Advance publicity built expectations high. The famous orchestra, The Clicoquot Club Eskimos, was on tour nationally, ahead of their NBC broadcasting season. The group was outfitted with new fur coats. Their manager said, "They are not really so warm as they look. I hope our music is a lot hotter." The place was packed with over 400 members and many out of town guests. The clubhouse was decorated all in green. Buffet supper was served from 11:00 to 1:00 in the billiard room, the tables elaborately decorated with all gold and green. The Eskimo band enlivened the dancing with their special acts. [258]

Right away the entertainment committee scheduled a new Easter event, a club tradition that still continues today: the first Easter buffet and Easter egg hunt for the children in the afternoon. A special program of Easter music, played by the Webber String trio was planned to follow the egg hunt. In the meantime, continuous spring rains had predictably shut the road to Oak Hill so that the big grand opening was postponed. It didn't dry out until June, but Buzan announced that the 150 memberships had been subscribed and they were getting the old place in shape. Hillcrest still didn't relax. In April, their regular

dance became a "prospective membership spring dance." There was a buffet supper, Campbell's Serenaders played, and Misses Elizabeth and Elise Seaton entertained with specialty dances. Trouble must have developed in the kitchen over the summer. A new chef and an experienced head waiter were hired. New cold storage was installed, and it was announced that the dining room would be open from 8:00 A.M. to 8:00 P.M. every day. [259]

There wasn't another peep from Oak Hill for months. Meanwhile, the HCC women's golf season got off to the same sort of active season they had enjoyed the year before. The Northeastern Women's Golf Association had bi-weekly matches at the member clubs. Mrs. Carl Wood was a finalist in the fall tournament of the regional ladies golf organization. Wednesday was ladies day at Hillcrest. Besides golf, there was also tennis play and a luncheon. The women's handicap tournament started in September. Mrs. Carl Wood won the final round, defeating Mrs. Paul Dahlgren and Mrs. A. C. Leike. Mrs. Fred Gleason won the consolation prize. The club women's championship ended with a surprise winner. Mrs. James Ball defeated Mrs. Wood at the last minute. Mrs. John H. Kane won the Class A flight, Mrs. W. E. Feist and Mrs. Callie Joe Lee won the consolation prizes. Awards were given at the final golf luncheon of the year. Mrs. Ball received the club cup. Mrs. Wood got the handicap cup and ringer cup, Mrs. Wickard received the improvement cup, Mrs. Dahlgren received Wednesday's low score, and Mrs. Carl got Wednesday's low putt. [260]

Men's golf tried to get underway in April with a special Nassau tournament of teams from Phillips, ITIO, Empire, and local businesses. Empire finally won after two weeks' delay because of rain. Hillcrest hosted a citywide tournament, including Oak Hill and Sunset in mid-July. The trophies were displayed at Laderer Clothing Store. Predictably, the final round on 11 August was a contest between Hillcresters, J. H. Collins and V. T. Broaddus. They had a tournament for the caddies. Clarence LaPrade was the winner. The club handicap championship play began in September. Tucked in the middle, Kiwanis shellacked Rotary in their annual golf tournament. V. T. Broaddus retained his title in the handicap tournament at the season's close. [261]

Rotary and Kiwanis had their usual banquets at Hillcrest during the year. One of the biggest civic events of the year was a visit by the Kansas City Chamber of Commerce "Goodfellows." Bartlesville rolled out the red carpet with a dinner-dance at Hillcrest. Buffet dinner was served in the main dining room and tables were set on the west veranda, with a magnificent view of the Osage Hills on the west and the city to the northwest." Rotary again sponsored a party for the schoolteachers at the club at the beginning of the school year. In October, Oak Hill was the site of the Lion's Club ladies' night program. The competition was still on between the competing clubs, but it appears that constituencies were beginning to emerge. AAUW had its state convention in Bartlesville in November. Hillcrest did its bit with a Friday night banquet, and Oak Hill entered in with a Saturday luncheon. Meanwhile, Oak Hill hosted part of the Armistice Day dance; the other parts were at the park pavilion and the Maire Hotel, with a dinner served at the Civic Center. [262]

The polish-up Bartlesville agenda was still functioning. At the September meeting of the board of the Chamber of Commerce, John Holliman gave the report of the good roads committee about the progress in paving the highway to Nowata, improving county roads and bridges. There was mention of the

work being done to secure a bridge connecting the country club district with the south end of Bartlesville.

Meanwhile, it was announced that the renovations that had been in progress on the Maire Hotel for the last year or two were finally concluded. The $150,000 rebuilding and redecoration included installation of a new coffee shop, dining room, kitchen equipment, new mezzanine balcony, refurnishing, carpet, and plumbing. The New Maire Hotel dining room was at last opened. The New Maire Hotel threw a splashy grand opening after Thanksgiving weekend. The elegant hotel was a definite part of the new cosmopolitan image of Bartlesville.

The most elegant parties were festooned with flowers. In this photo from the 1920s, the mezzanine opposite the fireplace is filled with flowers, and flowers are draped from the light fixtures and around the window treatments. *Courtesy Bartlesville Area History Museum.*

L. E. Phillips was that year's sponsor of the annual city beautiful campaign. The Boy Scouts were helping out with the city-wide clean-up, and Phillips had secured the cooperation of a Tulsa nursery to help with new plantings in town, a nice epilogue to the redecoration frenzy of a couple of years earlier. On Christmas Day, it was announced that Dana Reynolds' home at 1200 Cherokee was the winner of the first prize given by the Business Men's Association for the most attractive and original Christmas lawn display. Burdette Blue at 300 E. 11th was the second place winner. Finally, the regional planning board met and approved the location and route for the road and bridge that would connect the south of town to the country club. [263]

The 1929 fall social season began with a club dinner dance with a Japanese theme. Soon there was the beginning of a flood of parties that accompanied the wedding of Martha Jane Phillips to John Wilbur Starr on 26 October. The wedding preoccupied all Bartlesville social activity for a month. They did tuck in a regular dinner dance, and after the wedding, they had a big Halloween party. The ladies' bridge committee at Hillcrest scheduled a regular program. The big season opener was the formal dance on Thanksgiving weekend. The special entertainment was Gardiniere, Gardiniere, and Señorita Carmen, an Argentine dance act from New York. The Christmas season was the familiar round of big parties. The society editor summed it up:

The social calendar for the past week was filled with an unusual number of large affairs, most of which were dances and centered about Hillcrest Country Club.

The first, Monday evening, was a dancing party given by the Misses Corinne and Irene Gray. The younger college group and the members of the

young social set of the city were guests at the affair.

Tuesday, the club entertained the children of the members at the annual Christmas party, and Wednesday the members of the club gathered for a sacred concert.

Thursday evening John Miller Kane entertained about 200 guests at a dancing party at the club.

Friday afternoon Mrs. D. M. Tyler honored her daughter, Miss Helen Tyler, at a charming tea-dance, and Friday evening Mr. and Mrs. William E. Davis and their daughter, Miss Elise Rhett Davis, entertained with another dancing party at the club.

The last of the week's large parties was given Saturday evening when Mr. and Mrs. C. W. Doornbos and Miss Marie Foster were hosts to about 225 guests, including a number from out of town, at a dance at Hillcrest... [264]

The big fashion news of the season was that hemlines were going down – way down. After a decade that rose well above the knees, the winter styles were mid-calf length. Oak Hill and the American Legion cooperated to schedule two New Years' benefit dances for $1.00 admission. As usual, the Hillcrest New Years' party was the place to be. The 400 guests included many friends from out of town. The featured entertainment was another dance act, and the music was by Simmond's Recording Orchestra. The next morning, Mr. and Mrs. Carl Minnig hosted a goose breakfast for 125 guests, a carefree finale for "the most enjoyable decade in American history." [265]

The decade of the 1920s was one of the most prosperous and confident that America has ever experienced. The decade opened with the Depression of 1921, a natural economic correction of the industrial boom and inflation of the war years. The Depression was very sharp, and very short. Afterwards, the

Twenties saw the longest housing boom on record, the whole-cloth construction of the automobile industry and its attendant industries, including petroleum, also the home appliances and electronics industries, aviation, and broadcast, and the phenomenal growth of many existing industries as diverse as insurance and higher education. More than that, "during the 1920s, in fact, America began suddenly to acquire cultural density." [266] To match our industrial and technical prowess, we produced new serious literature, plays, art, and music all our own. The music of the 20th century rose from the American jazz age.

In this America, Bartlesville fully participated. It was a lucky city atop petroleum reserves, filled with an entrepreneurial spirit and citizens of imagination and boldness. By 1920, the smelter activity in Bartlesville was waning, but the children of the immigrants who worked at the smelters were employees in the offices of Empire Gas, ITIO, the new rising Phillips Petroleum Company, and dozens of smaller companies around town. The decade opened with Hal Price developing a new kind of pipe welding on which he would build Price Pipeline Company; and the decade would close with the development of Armais Artunoff's submergible pump that would be manufactured at REDA Pump Company.

All of this growth in industry was supported by an active Chamber of Commerce and two decades of social capital, built on an infrastructure of active civic, social, and religious clubs. The city eagerly took advantage of the prosperity to build progressive roads, neighborhoods, schools, public utilities and parks, and better government. One of these projects has been shown to be the country club. The country club has functioned as an important and primary instrument in building the social capital that undergirds business growth.

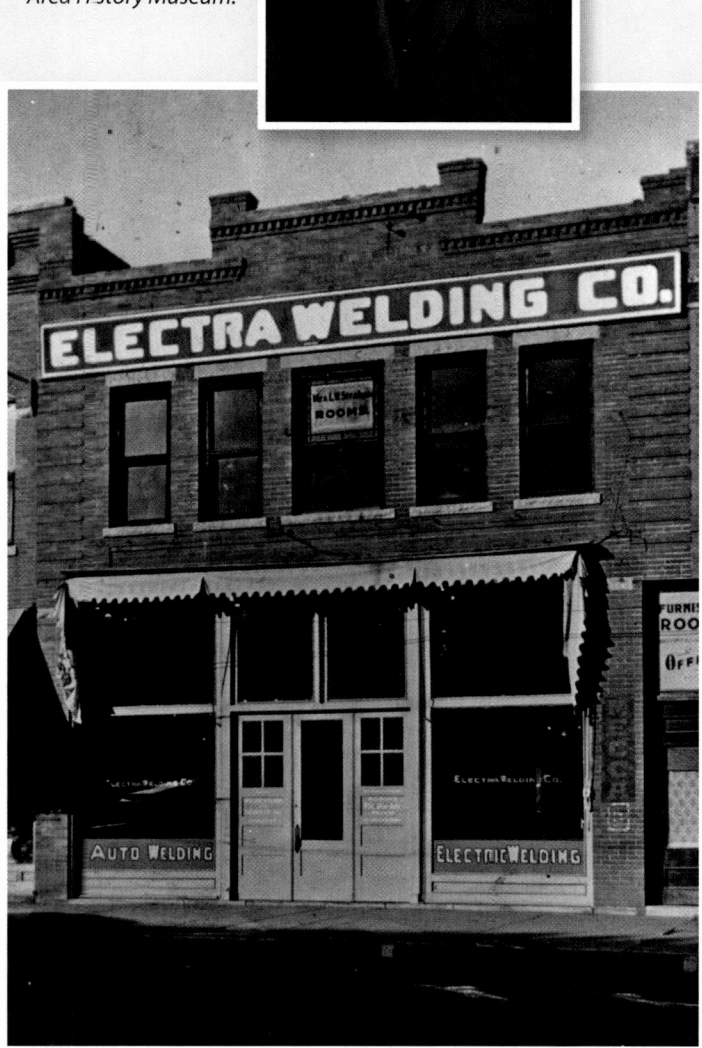

Harold Price developed a process of welding joints on pipelines, revolutionizing the industry. He established Electra Welding Company in 1921, the precursor to H. C. Price Company that became a Bartlesville growth industry in the 1920s. *Courtesy Bartlesville Area History Museum.*

The daring move from the old Oak Hill site to an entirely new country club at Hillcrest took advantage of the experience of fifteen years. The new club was on a thoughtfully selected site, with proper access provided by the nearby Old Tulsa Road, and the soon to be completed country club road; nothing was spared in selecting the best architects for the clubhouse and the golf course; the articles of incorporation and the by-laws took advantage of experience; and most important, it was for the first time properly capitalized.

From the vantage point of history, as the fateful day of 29 October 1929 approaches, there is a sense of foreboding. The crazy price-earnings ratios of the spring, the tremors in the market during September all take much more meaning from our perspective. To Americans in general, and to Bartlesville businessmen at the time, the crash in the market was indeed very grave. Some Bartlesville businessmen knew some of the eleven New York men who committed suicide because of their financial ruin. But, in fact, Bartlesville had toughed out other corrections. The fundamentals of the American economy were sound. As their friends enjoyed the sumptuous goose breakfast with the Minnigs on New Years' morning of 1930, they were surely concerned about immediate business prospects; still they reasonably expected things to work out in a few months.

4

HOLE NUMBER FOUR • 187 YARDS • PAR 3
Great par 3 with tough pin placements and well bunkered.
If pin placement is on the left side, do not give in to temptation.

HOLE NUMBER FIVE • 340 YARDS • PAR 4

Looks easy – can sneak up on you.

The secret is to place tee shot on top of fairway plateau 236 yards.

Ball must be in fairway for second shot; trees are left – out of bounds on right.

This will leave you with a short shot to a 5,000 square foot green with severe undulation.

Take 4 and go on down the road.

CHAPTER THREE

And the Band Played on: THE *E*ARLY 1930s

A frigid blast blew past the massive oak doors along with a teenage couple, both wrapped in winter coats and huge, expectant smiles. The young lady slipped out of her coat, turning toward the door on the right where she would find a place to hang it, as a gaggle of pretty girls giggled and whispered their way out of the rose and pale green sanctity of the ladies powder room. Their finger curls hairdos were all primped and their red lipstick refreshed, as one by one, they took the arms of their waiting dates who escorted them toward the portals of the ballroom. Every one of the girls wore her best dress or skirt and sweater, and high heels to this most prized social event; while the boys wore wool flannel slacks and starched white shirts and ties to one of the regular dances for teens that was sponsored by the Club of '35.[267] The youthful escorts paid their admission fees of 25¢ a couple to one of the Club of '35 members at the door. Quite a few stags drifted in the door in twos and threes.

Inside the great hall some of the 10 boys who were the members of the Club of '35 had already removed the furniture and were engaged in rolling the huge blue chenille carpet to the side in order to clear the ballroom for their dance. As they finished their task, some of the stags were already gathered around the jukebox in the corner, selecting the latest hot tunes while one of the Club of '35 was busily plugging the machine with nickels from the admission fee. Olga Foster, Hillcrest's manager, took a stern, eagle-eyed station between the entry hall and the ballroom for she would serve as the only chaperone that night. There was no expectation that a single one of the kids would require her censure, for every one prized the privilege of holding these dances, which were open to all the high school, and none would risk losing it.

The music was already playing from the juke-box. The funny pinched tones from the speakers of the times, a distortion of sound with lots of treble and no bass that we still recognize from old recordings and movies of the era, only added to the ambience, a sort of joy and innocence in the new Big Band sound that was sweeping the country. Soon the Hillcrest ballroom was jammed with youthful couples swinging to the Dorsey Brothers, or Ozzie Nelson's Orchestra, and to memorable pieces like King Porter Stomp, played by Benny Goodman's Band. They slowed down to Sunrise Serenade as played by Glen Miller, or Body and Soul smoothly intoned by Benny Goodman himself. The new music mode of Big Band Swing revolutionized jazz by eliminating the syncopation of the 1920s and simplifying the beat to a definite rhythm that was easy to follow. Musicologists say the changes in Swing made rather elitist jazz more accessible to everyone. It was certainly more danceable – music of the Big Band era was just plain fun. Dancing was considered a social grace and many Bartlesville teenagers had already taken ballroom dancing lessons from Irene Frank, mastering the box step, foxtrot, waltz, and even daring steps like the tango and Charleston. Soon they were adding new crazes like swing and jitterbug.

As the dance party began, the stag line formed. A stag boy could tap another guy on the shoulder and cut in to dance with a girl, until he too was tagged. Every girl kept a little list of "tags" to take them home and count them after the dance. Twenty or more was a nice, successful evening. The grand piano was also in the ballroom, near the fireplace, and sometimes the dance would break, while someone played the piano and a group gathered around to sing for a while. There were no refreshments, and curfews were strict so that the dance ended early enough to get the girls home in plenty of time.

It was the golden age of dance, brought to popularity by the Big Band sound. Bartian Mary Kane remembers a fun illustrative episode in 1935. She says David Burch had a brand new Hudson with the latest new accessory that year – a radio. David would drive over in his new car, pull up and park, and turn the radio up loud so that a group of friends could dance in the driveway to the Benny Goodman or Glen Miller broadcast on a summer evening. The music defined a generation.

Seventy years later, we are all well-schooled in visions of a grim age in American history: long gray lines of men wending their way to a soup kitchen; Henry Fonda as Tom Joad, driving his family into the migrant camp in California; a black duster roaring down onto the plains, the grit creeping into every crack; union violence and radical agitation; impending war. Certainly it was a hard, frightening time, but the music of the age belies the dark visions, and gives us a window into the souls of Americans then. Some say it was merely escapism, but the nature of music is too elemental for that answer alone. It truly is a window to the soul of an age. America's "greatest generation," the generation that weathered the Depression and won the War, has to be characterized by individual initiative, a sense of responsibility that reached out to help one another, and by a transcendent optimism that carried them through the economic, climatological, and political disasters that lasted 15 years. All of these elements are seen in Bartlesville during the period. When you ask that generation what they remember about the country club then, they all say, "Oh, it was the dances!"

1930

The new decade of the 1930s was opened with the usual big splashy New Years dance at Hillcrest. People generally expected the effects of the stock market crash last fall to level out soon and the good times would pick up again. Indeed, it seemed like the worst of the correction had to be under their belts and prices were beginning to recover. They were concerned when the Ochelata bank failed on 8 January, but they had seen bank failures resulting from such panics in the past. The big news in Oklahoma was the opening of the election season. Oklahoma politics was particularly lively that year. Political hounds were fresh from the impeachment show of 1929, the trial of Governor Henry S. Johnston and the outrageous scandal surrounding his secretary, Mrs. Hammonds. The 1930 race's front-runner, William H. "Alfalfa Bill" Murray,

the former chairman of the State Constitutional Convention, tossed his hat in the ring first. The field soon contained 7 Democrats and 3 Republicans, racing for the July primary election. Oklahoma automobile drivers had to get driver's licenses for the first time that March. President Hoover decided that his political future was with the "drys" as the Prohibition debate heated up, and so he ordered a vigorous enforcement campaign. Meanwhile, national conditions became tense. There were a series of nasty labor confrontations during the spring, followed by a call for a general uprising on May Day. Sure enough, on May Day there were huge demonstrations in major industrial areas. But, the newspapers reported that working Americans turned out in large numbers, more for curiosity and maybe for entertainment, not for revolution, to the great frustration of a radical core. New York police raided Communist Party USA headquarters and

By 1930, the clubhouse plantings were beginning to grow and a stylish awning was added at the entrance. There was some lawn furniture with sun umbrellas in the front lawn, allowing members to relax on the eastern, shady side and watch the putting on the green in the circle. This panoramic photo taken from the northwest shows the backside of the clubhouse, the front nine, and undeveloped countryside that was then south of town. *Courtesy Hillcrest Country Club.*

seized documents showing that the Soviet Union was actually funding the agitation in hopes of instigating revolution. To everyone's relief, the mood of ordinary Americans continued to one of optimism that times would get better.

In keeping with the hopeful expectations, Bartlesville had the vision and the nerve to invest in a new start-up industry that Armais Artunoff planned to locate in town. Initially, the little company, called Bart Manufacturing Company, was backed by Phillips Petroleum Company. Their first successful trial for the submergible electrical pump was at the El Dorado, Kansas field in 1928. Two years later, they reorganized the company as REDA Pump, and Bartlesville investors raised the necessary capital locally to insure

the company would stay in Bartlesville. Mike May says that Frank Phillips walked down the street, into the stores and businesses. When he came into May Brothers, he told Jake May that there was a new business that wanted to move to town, that would employ 200 men, and that he had Jake down for 100 shares. [269]

Social life at Hillcrest maintained a normal pace early in 1930. Kiwanis had a ladies night dinner dance the first weekend of January. The Koopman's were hosts of a big dance for 280 guests on 12 January, and many small dinner parties around town preceded

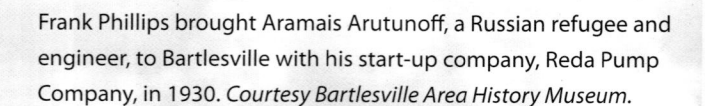

Frank Phillips brought Aramais Arutunoff, a Russian refugee and engineer, to Bartlesville with his start-up company, Reda Pump Company, in 1930. *Courtesy Bartlesville Area History Museum.*

the event. There was enough competing social activity on Valentines weekend that a big country club bridge party for members and out of town guests was postponed a week. The club threw a huge dance for St. Patrick's Day, with 500 showing up to kiss the Blarney Stone and dance to a famous New York orchestra, the Ipana Troubadours. Kiwanis had another ladies night on 27 March, this time a "tacky party" dinner-dance. Oak Hill managed to have a large dance on 4 March. The Lions had a ladies night in May at Oak Hill. The old club was having a little social success. At the end of the school year the junior-senior dance was held at Hillcrest. It was declared the best prom in years.

Hillcrest hosted an imaginative dinner party for representatives of the supply companies and oil companies in town. Seventeen men were enumerated on the guest list. The dishes on the menu were named after products being sold by the companies: Koolmotor soup (High compression, anti-knock), Semi-finished nuts – Continental green olives, Ex. Heavy, J. G. flanged onions (250 lb. W. S. P. – 400 lb. O. W. G.), Filet d'mignon ala Jarecki malleable, Std. N. R. S. F. E. potatoes w- C. F. B. O., L. H. R. P. knives and spoons, E. H. L. H. U. P. S. L. – rolls, Corn muffins – ASME code (Oilwell) Cities Service paraffin base butter), Hillcrest Surprise (8 1-2" O. D. 7.7 lb. Heatreated-exterior upset). Phillips 66 coffee (controlled volatility), Tom Moore Perfectos (plain laid Manila). The entertainment seems to have been some silly singing and a tongue-in-cheek speech. [270]

By far the biggest social event of the spring was the wedding of H. R. Straight's daughter, Harriet, to Elmer Tompkins Stevens of Chicago. For weeks in advance of the wedding the social calendar was jammed with parties for the bride. The wedding was held at First Presbyterian Church. Most weddings were still held in the home of the bride in those days,

though by the 1920s, really big weddings were at the churches. But, their small receptions continued to be held in the home of the bride. On this wedding day, the Straights entertained out of town guests at a breakfast at the Maire, then they were the guests of Jane Philips at the Woolaroc lodge for a luncheon, finally, before the wedding W. N. Davis and E. F. Walsh hosted a dinner at the Walsh house. The wedding was at 8:30. Afterwards, a new thing happened in the annals of Bartlesville society –fathers take note – they had a reception for 250 guests at the country club. The piano played in the background while the receiving line greeted the guests. There was no buffet, but there was a huge bride's cake and a groom's cake. Seating was on the patio and dancing followed the cake, lasting into the wee hours. [271]

The club manager, Tom Moore was very popular with the members, and without a doubt, the best manager they had ever had. He was very active in civic affairs. Moore had a fine tenor voice and was often the feature singer at civic luncheons, and mentioned at many parties. He was the brains behind some of the spectacular parties, and he was an important organizer of the social side of the very active women's golf program at the club. He kept the tennis program going. It was Tom Moore who conceived the idea of publishing a regular club newsletter. The predecessor of Hillcrest Happenings dates to Tom Moore's initiative in March 1930. It's too bad that no one had the interest to save them. Sadly, the economy finally caught up with Hillcrest by the summer of 1930. Moore, whose salary was probably relatively large, was an early casualty. He was hired immediately by the Elk's Club. [272]

Bermuda grass was planted on the front nine in 1930, in 1931 the back nine was put in Bent grass, then in 1932 the Bermuda in the front nine was replaced with Bent. [273]

Women's golf jumped the season a little early in 1930. Mrs. James Phillips made a hole-in-one during play on one of the regular Wednesday ladies days, 26 February. Of course, there was a lot of celebration at the luncheon that day. Regular play began on 1 March. Two women's teams represented Hillcrest in the Northeastern Oklahoma Women's Golf Association during the spring. As usual, they were quite successful. Mrs. Carl Minnig won the women's flag tournament on Memorial Day weekend. Meanwhile,

Oak Hill was very competitive with an early start to their golf activities in the Southeastern Kansas Golf Association. There was match play between the two clubs in May.

After Fred Spies' automobile accident in 1929, his doctors advised he give up tennis. Meanwhile, Hal Price was spending much of his time in California, developing his pipeline company. Bartlesville tennis went through a few years of languishing leadership. Tom Moore, Warren Spies, and Darwin Kirk formed a committee that organized an exciting exhibition match series at Hillcrest on 18 May 1930. Players from the University of Oklahoma were friends of Kirk, and Tom Moore was instrumental in getting some university champions from Arkansas and A & M through his Tulsa acquaintances. There was a huge crowd of 400 Bartlesville tennis fans to see the matches. [274]

In June, there were some big picnics at Hillcrest, not an especially surprising event in itself. Doherty Men's Fraternity held the Empire picnic for a massive crowd of 2,000. The entertainment was games, contests, and stunts. The menu included pop, near beer, Eskimo Pies, hot dogs, barbecued beef and pork, potato salad, and beans. The Junior Chamber of Commerce also held a substantial, though smaller, picnic. The menu and entertainment was similar, and they also enjoyed dancing to Claude Ross's Revelers. Kiwanis held a "fellowship hour" at Hillcrest on 20 June to coincide with similar gatherings of Kiwanis clubs all over the U. S. It may be that this is the point

The society wedding of 1930 was the daughter of H. R. Straight, Harriet, to Elmer Stevens. The Straights accomplished a social first for Bartlesville by holding the wedding reception, cake and dancing, at the country club, following a church wedding. *Courtesy Bartlesville Area History Museum.*

Leora Phillips (left), and Beulah Feist were two of the triumvirate of Hillcrest's women's golf for many years. The third, Lourah Wood, is not pictured. *Courtesy Bartlesville Area History Museum.*

when Tom Moore resigned, and that there were so many picnics because the clubhouse was minimally operative. On Fourth of July weekend the executive committee announced that the dining room would be open for the holiday weekend, but food service would then be discontinued for the rest of the summer. "But the fresh salad and sandwich service will be available daily from noon until 8 P. M." A few weeks later, Mrs. Ella Roach was hired. She had managed the Okmulgee, Muskogee, and most recently, Indian Hills Clubs in Tulsa. [275]

It was a hot summer. The central part of the United States baked in temperatures well over 100°. The work on the bridge over the Caney River that would connect south Bartlesville with Hillcrest was finally underway. Though no work had been done on the dirt road, and there were no approaches to the bridge, the abutments were up, and most of the tubes erected. They hoped to have it ready by fall. "The view of the river will be better than from any of the other three bridges…as at this point the river passes between steep shale cliffs not far distant and the absence of mud islands and drifts will add much to the attractiveness of the stream." The road would pass through some "beautiful hill scenery," and past some grand new homes that were being built, the beginnings of the country estates that Frank Phillips had envisioned growing up around the country club. Within two years, the John H. Kane home, Paul Dahlgren home, and H. V. Foster's La Quinta would spring up in the

2000 attended the Doherty Mens Fraternity picnic at Hillcrest on 7 June 1930. A gallery views the golf tournament on number 1 green. The boy facing the camera at center front is Tom Sears. *Courtesy Bartlesville Area History Museum.*

John H. Kane moved into the Kane home across from Hillcrest golf course in 1931. The house was designed by Edward Beuhler Delk.

Paul Dahlgren, H. V. Foster's brother-in-law, built another Delk-designed home across from the golf course in 1932. *Courtesy Bartlesville Area history Museum.*

neighborhood around the country club. Downtown, the modernization continued, with the installation of the first traffic lights at four intersections. [276]

With the clubhouse barely functioning, the summer golf season at Hillcrest bumped along at the usual pace. Women's golf slowed, probably as most of the wives made their annual migration to cooler climes. Mrs. Carl Wood represented Bartlesville at the Trans-Mississippi tournament in Tulsa. There was an intercity tournament with 50 Tulsa players, an 18-hole Nassau contest. The chairman of the entertainment committee, Tommy Matkin, admonished each contestant to be there early enough to take his opponent to a luncheon. The city open began early in August with contestants from Hillcrest, Oak Hill, and Sunset participating. Hillcrest boasted their champion, V. T. Broaddus, who had only recently broken the club

record score with a 72. Indeed, he was the victor of the first round of play. They must have suffered. Headlines on 5 August said that Bartlesville had one of the highest temperatures in the nation with 111 1/2° that day. The first junior golf tournament was held for the Sands trophy in the intervening week. Rain finally relieved the semi-finals round of the city open, with Broaddus again winning. Jimmy Gullane came in 6th in the OPGA in Miami. A week later, V. T. Broaddus claimed the city open championship. Right away the club championship began. Meanwhile the annual caddy championship was underway the last weekend in August. G. Resnick defeated G. Sas in the A flight, Johnny Meyers bettered Jack Lernertz in the B flight, Paul Sturm won over Loddie Szalla in the C flight, John Kemper beat Ervin Pugh in the D flight; LeRoy Berry beat Bill Fitch in the E flight. The contest that

H. V. Foster built the La Quinta estate, also designed by Edward Buehler Delk, in 1932. *Courtesy Bartlesville Area History Museum.*

emerged was between Orloski and Rinker. Tulsa champions came to Bartlesville on 13 September to begin a 72-hole contest with Jimmy Gullane and V. T. Broaddus. The Bartlesville team emerged the victors the following week. Broaddus also won the International Petroleum Exposition championship in Tulsa on 9 October. Cyril Tolley, and amateur champion from Great Britain with a remarkably long drive, and Joe Kirkwood, a solo trick artist, played one of those (high stakes?) exhibition rounds with Jimmy Gullane and V. T. Broaddus on 12 October. [277]

Ladies Day play cranked up again early in September with some strongly contested matches. The annual women's championship rounds began at mid-month. The Northeastern Oklahoma Women's Golf Association tournament was played at Hillcrest. Mrs. Carl Wood lost in the final round. The Hillcrest women's handicap championship tournament was played in October. Again, Mrs. Wood was a strong contender right down to the last round on 15 October when Mrs. W. E. Feist emerged as the new titlist. Hillcrest

women closed the season with the annual Hillcrest women's championship tournament. This time Mrs. James Phillips defeated Mrs. Wood in another closely contested final round. [278]

The clubhouse must still have been closed on 2 August when the Vagabond Club held a picnic at Hillcrest, despite the arrival of the new manager. By 17 September, a birthday dinner dance was held for T. B. Hudson, the first social notice in quite a while, indicating they were up and running again. A lot of the September social activity, as usual, was focused on the Washington County Free Fair, and also on the Cow Thieves and Outlaws Reunion at Woolaroc on 30 September. Economic conditions were not encouraging. Stocks hit their low of the year for the first anniversary of the big crash. Clyde Alexander reported to the Chamber of Commerce that the city was in dire need of low-income housing. In Southwest Oklahoma, the crop failure had been so serious that many farmers were in need of food for their families as well as for their livestock. Right after Bill

Murray was elected governor on 5 November, retiring Governor Holloway appointed John H. Kane to the Relief Board. The board was enjoined to formulate relief policy for the state in the face of the grave unemployment situation. Americans were acutely aware of ominous developments in Europe. In Bartlesville, an unprecedented 100 families needed Christmas Baskets. It would get worse. [279]

The economic bite on country club activity began to show by the fall social season. The civic clubs' events continued to utilize the club, but some that usually were held at Hillcrest moved to other sites. It was reported that the Jaycees had a fall dance, Eastern Star had a dinner party, Kiwanis had a Halloween dance and a holiday season ladies night, and Fortnightly Club had a dinner at Hillcrest. After the first of the year, the Jaycees had their annual dinner dance at Hillcrest. Meanwhile regular country club activities continued, but the numbers in attendance were diminished. Only 85 guests came out for the an-

nual Halloween dinner dance. The Christmas season party schedule was very curtailed. The Burlingames gave a big dance at the Hotel Maire, the Overlees gave a party at the country club, and the H. V. Foster daughters gave a very large Christmas dance for their friends at the club. In addition, Hillcrest had its annual Christmas dinner dance, and the children's party. That was the sum and total of Christmas entertainment around town, outside of small private parties in homes, a huge change from recent years.

1931

Dana Reynolds had a sizeable dinner party at his home before the annual New Years party at the club. Unlike every other year before, there was no glowing report of the New Years dance the next day. This was the pattern over the next few years, a notice that an event would be held, but no elaborate report, or at least an abbreviated account. It appears that, in part, the club was undergoing financial retrench-

A party house and swimming pool preceded the Burlingame mansion on Clarence Burlingame's property across from the Hillcrest entrance. The Dahlgren home (left) and La Quinta (right) are in the background. *Courtesy Bartlesville Area History Museum.*

ment, and in the face of so much want in the community, those who were still members didn't want to appear conspicuous. On 25 January 1931, they made an attempt to put a lighter spin on the situation with an informal "Poverty Dance." Campbell's Serenaders played, and Coney Island sandwiches and coffee were served at midnight.

The annual meeting of Hillcrest Country Club was held on 20 January 1931. Four directors were elected, one to fill the unexpired term of Floyd C. Brown who had resigned. The members elected the big dogs to deal with the gathering crisis. The men they elected were Frank Phillips, H. V. Foster, A. W. Ambrose, and Paul Dahlgren. That very day, Frank Phillips, John Kane, and Phillips directors, E. P. Earle and E. E. Loomis, met Obie Wing and some Phillips lawyers in the offices of Chatham Phenix in New York, signing a deal for $20 million in new funding to give the company some breathing room. [280]

Over the last three months of 1930, Frank Phillips had lived at his battle station in New York. The daring merger with Independent Oil and the acquisition of debt from the Phillips' pipeline project had been very costly. Frank kept up appearances, making additions to the Phillips office building and adding on the First National Bank, even doing major renovations on his townhouse in Bartlesville, as the local economy slowed to barely moving. Now his New York bankers were demanding their pound of flesh. Frank maintained control of the company only by the dramatic ploy of tendering his resignation (which was not accepted), but the bankers insisted on attaching a board watchdog as Frank's "personal advisor," Amos L. Beaty. The financing lifeline saved the company, but at the annual meeting in March 1931, the directors voted to pay no dividend, a situation that persisted to 1934. Crude oil prices sank to 20¢ a barrel and Phil-

lips stock sank from $16 to $3 a share in 1931.

Meanwhile, H. V. Foster had been negotiating with Henry Doherty to sell Foster Petroleum's interest in the Oklahoma City field to ITIO. After lengthy evaluation of the assets, the deal was finally struck, and on New Year's Day 1930, Foster agreed to transfer its lease holdings and working interests to ITIO, which in turn, were transferred to Cities Service for $20 million. Foster was in cash as the Depression settled in. Cities Service had accrued a large debt load. [281]

A week after the Hillcrest director's election, the board elected W. D. Reynolds president, Paul McIntyre vice president, C. B. Fowler secretary-treasurer. The new directors named were W. D. Reynolds, G. A. Thompson, Paul Dahlgren, C. B. Fowler, and R. L. Gordon. The membership committee had come to such prominence that it was part of the news release: M. B. Heine, E. C. McClintock, and Don Connoly. Evidently, Frank Phillips and H. V. Foster were not willing to serve on the country club board just then. They certainly had their own irons in the fire. Nevertheless, Hillcrest was clearly in trouble and the old corporate oligarchy agreed to come to their rescue. The directors mortgaged the country club property to ITIO, Foster Petroleum Company, Cities Service, and Phillips, each for 1/4 of $25,000 at 5% interest for 10 years. The trustees were W. C. Smoot of First National Bank and H. E. Hulen of Union National Bank. It isn't immediately clear why the huge debt, except that membership was obviously dropping. It is likely that they had taken a sizeable loan to build grass greens in time to attract the state golf tournament, and to build the Spanish Colonial style riding stables on the south side of the club property. At any rate, the mortgage specifically required that no new building projects would be started. [282]

There was relief for the stress in the local news. Governor Murray was already the joy of the political pundits. The day that he appointed new administrators at the McAlester penitentiary in order to break up some local corruption, he also hired his niece as the new cook at the governor's mansion and was anticipating a good mess of "biled turnips and hog jowl" for supper, to the general hilarity of the urbane urban press in Oklahoma. Bartlesville enjoyed a periodic show of federal liquor enforcement. Six people were arrested and alcohol was confiscated, mostly from some skid row denizens and a couple of bellhops. And there was the good news that Hillcrest had been selected to host the state golf tournament. [283]

By early spring of 1931, the relief need across the state had become very serious. Will Rogers did a tour of several state cities for a series of relief fundraisers. Bartlesville was very anxious to enjoy the performance of one of the great comedians of the era and a man they considered nearly one of their own. Tickets were sold for $2.00 regular admission, and $5.00 for patron tickets to the afternoon event at the Civic Center. It was a sign of the times that on the morning of the show, there were still seats available. Chairman Forrest Feist admonished, "Bartlesville must maintain its record of producing results in this, as it has in every other worthwhile enterprise." It was a worthwhile endeavor, but it was also a drop in the bucket compared to the growing need. Still, Bartlesville rose to the emergency in a characteristically remarkable way. The ad hoc association that was self-organized to meet the emergency during the flood of '26 was, at that time, a primary example of the fruit of Bartlesville's long-standing habits of many voluntary associations. Now in 1930, the spin-off of that very same Flood Relief organization became the Bartlesville Welfare Association. Once again, Bartlesville

leaders fell back on their long experience of working and playing together in numerous organizations to find the people and resources to thoughtfully furnish help to local families who had reached the desperate need of charity. A survey was made of unemployment conditions, and a plan was produced for relief of want and deprivation. As an early part of that effort, 41 unemployed men were hired by the county, through the Welfare Association, for highway maintenance, and immediately set to work on the Country Club Road and the Tuxedo bridge for 25¢ an hour. [285]

The Bartlesville Welfare Association board was headed by mayor M. E. Michaelson, while Ralph Morton, who was treasurer of Empire Companies and chairman of the Chamber of Commerce, was the vice president, F. A. Bisel, secretary of the Y.M.C.A., was secretary, H. J. Holm, vice president of First National Bank and representing the city commission, was treasurer, Mrs. H. H. McClintock, president of the Y.W.C.A., director of distribution, Dr. H. C. Weber, director of health and medical relief. They appointed a finance committee with R. J. Daugherty of Empire as chairman, L. E. Fitzjerrald of Phillips and Lee Robinson of ITIO. The board soon enlarged to include the representatives of the Salvation Army and Red Cross, county commissioner M. R. Puckett, and G. C. Clark representing the Federation of Catholic Men. Offices were opened in the Civic Center in December 1930, and a call was made for the registration of unemployed citizens. By February of 1931, there were 387 men and 60 women on the list, though the committee believed this was probably only about 75% of the actual number, affecting about 1200 people. Their study estimated that about $20,000 would be needed to relieve the need for the year of 1931. They organized a fund drive, calling for every employed citizen to donate one day's wages to the relief fund, through their company payroll. The proposal was an early version of the United Fund concept, funding the Salvation Army, Red Cross, Boy Scouts, and the Welfare Association. It is interesting that the city leadership evidently thought that the Boy Scouts were an essential of community relief. Of course, in the end the usual men shouldered the largest part of the load, but it was an emblem of the times that ordinary people considered it a duty and responsibility to share in the relief of their own community. [285]

Social activities in town retired to home entertainment again. Hillcrest had its Easter egg hunt for the children and an ever so small mention of the spring dance. Besides those, AAUW had its scholarship luncheon, the annual junior-senior reception for Bartlesville High School, and the Doherty Girls had a spring dinner dance. The women's golf team provided most of the spring's activities. Hillcrest women played Northeastern Oklahoma Women's Golf Association teams at McFarland in Tulsa, Muskogee, Okmulgee, Indian Hills in Tulsa, ending the season at Hillcrest on 15 May. On a windy field, Mrs. Carl Wood led the Bartlesville women to victory. Hillcrest men organized a club tournament with the men in the club organized into "Reds" and "Blues." The interesting thing is that the article claimed that "the majority" of the members were playing. There were 60 participants. If this is, indeed, a majority, the membership was down to 120 or less. [286]

Meanwhile, there was some very high stakes golf going on. Two notorious professional gamblers, Titanic Thompson and Ky Lafoon, were in town, challenging Jimmy Gullane and V. T. Broaddus to some big-money golf. The pair had relieved the Hillcrest stars of $1,000 the week before. Thompson was a reedy thin, dapper hustler who had worked links from Chicago to the Rio Grande, and the handsome Lafoon was considered one of golf's coming stars. Their hustle worked like a charm: young Lafoon would pose as Thompson's shabby-at-the-elbows caddie. After a little play, Titanic would declare, "hell, my caddy can beat you guys." Titanic had already cleaned out John G. Phillips in a poker game at the Maire Hotel in which the soused target bet, and lost, his house on Cherokee Avenue. Frank Phillips was in a purple rage when he heard, but bought back the house the next day, putting it in six-year-old John G. Phillips, Jr.'s name to prevent it from becoming gambling capital ever again. Unintimidated, Titanic and Ky moved to the country club. [287]

…He and young Ky Lafoon spent a lot of time out at the Hillcrest Country Club and worked the course like it was a violin they'd played all their lives. The country club was just south of town and too close for Titanic to try his sign scam…But playing golf by day and cards and dice by night was good enough.

Titanic and Ky hustled the members and they hustled the pro. They teased and tantalized their victims into thinking they were playing a couple of bumpkins and then they'd lower the boom. Titanic would set them up and Ky would shoot the dimples off the ball. Hillcrest was bubbling with money and the pair of gamblers came back for three seasons to reap their rewards. They got along just fine by observing a couple of simple rules – never play cards with John Phillips and steer clear of Uncle Frank. [288]

The club had infinite betting possibilities for a guy like Titanic. Dick Kane remembers a story that one day in the locker room, Titanic Thompson bet some of the men that he could throw a drive into a shoe that was several feet away. Immediately the betting scent was in the air, and of course there were

The golf course was in tip top shape for the tournament, sporting new grass greens. An aerial shot from the mid 1930s, pointing SW, gives a good view of the area around the clubhouse.

plenty of eager takers. Naturally, he tossed the ball right into the shoe.

Meanwhile, all were getting ready for the big state golf tournament. Bartlesville was already receiving praise from the state's sports writers for the condition of the course and the scenic beauty. The work crew completed the grading and widening of the curve on the country club road to finish the job just in the nick of time. (This is the curve at the bottom of Kane Hill where the fence still takes a beating several times a year; imagine how bad that curve must have been on an ungraded gravel road.) [289]

Bartlesville hadn't had a state amateur tournament since 1914. They were pretty proud of themselves in 1931, when they crowed that they were one of the smallest cities to host the event, and that they had Oklahoma's most beautiful golfing pasture. Amateurs began to show up in Bartlesville on 6 June to take advantage of three days free play to warm up. The out of town contestants were checked in at the local hotels and stashed around town in people's homes. There was a banquet at the club on Monday night, and the Jaycees were providing transportation for the participants out to the country club from the city. Several of the members at Osage Hills and Sunset Country Club also signed up for play. In the practice rounds, the Hillcrest champion, V. T. Broaddus, choked and came into the clubhouse without turning in his card. Mrs. Tom Wallace, a former women's state amateur champion from Sapulpa, took advantage of the free days to "fairly burn up the course." There was more unusual excitement for Thursday's semi-finals, when two youthful amateurs shot their way into the next to last round. Walter Emery, a high school senior from Duncan who was the state junior champion, was deadly on his drives, but inexperienced on the grass greens at Hillcrest. Henry Robertson, a tall lanky 21-year-old from Lincoln Park, Oklahoma City, was considered a steadier player. They met in the final round the next day. The flashy young Emery thrilled the gallery with his long straight drives, but repeatedly missed birdies on the greens. Robertson emerged from the Friday contest the new state amateur champion. [290]

Bartlesville was proud that its golfers fared well with the trophies. C. V. Johnson in flight A, Vic Burton in flight F, and T. H. Matkin in flight H led their fields. Also, W. E. Feist in flight C, C. B. Fowler in flight D, T. K. Willet in flight G, U. M. Stone in flight F, Bob Leisure in flight H, C. C. Dufford, in flight I took trophies. Dale Lott in the championship consolation class and Johnny Dahlgren in flight A consolation reached the finals, only to be eliminated. All in all, Hillcrest hosted 211 participants from clubs all over the state, and a gallery of 2,000 followed the contests. The officials, Jimmy Gullane, V. T. Broaddus, and Joe Dahlman of Tulsa Country Club, remarked at the good sportsmanship and respect for the well conditioned greens so that this gallery was the best they had ever dealt with. [291]

The Oklahoma State Amateur Golf Championship was played in Bartlesville for the first time since 1914 on 7-12 June 1931. Walter Emery. Age 19, of Duncan (left) embraces Henry Robertson, age 21, of Oklahoma City. Robertson, formerly a caddy, "plays in long trousers because he was superstitiously afraid of knickers." Emery was the state high school champion for 1931, but inexperienced on grass greens. *Courtesy Bartlesville Area History Museum.*

The gallery watches Henry Robertson on number 12 green. *Courtesy Bartlesville Area History Museum.*

The Oklahoma Amateur officials remarked that the Bartlesville gallery was the best they had ever dealt with. *Courtesy Bartlesville Area History Museum.*

The clubhouse in the distance, a small gallery follows the 1931 Oklahoma Amateur. *Courtesy Bartlesville Area History Museum.*

After a week's stay in Bartlesville, most of the tourney contestants headed home right after the final round. It was back to daily business. It is interesting to note that the new incarnation of Oak Hill had financially failed and been sold to the Means family by this time. It was being operated as Osage Hills Country Club. Wilkie's was organized that summer as Sunset Country Club and was functioning nicely. A year after resigning at Hillcrest, former manager Tom Moore, resigned at the Elks Club amidst some kind of hubbub for there were resignations on the board too. Two weeks later, he was hired to manage the newly organized Moose Lodge. He was mentioned around town for a few more months in civic activities, then seems to have moved on.

One more important social event took place before the heat of summer. The Washington County Bar Association hosted its annual banquet at Hillcrest. One hundred ten lawyers from Washington, Tulsa, and Osage Counties came for an afternoon of golf and to hear a speech by federal judge Franklin E. Kennamer at the banquet. [292]

There were some of the usual civic picnics at Hillcrest during a rather quiet summer. Only 30 attended the Junior Chamber of Commerce picnic, probably both a reflection of vacation season and of the poor economy. The Hillcrest hosted a lively Fourth of July picnic and fireworks. The club furnished barbecue and ice cream, and the members brought covered dishes. Lions Club held a picnic at Hillcrest the last week in August. The last picnic of the year was for the Fortnightly Club early in October.

Despite the quiet social season, the summer of 1931 was one of the most politically hilarious in Oklahoma history – though there was less humor expressed at the time. The national disorders planned for May Day were rumored to call for oil field stoppage and riots among unemployed Oklahoma miners. Governor Murray alerted county sheriffs to be on the lookout for trouble and various relief efforts were ramped up in some areas of the state. Murray arranged for possible mobilization of the National Guard, but fortunately, Oklahoma remained quiet. Oil prices continued to drop like a rock through the summer.

In mid-July, Governor Murray made good on a campaign pledge and got a lot of national notoriety. By then he had plans to run for president in 1932. His first escapade was in mid-July. At the time, there were privately owned bridges over the Red River that collected tolls. Murray declared the bridges must be opened to free commerce, but Texas got injunctions to protect the owners. Texas posted guards at the bridge at Denison to prevent anything from happening to it, in effect closing the bridge. Texas' governor Sterling then retired to Mineral Wells to review Texas National Guard troops, and would not respond to Murray's telegram. With this impasse, Alfalfa Bill declared martial law, called out the Oklahoma National Guard, and marched on Texas. At their Durant camp, the tobacco-chewing governor was packing a horse pistol and slept on a cot with his troops. It was not long before Texas passed legislation to build free bridges, and

in Muskogee, federal judge Nesbit issued a restraining order to keep Oklahoma from directing traffic to a hastily constructed free bridge nearby. Eastern pundits portrayed Alfalfa Bill as a dim-witted cowboy dictator and backwoods incompetent. "They did not know Murray. Whip thin with a craggy face, a cigar poking from the center of a sweeping black brushy mustache, Murray was an experienced orator and negotiator and perhaps the best informed politician in Oklahoma." [293] And, Bill Murray was one of the most knowledgeable Constitutional lawyers of his time. He coolly defied the federal courts, contending state's rights and saying the judge could be impeached if he goes through with his order. Soon traffic was passing over the free bridge and the toll owners were allowed to sue Texas to recover their losses.

No sooner was the bridge crisis resolved, than Alfalfa Bill turned to the crisis of oil prices in the Oklahoma fields. This was an on-going problem throughout his term, but in August 1931, he again declared marshal law, this time in the Oklahoma City oil field. He declared the wells shut in until the price of oil reached $1.00 a barrel and 100 guardsmen patrolled the oilfield. Oil operators were split in their opinions of the maneuver, but the big companies were eye-popping livid. The field didn't re-open until 10 October. There was plenty that summer to keep Bartlesville oil men busy.

Oblivious to the political melodrama, the tournament to determine the city golf championship was played the last week in July. The final round was played between defending champion V. T. Broaddus and H. Dale Lott on 2 August. Lott was the new champion for 1931. The annual caddy tournament was the last few days of August. Fifty-seven boys qualified for play. Four days later Dale Storie defeated Harley Hicks, the future assistant pro, for the medal honors.

Another important youth got a less visible start at Hillcrest that summer. Bill Spiller, an 18-year-old Black youth helped his father as a locker room attendant at Hillcrest in the summer of 1931. A year later, Spiller got an opportunity to play five holes with his father. "I wiffed eight times." The athletic Spiller went on to graduate from Wiley College in Marshal, Texas. He began playing golf in 1942 and in 1947 he became one of the early Black professionals. [294]

The Oklahoma Open was at Tulsa Country Club in September. Jimmy Gullane, V. T. Broaddus, and Dr. Paul Kincade represented Bartlesville. The Hillcrest club championship was played at the end of the month with V. T. Broaddus retaining the championship. Two other championships started up that same week. Play for the annual women's handicap started with 14 women. Mrs. Carl Wood won the Fred Dunn championship for the third year and permanent possession of the trophy. Play for the men's handicap Foster Cup was delayed by rain. Meanwhile, there was Wednesday ladies day play with an invitational meet with Independence ladies and a luncheon. A few weeks later, Jimmy Gullane and V. T. Broaddus won the team match at the southwest Kansas professional-amateur open golf tournament. Hillcrest sponsored what they hoped would be their first annual amateur invitational tournament at the end of October. Fifty-four men entered the tournament, including young Walter Emery of Durant who had been runner up at the state amateur tournament in the summer. Logan Van Zant of Tulsa Country Club won first honors. Jimmy Gullane finished out the season in a thrilling demonstration game with his partner Broaddus, and noted pros, Walter Hagan and Joe Kirkwood. "On his second shot," on number 17, Gullane "used a No. 7 iron, the ball going straight 90 yards to the pin, hitting the back lip of the cup and dropping in for an

eagle 2." Hillcrest ladies decided to play through the winter whenever possible and Mrs. Roach, the club manager, agreed to serve hot waffles to them on short notice during the cold weather. [295]

Social activity was again spare. Ruth Doornbos and her sister, Marie Foster, held a luncheon at a long table, set for 18, in honor of Harriett Straight Stevens on 24 October. Seven tables were set to open the bridge-tea season on 25 October. That same evening the Jaycees sponsored a charity ball for their project to raise money for schoolbooks for needy children. A large crowd filled the ballroom to dance to Ross Revelers. Some good club dances were held that season. The annual Halloween dance was held on Saturday night, the 31st, with decorations and merriment, dancing to Campbell's Serenaders. It was the first formal dance that fall and there were several buffet suppers preceding it, including one announcing the marriage of Louise Dixon to L. B. Armstrong. The dinner-dance club season opened with only 35 couples. There was a formal dance and midnight buffet for Thanksgiving on 28 November. Girl Reserves and their advisors had an outdoor breakfast on 7 December.

Though 40 couples came to the dinner dance club on 2 December, the local atmosphere was showing the financial constraint. One half dozen stores announced closing sales in the Sunday paper the next day. A special election defeated Governor Murray's "firebells" bills for economic reform. He wanted income tax revision, free textbooks, escheat of certain corporation lands, and changes in budget preparation. In Bartlesville, an anonymous woman provided a donation to pay for free meals for 500 needy single people and small families. The Christmas Cheer Committee provided Christmas baskets through the Bartlesville Welfare Association for 350 families. Mrs.

Effie McHam, the director of the Bartlesville Welfare Association office, said the basket contained potatoes, flour, fresh vegetables, corn meal, butter, coffee, sugar, and other items to prepare a Christmas dinner for those families. [296]

The ladies of the Kirk family had some teas and receptions at the club during the Christmas season to honor the bride of their son, Millard. Millard's new wife, Muriel Harris Kirk, had come to Bartlesville as an attorney in the Phillips legal department. Sophomores Alton and Kenneth Rowland, home from the University of Michigan, had a stag party a few days before Christmas. The annual children's Christmas party was celebrated with Santa stories and carols. [297]

1932

"The Hillcrest New Years Eve frolic is attracting even more interest than usual as it is the biggest affair of the quiet holiday season." Even with all that interest, there was little information about the party itself. The winter social season took a pattern of regularity, but the big private parties had largely disappeared, at least from public attention. One whopper that the newspaper didn't pick up was a birthday party for Hal Price. In the classic costume party format that seems to be a marker for pull-out-the-stops parties of the era, Bartlesville movers and shakers cut up at a long-remembered party. Dinner dance club which had been routine about every two weeks became irregular. The regular club dances continued with a Valentines dance and a Leap Year dance especially mentioned. The exciting dance of the season was on 1 March when Ted Fioretta's orchestra, recently from the Muehlbach in Kansas City played for a dance and midnight supper. [298]

Probably the most important dance series that year is one that seems almost insignificant in its news-

In January 1932, Hal Price threw one of those rollicking costume parties at Hillcrest. Here Stewart Dewer, John H. Kane, unknown, Clarence Burlingame, and O. K. Wing pose in the entry hall for a photo that Frank Griggs sent Marylou Price years later. *Courtesy Bartlesville Area History Museum.*

paper notice. The Irene Frank Junior Dance Club began its instruction series on Valentine's weekend. For a $35.00 fee, Bartlesville youths, ages 12 to 17, were invited to sign up for the 8 part series, modeled on Miss Frank's senior and junior dance clubs in Tulsa. This included seven club dances where Miss Frank herself demonstrated dances, and proper etiquette was suggested. The last dance was a guest party. These were the dance classes in which that generation of Bartlesville youth learned the love of ballroom dancing that marked their generation. Miss Frank went on to establish her own school of dance downtown by the next winter, and even to travel to California to learn new dances and hire additional instructors, a lucrative new small business popping up in the middle of depression retrenchment. [299]

On its usual January schedule, the Hillcrest membership unanimously re-elected G. A. Thompson, Paul F. Dahlgren, and M. E. Michaelson to the board. Dana Reynolds was elected to his sixth term as president of the club. [300]

One hundred University of Kansas alumnae gathered in February to hear Dean Olin Templin, and a program that included a roasting and some "snappy" KU songs. In May, AAUW gave a good old-fashioned scholarship dinner, and the annual junior-senior prom danced to the music of Everett Cobb's Commanders. There was little else in the way of organized social events for the season.

Most likely, the main reason for the inactivity was simply expense. But there seemed to be some compunction because of the pitiful financial circumstances of so many area families at all levels. Even the Miller brothers in Kay County, the famous 101 Ranch

Irene Franks' dance classes were a part of childhood in Bartlesville, and the foundation of all those avid dancers in the 1930s. Four of the children here were Burns, Phillips, Kirwin, and Sands. *Courtesy Bartlesville Area History Museum.*

family, could no longer keep up appearances. Once a destination for Bartlesville society, their historic 101 Ranch was auctioned in March. There was unquestionably one other reason for the low profile. Early in March of 1932, Charles Lindbergh's infant son was kidnapped from his nursery in his home. This was the most shocking of a series of sensational society kidnappings that were happening around the country. The danger was real in Bartlesville, and people like Frank Phillips were very aware of the risks. In 1933, Pretty Boy Floyd kidnapped Oklahoma City oil man Charles F. Urschel from a poker game in his own home. That same summer, Pretty Boy Floyd made a daring attempt to kidnap some of the Phillips family right in Bartlesville. It is little wonder that there was a lower profile on much of the social activity at the country club.

The profile of the golf season was not low. As usual, the women's golf got off to an early, enthusiastic start. There was golf and bridge and a luncheon planned for the regular ladies days on Wednesday. The annual men's city championship tournament began in early April. Thirty Hillcrest men, 30 from Osage Hills, and 35 from Sunset qualified for the tournament. The final round was played on 30 April. The microfilm for that day is illegible, but V. T. Broaddus won the city championship, playing Stanley Orloski, the local high school star. While this was going on, the women's team was busy in the Northeastern Oklahoma Women's Golf Association meets around the area. As usual, Mrs. Wood, Mrs. Feist, and Mrs. James Phillips were the stars. Mrs. Carl Wood qualified to play in the Trans-Mississippi Women's Golf tournament in June. Jimmy Gullane and V. T. Broaddus played in the men's tournament a few days later. [301]

The Northeastern Oklahoma Women's Golf Association played their monthly tournament at Hillcrest on 17 June. The winner was Mrs. Tom Wallace, the cocky lady from Indian Hills who turned in the withering scores at Hillcrest during the free days before the amateur tournament in 1931. Jimmy Gullane played in the OPGA tournament at the Conoco course in Ponca City on the Fourth of July weekend, then hosted a five-some of prominent golfers from Kansas on 19 July. [302]

The 1932 annual caddy tournament began the last week in August. Stanley Orloski defeated Harley Hicks to claim the Kincade trophy on 1 September. The very next day, practice rounds began for the second invitational amateur tournament. They hoped for, and came close to 100 entries in the tournament. V. T. Broaddus was the winner of the meet. [303] Broaddus was the city champ in 1932, and the winner of the invitational amateur match. Two weeks later he was defending his club championship, but lost it to Bill Feist. A month later, Mrs. Carl Wood and Jimmy Gullane were paired in a pro-amateur foursome at Oakhurst Country Club in Tulsa before the NEO women's golf championship. The same day, Sunset beat the Hillcrest men soundly at Hillcrest. On 10 October Jimmy Gullane won the Oklahoma open championship at Twin Hills in Oklahoma City. In Bartlesville, the same day, M. B. Heine tied John Cronin for the handicap championship. In the women's handicap, Mrs. James Phillips defeated Mrs. Ralph Harvey after a two weeks delay. Meanwhile, Mrs. Phillips also won the women's club championship. It was supposed to be the last of their regular feature golf play, but they voted to continue for another month.

Meanwhile, Jimmy Gullane was winding up a satisfying season. After winning the Oklahoma open championship on 10 October, he went on to play an exhibition game with British Open and National Open champion, Gene Sarazen, at Oakhurst Coun-

Jimmy Gullane was a remarkably talented pro. By the 1933 Oklahoma Open that was held at Hillcrest, Gullane had won the Oklahoma PGA championship 3 times in his 7-year tenure at Hillcrest. *Courtesy Bartlesville Area History Museum.*

try Club in Tulsa on 15 October, defeating the home team of pro Jack Guild and their club champ, J. W. Bryan. Two weeks later, Gullane and Jack Guild, teamed against Okmulgee pro Tom Cahill and nationally known trick shot artist Joe Kirkwood at Okmulgee. By December, the state rankings put Gullane at the top of Oklahoma's pro golfers, and Mrs. Wood as 9th ranked woman golfer. [304]

By the summer of 1932, social activity at the country club had resumed a regularity, though at a reduced level from in the go-go years at the end of the 20s. Phillips had a dinner dance for four departments at the end of August with 150 attending. The big news in town was the huge party that Frank Phillips hosted at Woolaroc for the Air Races. The Phillips airport was the congregating point for the Atlantic and the Pacific wings of the Cord Cup Transcontinental Derby. That evening 600 guests came to a classic barbecue at Woolaroc to entertain the contestants. Mrs. H. E. Koopman was the club social chairman in October, and was hopeful of an active calendar, culminating with the annual Halloween party. The Jaycees charity ball was the biggest event in the fall. Over 300 couples attended the fund-raiser for the Bartlesville Welfare Association to provide school lunches for needy children.

Feeding the needy families in the Bartlesville area had become a concern. Early in the year, the Chamber of Commerce organized a community garden, to be administered by the Bartlesville Welfare Association and by the county agent. Twenty acres was cleared and needy families could apply for 1/3 acre plots. The county home demonstration agent was making the rounds of schools and other meeting places to teach people how to can their produce and canning jars were donated to the project. Folks weren't in a humorous mood about their produce, and a touring car, full of Bartlesville teenagers, got a load of buckshot when they pulled off the Barnsdall Road near a watermelon patch. The kids swore they did not get into the watermelons. The fall Welfare Drive had ballooned to $40,000, the committee being run by the really big guns, H. R. Straight, Frank Phillips, H. V. Foster, and C. E. Burlingame. This time Bartlesville citizens donated 2 days wages to help their neighbors. Federal aid flour and cotton cloth were being distributed. [305]

It was election year. Oklahoma populist Democrat, Alfalfa Bill Murray, had one of the first hats in the ring for President of the United States, but Franklin D. Roosevelt soundly thrashed him in his opening primary in North Dakota. In the face of the Great Depression, Republican President Hoover

cast himself on the Prohibition plank of the party platform, while the Democrats nominated Roosevelt. Roosevelt stood for repeal of Prohibition, as well as a host of proposed remedies to the economic crisis. Murray actively campaigned against him in Oklahoma, labeling him a socialist.

The Roosevelt victory in November was glum news for Bartlesville oil men, but the fall social season at Hillcrest proceeded with a stiff upper lip. G. A. Tompson, chairman of the social committee, proudly announced that the Thanksgiving dance would feature Slatz Randall and his Brunswick recording orchestra. The band had recently played at the Adolphus in Dallas and the Muehlbach in Kansas City, among many other high fashion places. One of the few events of the Christmas season was the beginning of Hillcrest Junior Dance Club, begun under the sponsorship of the Seaton sisters, a new regular event at the club. But, the social committee canceled the annual children's Christmas party that year. The only large private party of the season was given by Marie Dahlgren Foster for 250 friends, several of them young married friends, visiting their families from out-of-town. Dancing started at 10:00 to the Campbell's Serenaders, and a supper was served at midnight. The New Years dance at Hillcrest was prominent in another quiet season. A number of parties preceded the club dance by Arlie Simmond's band. [306]

1933

The 1933 annual meeting of Hillcrest in January, elected new board members and the officers were selected. The board was Paul Dahlgren, H. V. Foster, A. W. Ambrose, C. B. Fowler, and G. A. Thompson. The new directors were H. B. Owens, Paul J. McIntyre, and H. E. Holm. V. T. Broaddus was elected to fill the vacancy of M. E. Michaelson. The new president was H. E. Holm, the vice president was G. A. Thompson, H. B. Owens was treasurer, and C. B. Fowler was secretary and assistant treasurer. Two days later, the directors of Hillcrest elected Dana Reynolds to honorary membership for life "in recognition of his seven years service as president and his work in organizing the club and the building of Hillcrest." The Depression was cutting deep. [307]

Despite the evident long diminution at Hillcrest since the 1929 Crash, the 1933 spring season was one of the most active in club history. Things started in a normal winter season with the usual big banquet for Kiwanis, the Junior Chamber of Commerce inaugural ball, and a late season start for dinner dance club. The regular club dance in January was touted for its unusual music – whatever that was - furnished by the Bennie Moten orchestra. The Paul Sell orchestra of Kansas City played for 50 couples at the Valentine's dance. There were two unusual events. The St. Ursula Guild of St. Luke's Episcopal Church sponsored a silver tea with a splendid musical program, featuring Mrs. William P. Ringo of Tulsa (formerly of Bartlesville) as soprano. On Inauguration weekend, Phillips Petroleum Company sponsored a 45-minute remote broadcast on KGGF, Coffeyville, from Hillcrest. After years of Republican administration, Washington County Democrats were in the mood to celebrate on 3 March. There was a big parade, a community sing at the Civic Center, special programs with the president's inaugural address broadcast live over loud speakers, the Business Men's Association threw a "monster free barbecue," more parades, and even a square dance at the Elks' hall. This was certainly more celebration for an inaugural than had ever happened before. The new president lost no time at all in initiating his program. Within days a currency reform was announced, and Congress was

anxious to get into the act. One of the first initiatives was action on repeal of Prohibition. Oklahoma had beer hearings by the end of the month. The push was to limit Oklahoma to 3.2 beer.

The social news in town was the announcement of the engagement of Marie Dahlgren Foster, the daughter of H. V. Foster, to John Miller Kane, the son of John H. Kane, that presaged the near total dominance of Bartlesville social activity for the entire spring season. The 14 June date was chosen on 7 May, and afterward there was a whirlwind of wedding parties, daily for the ensuing six weeks. One or two showers were given, but most parties were dances, or luncheons, or teas, and of course many of them took place at the country club, even though the wedding and reception were at the Foster ranch. [308] All the while, it was hardly noted that in Germany, the Third Reich was already moving against Germany's Jews.

Hillcrest seems to have built stables on land southeast of club property, leased from Cela Gray before 1930, probably about the same time they built the grass greens. The stables were constructed in a Spanish Colonial style reminiscent of the clubhouse. The adjacent show ring was completed in May of 1933, approximately north of the present site of 1800 Wayland Ct. in Kenilworth, including the south part of the present driving range. Several members who were riding enthusiasts boarded their horses at the stable. In the spring of 1933, the Hillcrest Saddle Club decided to be active in the life of the club. The earliest sign of this activity was a buffet dinner at the John H. Kane home on Kane Hill for the annual meeting of the Hillcrest Saddle Club. The saddle club subsequently hosted a large pre-party before the Hillcrest spring dance. A few weeks later, it was announced that the Saddle Club would host a horse show in May. [309]

Meanwhile, the golf season opened very early with balmy spring weather in January. The first ladies day in March featured an "elephant hunt," in which sixsomes of ladies played, all making as much noise and disturbance as possible during shots. On 15 March, the women played one ball one club foursomes, and on April Fool's Day they had special events. The regular Northeastern Oklahoma Women's Golf Association play began in Tulsa on the same day. There was no need for special events for April Fools because the high winds that day played havoc with the games. [310]

An exhibition round was played at Hillcrest before the city championship tournament. Jimmy Gullane and Charlie Fowler of Hillcrest lost to Paul Jackson and Joe Matthews, Kansas City pros who were promoting the Heart of America tournament. Jackson returned in June on business and played another round with John Cronin as his partner, to beat Gullane and Charles Smoot. Doubtless these matches were both among the storied high-stakes games of the era. The Doherty Men's Fraternity golf tournament played on city courses, began and ended at Hillcrest. The play off rounds for the city golf championship began 11 May with 80 citywide entries. Charles B. Fowler won the hard fought series on 30 May to become the new city champ. They wound up the rainy month of May with a blind bogey tournament, part of a state-wide tournament to raise funds for the grass experimental station in Tulsa, to research various grasses and soils in the development and selection of grasses for grass greens. [311]

There was plenty of excitement as the date of the first Bartlesville horse show drew near. The chairman of the horse show committee was R. M. Riggins. Jake May was chairman of the program committee, and his committee was Mrs. P. F. Dahlgren, Mrs. H.

C. Price, Mrs. H. J. Sherman, Mrs. O. K. Wing, Phil Phillips, and Dudley C. Phillips. The reservations and tickets committee was Mrs. H. C. Alexander, Mrs. C. E. Burlingame, Mrs. G. S. Coburn, Mrs. C. W. Doornbos, Mrs. Clyde Fowler, Mrs. L. H. Fitch, Mrs. John H. Kane, Mrs. C. J. Minnig, Mrs. R. M. Riggins, and chairman Mrs. R. L. Morton. The parking and seating committee was C. E. Burlingame, C. W. Doornbos, H. E. Holm, J. T. Sweeney, and chairman H. L. Montgomery. The publicity chairman was R. C. Jopling, with R. L. Morton, P. J. McIntyre, C. E. Murray, and O. K. Wing, his committee. The pressure was on. As the newspaper reported entries of famous horses in mounting excitement, with animals from the surrounding area and from Kansas City, Wichita, and Oklahoma City. The social column reported every one of the reservations for boxes at the show. General admission to sit in newly constructed bleachers was 75¢ for adults and 25¢ for children for the evening shows, and 25¢ and 50¢ for the afternoons. Horses were shown in military jumping and polo events, three and five-gaited classes, harness, hack, youth, pony, and trick riding groups. [312]

Eighty-one horses competed in the show, with 20 of them from Bartlesville. The two Bartlesville mares which were most noted were Mrs. John H. Kane's black Nancy McDonald, and Mrs. R. L. Morton's sorrel Red Top. Jacque Elaine Phillips, the daughter of Fred Phillips, Frank's brother, brought her winner from the Tulsa Horse Show the week before. [313]

It is odd that the Kanes would be seized with the desire to instigate a big horse show only weeks before their son's big wedding. Most likely, the horse show was one of those Frank Phillips directives. The listing of box reservations was weighted with at least 2/3 Phillips employees. The interesting question is what was going on? Frank had certainly observed that fancy shows were a part of society activities around the big Eastern country clubs, and in Kansas City. Possibly he was beginning to see light at the end of the long financial tunnel. Phillips Petroleum Company lost money for the first time in its history in 1931. The next year profits had struggled to $776,000, and in 1933, with news that the economy seemed to have finally turned the corner, the company's earnings doubled to $1.5 million. It was time to make a splashy statement that Bartlesville was back among the movers and shakers. [314]

Of course, numerous social events were planned for the horse show weekend. Not since the grand opening ball for The Bartlesville Country Club in 1911 had the newspaper given such a full description of the fashions worn by Bartlesville ladies. Mrs. Frank Phillips made first note with an ashes of roses dress and jacket, worn with a sand turban and accessories. Mrs. G. C. Clark wore a white spectator sports ensemble with a white hat. Mrs. D. V. Swing had a becoming blue, green, and white print crepe dress with a full length navy blue coat and a white turban. Miss Marie Foster wore a crinkly cotton two-piece dress of Eleanor blue with a pin check of white, a flat tailored white bow at the neckline, repeated at the waist, and a white hat. The fashion chronicle carefully described the regalia of 15 Bartlesville women, before going on to describe several visiting ladies. The entertainment committee scheduled a spring dance for the horse show weekend, with Campbell's Serenaders playing for the members and out of town guests, along with the horse show visitors. Other entertainment included a luncheon for the women, and steak fry for dinner at the Burlingame estate across the road. [315]

Earlier in the same week, Ruth and Chuck Doornbos hosted a huge dance for 300 guests to honor Ruth's sister, Marie Foster and John M. Kane. The

high school junior-senior prom was the night before the horse show. Immediately afterward, the Kane-Foster wedding totally preoccupied social activity, but nothing could preclude the golfer's maniacal pursuit of the ball. On 11 June, Bill Feist and Jimmy Gullane played an exhibition round against Paul Jackson, Kansas City's amateur champion, and C. V. Johnson. Johnson turned in one of the best amateur rounds of the season, with a 74. The next day Jackson and Gullane left for the pro-am in Oklahoma City, while qualifying rounds for the annual Hillcrest championship continued. The club championship began on that weekend. Some of the most exciting play of the series happened that first week, when Boots Adams, "playing the best golf in his career," beat C. V. Johnson and made a hole in one, the first ace in tournament play ever shot at Hillcrest. It was an ace season. V. T.

V. T. Broaddus was one of Hillcrest's hopeful amateurs. A champion of many a tournament and exhibition game, he also had a tendency to choke. *Courtesy Bartlesville Area history Museum.*

Broaddus shot one in an exhibition game with Jimmy Gullane at the new Perry Maxwell designed Hillcrest Country Club in Coffeyville on 19 June. On the 22nd, C. V. Johnson turned in a new best local amateur score for the year to become a finalist in the championship. But, C. B. Fowler emerged from all the excitement, the 1933 club champ. [316]

Right away, the men golfers turned to team play, starting with Tulsa Country Club. The woman continued their popular feature golf on Wednesday ladies' days. While Jimmy Gullane left for the state PGA tournament in Oklahoma City, early in July, the Hillcrest women whooped it up with Scotch foursomes. On 13 July, Jimmy Gullane won the state PGA for the third time in seven years. Then, all attention turned to the state open tournament on August 4, 5, and 6. There was high expectation with Bartlesville's fine amateur golfers, V. T. Broaddus, C. V. Johnson, and Charlie Fowler, and with Jimmy Gullane already holding the state professional title. To sweeten the purse, a number of Bartlesville men entered the tournament and paid the fees, without actually intending to play. Gallery tickets for three days were 75¢ or 35¢ for one day. Oscar Bowman, head greens keeper at Tulsa Country Club and director of the grass greens experimental station there, came to consult in order to make sure things were in tip-top shape. Hillcrest already had several Seaside Creeping Bent grass greens, and a few Bermuda ones, but was in transition to all Bent grass. There had been a recent 1.5 inches of rain which added the finishing touch to make the condition of the fairways the best in club history. Ben Hogan, then 21 years old and a friend of some of the youthful Oklahoma City entrants, arrived from Ft. Worth late on the 2nd. [317]

With 86 players entered in the tournament, Ben Hogan and Bartlesville's Charlie Fowler opened by winning the pro-am play on the first day. Gullane had prognosticated that four rounds of 72 would be good enough to win the tournament. After the pro-am play, he revised his figures:

This is the largest and the fastest field in the history of the state open which was started back in 1910. It will take four rounds of 71, a total of 284 to win. [318]

"Smiling" Jimmy Gullane, the defending Champion, fought yawning sand traps throughout the forenoon to finish the 18 in 75" half way through the week of play for the 1933 Oklahoma Open. His victory that week over Ben Hogan for the championship was a real cliffhanger. *Courtesy Bartlesville Area History Museum.*

Gullane's assistant pro, Pete Nossent, and club president H. E. Holm, had their hands full, behind the scenes, while the Bartlesville favorite thrilled the gallery.

Smiling Jimmy Gullane of Hillcrest, the defending champion, fought yawning sand traps throughout the forenoon to finish the 18 in 75 which is hardly average for Jimmy. He fared no better on the front nine in the afternoon, driving one out of bounds on eight and taking a six on the hole, then taking five on number nine for another 37. On the back nine which he always maintains is the easier to score on, he finally got going and turned in a 34, two under par. The 71 gave him a total of 146which leads the field at the half way mark. [319]

On the last morning of the tournament Gullane shot another 75, then blew his chance for a 294 on the sixteenth, wasting a stroke in a shallow trap. He finished the tournament with a 296, Dallas pro, Bill Robinson, and Ft. Worth pro, Ben Hogan, breathing down his neck. Gullane was whisked to the Bartlesville airport just in time to catch a Braniff flight to Chicago. As he made his dramatic departure, he learned by telephone just before boarding his airplane that he was still ahead. Meanwhile, the Bartlesville gallery was breathless as Ben Hogan stepped up to number 11 with 2 under par. He was even par as he made his drive from number 17, but his drive caught the tops of some branches, winding up with a 5 on the hole.

Hogan's drive was short on number 18. He hooked a second out of a bad lie and went into the tail rough. He sacrificed out into the fairway with a mashie and had a long iron which cut the corner of the green and rolled four feet into the corner of the uncropped crab grass at the extreme upper left of the green, some 35 feet from the cup. He was there in four and needed a five to win. Apparently deciding to attempt to tie Gullane's score by taking two more strokes he was overcautious and fell short of the cup seven feet. [320]

Gullane learned, again by telephone, while changing flights in Kansas City, that he had won, and he journeyed on to Minneapolis to enter the PGA tournament.

In the midst of all the summer's excitement, there were some other important developments. A. H. Riney, chief engineer for Phillips Petroleum Company was in Washington to confer with Congressman Wesley E. Disney and with the Corps of Engineers about a proposed Hulah dam project on the Big Caney River. Don Tyler and the Bartlesville Chamber of Commerce had been working for several months to get a Corps of Engineers survey on the watershed. It appeared to be on track to approval, to get in queue with many other such public works of the era, if the money could be obtained. The proposal was on Harold Ickes desk in the Public Works Administration by the end of the year. On 11 July Oklahoma voted to permit sale of 3.2 beer in a state referendum. Immediately, beer sales soared well beyond all expectations. Trucks made deliveries to Bartlesville dealers who sold the stuff at $3.60 a case or 15¢ a bottle, as county and federal officers carefully monitored the first day of legal sales. The Prohibition forces immediately rallied to the defense of the Eighteenth Amendment. In November, numerous state referendums voted out the 14-year-old failed effort at social engineering. Bartlesville passed a bond in December to fund its first sewage treatment plant. A. H. Riney and Billy Parker also succeeded in getting the Civil Work Administration (CWA) project to light the Bartlesville Airport, and install a radio beacon system. [321]

Local crime was up. There were daily newspaper reports of chicken thieves, and occasional prosecutions. On Thanksgiving weekend, several south Bartlesville homes were burglarized. The thieves were so bold that they broke into an upstairs bedroom window at the Chester Brewer home while a bridge party was going on downstairs. The culprit rifled all the ladies purses and stole about $16 in cash.

The annual drive to fund the Bartlesville Welfare Association was in September. In 1933, the goal was $30,000, mostly because of some increased employment through the National Relief Administration (NRA) and slightly better local economic conditions. The organization was funding clothing for needy school children, and food for indigent families. The Jaycees moved their third annual Charity Ball to the Civic Center, hoping to raise even more money to buy school textbooks for needy children.

Even though the Oklahoma Open golf tournament had come and gone golf enthusiasm continued unabated. The newspaper reported that Joe E. Musgrave, brother of C. R. Musgrave, who was visiting from Tulsa shot a hole in one on number 5 on 15 August, and Charles B. Fowler shot an eagle on number 3 on 19 August. Sixty caddies teed off for the annual caddy tournament the last week in August. Alton LaPrade was the medallist. Team play and the ladies feature play continued. J. C. Fowler won the annual handicap tournament. W. B. Engelbrecht won the flag tournament on Labor Day weekend. Mrs. H. A. Gardner won the women's handicap tournament. Mrs. J. W. Phillips successfully defended her club championship. V. T. Broaddus won the third annual amateur invitational tournament in mid-September. [322]

Heady with the victories of the spring, the Saddle Club announced a show for the fall, "La Petit Horse Show." Hoping to inaugurate a series of small

shows, and dinners at the club. A few days later, it was postponed for a week because of "conflicting activities." The plan just didn't seem to gel and there were no fall shows. [323]

Mrs. James Phillips placed in the Northeastern Oklahoma Women's championship in Tulsa, then returned home to make a hole in one on number five the next day. Everyone wound up the season with a mixed Scotch foursome. Jimmy Gullane closed out a great year with a new course record of 66 in the Foursome play. [324]

The fall social season began with ladies nights for the Lions and the Kiwanis clubs at Hillcrest. Chuck Doornbos was the chairman for the annual Hillcrest Thanksgiving dance, and he hired the Charlton Coon orchestra from Kansas City to kick off the season. A smattering of routine luncheons, teas, and college kids' dances began to appear at the country club during the Christmas season for the first time in a couple of years. [325]

Finally, some faint signs of restored economic health appeared with a big New Years party and all the trimmings. There were several pre-parties on New Years Eve, the fanciest being at the Russell Riggins home. The Hillcrest party started late, as usual, and featured the Red Blackburn dance orchestra.

1934

The morning after the New Years holiday, a Civil Work Administration (CWA) crew of 25 began work, grading down the hills on the east-west portion of the Country Club Road, just north of the club property. It was a much-needed improvement to the steep, roller coaster gravel road that journeyed out from the city. Though such public works, along with local assistance, had helped the most distressed families weather the prolonged depression, there was finally substantial improvement in the economy. In February, the Bartlesville Welfare Association's rolls were down to 352 families, half that of two years previous, and Phillips announced that their gross income and jobs were at new peaks. Notwithstanding the nationwide improvements, President Roosevelt unveiled his massive expansion of federal intervention in his "New Deal" speech on 4 January. A few weeks later Governor Murray, at the end of his term and barred by the constitution from succeeding himself, began campaigning for his preferred slate of candidates for the 1934 state elections. With characteristic directness he sputtered, "nobody south of the Canadian knows Marland," as he pitched Tom Anglin for governor. Further portents for the coming year were buried in a small article about the weather. The Bureau of Mines petroleum experimental station kept weather records

for Bartlesville. The long-term average rainfall was 36.5 inches. Between 1926 and 1931, average was rainfall was just short of 42 inches a year, but in 1932 and 33 the rainfall average was only about 29.5 inches. [326]

January society was off and running in 1934, beginning with the annual Kiwanis induction banquet. The banquet, attended by 150, was followed by vaudeville-style skits. One skit was a silent pantomime, accompanied by a trumpet and a laughing phonograph record. Campbell's Serenaders played for the dance that followed. The Jaycees followed two weeks later with 300 at their installation banquet, afterwards dancing to Ross Revelers and playing bridge. (One wonders if in this context "bridge" was an euphemism for "poker.") Jess Overlees gave an address, recognizing Frank Phillips as a city-builder, A. H. Riney for his Hulah Dam work, and H. H. McClintock for his work securing the Highway 60 route through town. The Joplings threw a private party for 150, entertained by High Grade Cunningham, a KVOO radio star, and dancing to Campbell Serenaders, before a midnight buffet – shades of the good old days. The biggest social event of the month was the birthday bash in honor of President Roosevelt at the Legion Ballroom and the Civic Center, part of a national efforts benefiting polio research. As in the 1933, it was not an overtly partisan event. Henry L. Doherty, himself, took the lead for Cities Service and all the major Bartlesville businesses followed suit in planning the big dance. The excitement of the evening was that the American Legion was going to use its newly acquired public address system for the first time. [327]

In mid-January, Hillcrest had its annual stockholder's meeting. H. V. Foster, A. W. Ambrose, and C. B. Fowler were re-elected to the board, and F. E. Rice was elected to fill P. J. McIntyre's un-expired term. An improved financial condition was reported. Amidst

In the 1930s and 1940s, the Campbell Serenaders were the Bartlesville dance band of choice. *Courtesy Bartlesville Area History Museum.*

the improved prosperity and big parties, right after the director's election, smaller social events such as bridge parties and ladies day luncheons fell off drastically and many parties moved to people's homes. Probably about this time Ellie Roach, the club manager left, leaving Hillcrest for a while without anyone filling that important function. It seems possible that the new manager, Olga Foster, was actually the suggestion of Jane Phillips. Mrs. Foster was a socially active local woman who would have known Jane or some of her close friends. It is not clear when Olga Foster was hired. Her daughter, Dorothy, gave a party for friends at Hillcrest on 5 July, the first confirmation that Mrs. Foster was serving as the new manager. It is probable that she was on the job well before the all-important horseshow festivities in June. [328]

Other important social milestones of the late winter of 1934, were the Lion's Club ladies night on 7 February, the Business Men's Association banquet on 16 February; a dinner for some executives of the United Drug Company on 25 February, a big dance for the Eastern Star on 11 March, an O.U. alumnae banquet on 31 March, and the Junior-Senior Prom on 19 May. The club put on dances for George Washington's Birthday and St. Patrick's Day. The attendance for these was about 200. Before the first of April, the number of ladies' parties began to pick up, an indicator that things were running more normally at the clubhouse.

Women's golf shows a similar pattern. The women's golf association held its spring organizational meeting at the home of Mrs. Gerald Coburn on 7 February, and another meeting at her house two weeks later, but 40 guests attended the opening ladies day at Hillcrest on 15 March. This may be about when Mrs. Foster came on duty. [329]

The golf season was up and running early in April, with mixed foursome play on 7 April. Despite the early portents of drought, Jimmy Gullane turned in a par score in play with T. K. Willet on rain-soaked greens. The Hillcrest men's and women's teams had an active April, playing in matches in the area. The D. M. F. (Doherty Men's Fellowship, the Cities Service men's organization) tournament was played at Hillcrest at the end of April. The annual city tournament qualifying rounds began on 1 May for the tournament the next weekend. Jimmy Gullane tipped off the big golf weekend in an exhibition match with Kansas City pros Benny Torpey and Ed Guetell. Like the Titanic Thompson - Ky Lafoon game in 1931, this match was probably part of high stakes gambling matches at the club. Pros at the time were poorly paid, and often augmented their incomes with winnings from these exhibitions. The weekend's tournament had some excitement with high school sophomore, Tommy Trower, three up on V. T. Broaddus for the semi-final round. Of course, the seasoned champ emerged victorious the next week with a course record score of 71, defeating Trower 3 and 2. Meanwhile, 187 women participated in the Hillcrest women's invitational the next week. The ladies outdid themselves entertaining the visitors, hoping to win sentiment for the state championship tournament at Hillcrest. Rotary held a district golf tournament on 20 May. The golfing set rounded out the month with more mixed Scotch foursomes, and a flag tournament won by C. V. Johnson. [330]

Somehow Governor Murray got the impression in April, that Washington County was going to have a tax resale of state-owned land, turning untold numbers of little guys out on there ears. No protestations of fact by County Treasurer Wade Hampton could convince him that there was not going to be a sale, and he determined to march on Washington County with the militia. By the time Alfalfa Bill's expedition assembled, it consisted of 4 men arriving by car on 16 April, dumbfounded by the complete fiasco. Osage County ranchers declared that the spring was the best grazing season in history, with 100 train carloads of cattle arriving in the County on 16 April from South Texas. Though Washington County crops were in good shape, the Department of Agriculture declared the winter wheat condition the worst since 1885, with futures soaring to 90¢ ($14.27 in 2007 dollars). On the morning of 11 May there was a good rain, followed by a dust storm.

The Chamber of Commerce was worried about Bartlesville school system's finances, but otherwise things were looking up. Chamber membership was nearly doubled in one year, the Boy Scout fund drive was nearing its goal, and the Chamber was deeply involved in the bigger and better 1934 horse show. The Hulah Dam project seemed to be on track. Seven hundred Rotarians held their district convention in Bartlesville on the weekend of 20 May. Hillcrest did due diligence for the civic extravaganza with ladies luncheons and teas for the Rotary Anns, and the Governor's Ball grand finale held at the clubhouse. The Hillcrest Saddle Club met for dinner at the John H. Kane home on 7 April, an organizational affair preceding the 1934 horse show. They were the sponsoring committee, an interesting juxtaposition with the Chamber of Commerce interest in the show. It is another example of the mixture of organizations in a large civic effort. The Chamber subsequently appointed a citizens advisory committee, the real heavy weight interests, and a publicity committee to assist the show committee. The baseball schedule for the week was adjusted to make the stadium available for the horse show. At the time the saddle club had 35 members, but the Hillcrest stable only had facilities to accommodate 22 horses, though they hoped to double the stable size in the coming year. [331]

As a drive to raise prize money was started to augment the funds from entry fees, it was proudly announced that the purses would significantly exceed those at the American Royal. Frank Phillips, L. E. Phillips, and H. V. Foster each donated $500 to the effort, the remainder of the $4,000 in smaller donations coming from city businesses and individuals. The fund was capped off by a donation of $400 each from John H. Kane and C. E. Burlingame. On 21 April the Saddle Club engaged Eugene Cawley as trainer and riding instructor. Cawley was from a stables in St. Louis. It is a guess that he was recommended by Frank Phillips' good friend George Vierheller, the director of the St. Louis zoo. Cawley had managed large horse shows in St. Louis, Indiana, and Illinois. As the prize lists were announced, five major stake prizes headed the 40 classes at $2,200 ($35,000 in 2007 dollars). The judge was to be Charles W. Green of Sedalia, Missouri, and Major Phil Clayton was chosen ringmaster. Cawley was already helping them out, for Green was a nationally respected horseman who had judged at the National Horse Show, and manager of the Missouri State Fair. Maj. Clayton was from Oklahoma Military Academy. [332]

Ticket sales opened on 6 May, and the newspaper carried daily reports of large sales, and spectacular horse entries for the show. Room reservations at the Maire were quickly filling up by mid-month. The publicity committee did a spectacular job, not just in the local press, but Saddle and Bridle magazine wrote, "the Bartlesville Horse Show is absolutely the greatest in the southwest this year." Meanwhile, the Hillcrest Saddle Club represented Bartlesville at the horse show for the oil exposition in Tulsa on the weekend of 19 May. In the end, 109 exhibitors brought 250 horses to be shown on 8 and 9 June. With a million dollars in horseflesh headed for Bartlesville, additional stable facilities were hurriedly constructed in a tent city in Johnstone Park, while work was underway for the 200-foot exhibition ring. [333]

The members of the Hillcrest Saddle Club provided the backbone of the organization for the 1934 Bartlesville International Horse Show.

SADDLE CLUB OFFICERS FOR 1934

C. E. Burlingame
President

R. M. Riggins
Vice President

Phil Phillips
Secretary-Treasurer

TRUSTEES
C. E. Burlingame
John H. Kane
H. A. Trower
F. K. Haskell
A. M. Hughes
C. E. Murray
C. W. Doorndos

COMMITTEES *(chairmen named first)*
HOUSE,
R. L. Morton
K. S. Adams
H. E. Holm
• BRIDLE PATH
Mrs. R. L. Morton
Mrs. R. M. Riggins
John H. Kane
P. F. Dahlgren
R. C. Jopling

HORSE SHOW
R. M. Riggins
Rigby Slight
H. A. Trower
MEMBERSHIP
Mrs. Carl Minnig
Mrs. Don Freiday
Mrs. H. C. Price
SUPERVISE
MANAGEMENT
OF STABLES
F. K. Haskell

The next day Russell Riggins, chairman of the show committee, appointed sub-committees whose members were not necessarily members of the Saddle Club.

LOCAL CLASSES
K. S. Adams
GROUNDS
H. E. Hewitt
RAILWAY TRAFFIC
E. C. Kitching
TICKETS
R. L. Morton

PRIZES
J. F. May
HOTELS
Rigby Slight
PUBLICITY
H. A. Trower

RECEPTION AND
ENTERTAINMENT
O. K. Wing
SHOW
SUPERINTENDENT
F. K. Haskell
STAKES
P. F. Dahlgren

CITIZENS ADVISORY COMMITTEE *(appointed by the Chamber of Commerce)*

Clyde Alexander
C. E. Burlingame
H. F. Cameron
H. G. Ellis
R. J. Daugherty
H. V. Foster
Bert Gaddis
W. H. Gill

H. E. Hulen
J. H. Kane
J. S. Leach
H. H. McClintock
J. L. Overlees
Frank Phillips
L. E. Phillips
C. E. Perkins
M. E. Perser

A. F. Potter
H. R. Straight
D. M. Tyler
H. C. Webber
N. D. Welty
M. I. Zofness
W. C. Smoot
Ralph Taylor

PUBLICITY COMMITTEE

Ralph Taylor

A. F. Potter

C. E. Perkins

The program for the 1934 Bartlesville National Horse Show, held on 8 and 9 June. The horse show was a development of the Hillcrest Saddle Club local shows. *Courtesy Bartlesville Area History Museum.*

As the show opened, Bartlesville society prepared a whirlwind of social activities to entertain the horsey crowd. Dozens of out-of-town guests and exhibitors planned to stay with local friends, the hostesses planning numerous events for them. The highlights of the weekend were a garden party for 500 around the Burlingame's pool, and a big dance at Hillcrest. As in the previous year, ladies fashions were an important sidelight to the various events, dutifully reported by the newspaper social column. [334]

For the rest of the town, grandstand seats were going for 55¢, children 25¢. A loudspeaker system was installed, and KVOO broadcast from the show, live on Friday and Saturday nights. Claude Ross and his band, "Bartians," played during the show, while Harry Jones manned the loudspeaker and R. J. Daugherty served as master of ceremonies. Hundreds of curious Bartians poured into Johnstone Park to examine the tent city and the prize horses before the opening of the show. The Ransom Art Gallery of Oklahoma City arrived with a truckload of paintings to be displayed for sale in the tent city. The Oklahoma Press Association caravanned over to Bartlesville for the weekend, after their state meeting in Claremore. They were entertained at Woolaroc, though Frank Phillips was absent, and then attended the horse show. *The Enterprise* anticipated a crowd of 10,000 to view the show. The spectators were thrilled with the show of horseflesh and horsemanship in the 100° afternoon heat. Highlights of the local classes were the five-gaited champion won by Wilbur Barr on Rexora, and three-gaited mare and gelding classes won by Russell Riggins and Mrs. Riggins. The very next week, R. L. Morton spoke to the Chamber of Commerce about the success of the show and a comprehensive plan for the next year's show, still sponsored by Hillcrest Saddle Club and headed by R. M. Riggins, but with the addition of a tri-county stock show. [335]

It is interesting to see who the local horses and exhibitors were: In Western Class R. L. Morton brought *Pippin's Choice*; Sally Wallace brought *Wallace Brown*; Stewart Dewer entered *Flash*, Fred Haskell entered *Prince Dare*; Mrs. Van H. Montgomery entered *Lady Ghost*; Bill Hale Montgomery brought *Pinto*; R. C. Jopling brought *Pecos*; Mrs. Clyde Fowler rode *Lassie McDonald*, Mrs. R. M. Riggins brought *Blue Heaven* and *Aletha Highland*; Al Gililand entered *Zed*; L. E. Sheridan entered *High Hat Jimmy* , *My Pal*, and *Tony Boy*; Billy Dancer rode *Tony*; Grace Koster rode *Button*; Belle Meade Academy entered *Blackie*; S. N. Van Wort entered *Pin Toy*; Vicki Kerr entered *Tony*, Wallace Brown rode *Sally*; Loren Nye rode *Silver*; Oren Mair entered *Pal*; Morton Murray entered *Blue Bell* and *Spot*; Jimmie Potts rode *Major Kickapoo*; Mrs. H. V. Foster entered *Jean Bourbon*; Mrs. H. C. Weber entered *Rex*; G. C. Clark entered *Duke Macdonald*; and Wilbur Barr entered *Margaret Marie*.

While the city was consumed with the horse show excitement, the rest of country club life continued apace. The Doherty girls held a banquet, and the Kilkare Club had a picnic and bridge party. Forty-two contestants got in a mixed Scotch foursome the weekend before the show. On ladies day, the women golfers chose delegates to a women's golf association luncheon in Tulsa to try to bring the state tournament to Bartlesville. By the end of the month, qualifying rounds for the annual club championship began. On 8

July, C. V. Johnson defeated V. T. Broaddus to become the 1934 champ. [336]

The city was already getting set for the next big summertime event, a three-day revival held by Aimee Semple McPherson. Hot winds caused crops to curl, as day after day, new high temperatures were set. Wheat prices soared, but there was nothing to harvest. Drought gripped the plains, with temperature hovering just over 100° by 1 June, and nearer 110° by the end of the month. Bill Murray made a campaign swing through Pawhuska on 20 June, receiving cold welcome there for his candidate, Tom Anglin. On 3 July, Ponca City's E. W. Marland won the Democrat primary by a landslide.

Federal Emergency Relief Agency (FERA) shipped 5,000 cattle from "drought regions of northern states" to Oklahoma. Ramona received 2,200 head, 900 at Bowring, 300 at Opah, 400 at Bartlesville, 575 at Shrohm, 200 at Wynona, 175 at Nichols, and 240 at Burbank. Some of the animals were so poor they were just killed and processed, the rest were distributed to needy farmers. On 14 July, the first county record of the season was set - for 26 days over 100°. As area communities began to report water shortages, Bartlesville announced that the Caney Dam, just below the Cherokee Avenue Bridge, provided a five-mile water reservoir, and that there was plenty of water for the city. City engineer Gene Perkins commented that water usage on lawns was down since 1930 because of the Depression. As federal programs began to multiply, the long city's tradition of local relief efforts flagged. The Bartlesville Welfare Association was out of funds by the first of July, by then servicing a much-reduced load of only 200 families. [337]

Since early in the year, newspapers had been reporting sensational scandals about nudist colonies popping up all over the United States, especially by

a big one near Chicago. As summer temperatures soared, five Bartlesville teenagers decided to go with the times, the four boys and one girl being arrested on 4 July for disturbing the peace with their own little colony. Justice Clarence Kahle's steamy courtroom was jammed with 300 spectators on 12 July to hear the case. It's probably no wonder. It had been a long time since the city had a good old time revival. Aimee Semple McPherson was nigh on as sensational as the nudist colonies. She was the founder of the Foursquare Gospel Church, and one of the most successful evangelists of all time. For many years the minister of the 5,000-seat Angelus Temple in Los Angeles, emphasizing faith healing and speaking in tongues as the evidence of baptism with the Holy Spirit. After an alleged kidnapping incident in 1926, she deteriorated in mental health, finally having a nervous breakdown in 1930. She was so controversial that Frank Phillips demurred from throwing the *de rigueur* party for visiting celebrities at Woolaroc, instead offering a quick tour and small luncheon for the committee. The revival opened on a 104° afternoon of high winds and a sand storm. Yet, 2,000 undaunted Bartians crowded the Civic Center on the evening of 30 July to sing hymns, hear the local soloists, and receive Reverend McPherson's sermon, "Redemption." Crowds in Sunday dress filled the baking-hot Civic Center for the three days' services. [338]

By the first of August, Oklahoma drought conditions were every bit as extreme as the northern plains. Frank Phillips was out of water and out of grass at Woolaroc, but there was absolutely no market for either beef or buffalo. He began slaughtering a few of his prize Brahmans and buffalo to be distributed each week to the needy through the Bartlesville Welfare Association. The first was on 31 July. The 8 steers were butchered by the Cooperative Grocery,

Landers, and Packing House Market, stored at the Crystal Ice Plant, and distributed to 318 families at the Salvation Army headquarters, all directed by Bartlesville Welfare Association's Effie McHam. The state was finally put in the primary drought list about that same time. FERA received approval to construct seven large ponds around the county to supply water to distressed stock. But, of course, there was no rain to fill the ponds. Only weeks earlier, Oklahoma was receiving droughted-out cattle from the government buying program - now the government was buying Oklahoma livestock. Then, another bizarre govern-ment decision – they decided to give the cattle to the Indians who were also suffering drought. [339]

In Bartlesville, majestic Maple trees, planted back in the 1912 booster era, lined the streets and shaded the sun-baked lawns. Stressed with the drought, they were attacked with borers and in short order, one by one, died. Frank Phillips' secretary made a plaintive notation, "117° today," at the end of the 12 August entry in his appointment book. Bartlesville families moved to their backyards, as their stifling homes were too hot to inhabit. The gracious old veranda at Oak Hill Country Club, west of town, became the most desirable sleeping place in town, catching cooling stray breezes on the high knoll. "Hank Carson, genial boss of the club, awakens the sleepers each morning in sufficient time to allow them to hie to their homes, taking their morning shave and coffee and get to their desks." Folks took to going by Glencliff for ice cream, then taking a drive out Nowata Road in the evenings – it just seemed a little cooler. The city denied rumors that there was an emi-nent water shortage, though the reservoir was quickly receding. Already many home cisterns were dry, and the giant cisterns at Phillips and Empire were close to dry. Finally, on 23 August, the weather broke with an inch of rain and a drop of temperatures. It had been 64 days, with temperatures under 100° only four times, and no rain. The low water had highlighted another problem, and the city began soundings for a sewage treatment plant right after Labor Day. [340]

In the summer heat there was hardly energy to wiggle. The Lions Club did hold a ladies night at Hillcrest. They were made of tough stuff in those days. The Lions had a full installation program indoors with speakers, and entertainment, and cutting up. The intrepid golfers had a mixed foursome for the Fourth of July. Otherwise, the big event of the dog days of summer was the annual caddy tournament. Qualifying rounds began on 31 July. The next day, Rookie (Ru-dolph Schmidt) Smith, Dale Storie, Walter (Loddie) Szalla, and Forrest (Fuzzy) Thompson went into a 36-hole semi-final round. Smith was Jimmy Gullane's protégé, winning with a 37-41-78 on a day of high southwest winds. On 30 August, Mrs. Carl Wood shot the women's record on the Hillcrest course with an 81. [341]

Even though it was still pretty warm, social activity got going in mid-September. The major civic clubs in town planned a huge reception and dance at Hillcrest for C. C. Harberson, the newly-elected Oklahoma division commander of the American Legion. St. Luke Episcopal Church hosted visiting church dignitaries at a dinner at Hillcrest. The Busi-ness Men's Association had a big banquet on 27 Sep-tember. The Traffic Club was in town for the weekend of 27 September. Of course, Frank entertained the 350 railroad magnets at Woolaroc, and Hillcrest served its civic function with golf and a luncheon. [342]

The Men's handicap tournament got off on the week of 11 September. By 2 October, Tommy Trower and Frank Finney, Jr. were finalists for the tournament, a high school junior and senior, sons of club golf

In the fall of 1934 the Oklahoma Wolf & Fox Hound Association hosted the Southwestern Fox & Wolf Hound Association meet at a site 4 miles northwest of Buck Creek in Osage County. There were 500 hounds entered. It was an extravaganza of Okesa fanciers, Woolaroc neighbors such as Henry Wells, Dave Ware, and M. J. Murray. The meet was held annually for several years, into the 1940s. *Courtesy Bartlesville Area History Museum.*

enthusiasts. Trower was the winner on 16 October. Meanwhile the women's handicap was underway at the same time. Mrs. J. W. Phillips defeated Mrs. A. A. Hopper in the final round. The women's club championship was played on 25 October with Mrs. James (Leora) Phillips emerging champion for the third year. At the end of the season, the women voted to continue weekly play through the winter. [343]

After the stifling summer was past, the county began to oil three-fourths mile of the country club road, south from the city limits. The rest of the road awaited arrival of a new supply of oil. The city continued to modernize with a new ordinance on 1 October, requiring indoor toilets. Meanwhile, October brought area sportsmen a thriller, ranking right up there with the spring horse show. The annual meet of the Southwestern Fox and Wolf Hound Association was held four miles northwest of Buck Creek Ranch in Osage County. Five hundred of the finest field hounds in the nation assembled for the event. This section of the Osage was deemed especially suitable for the meet because of an abundance of "wolves" (coyotes) and the lack of trees. Local fanciers who entered were M. J. Murray of Buck Creek, Dave Ware, Lee McClain, and D. K. Walton of Ochelata, Henry Wells of Okesa, and John Taylor of Barnsdall, among others. The camp consisted of 100 tents, and a restaurant, a Farm Women's Club headquarters, and a barbershop. The thrill of the chase brought contestants from as far as Kentucky and Georgia, and 1500 spectators from Bartlesville for the night program on the first evening to enjoy a fiddlers contest and a vocal program. [344]

As was usual, ladies and civic social activities were well under way at the country club by the end of

September. Some of the high school boys organized a notable club, the Club of '35. At their second meeting on 4 October, at Frank Heller's house, they took in a new member, bringing their membership to its quota: George Bunn, Frank Finney, Lucius Hubbell, Dick Kane, Alex Nagel, Lloyd Rowland, Bob Trippett, Ed Watkins, Frank Heller, and Leo Johnstone. They planned their next meeting at the Hubbell home, and a picnic dance on 13 October at Dick Kane's. This self-organized (boy's) club was an important social nucleus for the high school set that year. It is interesting to note that because of this early association in these young men's lives, as they matured into leadership, tapping each other and extending to new contacts during the growth years after the war, the community benefited from their accrued social capital. Of the young men who came back to town, the club produced a vice president of Cities Service, two attorneys, a president of Phillips Petroleum Company, and a leader in engineering research, all active in the life of the community. This is a good example of long-term investment of social capital. It is still playing out with the last of these men. [345]

As usual, the annual Halloween dance opened the fall season at the club. At Hillcrest, the Bartlesville Clearing House Association hosted "The New Deal Luncheon" for the board of directors of the Federal Reserve Bank in Kansas City, who were on a short visit to town on 3 November. John Cronin planned a menu for the luncheon, tagging each dish with a New Deal-style alphabet acronym. The directors had a high old time, and as they left for Tulsa, quipped that the headquarters ought to be in Bartlesville, to the glee of the local boosters. The election two days later was a national landslide for the Democrats, sweeping the Republicans nearly from existence in Oklahoma. As popular as Roosevelt's tinkerings were, the economic problems persisted. The Bartlesville Welfare Association's annual campaign had a goal of $21,520 in December. When the campaign closed, they were happy to announce that they were $800 over their goal. There was more good news by year's end. The Hulah Dam project was approved among the Arkansas River projects presented to President Roosevelt. [346]

During the fall season several high school hosts held dances at the country club for groups of their

CLUB OF '35

The Club of '35 was a high school boy's social club. It may have been the first of many self-organized high school social clubs that became a mark of Bartlesville youth leadership development. The young men in the photo (left to right) are: (back row) Edwin "Eddie" Watkins, George Bunn, Frank Finney, Leo Johnstone, Richard "Dick" Kane, David Burch, (front row) Robert "Bob" Trippet, Alex Nagel, Frank Heller, Lucius Hubbell, Lloyd Rowland.

friends. The dance held by the Club of '35 boys on 30 November fit right in with the trend. The next night, Hillcrest opened the holiday season with the annual Thanksgiving dance, replete with out-of-town guests, pre-parties, dinners, and bridge. As usual, Campbell's Serenaders played. Immediately the gauntlet was down and the party schedule jammed the society section until after the New Year. Hillcrest was the site of at least one dance, and sometimes also an afternoon event, every day. The parties were not as big or as splashy as they had been before the Crash, but they were certainly as persistent. Squeezed in, the Sub-Deb club of high school girls threw one of the biggest parties of all. The Jake Mays scheduled a breakfast bridge for the morning before New Years Eve. The seasonal crescendo was the New Years Eve formal dance where the Bernie Cain orchestra (Tulsa's Cains Ballroom) played for a poinsettia-festooned gala at the clubhouse. Preceded by dinner parties, more open houses between the hours of 9:00 and 11:00, the big party was followed by New Years Day open houses around town. Not to be short-changed, the Club of '35 invited 22 friends to a supper dance at Frank Heller's house to welcome in the New Year of 1935. [347]

1935

By the mid years of the Thirties decade, there was a noticeable new element in Bartlesville social structure, and the country club had played an important formative role. Early in the century, there were no evident social or civic provisions for youth in the community. The first Boy Scouts troop in Pawhuska in 1908, and the Bartlesville troop in 1910, were enthusiastically embraced by Bartlesville civic leaders who immediately saw the organization as a good way to foster character and civic virtues. Not much later, the YMCA, and then the YWCA, came to town. The

high school began to provide athletic opportunities and other limited extra curricular activities about the same time. Boy's football, and boy's and girl's basketball teams were part of the high school program by the '10s. College age youth gave dances and teas in the '10s, and by the '20s there were a few chaperoned dances for high school youth at the country club. Russell Davis confirmed that in those years there was a great deal of social stratification by age. Children simply were not included in much.

By the middle years of the '20s, the country club was at the vanguard of providing new social and civic opportunities for youth. Member's children used club facilities to entertain their friends, and they learned the games of golf and tennis, and the senior prom and honors dinners were held at the club. After World War I, local boys began to earn a little cash by caddying at Oak Hill, and in the process learned the game of golf, while rubbing elbows with the city's most prominent citizens. The first caddy tournament at Oak Hill in 1924, is evidence of the club's encouragement of the caddies and the enthusiastic participation of those boys. By the end of the '20s, Bartlesville high school had very active golf and tennis teams competing in the area. The best golfers were boys who had learned to play while caddying. By the 1930s, civic and social organizations for youth were an important part of life for Bartlesville young people, many emulating the voluntary associations of adult society and enthusiastically supported by Bartlesville's leadership. The country club participated actively, doing its part. The Club of '35 dances were an emblematic example of this modern social development. It is an interesting phenomenon to observe, not unique to Bartlesville, but certainly important to the character of the city. Recently a city visitor told of her undergraduate years at University of Kansas in the 1950s.

She was from a small town in Missouri, and like most freshmen, felt pretty overwhelmed by the big university. She mused that the Bartlesville kids were a different story. Though they were living all over campus in several different sororities and fraternities, and not clumped up and clinging together, they remained in close contact with their Bartlesville friends, confidently using the social skills they had learned at home to build networks from their contacts around campus, often quickly rising to leadership. The same pattern was evident at places like the University of Oklahoma or Oklahoma A&M, where there were significant representations of students from Bartlesville. Development of civic skills in city youth is an important contribution to the next generation of civic leadership, a very valuable source of social capital. This method of developing youth was born in the social habits of the community and fostered in the civic organizations, not the least of which was the country club.

As usual the annual meeting of Hillcrest stockholders for 1935 was held in mid January. It was preceded by the usual stag dinner at 6:45. Guy Thompson, Paul Dahlgren, and Melvin Heine were elected the new directors. A few days later, the board elected H. J. Holm, president; Guy Thompson, vice president; H. B. Owens, treasurer; and C. B. Fowler, secretary. [348]

Civic life at the club continued apace. The Junior Chamber of Commerce held its annual installation banquet and dance on 19 January. To the delight of all, the state president declared the Bartlesville organization was the best in the state. The Rotarians opted for "old-fashioned" dance music for their winter event. Also, that month, PEO had a big founders day luncheon. Meanwhile, the big Bartlesville social event for January was another charity birthday extravaganza in honor of FDR. Four hundred couples crowded the American Legion ballroom and the Civic Center, while other parties were held for city youth in several places around town. [349]

The spring civic calendar at Hillcrest included a Sons of the Legion dance, an area Lions banquet, and a DAR Valley Forge luncheon on George Washington's birthday. The Phillips comptrollers department tied one on at a big Hillcrest party with a Ross Revelers dance and a floorshow. The Order of the Eastern Star held a big benefit dance complete with bridge games and prizes. The biggest holiday season dance was the Jaycees' spring dance. The League of Women voters, the Junior-Senior Prom, the annual scholarship banquet, the University of Kansas Alumnae Association dinner, and several smaller clubs also held events. While the civic clubs held their spring parties at Hillcrest, the Glenoak Pavilion, out by the Foster estate, was open again to the public with music by Bob Wills and his Texas Cowboys on 22 May, playing from 9:00 P.M. to 7:00 A.M. for a hefty 75¢ a couple. There were two or three other public dance places around town that were busy every weekend. [350]

Club social events included the annual Valentine's Day dance, which was, as usual, preceded by several dinners and receptions. Early in March, they held a Monte Carlo dance with "unusual amusements." Campbell's Serenaders played for the annual St. Patrick's Day dance. Boots and Blanche Adams hosted the biggest private party of the spring season, and all of "smart society" was invited. Mrs. Paul Kinkaide and Mrs. T. B. Hudson had a "smart" luncheon and bridge game just before Easter. The annual children's Easter egg hunt had been suspended at Hillcrest since the 1931 financial crisis, so it was a good sign that in 1935 that it was again part of the spring calendar. Several high school youth held dances for their friends, the biggest of these seems to have been hosted by

Frederick Dimit and Warren Ambrose. The perennial luncheon bridge met regularly as did ladies day golf functions. The Bernie Cain orchestra (of Cain's Ballroom) from Tulsa played for the final club dance of the spring season on 4 May. [351]

After nearly a year's illness, Phillips Petroleum Company's promising young secretary-treasurer, Obie Wing died in Baltimore. Bartlesville closed for his funeral on 25 April. The city was rocked again with the news on 9 May that H. V. Foster had resigned as president of ITIO. Burdette Blue was chosen as his successor. It was a tough spring. High winds all day on 22 February, blew in a pall of dust that obscured the sun by late in the day. Each spring cold front brought high winds and more dust - on 5 March, 16 March, 21 March, and 31 March. On 21 March, the newspa-

per wrote, "The mustard colored fog that descended on Bartlesville and vicinity was the worst here in history." The storm that blew through on 10 and 11 April was even worse. By that time, the western wheat crop was gone. Drought reigned. [352]

On the night of the big dust storm, the Saddle Club hosted a "rube" party and box supper at Hillcrest. The 50 guests wore appropriate costumes and part of the entertainment for the evening was a spelling bee. The Saddle Club was already looking forward to a very intensive year. Frank Phillips, probably induced by his friend J. C. Nichols, planned to take the Alf Landon campaign for President of the United States national by announcing his candidacy at the Bartlesville National Horse Show. Already in March, the plans were being laid. The Chamber of Commerce appointed commit-

The Hillcrest Saddle Club held a Rube Party at Hillcrest on 10 March 1935. It was part of building the team for the fall horse show. Some of the people identified in the photograph are: (back left) L. A. Rowland, Clay Smoot, Frank Stradley, Clyde Alexander, John H. and Louise Kane, Leota Coleson, Boots and Blanche Adams, Budge Welty; (front) Stewart Dewer and Rowena, H. C. and Marilou Price, Bob Kidd, R. L. Morton, Wilbur Starr, Nodie Phillips, Lloyd Lind, Nobe Welty, John Cronin. *Courtesy Bartlesville Area History Museum.*

tees to work with the Saddle Club on the Bartlesville National Horse Show planned this year for the fall, saying it would be "in conjunction with some other activity." The next week, the Saddle Club women agreed to schedule a weekly ride and luncheon, and a monthly picnic for the summer months. People who remember those days say the golf crowd really grumbled about the horse manure on the golf course after the twelve Saddle Club ladies' rode on the nearby bridal path. C. E. Burlingame, the out-going president of the Saddle Club, hosted the annual banquet at the cleverly decorated dining room of the Maire. It was a socially significant event so that the entire guest list of the dinner was published. At the May board meeting, the Saddle Club decided to hold monthly local horse shows through the summer for all Bartlesville owners and riders and they announced the Bartlesville National Horse Show on 2 and 3 October. [353]

Saddle Club committees were appointed. Local horse show was: Budge Welty, Mrs. D. E. Lounsberry, Mrs. S. N. Van Wert, and H. A. Trower. Membership was: Mrs. K. S. Adams, Mrs. A. W. Hubbell, Mrs. Carl J. Minnig, Mrs. G. C. Clark. Stable management was: Fred K. Haskell, G. C. Clark, Charles R. Musgrave, Arthur M. Hughes. House committee was: Ralph L. Morton, H. E. Holm, Mrs. H. C. Price, Mrs. John H. Kane. Entertainment: Mrs. Don Freiday, Mrs. J. C. Fowler, Mrs. Budge Welty, Mrs. C. E. Burlingame, Mrs. C. R. Musgrave. Bridle path: Mrs. R. L. Morton, Mrs. R. M. Riggins, John H. Kane, H. I. Montgomery. Gene Cawley, the manager who had so successfully run the 1934 show, had already moved on to Oklahoma City. It was hoped that he could be hired back for 1935, or perhaps the choice would be Barney Schilling of St. Louis who had been the ringmaster last year. On 9 May, it was announced that Maryin Couch of Spindletop Stables in Beaumont, Texas had been

hired as the new Hillcrest Saddle Club trainer. [354]

The first of the monthly local shows was advanced to 18 May to avoid conflict with the Bartlesville Reds – Hutchinson Larks double header ball game on the 19th. Wouldn't you know it, after a withering spring of dust storms, torrential rains forced the last minute postponement of the first show to 26 May. Cinders were added to bring the show ring back into condition, and the public was invited, but the weather was again questionable for the six-class show the next week. Despite all, the little show was great fun, and heady with success, the Saddle Club announced a few days later that the October show would be one of the best in the United States. A $10,000 ($153,365 in 2007 dollars) purse and $1,000 championship stake classes were announced, along with expanded class offerings. [355]

While all the horse show activity was going on, the golf season moved right along. The women's golf association had been able to play through the winter. They did have to do indoor putting for feature play on 16 January, but week after week, they held their regular ladies day, or played other clubs. The men's first meet was with Osage Hills on 14 April. Over the winter several improvements were made to the grass greens of the back nine, and the fairways were carefully cultivated for the opening of the official golf season on 21 April. Jimmy Gullane and V. T. Broaddus, who was O. G. A. president that year, hoped to win one of the big state tournaments for Bartlesville. [356]

It was the golden age of golf in Bartlesville. Chuck Smoot won the Jaycees tournament on 30 April. The same day, 216 men entered the qualifying rounds for the Phillips Petroleum Company golf tourney for the next week. V. T. Broaddus won that tournament two weeks later. Meanwhile, the women's golf association held a dance to raise funds for the state tournament to be held at Hillcrest the next month. The women played a flag tournament of 29 May to make final plans for the State tournament. Mrs. Carl B. Wood became the flag play champion, as usual. They planned a banquet for the state tournament and a tour of Woolaroc for the out of town guests. On 30 May, Chuck Doornbos and W. J. Neumann tied the men's flag tournament. [357]

The next day, Mrs. James Phillips brought in low score for the first practice round of the state women's tournament. Miss Barbara McClintock was president of the state women's golf association, Mrs. T. B. Hudson was the secretary, and Mrs. Frank Stradley was the treasurer. They, and Mrs. W. E. Feist, were the hostesses for the tournament at Hillcrest. The women began play with Scotch foursomes on Sunday, and qualifying rounds began on Monday, the final matches to be played on Friday. The newly elected president of the state association, Mrs. Estelle Drennan of Tulsa, emerged the state champ in a close match with Mrs. Mrs. Lucy Wallace of Claremore. [358]

Immediately, the men began qualifying rounds for the city tournament. The eight-man Bartlesville high school team automatically qualified for the tournament. Medalist rounds were played in high winds and rain, but C. V. Johnson won the city championship on 25 June, in fine weather. [359]

The summer droned into the dog days. Remembering 1934, most of the wives fled north. Roosevelt's New Deal proposal provided plenty of controversy, as the Supreme Court found the NRA was unconstitutional. Walking between holes or at the poker table, discussions must have been heated. Hillcrest marked the Fourth of July with a golf tournament. There were so few families in town that the golf was followed by a stag barbecue at 6:00. They had a tug of war at 7:00 and the losing team was required to take a plunge into the lake. Jimmy Gullane turned in a new course record that day: a 32 on the front nine and 37 on the back. There were also several no-host picnics planned on the grounds that evening. If the celebration in Bartlesville was fairly simplified, Pawhuska began a bang-up tradition with a huge rodeo and street dance, the forerunner of their Cavalcade. The Doherty Men's Fraternity held their annual tournament late in the month. Ed White won that title. Woody Wilson won the "Keeler Avenue Championship" on 28 July by shooting a 76, his lowest score ever, playing with A. Hopper, G. A. Thompson, and C. Julian. [360]

Mrs. Estelle Drennan (Tulsa) was winner, and Mrs. Lucy Wallace (Claremore) was second at the Oklahoma Women's Golf Association State Championship, at Hillcrest 2 June 1935. *Courtesy Bartlesville Area History Museum.*

The men had a fun exhibition round to bet on. Paul Johnson, runner-up in the state amateur championship, played with H. J. Holm against V. T. Broaddus and John Cronin on one day, then he teamed up with V. T. Broaddus against Jimmy Gullane and Charles Smoot on the next day. That fall they had an even more rarified opportunity for some serious gambling. Ky Laffoon was back in town, this time with George Coleman, an amateur from Miami. The summer of 1935, marked another notable milestone. On 29 July, a new law came into effect outlawing slot machines in Oklahoma. The machines that were in the men's locker room downstairs were not removed though, for old time members vaguely remember that they were always there. It is remembered that Harry Burlingame was in charge of the slot machines. The Sheriff's office would let him know an inspection was impending, and he would take the machines across the road to his garage until after the sheriff's visit. [361]

There was the usual summer social slump. After heat of the summer of '34, the town was pretty much evacuated in the hot season of '35. Nevertheless, the Jaycees held their annual picnic in 23 June. As the temperatures soared, the intrepid Lions held their ladies night banquet in the clubhouse on 26 June. The Oklahoma Florists Association held their convention in Bartlesville 1 through 3 July, and of course, they closed their meeting with a banquet and dance at Hillcrest. The buildings must have been stifling, but then, so was home. We are told that all the windows and French doors were thrown open on hot summer evenings and guests often wandered outside to the cooler evening. The sizzling summer reached 115° on 8 August. At midnight that night the temperature still stood at 91°. Nowata recorded 119°, but their ("shaded") thermometer was atop a downtown building. The hottest news of the summer came when Congress passed the Social Security bill just before adjourning for their August recess. The next day, on 16 August, the devastated nation learned that Will Rogers and Wiley Post had been killed in a plane wreck in Alaska. [362]

The worst of the heat wave was past by the Friday feature play for the women on 23 August, scheduled to be a medal round for the Tulsa district women's association. Rain and a wet course on that day turned in scores that did not break 100.

The city's official thermometer had been on top of the tar roof of the Empire Building at one time. The Chamber of Commerce thought the astronomical summer temperatures that were often reported were bad publicity, and so the thermometer was moved to the airport. The date of this move is not known, but newspaper reports from the 1930s heat waves specifically mention that the thermometer was at the airport by that time.

The annual caddy tournament began the last week in August. Lyle Reed and Rudolph (Rookie) Smith fought the final round on 1 September, Smith emerging champion. Broaddus and Smoot represented Hillcrest in a lowball match with Sunset's Don Wilkie and M. E. Bartlett, half on grass greens and half on sand. Rain halted the match at Sunset. [363]

Through the summer's scorching heat, the horse show committee diligently worked on its organization. They opened offices on the mezzanine the Maire Hotel on 18 June. Soon it was announced that Barney Schilling would be the ringmaster, but four judges would be necessary to handle all of the classes. Col.

E. A. Keyes of Oklahoma City was tapped to judge hunter jumper classes, Ross Long of Lexington, Kentucky was called to be head judge. In keeping with their expected national visibility, Bartlesville viewed the show as a milestone civic event. It was a new expansion of the social capital the community had so persistently accrued over many years and they were quite conscious of the fact: [364]

> *It is generally conceded that the staging of a great civic enterprise like the Bartlesville National Horse show, which will be held at the municipal stadium on October 2 to 5, inclusive, and which will be the largest horse show ever held in the southwest with the exception of the American Royal in Kansas City, is not a on-man (sic) job but requires the energetic and enthusiastic efforts of each and every citizen of Bartlesville in one way or another.* [365]

R. M. Riggins, the chairman of the horse show, appointed 15 committees to handle the workload and fundraising. Phillips' publicity guru, R. C. Jopling assumed the responsibility of "making Bartlesville a horse barn word from coast to coast and from gulf to Canadian border." They were especially proud of the new hackney classes, and the locally popular cowboy classes that had been added. By the middle of August, box seats were going fast at $6.66 or $4.44. [366]

Undeterred by the hive of horse show activity, Labor Day was the beginning of the regular fall golf activities. The men played a flag tournament for Labor Day, and the women played one right after the holiday weekend. Qualifying rounds for the club championship began right away. V. T. Broaddus eventually defeated Tommy Trower on 24 September. Several Hillcrest women played in an invitational tournament at Twin Hills in Oklahoma City. Mrs. J. A. Lernertz won the B flight trophy. Meanwhile, 100 hopeful city golfers signed membership cards for a proposed Perry Maxwell grass greens municipal course about a mile east of Tuxedo. A mixed Scotch foursome tournament began at Hillcrest on 22 September. Ruth Doornbos and Austin Allen won the low gross prize, but four teams tied for the low net and Mr. and Mrs. T. B. Hudson won on a draw. With the horse show opening downtown, on 2 October, Mrs. James Phillips won the 72-hole medal tournament that had been going on all month. The annual men's handicap began on 28 September. That same weekend, Charles Smoot won the Jaycees' tournament that was played on all three city courses. V. T. Broaddus won the men's handicap on 6 October, while the Northeastern Oklahoma Dental Association played a tournament during their convention in Bartlesville right after the horse show, and the women began their handicap championship. Leora Phillips was the handicap winner, and a month later, she also won the club championship. [367]

The usual pace of civic activities continued at the club. The American Traffic Club was hosted in Bartlesville by the local traffic club. Hundreds of railroad executives, pipeline, steamship and barge, warehousing, mechanical and purchasing, trucking, and air transportation officials assembled in town for their annual meeting. For entertainment they had a golf tournament and luncheon at Hillcrest, then Frank Phillips held the blowout *grande finale* barbecue at Woolaroc. Lions had a ladies night dinner-dance, complete with a radio show burlesque for entertainment, on the same night as the Traffic men were at Woolaroc. The Business Men's Association celebrated the presentation of their new charter with a banquet for 200 only a few days later. [368]

Box seat sales for the horse show to out of town luminaries elicited breathless excitement about the social gala for that week. The name of every one of the box holders was published. By 10 September, there were still a few advance $4.44 ringside boxes available, but the price was going up to $1.67 a performance. The Wednesday night opening of the show was designated "Oklahoma Night" in honor of Governor Marland who officially opened the show, then Thursday night was designated "Kansas Night" in honor of Governor Alf Landon of Kansas. Frank Phillips sent the company plane to Oklahoma City, and to Topeka to pick up his distinguished guests. The last day of the show, devoted to "cowboy" riding classes, was designated "Bartlesville Day." Bartlesville hostesses geared up to have all bunks filled, entertaining distinguished out of town guests. While all the hype was going on, the Southeastern Fox and Wolf Hunters Association ran an ad, inviting the horse show attendees to stay for their annual hunt, beginning 7 October. Horse show parties were planned at the country club after the nightly events, and a *finale* dance at Hillcrest on the last night. Frank Phillips planned a Woolaroc extravaganza barbecue on "Kansas Night" with everything to be broadcast on KVOO and KGGF. [369]

A crowd of 1,000 waited at the airport for Governor Marland to arrive at 5:15 P.M. on Wednesday, 2 October.

While waiting for the arrival of the dignitaries aboard Frank Phillips new plane, they will listen to pilot Billy Parker and possibly other occupants of the plane – including the governor – to talk to them.

The planes (sic) two-way radio communication system will be hooked to a loud speaker at the airport…" [370]

The Pawhuska High School and the Oklahoma Military Academy bands struck up greetings as the governor's party of eight state dignitaries, including Washington, D. C. social arbiter Pearl Mesta, disembarked the Phillips Petroleum Company airplane, and were whisked to the Phillips' town house for dinner. At the stadium, a platoon of O. M. A. cavalry escorted the governor to his bunting-draped box, where a steady stream of hand shakers filed by. He met the Sea Scouts, Oklahoma Military Academy cadets, Rainbow

Frank Phillips takes the KVOO microphone at the horse show to introduce Governor Landon on "Kansas Night." *Courtesy Woolaroc.*

Governors Marland and Landon flew into the Phillips Petroleum Company airfield on 3 October 1935 to take part in the Bartlesville International Horse Show from which Alf Landon would announce his Republican candidacy for President of the United States. Shown at the hanger in front of Frank Phillips' limousine are (left to right) Oklahoma Governor E. W. Marland; Kansas City developer J. C. Nichols; Kansas Governor Alf Landon; John H. Kane, Frank Phillips, and Boots Adams. *Courtesy Woolaroc.*

Girls, and a delegation of Campfire Girls. He only took time from the handshaking to closely watch the five-gaited classes. [371]

Kansas governor, Alf Landon, arrived aboard the *Woolaroc III* the next morning at 11:45, amidst similar hoopla to that of the day before. The Coffeyvillle high school and the Bartlesville high school bands greeted him as he stepped from the airplane between the national emblem and the Kansas state flag. Oklahoma Military Academy paid him honors, and the governor was quickly taken to Woolaroc Lodge where he would be a guest along with Governor Marland. Pawnee Bill and a contingency of Osage guests added some Oklahoma color to the Woolaroc barbecue. KVOO broadcast for 45 minutes from Woolaroc. After some remarks, Frank Phillips introduced first Governor Marland, then Governor Landon over the radio, and then other notables such as Pawnee Bill. The Democrat and Republican governors engaged in constant good-natured political repartee all evening, to the delight of reporters. At the horse show, Governor Landon presented the prize

for the Kansas-owned three-gaited event, and had an opportunity for a few personal words to the crowd, following a presentation by Frank Phillips. [372]

They were very lucky the first two nights. On Friday it rained so hard that part of the show had to be postponed to Sunday night. The country club took

Governors Alf Landon and E. W. Marland embrace at the Bartlesville horse show. *Courtesy Bartlesville Area History Museum*

The judging of a driving class at the 1935 horse show.
Courtesy Bartlesville Area History Museum.

up the slack in the social schedule, created by the bad weather extension of the show. The show committee entertained 500 guests "informally" at the clubhouse. Several dinner parties preceded the dance that climaxed the show festivities on Saturday night. All in all, the committee claimed that 12,000 attended the show, and proclaimed it the best of 1935. [373]

Horsey enthusiasm was not quite over after the big national show. Within weeks they were all caught up in polo. On 3 November the Bartlesville National Horse Show Association planned to sponsor a polo match between Tulsa and Independence in the municipal stadium. They even proposed a loudspeaker truck to call the match for the crowd. The game was rained out three times, but finally played on 26 November. [374]

The national economy had been better, but still very sluggish. Yet, Bartlesville had good news right after the horse show. H. C. Price Company announced

a series of big contracts. The Bartlesville pipeliner moved into position as the most important company of its kind in the nation. Frank Phillips grabbed headlines when he "struck out at office seekers who assail capital." He was a prophet, for the soaring tax rates in the midst of a depression soon brought the nation a "double dip" in 1936. Frank would soon pay for his high visibility chutzpah with a high visibility antitrust trial. It was a scary time. As Hitler consolidated his hold with German militarism, Mussolini grabbed Ethiopia after months of alarmed clucking from the impotent international community. A radical professor from the University of Arkansas made headlines that echo our times by criticizing patriotic organizations such as DAR and American Legion on grounds of academic freedom because the patriots objected to his Marxist critique of American founding documents. [375]

A few more significant civic events took place

at Hillcrest in the last part of the year. The North-eastern Oklahoma Dental Society held its convention in Bartlesville right after the horse show. They held a golf tournament and stag dinner at Hillcrest, and a musical tea and a dinner-bridge for the wives. The Musical Research Society gave a big musician tea about the same time. Dr. E. E. Dale of the University of Oklahoma history department was the speaker for an OU alumnae association dinner at Hillcrest on 30 October. The Federated Women's Clubs statewide convention had a banquet at the club before the holiday season.

The annual Bartlesville Welfare Association fundraising drive late in November had a goal of $20,575. As usual it was well organized through the several local civic groups. The drive was finished in a week and the goal was over-subscribed, reaching $21,623. During the Christmas season the Welfare Association prepared Christmas Cheer baskets to 495 families, and the Jaycees delivered them. The Salvation Army prepared Christmas stockings for needy children and the Lions distributed several hundred boxed toys. [376]

Ordinary social life at Hillcrest followed a familiar pattern. There was a Halloween dance and a Thanksgiving dance. Music recitals for children became a social event of sorts and a few of them were held at Hillcrest. Musical teas were popular. As the Christmas season approached, local clubs had their usual round of Christmas luncheons and dinner-dances. Some of the high school set had dances for their friends, as did college kids, having returned from school. The annual Christmas party for Hillcrest children on 20 December, featured a recital of Christmas music by students of June Runyon school of piano. The most elegant dance of the season was given by Mr. and Mrs. H. V. Foster, Mr. and Mrs. C.

W. Doornbos, and Mr. and Mrs. John Miller Kane on 28 December with a long list of out of town guests to dance to Herman Waldman's orchestra. Hors d'oeuvres preceded the party, and a buffet was served. Several other smart parties and dances kept the season active until after New Years. As had been the case for several years, the Tyler Christmas Party on 29 December, was the rip-roaring event of the season. Dick Kane recalls that part of the fun was a game in which they dangled stuffed toys on fishing poles from the mezzanine. The young men jumped up to grab the prizes for their ladies. From the 1938 Tyler dance, Mary Kane's family still has one of those elegant little Steiff bunny rabbits, wearing a jacket. The Campbell Serenaders played for the dance, sporting their new vocalist, Jo Ann Travis, while that night Bartlesville was blanketed with 3 inches of snow. [377]

Though the times were still very straitened, business profitability was rapidly improving and Bartlesville companies were aggressively in the market. Employment was improving locally and the relief rolls were down significantly from their peak. Social and civic activity was assuming a normal appearance. The attitude of optimism that undergirded all the hard work in the bleak last few years seemed well warranted. Bartlesville was feeling fat and sassy.

6

HOLE NUMBER SIX.

163 Yards, Par 3. Not too difficult to 4,000 square foot green.
Avoid right front bunker.

HOLE NUMBER SEVEN.
502 Yards, Par 4. You can make an easy birdie or easy bogey.
This double dogleg right should be approached with a long tee shot down the
left side – trees and OB right.
If driven perfect, long hitters can cut second dogleg with 180 or 190 shot to a 5,000 square
foot well bunkered green. If not driven perfect, second shot must be layed up at the second
dogleg with a 100-yard shot to the two-tier green.

CHAPTER FOUR

Brave New World: THE *M*ADISON ERA

Frank Phillips looked haggard, with a cigarette drooping from his mouth, a rumpled overcoat over his arm and his hat pulled down as he emerged from the courthouse in Madison, Wisconsin. He was swarmed with newspaper reporters, yelling questions amidst frenzied photographers pointing their cameras with big blinding flashes over their heads at the beleaguered oilman. The resulting newspaper copy vividly shows the staggering personal toll that was being exacted on Frank Phillips, and on other Phillips executives who were swept up in the anti-trust indictments that accused 23 oil companies, 3 trade journals, and 58 individuals of price fixing conspiracy. The grand jury returned indictments 28 July 1936, that named Bartlesville's Phillips Petroleum Company, Frank Phillips, A. M. Hughes, and also Cities Service among the conspirators. Over the course of the ensuing trials, dismissals trimmed those numbers to 16 companies and 30 individuals. Frank Phillips was personally embroiled in the trials into the summer of 1938, when he decided to plea nolo contendre and pay $30,000 dollars in fines in order to be free of the harassment.

It is acknowledged by many scholars of Franklin Roosevelt that he was politically vindictive. In fact, Alfalfa Bill Murray was the first Oklahoma victim of the Roosevelt vengeance. Murray was an outspoken opponent of Roosevelt from the beginning. His memoirs claim that his object in campaigning for president in 1932, was to gain a forum to warn the nation of Roosevelt's socialist inclinations. In true Murray style, some of his accusations were really over the top. Two years later, the President of the United

A newspaper reporter shot a photograph of an exhausted, haggard Frank Phillips as he emerged from hearings during the Madison Trials in Wisconsin. *Courtesy Woolaroc.*

States journeyed to southern Oklahoma to campaign against the handpicked heir-apparant of the crusty governor in the Oklahoma Democrat *primary*. In a speech given at Ardmore, he specifically endorsed Gomer Smith, one of the opponents of Murray's man, and attacked – not Murray's candidate, Tom Anglin - but Murray. Though F.D.R.'s recommendation was not eventually selected, Murray was handed a political defeat. In November, the result was the election of Ponca City oilman E. W. Marland, who claimed to be a New Dealer. But, Murray was not finished. Thus, during the 1936 Alf Landon campaign the quintessential Southern Democrat threw his support behind the Kansas Republican. It was in this milieu that Frank Phillips had the chutzpah to orchestrate the Landon announcement from the Bartlesville horse show, and subsequently hit the trail with a series of high-profile business speeches attacking socialism. There is reason to suspect that he paid dearly for his opposition to the Roosevelt re-election.

Though Phillips Petroleum Company earnings were up 100% in the first quarter of 1936 over the previous year, there was plenty to be worrisome in the business environment. In the 1935 legislative season, the National Labor Relations Act (Wagner Act) was passed, climaxing a drive by Roosevelt to empower labor unions at the expense of business. The act gave unions the right to organize and to strike, and set forth unfair labor practices of employers – but there were no unfair practices set forth for unions. Over the next few years union membership quadrupled and union disruptions and violence steadily rose to a peak in 1937. Phillips Petroleum Company already had experience from East St. Louis, beginning in 1930. After two years of sporadic violence, an eventual scandal and an unsolved murder at the East St. Louis plant, the company finally negotiated an agreement with local organizers to hire only union labor. Meanwhile, Frank was personally moved by the human desperation he observed there among needy families who were thrown out of work. Over the next few years, though his personal finances were not liquid, he donated beef to the East St. Louis Salvation Army for distribution to families without income during the labor halt. Phillips was not alone in its troubles. ITIO and Cities Service struggled with strikes and threatened violence at the Seminole field holdings, and the Oklahoma City field was the center of a political firestorm focused on slant drilling under the capitol buildings. It's no wonder that Bartlesville oilmen feared labor organization and government interference.

There was also a genuine fear of kidnappings. It is well known that the Frank Phillips home had a safe-room and escape tunnel, but less well known that several Bartlesville homes had secret rooms and escape routes. Other incidents of attempted kidnappings came close to home since the attempt to abduct the Phillips children in Bartlesville in 1933. As late as December 1939, there was an attempt to snatch John G. Phillips while he was on business in Chicago. It was probably not overblown watchfulness to downplay big social events. These elements coalesced to profoundly change the civic landscape in Bartlesville.

1936

As usual, the New Years celebration of 1935, was preceded by several "informal" affairs, beginning at 5:00, and some dinner parties. The most notable was a pre-party for 80, given by the H. R. Straights, A. W. Ambroses, and E. F. Walshes at Hillcrest. There was also a large dinner for Stewart Dewer's birthday at his home, before the dance. Red Blackburn's orchestra from Kansas City played for the large crowd of members and their out of town guests at the annual Hillcrest New Years event, followed the next morning by a big open house at Burlingame Place, the C. E. Burlingame country retreat across from the club. [378]

The New Year's newspaper trumpeted a building boom in Bartlesville. According to the paper, 1935 broke all records and 1936 was off to an auspicious start. The next day, the Washington County Medical Association had its annual banquet at the club. Just as in 1935, the Saddle Club had a rube party, being one of the biggest post-holiday gatherings. Dancing was to the Babe Calloway orchestra followed a dinner and floorshow. The monthly musical teas resumed on the 16th, with a distinctly highbrow program. [379]

The annual stockholders meeting took place on 21 January, electing H. B. Owens, H. E. Holm, and A. W. Ambrose directors, preceded by the usual stag dinner. H. E. Holm was elected president and M. B. Heine was vice president. [380]

The Doherty Girls Club planned a leap year dance for 250 couples on Valentines Day, dancing to Ross Revelers and playing bridge. Boots and Blanche Adams gave a birthday dance for their high school-age daughter, Mary Louise. Ken Moyer and his orchestra played for the St. Patrick's Day dance at Hillcrest, a party that was preceded by several

Stewart Dewer's birthday was New Year's Eve, so in 1935, one of the Hillcrest pre-parties was obviously a stem-winder at Dewer's. Pauline Johnstone (striped socks, on the floor) is the only person identified in this photo. *Courtesy Bartlesville Area History Museum.*

pre-parties. T.W.T. Club of high school boys hosted a dance on 11 April, continuing the youth dance activity that marked the era. The spring club dance was a '49-er costume party. Featuring square dancing and a floorshow. The final club dance for the season was given 1 May, dancing to the Stan Hall orchestra. [381]

The Rigginses planned a dinner at Hillcrest for the Saddle Club on 2 April, but illness moved the gathering to a luncheon at the Don Freiday home. A few weeks later, the Saddle Club had its annual dinner meeting with 75 members in attendance. R. L. Morton was elected the new president, Phil Phillips was vice president, and D. A. Beger was secretary-treasurer. C. E. Burlingame, Don Freiday, Fred Haskell, John H. Kane, as well as Riggins, Morton, and Phillips were trustees. Frank Phillips, H. V. Foster, Burdette Blue, and Cities Service president W. A. Jones from New York were new members. Clearly, at this date the Saddle Club intended to continue to function at the leading edge of Bartlesville again in 1936. [382]

The spring horse show was announced early in May, but under the auspices of a newly formed organization, headed by H. H. McClintock and closely associated with the Chamber of Commerce. The huge committee was salted with civic heavy-weights: Paul Dahlgren, H. V. Foster, Chuck Doornbos, John H. Kane, Frank Phillips, L. E. Phillips, H. R. Straight, Don Tyler, and C. E. Burlingame. Suddenly the civic influence had shifted to a more egalitarian format. The show was to be held at the Dewey fairgrounds on 29-30 May. It was billed as a horse and livestock show, on the heels of the market crash of the previous week, the show was now heavily weighted toward Western stock horses, and away from the emphasis on English saddles and highbrow driving classes. "We are sponsoring the spring show to introduce the horse show world to the home of the Bartlesville National Horse show…" [383]

Admission for the spring show was aimed at a more broad-based audience: 25¢ general admission and $1.00 for boxes. Entries were soon pouring in, according to the puff piece in the newspaper. There were 63 entries for the first evening's performances and 90 on the last evening. Still, the newspaper was most impressed with the gaited horses and fine harness entries, but the Western horses were popular with a much wider Washington County audience. The horse show committee hosted a party at the country club for the show guests and club members to dance to Campbell's Serenaders. But, a month later the association decided to abandon plans for the 1936 Bartlesville National Horse Show. It is also probable that the appearance on the committee of the civic heavyweights was an indication of a felt urgent need for a change of direction. A guess is that the local leaders thought Bartlesville high society had become too visible, too fat and sassy, and in the national political scopes – they wanted "heads down." [384]

Bartlesville social life in the winter of 1936, was as healthy as it had been for several years. It was also a healthy sign that the country club was a regular part of civic activity. As usual, the Jaycees held their annual dinner at Hillcrest in mid-January. It was a very cold winter, but that only put a slight damper on the annual president's birthday ball at the Civic Center on 29 January. The cold weather that year ushered in a frightening meningitis epidemic around the state, with a few cases in Bartlesville, and a smallpox outbreak at Newkirk. Still, small normal civic events continued. The League of Women Voters held a benefit bridge, and PEO held a dinner for their husbands at Hillcrest. Girl Reserves held a big tri-state conference in Bartlesville, with workshops on etiquette, clothes, racial problems, family relationships, jobs, religion, hobbies, and Y.W.C.A. The climax of the meeting was a banquet at Hillcrest. The same day, the V.F.W.

brought Admiral Byrd to town for an afternoon talk at the Civic Center to be attended by Bartlesville school children, and also an evening lecture. [385]

Bartlesville got its first dust storm of the season on 12 March, with the evening sky obscured and a slight dusting on the city. Dust notwithstanding, drilling fever gripped Oklahoma City. A standoff between Governor Marland and the Oklahoma City city commission held the boomtown at bay over leasing rights around the capitol. Business Women's Week opened with a banquet at Hillcrest. Bartlesville Business and Professional Women's Club hosted the ladies with a program of music, singing, and costume dance. On 24 March, the Lions entertained their wives with dancing and cards at Hillcrest, the same night as a record dust storm in Bartlesville. The American Business Club held a charter dinner with Ponca City and Tulsa delegates in attendance at Hillcrest on 16 April. Temperatures were already soaring, reaching 98° the day before. The Sigma Chi alums held their annual dance that evening – the French doors must have been open wide. On 28 April, the stock market crashed preceding the second dip of the Depression and commodity prices tanked with drenching rains in the Southwest. The next day Phillips announced its excellent first quarter statistics that must have been an encouragement to Bartlesville at a scary time. [386]

Hillcrest golf forged right on through. The women's golf association met through the winter, though the weather was frigid, windy and dusty. Mrs. H. K. Hudson was elected president 16 January. Jimmy Gullane was elected vice president of the Oklahoma Professional Golfers Association at their Tulsa meeting in February. Between dust storms, V. T. Broaddus and C. B. Fowler tied for low score honors on 21 March as men's play got underway. Hillcrest succeeded in getting the OSGA amateur championship tournament for 1936. Spring play looked forward

to the big tournament in June. In honor of Obie Wing, Phillips offered the O. K. Wing trophy for the annual Phillips Petroleum Company championship tournament. Meanwhile, Hillcrest began mixed foursomes. V. T. Broaddus was in top form when he carded the low amateur score for the course, one under par 69 on 24 April. The same day Tommy Trower made an impressive showing at amateur play in Tulsa. Trower went on to win the championship at the Oil Expo Tournament in Tulsa, and the city championship as the amateur tournament loomed. Bartlesville was looking competitive for the tournament. Bartlesville women continued their usual active spring golf. After weeks of play, Mrs. J. W. Phillips retained the city championship in May. Mrs. Phillips and Mrs. C. E. Wood went on to compete in the Southern Women's golf tournament in Oklahoma City a week later. Another impressive performance was by 11-year-old Keith Fowler who won the Memorial Day flag tournament. [388]

While golf competition and the horse show occupied the town in May, annual graduation activities took their usual course. A. A. U. W. kicked off the season with its annual scholarship luncheon. Campbell's Serenaders played for the Junior-Senior prom at Hillcrest on 8 May. Emulating adult practices, Lesley Pinkerton gave a dinner at Hillcrest for some friends before the prom. Lieutenant Governor Walter Davidson was the guest speaker at the Kiwanis banquet at the club. Only 100 Kiwanians and their wives attended the event, probably because the summer exodus was already underway. Hillcrest also hosted some piano recitals and high school parties in May, winding up the school year for Bartlesville high school society. DAR held its annual Flag Day luncheon at Hillcrest on 7 June. Doherty Girls planned an annual banquet as a last social event before the summer season. Despite soaring temperatures, three more civic banquets were held at Hillcrest early in the summer. Fifty attended the Rotary Father-Daughter banquet, Business and Professional Women held their installation dinner, and Lions held a ladies night. [389]

Alf Landon was nominated for president at the Republican Convention in Cleveland, Ohio in June. The hopes of Frank Phillips and his friends soared. Surely the people would be persuaded by this Republican voice for a more moderate deal. As late as 28 October, E. P. Earle was writing Frank Philips thanks for the gift of an election ham, "Why don't you put a little arsenic in one of the hams and send it to F. D. R.? However, I hope the suggestion is not going to be needed and that next Tuesday we are going to put your friend Governor Landon, over and get rid of F. D. R. and the 'brain trust' forever." [390] Meanwhile, by mid-July the summer of '36 rivaled 1934 for drought. The nation's heat-related fatalities rose to 3800 in a heat wave that extended well up into Canada. Bartlesville and Nowata registered the nation's high temperatures at 117° on 16 July. A cold front swept through just in time for the primary run-off election, dropping temperature to more normal summer highs. The Spanish Civil War clash between fascist and communist forces grabbed headlines that dragged on for years when rebels marched on Madrid. But, the big headlines of the summer explain why the new civic emphasis on low profile emerged earlier in the month. The Madison indictments were handed down on 28 July. [391]

Amateurs began pouring into town for practice rounds before the big Oklahoma State Golf Association amateur tournament on Thursday 11 June. Tommy Trower was slated to play with Jimmy Gullane in the opening feature of the tournament. [392]

The maniacal soccer moms of our era have nothing on the ambitious golfing fathers of the '30s.

A phenomenon of the time was younger and younger tournament participants.

The gallery lounging around under trees on No. 18 green sat up and took notice as a pair of really freshman golf players came over the rise at the near end of the fairway. The tiny little black-haired, blue-eyed youngster found his next shot in the deep ditch that parallels No. 18. He is the youngest player competing in state amateur, and, while we have no records on it, he is possibly the youngest competitor ever to play in a tournament of a ranking as high as this. [393]

The little kid was 10-year-old Jack Van Zandt of Tulsa, and he scored 148 that day. Jackie's partner that day was D. C. Phillips, age 13, son of Dudley Phillips. The Bartlesville city champ was Tommy Trower, a ninth-grader, and he was showing very well against the amateur men, only losing out at the quarter finals round. [394]

The Oklahoma Amateur in 1936 was played at Hillcrest. Handsome young Billy Simpson was the heart-throb of the local girls, even though he came in second to Walter Emery in the tournament. *Courtesy Bartlesville Area History Museum.*

The tournament is remembered by Bartlesville girls of the era. Nowata heart-throb, Billy Simpson, was so handsome that all the girls were giddy about him. One young lady remembers that she made a brand new stylish sundress to wear in the gallery packed with girls that was following the former OU golf star during the tournament at Hillcrest. In the end Walter Emery of Oklahoma City defeated 21-year-old Billy Simpson to emerge state amateur champion on the sweltering evening of 20 June. The girls only remember how handsome Simpson was. [395]

Heat reigned, and golf was one of the pleasant activities out side of the swimmin' hole. Four days after the tournament, the women held a district meet at Hillcrest. Somehow Hillcrest managed two tournaments on 27 June. Phillips Petroleum comptrollers department met the Skelly Oil accounting department in the morning, on the same day that the Jaycees began their qualifying rounds for their tournament in the afternoon at the club. Skelly Oil beat Phillips two days later. Doherty Men's Fraternity began its tournament on 11 July. The day Einar Hofstrom won, it was 109.5°, in a stretch of 13 days well over 100°. By 5 August, the newspaper was reporting golf scores for Tommy Trower and John Dahlgren from the Broadmoor invitational tournament. But still, regular play was reported weekly, while scorching temperatures continued through most of August and September.

Water became a pressing local issue. C. E. Perkins, the superintendent at the Bartlesville Water Company, claimed that there was plenty of water in the Caney River on 12 August, but a week later it was lower than the same date in 1934. The county proposed water wells, but most of Washington County has no fresh ground water, and there is only poor quality seepage from near the river for wells. Jerry Hackney says that his father worked for the city in

1936, and talked about pumping from hole to hole to get water to the city that year. Hillcrest probably pumped from the low river downstream from Bartlesville to keep the greens going. Superintendent Eddie Brookshire says the old greens were susceptible to all kinds of funguses before they quit pumping from the river – it's no wonder – but it was the only water there was. Notwithstanding, as usual, the caddy tournament was the last weekend of August. Loddie Szalla, and three Smith brothers, Rookie, John, and Fred were the stiff competition. Rookie Smith beat his brother, John in high crosswinds on 1 September. [396]

A three-inch rain broke the drought on 16 September, just in time to freshen up the greens for the Traffic Club outing in Bartlesville. Three hundred railroad, and other transportation executives met in Bartlesville at their annual meeting on 24 September. Highlights were a golf tournament at Hillcrest and a barbecue at Woolaroc. Hillcrest women made impressive showings at the state women's championship in Oklahoma City Mrs. Carl Wood and Mrs. James Phillips were finalists. The women's club championship was postponed by the big rain, but the men began their championship play on water-soaked greens. Mrs. Carl Wood eventually won the 1936 championship. The women's handicap champion was Mrs. W. E. Feist. Charley Fowler won the club championship, but the men's handicap winner was F. W. Alexander. The fall golf season was frigid and wet, but play extended into November. [397]

Saddle Club members made another stab at supporting interest in their horsey activities. Late in November The Miller School of Horsemanship held an open house at the Dewey fairgrounds. Riding masters, Harry Miller and Hugh Dempsey opened their new venture in Dewey. Hugh Dempsey became a long time fixture with Bartlesville riding enthusiasts and the horse show set. [398]

The hot news for December was the announcement that British King Edward was romantically involved with an American divorcee. In Bartlesville, the Welfare Association finished the year with a surplus, and the annual drive goal was set at $14,430. It was announced that other welfare associations in the region were still asking for higher budgets, but improved employment in Bartlesville allowed a much lower budget for 1937. At Christmas the Jaycees' Christmas Cheer Committee distributed 400 turkeys. The Garden Club gave the A. H. Rineys first prize for the most artistically decorated house. There was very sobering news from Germany that Hitler's pagans were attacking Christians, and Nazis were making shocking statements, "Christianity is the only enemy of national socialism and of its reconstructive work among our people." Two days before Christmas, a new federal judge returned indictments in Madison, Wisconsin. [399]

With the weather turned cold early, it was a perfect season for social activity at Hillcrest. The popular musical teas opened the social season on 14 October. Don Colebourne and his orchestra played for the Halloween dance, with lots of pre-parties and out-of-town guests. [400] Inactive for the last few years, Hillcrest dinner-dance club kicked off its season in November. The social notice gave some interesting additional information:

Helen Tyler married Scott Beesley in a home wedding 18 December 1936. Here the wedding party is: (left to right) John Tyler, Mary Jane Phillips, Helen Tyler, Scott Beesley, Jean McKeen (Topeka), Glen Alexander. The wedding reception was a big party at the country club, with a huge wedding cake and dance by the Campbell Serenaders. Ten days later, the Tyler's hosted their usual holiday season party at the country club. *Courtesy Bartlesville Area History Museum.*

The membership is limited to forty couples and the parties will be held once a month. Members unable to attend may send guests as their substitute as in former years. Only local orchestras are to be employed. [401]

The Saddle Club was still busy and had a steak fry at Burlingame Place on 4 December, just ahead of the holiday season. Through thick and thin the Fortnightly Club and the Kilkare Club continued to meet regularly at Hillcrest. The Musical Research Society had a luncheon. The Children's Program notice listed all the little socialites by name and absolutely no other information about the party. The club had a Christmas dance for the high school and college age set. [402]

The holiday party season was brilliantly launched with several parties for Helen Tyler, bride of Scott Beesley. The wedding was in the Don Tyler home on 18 December, followed by a huge reception at the country club. Amidst a forest of flowers and candelabra, the guests enjoyed a spectacular three-tier wedding cake, and danced to Campbell Serenaders. [403]

The Gordons planned a dance for the 22nd, but evidently got bumped by a bigger dance given by the K. S. Adamses, Rigginses, Dimits, and Linds. Parties were back in high style with lengthy lists of out-of-town guests and careful descriptions of the elaborate floral decorations being the sign of the most prestigious affairs. Hostesses of parties, and even some club meetings, customarily mailed out elegant engraved invitations, requiring a hand-written formal responses. The R. L. Gordon dance to celebrate their daughter's engagement announcement took place on the 23rd. The L. E. Phillipses gave a dance on the 26th, but the social notice was notably understated. Even though the Don Tylers had entertained royally for Helen's wedding only ten days earlier, their second round was their annual holiday dance extravaganza, this year in

the young couple's honor. A black duster blew into the Panhandle on New Years Eve, ahead of snow and a sharp drop in temperature that greeted the New Year in Bartlesville. The Matt Betton orchestra from Chicago played for the annual New Years party, but much of society was out at Frank Phillips' town house where he was entertaining the Frank Bucks, Pearl Mesta, and the Vierhellers. [404]

1937

All the signs of the improved local business environment were evident through the year 1936. The activity at the club picked up steadily through the year. Civic events, regular club activities, and lots of big, extravagant parties, even the state amateur golf tournament were all markers that Hillcrest was finally having a good year. A record bears this out. On 12 November, John H. Kane and Hillcrest exchanged small tracts of approximately 7 acres, giving Kane a little piece of adjacent acreage, and the club some property between numbers 11 and 12 greens, with access down to the river. The same day, a banner day indeed, they paid off the mortgage to Phillips, ITIO, and Empire from the 1931 loan. [405]

The annual stockholders meeting was held after dinner on 19 January 1937. Eight new directors were elected: Frank Stradley, C. E. Burlingame, Stewart Dewer, J. E. Rice, C. W. Doornbos, C. E. Murray, Lloyd Lynd, and John F. Cronin. An amendment to the by-laws passed, increasing the number of directors from 8 to 11. A week later Chuck Doornbos was elected president, John Cronin was vice president, H. B. Owens was treasurer, and F. L. Feist was secretary. [405]

After a second beastly summer in 1936, prosperous Bartlesville businesses decided to follow Frank Phillips' lead from the year before when he air conditioned his house. Air conditioning was installed at the Empire building, Phillips Petroleum Company, and the First National Bank building. Better times also brought new pressure to finish paving sections of US 60 in Nowata and Osage Counties, and to try to raise $1,000,000 in local money to match government funds to get Hulah Dam on track. A treasury report to Congress revealed that Frank Phillips' salary for 1935 was $91,000, the highest in Oklahoma. At that very time Empire was engaged in stiff talks with the Oil Workers Union at Seminole, and in Michigan, there were riots at the General Motors strike. These were portents of the period just ahead. [407]

The winter civic agenda was usual, with the Chamber of Commerce, Jaycees, and the Medical Association having banquets at Hillcrest in January. As had become customary, the president's birthday dance was held at the Civic Center. It was announced that the fall horse show was to be put on the back burner. "Of course, the whole thing is up to the citizens, but, if they want it, Bartlesville can have one of the greatest – if, indeed, not the greatest – of the 1937 horse shows." A polo club was formed. The Saddle Club continued meeting and had a "tacky party" in February. Eventually, the Chamber of Commerce announced that there would be a three-day rodeo at the Dewey fairgrounds on the Fourth of July weekend. The full-circle democratization of Bartlesville's horsey episode was nearly complete with the re-emergence of the Dewey Round-up. [408]

Normal Hillcrest social events continued to be active. Dinner dance club was regular, the annual Valentine's dance was postponed but came off a week later, there was a "tacky" club dance in March, the musical teas remained popular, and the final club dance of the season was held on 8 May. There was the usual crowded schedule of parties and social affairs. The major social preoccupation during January was the wedding of Frank Phillips' daughter, Jane Phillips, to Frank Begrisch in New York. Several luncheons, breakfasts, and dinner parties were held in her honor while the bride was in Bartlesville before the wedding. The spring was busy, with numerous dances and parties given by individuals and clubs. The season closed, as usual with the junior-senior prom. C. E. Burlingame threw a huge birthday dance for his wife on 12 May, and the Empire legal department gave a big dinner in honor of Judge Finley. What is notable about these social notices is that they became generally more circumspect than they had been a few months earlier. In the meantime, Olga Foster, the manager since 1934, who is to this day well remembered, resigned to take a job at Winnwood School at Lake Grove, Long Island. She was replaced by Mrs. Jeanette Hawks Stewart from Twin Hills Country Club in Oklahoma City. Mrs. Stewart was a divorced mother who was one of the early female professional club managers. She had started her career managing the University of Oklahoma Student Union before going to Twin Hills. [409]

Mrs. Stewart arrived from Oklahoma City only weeks ahead of the annual Easter egg hunt. Her son, Bill, who was in the sixth grade, still remembers that event with youthful awe undimmed by the passage of years. He says that they dyed hundreds and hundreds of real hard-boiled eggs and hid them on the golf course. He thought the eggs may have extended four blocks distance from the club house. It was a sight to behold even as you approached the club along the road. The rolling fairways were dotted with brightly colored eggs. Among them were about a dozen golden eggs. These were duck or goose eggs that were painted gold. They were the eggs that won prizes of money or even a live bunny. He was privy to the secret knowledge before the hunt of where those special eggs were hidden. Of course, he was sworn to secrecy.

Remembering the life in the clubhouse in those days, Bill remarked about the fine quality of the Hillcrest staff. He remembered that his mother had a gift for hiring good people – always a mark of good managers. Almost all of the staff working in the clubhouse was Black and their jobs were considered prestigious. He especially remembers the *maitre d'*, Joe Brooks, who eventually moved to Oklahoma City and continued with a notable career there in city clubs. [410]

It was an eventful spring. Amelia Earhart took off on her fateful last adventure. For months, the newspapers carried excited reports of her stops, until she was reported missing on 3 July. Hiltler's pagans declared him "the son of god," in a fight for control of the Protestant church in Germany. That grabbed headlines for sure! F. D. R. made his move to attempt to pack the Supreme Court, thereby politicizing court appointments into the 21st century. Eleanor Roosevelt made a visit to Pawhuska under the auspices of the Tulsa Business and Professional Women's Club on 16 March. A few days later, another spring dust storm blew in on strong west winds. Only 5 days passed before a worse storm blanketed the city, followed by a rising river. Easter was cold, but by 2 April a heat wave roasted the state. It was perfect weather for chicken stealing and a crime wave swept the area. Six were arrested. The Chamber of Commerce continued to try to move the Hulah Dam initiative. Bartlesville attorneys, Dorothy Young of ITIO, Darlene Anderson of Phillips, and Lois Straight of Empire, and Chloe Passley (who was the district court reporter) were prominent in the state banquet of women lawyers, bringing the planned June meeting to Bartlesville. Of course, Hillcrest helped put Bartlesville's best foot forward when the 35 professional women enjoyed a club breakfast before touring Woolaroc during their meeting. [411]

The Oklahoma City Golf and Country Club was raided for slot machines by Oklahoma County sheriff's deputies on 4 May. Washington County sheriff, J. W. Masters, established a more circumspect precedent in response to an order received from the attorney general by advising the newspaper that he planned to begin his work on Monday. "In the mean time many of the owners were expected to have their machines moved out by Monday morning," giving C. E. Burlingame plenty of time to get Hillcrest cleaned up. The slot machines weren't the only new enforcement initiative. Under age youths, boys below 21 and girls younger than 18, were barred from the local dance halls. [412]

Hillcrest women began golf play early in January, despite cold weather. Mrs. Gerald Coburn was elected president of the golf association, along with other officers on a day that featured indoor putting on 14 January. Despite the enthusiastic start, the crummy spring weather put a damper on activity until April. As usual Hillcrest women participated in the district meet at Indian Hills. Jaycees played a sand greens tournament at Osage Hills. Both men and women played sweepstakes tournaments in April at Hillcrest. Jimmy Gullane was happy to host 100 golfers from the Tulsa District Golf Association in an inter-club relations meet in May. There was a flag tournament for Memorial Day. Though golf activity seems to have been sprightly, as with social notices, newspaper golf notices became more circumspect as the season wore on. [413]

Around town, tennis enthusiasts resurrected the Bartlesville Tennis Association after several years hiatus. The Jaycees sponsored a polo meet at the Dewey fairgrounds. The wide popularity of golf brought mass-market golf clubs to Montgomery Ward. A set of eight irons was $38.95, and four woods for $23.45.

Golf balls were on sale: 75¢ liquid center balls with vulcanized covers were 59¢, and 50¢ semi-plastic centers with vulcanized covers were 39¢. [414]

Assistant pro Harley Hicks was left in charge of a foursome tournament while Jimmy Gullane attended the state amateur tournament in Ardmore the first week in June. The winners were Mrs. C. W. Hubbell and Chuck Hyatt. A good rain soaking put off the Phillips and the Doherty Men's tournaments to late June. The National Indian Gold Tournament was scheduled at the Pawhuska Country Club the same weekend. [415]

Probably, while Gullane was still out of town, Hillcrest's caddies caught the national atmosphere of union unrest on the same weekend as the caddies at Southwest Park Country Club in Oklahoma City by attempting to organize for bargaining. Harold Smith was chosen spokesman for the caddies who demanded a raise of 20¢ for 18 holes. The wage scale at the time was 60¢ for novice caddies, 70¢ for intermediate caddies, and 80¢ for top-notch caddies. (Oklahoma City caddies were earning 25¢ a round.) Harley Hicks, whose duties included being the caddy master, instantly fired the lot. The caddies resolved to take the issue to the Hillcrest directors, while golfers were left to tote their own bags. The episode must have been short-lived because no one recalls the incident. Humorous as it all sounds, this was very frightening stuff in the context of the times. When ideas of collective bargaining managed to filter down to a lot of adolescent boys in Bartlesville, it was a sign that there was change in the wind for Bartlesville businessmen. For the next couple of years, it was "heads-down" for Bartlesville society, while civic leaders shifted their emphasis toward a more common touch in community events. [416]

While the caddy crisis was still fresh, young Tommy Trower shattered the course record for the front nine, shooting 30 on 16 June. At the time Tommy and state amateur champion, Bob Conliff, shared the course record. One hundred golfers turned out for the Doherty tournament qualifying rounds, including young ace Tommy Trower, and 11-year-old Keith Fowler. Interest was intense because Ed L. White, who was the DMF champion the last two years, was again in contention for the title. Should he win, he would have permanent possession of the H. V. Foster trophy. George Roach finally turned in the winning score. Immediately play began for the O. K. Wing handicap trophy in the Phillips tournament. A week later, William R. Lund emerged the Phillips tournament champion. The city sand and green championship was postponed again on 18 July, after repeated delays because of rain, and Hillcrest was closed for a few days because of soggy greens. Jimmy Gullane and Harley Hicks, along with Tommy Trower, Marvin Mesch, and J. W. Phillips went to the Oklahoma Match Play tournament at Indian Hills. [417]

Meanwhile, Hillcrest women showed well in the state tournament in Tulsa. Women's golf settled in to an active summer season. The club planned a mixed Scotch foursome before the Fourth of July holiday. On 1 July, Lions Club held an unusually large annual installation banquet. Ruth Doornbos shot the low score of her career on 3 July. H. C. Charles won the Fourth of July flag tournament the next day. The women's association had a busy summer with ladies day tournaments and mixed foursomes regularly. Mrs. J. W. Phillips and Mrs. C. W. Hubbell were finalists in the Tulsa District Women's championship tournament. [418]

Right after the Fourth, a handful of cases of infantile paralysis began to show up around the community. People were frightened. In a single week, 621 cases were reported in the United States that summer. The Bartlesville medical community was at a loss to explain the local outbreak. They fought back with their best guess effort, by quarantining the families of the victims. The American Legion responded immediately, purchasing an iron lung for the Memorial Hospital. The medical marvel was on display in the Hotel Maire lobby on 15 August.

As usual the caddy tournament marked the end of the summer season. Evidently the incipient labor movement was soundly suppressed. Rookie Smith defended his championship for the second year. Young Bob Finney won the Labor Day blind bogey tournament. Indian Hills visited Hillcrest and Hillcrest women cleaned up at an invitational in Nowata. The final round of the men's club championship included a match between young Keith Fowler and his father Charley, the defending champion. C. V. Johnson became champion a few weeks later. S. C. Warren shot a hole in one on number two. Mrs. C. B. Hubbell won the women's championship, and Mrs. W. E. Feist was handicap champion. W. B. Englebrecht was the men's handicap champion. [419]

ITIO had the clubhouse for a company party, with a dance and midnight supper, and bridge tables on 23 September. 450 Traffic Club men attended the fourth annual fete, starting 6 October. Hillcrest hosted a golf tournament and luncheon as their part of the event. It was followed immediately by the Jaycee's state convention the next weekend. One highlight was a golf tournament, and activities for the wives that were held at Hillcrest included a fashion revue, breakfast bridge, and the inauguration ball. [420]

The City continued to struggle with its water situation. Bartlesville was one of only two cities in the state that didn't own its own water plant. Public pressure was growing for an election about purchasing the plant. Meanwhile, the Hulah Dam initiative languished on Harold Ickes desk in Washington.

C. E. Burlingame decided to raze the country home on his property across from Hillcrest – the site of so many fancy parties and steak fries over the years - and build the handsome English Tudor house that stood at Burlingame Place until after it was sold in the 1970s and torn down to make way for the Glynnwood development. The Burlingames intended to move from the Cherokee Avenue residence to the new country estate home by spring. The architect was Walton Everman. [421]

One of the most significant instances for the community passed quietly, attended with concern of his many friends. H. V. Foster was suffering from recurring effects of a leg infection on 6 October. While many of his old friends were involved in the Traffic Club convention, he was at home in bed for an extended period, fighting off some infection in his leg. We know today the importance of moving about and mild exercise to prevent blood clots in bedfast medical patients. Possibly the leg infection was the genesis of a stroke that Foster suffered a few days later. It was the beginning of a steep decline until his death 6 June 1939. [422]

The Madison Trial heard the first testimony of witnesses about that same time, beginning a winter of frequent reporting of the progress of the trial. For the times, there was some degree of rancor among the defense attorneys toward the prosecutors, who they thought were trying to conceal from the jury the facts of the NRA code under which the oil industry operated at the time of the alleged infractions. During the Christmas break of the trial, Frank Phillips gave a major speech to the Tulsa Chamber of Commerce about the economic conditions in the oil industry. With a stab at humor, he explained the Gorgon's knot of laws, taxes, and regulations that were restraining free trade in the industry. "This constructive program which originated under the oil code was abandoned when…Now I come to the best part of my speech, but its been deleted by my lawyers." [423] Bartlesville leadership was feeling in the crosshairs, but civic life continued as usual. The annual welfare drive began in November with a goal of $14,200. It was including support for the Salvation Army that also had responsibility for the local transient problem. The drive was complete in only one week, and attention was turned to the Christmas Cheer Committee fund drive. $1,500 was raised from city businessmen with the remainder of the $2,165 goal to be finished by an anonymous donor (Frank Phillips). The Enterprise crowed that Bartlesville businesses would pump $800,000 in Christmas payrolls into the local economy.

Despite the continuing national economic distress, Bartlesville thought a corner was turning. In the fall, the social season opened with a series of parties all over town, as Bartlesville was feeling like celebrating even if they needed to keep their heads down. Clyde Byson's twelve-piece orchestra from Kansas City played for the country club Halloween dance. Usually a major party of this order would have had a big write-up, but this one gave no more information. The same night, Joanne Riney had a weiner roast for a number of her high school friends at the picnic grounds. The Dinner Dance club kicked-off the season on 9 November, with the Ross Revelers playing after dinner. Campbell's Serenaders played for the Thanksgiving dance. Notices for all of these events gave little extra information. This may have been a reticence from the kidnapping fears and political factors, or it may be due to a less energetic society editor. [424]

Christmas season was very active, but not evidently so splashy as society had started to become

in the last year or so. "The larger social events will center as usual at Hillcrest Country Club which is to be decked in its usual holiday attire to provide an attractive setting for the many gatherings which will be held there." [425] The high points were expectantly recited by the society editor: dinner-bridge, Fortnightly Club, then the first big holiday party, given by the Burlingames, followed by the annual children's party and a youth dance, then the really big parties given by L. E. Phillips and the Tyler's party, and a Phillips legal department farewell dinner for John H. Kane, and the annual New Years bash. All of this was interspersed with lesser highlights. The children's party must have been stultifying. Children gave recitals from their various dance and music schools, and even the debut of Verian Cheney's elocution class (which became a social fixture for the next 40 years). The youth dance emulated the adult parties with a large dinner party preceding the dance given by the Rammels, and a breakfast after the dance given for the DDD club by Louise Miller. [426] The Tyler party drew the big attention.

> *Another long line of automobiles will wend their way southward toward Hillcrest Country Club early this evening when guests begin assembling for the large holiday dinner at 7 o'clock at which Mr. and Mrs. Paul F. Dahlgren and Dr. and Mrs. H. C. Weber are to be hosts. Both the older and younger groups will be represented in the one hundred and fifty guests invited for the party.*
>
> *The dinner will be followed by an even larger social affair, the dance which Mr. and Mrs. D. M. Tyler, Mr. and Mrs. Scott Beesley, Jr., and John Tyler are giving as their contribution to the holiday gaiety this season.* [427]

The article has none of the elaborate enumeration of out of town guests, the full recounting of the flowers and candles, or even the name of the band. This sort of restraint is characteristic of the high society reporting of the time, despite the evident prosperity of the club.

As usual 1937 was rung out and 1938 came in at the annual "New Years Eve carnival ball." Don Colebourne and his Commanders from Oklahoma City played for the Hillcrest dance. With H. V. Foster sick in the hospital, unable to give his annual New Years open house, others took up the slack the next afternoon. Couples hurried between affairs at the John H. Kane home, the M. E. Foster home, and one at the country club hosted by the Minnigs and Fridays. [428]

The season was not over yet. The Artunoffs gave a party that is so legendary that it is still breathlessly remembered. Reda Pump was not under federal indictment and Kyra Artunoff did not feel pressure to curb anything. The whole of Bartlesville society was invited. Out-of-town guests included Armais Artunoff's brother from Detroit, Suren, who is remembered as the one who could do Cossack dancing, and the C. E. Stouts from Santa Monica. Of course, many from Tulsa, Independence, and Ponca City were on the list. It was as elegant a party as anyone ever remembered, with dancing beginning at 9:30 to music furnished by the Reggie Childs orchestra from New York City. [429]

The day before the party, Mrs. Artunoff used a Kansas City florist to decorate the clubhouse with the very latest festive and elegant appointments, including brightly colored helium-filled balloons. The next morning she dropped by the club to check on last minute instructions, where, to her wide-eyed horror, the balloons had wilted. In the lyric tones of a Romantic opera she shrilled, "Zee balloons, zey are like leetle peas!" That plaintive has been passed with a chuckle to three generation of Bartlesville women.

Within minutes she was on the telephone to the florist in Kansas City, "send some more balloons immediately." The florist responded in alarm that it was too late to catch the train to Bartlesville. She returned, "Well, send a driver." The florist's sinking reply was that there was no car available. "Then send them in a taxi cab." And, indeed, the party was festooned with helium balloons that very evening, freshly arrived from Kansas City by taxi.

The ballroom, dining room, and gallery were hung with garlands of smilax and huckleberry, and each of the wall lights was clustered about with an arrangement of white Garcia mums, carnations, and calla lilies with eucalyptus for subtle greenery. There was a mound of white calla lilies on the mantle in the ballroom, and each table had a centerpiece of callas and white tapers. The many-colored balloons were attached to the ceiling fans, and in eight huge balloon shells that were to release the orbs at intervals during the party. Attached to these balloons were lovely scarves that were the party favors. Other dance favors were small Russian dolls. During an orchestra break there was a floorshow that included Vernon and Rascoff, a novelty dancing team most recently from an engagement at the Meuhlbach in Kansas City, and special songs by the orchestra's singers. Tables were arranged in the balcony and in the dining room, and a midnight supper was served at 12:30. [430]

1938

It was the last really big party for months. Regular events such as dinner-bridge, dinner-dance club, and Fortnightly club met as they had for years. The medical society held a banquet and installed officers on 12 January. Jaycees had their big annual installation banquet on 21 January. The high school French club had a high profile banquet at Hillcrest on 29 January.

June Runyon's dance studio began a series of dancing parties on Valentine's Day, similar to the dance classes held by Irene Frank earlier in the decade. [430]

The annual membership meeting, preceded by the traditional stag dinner was held on 18 January. Though the total membership was 231, 50 men were present at the meeting. The new directors elected were D. L. Connelly and C. F. Beecher. M. B. Heine was re-elected for another term on the board. [432]

The city bond election on 19 January narrowly voted water bonds to finally purchase the city water plant. After years of struggling with water problems, it was a first step toward dealing with the chronic nuisance and occasional crisis. The most substantial help was still ten years in the future, as the Hulah Dam project still turned on a thread in Washington.

Of course, the now annual FDR birthday fundraiser for polio was held on 29 January at the Civic Center. The new populist mood enjoyed a new local sport, introduced by the Bartlesville Coursing Club. Wolf roping was held at the club ground west of town. "The wolf rodeo will be a prize event with the winners judged on the time they take in roping the wolves." [433]

The spring golf season was sprightly, starting in March. Pairing for the women's annual handicap feature event on 12 April was the first of the tournament season. There was mixed Scotch foursome play regular all year. On 5 May high winds didn't prevent enthusiastic play. As usual, the women engaged in tournament play around the state. Floodlights were installed at the practice putting green in time for the start of the D.M.F. tournament. Billy Simpson, by now a young ITIO employee who commuted from Nowata, was the tournament champion a few days later. Immediately, the Phillips Petroleum Company O. K. Wing handicap tournament got underway.

George Hanks emerged the champion. In shades of the old Oak Hill days, Hillcrest men fought a match between the red and the blue team for the prize of the losers treating the winners to a dinner party. The women divided up into 100% handicap teams for play that was intended to run for the summer. [434]

The Phillips annual meeting was held in Bartlesville on 26 April. It was a milestone year. The company showed $2.3 million in profit in 1937, producing 52¢ a share for stockholders, a continuation of the healthy growth trends of the last few years. There were big new management changes in the company, announced after the meeting. After the retirement of Executive Vice President John H. Kane at the first of the year, Frank Phillips retirement as president was announced at the board meeting, clearing the way for Boots Adams as the new president. C. P. Dimit, A. M. Hughes, F. E. Rice, and M. P. Youker became new directors; C. O. Stark, A. H. Riney, and R. C. Jopling became vice presidents. The new Phillips Petroleum Company research laboratory at Fifth and Jennings was completed three weeks later. Yet, The Madison pall hung over much of the city throughout the spring. Frank Phillips gave his usual party at Woolaroc for the directors on Sunday night before the board meeting, and Mrs. John H. Kane held a huge luncheon for the directors after the Monday morning directors meeting. The country club was not one of the usual highlights of the 1938 meeting. The omission may have been an attempt to disentangle perception of Phillips' troubles from civic Bartlesville. [435]

The National news was sobering. Mexico expropriated the holdings of foreign oil companies, to nationalize Mexican oil. In Europe, the Spanish Civil War took an ugly turn with Hitler's intervention. While in Eastern Europe, one nation after another began to fall to German machinations. Yet, American optimism and imagination was irrepressible. One happy example from the era was release of Walt Disney's animated movie, *Snow White*, a technical milestone of the time, and still a beloved classic.

At the end of May, 14 oil companies and 11 individuals involved in the Madison trials agreed to plea *nolo contendere* and pay $400,000 in fines. This included Empire Refining in Tulsa, Phillips Petroleum Company, and Frank Phillips. Upon his return to Bartlesville from the Madison, Wisconsin trial Frank Phillips gave a local interview,

> "I thought and still think that the conduct of my company in its efforts to help restore prosperity by correcting trade abuses was its patriotic duty and cannot be a violation of the law. After the government invited cooperation and the industry had generously responded, it was shameful persecution to procure the indictments at Madison." [437]

About the middle of July, the Madison trial judge finished his review of the evidence from the trial, revising the sentences of one corporation and 10 individuals. Frank Phillips was acquitted after the review, and A. M. Hughes and Phillips Petroleum Company were granted a new trial. But, 64-year-old Frank Phillips' health was wrecked. [438]

William Lund was social chairman for Hillcrest in 1938. He planned a spring schedule that was both robust and spare. The annual children's Easter egg hunt was a bigger and better event. Prizes were given for finding the six "golden eggs," and for the most eggs. The Henry Durst band played for the spring club dance on 23 April. There was a barbecue on 7 May at the picnic grounds. Otherwise, necessary civic events used club facilities. The Lions wives, Lion Tamers, had a big dinner party on 30 March. Phillips Men's Club held a dance on 25 March, and

The Lions Club held their state convention in Bartlesville. Their banquet was 27 May 1938 at Hillcrest. The banquet was held in the ballroom. The mezzanine can be seen on the right side of the photo; the doorway into the dining room can be seen on the left where overflow guests were seated. *Courtesy Bartlesville Area History Museum.*

the Doherty Girls held a Mexican dance on 27 April. Mrs. H. R. Straight honored Mrs. David Phillips of Bradford, Pennsylvania at an unusually large tea on 3 May. The social event of the spring season that got the most publicity was the politically safe junior-senior prom. [439]

With relief in sight from the Madison wet blanket, the social activity at the club was unusually busy. The season started with one of the June Runyon children's dances, that even included a buffet supper for the younger set. The Fourth of July celebration was quiet around town, but Hillcrest held a box super and fireworks display. A week later, the Benny Meroff band, which had a lengthy list of important engagement to their credit, played at an unusually large summer dance at Hillcrest. Bartian, Ruth Burlingame Gast was Moroff's sister-in-law, so Bartlesville was taking the opportunity to celebrate the success of one of their extended family. There were several pre-parties around town, and Chuck Doornbos even hosted a swimming party at the Foster Ranch. A number of luncheons and teas, of the sort that had been held discretely in private homes over the last few months, popped up at the club, even in the summer heat. [440]

The state Lions convention was the major civic event of the early summer. About 600 men and their wives attended. Harley Hicks issued an emergency call for caddies the week before, for the Sunday and Monday Lions golf tournament to be held at Hillcrest. The Club also hosted a banquet for the district governors and the governing board before the convention. Most of the meetings were held at the Civic Center, but the governor's ball at the close of the convention was at Hillcrest. A month later, the Dewey Roundup, which had been resuscitated to replace the horse show, drew 12,000 over the Fourth of July weekend. [441]

It was an interesting election year summer. FDR toured the nation in behalf of his favored candidates. In Oklahoma he had a long-lived duel with the indefatigable former governor, William H. Murray. Lifelong, dyed in the wool, yellow dog Democrat Bill Murray was so enraged at Roosevelt's political agenda and personal attacks on him that he had finally endorsed and campaigned for Alf Landon in the 1936 election. Roosevelt was not inclined to allow the insubordination to go unpunished. The axe fell in Oklahoma City on 9 July. Old time Oklahoma City residents can still describe the spectacle, as the President of the United States slowly circled the fairgrounds, waving and grinning at the frenzied crowds from the back seat of his huge limousine convertible. On the podium the Eastern aristocrat intoned the poison pill, "Of course some people are not even 'yes but-people.' For I notice that one of the candidates on the democratic state ticket this year is nationally known as a republican." [442] All the other Democrats were busily jockeying for favor during the presidential swing through Oklahoma. In the end, FDR did not endorse any of the men after his verbal assassination of Murray. The primary was held a few days later. After a close vote and a recount, Leon "Red" Phillips emerged the Democrat nominee for governor. The man who became Governor Phillips was good news to Bartlesville, for he was the brother-in-law of W. R. Smoot.

Just before school started, Frank Phillips decided to "throw a circus party" for all the Bartlesville school children. It was a brilliant stroke in his new more common touch image, coming in the wake of the Wagner Act and the Madison debacle. Suddenly he became "Uncle Frank" in the press releases. The public had already voted loudly about their entertainment preferences by their enthusiastic attendance at the Dewey Roundup in the summer. However the decisions were made, Hillcrest executed two real estate instruments in the fall that appear to have been a move to assuage the public sentiment and to appear more public spirited. At the end of September the Hillcrest Saddle Club and the board of Hillcrest filed a quit claim deed to Cella Gray's property where the stable and riding ring stood. About 2 weeks later, Hillcrest leased the river property they had acquired from John H. Kane the year before to the state Game and Fish Commission for a game refuge. The lease required the state to stock the property with quail, to provide cover for the birds, and to control predators, a popular movement at the time. [443]

Summer golf began with the Phillips-Skelly golf tournament at Hillcrest. Phillips was the victor on 4 June, just as the Lions came to town. Hillcrest golfers were out and about. Mrs. Wood played in the Trans-Mississippi tournament; and T.K. Willet, Billy Simpson and Jimmy Gullane went to the pro-am in Oklahoma City; 7 men went to the state open tournament; Bob Finney won the class A championship at the Tulsa District junior golf tournament. Keith Fowler, barely 13, won the club championship, and Mrs. Carl Wood won the women's championship. The Phillips engineers held a handicap tournament with W. B. Boggs the winner. Later in the summer, the Phillips comptrollers beat the treasurers in a friendly match. One hundred and seventy-five women descended on Hillcrest for the women's invitational tournament. Mrs. Tom Wallace of Tulsa and Mrs. C. B. Wood tied for low gross scores. On 24 July Mrs. Wood shot the new women's low score of 80. [444]

As usual, the caddy tournament was the last event of summer. Hillcrest members made donations to be divided as prizes for the boys. Harley Hicks explained, "any caddy can maintain his amateur rank

up until the time he reaches the age of 18 years even though he accepts cash prizes." Loddie Synos was the new caddy champ. Hillcrest caddy Fred Smith won the city championship a few days later. At age 19, the brother of Hillcrest caddies, John Smith and Rookie Smith, had been lugging bags for 7 years, but this was his first ever championship. Mrs. James Phillips won the women's handicap tournament and the women's championship. In mid-October the Rotary-Kiwanis tournament returned after several years. Rotary won. Hillcrest women kept up play long after the annual awards banquet on 3 November. Mrs. Opal Hill, Kansas City amateur turned professional was in Bartlesville for an exhibition game with Mrs. J. W. Phillips and Jimmy Gullane on 1 December. [445]

Signs of an improved local economy continued. Dewey Portland Cement re-opened 300 jobs in the Dewey plant in August, anticipating improved demand from better business conditions. H. E. Wilkins announced the opening of the new Southview Addition with 80 lots. [446]

Frank Phillips hosted the national conference of governors, along with 30 state governors and the interstate oil commission, at a Woolaroc shindig on 20 September. The event was a plum from Governor Marland, an opportunity for oil industry spokesmen to talk informally to an influential group of politicians. Two weeks later, the Traffic Club held their annual meeting. Hillcrest held a get-acquainted social and golf tournament on the morning the 500 guests arrived, then after a luncheon, the guests headed out to Woolaroc. The one-two punch of Hillcrest and Woolaroc was proving to be an effective method of dealing with very important large events. [447]

Plans for the new high school were moving forward rapidly in the fall. Late in 1937, local leaders approached John Duncan Forsyth, a Tulsa architect,

The Bartlesville Chapter of the Traffic Club hosted the national annual meeting in Bartlesville for several years in the 1930s. The Traffic Club was a trade association of transportation executives: railroads, pipelines, steamship and barge, air transport, mechanical and purchasing, warehousing, and trucking. Entertainment for the meetings was a luncheon and golf tournament at Hillcrest, they moved to Woolaroc for a huge evening party. On 5 October 1938, Business executives (left) enjoy a leisurely luncheon on the veranda of the clubhouse (Courtesy Woolaroc), later Frank Phillips (third from left, below) is photographed with some unidentified executives on the putting green in front of the clubhouse *Courtesy Bartlesville Area History Museum.*

about plans for a new high school. Forsyth was highly respected in Tulsa, and had done several notable buildings in Ponca City, including the Marland Estate. Most recently, in Tulsa, he did the Art Deco Daniel Webster High School that was completed in 1937. Bartlesville had woefully outgrown the old Central High School, and with the local economy improving, it was time to consider a new building with a Bartlesville statement. Forsyth's early plans were for a brick building in the Streamline/Moderne Art Deco style that was all the rage at the time. Dewey Portland Cement employees responded with a petition for a concrete structure. By late in 1938, plans had expanded to include a Manual Training and Field House building as part of the complex. The Frank Phillips Foundation gave $55,000 toward the construction of the industrial arts building. It was a masterful stroke. Frank gave his usual big closing dona-

tion toward this latest civic initiative. This time with the aid of the foundation arrangement he was able to make a much larger donation. In addition, he was able to foster his more democratic image by funding manual arts, and at the same time further his conviction that job skills were of key importance in the struggle against the threat of socialism. The new high school was designed to house the six-year program that included a two-year junior college, hence the eventual name *College High*. The new Art Deco high school building was in keeping with Bartlesville's long tradition of architecturally significant construction. The city educational establishment was ready to celebrate, which they did at the teacher's banquet held at Hillcrest on 30 November. Amidst the high school fund-raising, the annual Welfare drive got underway. The goal was $13,710 to fund the Welfare Association and the Salvation Army. [448]

The power base of civic structure, especially in women's organizations, was subtly changing. Before World War I the bridge clubs, Musical Research Society, and Tuesday Club held the clout in Bartlesville Society. By the late Depression the Musical Research Society and Tuesday Club (alternatively called Fortnightly Club) remained in the Bartlesville hegemony, while national organizations – Y.W.C.A., American Association of University Women, DAR, and League of Women Voters – were the most powerful sources of social capital for woman. The trend away from local organizations, toward big national organizations was nationwide. They had considerable influence outside of their immediate communities. The most influential men's clubs were the Chamber of Commerce, Lions, Kiwanis, Junior Chamber of Commerce, Rotary, and the American Legion. The country club is never mentioned as a civic organization, but in fact, as envisioned by the early founders had long functioned as the social wing of civic Bartlesville, the common ground and unofficial meeting place of all the organizations. [449]

In keeping with the steadily improving economy, social activity at the club increased substantially in the fall with numerous small teas, breakfasts, luncheons, and meetings. At the end of October, it was announced that the Mrs. Stewart, the manager, was resigning, and that Mr. and Mrs. Harry Claudy from St. Louis would be the new managers. Dinner-Dance Club opened its season in mid-November with dinner at 7:00, followed by dancing. They contracted with Ross Revelers to play the whole season. Beta Sigma Phi held a big breakfast party for pledges, the League of Women Voters held a large dinner to hear Dr. Benson of OU lecture on "Neutrality," and the faithful Fortnightly Club began its season of get-togethers. The Marshal Poole orchestra played for the opening club dance on 19 November. [450]

The annual children's Christmas Party actually started off the holiday season. As in the previous year, the party sounds stultifying. [451] The big party season started a few days later. The newspaper writer set the scene:

> Seldom is the club house more attractive than
> it is at present with its huge Christmas tree in the
> lounge with blue as the striking note, and the many
> large wreaths of green tied with red satin bows.
> Some hang from the balcony, there is a large
> one above the fireplace, and others at the door.
> The entrance is decked with Christmas lights. The
> tree is a particularly lovely sight with its blue-green
> foliage dripping with blue icicles and decorated
> with snowballs which shine realistically under the
> gleam of many blue lights. [452]

The Burlingames and their children started off the parties with a dance for their friends. All was festooned with balloons and Oklahoma mistletoe. Mr. and Mrs. K. S. Adams and Mr. and Mrs. Don Emery had a party for several hundred guests on 19 December. Several parties were squeezed in by the younger set. Jacques Collins, home from UCLA for Christmas break, had a big one with his younger sister on Christmas Evening; and a high school girls club called AKA had a very prominent dance. The Tyler party was on 30 December, but information about the party is very short. [453]

Mr. and Mrs. Donald M. Tyler

Mr. and Mrs. Scott Beesley, junior

Mr. John W. Tyler

request the pleasure of your company

on Wednesday, the twenty-ninth of December

at ten o'clock in the evening

Hillcrest Country Club

The favour of an answer is requested

Dancing

An actual invitation to the Tyler's annual holiday party, 29 December 1938. The Steiff bunny was the favor at the party. Stuffed animals were dangled from a fishing pole, piñata-style, for the men to knock down and give to their dates.

1939

As had been the custom for several years, there were some installation banquets for several civic organizations at the clubhouse after the holiday season. Kiwanis was on 3 January, and the county medical association was a week later. The Jaycees had a large inaugural banquet and dance on the 20th at which Stan Learned received a national service medal. The Hillcrest Women's Golf Association met and organized for 1939, a few days before the annual stockholders meeting, electing Mrs. C. B. Wood president. The new Hillcrest directors were John M. Kane, D. B. Dow, Forest B. Plank, and Harry B. Owens. Chuck Doornbos was the out-going president who announced the election of new officers the following week. [455]

Dinner-dance club continued its regular party season with a dance the day after the board elections, but other social activity was sparse for January. The president's birthday dance for the benefit of infantile paralysis was held at the Civic Center as usual, but the hoopla surrounding it was fading. The informal club dance reappeared after several years absence. On 28 January a buffet supper was served at 7:30, then a

The New Years party was the season event that it usually was. The party was preceded by an open house at the John M. Kane home on Delaware, then on New Years Day, there was an open house at the John H. Kane home. [454]

Throughout the fall and holiday social season there seems to have been a pent-up desire to really cut a rug. But, in fits and starts, the society editor seems to have been constrained in reporting the happenings. The pretty little picture of the Christmas decorations is something of a substitute for the usual detailed recounting of the flowers and tapers, bands and floor shows, favors, and midnight suppers that characterized the big parties. Questioning people who were at these parties, even if they can't recount specifics, the impression is that the delightful, rip-roaring parties rolled right on. Yet, at the end of 1938, there seemed to be some new concern in the air even as they passed through the holiday celebrations.

"colored" swing orchestra from Tulsa furnished the music for the 9:00 dance. On the same evening, the Burlingame's daughter, Mrs. Norman Gast, invited 60 guests to a housewarming party for their parents at their grand new country estate home across from the country club, the latest addition to the original vision of elegant country estates surrounding the country club. The beautiful English Tudor home that replaced the earlier house on the estate was an impressive landmark on the northwest corner of Country Club Road and Silver Lake Road until it was demolished in the 1970s to make room for the Glynnwood housing development. [456]

An important party in February was a sign of the times. For the first time since World War (I) days, for National Defense Week a formal military ball was held by the Bartlesville chapter of Army Reserve Officers. A receiving line of officers and their wives, including some from out of town, greeted the guests. The social pressure was on for the show of patriotism with a list of all the town's social heavy weights in the published guest list. The ballroom was decorated entirely with American flags and tri-colored buntings. Campbell's Serenaders played for the occasion and there was a grand march at 10:20. The dinner-dance club continued the theme a few days later. Names of dinner partners were found by matching names of presidents to vice presidents, which were found hung on a cherry tree in the living room. The following weekend the club dance continued the patriotic emphasis with the theme of George Washington's birthday with the music played by the Lloyd Hanson orchestra from Des Moines, Iowa. [457]

A new salvo hit very close to home on 2

Clarence Burlingame decided to raze the little country house, site of many swimming parties and steak fries, and built Burlingame Place on the estate directly across from the country club entrance. The housewarming party was held on 29 January 1939. *Courtesy Bartlesville Area History Museum.*

March, in an article in the *Oil and Gas Journal*, in which Amos L. Beaty, an oil man and attorney from Texas and New York who had been the New York bankers' watchdog appointed to the Phillips board to keep tabs on Frank Phillips back during the 1930-32 financial crunch, advocated "modified" federal control of the oil industry. The Madison trials were partly political vindictiveness, but they were also immensely useful rhetorical tool to remind the American public of the felt outrages committed by oil tycoon John D. Rockefeller in the 1880s, that lead to the trust-busting frenzy in the 1890s. These were no more remote to the people of the 1930s, than the Vietnam era is to us, and equally emotion-fraught. Now there was a move afoot to follow the Mexicans in nationalization of the oil companies. No wonder Bartlesville's fat and sassy attitude of the horse show era came to a screeching halt. No wonder many of the small parties that were usually held at the country club were moving to homes, and civic affairs were being held at the Civic Center or the Jane Phillips Sorority rooms. [458]

The March quarterly earning reports began to come out. It was announced that Phillips earned $2.32 a share in 1938, Reda Pump earned $1.12, and Cities Service earning were also down. All pointed out that oil prices were down substantially from 1937 and taxes were up substantially, nevertheless they all felt they were in good financial condition. Sandwiched in between those repots was a reminder of the continued general economic distress in which Congressman Woodrum of West Virginia asserted that needy Americans were not getting all of the relief funds being appropriated for them. The sobering effect of the double dip had hit. [459]

Social events at the club remained fairly active in March. There was a series of parties for five ladies who were visiting from Shawnee. There was a breakfast and a luncheon for them, given by several Bartlesville ladies. The Doherty Girls gave a big dance on St. Patrick's Day. The geologists' wives gave a dinner-bridge for wives of Phillips geologists whose husbands were in town for a geologists' convention. Easter decorations were up for the Dinner-Dance Club, who ate dinner at four-top tables before the Ross Revelers played for their dance. The Women's Golf Association dance was preceded by several small parties. The Ernie Williamson Orchestra from Pittsburg, Kansas played from 10:00 to 1:00 for the lady duffers. Lindenwood College alumnae had a big student recruitment dinner party. [460]

The season began to wind down in April. The Doherty Girls had a breakfast meeting at Hillcrest. Not to be outdone by the women, the men golfers had a stag dinner. The last Dinner-Dance club was an informal dance. The Sigma Chis gave a very large party with many out of town guests, active members and rushees. The last formal club dance of the season was on 29 April, followed in short course by the biggest event of the spring. Jane Phillips Sorority brought in a series of big-name bands, the last dance being the biggest with 600 couples. Vincent Lopez played the piano and his swing band packed the Hillcrest clubhouse with a capacity crowd. Part of the program was broadcast over KVOO. Lopez' featured artists included Betty Hutton. [461]

While the Sorority cut a rug, the Phillips men began pairings for the O.K. Wing trophy in the company handicap tournament. Play started as scheduled on 6 May, but microfilm quality is too bad to be able to report the results. The Doherty Men's Fraternity began their golf meet on 20 May, but the newspaper microfilm was again too poor to report the results. Fortunately, it was mentioned in a 4 July article that Keith Fowler was the J. M. Sands trophy winner. The spring golf season was active with numerous feature play and Scotch foursome tournaments, but readable results of club tournaments are spotty for the whole year. [462]

A general coal strike began in May mostly in the East, but also including Oklahoma miners, a sobering sign that the labor unrest that peaked in 1937 had not been resolved. At the University of Tulsa, a student came down with smallpox, and sent a fright through the public health community. But, most of the medical news was exciting almost beyond imagination. The new class of drugs, called sulfas, were the first effective antibiotics, the forerunners of the life saving medications that poured onto the market in the late 1940s, giving overweening hope of total conquest of infectious disease. In Bartlesville, the school board voted to only hire teachers who were not married, a reminder that some old fashioned practices persisted in a rapidly changing world. Nonchalantly, the newspaper reported that liquor prices were going up locally because of a big liquor seizure at Sulphur Springs, Arkansas that was making it difficult for local dealers to get a supply. They reported that cheaper grades had gone from $1.50 a pint to more than $2.00. [463]

A few of the civic clubs closed out the spring season with some banquets at Hillcrest. Beta Sigma Phi and Business and Professional Women's club had installation banquets. Kiwanis had a wives party for Mother's Day and the county Bar Association had its final dinner meeting. Lions had their recently usual installation banquet the last of June. Nellie McCready Wilson upped the ante among the various competing music teachers by holding her end of the year recital at Hillcrest on 21 May. Most of the other recitals in town were held at Garfield School. [464]

It was a hot, dry summer, and most activity around town, except for golf, slowed to a crawl. The women's golf association had a picnic on the back nine after their regular ladies day activity on Wednesday, 25 May ahead of the big golf tournament. In response to the reappearance of a junior boy's golf association, a junior girl's association, sponsored by the women's association, was in the process of being organized. It was announced that Jimmy Gullane would be giving lessons to the girls on Saturday mornings. The phenomenal success for high school age boys in the men's tournaments around the state had finally forced a loose organization of junior golf. In fact the various clubs' programs went by fits and starts when there was someone interested in promoting it. Formal organization was many years in the future. M. R. Heine won the Memorial Day flag tournament. A busy summer of four ball, Scotch foursome, and other little contests was scheduled. [465]

Immediately entries began to come in for the Oklahoma State Women's Golf Championship tournament, June 4 to 10. On the first day, Mrs. Tom Wallace of Tulsa Country Club, the defending champion, announced that she would not be entering the tournament. Interest was running high. Hillcrest entertained the women at an evening buffet and a banquet. A Wednesday evening picnic was held at the Foster Ranch. No wonder the junior girls association was organized: in the last round, 18 year-old Pat Grant of Cushing came from behind to defeat Bartlesville's Mrs. Carl B. Wood for the state championship. [466]

It had been a jolting week for Bartlesville. On 6 June, H. V. Foster died after months of illness, traveling from medical center to hospital, looking for help after his 1937 stroke. He died from a stroke, following a broken hip, in a Beverly Hills, California hospital. Three days later, he was buried in Bartlesville after a simple private ceremony held at La Quinta. His death set into motion a new series of events that would deeply effect the city.

The men's club championship was off to a good start by 11 June, with the state open champion, Billy Simpson, looking like the favorite. A few days before the final round, Simpson and Stewart Dewer played the new state amateur champion, Walter Emery and Frank Pryor of Tulsa in what appears to be one of those storied high stakes special matches at Hillcrest. Simpson took the club championship the last weekend in June. [467]

Meanwhile, the junior championship was in play, to be wrapped up on the Fourth of July weekend. Despite the heat, a big holiday was planned for Bartlesville - and sure enough, it rained. Bob Wills and his Playboys were scheduled to be the big show for 3 July in Dewey. The grandstand overflowed as a capacity crowd watched calf roping, bronc riding, bulldogging, steer roping, steer riding, half mile horse race, and a cowgirl exhibition. The same day Keith Fowler won the junior golf championship. On 19 July, V. T. Broaddus, owner of Bartlesville Stationary, and many times golf champion, died suddenly at age 39. On 20 July, J. H. Tippit shot a hole-in-one on number 12 hole. [468]

The slow pace of social and civic use of the club can be explained by the hot summer, but there was probably another factor. The Madison Trial was back. The U. S. Circuit Court of Appeals ordered the case retried, holding Federal Judge Patrick T. Stone's instructions to the jury contained an error. The government also filed a mandamus action in the circuit court, which was carried to the Supreme Court, which granted it a review. The action affected both Empire and Phillips. About a month later, a group of independent oil operators notified Interior Secretary Ickes to keep "hands off" the oil industry, in a stand-off in which the Secretary threatened to take control of the

industry. In Danville, Illinois, another federal grand jury had been meeting from 6 to 23 June on more anti-trust charges. The government said its "anti-trust campaign was necessitated by indications that practices on which the oil trial at Madison, Wisconsin, in 1936, were based have not been wholly abandoned in the oil industry." [469]

Despite the worry about the Madison resurrection, and about impending war in Europe, Bartlesville was arriving at another of the important civic milestones envisioned nearly 20 years ago when the polish-up Bartlesville move first started. The drawings for the beautiful new high school were splashed all over the back-to-school section of the Sunday paper. The building was about 65% done. Enrollment for the junior college was nearly tripled to 85 students. [470]

People woke up on the morning of 1 September to read the news that Nazi troops had rolled into Poland. The same day, Frank Phillips arrived back in Bartlesville after 2 months abroad. He said he was, "darned glad to be here," and that the Europeans were left guessing what was going on. After his interview, he headed out to Woolaroc to view the new construction that had doubled the size of his museum. The war gloom was offset by some good news. A grand jury that had been convened at Danville for another locus in the assault on the oil industry was dismissed by the court. The stock market began to rally. [471]

Qualifying rounds for the caddy tournament began 6 September. Harley Hicks announced that Loddie Synos would not defend his championship. After battling away for four days, Fred Smith became the new caddy champ. The men's handicap championship began immediately. Second round matches were reported, but then the microfilm became illegible so that results of the handicap can't be read. Mrs. J. W. Phillips won the Tulsa District title on 30 September, and became the Hillcrest Women's Handicap champion 17 October just as temperature were recovering from one last stint in the 100s on 7 October. Illegible microfilm obscured the women's championship tournament, but in the report of their awards banquet it is learned that Mrs. J. W. Phillips was the champ that year. [472]

Fall social activity was sporadic at Hillcrest as the summer heat dragged well into October. The first dinner-dance club was on 17 October. Right away things got going. There was a large tea in honor of several Tulsa ladies and Lindenwood College alums did another recruitment luncheon. The first club dance was a Hill Billy costume dance just before Halloween, and there was a dinner bridge party about the same time. A new kind of event was a buffet dinner and bingo party announced on 2 November. The usual meeting of the dinner-dance club in November was postponed a day so that the Doherty Girls could have their final meeting banquet at Hillcrest. [473]

On 4 October, the Traffic Club met in Bartlesville for their sixth annual visit. As was their practice, there was a golf tournament at Hillcrest in the morning, followed by a luncheon. Of the 126 participants, Lew Dunn shot low score with 40 on the front nine, and Neal Barrett was medalist with a 41 on the back nine. The winners were awarded blankets at the Woolaroc party that evening. The new egalitarianism was even out at Woolaroc with a Hill Billy band being the feature entertainment. The folksiness continued right on into the next local event, the Southwestern Fox and Wolf Hunters association field trials. The wolf hunters celebrated at Sunset Lake with a country band from Oklahoma A&M, a barber shop singing group called the Bar Flies, and a "Negro tap dancer." The city threw a kid extravaganza for 4,500 attendees on Halloween with a big parade and a costume party

at the Municipal Stadium, sponsored by the American Legion and downtown merchants. The Kansas University alumnae dinner drew quite a bit of civic interest with their first dinner meeting at Hillcrest. The Bar Flies quartet kept them on the populist track. The Welfare Association drive met its goal of $13,910. [474]

The event of the fall was one of the biggest in Bartlesville history – the sixty-sixth birthday of Frank Phillips on 26 November. The whole city turned out for the parade and many presentations during the daylong celebration. Frank Phillips used the event to announce a $66,000 gift to the newly formed college scholarship fund for the children of Phillips employees – another labor-sensitive initiative. But, the night before, 150 of his close friends turned out for a cocktail party at the G. C. Clark home, followed by a stag dinner at Hillcrest to pay tribute to "Bartlesville's No. 1 citizen." Speakers and toasts and impromptu remarks were the fare for the evening. The city's leaders heaped praise: H. W. Trippett who was president of the Chamber of Commerce led off, Clyde Morrison the president of Rotary spoke for the civic clubs, John H. Kane, L. E. Phillips, Burdette Blue, H. E. Hulen, Judge I. T. Shipman, H. R. Straight, L. A. Rowland, John Miller Kane, Clarence Burlingame, Don Tyler, and Boots Adams all held forth. It was an old-fashioned banquet with no nod to new inclusive trends. Frank Phillips' real birthday present came three days earlier when the Supreme Court affirmed the judge's ruling to dismiss indictments against 11 defendants in the Madison trial. [475]

The Christmas Cheer Committee Drive to furnish Christmas baskets for needy families lead off the holiday season on 17 December. The same day dinner-dance club had its December party. Just ahead of the social rush, the Land and Geology Department at Cities Service held their annual banquet. The first

Bartlesville celebrated Frank Phillips' 66th birthday in grand style. The events were capped of by a stag dinner with his close friends at Hillcrest, 25 November 1939. Those identified below: (left to right) obscured by the waiters arm is L. E. Phillips, right of the waiter is Clay Smoot, Frank Phillips, John Cronin, C. E. Burlingame, John H. Kane, Boots Adams, H. R. Straight, Noble Welty, H. C. McClintock, John M. Kane.

of the big holiday parties was a tea dance for 300 on the 22nd. The A.K.A. high school girls put together a very big dance on 27 December, complete with detailed description of all the decorations and flowers, hostesses, and important guests – just like the adults. Except, most of the adult parties were receiving only circumspect social notices, and there were decidedly fewer parties this season. The Tyler party saved the season on Saturday night. Party-goers passed through the Spanish Colonial portals at the front door only to arrive into a gay Japanese garden. Smilax was every-where, garlanding the walls, covering the windows and stairways. Japanese lanterns were suspended from the ceiling along with masses of balloons in silver and pale blue. A golden Buddha, Japanese fans, parasols, and antique candelabra were set about as decorations. French dolls and panda bears were the favors for the guests. The Eddie LeLange orchestra played for the dance. [476]

Preceding the New Years dance, the John Miller Kanes were "at home" to their friends. As usual, the big party in town was at Hillcrest where the Sternie Sternberg orchestra from Omaha, Nebraska played for the annual dance that began at 11:00 and ended with a breakfast at 3:00. It was the end of a very eventful decade, but it was not yet the end of the era of the Madison trials and the practices of political intimidation, or of economic troubles. [477]

The 1930s, were a storied era of hard times, a decade-long double-dip depression. It took several months for people to realize that the Depression that was more or less signaled by the stock market crash late in 1929, was not going to turn around quickly, but in fact continued to worsen. In Bartlesville, unemployment lists grew and small businesses failed as local community leaders found themselves in severely straitened financial condition. Frank Phillips found that he had a tiger by the tail, trying to raise the financing to keep the company afloat. The local relief rolls ballooned in 1930, and continued to grow worse for a couple of years before leveling off and then declining for the rest of the decade. Civic Bartlesville quickly organized to meet the relief emergency. The region suffered a storied drought that reigned for thirteen years, compounding the financial market collapse with agricultural failure. The successful entrenchment of Communism and its mirror twin, Fascism, in Europe encouraged leftist agitation and union violence in this country that sent chills down the spines of American businessmen. New socialism-lite initiatives from the Hoover and Roosevelt administrations, intended to meet the crisis and assuage political pressure, arguably prolonged the Depression. The oil industry (and others) endured a period of legal persecution for reasons of political revenge and policy advantage.

Bartlesville leaders drew on stores of social capital, first to meet the local emergency, then to rebuild, and finally protect the community from radical organized labor and from political attacks on the oil industry. The country club had another close brush with financial failure in 1930 and 1931, and was rescued by the old oligarchy of ITIO, Phillips, and Empire. Though Hillcrest membership dwindled drastically in the early 1930s, by the middle years of the 30s the club was in the forefront of the drive to reassert civic Bartlesville as a leader among the communities of the region. The horse show era failed to move Bartlesville socially into the first ranks of cities in the region much because of overreaching the local population, but also largely because of the populist ideology of the times, fears of radical big labor, fears of kidnappings, and the social rerouting in response to the Madison era. Nevertheless, the country club and Bartlesville businesses emerged from the 30s in reasonable financial condition, though civic functioning was permanently impacted by the new nationalization mentality.

During the period, there was a remarkable rise of youth oriented activities and Bartlesville enthusiastically embraced the social change. Before World War I, early moves, especially for boys, such as the Boy Scouts, were quickly encouraged in Bartlesville first by L. E. Phillips who saw the organization as a needed constructive activity for youth. They especially wanted to divert the boys from the dives on Second Street. Not many years later, the YMCA and then the YWCA were organized in town, and they too provided some new wholesome youth activities. The country club did its part with the development of junior golf and tennis that quickly became rewarding youth activities, as well as a vehicle for upward mobility especially for the boys who worked as caddies at the clubs. The youth organizations and programs in Bartlesville have proved useful toward fostering the development of the next generation of civic leadership. The rise of Big Band music ushered in the golden age of social dancing. It was a common denominator between kids throughout the whole community and once again, the country club did its part.

1940

There was snow for New Years 1940, and right after the first of the year the weather turned very cold. The advent of the cold and precipitation in the early months of 1940, did not put a chill on the usual round of civic installation banquets held at Hillcrest. The Kiwanis banquet was held on 4 January, the Washington-Nowata County Medical Society on 6 January, the Jaycee's Inaugural Ball on 14 January. There was some enthusiasm when John H. Kane took the reins as the new president of the Chamber of Commerce in their weekly luncheon at the Maire, seeking a new consensus for the direction of the flagship civic organization in the coming year. The Chamber had been suffering diffusion of direction since the horse show implosion, and there was a new imperative on the horizon toward cooperation between government and business. The new emphasis was patriotism. The Welfare Association announced the good news that their caseload was down to 189 in January. [478]

A blizzard roared into town, dropping three feet of snow on 14 January. The bad weather put a damper on much social activity outside of private homes in Bartlesville during the rest of the winter. Snowmen were the decorative theme for dinner-dance club two days later. Despite the weather, the Women's Golf Association held their organizational meeting on 18 January. Bartlesville ladies put their best foot forward for two large luncheons at Hillcrest, given by the Mesdames Straight, Ambrose, and Murray for Mrs. W. H. Merrit of Chicago, while the annual president's birthday dance at the Civic Center still attracted some interest. [479]

On 30 December 1939, the city released the first water from Bar-Dew Lake into the Caney River. On 18 January 1940, it was gleefully announced that that salty taste would soon disappear from city water,

a milestone in the long history of the Bartlesville water system. Only a few days later, the Department of Justice abandoned its pursuit of a rehearing of the Madison trials. The city was feeling better, with a little building boom going on. The spectacular new high school, a new Osage theater, the fancy Ritz apartments in the south part of town, and the Foster Petroleum Building at Third and Johnstone gave the impression of civic progress. Still, legislation to give the federal government control of the oil industry was working its way through Congress. Hearings on the Cole Bill were held in February and fortunately opposition was mounting. [480]

Despite the toughest winter in years, and the pall of threatened nationalization, social duties continued. The club dance on 10 February brought only the briefest notice, though it is learned that Hayword Marsh was the entertainment chairman at the time. Mrs. Paul Dahlgren and Mrs. H. C. Weber accomplished a true social feat by co-hostessing two luncheons at Hillcrest on the same day. Another military ball was held by the Reserve Officers as part of a second annual National Defense Week observance. That show of patriotism was the commanding social event of the season, drawing repeated publicity for weeks. On George Washington's Birthday, the dinner-dance club continued the theme with decorations of flags and bunting, cherry tree logs for candleholders, and cherry pie for dessert. Dinner-bridge had a St. Patrick's Day get-together, Dinner-Dance Club had a special guest night with Jackson's Orchestra from Tulsa on 19 March. The annual children's Easter egg hunt was early that year, on 23 March. The spring club dance was on 31 March. The final dinner-dance club of the season was scheduled to be informal with guests invited. It turned out to be their biggest dance of the year. On 4 May the final club dance of the season was informal. Phil Phillips entertained the national champion Phillips 66 basketball team with dinner at his house on Cherokee that evening, then brought the lot to the club dance. On Sunday afternoon, 5 May, the Musical Research Society sponsored a public concert at Hillcrest for National Music Week. Frances Fritzlen Ebright of Bartlesville and Alice Campbell Wrigley of Wichita University presented a dramatic musical. The Lion's Club held a ladies night at Hillcrest. Mrs. Billy Parker and Mrs. J. M. Sands held a very large, elegant, ladies luncheon, complete with the forests of flowers that marked an important affair. [481]

A break in the weather brought out 175 ladies for a Women's Golf Association benefit at the end of February. On the following Wednesday, the women were able to play outdoors for the first time in months, beginning the early season reporting of matches. By the end of March the tournament season schedule was compiled. The season opened with a mixed Scotch foursome breakfast before Friday play the first week in April. But, the kick-off was only a whimper, when within days rain postponed the schedule for the first time in the season. Women's play was coincidentally not hampered. The annual "remorseful" team play tournament between Chuck Doornbos Daffy Divoteers and John Cronin's Crackpot Cronies got off on 13 April, with the Doornbos team triumphant the next day. The Divoteers were treated to a stag chicken dinner by the Cronies. That day Dr. Kinkaide and H. E. Gibbs scored deuces on the number 16 hole. From the newspaper report of the incident we learn that the water hole at number 16 had just been remodeled. [482]

> *Ted McCaslin, greens keeper at the club, has done a nice job in making No. 16 one of the sportiest holes in the lay-out. The green has been moved to the left and raised even with the tee, requiring a well-hit shot to land on it.* [483]

Qualifying rounds for the Phillips Petroleum Company championship began on 20 April. Billy Simpson was the champion on 5 May. In between heavy rains brought flooding that finally flushed out the salty taste in the city water. The Tulsa District Women's Golf Association met at Hillcrest on 3 May with Mrs. J. W. Phillips and Mrs. F. W. Bleakmore of Tulsa the blind bogey winners. Doherty Men's Fraternity began its annual golf tournament on 18 May. While the DMF tournament progressed, for a little fun, Hillcrest pro, Jimmy Gullane, and M. E. Foster, the city archery champion, staged a golf-archery meet. Foster beat Gullane 67 to 71. [484]

The civic program was quickly coalescing. The new high school had been referred to as Hillcrest High since fall, but at the dedication ceremonies on 31 March it came to be known as College High School. Union National Bank crowed the sentiments of the city:

> *The dedication today of Bartlesville's fine new $500,000.00 Senior High-Junior College is just another testimonial to the foresight and confidence of our civic builders. It takes Confidence and Fore*

Planning for the Art Deco Bartlesville High School began in 1938 by Tulsa architect John Duncan Forsythe. The school, which included a junior college, was completed early in 1940 and was named College High School. It was another example of Bartlesville's interest in architecture and a new step in the build-Bartlesville civic tradition. *Courtesy Bartlesville Area History Museum.*

*sight to build a community. It takes courage to put
your city out in front. Bartlesville and its civic
leaders deserve upon the completion and dedica
tion of one of the finest school plants in the country.* [485]

The Chamber had a number of committees working, the most pressing were city beautification, housing, the Hulah Dam, and better highways. The Jaycees sponsored "Silver Dollar Day," a sort of citywide open house with parades, games, prizes, and so forth. It seems to be the origin of the famous Frank Phillips silver dollar give-away events.

It was election year and Vice President Garner had been loudly joining the fray, since early in January the only Democrat to challenge President Roosevelt in his unprecedented third re-election bid. By May, Roosevelt had already brought the party to heel and Garner was far back in the spring primaries. The Bartlesville Chamber of Commerce was already positioning the city in the face of the inevitable. On 7 May Governor Red Phillips flew in to give a speech at the first annual "head-up" dinner, a climax to the "Manpower Rally" that afternoon. The Governor spoke on the city's recently organized industrial council. Continuing the momentum, the Chamber immediately shouldered a program to help with the closing of the 1940 census drive. By the first of June the city boasted a little over 16,250 residents for the census. [486]

The Junior-Senior prom was held at Hillcrest on the night of 10 May. Did the party-bound youngsters muse at all as they perused the evening newspaper headlines: "Holland, Belgium, Luxembourg Are Invaded by Hitler Forces Moving in To 'Safeguard' Them." It was quite timely that the Traffic Club met on 12 May instead of their usual fall gathering. As they held their accustomed golf tournament and luncheon at Hillcrest before the barbecue at Woolaroc during the meeting, there must have been an awareness of the immediacy of the need to mobilize American industry. Indeed, only a few days later the headlines announced the pledges of full cooperation by the much-abused "Big Business" engine of the American economy. The shoe had finally dropped. The last of the Madison Era was in sight. [487]

HOLE NUMBER EIGHT.

344 Yards, Par 4. Be careful – the fairway 29 yards wide;
out of bounds right – lateral hazard left.
Fairway slopes left. Score on this hole is determined by tee shot. Forget the driver.
Use a long iron or fairway wood. Hit the club it takes to carry the ball to the landing area
125 yards from the green. Green is 4,500 square feet with severe bunkers.

9

HOLE NUMBER NINE.

502 Yards, Par 5. This dogleg right par 5 is not a difficult hole as long as you avoid the out of bounds and trees on the right side.

The only fairway bunker on the course is placed 257 yards off the tee – straight away.

You can reach the putting surface in two if you can avoid the left front bunkers.

This green measures 6,000 square feet.

CHAPTER FIVE

Where Have All The Young Men Gone?
THE *War* YEARS

The low rumble of an idling diesel locomotive mingled with the busy mid-morning sounds of downtown Bartlesville. Dark gray scut clouds hurried north across the face of an early morning thunderstorm that was exiting to the east, as sparkling April sunshine began to bathe the dampened bricks and running gutters of Bartlesville streets. At the back of the short train, a little Black kid with a huge smile popped off the stairs of the last passenger car, his punched ticket on a string around his neck, twirling in the gusty breeze. The conductor was only a step behind him, waving good-bye to Eugene Carney who was a frequent rider visiting his grandparents in Kansas City.

The conductor quickly busied himself with his duties, keeping an eye on the baggage and extending a hand to help two stylishly dressed ladies who were stepping out of the next car. One lady wore a closely tailored suit and the other a dress and contrasting jacket, both with padded shoulders and hems just below the knees. Their high, but substantial, heels were laced up with jaunty bows. One lady's hair was curled and topped by a small hat with a bow in the back, the other wore her hair swept up with a jaunty little topper like a small fedora with feathered wings against the sides. Two young gentlemen in striped business suits, tipped their hats as they met the women and helped them carry the fruits of their Kansas City shopping spree and their luggage, from the station to their waiting cars.

A small crowd of people milled around the station area to watch the train come in since the rain had begun to clear. A small boy jumped in a puddle, splattering his spick and span knee socks with muddy rainwater. A handful of cars were double parked at the curb on Keeler with trunks opened, disgorging or loading bags. Four young men, dressed in shiny new Army uniforms, slowly edged toward the train, wishing good-bye to friends and family. Donald Clark Fitch, Gene Bolser, Nelson Brady, and Russell Case were headed back to Camp Barkley at Abilene, Texas after two weeks leave. [488]

Only a week before, an Examiner *frontpage story reported that three of Bartlesville's prominent young businessmen who were reserve officers had also been called up. Since passage of the peacetime conscription act the last fall, each month Bartlesville had sent between 10 and 30 local men off for a year's military service. Young Jack Leonard, a reserve infantry officer and very active in the Junior Chamber of Commerce, was the first Bartlesville reserve officer to be called up on 22 April. Bob Neptune and Bill Simpson were ordered to report to Ft. Sill about two weeks later.* [489]

Bob Neptune, the county attorney for the last two years, stood near the first passenger car, a small valise in his hand. His father shook his hand and patted his shoulder, while his mother stood by with a crumpled hankie in her hand. Everyone smiled stiffly as they put their son on the train to Tulsa. Right behind him was Bill Simpson, the state open golf champion and former state amateur champion. His lovely wife of only two months was waving through a tearful smile as he hefted himself aboard the 9:30 (A.M.) train.

The United States was not at war, but Europe was. There was considerable vocal anti-war and isolationist opinion with some prominent voices, including all-American hero Charles Lindbergh and even Oklahoma's own Alfalfa Bill Murray. German subs had already attacked many American merchant vessels and Japanese predations in the Pacific were becoming increasingly ominous. The United States was attempting to supply Britain with new arms and aircraft. Military service was an inconvenient disruption of ordinary life, but these men were very patriotic. The wives and families, standing at the Bartlesville railroad station, knew there was a very real likelihood their young men would also see war service. The conductor, leaned out to take his survey of the area, "bo-o-ard," as the train lurched and pulled slowly out of the station to the sound of a revving diesel engine.

The changes wrought by the promised end of the Madison persecutions in May 1940 weren't immediately evident in civic Bartlesville. Life proceeded with a routineness that belied the disquieting headlines from overseas in the morning newspaper. The planned opening of Bar-Dew Lake was postponed at the last minute because city water shortages had forced Bartlesville to draw the lake down, preventing timely filling for the opening. Bob Matthews won the D.M.F. championship trophy at Hillcrest. The club began its annual championship tournament on Memorial Day weekend. Right after the holiday, the county Bar Association concluded its monthly meeting schedule for the summer with a banquet at Hillcrest, featuring state supreme court justice Thurman S. Hurst as their speaker. That weekend, on a campaign pass through Kansas, presidential hopeful Wendell Wilkie called Roosevelt a "piker." The same weekend, at a Woolaroc retreat, Archbishop Francis Spellman teased K. S. Adams that he was wearing the first "Wilkie For President" button that the bishop had seen. [490]

The sobering international situation was reported from Paris, where a correspondent wired the Associated Press that Nazi flags flew from every monument in what appeared to be a "dead city." Yet, the same page reported, "under cover of the exciting events in Europe a change occurred this week in business and speculative psychology which may mark a turning point in the American chapter of the economic history of the world struggle." President Roosevelt asked the oil industry to operate on a 24-hour basis in readiness to meet the international crisis. On the same day, he proposed institution of a military draft. A new tax bill passed, raising taxes to their highest since the Great War, and new national defense plans were announced to expand the naval fleet and provide additional officers for the military. All of this was none too soon, as German aircraft were already pounding Britain in nightly bombing raids, the beginning of the Battle of Britain that raged through September. [491]

In Bartlesville, while the semi-final round for the club championship at Hillcrest was finishing up, Bill Simpson, H. E. Gibbs, Jr., and Keith Fowler, along with Sunset ace George Hanks, entered the state amateur championship tournament at Oakhurst in Tulsa. It was the beginning of another active summer of golf at Hillcrest. Mrs. Carl Wood and Mrs. James Phillips took second and third in the Muskogee Women's Invitational tournament. On 16 June, the 1939 club champ, Bill Simpson, met Charles Hubbell in the battle for the 1940 championship, retaining his title. ITIO began its championship contest on 22 June, with H. L. Miller emerging the victor two days later. The Frank Phillips Men's Club began their championship on 25 June. Meanwhile, ordinary play proceeded at Hillcrest. On 28 June, F. W. Alexander, playing with E. E. Beechwood and Joe Glason, shot an eagle on the first hole, which was 365 yards. The week before, his son, John, had scored the same trick on number 17. The month ended with Mrs. James Phillips losing in the final round at the state women's

golf championship at Indian Hills in Tulsa. [492]

Social activity continued to be anemic, even for the usual early summer slump. Joanne Riney and Emily Ann Emery gave a dancing party to say farewell to their friends, Geraldine and Charlotte Wrinkle, who were moving to Oklahoma City. Doherty Girls ended their social season with a breakfast at Hillcrest on 11 June. [493]

The Fourth of July celebration was focused on the Dewey Round-up again. Bob Wills' band played on all three days. On the Fourth, Hillcrest members had a box supper of fried chicken at the clubhouse, then a fireworks display in the evening. The local news was fairly good. Money had finally actually been appropriated for engineering on the Hulah dam. The primary elections were held on 9 July, with Oklahoma sending a national defense delegation to Congress, and the local welfare rolls were reduced to 164 cases in July. Richard Kane and Mary Muder's wedding was the total of social activity in town for the rest of the summer. Some of their pre-wedding parties were held at Hillcrest. [494]

Golf and politics provided the entertainment in the dog days of summer. Ahead of the Democrat's national convention, Alfalfa Bill Murray declared an isolationist stand, and sniffed at fears of German invasion. But, Roosevelt's audacious run at an unprecedented third term as president was firmly built on the recovering economy and war fears. Socialist Henry Wallace was nominated for vice president. Jilted, Vice President Garner led a movement of party bolters, including Bill Murray. The Ku Klux Klan reappeared in national politics, metamorphocized into a radical, fascist organization, closely allied to their communist cousins of the anti-war activists left. This was a new and future phenomenon that was different from the traditional isolationists that had opposed all of our wars since the Revolution. Still, Bartlesville celebrated National Defense Day on 19 July, in a big way. Army recruiters were in town, and a big parade was climaxed with patriotic speeches and band music at the municipal stadium. Judge Hudson's oratory rose on the fears of the era, "This is a time when every man should know his neighbors and report to the proper authorities when he finds any communists or Nazis." [495]

Bill Simpson won the Frank Phillips Men's Club championship trophy on 9 July. Hillcrest golfers settled in for a leisurely deep summer season. Following the regular Scotch foursomes, at 4:30 on 23 July, the women's golf association held a picnic and putting feature for non-golfers. Keith Fowler, James Bailey, Johnny Alexander, and Bob Finney entered the Tulsa District Golf Association junior championship at Tulsa Country Club and made a good showing. An Oklahoma City guest of R. E. Boggess and F. I. Thompson, Clyde Davis, capped off the summer with a hole-in-one on the sixteenth hole on 23 August. During the summer, the city was enjoying a little renaissance of tennis interest, though there was no tournament play at Hillcrest. The tennis courts had fallen into general disrepair during the long neglect of the 1930s so that they were in no condition for tournament play. The member's kids piddled at the game on the old courts that were even cracked during the drought of the 1950s. It was many years before tennis was enthusiastically rejuvenated at Hillcrest. [496]

Bartlesville's labor unions organized the Labor Day festivities on 1 September. Since the fear-full days of the middle 1930s, a great deal of effort had gone into fostering "an harmonious solution to labor's problems." [497] This was the second year that the union's Unity Council had been in charge of the holiday observance in Bartlesville. The successful efforts of local civic and labor leaders had the object of averting the tension and violence of labor action found elsewhere in the state. While the parade and baseball game were going on, two social events popped up at the country club. Mrs. A. W. Neal surprised a visiting niece with a dinner bridge, and the Dimits entertained a number of young people at a dinner party for some visitors from Pennsylvania. [498]

Rains over the next few days postponed golf and softball games around town. By Wednesday, there was wide spread flooding in the state and, of course, the Caney was also flooding, limiting access to the country club. Bartians' entertainment for that soggy week was the official opening of Martin's Department Store in the new Foster Petroleum Building on the corner of Third Street (now Frank Phillips) and Johnstone. The old store there had been Degans, but in the new building, Martins welcomed a curious mob of 4,000 from 7:00 to 10:00 on the evening of 5 September, with balloons, flowers, and music. Not to be outdone, Koppel's was newly ensconced in quarters a few doors down the street, holding a similar open house on 12 September. In those days much shopping in downtown Bartlesville was very upscale, with Montaldos across the street, Swing's shoe store and Zofnness next door, and May Brothers across Third Street. Only a few ladies went off to Miss Jackson's in downtown Tulsa for even more exclusive fashions. [499]

Shortly following the flooding, there was a typhoid outbreak and it was feared that it was caused by seepage into cisterns and wells, a problem that had not occurred in better than ten years. Public health was immensely improved, and the local problem was quickly contained. The Chamber received a report that the City was testing any suspect water supply, but a few days later it was determined that the source was actually unpasteurized milk that some families were purchasing from Linn Dairy in Dewey. At their first fall meeting they also heard about progress on the Hulah project, national defense, the local housing situation, and a proposed new $50,000 bond to build an addition on the Memorial Hospital. After several years' retrenchment, it was beginning to sound like Bartlesville was again setting its sights on aggressive civic progress. Still, the most influential event of the fall was Congress' passage of the military draft on 12 September. Men between ages 21 and 35 were liable for one year's service. It would change the face of Bartlesville. [500]

National policy toward the oil industry continued to improve. The National Defense Commission clipped Attorney General Jackson's wings by issuing a report that another planned anti-trust suit against the major oil companies would hinder the defense program. Yet, Harold Ickes threatened a new scheme to bring the industry under federal control, this time under the guise of national defense. Wendell Wilkie immediately attacked the proposal in his campaign, gaining the support of most oil country executives. [501]

September was frenetic with fall season golf activities at Hillcrest. A leisurely breakfast and Scotch foursome on 7 September was the last of the summer season for the women's golf association. The next day, the men began their annual intra-club match, that year between R. L. "Captain" Kidd's Pirates and W. R. Lund's Outlaws, followed by a picnic. Things got much more serious with the last round of the caddy tournament, Loddie Hambie the winner. Loddie was also the winner of the Tulsa District caddie championship. Jimmy Gullane made him the new caddie master. The women's championship tournament began on 16 September, and men's handicap began on 15 September. Mrs. Phillips again won the club championship on 19 September. During men's handicap play, Jimmy Gullane had a good day, besting his former re-

cord of 69, with a new club record of 68 strokes. Mrs. Phillips took honors at the invitational tournament the women's golf association held on 26 September. [502]

The excitement for the fall season was the Oklahoma State Open Golf Championship tournament held at Hillcrest the last weekend in September. Jimmy Gullane and greenskeeper Ted McClaus were busting their buttons at the good condition of the course after a summer of good rainfall. A call went out for 50 additional caddies. Golf enthusiasts anticipated a very competitive tournament with many of the state stars in town, and with our homegrown lights. Sure enough, Hillcrester Bill Simpson and Walter Emery

Bill Simpson shakes hands with Hillcrest caddie master Rookie Smith his win at the Oklahoma State Open Golf Tournament, 1940. *Courtesy Bartlesville Area History Museum.*

of Tulsa Country Club put on a great show for the crowd. Bill Simpson, who also won the state open in 1938, went six over par to take the 1940 championship. Simpson and Jimmy Gullane tied the pro-am event with Bill Oliver and Labron Harris of Oklahoma City. [503]

Mrs. James Phillips retained her title in the handicap championship on 8 October. The season was becoming chilly early, so that there was some question if it would be too cold for an exhibition match on 13 November, featuring professional Denny Shute. He was in town to promote Montgomery Ward's golf equipment, and was scheduled for a full agenda in town. Besides the exhibition match with Jimmy Gullane, Shute and Stewart Dewer planned to play Gullane and John Cronin, probably in one of those legendary high stakes rounds. Sure enough, the Hillcrest appearances were "frozen out." He gave a thrilling talk and demonstration to the Frank Phillips Men's Club before leaving town. The women's golf association closed out their season with their annual awards banquet on the same day. [504]

As usual, Dinner-Dance Club kicked off the fall social season in mid-October. The membership of 50 was quickly filled and everyone looked forward to dinner at 7:00 and dancing once a month to Jackson's orchestra from Tulsa. The first club dance of the fall was a costume party a few days before Halloween. Members could invite both town and out-of-town guests and dancing was to the Art Davis orchestra. Several dinner parties preceded the dance. In between dance parties, Beta Sigma Phi fit in a banquet for its pledges. Doherty Girls held an even more ostentatious annual banquet with a birthday party theme. Twelve tables were each decorated for the month's birthdays it represented. Dancing and a floor show followed. Dinner-dance club followed right along

with a Thanksgiving theme (probably inspired by the new Disney movie, *Cinderella*) a few days before the holiday. Five long tables were decorated with fanciful pumpkin coaches with rotund drivers fashioned from vegetables. "Their plump purple bodies were eggplants, with turnip heads and mango hats. Their string bean arms were extended to hold the reins to guide large turkey gobblers." The decorations didn't warrant a detailed description for the Thanksgiving club dance on 23 November, but it was noted that very large party was preceded by several "cocktail" parties around town, including a particularly interesting one at the Artunoff home. While the big parties for the season were off to a roaring start, private events were quite lacking, except for a dance given by the Beesleys for 40 junior high kids to celebrate Celeste's thirteenth birthday. [505]

The city enjoyed another big Halloween costume parade again. Afterwards there was a show, band music, and prizes at the stadium to keep Bartlesville kids out of orneriness that night. Some kids did escape the round-up, and the police reported a number of pranks around the city. The town was finding a racial consciousness, and for the first time special provisions were made for Black kids to participate. The Bartlesville Welfare Association kicked-off its annual drive, this time with a goal of $14,060. As had been the practice since its inception, every employed person in the city was asked to contribute a part of his or her income. In 1940 it was 2/3 of a day's wages. Local businesses and civic leaders finished the goal at the end of the drive. There was quite a bit of social pressure, and some resentment of the coerced donation, but Bartlesville continued to provide for its needy citizens. The Jaycees headed up their annual Christmas Cheer Committee drive a month later to deliver baskets to 375 needy families on Christmas Eve. [506]

The presidential election of 1940 was on 6 November. Close to 14,000 voters in Washington County gave Wendell Wilkie a majority of 1,000 votes. F. D. R., of course, comfortably won his third term, but not with the margins of his second term. Still, Americans were unwilling to change horses in such dangerous times. At a Tulsa Chamber of Commerce forum, Oklahoma congressman Disney said the bill to establish federal control of the oil industry was bottled up in committee. Yet, only weeks later, Secretary of Interior Ickes said, "Both the Navy and the Interior Departments believe that oil belongs to the government, - or ought to be." [507]

The early Christmas season at Hillcrest was kicked-off by an ITIO banquet with awards going to 213 employees at the event. The Sigma Chi's held a sweetheart dance early in December. A bridal shower for Mildred Easter was held in the mezzanine at Hillcrest with a dessert of ice cream molded in frozen lovebirds, served on crystal plates. It was the very latest – virtually haute cuisine – at the time. Mmes. Coburn and Fowler held a Santa Claus luncheon and bridge party for 69 friends. [508]

Dinner-dance club opened the high holiday season on a Tuesday night, 17 December. The club was decked out in its Christmas finery:

The 1940 Christmas Season was kicked off by the ITIO employees banquet, 4 December 1940. *Courtesy Bartlesville Area History Museum.*

The club house itself is in holiday attire and made a beautiful setting for the affair. Holiday greens have been hung throughout and the alcove is the highlight of the decorative scheme. Here stands a huge decorated Christmas tree and snow scene. Beneath the tree is a village with lights in the windows of the tiny church and houses. At an other point is the stable scene with the Christ Child and at some distance stands a miniature army camp suggesting one of the major interests for the world for the 1940 Christmas season. [509]

Mmes. Barton E. Witchell and E. B. Emenhiser were the hostesses of a large Christmas tea for two shifts of ladies on the afternoon of 18 December. The annual children's party was held on 21 December. Musical Research Society held a Christmas luncheon for 100 members. The AKA girls had another huge dance for the college age set. Mercedes Freiday had a reception for friends and a number of out-of-town guests in two shifts from 5:00 to 6:00 P.M. and 8:00 to 9:00 before the AKA party. [510] The girls augmented the Christmas decorations at the country club with a patriotic theme:

Cellophane streamers of red and white extending from the sides of the room formed a canopy in the large ballroom and dozens of red, white and blue balloons contributed to the setting… Above the fireplace hung the large letters forming the club's monogram which has been used at the Christmas dance each year. This year the background was an American flag. [511]

Greeting their guests in a receiving line and dancing to the Chuck Angevine orchestra, these young *arbiters elegantiae* had certainly learned how

AKA was one of those self-organized high school social clubs that was popular with Bartlesville high school kids right through the 1960s. Marie Pinkerton Freiberger says AKA does not stand for anything. By 1940 some of their members had moved on to college, so they had a Christmas dance that included the college crowd. Like the Club of '35, this club produced a number of local leaders. The girls are (left to right) back: Dottie Gleason, Peggy Fierce, Joann Johnson, Jane Stites; middle: Louise Rodgers, Anait Arutunoff, Mercedes Freiday, Babette Bateman; front: Beverly Ann Duston, Marie Pinkerton, Martha Fitzjarrald, Mary Louise Adams, Helen Gardner, Virginia Hoffman. *Courtesy Marie Freiberger.*

to throw a bash. The annual Tyler holiday party kept up social standards on the following evening. Gone were the Christmas decorations in favor of masses of smilax, draping the windows and completely screening the walls, with poinsettias and palms appointing the fireplace. One o'clock supper was served with an Hawaiian beach theme. [512]

As usual the Hillcrest New Years party was preceded by a number of dinner parties and attended by many out-of-town guests. The Stan Stanley orchestra played from 11:00 P.M. to 3:30 A.M. and dancing was followed by breakfast. It was one of the biggest parties of the old year and anticipated an active social year for 1941. [513]

1941

Right after the beginning of 1941, the usual round of civic events began their annual banquets, about half of which were held at Hillcrest. Kiwanis installed officers on 6 January, with 122 at the dinner. The Jaycees topped them with better than 200 at their installation banquet and dance on 17 January. The theme for the dinner-dance club party on 20 January, was a "children's party" with pastel tints and dolls for decorations. Dinner was at 7:00 P.M., and Jackson's orchestra from Tulsa played the dance music. The next night was the annual meeting for the country club. C. E. Beecher, M. B. Heine, and D. L. Connelly were re-elected as directors. A week later Forrest Plank was elected the new president, J. F. Cronin was re-elected secretary, and Ed L. White was re-elected assistant secretary and treasurer. [514]

The Chamber of Commerce sponsored a smoker at their office downtown with free soda pop and cigars for an organizational meeting of the Round-up Club. It was attended by 46 local cowmen and business leaders. The club was a new initiative that the Chamber hoped would continue to draw Western events to the area and to provide an infrastructure for the spectacularly successful Dewey Round-up. Of course, the FDR birthday benefit party was held again at the Civic Center. [515]

February was the most active in a few years at Hillcrest, despite heavy snowfalls and cold. The luncheon bridge club was held at Hillcrest on 5 February, but they played cards the rest of the afternoon at the home of Mrs. Forrest Smythe. The February club dance was an informal dinner dance on 7 February, which was a smashing success. The 150 members and out-of-town guests danced to Strenie Stromberg's orchestra from 9:30 P.M. to 1:00 A.M. and enjoyed an "imported" eight-act floorshow. The Doherty Girls annual club dance featured the Hal Brown orchestra on 8 February. On 9 February, Mrs. W. P. Ringo and Mrs. G. V. N. Yates played a piano concert. Two concert grand pianos were brought in from Tulsa for the event. The music was billed as "lighter" and suited to a more general audience. *The Blue Danube*, *Rush Hour in Hong Kong, South of the Rio Grande*, and Rachmaninoff's *Lilacs* were the draw that afternoon. Dinner-dance club's monthly dance on Tuesday, 19 February, celebrated George Washington's birthday with a patriotic theme of decorations. The reserve officers held their third annual ball, with several out-of-town couples invited, and any active duty officers invited. There were small dinner and cocktail parties preceding the 9:30 reception. The numbers in attendance were somewhat depleted from the previous years, as young officers were already being called up for six month's training. Forty couples attended to dance to the Harold Brown orchestra. On the same day the ball was announced, the newspaper article immediately below that about the reserve ball proudly announced a new enlistment each day for the month of January. Along with the pick up in large social events at Hillcrest, small club meetings and luncheons were also busy during the spring. [516]

Heavy snowfall fostered another kind of social activity at Hillcrest. Bartlesville children fondly remember sledding and skiing down the best hills in town – on the fairways. Bill Yinger joyfully retold of "skiing" on the 18th, using slabs from a barrel for skis. [517]

Family night was a new successful sort of party at Hillcrest. After dinner, bingo, ping-pong, cards, and other games were the featured entertainment. It is interesting to remember that table games were very popular entertainment in the world before TV and before the extreme individualization of our time. Getting out the game board, or whiling away an evening at the ping-pong table were the standard ways that families and friends relaxed together. These family parties at the country club were so successful that they became regular mainstay events. [518]

There were other portents of the end of an era with the announcement of the huge taxes paid by the Foster estate on 11 February. The effect of the statist Robin Hood confiscating wealth through estate taxes would soon ripple through the city economy, costing many Bartian's jobs, and costing the city one of its key oil companies. [519]

A few days later, the Chamber of Commerce decided they would not seek to bring conventions of more than 250 delegates to town the next year. In another milestone decision, the Chamber endorsed a new group hospitalization insurance plan, Bartlesville's beginning of the costly third-party payer system. [520]

One of the biggest civic events of the spring was the state DAR convention on 4, 5 and 6 March. Most of the meeting sessions were held at First Methodist Church, and the officer's banquet was at

the Maire, but the big banquet was held at Hillcrest in honor of the visiting national president, Imogene B. Emery from Iowa. In her address to the leading women in Oklahoma, Mrs. Emery stated, "As originally presented it [the lend-lease act] is a dangerous act, abrogating all powers of Congress to the chief executive- a peacetime measure with power conferred beyond that given to dictators, or such as are given to the executive only in emergencies, drastic emergencies." Pretty strong stuff for women we moderns would presume to be unemancipated. But then, the national workforce already consisted of 40% women. [521]

In March Phi Delta Theta had a dinner, Beta Sigma Phi had a dance, and the Sigma Chi's had an alumnae dinner. Heavy snows postponed the annual "Spring Opening" of Bartlesville merchants' Easter merchandise on the evening of 13 March to 20 March. Easter bunnies and eggs decorated the dinner-dance club party on 20 March. Toastmasters officially became an organization at an installation banquet at Hillcrest on 29 March. By April the social activity pulled into full swing. The Hal Brown orchestra played for the club dance and there was a floorshow, but it was all over early, at midnight on 12 April. That was because the next morning was Easter. The annual children's egg hunt was on Easter afternoon. Dinner-dance club held its last monthly dance of the season on 16 April, decorating the tables with toy cars for an auto show theme. The Sigma Chi's held their annual spring dance on 19 April. Boots Adams was the alumnae president that year, inspiring 130 members and guests to turn out for the event despite torrential rain and a rising river. Oklahoma oil accountants, some 200 strong, held their convention in April, with golf and their final banquet at Hillcrest. They dined on Hillcrest's famous steaks and the program for the evening was a humorist. [522]

In May the Business and Professional Women held a Mother's Day banquet at the country club. The junior-senior prom was the following weekend. Bartlesville put on its best show for the Oklahoma Press Association convention in mid-May. Sessions at the Maire Hotel, golf and banquets at Hillcrest, an open house at Burlingame Place, and a barbecue at Woolaroc kept the newspapermen entertained like royalty. Several of the smaller ladies' civic clubs had luncheons at Hillcrest during the spring, a refreshing trend from recent years. The biggest was the Sorosis musical tea in May. [523]

Right after Easter, an unusual series of fashionable ladies luncheons and teas kept Bartlesville socialites on their toes. Mrs. C. O. Stark and Mrs. E. C. Kitching were hostesses of a luncheon for 30 quartet tables, decorated with hobnail vases of spring flowers, then an afternoon of bridge in the living room that was decorated with tulips, apple blossoms, and lilacs. That set the stage. Mrs. A. H. Riney and Mrs. Stanley Learned were hostesses of another spring luncheon on 22 April. Another luncheon by Mrs. J. Sam Williams and Mrs. L. T. Huffman was on 26 April. Mrs. F. N. Duston, Mrs. Clint Rogers, and Mrs. George Baird gave a large tea on 30 April. Mrs. E. F. Walsh gave a "thimble party" tea for bride-elect Mary Martha Sellers who would be marrying Walter Evans in June. Mrs. J. F. Cronin and Mrs. H. K. Kirk held two luncheons on Monday and Tuesday, May 26 and 27, to accommodate their guest list. Mrs. W. B. Engelbrecht and Mrs. W. A. Hensley entertained more than 100 ladies for luncheon and bridge on 5 June. [524]

The society maneuvering continued through the June wedding season. Mrs. H. H. McClintock and Mrs. H. E. Hulen had a wedding breakfast in honor of Katherine Goddard and Mary Martha Sellers. The Don Emerys had an important dinner party to entertain the Frank Begrischs while they were in town visiting Frank and Jane. The Doherty Girls held their annual breakfast. Mrs. J. Wood Glass and Mrs. H. W. Read, Nowata members, held a goodly sized luncheon at mid-month. A week later, the Don Tylers and Scott Beesleys gave one of their big dances for Margaret Swain, John Tyler's fiancé. As was fitting for the most social parties, the country club was festooned with flowers and decorated to the teeth. There were several pre-parties and refreshments were served at 1:00 A.M., while Campbell Serenaders took a long break. It was the finale for the busiest summer social season in memory. [525]

Hillcrest may have been quite interested in the report that members of Tulsa area, Oakhurst and Indian Hills country clubs were arrested in slot machine and liquor raids by state officers. Local Bartlesville officers had a more heroic image when Officer Fishburn hurried to a call at the sidewalk in front of the Union National Bank and there grabbed a large snake by the tail and stepped on its head. These were lighter affairs, while civic life continued in the unusual environment of impending world war. The Chamber of Commerce became preoccupied in the spring with community participation in the national defense initiative that was a growing concern. At the convention in Bartlesville of the Oklahoma Association of Commercial Secretaries, the statewide chamber organizations wrestled with the looming commercial changes. Of course, Bartlesville feted the Chamber leaders with their best foot forward. Finally, that month the U. S. Senate passed the necessary legislation for construction of the Hulah Dam. The following morning the news was that The American Boy Academy had purchased La Quinta, the Foster mansion near the country club, for a military boarding school. [526]

The Foster estate sold the La Quinta property to The American Boy Academy, a military boarding school, in May 1941. By the end of the war, the school was closed. *Courtesy Bartlesville Area History Museum.*

The winter and spring months were burdened with heavy precipitation that suppressed golf activity at the country club until after the middle of March – just in time for the last heavy snow storm of the season. To kick things off, Don Wilkie arranged a demonstration round of golf on 16 March, including Sunset champ Bill Emerson and medalist Dave Lhuillier and Hillcrest pro Gullane and champ Bill Simpson. The snow cancelled the demonstration, but all three golf courses in town reported play two days later. Near the end of the month Osage Hills Golf Club was feeling enough new life to apply again for membership in the area organization of golf clubs

called Sekanokla, and we learn that at the time Hillcrest was also a member of this southeast Kansas and eastern Oklahoma association. For the first time in years, Hillcrest hosted a high school golf tournament with several area teams in town on 9 April. [527]

Tournament play began on 26 April with the annual club team match between Peyton's Punks and Julien's Jug Heads, the losers footing the bill for the stag dinner afterwards. Qualifying rounds for the annual Phillips O.K. Wing trophy began on 18 April. Jack Calvert, an Osage Hills member, won the tournament on 4 May. "First time I ever broke a hundred at Hillcrest," he told the newspaper. Qualifying rounds for the DMF tournament began on 6 May, with 100 men entering. Bob Matthews eventually retained his title as DMF champ. Memorial Day weekend was very active. ITIO began qualifying rounds for their championship at Hillcrest, the qualifying round for the club tournament began, and the women began a flag tournament. Slipped in between the major annual tournaments, area bankers held a tournament and luncheon on 22 April. Meanwhile, Jimmy Gullane and Keith Fowler ventured down to Southern Hills to enter qualifying rounds for the National Open. [528]

When H. V. Foster retired as chairman of ITIO back in 1937, which long had been a subsidiary of Cities Service, it signaled the impending complete merger of the two entities. Soon all of Foster's remaining personal business interests were vested in Foster Petroleum Company, but the employees of ITIO faced the prospects of the process of merger. Time passed, and as the economy recovered, merger fears slipped into the background. On the morning of 10 June 1941, Bartians woke to the announcement that ITIO would be completely merged with Cities Service. Burdette Blue tendered his resignation. The sober news was cloaked in patriotic rhetoric that the move was to position the company to serve the national defense. Within months the Burdette Blue family had moved to Tulsa. [529]

When the final announcement was made on 2 August, most ITIO employees were absorbed into Cities Service, but many lost their jobs. Bartlesville endured a prolonged period of contraction. It was a period in which the leadership of one of the major industries in town was lost forever, full recovery from the Great Depression was only beginning, the old, stalwart leadership was retiring and dying, and the new generation was absent, serving in the war. John Hughes described the impression of the time, "Half the houses in town were for sale." [530]

The 1940 I.T.I.O. golf champion, M. F. Broaddus stoutly defended his title early in June 1941, but was bested by Dick Booker on 3 June. Booker was the last I.T.I.O. golf champion. The company and H. V. Foster had been stalwart supporters of Hillcrest Country Club and its antecedents, but were already entering into the realm of hallowed history. [531]

It was an active month for golf at Hillcrest. With Bill Simpson, last year's club champ, off to military service since that April morning only a few weeks ago, the field was wide open for the qualifying rounds that began on 1 June. Hillcrest women were quite active too, with the first Scotch Foursome play and a breakfast on 1 June. Five Hillcrest women were in Coffeyville a few days later for an invitational tournament where they took top honors. Heavy rain forestalled all of the sports events in town the next day, including the "mashed potatoes" inter-civic club match at Hillcrest, though the men still held their stag banquet. Harley Hicks, the assistant pro, announced the next day that the first round of the club championship would begin at 1:00 P.M. that day. The prospective favorite, Chuck Hyatt, was playing in the state amateur championship in Oklahoma City, on the day of the opening round, so that the match between him and Chuck Doornbos became a three-way contest. While the men chipped away on the club championship over the next weeks, women's golf continued apace with their usual luncheons and Scotch foursomes. Mrs. J. W. Phillips was in second place at the state women's amateur championship. Fifty-eight qualified for the FPMC championship, beginning 22 June, with another wide-open field because of the absence of Bill Simpson. Chuck Hyatt took the club championship on 23 June. [532]

On the Fourth of July weekend all three Bartlesville golf courses scheduled flag tournaments. The country club had a large turnout, with J. O. Turner winning the tournament and Chuck Hyatt winning the driving contest afterwards with three drives averaging 247 yards. The usual Fourth of July box supper began at 5:45 P.M. and the annual fireworks display began at 8:30 P.M.. It was reported that the local bootleggers had been locked up under the close eye of the sheriff. Liquor was not available at any price and the "local gentry" resigned themselves to a sober weekend. (Presumably there was hooch available in the river bottoms if a man was desperate.) The Dewey Roundup on that weekend was one of the best ever. Some RAF pilots were the special guests. The crowd topped out at 27,000 Saturday night for the last bull riding event, followed by Bob Wills and his Texas Playboys playing for another dance. The annual holiday blowout was bigger and better than ever and planned to best that next year. The civic move to capitalize on the popularity of Western events was manifesting in other events through the year, such as the Round-up Club rodeos, the fat stock shows, the coyote hunts, dog trials, and success of Western Swing dances at the local clubs. [533]

The FPMC tournament began the next day. Again Bill Simpson's absence presented an open field to the contestants. L. H. Huffman and Larry Timmons tied the contest on Sunday. Timmons finally won the playoff two weeks later. Not to be outdone, the women's golf association had a driving contest as its feature after the holiday weekend. Club manager, Mrs. Claudy, took reservations for the large turnout who also attended the luncheon bridge that followed. The next week the Tulsa District Women's Golf Association met at Hillcrest. Mrs. Phillips was Hillcrest's champion, tying the state amateur medalist, Margaret Thompson. The same week, Hillcrest's showmen staged an exhibition match. Tommy Trower

was paired with Keith Fowler and Chuck Hyatt with Jimmy Gullane. Reda Pump opened its annual tournament on 19 July. The "mashed potato" civic clubs tournament finally got back on the schedule. The Kiwanis "Happy Hookers" defeated Lions "Slick Slicers" and Rotary "Divot Diggers." The first city junior open golf tournament began immediately. Keith Fowler was the winner of a hard fought contest. After a five-year hiatus, Hillcrest and Sunset announced resumption of an inter-club tourney. Jimmy Gullane took seven Hillcresters to the state open golf tournament at Tulsa Oakhurst, and two foursomes to the incidental pro-am contests. Jimmy's team was Gullane, Chuck Hyatt, Tommy Trower, and Keith Fowler; Harley Hick's team included Jim Phillips, C. C. Custer, and Johnny Alexander. Regular play rounded out the summer, but as the city tennis tournament took center stage for a few weeks, golf enthusiasts looked forward to a Labor Day rematch of the local all-stars. The young bucks hoped for revenge on the old goats that had bested them a month ago. [534]

The only social function at Hillcrest noted during the summer was a dinner party given by Mrs. H. R. Straight and Mrs. E. F. Walsh in honor of Martha Good who was leaving after seven years as secretary of the Bartlesville YWCA. The same day it was announced that the dining room would be closed for the rest of the summer, though women's golf luncheons would be provided. According to the article this was the custom of several year's standing. [535]

The world news continued to grow worse. The Germans were at the gates of Moscow. The Japanese agreed to alliance with Germany while they continued their march through Southeast Asia. For some reason, Harold Ickes appointed Frank Phillips to the newly formed oil defense board. It was a committee of five industry leaders, intended to advise Ickes on what would soon develop into near full government control of the oil industry with an eye to nationalization. Phillips only lasted a few months on the board before resigning, but he had tried to do his duty. With the Russians fighting in the streets of Leningrad in the last days of August, the United States government tried to minimize the importance of a U-boat attack on an American destroyer during Labor Day weekend.

The Maire Hotel, a Bartlesville landmark and social center since 1914, disappeared forever when the name was changed at the end of the latest round of refurbishments. A new neon sign announced that it was now the Burlingame Hotel. Rigby Slight, the manager since 1929, said that the problem "might have daunted anyone except one who had the greatest faith in the future of this community." After the redecoration of the ground floor, one important change in the old hotel was the addition of bathrooms since half of the rooms didn't have them. In 1937, Mr. Burlingame built an apartment building adjoining the hotel across the alley with a bridge to the hotel. Significant to the social life in Bartlesville, the renovations included an air conditioning system on the ground floor and the first two floors of guest rooms as well as the apartments. All that cool air sure sounded good when the announcement was made at the end of a long hot summer, especially since the Hillcrest clubhouse was still not air-conditioned. [536]

That same week, the bond for a new addition to the Memorial Hospital passed. There was a rumor that the Hulah Dam was again shelved, even though the Chamber of Commerce was assured by Senator Thomas that it was still on track. Attention turned to normal end-of-year activities. Don Freiday was appointed to head a committee to see that Bartlesville Christmas decorations were the best ever. Meanwhile,

most of the ladies clubs in town began their season in October as usual. The Traffic Club held its eighth annual meeting in Bartlesville. As it had in the past, they began the day with a golf tournament and a luncheon at Hillcrest on 8 October, before going out to Woolaroc for the annual whingding. The Chamber of Commerce moved headquarters for the annual wolf hunt to Sunset Lake, though a rainy spell dampened the festivities. The main purpose of the move "was to give those who wished to attend the assurance of a good road all the way out no matter how much it continues to rain." The American Legion again sponsored the Halloween parade, and a party at the municipal stadium. [537]

Despite the concern of impending war, fall social activity was lively around town. As always there were numerous club meetings, bridge games, teas, luncheons, and parties in homes. Hillcrest's season was busy too. The first family night dinner was held on 2 October. Dinner-Dance club was reorganized early in October for the first party 21 October, though the successful format wasn't changed at all. The opening club dance was scheduled well before the usual Halloween party. They added a supper in the dining room before the dance. The Beta Sigma Phi girls went all our for a rush party, decorating with a trendy Western theme. Of course the season included a number of ladies parties, the most important was probably a luncheon given by Mrs. A. H. Riney for bride-elect Jane Mancill. [538]

The fall golf season continued apace. The Labor Day all-star match saw Jimmy Gullane and Chuck Hyatt defeat the kids again. That day Ed Buddrus shot a hole in one on the 19th [sic] to take first place in the flag tournament. The next day James Bailey and Keith Fowler represented Hillcrest in the Tulsa District junior tournament at Indian Hills. Fowler became the champion and Bailey was the class A titlist. The caddy tournament began immediately after the holiday. Earl Bennett won the title on 5 September. Indian Hills Country Club journeyed to Hillcrest for an inter-club tournament. The home team won handily, and there was a large turnout for a feature match between Jimmy Gullane and Chuck Hyatt and Indian Hills' pro George White and their champ Walter Emery. The annual handicap tournament wound up on 30 September, with F. E. Rice taking the title. Hillcrest Women held an invitational tournament with women from Tulsa, Ponca City, Independence, Cushing, Nowata, Muskogee, Coffeyville taking part. Leora Phillips was the winner. The City championship was played in mid-October. Keith Fowler was the 1941 city champion. It was the women's handicap championship that became a closely fought contest. The bad October weather held up the semi-final round. But finally, Mrs. John Miller Kane played Mrs. F. B. Plank. Beulah Plank defeated Marie Kane 2 up in a seesaw battle. Mrs. Plank also won the women's club championship that year. [539]

On 22 November 1941, the Oklahoma Tax Commission issued order number 11.328, directing the suspension of the right to do business in Oklahoma by Hillcrest Country Club. The State, erroneously believed that Hillcrest was a for-profit organization and therefore not in compliance with the Oklahoma License Act. It isn't clear what response, if any, the country club made to the order. It was 1950, before the matter was attended to, though the club continued business as it always had. [540]

Shortly before Thanksgiving in November, Dinner-Dance Club held a more gala than usual party with the Hal Brown Orchestra and a floor show. Mary Louise Adams held a dinner party for some Kansas City guests and the Don Tyler's held a wedding party for Mrs. Tyler's niece on 22 November. Mrs. H. W. Trippett held a smashing tea for the fiancé of her son on 2 December. Mrs. A. N. Horne and Mrs. W. A. Fisher entertained 75 ladies at a luncheon, decorating with poinsettias, the first sign of the holiday season. Mrs. H. E. Koopman, Mrs. K. S. Adams, and Mrs. R. M. Riggins held an important tea that received several social notices. Mrs. Osa Johnson, Frank Phillips' big game hunter friend, was one of the feature guests. [541]

Dinner-Dance Club opened the Christmas holiday season on 14 December, a week after the Japanese attack on Pearl Harbor. What had begun as a lively social season, slowly lost steam. It was hard to carry on business as usual with the very real alarming concerns that season. There was genuine concern that the United States would be invaded. That generation well knew the costs of war and began to gird themselves for the ordeal. Some parties were already on the books. The Beechwoods went ahead with a dancing party for their kids, the Collins held an open house for their family who were visiting from California, and the Musical Research Society held their annual Christmas luncheon. The annual Hillcrest children's Christmas party was held on 21 December. [542]

Civic leaders tried to make sure the city's needy had an especially good Christmas provision. The Bartlesville Welfare Association's annual Christmas Cheer drive provided generous Christmas dinner baskets to 250 needy families. John Cronin was elected president of the Chamber of Commerce. He said the objectives of the coming year would be support of the war effort and a long-range view to rebuilding after the war. They feared there might be an invasion or bombing and they were steeling themselves for the job. Already tires were being rationed. [543]

"Each holiday season since Hillcrest Country Club was built members have gathered there on New

Year's eve for the annual ball…This year is no exception. The arrival of 1942, is to be celebrated just as warmly as was 1941." There was a sons and daughters dance preceding the ball, from 3:30 to 6:30 in the afternoon. The Rene Hartley orchestra played for the ball from 10:00 P.M. til 3:00 A.M. Following the ball a few people had open houses. Elsewhere in town, there were the usual parties "which to a great measure were tempered by sober thoughts of the war effort ahead." Nevertheless, the New Year was ushered in by blowing whistles, car horns, assorted noise-makers, and an occasional pistol shot into the air. [544]

1942

Right after New Years, there was a good snowfall, followed by zero temperatures, the beginning of a cold winter. Already the Ration Board in Bartlesville was meeting about tires and inspectors were selected for the work. The Japanese were moving on the Philippines. The Roosevelt administration was moving quickly for $9 billion in new taxes. They planned to raise the extra revenue by raising the minimum tax rate from 10% to 25% and a dramatic tightening of the excess profits tax on corporations. While Bartlesville businessmen were still reeling from that announcement, Ickes' Office of Production Management slapped new senseless restrictions on the industry: no new gas stations, and a rule requiring the consent of adjacent property owners before new drilling. By May some in Congress were toying with a 100% excess profits tax! A flat 90% tax is what actually passed, up from a sliding scale that went from 35% to 60%. [545]

For a few weeks people struggled to find the most appropriate attitude in a time of war. The Tylers were hosts for the second dinner bridge club meeting of the month on 17 January. They had a hillbilly party with red and white check table clothes, a very

low-key affair by the Tyler standard. Lt. John Tyler left the next week for Ft. Sill. Dinner-Dance club met as usual on 19 January, the day before the annual club meeting. Theirs was a patriotic party with flags and red, white, and blue candles for decorations. A high school party, given by John Kirwan, featured a spaghetti supper and a square dance. On 16 January, Tulsa Democrats cancelled their annual Jackson Day dinner because of the war, signaling the direction that social activity seemed to be drifting everywhere. [546]

On 20 January, Hillcrest held its annual meeting for 1942. D. B. Dow, F. B. Plank, R. P. Reid, C. V. Sellers, R. L. Kidd, and John H. Kane were elected directors. A few days later all but two of the Hillcrest dances were cancelled. The 14 February, Valentine's dance was one of the two exceptions, but it was moved to 21 February, George Washington's Birthday, which made it seem more appropriately patriotic. [547]

By 17 February, the board of the club was beginning to resolve its leadership problems for the year. The call-up was draining off a whole generation of young leadership from the city. The board re-elected all of the officers: F. H. Plank again served as president, M. B. Heine was vice president, John F. Cronin was secretary, Ed. L. White was treasurer and assistant secretary. R. L. Kidd was appointed chairman of the house committee, C. W. Doornbos the greens committee, John Miller Kane the membership committee, and Hayward Marsh the entertainment committee. [548]

Nodie (Mrs. L. E.) Phillips did manage to bring off a whopper social event on 4 February, a Red Cross benefit tea and bridge party. The newspaper social column encouraged attendance from the whole community. They said the club's management hoped to tax its capacity. There was a prize drawing for defense stamps. Other ladies clubs in town cancelled their activities for that day so that there were 300 women in attendance on a day with perfect weather. Nearly everyone played cards, with tables in the living room, crowding the balcony, and overflowing to the downstairs rooms. They raised $425 for the Red Cross. [549]

The women's golf association had its usual annual organizational meeting on 21 January, electing Mrs. H. A. Gardner chairman. Hillcrest women fielded a bowling team for the annual women's city bowling tournament. The Hillcrest women led with Leora (Mrs. James) Phillips high scratch total score. [550]

For the time being, civic activities were not remarkably repressed because by their nature they had a patriotic reputation. Kiwanis had its usual ladies night on 3 January, at Hillcrest. The Jaycees banquet at the club was on 16 January. Already, the Junior Chamber was being impacted by members leaving for military service. Loren Steel and Bill Province were elected to fill vacancies, and several alternate directors were named, while at their meeting the Chamber of Commerce "pledged the organization's membership and facilities to civilian and government defense agencies." Kiwanis had a big, successful banquet at the club on 7 January. The county medical association banquet at Hillcrest heard L. A. Rowland, an attorney, speak on "three learned professions." The Doherty Girls had their annual banquet on 14 February, dancing to Hal Brown's orchestra. There was effort to keep up the civic progress of the last few years. Round-up Club elected new officers and began a 1942 membership campaign in preparation for regular activities, and of course, the president's birthday ball came off on 29 January, at the Civic Center as usual. [551]

The times were becoming very strange. Earl Reddy, the route man for Heck Bakery, was proud to make his contribution to the war effort by beginning deliveries with horse and wagon. Phillips Petroleum was expanding so fast it had to find new office space in three other downtown buildings. Elsewhere, 20 Japanese and Italian aliens in Vallejo, California, who the F.B.I. found with signaling flags, guns, radios, cameras, and other contraband, were arrested on charges of espionage. People were becoming pretty jumpy when President Roosevelt warned of likely attacks on U. S. cities. [552]

Dinner-Dance Club carried on bravely to finish out the season with parties on St. Patrick's Day and 21 April. The Newcomers Club, a national organization and a project of the Bartlesville Chamber of Commerce, was a new club in town, only two years old, that began holding monthly meetings at Hillcrest in March. They had been meeting in private homes. It is possible that the Chamber wanted to promote the country club by meeting at HCC in order to attract new leadership for Bartlesville organizations and to keep the country club active. The club did relent on its dance cancellation to hold one more informal dance on 15 April, with the most circumspect social notice in the newspaper. [553]

Rotary continued the annual civic banquets with a good-sized spring party on 31 March. The Sigma Chi's once again had a big spring party, this time under the sponsorship of Kenneth (Bud) Adams who brought a contingency of fraternity brothers down from the house at KU for the bash. More restrained community groups that held events at the club in those months included the Presbyterian Church choir. The Musical Research Society gave a huge coffee and program on a rainy Monday morning with low land flooding complicating the trip out from town. Nevertheless, 90 women came out for the end-of-year event. The American Legion Auxiliary held an unusual luncheon at Hillcrest to entertain some state officers who were in town on 7 May. Unspoken social constraints judged that it was okay for young people to kick up their heels, and they did at a large party given by the C.D.G. club. After the party the club members went to the home of Jo Ann Whitcomb for a slumber party. [554]

After a cold, wet winter, golf was slow in getting underway. Sixty men turned out on 14 April, to get in a round. It was the first report of the spring. But the rains continued so that by the day of the Musical Research coffee, the river was at 15 feet. Things dried out sufficiently to begin pairings for the annual inter civic club tournament on 30 April. They had trouble with a shortage of members on the Rotary team probably because of the military service of the younger men. Kiwanis won the tournament on 5 May. Finally the season opened on 2 May, with the annual team play at Hillcrest. That year it was Art Levan's Reds battling Larry Calkin's Blues. The Blues won, so in keeping with long tradition, the Reds were obliged to buy dinner for the winners. It was probably a very exciting evening, not because of the good company, but because of a large tornado that passed through the north of town and destroyed Wayside community. Once again, Bartlesville rose to the occasion. The Boy Scouts and American Legion were out immediately to help people and to guard the area, the Red Cross was immediately ready for blood donors if needed. The next day the Smelter Union voted aid to their men who had been hit by the tornado. [555]

The city was doing quite a bit of work on streets and gutters downtown that spring. In lowering the street to the level of the gutters at the southeast corner of Third (Frank Phillips Boulevard) and Dewey they removed a four-foot square iron plate that had bridged the gutter for time out of memory. It was called "the Bridge of Sighs" but no one knew why. Hillcrest had a good turnout for the annual Business and Professional Women's Mothers Day banquet,

which also had a patriotic theme of decoration. The junior-senior prom at Hillcrest kicked off graduation week activities as usual. The Round-up club sponsored a Festival that included a parade and rodeo and horsemanship events in the Municipal Stadium. There were 500 horses in town for the meet. The Chamber of Commerce hosted a third annual "heads up" banquet at the Civic Center. For only 75¢ civic-minded Bartians could enjoy a banquet "with all the trimmings" to celebrate the silver anniversary of Phillips Petroleum Company, and boost Bartlesville civic activity. The same day the Federation of Women's Clubs held a big luncheon at Hillcrest, organized by the Tuesday Club and the Indian Women's Club to host the General Federation fine arts chairman. A thousand people turned out for a dance review benefit program at the Civic Center put on by Jane Runyon's dancing school to raise money for the Navy relief fund. Summer lightened up civic activity, with the annual Lion's banquet at Hillcrest ending the season. The Dewey Round-up once again was a huge success. Contestants who hadn't been drafted sent their entries by telegraph. It was a big event and a chance for Washington County to strut its patriotic all-American stuff. [556]

You never saw so many weddings! The entire war period was filled with weddings and their associated showers and parties. A new convention was that most wedding announcements were carried in the society column. It the past, it was only the most social weddings that received attention. Most weddings continued to be at home with a small reception, but increasingly weddings were held in the churches, though even most of the very social weddings still held small receptions in the bride's home. With young people going off to college and so many men away from home while in military service, many fiancés were not from Bartlesville. Before the wedding there were often showers, teas, luncheons, and parties for the couple. Many of these, and a handful of very prominent wedding receptions were held at the country club. An important pre-wedding party at Hillcrest in the early summer of 1942 was a dessert bridge party for Miss Betty Jean Killian who was marrying a Wisconsin man. In July, there was a luncheon and crystal shower for Martha Louise Fitzjarrald. The rehearsal dinner for her wedding a month later was also held at Hillcrest. [557]

Jim Collins won the annual DMF tournament on 19 May after two weeks of dodging rain in the tournament rounds. The city golf tournament began on the same day as a city archery tournament for Memorial Day weekend. The Memorial Day feature was a match between Keith Fowler and his father C. B. Fowler. The first round of the club championship was complete the first weekend in June. For a second year the title was undefended, since Chuck Hyatt was on vacation during the tournament. Play was held up the next week because of heavy rain and a damaging windstorm. The groundskeepers were busy cleaning up downed branches. John Cronin took the championship for the year. Don Wilkie at Sunset and Hank Carson at Osage Hills courses were complaining that "the army, defense work, and victory gardens" as well as tire rationing were thinning out the numbers of golf enthusiasts at their clubs. It was probably also the case at Hillcrest. There was even worry about a golf ball shortage. Leora Phillips made a good showing in the Oklahoma Women's Golf Association tournament in Shawnee in mid-June. They hosted a Women's Invitational Tournament at the end of July. [558]

Five Hillcresters, Keith Fowler, Bob Plank, Jimmy Gullane, C. B. Fowler, and W. C. Feist, went to Muskogee for the State pro-am. Chuck Hyatt, the 1941 club champion and former Phillips 66er coach,

went to the Army that week. Keith Fowler got a lot of glory by beating Walter Emery, the former national intercollegiate champion, but he was knocked out the next day. The Bartlesville Wildcat's golf hero bested Jimmy Gullane's course record from the previous year at Hillcrest on 1 July, with a 67. "The lowest score ever made on Hillcrest was a 66 several years ago but since then a number of holes have been remodeled to make the layout tougher." It was also pointed out that the lowest competitive score ever made was by Fred Smith, a former caddie, who carded a 69. [559]

Jimmy Gullane announced that the membership wanted to celebrate the Fourth of July in a grand fashion this year. The plans for the day included a flag tournament, putting and driving contests, a special feature (the prize was a dozen golf balls), a Scotch foursome, besides dinner, dancing and cards in the evening. Chuck Doornbos had a big day, winning both the flag tournament and the special feature, Dr. O. C. Omohundro won the putting and Bob Gates won the driving contests, Mrs. W. E. Feist and C. B. Fowler won the low net in the mixed Scotch foursome and Mrs. J. W. Byrd and John Profitt won the high net. Wayne Smith won the annual Reda tournament in mid-July. Young Keith Fowler tried his hand in the big time, entering the All American Amateur and the Tam O'Shanter tournament in Chicago, but he declined to defend his city junior title. James Bailey subsequently became the junior champion at a tournament played at Sunset course. [560]

Busy plans were made for the usual Labor Day golf weekend. Bill Martin won the handicap tournament that day, while the FPMC continued their tournament, and qualifying rounds for the club handicap championship began. The women's association had to change the time of their weekly meeting to 1:00 P.M. because the caddy shortage had become very acute.

Near the end of September, George Wickersham won the FPMC – OK Wing trophy for 1942. H. C. Peyton won the club handicap championship early in October. A Red Cross benefit golf tournament was played at Hillcrest the second week in October. It included driving and putting contests, open to anyone in the county. The women's handicap championship ended on 15 October, with Mrs. W. E. Feist the winner. The late fall weather turned bad early, but the women held their annual awards luncheon on 18 November. Unfortunately, the microfilm was illegible so that there is no record of the women's champion that year, nor is there a name on the trophy in the women's locker room. [561]

The war news during the summer and fall was hopeful, but there was still not a feeling of assurance that America could prevail. The Japanese were poised to invade Australia after our debacle in the Philippines. We began to laboriously retake ground in the South Pacific and Burma. In Europe we joined the British in bombing Germany and began operation in North Africa. People were only minimally interested in the elections that summer. Oklahoma Republicans lost all hope of sending a senator to Washington when their candidate, former Senator William Pine died suddenly. Oilman Robert S. Kerr was elected governor in November. Harold Ickes appointed Dr. John W. Frey, one of the government's Madison, Wisconsin consultants, deputy petroleum coordinator. It's no wonder Frank Phillips resigned from the board. Manpower shortages began to grow acute by fall. A peculiarity of the times was that the newspapers began to publish photographs of 2 or 3 bathing beauties in every edition. This practice continued through the war years.

Rationing became a full-blown reality right after the elections. Tires and gasoline were already early items to be rationed. That was impacting travel in general and the country club saw a drop in utilization. The list of rationed foods began to grow: coffee, meat, sugar, and butter. Food rationing would quickly become a tangled points system. It soon began to impact restaurants, and the country club was no exception. By the end of 1942, the war effort was deeply effecting the ability of the country club and other civic organizations to operate. The general sense that partying (except for kids), while our men were at war, was unseemly was there from the beginning. Tires and gasoline shortages prevented travel and required carpooling and other measures to move people around. Food rationing made it difficult to entertain at home or eat out. Manpower shortages made it difficult to staff the clubhouse and golf course.

The emphasis of civic activity remained important. The Town Hall program that had brought good speakers to Bartlesville for many years was beefed up. Working in the summer of 1942, they were proud to announce their schedule for the winter season, especially their final speaker, Fulton Lewis, Jr., a highly respected radio commentator of the time. Fall enrollment at the junior college dropped to only 15 students. The Business Men's Association returned to Hillcrest for their annual banquet on 7 October. In October civic attention turned to the annual Halloween parade and party, and to the organization of the annual Welfare Association drive, both cut back somewhat because of the war effort. The welfare drive was "streamlined and cut to the bone," with a goal of only $12,030. The war transportation committee was pushing a plan to carpool called "swap-ride," but most people were already very mindful of picking up other folks and giving them a lift. As early as Labor Day, Hillcrest had already resorted to organizing rides to big events, starting from the YWCA downtown. It could be worse, the newspaper had a photograph of an old-fashioned four-in-hand coach that the Tan O'Shanter Country Club in Chicago was using to meet members at trains and buses to take them to the clubhouse. [562]

At the end of August, Mrs. H. C. Claudy, the club manager, had some elective surgery at Memorial hospital and wasn't dismissed for almost three weeks. Shortly afterward, the club announced that it would be moving the bimonthly family night informal suppers from Thursday nights to Saturday nights. They said, "they seemed to fill a need for informal gatherings for weekends during the period when elaborate social affairs are in the eclipse." Meanwhile, the first graduating glider training class was hosted by the American Legion for a luncheon at Hillcrest on 27 September. For that party, Harry Sauer, the chairman of the Hillcrest house committee, had charge of the arrangements, probably a sign that Mrs. Claudy was still not able to resume all of her duties. Near the middle of November, it was announced that the Claudies would be leaving the club at the end of the month – not a good time to be without a manager. [563]

Dinner-Dance Club was one regular Hillcrest social event that persisted for quite a while through the pervasive social black-out. They opened the social season, such as it was, on 20 October, as usual on Tuesday night with dinner at 7:00 P.M. and Jackson's orchestra from Tulsa playing for the dance. In past years Dinner-Dance Club had limited its membership to 50 members, but for the November dance there were 100 members at the dance. Since there was virtually nothing else going on, they seem to have expanded the program. There was another buffet supper and dance on Sunday night of Thanksgiving weekend that attracted a large Hillcrest crowd. As a sign of the times, the entertainment committee arranged a juke-box dance for the evening. This is probably a sign of another reason that there were fewer dances. The next week, Jackson's orchestra notified the dinner-dance committee that they would be there as usual. Probably there was a problem with transportation from Tulsa and maybe also the manpower shortage was affecting their ability to pull together an orchestra. [564]

Small social affairs and meetings almost disappeared from Hillcrest. Most things took place in peoples homes, and more formal events were mostly at the Burlingame. The Beesleys had a dance for Celeste's fifteenth birthday, and the Dahlgrens entertained some visitors from Wichita for the sum of the fall occasions at Hillcrest. Whether it was difficult to entertain or not, the FPMC held a dance for 350 couples of adoring Phillips employees on Frank Phillips birthday. Frank was upbeat in his lengthy oration for the gathering, saying, "that one of his prime purposes in life had narrowed down to the welfare of every Phillips employee; that he planned expansion of the company's activities which would assure a greater Bartlesville and a larger independent oil company." December saw an alumnae dinner for Colorado School of Mines, and a Christmas Eve reception for newly wed Lt. Scott Rice and his bride. Two young ladies were the hostesses of dances before New Years: Marilyn Walker had a birthday party on 28 December, and Nancy Ambrose entertained 75 friends on 29 December. The wedding of Helen Trower, daughter of Harry Trower, and Dean Walker on 30 December was the society wedding of the season, with the reception at the country club. [565]

The city resolved to welcome the New Year in a more sober vein. Hillcrest had its usual New Years party. There was another sons and daughters dance at tea time on New Years Eve, and several homes "open for the gathering of friends before the dance at Hillcrest." The Wayne Wills orchestra was the dance band that evening and there was a breakfast served as usual. Otherwise the city seems to have been quiet. Early risers were met with dour headline, "Civilians Told To Prepare For Toughest Year." [566]

1943

The Hillcrest annual meeting was held on 19 January, reelecting John Cronin and Frank Stradley, and electing new directors J. H. Collins and W. R. Lund. The following week, the board elected R. P. Reid the new president, W. R. Lund vice president, John Cronin secretary, and E. L. White treasurer and assistant secretary. [567]

There was scant activity in town that winter. The weather was very bad on top of all the war constraints. Kiwanis held its annual banquet at the club on 8 January, with a good turnout. Boots Adams got out a significant crowd for the Sweetheart of Sigma Chi dance on 12 January, leveraged with an old-fashioned published guest list. Of course, the president's birthday ball was again held at the Civic Center. Saturday night family nights returned to Hillcrest on 6 February. People were delighted and they invited many friends, so that the always-popular gathering was quite large. Joe Boyd hosted a group of 60 high school friends for a dance the night before. Over the next month only one ladies luncheon and some Newcomers meetings were the only activities that were not sponsored by the club. Another big family night was on 21 February. It was the Dinner-Dance Club that came up with the most imaginative party theme in a long time, showing that people still had their sense of humor. As usual their Tuesday night dinner was served at 7:00 P.M. This time each table was decorated with "suggestion of the several important items which the public is learning to do without or to be satisfied

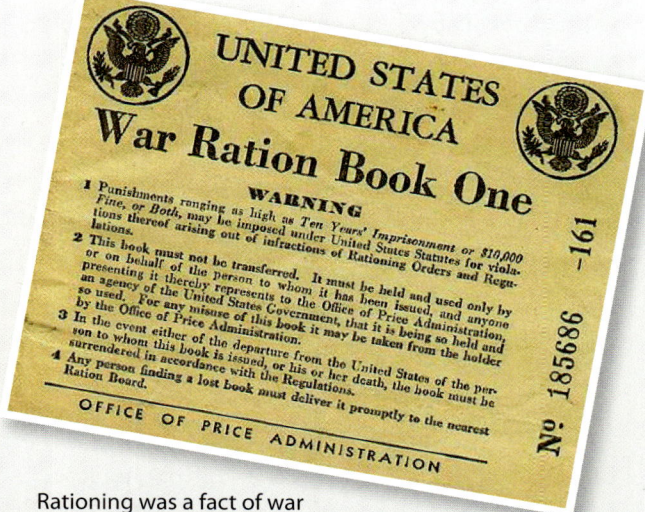

Rationing was a fact of war policy within the first weeks of World War II. It quickly became a tangled knot of managed economy, alternating shortages of goods with shortages of ration tickets. It made food service at the country club a near impossibility. That along with labor shortage and no construction materials made operation very difficult. *Courtesy Bartlesville Area History Museum.*

with smaller portions. Dinner partners were found by matching ration cards." [568]

In fact, rationing was cutting deeply into the quality of everyday life. Meat, fish, fats and oils, and cheeses were severely rationed, using a points system. Virtually all food items fell under a similar system, the points allotted changing regularly. 40% of foodstuffs were taken off the top for supplying the military and for Lend-Lease, the rest was portioned out by a bureaucracy that was impervious to market forces. Price controls drove many products off the market. For a while restaurants had reasonable supplies of needed goods, but as time passed they fell under tightening and irrational constraints too. Everybody thought it was his or her patriotic duty to make fair sacrifices for the war effort, but some found ways around rationing. People began to raise their own chickens, but baby chicks in the spring soon hit nearly $1.00 apiece (about $14.00 in today's money), an exorbitant price for a high mortality commodity. Few people had home freezers in those days, and it wasn't long before Department of Agriculture agents took to raiding cold storage lockers to root out illegal private stockpiles of beef, lamb, poultry, and pork. Many people began victory gardens and learned from the home demonstration agent how to can their produce. Sugar was a big bugaboo. Some years people couldn't get enough to can fruit or make jams. Imagine the difficulty of running the kitchen at Hillcrest in those conditions.

There were a number of civic adjustments. The Oklahoma State Golf Association board of directors decided to cancel the statewide tournaments, but was ready to sponsor war benefit tournaments. The American Legion held a series of dances for local and visiting servicemen at the Civic Center. Paul Endicott, C. V. Sellers, and John Cronin incorporated the first United Community Fund in town through the Chamber of Commerce. It was a consolidation of the several local and national fund raising drives that took place each year. Since a major fund-raising emphasis during the war years was repeated war bonds drives, it was immensely helpful to keep the other needs viable. The school board decided they would have to drop the junior college program. [569]

For the next month's Dinner-Dance, family night, and Newcomers Club were virtually the only social activities taking place at Hillcrest. The Musical Research Society held its annual spring morning musical at Hillcrest on 18 April, as nearly all of the city ladies clubs began to end their year early. Late cold and wet weather kept the golfers at home into April. The high school team finally started its season on 8 April, on muddy fairways. The first notice

of regular golf rounds at Hillcrest were on 25 April. The women's golf association did not have its annual organizational meeting until 5 May. The meeting was poorly attended and re-organization was not accomplished. They were having trouble getting members. Dues were decreased from $2 to $1. They were seldom heard from thereafter for the duration of the war. Probably the most important reasons were transportation, loss of younger wives of servicemen from their membership, and caddy shortage. [570]

The competitive golf season opened with the annual team match, Walt Kinderman's team against Charles Julian's team, on 15 May. Julian's outfit was the winner. The DMF Championship was finished on 25 May, with Carl Drath the winner. C. V. Johnson took first in the annual Memorial Day flag tournament. Johnson again played well in the club championship rounds, but W. B. Englebrecht took the title on 13 June. Prizes were paid in war stamps. Meanwhile, young Keith Fowler, too young for the draft, qualified in an invitational tournament at Oklahoma City Golf and Country Club. Jimmy B. Collins took the match play tournament on 15 June. W. F. Neumann won the blind bogey on 27 June. Hillcrest women did emerge to plan a Scotch foursome and fried chicken dinner for the Fourth of July. [571]

The first weeks of May were relatively active in town. There were 700 persons at the Central High band concert on 1 May. The music program of the public schools was very well supported by the community and the several concerts that took place through the year were always well attended. The performances were within walking distance for most people's homes then. Lions held its ladies night at Hillcrest on 4 May. The fine new wing for Memorial hospital and renovation in the old part was open for an open house the next week. The spring had been constantly rainy and a 6 1/2 inch rain on 10 May, was the beginning of lowland flooding with the river at 15 feet on 11 May. Despite the flooded roads, AAUW had their spring banquet at Hillcrest on 16 May. The evening program was Herman Larson, a tenor from O.U. A new 3-inch rain on the 18th returned the Caney to a flood of 17 feet on the next day. A Vagabond Club tea planned for that day at Hillcrest had to be cancelled, as was a family night on 22 May. It was the worst flood on record for northeastern Oklahoma. Though Bartlesville was hard hit with a high water mark of 20.4 feet, it was not our record flood by any means, but it was a bad one. The flood evacuees were promptly cared for by the Bartlesville Welfare Association, the organization erected on the infrastructure built by the Flood Relief Committee of 1926. Though most evacuees were taken in by friends and relatives, a number were housed in the Elks Club downtown. The Red Cross furnished cots. Once again Dr. Elizabeth Chamberlain manned the public health station, this time at the Elks Club, giving typhoid and tetanus shots. The home demonstration agent, Ruth Wheeler, and Grace Smith, the Central High School home economics teacher, organized the food preparation for the evacuees. It must have been a trick with rationing going on. The Salvation Army headquarters was flooded, but Major Martyn Richard was busy organizing the relief effort personnel. It was another striking example of the quick response and efficiency of the local organization accustomed to working together on many community needs. [572]

The flood emergency was passed by the Memorial Day weekend. Four parties at Hillcrest on 4 May, relieved the backlog of social commitments. Through June there were a few small dinners and luncheons, and two family nights. Lions Club had their banquet right after the Fourth of July. The Fourth celebration at Hillcrest consisted of the usual flag tournament, with evening activities being a softball game, mixed Scotch foursome, archery contest, and horseshoe pitching. Society parties, golf tournaments, and civic events were subdued in this summer. There was even a small opening crowd at the Dewey Roundup. When a heat wave hit the second week in July, the city sizzled as the temperature hovered near 110° for 6 weeks. Everything but golf pretty much dried up. [573]

Undauted by heat and sun, the golf enthusiasts played on through July with regular play reported. The Reda Pump tournament ended 13 July, with Verle Judson the winner. F. C. Donaldson won the Frank Phillips Men's Club Championship on 11 August. Frankly, it was hot, and the golf was just not that competitive with the young hotdogs off to war. On 14 August, there was a little rejoinder with Capt. William J. Simpson in town on leave. That day he tied Keith Fowler's course record, set in 1942, with another 67, playing in a foursome with Cpl. Dick Booker, J. H. Crook, and Jimmy Gullane. His score wasn't quite that good the next day, but it was well ahead of everyone else on a day when only 43 players came out in the excessive heat of August. [574]

The discovery of penicillin was announced on 1 August. Sulfas had been the wonder drug only a few years ago, but had proven to have limited success and some serious problems. Now penicillin was being used to miraculously save the lives of wounded and sick American soldiers. It was a medical revolution and a milestone step into a new world of effective treatment of infectious disease.

By the summer of 1943, Allied commanders were confidant that the tide of war had turned. Americans were heartened that North Africa was almost entirely in Allied hands, with British General Montgomery fighting the last battles in Tunisia. America's hero, General George Patton, raced across Sicily and Americans advanced into southern Italy. In the South Pacific slow gains steadily moved toward recapturing the Philippines. At home, people were beginning to feel a little more confident.

The usual Labor Day flag tournament opened the fall season. Only 66 players came out in the heat, but H. C. March had low net score. Chuck Doornbos won the handicap tournament a few days later. The handicap championship began a few days later. There was another Red Cross benefit tournament with 130 men paying $1.00 entry fee. [575]

Better weather in October benefited other civic activities. Despite the draft and transportation problems the annual Osage Hills wolf hunt took place. The numbers were down, and the hoopla was restrained, but the wolf hunters were irrepressible. The Osage County ranchers were glad to see them, saying coyotes were plentiful and that they had been making raids on chicken houses and that they were worried about pigs and calves. The United Community Fund drive was organized, combining all the big drives in Bartlesville, except the Red Cross and 17 national war relief programs, and ready to do a one-day blitz to raise $85,000. There was bad news on 12 November. Sgt. Tommy Novak, a former Hillcrest caddy and a golf professional, was killed in action in Italy. [576]

The first family night dinner in September brought astounding information. The Henry Thompsons, who had been the first managers when Hillcrest

You never saw so many weddings as during the war years! Mary Louise Adams, daughter of Boots and Blanche Adams, married Edward Allis on 30 October 1943. Here the bride and her father. *Courtesy Bartlesville Area History Museum.* In a great illustration of social capital at work, Governor Robert Kerr visits with Frank Phillips at the reception. One of Kerr's first acts when Truman became president a few months later, was to call and ask for action on the Hulah Dam. *Courtesy Woolaroc.*

first opened back in 1926, had evidently been enticed out of retirement until a permanent manager could be found. The Thompsons announced that there would be no family night dinners while they were on the job. It seems that the club had been without a manager for 9 months. The tempo of social activity did not especially pick up. There was some kind of party for the Red Cross benefit tournament but the microfilm was too bad to read. Seven wedding showers were reported on 8 October. One of the big weddings of the season was Mary Louise Adams, daughter of Boots and Blanche Adams, to Edward Allis. Of course, there were several important parties held for her at Hillcrest. The Adamses hosted a beautiful rehearsal dinner at Hillcrest, and a reception was held the next day at Hillcrest. There were a few ladies parties in the fall, and the Jaycees had a members' dance on 20 November. [577]

The Christmas season was light again as it had been in 1942. There were a few more dances, and the wedding of Grace Baird to Benny Parr generated several parties. The Phillips research department held a Christmas dance on 17 December. The next night the Doherty Men's Fraternity held their Christmas dance. Dinner-Dance club held its first gathering of the season 29 December with more than 100 members present. [578]

The annual New Years party was preceded by an open house at the John M. Kane home on Delaware. Steve Steven's orchestra played for the ball at Hillcrest that was followed by a breakfast at 3:00 A.M. It was an even quieter New Year that the last one. "There were no large and expensive parties this year as social activities in the city throughout the winter have been kept simple and unpretentious because of the war clouds…" [579]

1944

Right after the first of the year, the Chamber of Commerce joined a national Chamber program to plan the post-war period. Already committees were at work and had produced a five-year agricultural plan. One wonders if they were aware of aping the failed ideas of Stalinist Russia. Meetings were already ongoing with local merchants to acquaint them "with changes in price regulation and ration points." In general, the idea seems to have been to emerge from the war with a managed economy. Not all Bartlesville leaders were enamored with the new thinking mode. A few days later John M. Kane accepted the chairmanship of the Chamber's planning committee. It wasn't long before future plans were following more classic economic ideas. The committee was emphasizing Bartlesville's water supply, better highways, downtown street lighting, street improvement, and encouraging new industry. Soon there was a new committee report with two goals: jobs for willing workers, and an effort to diversify the area's economic structure. "The post war job is everybody's job," said Kane, "It doesn't belong to the Chamber of Commerce alone – and it certainly doesn't belong to the governmental agencies which have neither intimate knowledge of nor personal interest in our community's problems, hopes, and wishes." [580]

W. R. Lund was the president at Hillcrest in 1944, evidently elected at the annual January meeting of the newly elected board. Mr. And Mrs. Charles Lunkley, from Tulsa, were hired as managers at Hillcrest, but it is difficult to determine when. The return of family nights at the end of February seems to signal that they were on the job. [581]

The Newcomers Club continued to meet at Hillcrest monthly. The family night dinners returned 27 February. FPMC sponsored a leap year dance at Hillcrest on 26 February encouraging the single women in town to compete for the handful of single men to take to the dance. The dance was cancelled for bad weather, but when it reorganized on 3 March, it was a square dance at the Civic Center, sponsored by both FPMC and the Jane Phillips Sorority, and Frank Phillips was the caller. The Bartlesville Civic Band reorganized for the year in February. Band concerts were a popular civic social activity in those years, and the American Legion resumed sponsorship of its dances for military personnel. Young Jack May and Dick Holbert were the hosts for a big dance party at Hillcrest for their high school friends. The Jake Mays, G. V. Holberts, and Stan Learneds were the chaperones that evening. [582]

There were signs of the times. People were beginning to get tapped out and the annual Bartlesville Red Cross drive had a hard time making its goal. L. E. Phillips died on 16 April, after lengthy illness. The town shut down on Tuesday 18 April, in his honor. Other Bartlesville pioneers had been passing on in recent years, but somehow this seemed like the passing of an age. That same day H. R. Straight announced his resignation as president and director of Cities

Service Gas Company, though he would continue as president of Cities Service Oil Company. It was an interesting political year. Roosevelt was audacious when he ran for a third term in 1940, now with the war, there seemed little question that he would run again, but it was not sitting well with many people. In April, Wendell Wilkie dropped out of the Republican race, leaving the momentum with Thomas E. Dewey. Dewey was nominated at the convention in June, declaring (it was) "no time for tired old men – we learned that in 1919." [583]

Rainy weather pushed the annual children's Easter egg hunt at Hillcrest indoors. It was another cold and rainy spring. Right after Easter, heavy rains brought on another major flood with the river cresting at 21.1 feet on 11 April. For Hillcrest, the only social activity for the rest of the month was a rehearsal dinner and wedding reception for the marriage of Mary Louise Koopman to Clifford Armstrong. The month of May was equally slow. The junior-senior prom was the only major event, and some small wedding parties. [584]

Another wartime wedding, Mary Louise Koopman married Clifford Armstrong 30 April 1944. Some of the wedding party are identified: Louise Rodgers Adams (2nd lady), Margie Lou Ulrich (3rd lady), Mary Louise Armstrong (bride, 4th lady), Cliff Armstrong (groom), Betty Sneed (5th lady, groom's sister), Jodi McCready (6th lady), Dottie Gleason (7th lady, end). *Courtesy Bartlesville Area History Museum.*

By then things were dried out enough to try to start the Reda Pump golf tournament. It was the first activity of the cold wet spring at Hillcrest. But it was washed out that very day. Carl Lee was the winner on 7 May. [585] In the meantime, Don Wilkie placed a notice in the newspaper:

Effective Monday, May 1, 1944, Sunset Golf Course will be closed to golfing play. This step is necessary for the complete coordination of our new construction program. Beside the remodeling of our golf course to a par 34 front nine and a par 37 back nine with bent grass greens, we find it necessary to increase the fertility of the course's soil with the addition of needed chemical elements. This in itself makes it an economic necessity that both nines are developed together.

We feel honored to have 186 former members and golfers in the armed forces as well as 31 of our former caddies. Every effort shall be bent to insure these boys have a better golf course with additional clubhouse facilities available for them upon return [586]

Both Sunset and Osage Hills were unable to continue operation by this time. Sunset remained absent for the duration of the war. In short order several of the most active Sunset golf enthusiasts appeared on the Hillcrest course.

Club member, Frances Emerson, says that she and Bill joined then. Bill was from Independence, Kansas and had grown up playing on that good golf course. He was a terrific young golfer who had been the Independence city champ before moving to Bartlesville. The $250 for full stockholding membership at Hillcrest was expensive at the time, so Bill had been making due at Sunset. When Wilkie closed Sunset, Frank Tollman, Frank Phillips' nephew, who liked playing golf with Bill, recruited him for Hillcrest membership, and Scott Ambrose put up his name. A

sweet memory: Frances' mother, Elsie Wyant, gave them the money to buy their Hillcrest stock. Hillcrest gained one of its best young golfers of the era. [587]

Immediately, the high school team began play at Hillcrest. Virgil Daniel's team defeated J. H. Crook's team in the annual stag dinner tournament. The DMF tournament was rained out on 20 May. Jim Collins won the tournament in the beginning of the Memorial Day holiday. Bill Emerson, one of the new Sunset transfers, won the Memorial Day flag tournament. The new men were adding some excitement to the golf season already. [588]

The summer saw slow, but steady social activity at Hillcrest. The Washington County Bar Association held their banquet at the clubhouse in the end of May, the end of the civic banquets for the season. There was more good news for club life when Olga Foster agreed to return as club manager. Mrs. Foster was the manager at Hillcrest from 1934 to 1936, when she left to take a job in Pennsylvania. She was the very popular manager who had encouraged the young people's dances at the time. She had been back in town for a few years and was active in civic circles. Miss Emma Grosmeyer, a Montaldos (very fine ladies clothing chain) employee, would be assisting her. Many people still remember her tenure happily. The club dining room had been closed for a few weeks while there was no manager. It was a good sign to see family night, Newcomers meetings, and small luncheons sprinkled through the rest of the summer. [589]

The club golf championship started on 3 June, with Jim Collins defending his title. It was an exciting tournament from the first round. E. H. Lyon just beat Bill Emerson on the 19th [sic] green. Dr. P. A. Kincade won the title on 11 June. There were 117 players for the flag tournament of the Fourth of July. George Roach shot a hole in one on No. 4. The pairings were made to begin the FPMC tournament right after the holiday. Harley Hicks, the former assistant pro at Hillcrest, had the low score on the first day. The tournament between the Chamber and Junior Chamber of Commerce began on 16 July. [590]

There was an unusual amount of civic activity for the hot summertime. The Chamber was actively working with the war production board to assure supply of essential goods locally. Such things as farm implements, hospital supplies, dry goods, work clothing, medicine, dairy and industrial equipment were being carefully watched by the Bartlesville Chamber. Phillips hoped to start construction locally of 50 new houses with approval of the national housing authority. A survey of the local churches found them to be prospering, with increased attendance and improved financial standing. Resumption of bus service to Bartlesville was a big help to the transportation problem. A huge fire in the 200 block of East Third Street (Frank Phillips Boulevard) destroyed Bartlesville Stationary, Ideal Food Market, Nathan Barber Shop, and Standard Auto Parts on the morning of the Fourth of July. After the primary election, the Oklahoma senatorial race was between William Otjen, the Republican, and incumbent Senator Thomas, the Democrat. As the national Democrat convention opened in Chicago, President Roosevelt let it be known that he wished to keep socialist Henry Wallace as his vice presidential candidate. Southern delegates fumed at the "communist domination" and the convention balked. Wallace was forced out by convention chairman Senator Samuel Jackson of Indiana. Quickly, Harry S. Truman was picked, the favorite of the big city bosses. It was a convention of surprise and intense behind-the-scenes activity and high drama and it was all over by 20 July. [591]

C. V. Johnson defeated E. R. Holt on the 19th [sic] green in the Labor Day Flag tournament, as the golf season went into its closing days. "Shooting the best two rounds of his golfing experience, R. E. Arnold won the championship of the Hillcrest handicap tournament" near the end of September. W. J. Hayes and C. C. Custer won a 36-hole lowball handicap twosome tournament on 10 October. The entrance fee was $1.00, with prize money distributed 25, 20, 15 and 10 percent to the twosomes finishing from first to fifth. In probably the very last round of the golf season on 12 November, Charlie Leathers shot a hole-in-one on No. 16. [592]

The fall social calendar was much busier than it had been in years, mostly from some high profile weddings. The marriage of Beverly Ann Duston to Brooks Spies, and the marriage of Anne Caldwell to Carl Rawlins both generated several Hillcrest parties in September and October. The Dustins entertained the families at a rehearsal dinner on 6 October. A reception dinner honored newlyweds, Mr. And Mrs. Charles Selby. There was a rehearsal dinner for the wedding of Helen Gardner to Lt. Dimit on 11 November.

Otherwise, there was a big tea given by the wives of Cities Service Oil Company as a farewell courtesy to the wives of Cities Service Gas Company who were moving to Oklahoma City and Wichita. Bartlesville would be losing several more leading families. The Doherty Girls gave a festive, patriotic annual banquet in honor of their departing members on 25 October. Along the way there were a half dozen normal-times parties to honor out-of-town guests of various people. [593]

At the end of November, Phillips moved to take up the slack in corporate hegemony with another big birthday bash for Frank Phillips. The various events in town were kicked off on 22 November by a FPMC banquet at Hillcrest. Bill Cross from Chicago brought an eleven-piece orchestra and vocalist Margie Fields to play for the dance. Tickets were limited to FPMC members only, because of a big increase in new members, hired from the Cities Service transition. [594]

Elsie Parker told a funny story that was probably from this FPMC party. She says that Paul Parker was a young lawyer at Phillips and they were fairly new in town. On the evening of this party which was in honor of Frank's birthday, the aging patriarch was sitting in a chair facing the entry, so she went over to greet him, as would be appropriate for his birthday. She had never met him before. She says the first thing she knew he pinched her on the bottom. She was so shocked, she said nothing, and just moved away. The stories of Frank's fanny patting proclivities are many, so that in itself, Elsie's story is not remarkable. But, it gets better. As she realized the indignity, Elsie resolved revenge. All the other young wives, wide-eyed, cautioned her that Paul would lose his job if she did anything. Months went by before they were invited by Bill and Puella Hodges, and Rayburn and Alma Foster to another Hillcrest party where Uncle Frank was present. Elsie didn't hesitate. She sidled right up to him and pinched him right on the tooche. Frank turned around, a twinkle in his eye, and responded, "Now we're even." [595]

On the morning of 8 November, President Roosevelt had won his fourth term. The Allies landed in Normandy in May. Since then American and British armies slowly fought their way across northern France and Belgium. In December, Hitler launched his last big counter-offensive at Ardennes, the frozen hell of the Battle of the Bulge. By January, the victorious Allies were preparing to cross the Rhine. Bartlesville civic leaders continued to do their part for the war effort. The fall United Community and War Fund drive was conducted in October. Washington County passed its quota for E bonds in the December drive.

It was another slow Christmas season. The newspaper even noted the dearth of toys in the store for Santa to buy for good little children. The new president at OU, Dr. George L. Cross, appointed after a leftist purge by the legislature's un-American activities committee, spoke to the organizational meeting of the Bartlesville alumnae association at Hillcrest on the evening of 15 December. Dinner-Dance club had one of the few holiday parties at Hillcrest on 19 December. Their regular meetings had been discontinued. The only other country club party of the season was a dance given by the Kelita Klub, another of the high school girls clubs of the era. Afterwards, the hostesses had a slumber party. FPMC and JPS held their annual Christmas parties together at the Civic Center on 22 December. It was a giant bash, so big that 700 persons were left outside when the doors were closed on the first night, and the show had to be repeated on the following night. Employees staged a "minstrel" show that rocked the house with belly laughter. [596]

1945

There was no mention of the annual New Years ball at Hillcrest in the newspaper. In fact, there was no mention of any New Year's celebrations in town. It is hard to believe that there wasn't one. There is simply no explanation. The first recorded activity at Hillcrest for 1945, happened to be a golf round reported on 14 January. A mid-January break in the cold brought 74 devoted duffers out, Dr. Kincade turning in the low score of the day. [597]

Family night resumed as a regular event after a holiday season break. There seemed to be a real desire to get things going again. Dinner-Dance club decided to resume regular parties on 23 January, but that party was cancelled at the last minute and there were no more dances that winter. New directors were elected on 16 January at the annual meeting. They were: A. F. Potter, F. B. Plank, C. W. Doornbos, J. M. Nisbet, and W. W. Neumann was elected to finish the term of W. R. Lund who had gone into the service. There were only two small parties and no civic banquets at Hillcrest in the month. In town, the president's birthday party was again well-attended. [598]

February was similarly slow. A wedding rehearsal dinner, family night, a George Washington's birthday ladies tea, a high school age dance, and a big FPMC Valentine's Day dance were the events for the month. The March calendar was not much better. Mercredi Club met early in the month, Sally Drew had a dancing party for some visiting friends, there was a dinner party for the Gasts, and the McGinleys had a St. Patrick's Day luncheon. Dinner-Dance Club finally made another attempt to put together a dance. Part of their problem may have been the acute manpower shortage. They mention that they had to start dinner early so that the room could be cleared for dancing. The Bartlesville Community Concert Association and Town Hall both did highly successful spring membership drives. [599]

Food shortages due to rationing were so pervasive that it became comical. On 25 March, it was pointed out:

> Last weekend and the week before there was an acute fresh beef and pork shortage, and the women had plenty of points. This weekend the fresh meat supply is fairly simple, but the women had run short of points and much good meat went begging for customers on Saturday. [600]

Women's slacks had hit the fashion mainstream, so of course, there was a shortage, and men's undershorts, shirts, and pajamas were in short supply too. Ususally,

as long as an activity didn't require food, they could get it done.

The national situation wasn't so funny. Meat supplies were so short that there was concern there wouldn't be sufficient supply for the military. While a special Senate committee held hearing to investigate the shortages, the banking committee was considering legislation to extend price controls. No one seemed to figure out the connection. [601]

In the midst of all the shortages the N. G. (Budge) Welty's were building an unusual house on the northeast corner of old Tulsa Road (now Silver Lake Road) and Hillcrest (now Price Road), directly east of the Burlingame estate (now Glynnwood). Charles Dilbeck, a noted Dallas architect, with Tulsa roots, styled it a "Mission Ranch House." Dilbeck took credit for designing the first Texas ranch style and had designed some fine Tulsa homes that Welty would have been familiar with. The house was deliberately built to look old, with uneven floors and an ancient-looking exterior. The Weltys wrote, "in this year of material shortages and reluctant labor, it meant a headache for every stone and rafter." Though constructed on only a few acres, it was the continuation of building estates surrounding the country club. The year after the war, the Weltys moved and sold it to A. H. Buell. The singular house is still there, standing quietly aback from the road. After the Weltys moved, it really wasn't appreciated locally until the middle 1950s when ranch style architecture became all the rage. [602]

By April, the war in Europe was very near the end. V-E Day was only days away. Though their situation was hopeless, the Gestapo organized terrorists called "werewolves" to harry the Allied occupying forces, hoping to sow anarchy and fear. (It took a year to root out the last of these regime holdouts.) On

The Budge Welty Texas Mission Ranch style house was built during the last months of the war. It was the first Ranch Style in Bartlesville, foreseeing a style of architecture that would dominate for a generation and capitalizing on current trends of Western enthusiasm. *Courtesy A. H. Buell.*

13 April, Bartians awoke to the news that Franklin Roosevelt was dead. Only three weeks later, President Truman announced to the nation in a radio address that the war was ended in Europe. In the Pacific, U. S. troops were preparing in Hawaii for invasion of Japan, while the bloody battle for Okinawa was in progress. As V-E Day got closer to reality, people seemed to loosen up. Spring was always a more active time at Hillcrest in any times. Family night continued. Some small ladies clubs returned for meetings. By the end of the month there were a half dozen dinner parties or luncheons given for out-of-town visitors. By May, activity began to approach normal: Luncheons, open house, wedding parties, and even a Colorado School of Mines alumnae dinner on 30 May. Dr. John G. Hervey, dean of the OU law school, talked to OU alums for their association meeting at Hillcrest on 23 May.

The golf season was a little slow getting off because of the weather, but the Bartlesville high school team was actively practicing at Hillcrest by 31 March.

The dining room at Hillcrest was not the only suffering in the club. A pre-war golf ball was worth nine times its weight in silver. A ball that was only $1.00 in 1941 was $10.00 ($116 in 2007 dollars; a real exercise in supply and demand) by the spring of '45. Despite the hardship the tournament year began as usual with the stag tournament. This year it was Charlie Leathers team against O. D. Sackman. Leathers' team won the match. [603]

The local business news was good. Cities Service was in a management shake-up. R. L. Kidd became the new vice president of the land and geological division, while the company proudly announced building a new $20 million toluene plant in Louisiana, as part of the war effort. Phillips reported first quarter earning at a new high. With plenty of money in the economy and a shortage of goods, inflation was a new worry as reported by John H. Kane in a speech to the Chamber forum. A happy capacity crowd heard the Bartlesville high school spring concert at the College High field house. The gasoline ration was increased

50% as a result of the European victory. Hopes were buoyed. The city finally tried to deal with Bartlesville's chronic water problems by a bond to build a Butler Creek reservoir. The local Welfare budget was submitted to the directors with nearly $12,000 of $36,000 for indigent medical care, a new program for the Welfare Association. [604] But, the war was not over and the Jaycees found themselves driving the local trash trucks because of the manpower shortage.

The golf world was buoyed too. The state golf association decided to resume the state amateur tournament. The Hillcrest season was chugging right along. The Reda tournament was played for $107 cash prize on 26 May. A blind bogey was played on Memorial Day. Qualifying rounds began for the club championship that weekend. The Round-up Club staged a big spring show in the first week of June, a prelude to their hopes for a bigger and better Dewey Round-up this year. Meanwhile, the DMF tournament finished with Odis Everett the winner. Heavy rain washed out most of the first round of play for the club championship on 16 June. The club championship round between Dr. Kincade and Bud Browning was played a week later. The women's golf association had not been organized since 1942, so it was good news when they resumed meeting before the Fourth of July. [605]

Except for several parties given for the wedding of Dottie Jean Gleason and Jack Petrie, June was socially quiet, as usual. For the Fourth of July holiday, the club planned a flag tournament, a mixed Scotch foursome, and a putting contest after a picnic supper. There were special games planned for the children, but there were no fireworks that year. The picnic may have been somewhat problematic because the killjoys at the OPA announced that the rations of meat, fats, canned fruit and vegetables, and sugar would be cut. Slim

rations did not keep J. V. Wood from winning the flag tournament. Harley Hicks won the Frank Phillips Men's Club tournament on 10 July. [606]

The old First Presbyterian Church, downtown, was in the style of a beautiful real old Scottish parish kirk. The congregation and its ministries had been growing rapidly over the last several years. With the end of the war in sight, their board voted to do a $100,000 expansion of their facilities, one of the first post-war civic augmentations. (Almost $1.2M in 2007 dollars.) In southeastern Oklahoma, the U.S. Public Health Service began a spraying program of 1,000 square miles with DDT in an experimental program, one of the modern miracles that came out of the war.

On the morning of 7 August, the newspaper had a front page spread on atomic energy, "unlike any force ever before released on Earth." The nation waited the next day for a report. Communication was slow. It was on 8 August, that the story of the Hiroshima bomb filled the papers. The Americans were dumbfounded, as were the Japanese. It was something incomprehensible. Even after the Nagasaki bomb the Japanese responded with impotent threats that they had a bomb too, but in a few slow-motion days they began to realize the ghastly truth and surrendered. Finally the long-awaited V-J Day came. On 15 August, Bartlesville took a holiday. All city offices and businesses were closed and the churches were filled. The country club, too, was closed that day. [607]

On 12 August, Ted Lyons set the low score for the season, a 71 on an August day when 94 men toured the golf course. Near the end of the month the Junior and Senior Chambers of Commerce met again in their annual tournament. The old guys won again. By Labor Day, the new ebullience was evident with 204 players out for the annual flag tournament. H. E. Mayo, two inches from the cup on the 20th, won that day. C. B. Fowler won the driving contest; R. C. Pipes, H. E. Kaiser, and Jack Kinslow tied on the putting contest. At good ol' Osage Hills Golf Course activity reappeared. [608]

The Hillcrest handicap championship was started 21 September, and that evening there was a Calcutta stag dinner in honor of Jimmy Gullane who had been at Hillcrest 20 years that day. The men turned out in mass for the celebration, with Stewart Dewer the master of ceremonies. Dewer enjoyed credit for being the last surviving member of the committee that went to Colorado Springs in 1925 to persuade Gullane to come to Bartlesville. Jim Collins and Don McBride had praises for Jimmy, Harry Hall sang a brace of songs, Harry Lander cracked a few jokes, and everyone wheedled Jimmy to sing "A Wee Drap" - pure joy in his Scots brogue. They presented a plaque that was personally signed by every single guy. Somehow the handicap proceeded the next day unabated. In fact T. R. Cobb turned in his all-time low point gross in the opening round the next morning. Predictably, there was heavy rain the next few days and the river flooded. The river was at 12.8 feet on 25 September, and 18.3 on 2 October. US 60 east of Bartlesville, and US 75 north and south of town were closed. Golf play wasn't resumed until 9 October. [609]

One of the first acts of Governor Kerr when the Truman administration came in, was to call him and talk about the Hulah Dam, among other things. By the time of the fall flood, it looked like the program was again back on track. Not everything was going so smoothly. The entire war period had been filled with continuous strikes and union violence. The CIO was infested with communists and impossible to deal with. On 5 October 1945, President Truman ordered the Navy to take over refineries that were striking. Two of them belonged to Phillips. Truman had immediately stopped rationing of meat right after coming to office, but it was only a short time before meat was back on the list. The truth is they couldn't figure out how to disentangle themselves from the managed economy without causing wild swings in the market and roaring inflation. By the end of October, Truman asked Congress to continue wartime controls. It was becoming clear that we had won the war but now had the occupation of two nations on our hands and the rebuilding of a devastated Europe. The Chinese communists were taking advantage of the

Senator Elmer Thomas had worked a long, frustrating time on the Hulah Dam project. Here Sen. Thomas goes over the map of the Hulah Flood Control watershed aboard a Phillips aircraft, (right) A. H. Riney and C. E. Burlingame, (left) Maj. H. A. Montgomery are looking on. *Courtesy Bartlesville Area History Museum.*

weakened government to challenge the nationalists. It was evident that military conscription would continue for a long time. Truman did sign a tax cut bill on 10 November, the first since Herbert Hoover.

In Bartlesville, life was assuming a more normal tempo. In a comic episode, Edward Hoog, one of the town drunks, was sentenced to prison for stealing Boots Adams' suitcase. Hoog gave some heirloom cufflinks, belonging to Adams, to a truck driver who gave him a lift to Pawhuska, and one of Adams' shirts to a fellow jailbird. He admitted it was stupid to steal a big suitcase like that. The annual Halloween parade and party ballooned to a combined Victory loan – high school celebration – Halloween event. "Uncounted thousands" lined the streets for the torchlight parade and Wildcat pep rally. Mounted members of the Round-up Club led the parade of floats, Halloween costumes, returned servicemen, the College High and Central Junior High School bands to a bonfire in the College High football practice grounds. The high spirits of the evening kept the police jumping with pranks all over town, and a handful of arrests. The Jaycees decided to sponsor a program to boost church attendance in Bartlesville. "Leaders decided that the Armistice-Thanksgiving period, when people are in a mood of thankfulness, and conscious of the duty to divine prayer, was the time to put on this church going campaign." [610]

Truman naively toyed with the noble-sounding idea of sharing American atomic secrets with other nations, especially the British, and even the Russians. And finally, in time for Thanksgiving, it was announced that all rationing (except sugar) was ended. Most ordinary activities were resuming. The Lions held a zone meeting in Bartlesville, and the reception dinner-dance was at Hillcrest. The first of the postwar housing boom was underway despite an early

winter season, with seven new houses in Oak Ridge Heights addition near Limestone School. [611]

Throughout the fall, a handful of little social events at Hillcrest demonstrated that people were loosening up. Newcomers Club, which had been meeting at the YWCA for about a year, had a luncheon meeting at Hillcrest in September. Luncheon-sewing club decided to open their year at Hillcrest. One of the PEO chapters did the same. There was a birthday dance for Beverly Phillips, who was visiting the Rowsons, and Mrs. John Guardiola had a luncheon for some out-of-town visitors. The actual social season at Hillcrest began just before Halloween with a family night. There were several post-nuptial parties for Mary Lou and Bob Emery who were visiting for a few days. Doherty Auxiliary heard a book review by Tulsa bookstore owner, Lewis Meyer, at a tea on 11 November. The Doherty Girls had their annual banquet at Hillcrest a week later. An important old-times luncheon was given by Mrs. Paul Dahlgren for Mrs. S. G. Weber when she were visiting in town during Thanksgiving. [612]

The Jaycees opened the Christmas season by heading up the Christmas fund drive for needy children, the latest incarnation of the old pre-war Christmas Cheer Committee. Despite a widespread flu epidemic in December a number of teas and coffees were planned at Hillcrest in early December, and several of the ladies clubs held their Christmas meetings for the first time since Pearl Harbor. Mrs. L. A. Rowland held a particularly important tea for her new daughter-in-law, Vi, the bride of Lt. Alt Rowland, newly returned to Bartlesville to live. On the 19th, a beautiful snow enhanced the decorations for another important tea given by Mmes. Kitching, Charles, and Cunningham. The 22nd was the day for children's Christmas parties at the club. The annual children's party with refreshments and entertainment was from 3:30 to 4:30 P.M. that afternoon, and the older children had a dance from 9:30 P.M. to 12:00 midnight, the Down Beat orchestra furnishing the music. On 29 December, there was a high school holiday dance. The great anticipation was for the New Year's party that year. It would be the biggest since Pearl Harbor, no doubt about that. Bob Anderson and his "Chimes of the Times" came from Chicago to play in the New Year, beginning at 10:00. The dance was semi-formal which was a change from recent years, though no return to the rollicking habits of the years before the war. Novelties were provided to enliven the welcoming, and breakfast was served in the wee hours. Afterwards, there were several open houses around town, resuming the old pre-war New Years Day celebrations. [613]

The war years in Bartlesville had been very difficult, more difficult than those of the Great War a generation earlier. Still, they were a time of economic recovery when many of the local large industries, Phillips Petroleum Company, Cities Service, Reda Pump, and Price Pipeline prospered, despite the climate of confiscatory taxes. The end of the Madison era was a great relief to the oil industry, even with continued threats of nationalization. The pioneer generation was beginning to pass on and many were also retiring and handing the reins to a younger generation of leadership. During the Depression strictures the town had continued to make civic progress and the city leaders had new visions for improvements in the community now that the economy showed new promise.

People had been uncomfortable with international developments for years. Small provocations against American interests abroad had become more and more frequent with the passage of time, as the Japanese gobbled up the western side of the Pacific Rim, and the Nazis began to grab chunks of

Europe and Africa. Almost by instinct, Bartlesville sons seemed to have acquired the inclination to go to military schools and take ROTC at university in the late 1930s. By 1940, the military recruiters were busy in town, and the newspapers were reporting the patriotic young men who were joining up every week, while the young reserve officers were being snatched off, one-by-one, to active duty. Even our local aviation hero, Billy Parker, was one of the earliest, serving in the RAF.

The attack on Pearl Harbor that Sunday morning in December 1941 was shocking – yet in some way, expected. Immediately, *everybody* understood what was required. Many had lived through World War I and already had a sobering idea of the cost, though none could imagine the staggering effort ahead. There was fear of invasion, attacks on our coasts, saboteurs, and even of the ravages of war in this country. Almost immediately rubber was on the ration list.

War shortage problems appeared almost immediately. The earliest manifestation was a crisis of leadership. The younger leaders were rapidly siphoned off to form the needed new officers corps. Bob Neptune and Jack Leonard, two of the first local men called up, both spent their early months in service training troops. We can chuckle about the slow golf games at Hillcrest after Bill Simpson left, but that spirit was a problem in every part of civic activity in town. It sucked the wind out of the town's ability to get things done, both in spirit and in available manpower. The older, experienced leaders stepped into the breech and effectively met every demand, but new initiatives were impossible to bring off. Rationing of food cut down almost all entertaining in town, and the country club was affected too. Rationing of gasoline and tires made travel out to the club more difficult. Even golf balls were in short supply. Manpower was a chronic problem. Frank Phillips had to convince the War Manpower Commission and the Petroleum Administration that the military should not draft his engineers and chemists so that the company could continue vital research. The Hillcrest women's golf association finally had to disband partly because there were not enough caddies. The demands of the war economy must have made it hard to keep staff in the clubhouse and on the golf course.

Building materials were in short supply so that new projects could not be started and ordinary maintenance was difficult – if you could find the tradesmen to do the work. There was an acute housing shortage.

A less tangible factor, but a demonstrably compelling one was the attitude that extravagant entertaining was not appropriate when so many young men were risking their lives for those at home. There were exceptions. Anything patriotic needed to be done in grand style, and it seemed to be agreed that it was all right for young people to have reasonably nice parties. The attitude was sort of a barometer of people's feelings about the success of the war. Nevertheless, the usual civic clubs continued to work. They were devoting most of their activity toward postwar hopes and towards support of the war effort. Remarkably, they kept up the important programs for youth, welfare, round-up club activities, music and speaking series, and new outreach for area military service personnel.

The merger of ITIO into Cities Service, and then their subsequent reorganization caused a loss of jobs. Phillips quickly absorbed many of those good employees. Still, the town was substantially affected by the changes. Natural disasters, especially the annual flooding, and one serious tornado in 1943, were managed remarkably well considering the problems of manpower and construction materials in those years.

The country club was also stressed during the war years. Besides rationing and manpower problems, there was a loss of younger membership. In the unsettled times, and with the difficulty is transportation to the club, it appears they were not attracting many new members from the community. After Sunset Country Club closed, they did have an enlivening spurt from their golf devotees who decided to take the financial plunge. They managed to keep up appearances.

People who remember the day of the first atomic bomb say the best description was that they were just dumbfounded. V-E and V-J Days were not the end. There were many more months needed to pacify the war torn lands and begin the process for rebuilding. Some of the men began to return pretty quickly, but most began to return home and be discharged after the first of the year. Bill Simpson was the first to return, in December 1945. He was a captain, serving stateside during the war, in intelligence, and as a security officer at the Los Alamos project in New Mexico. Bob Neptune who left Bartlesville at the same time, was discharged in February 1946, having served in the 82nd Airborne Division as a parachute battalion commander from North Africa to Italy to Normandy. After the war he returned to the Philippines and Japan as a civilian war crimes prosecutor until 1950. Jack Leonard, the first of the young reserve officers to be called up in 1941, returned in March 1946. He had seen combat throughout Europe with the Army Air Corps.

10

HOLE NUMBER TEN.

500 Yards, Par 5. This is the start of the famous Hillcrest back nine.
Every hole is tree lined with oaks and pines, with every shot being very demanding.
The tenth hole is a dogleg right at 275 yards off the tee and a 225 yard second shot
if you can stay in the fairway.
The green is well bunkered with the right front being a difficult bunkered shot.
Green size 5,000 square feet.

HOLE NUMBER 11.

Hillcrest Country Club's signature hole.

This hole was voted the best 11th hole in the State of Oklahoma by PGA golf professionals in 1975. Forget the driver.

The perfect tee shot is a driving iron which will leave you 130 yards from the small split level 3,500 square foot green.

Be sure to hit the green. Bunkers are short – Caney River long.

CHAPTER SIX

Triumph Of The Modern:
THE YEARS AFTER THE WAR

There was a muffled, rapid tick-tick-tick-tick, barely discernable from the projection room, drowned out by the rollicking music and raucous voices coming from the scene on the great screen spread across the front of the theater. In the pitch black room a faint blue light reflected from the picture on hundreds of rapt faces, young and old, packed into the mohair upholstered theater seats, munching popcorn and candy bars, and sipping Dr. Pepper and Coke from 4 ounce paper cups, all purchased with the dime spending money their parents had given them for the event. "Zippity-do-da" sang a delightful, grandfatherly old Black man in a basso voice, played by James Baskett, as he stepped across a scene of animated trees and flowers to tell the tale of De Tar-Baby to the gathered crowd. Soon an animated Brer Rabbit came hopping down the road just in time to fall into the trap set by animated characters, Brer Bear and Brer Fox.

"Three!" yell Brer Rabbit. Now he mighty mad. He draw back his fist, and blip! He hit De Tar-Baby smack in de nose. But dis fist stuck der in de tar too. He can't pull it loose.

Now Brer Rabbit turrible mad. "Let go my fist!" he holler. Wid dat, he draw back his other fist, and blip! Again he hit de Tar-Baby smack in de nose. But dis fist stuck der in de tar too. He can't pull it loose.

De Tar-Baby, he say nothin', an Brer Fox an Brer Bear dey sorter chuckle in der stummocks.

"If you don't let go my fists," holler Brer Rabbit, "I'm goin' ter kick your teef right outer your mouf!"

Wel suh, Brer Rabbit kicked. First he pull back one

behind foot, an pow! He hit de Tar-Baby in de jaw. But Brer Rabbit's behind foot stuck der in de tar. Den, pow! He hit de Tar-Baby wid de other behind foot. Dis foot stuck der in de tar too.

"If you don't let go my behind foots," squall out Brer Rabbit, "I'm goin' ter butt you wid my head till you ain't got no bref left in your body!"

Brer Rabbit butted, but his head stuck der in de tar. Now Brer Rabbit's two fists, his two behind foots, an his head wuz all stuck in de Tar-Baby. He push an he pull, but de more he try ter get unstuck-up, de stucker-up he got. Soon Brer Rabbit is so stuck up he can't skacely move his eyeballs. [614]

To the bleary-eyed children pouring out the front of the Osage Theater after the early matinee of The Song of the South it seemed like only minutes had passed. The afternoon sun made their eyes squint as they returned to the real world of March 1947, from the delightful, joyous world created in Walt Disney's marvelous animations. Outside, cars were pulled into the angle parking spaces on Johnstone, their occupants simply enjoying the comings and goings as the movie let out. It seemed that John and Amelia Cronin never missed this spectacle. Other cars double parked along the street, motors running, waiting to pick up loads of kids. Some parents, who had accompanied small children, loaded their still-enraptured cargos into their vehicles. Little girls skipped down the sidewalk toward home, singing in chorus, "Zippity-do-da," and little boys grabbed up bikes that were leaning against Koppel's storefront and sped up the street. Going to the movie in the 1940s was a social event, even for children.

Bartlesville businessmen like banker John Cronin had reason to reflect on "De Tar-Baby" that year. Just how do you let go of the tar baby? The recovering economy of the war years had only complicated the policies that everybody but the planners knew would be dangerous. Already high taxes before the war had soared. Labor problems had intensified. Wage and price controls, along with rationing imposed a lid on the most powerful economic engine in the history of the world. Wartime full employment greeted the newly returned veterans with no place to work. A crisis-level housing shortage grappled with extreme shortage of building materials, and no place for all those wartime newlyweds to set up housekeeping. New ominous expansionism from our recent war ally, the Russians, and in the wake of war, opportunistic communist uprisings all over the globe from Chile to China, financed by the Soviets, made the new post-war world even more dangerous than the one so recently past. It was already clear that American boys would be serving overseas for a very long time, and the military draft would continue too, as we began the job of reconstruction and stabilization after the devastation in Europe and Japan. Already the seeds of the 21st century were being sown in the Middle East as boatloads of Holocaust refugees fled to Palestine to join an earlier generation of Zionist cousins who had been settling kibbutzim in the Land since the Napoleonic era. Stalin was already moving to seize Iran with her oil fields, and her warm water ports, and Turkey at the mouth of their Black Sea outlet, and the ancient key to control of the region. How do you let go of the tar baby of rationing, wage and price controls, taxes, war politics, and antiquated racial notions? All of this in a zippity-do-da, "we're headin' for the Laughin' Place," time to really live now, post-war America.

1946

It was a Zippity-do-da New Years for sure; the happiest in years, even if there was a shortage of sugar, and beef, and so forth. People gathered downtown, drove around, went to some of the cafes for late dinner, or went to the midnight movie; the various clubs outside of town had lots of revelers, and Elks had a notable party. Still, there was only one police call for a fight and only one accident in which a car overturned on the curve at Irwin corner. At midnight horns honked, sirens and whistles blew, but for the first time, there was no mention of guns being fired into the air. For some reason that venerable old tradition disappeared in 1946.

At Hillcrest couples danced to Chimes of the Times band into the early morning hours and on New Years Day resumed the round of parties with important afternoon receptions at Burlingame Place and at the M. E. Foster's home.

After all the celebration, the New Year remained slow. Many civic activities were still at the College High cafeteria, or the Civic Center, or the Hotel Burlingame. Only the Jaycees' banquet was held at Hillcrest. The new Chamber of Commerce program for 1946 was not remarkably ambitious, except for a new initiative to improve the airport and lure commercial flights to Bartlesville once again. There was a G. I. Clinic in the American Legion rooms at the Civic Center to discuss the rights of veterans. Veterans were returning home without jobs or places to live. Eisenhower advised that they should go to college – and many did. A generation of youthful leadership was still not back in Bartlesville. Meanwhile the Bureau of Labor Statistics announced that wholesale prices were up 31% since September. There was a rash of labor strikes and unrest, vying with price ceilings

to keep supply and demand tied in knots. Churchill's speech in Fulton, Missouri on 27 January, warned of the dangers of Soviet imperialism, a pronouncement that fell on deaf ears. Folks were not in the mood for a new struggle. [615]

Hillcrest stockholders had their annual meeting on 15 January, electing J. H. Collins, L. S. Ambrose, J. F. Kinshaw, and Stanley Learned directors, while R. L. Kidd was elected to fill the unexpired term of J. M. Nisbet. Collins was re-elected president for 1946. Otherwise, there was precious little social activity in evidence at Hillcrest, just three small events for January and only one in February. Mrs. Ringo finally stepped up in March with a luncheon for 50, proposed to be the first of a series of spring parties. It was followed 2 weeks later by a big ladies luncheon for the purpose of reorganizing the women's golf association. Mrs. A. H. Riney finally had a large May Day luncheon with the telltale flower decorations that marked a major social event. The entire season had passed with only a handful of small social events – no club dances; no dinner-dance club. Finally an announcement came that the dining room was closed for some repair - actually in the kitchen. They did make a concession for the junior-senior prom, but even the women's golf association had to forego luncheons. Whatever they may have gotten done must have been almost impossible. In March the Civilian Production Administration tried to speed up construction of new homes for veterans by clamping drastic restrictions on building or repairs on virtually all other structures. It appears the restrictions all but closed the clubhouse at Hillcrest for months. [616]

After the stopgap kitchen repairs, business picked up somewhat in May, but it was clearly only a patch. A handful of teas, dinners, and a Doherty Auxiliary luncheon finished out an anorexic spring season.

Mrs. George Bunn and Mrs. Barton Witchell gave a luncheon on 23 May, but the second round was a tea at the Bunn's home the next day, demonstrating that there was a persistent problem. The summer schedule was even thinner than usual. A series of parties near the end of June, given by the college set for various visiting friends, featured only one luncheon at Hillcrest. All of the other parties were in the girl's homes. On 8 August, there was a family night supper at the club preceded by a Scotch foursome as the feature event of the evening. The event was won by Mr. And Mrs. Brooks Spies with low net scores of 31; high net was taken by Miss Dottie Gleason and Bob Neptune with 44. Then as usual, the clubhouse was closed until September. Even after the summer vacation the club-

house saw little significant fall season utilization. [617]

In the summer of 1946, H. C. Price began to develop his estate immediately east of the country club. The Prices held some notable summer parties in the best barn in Washington County at the new Star View Farm. The biggest social news for the year didn't even happen in Bartlesville. K. S. Adams remarried to Dorothy Glenn Stephens in San Antonio, Texas the first week in November. The same weekend, the Dahlgrens and Webers rescued the Bartlesville season with two huge dinner parties for 75 on Friday afternoon and Saturday night. Doherty Auxilliary had a November tea. Even in December, there were only a few small parties. The holiday season culminated with a dance for the high school age children on 23

The loft in the barn at Hal Price's Star View Farm, across the road east of the country club, was the scene of some great square dances in the summer of 1947. *Courtesy Bartlesville Area History Museum.*

December. Mrs. G. C. Clark and Mrs. D. C. Hemsell entertained 200 ladies at a tea. Fortunately, the Tylers resumed their extravagant after-Christmas party tradition after a war-years recess. The whole interior of the club was decorated with greenery, poinsettias and garlands of smilax were arranged at vantage points. The George Olson orchestra from Chicago furnished the dance music, and a buffet was served after midnight. Of course, the New Years Eve ball was a big party. [618]

Even with the pitiful social performance of the country club in 1946, civic Bartlesville putted right on. None of this civic activity took place at Hillcrest either. Despite icy roads the sheriff and state officers raided the Clover Club, 6 miles south of town on 13 February. For the second time in only a few months that nightclub was closed down for liquor and gambling infractions, surely chilling to the other clubs in town, as well as Hillcrest. [619]

At about that same time, an article in Survey Graphic persuaded the local librarian, Miss Ruth Brown, that a small local organization, Committee on the Practice of Democracy (COPD), ought to be affiliated with the new national organization, Congress on Racial Equality (CORE), setting in motion new forces that would try the principles of social capital. COPD was an evolution of a circle of local people who were interested in social justice. Don Sheridan, the minister at First Christian Church, was the president, Roosevelt Gracey, the principal of Douglass High School, was vice president, and Miss Ruth Brown, the Bartlesville librarian, was secretary. One of their first actions was an excellent survey of the Bartlesville Black community, which was published in May 1947. [620]

By April, a series of community improvements were on the boards. An open house to view the remodeled Union railroad station was announced not long after the government moratorium on commercial construction. A big banquet was held at the Burlingame Hotel for Railroad Appreciation Day. St. John's School announced plans for their modern new school building. Juggling the burgeoning school populations at Central and College High, it appeared that the school board would have to sacrifice the junior college that was just recovering from closing down during the war. The long planned addition to Memorial Hospital held an open house on 12 May. [621]

The biggest civic event of the year was a crow dinner sponsored by the Chamber of Commerce in May. Finally, in February, the resignation of Interior Secretary Harold Ickes from the Truman cabinet seems to have cleared the obstacles that had frustrated the Hulah Dam project since 1933. The Morning Examiner crowed that the 31 October 1945, editorial did the trick, "When and if Thomas or Kerr get Hulah started we'll eat crow." So, Thomas and Kerr took up the challenge on 20 April, with the Chamber of Commerce serving the meal. The Jaycees got into the game, announcing that they were in charge of the crows, "Twelve Caney Valley crows have been captured and are on exhibit in the windows of the Chamber of Commerce office." It was a huge Chamber banquet for 300 at the Civic Center on the evening of 3 May; crow for the editors and other fare for the rest of the mob. Senator Thomas and Governor Kerr were the guests of honor, ostensibly for getting the dam on track, but Kerr used the event for a little campaigning for his upcoming 1948 senatorial race. The *Examiner* editors, N.D., Don, and Budge Welty, arrived at the affair with their "crow-eating paraphernalia" which included:

(1) a food grinder, (2) a meat cleaver, (3) a hack saw, (4) shakers labeled "sulfa" and "penicillin," (5) a box of soda, (6) a bottle of patent medicine

indigestion remedy, and (7) a stone jug labeled "Old Crow" and "Not Molasses Sorghum" on the other. [622]

Of course, the whole evening was one rollicking spoof after another. It seemed as though at last happy days were here again. [623]

H. C. Price Company was landing big new pipeline jobs. Phillips and Cities Service spring meetings enjoyed news of even greater profitability. Nearly 250,000 head of cattle poured into the Osage and Flint Hills country for the spring grazing season.

After 13 years, work on the Hulah Dam finally got underway in May 1946. Bartlesville's water problems have never been solved, but the Hulah Dam went as long way toward assuring adequate water. *Courtesy Bartlesville Area History Museum.*

But, there was also sober news. Finally the list of Washington County's war dead and missing was published. A Black student filed a petition in district court on 6 April, challenging the University of Oklahoma ban of Negro students, the beginning of many legal actions, a struggle that would eventually lead to the desegregation of American public schools and universities in 1958. In the face of an U.N. committee report on the Holy Land, Arabs warned that immigration of Jewish Holocaust refugees to Israel would elicit violence. Amidst voter apathy for the mid-term primaries, Roy J. Turner was finally picked as the Democrat candidate for Governor at the end of July. 1946 was plagued by on and off again economic controls in the face of raging inflation and shortages of goods. An election year is no time for a congressman to look like he isn't doing something. Industry after industry was hit by labor strikes. There was another scary summer of polio. No one knew what was causing the plague. So the public health authorities fell back on what they knew – sanitation and insect control. The Jaycees headed up a clean up Bartlesville program in hopes of getting some sort of control on polio. H. C. Price Company celebrated its 25th anniversary in November. But, at this auspicious civic milestone, a banquet for company employees was held at the Burlingame Hotel, not Hillcrest. [624]

Fortunately, there was plenty of golf activity in 1946. As usual the women's golf association opened the spring season with an organizational meeting on 27 March. Dues for 1946 were $3 and Agnes Foster was elected president. The back nine (sand greens) of Sunset finally reopened that same weekend, but the front nine of new grass greens were not ready for play yet. Wilkie aggressively pursued the local golf market by offering five free group golf lessons to everyone. The high school golf team continued to play

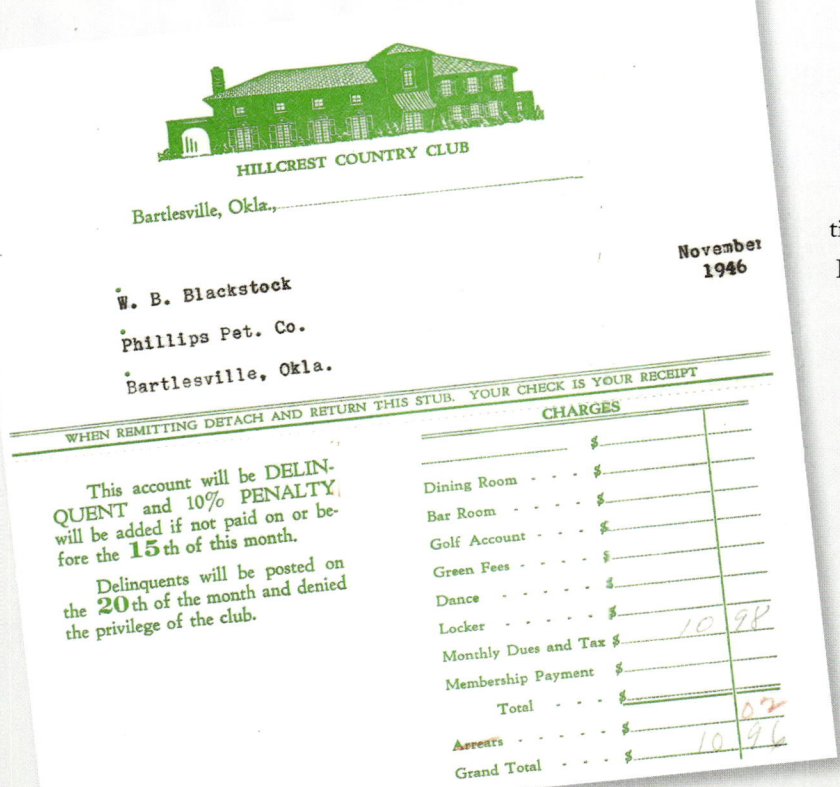

HILLCREST COUNTRY CLUB

Bartlesville, Okla., _____

November 1946

W. B. Blackstock

Phillips Pet. Co.

Bartlesville, Okla.

WHEN REMITTING DETACH AND RETURN THIS STUB. YOUR CHECK IS YOUR RECEIPT

CHARGES

This account will be DELIN-
QUENT and 10% PENALTY
will be added if not paid on or before the 15th of this month.

Delinquents will be posted on
the 20th of the month and denied
the privilege of the club.

Dining Room	$
Bar Room	$
Golf Account	$
Green Fees	$
Dance	$
Locker	$ 10.98
Monthly Dues and Tax	$
Membership Payment	$
Total	$ .02
Arrears	$ 10.96
Grand Total	$

In 1946 this monthly bill was $10.98. Dues were $3.00. Evidently Mr. Blackstock paid $11.00 (easier to subtract) in October.

at Hillcrest. It was mid-April before the golf season really got off. Jimmy Gullane shot a 65 in one of those high-roller rounds with C. A. Elliott of New York City, W. T. Lynn of Kansas City, and Ted Lyon, on a Palm Sunday when 105 golfers played the course. [625]

The annual membership golf match (and stag dinner) was on 27 April. Dr. Paul Kincade's team defeated the Bill Simpson team soundly. Oudrey Nelson won the Reda Pump golf championship on 21 May. Dave Lhuiller won the D.M.F. championship in mid-June. Amidst the summer tournament play, on 21 June, M. C. Wood shot a hole-in-one on the second hole while playing with his wife. While the Hillcrest club championship was being played, Jimmy Gullane was showing well at the PGA in Muskogee. Bill Simpson emerged the 1946 Hillcrest champ just before the Fourth of July. [626]

A special match between the National Bank of Tulsa and First National Bank of Bartlesville teams came to a tie at Hillcrest on 3 July. The annual Forth of July flag tournament was won by M. W. Conn. The annual FPMC tournament was played early in July with Jack Kinslow the winner. The American Legion held its district tournament at Hillcrest late in July. Bill Martin was the James H. Teel Post entry. [627]

Qualifying rounds began for the annual handicap championship just before Labor Day. A stag dinner on 13 September kicked off the golf weekend. It was an exciting tournament. In the final round Jack Maddox (handicap 16) and H. E. Mayo (handicap 14) tied with 137 net each, forcing a play-off round. Maddox was the winner. A few days later there was a match in Tulsa between Hillcrest and the Oaks Country Club. DMF was victorious in a return match with Ponca City at Hillcrest on 28 September, the next day the Jaycees and the Chamber of Commerce had their annual match at Hillcrest. [628]

While Jimmy Gullane was at the state open tournament in Oklahoma City, the Hillcrest women played their handicap championship tournament. Mrs. C. W. Hubbell became the handicap champion for 1946. Gullane made a good showing at Oklahoma City Golf and Country Club, winning his matches even though the Texas team carried the day. For the first time in Hillcrest Women's Golf Association reporting in the *Examiner*, early in 1946 an article appeared using most of the women's first names instead of their married names. It may have been a sign of the times. The married names were evidently an expression of social status, but it's too bad that women who were such high achievers in the sport lost their personal identity along with their first names for so many years. [629]

1947

The New Years ball at Hillcrest was the biggest in several years. Decorations were held over from the Tyler party two nights before making the clubhouse unusually festive for the ball. There were several important parties preceding the ball, and open houses the next afternoon. Otherwise, downtown Bartlesville was quiet at the stroke of midnight on a frigid evening. No guns fired, no whistle at the smelter. President Truman greeted the New Year announcing a presidential order relinquishing many of the war powers, declaring "hostilities of World War II ceased at noon today." During 1946, 251 new houses were completed in Bartlesville, mostly in the new Jane Phillips addition. [630]

January at Hillcrest was unusually quiet, but the January weather was very cold and people may not have wanted to get out. On the 31st, tornados swept all across the South along a sagging cold front, but that stormy night the Jaycees held their annual awards banquet and ball in high style at Hillcrest. H. C. Price, the new president of the Chamber of Commerce, presented the awards for the Junior Chamber, congratulating past effort and encouraging renewed enthusiasm. February saw a resurgence of social and civic activity in town and more normal activity in the clubhouse even though the kitchen had only had stopgap repairs. There was the usual smattering of small luncheons and teas during the winter, but for Valentine's Day, Hillcrest finally got its act together to resume club dances. Dinner-Dance club reappeared, complete with Jackson's orchestra, on 25 February.

With the kitchen out of commission, it is not clear how dinner was served to such a large group. Private dinner parties and luncheon activity picked up in March, and Dinner-Dance club held its next party on 25 March. [631]

Sweet Adelines, the women's barber shop quartet club, organized in town. Local men had been enjoying S.P.E.B.Q.S.A. (the men's national barber shop quartet organization) for several years. Barbershop quartets were a very popular activity in the era, especially for those with the vocal talent to participate. There was an open house for the new Y-hut at the Y.M.C.A., a new Hi-Y and Y teen (teen-age) dance hall at the Y. The Y continued to benefit from concerted community interest in their program, especially for local youth.

One of the most important social events of the season was the observation of the golden wedding anniversary of Frank and Jane Phillips on 18 February. The Phillipses celebrated the anniversary at a private party with 118 family members and close friends at Woolaroc Lodge. That evening, Jane Phillips presented her husband the Bryant Baker bronze statue of Frank Phillips that is still in the Woolaroc rotunda today. [632]

Commodity prices surged again at the beginning of March, foreshadowing continued inflation pressure on the economy. The absurdity of the situation was illustrated when Dr. Pepper officials were indicted for fraudulently diverting sugar stamps in 8 states. The sugar controls persisted until almost 1950! Overseas, instability in Palestine was growing more intense. But, there was the good news that a huge Nazi underground movement in Germany was cracked, and at last the Nazi resistance was broken.

The city of Bartlesville began activities that would culminate in the 50th anniversary celebration on 1 April. The *Examiner* ran daily stories about the old days in Bartlesville, preparing for the anniversary celebration. Interviews with old timers, or their children, made the history of a world then entirely gone, but in living memory, live in the imaginations of a post-war generation. A thunderstorm greeted the early morning of 1 April, but by parade time 40,000 people assembled to see the spectacle and participate in the many special events of the day. [633]

The president of the Chamber of Commerce, H. C. Price, was unusually aggressive in touting the Chamber program of the past year. There was extensive publication of Chamber activities, and their growing membership. A major Chamber forum on 18 April, with former president John H. Kane as moderator, was dedicated to a "multi-sided review of the organization's scope and accomplishments." Bartlesville civic leaders planned aggressive growth of Bartlesville business, and set their sites on ambitious new civic improvements. They weren't alone. The new governor, Roy Turner, began pushing construction of a turnpike between Oklahoma City and Tulsa, despite a populist uproar from his own party and civic outrage from the little towns along Route 66. Oklahoma needed a modern highway system. [634]

The Frank Phillips Men's Club sponsored an Easter egg hunt for all the children under 12 in town in the field southwest of Jane Phillips addition. 2400 eggs were put out, and 12 turkey eggs for special prizes, which were colored baby chickens and baby Easter bunnies. The country club had a spring dance on Easter eve. The membership was dealing with the dysfunction in the kitchen by going out to dinner elsewhere before the dance. On the other hand, things were running well enough that there were several teas and small luncheons that spring. [635]

At the end of April, Song of the South came to the Osage theater for a four-day engagement. There were 4 showings a day, two of them matinees. [636]

The Woolaroc museum opened on 4 May after 15 months of expansion and renovation. The beautiful octagon-shaped rotunda became the spectacular new entry. A paved parking lot, air-conditioning, offices, and expansion of the basement level were featured new structural additions. Special public tours of the ranch and museum began 3 days a week. [637]

The golf season was slow in getting off because of spring weather. The school golf teams were back at Sunset for their practices in March. That year young Fos Doornbos was the king of the Central golfers. The annual Hillcrest club tournament began on 26 April. Dr. Kincade and Bill Simpson were captains of the teams, and Charlie Selby was in charge of arrangements. Kincade's team was victorious. That weekend 306 men toured the golf course at Hillcrest, a real revival. The Society of Automotive Engineers played a blind bogey golf tournament at Hillcrest on 8 May, while holding a district meeting in Bartlesville. The final round of the club championship was played on 31 May. Bill Simpson was the winner. [638]

The wedding season saw many parties, and some rehearsal dinners, and receptions at Hillcrest. The wedding of Marie Pinkerton to John Freiberger was particularly prominent on the social calendar in May. As usual, the junior-senior prom was at the country club early in May. For the Fourth of July, the kitchen somehow managed a buffet supper before the fireworks. There were another half dozen weddings in the summer, otherwise the season was very quiet. The club dining room closed on 30 July, and remained closed until September. Finally, needed repairs and installation of new equipment in the kitchen was addressed. The war shortages had provided an instructive demonstration of the importance of the nuts and bolts infrastructure to the functioning of the club. It was an immense relief to be back in action in September, in time for several wedding parties, rehearsal dinners, and a reception. [639]

It was a quirky summer. As if the fireworks on the Fourth weren't enough, there were reports of flying saucers in 28 states that weekend. The engagement of Princess Elizabeth to Prince Phillip was announced, assuring lots of royal-watching for the next few months. Only weeks ahead of passage of the Taft-Hartly Act, the smelter workers local voted to strike on 9 July.

Dick Booker won the DMF tournament on 10 June, also capturing the Cities Service regional title. The victory won him a trip to the company's national tournament in Springfield, New Jersey. Keith Fowler and Bill Simpson showed well at the Trans-Mississippi tournament at Wichita Country Club. Meanwhile, the Hillcrest women hosted the Tulsa district tournament on 19 June. Jim McCall won the Fourth of July flag tournament. Hillcrest had an impressive representation at the Broadmoor invitational tournament: Charles Fowler, Keith Fowler, John Cronin, Jim Cronin, Stewart Dewer, and W. B. Engelbrecht. Keith Fowler was the runner-up medalist behind Ardmore's Charles Coe. Sunset golf club reorganized as a country club with 150 charter members, and elected officers in August. [640]

The summer finished with a scorcher on Labor Day weekend. Joe Carle was the winner of the flag tournament that was the feature of the holiday weekend play, though the crowd was a little thin. Everybody signed up in the golf shop for the Thursday evening handicap dinner before the start of the annual tournament. J. W. Proffitt was in the lead with a 69 on the first day of play, but there was a stiff wind and heavy rain on Saturday so that the final round was put off a week. Finally on the first weekend in October, glorious weather brought out 250 players for some fine golf. Independence was at Hillcrest for an inter-city match the next weekend, while the women's handicap got underway. Mrs. H. A. Gardner took the women's handicap championship on 22 October. Mrs. C. W. Hubbell was the Hillcrest women's club champion for 1947. The women had their awards luncheon on 29 October. The weekly luncheon had grown in popularity to include a number of women who didn't play golf, but stayed for bridge afterward. Mrs. Foster had to cancel the old permanent list for the luncheon and start all over. The women played a Scotch foursome in tacky costume that day. Mrs. Jim Hatfield and Mrs. O. P. Nicola won first and second prizes as the tackiest bums. Mrs. H. A. Sanders won third, as an 1890s bathing beauty. Others came as a ballet dancer, several floozies, Santa Claus, grandma in an outing nightie, bobby soxer, Joe Dude, and a baby with a bottle. Bartlesville and Ponca City Cities Service golf teams played a match on 1 November. The weather remained decent late so that the last recorded weekend play for 1947 was 23 December. [641]

The situation in Palestine began to degenerate into frank terrorism. The British had appointed a Grand Mufti as the head of state there, but during the war it became clear that he was in fact a Fascist when he allied with Germany. He fled to exile, but he became the sponsor of terrorist action within the proposed state, while the Arab nations threatened to attack if the Jewish state was actually formed. At home, the House Un-American Activities Committee for some time had been investigating shocking revelations of Communist infiltration into the United States government and many American institutions. By fall, House investigation into the Hollywood left was grabbing headlines. The Administration was grappling with high inflation and the necessity of high taxes to fund the Marshal Plan. "Cries of 'socialism' rang out on Capitol Hill," as administration spokesmen went to Congress with the president's economic plan. The Supreme Court agreed to hear Ada Lois Sipuel's racial discrimination case against the University of Oklahoma. The landmark case was at the forefront of a new civil rights awareness, and it was taking place right here in Oklahoma. The good news for the season was the royal wedding of Princess Elizabeth in England on 21 November. [642]

Civic Bartlesville had some big things on its plate for fall. The Chamber's airport project came through. A master plan for development of the airport to handle commercial flights was produced in October. Then in December, Frank Phillips and Boots Adams announced the company's gift to the city of the Phillips airfield west of town, and $204,000, to be matched with $204,000 in federal funds, for the needed improvements. While this was being negotiated, the mayor appointed a planning committee. The leadership is a good snap-shot of the changing of the guard since the war. W. C. Smoot (1st National Bank) was chairman, Don Tyler (Portland Cement) was vice chairman, and members were H. C. Price (Price Pipeline), Sam Harlan (Cities Service), and Paul Endacott (Phillips). Bartlesville was bursting at the seams, and this committee was charged with planning for real present and foreseen needs for community growth. Committees were organized in a few weeks. The roster was very similar to the spring member golf tournament at Hillcrest, a good example of the mechanics of social capital. [643]

The first club dance of the season was held on 1 November. Though no food was served at the dance, a number of members had dinner in the dining room before the 9:30 P.M. dance. The Rhythmaires played "sweet swing' for a night club theme dance. The Business Men's Association held their annual banquet a few days later at Hillcrest for the first time in years. The Doherty Auxiliary was also back with a tea and a banquet in November. Dinner-Dance club resumed its regular schedule after meeting only occasionally during the war and during the kitchen crisis. Dinner was served at 7:00 P.M. and dancing to Jackson's orchestra began at 9:00 P.M. The tables were decorated with baskets of fruit and miniature turkeys. The entire membership of 50 turned out with some guests, too, so that more than 100 people were at the dance. The reinvigorated clubhouse had a number of small, but socially important, luncheons, dinners, and teas during the month. A "son's and daughter's" dance on 27 November, Thanksgiving evening, was preceded by Thanksgiving dinner for the members at the dinner hour. This was the most activity at the clubhouse in November, perhaps, since the 20s. [644]

November 2, was the 50th wedding anniversary of the J. L. Overlees and it was celebrated at Hillcrest with all of the genteel hoopla for a couple who had lived their entire married lives in Bartlesville as active members of the community. The clubhouse was completely flower-bedecked in white chrysanthemums and smilax, and the tea table had arrangements of golden roses. A violin and piano played old-fashioned love tunes, and all the right guests were in attendance, a who's who of Bartlesville society. The old community leadership was aging and a new generation was taking the reins. [645]

The holiday season started early. FPMC held two holiday dances at Hillcrest on 28 and 29 November, to kick off the season. The Spies and Frank Phillipses entertained visiting relatives from Creston, Iowa at a dinner party at Hillcrest, a very unusual thing for both families despite their long interest in the country club. [646]

The J. L. Overlees 50th wedding anniversary party was a gala tea dance at its most elegant. *Courtesy Sissy Overlees.*

C. E. Burlingame and John Phillips just happened to have the same birthday, and over the years, they had periodically celebrated with a joint party.

Mr. Burlingame had given a party here when he was forty and Mr. Phillips twenty, the only time when one of the celebrants would be twice as old as the other. Ten years ago Mr. Phillips entertained with a "centennial" dinner-dance at Southern Hills in Tulsa when their combined ages totaled 100 years. [647]

On 3 December, Clarence Burlingame was the host for a birthday bash celebrating his 70th and John G. Phillips' 50th birthdays. The party list read like the good old days with hundreds attending and a good portion of them from all over the state and the United States.

There was a sprightly succession of wedding parties and Christmas teas, luncheons, banquets, and dances. The Hillcrest Christmas dance was scheduled for 13 December, and once again members were reminded there would be no food at the dance. There was plenty to buzz about at Dinner-Dance Club on 20 December. That afternoon there had been a serious fire in the Phillips Building downtown. Motors for the elevators in the top of the building were the cause of the fire that took 2 hours to control. The full membership and a number of guests once again made Dinner-Dance that evening one of the best parties of the season. The L. A. Rowlands had a large dinner party in honor of their newlywed son, Lloyd, and his wife, Jane, who were visiting for Christmas from New York City. As usual, it was the Tyler-Beesley party that stole the show on the 30th. The clubhouse was awash with flowers and the guests danced to the Buddy Moreno orchestra from Chicago. The party was every bit as extravagant as their parties had been before the war. The next night, club members expected to turn out for the annual New Years ball. The Gene Pope orchestra was engaged to play into the wee hours for the party beginning at 11:00 P.M., with breakfast served from 2:00 A.M. to 3:30 A.M. [648]

1948

"Shivering Bartians welcomed the New Year in last midnight on the heels of one of the worst rain and sleet storms in years, which swept through the city yesterday and early last night…" [649]

The ice was followed by 8 inches of snow. New Years festivities were canceled all over town and folks hunkered down.

Ice and sleet on the streets and roads which began to slow up traffic during the afternoon, expected to cut down attendance at the New Years ball, but it seems that about everyone who had planned to attend risked disaster to make the drive to the club house for there was a large crowd and sprinkled among the club members were a few out of town guests. [650]

John G. Phillips and C. E. Burlingame had the same birthday and sometime had a joint birthday party. On 4 December 1947, they joined in a huge formal celebration, held at Hillcrest. Clarence Burlingame and Frankie Burlingame, Mildred Phillips and John G. Phillips. *Courtesy Bartlesville Area History Museum.*

The spirit was irrepressible - the New Years ball at Hillcrest was the brightest spot in Bartlesville that night. "Novelties were furnished and the usual din provided a hearty noisy welcome for little New Year at the midnight hours." [651]

Despite the snow on New Years, only a few days later the newspaper carried a cute photo of 4-year-old Gary Grover fooling around with a golf club at the snowless Sunset golf course. On the weekend of 10 January, 130 men played rounds at Hillcrest. The women's golf association elected officers at their luncheon on 20 January. [652]

Kiwanis had their annual installation banquet on 9 January. They proudly announced that the Kiwanis club roster was the largest in its history. It was another indication of the renewed health of civic life in Bartlesville. The medical society also had a robust installation banquet at the country club. The Chamber of Commerce began to lay its groundwork for their 1948 program. It was not quite as extensive as the program that H. C. Price had spearheaded the year before. The accomplishments for 1947 were formidable, in many cases the culmination of many years of patient diligence by the civic leadership in Bartlesville. There were 262 new houses built in Bartlesville in 1947, a traffic safety council was formed, downtown streets were resurfaced, new street lights, established a city dumping ground, started work on the new highway approach to the city on the east over a new bridge, water improvements as a result of the Hulah project. The airport expansion and subsequent commercial airlines flights to Bartlesville were the feathers in the Chamber's cap. The specific programs proposed for 1948, mostly centered on the new water treatment plant and completion of the Hulah project. Otherwise the list was to promote growth in various areas of civic development. [653]

New Hillcrest directors were elected on 20 January. They were Chuck Doornbos, M. B. Plank, Al Potter, and A. K. Wilhelm. Chuck Doornbos was re-elected president of the board a few days later. [654]

The club jumped the gun with the first dinner-dance of the new year, calling it a leap year dance. To secure dinner partners, balloons carrying the women guests' names were released and caught by the men. Their regular meeting day was changed to Friday. The February Dinner-Dance was on Valentine's Day. There was a club dance on 21 February. Dinner-Dance decorated for Easter at their 12 March party. They closed their first full season in several years with the last party on 9 April. The last club dance for the spring was later than usual, on 15 May. [655]

For several years Bartlesville had been developing a racial awareness. Though the measures of the time seem meager to us now, there was movement. Civil rights pushed to the forefront of American political consciousness in 1948 with a message to Congress by President Truman on 6 February. In Oklahoma, the state attorney general advised the Board of Regents to deny entry of Black students to O.U. "Separate but equal" became a more conscious goal for the segregated schools in the state. Bartlesville's Douglass High School received North Central accreditation. In a world that was conflicted on the notion of segregation, the community was at least serious about providing a good school for its Black citizens. That same month, Ruth Brown, the public librarian, who had been reading stories at Douglass school for several months, resolved to request permission of the library board to try an interracial story hour at the Bartlesville Public Library. The board agreed to the idea, but the city commission found it too politically controversial. The proposal was abandoned. [656]

The city was again reminded of the changing

of the guard. On 1 February, H. R. Straight announced his retirement as Chairman of the board of Cities Service. Straight came to Bartlesville in 1911 to work for N. T. Barnsdall and upon the purchase of Barnsdall's interests by the Doherty Group, became manager of the local group. He was a graduate of Stanford University and a geologist, while Katherine Straight was a Vasser graduate. He had always been one of the prime movers in Bartlesville civic activity. [657]

The 1948 election year began to form up. General Eisenhower had been touted as a possible candidate, but he declined to run. General Douglas MacArthur opined that if called by the American people he would run, but he was not seeking the nomination. Meanwhile, former Governor Robert S. Kerr formally announced his bid for the Oklahoma seat for United States Senate, as had been long expected.

Golf began to come to life at Hillcrest in March, alternating with intermittent bouts of severe weather and even a blizzard. The Wildcats golf team was back on the Hillcrest course for the spring season. C. C. (Lefty) Custer retired as Bartlesville Public School's athletic director after 21 years. He was the beloved mentor of Bartlesville boys in football, basketball, baseball, and golf over those many years. His former students smile when they remember his raspy voice, and the way he poured himself into his young athletes. How many boys had he loaded into his own car to transport all over the state to athletic events? His high school golf teams had dominated play in the region since 1930, with 203 wins, 22 losses, and 2 ties. Most of the young men who earned that stellar record had originally worked as caddies at Hillcrest; Tommy Trower, Keith Fowler, and John Alexander were sons of HCC members. Custer, himself, had been a Hillcrest member since 1943. [658]

The women's golf association began regular Wednesday ladies day meetings the first week in March. They emphasized that the luncheon, bridge, and gin rummy were open to all the club ladies. The popularity of ladies day was increasing. Despite a blizzard on 10 March, 35 ladies came for lunch and cards. In April, the women began handicap team play the first Wednesday of each month. [659]

Charlie Selby was again in charge of organizing the annual stag team matches. For 1948, L. C. Trapp's team enjoyed a steak dinner provided by S. P. Kelly's defeated team. Cities Service again held its district tournament at Hillcrest. It was a spring for aces. S. O. Criswell made a hole-in-one on number 2. It was noted that he was playing that day with Charlie Selby and Dr. Kincade who were also members of the Ace Club. Only 6 weeks later, Dr. Kincade got another one on number 16 hole! [660]

The clubhouse was nicely active over the spring. Rehearsal dinners and wedding receptions for club members had become common, though not necessarily usual for weddings of the time. The Jane Phillips sorority held its annual installation banquet and dance at the club on 17 April. The Children of the American Revolution held a morning state board meeting, followed by a luncheon. Mdmes E. F. Walsh, H. H. McClintock, L. A. Rowland, and H. R. Straight, all former presidents of the Tuesday Club, held a past presidents luncheon on 28 May. The County Bar Association held their annual banquet, inviting their wives (even though Lois Straight was a member of the committee). The club held a buffet supper on Monday, Memorial Day, from 6:00 P.M. to 8:00 P.M. in the dining room. We learn that by this time, the club was normally closed on Mondays. [661]

The American Military Academy had faded from Bartlesville after the war, and the junior college at College High was struggling, while there was growing pressure to use the space for high school classrooms. Higher education had been a long sought dream in Bartlesville. If there was any town in Oklahoma that had a need and vision for an institution of higher education, it was Bartlesville. The announcement of the establishment of Central Christian College in Bartlesville, at the La Quinta estate of H. V. Foster, was good news. The Chamber of Commerce held the announcement ceremony at the College High auditorium (where, unlike Hillcrest, alcohol was not served). The speaker was Dr. George S. Benson of Harding College in Arkansas, a Church of Christ institution, and the sponsoring denomination of the new school. Dr. Benson was a well-recognized evangelist in the region and a nationally known anti-communist. Bartians were very interested in the talk and enthusiastically came out to hear Dr. Benson's comments. The new college foresaw construction of 3 new buildings on the 152-acre campus. Benson left no doubt of the theory of education that was envisioned.

> *…that our young people in college and high schools should know the following:*
>
> *That our national income is five times that of Russia.*
>
> *Why our national income is so much greater than any other nation in the world.*
>
> *What the Russian system is which would stop some of our young people from believing in the Soviet pattern of government.*
>
> *What the various isms are and what would happen under a nationalized economy.* [662]

After so many years without new development of estates around the country club, the H. C. Price family moved from their home on Johnstone (the former H. V. Foster house) to the caretaker's 5-room house at Star View Farm just east of the country club, because their new house was nowhere near finished

and Phillips was ready to occupy the Johnstone property to begin construction of the Phillips Apartment Hotel. The move by the Prices was a continuation of the original vision of an elegant country club surrounded by country estates. The Prices were trendsetters and were building a California ranch-style home. The house was designed by Cliff May. He was a highly noted architect who developed the new design he called Contemporary Ranch Style. May designed many homes in Los Angeles and in Hollywood, for example the home of Gregory Peck. Hal Price had come to know him through his work with liberty ships in Southern California. Cliff May's designs enjoyed a continuity with the indoors and outdoors and had a feeling of openness. Since the Art Deco Forsythe-designed high school in 1939/40, there had not been much building in town because of the war effort until 1947, when there was a boom in new construction, especially in the new Jane Phillips addition. The Welty house in 1945, and Hal Price's house were the first new large homes in several years. The Price home took the lead of the trend toward the new modern low rambling style. Despite the continued construction, they began to hold important parties at Star View Farm. [663]

Mary Lou Price was one of the old core group of social doyens. She had been a Bartlesville schoolteacher when she married Hal Price. The Prices were world travelers. She was a generous woman. One story about her is that she made a practice of giving away all of her clothes to the maids on her travels to come home with an empty suitcase. An adept hostess, she once advised a young friend to never serve red wine or coffee at a large party (because the guests would just spill them and spot the rug). Of course, she continued to be very active with her fine show horses for many years. Their closest social circle was liberal, intel-

The H. C. Price home, Star View Farm, was constructed in the Price family compound property directly east of the country club and finished in 1948. It was designed by California architect, Cliff May, the originator of California Ranch Style, and architect for many notable homes in Southern California. The compound eventually also sported Harold Price's home designed by Frank Lloyd Wright, and Joe Price's Shin'enKan designed by Bruce Goff. The Price compound was the last of the great estates built around the country club. The May house was demolished in the 1980s and Shin'enKan burned in 1996. *Courtesy Frank Phillips Home.*

lectual, cultivated, and Modern, in keeping with the business and artistic acumen of H. C. Price who was then clearly assuming the mantle of elder statesman of Bartlesville business. Carolyn Price describes Hal Price lovingly as "roly-poly, huggy, and always interested." He too was a man with a generous spirit – it was a common characteristic of the first generation of Bartlesville leaders. Carolyn says nobody knows how many kids Hal Price put through college.

Just across the road at the country club, the summer season was getting under way. The Memorial weekend saw 230 players touring the golf course, setting the pace for an enthusiastic summer. Play began immediately for the annual club championship. Bill Simpson once again won the laurels on 22 June. Meanwhile, Mrs. C. W. Hubbell showed well in the Oklahoma Women's Amateur Golf Tournament in Tulsa. The women's association was very active during the summer at invitational meets in the area. Five

Bartlesville men, including Keith Fowler, Charlie Selby, and Bill Simpson qualified for the Oklahoma Men's Amateur golf tournament at Muskogee, and showed well. While the Hillcrest "hotdogs" were in Muskogee, Cities Service played its district championship tournament at Hillcrest. Dick Booker, last year's national champ, again won the district championship. Rain at the end of June and in early July and subsequent flooding slowed down the golf enthusiasts. Only 13 hard-core men played on 27 June. A Scotch foursome was played for the Fourth of July weekend celebration. The club had its usual buffet supper and fireworks afterwards to observe the holiday. The FPMC tournament was put off nearly a month because of the mid-summer rain, but Charles Keller won the tourney on 25 July. In August, Keith Fowler won the Pikes Peak golf tournament in Colorado Springs. In the team match between Hillcrest and Sunset, Fowler turned in a "sizzling" 69. Hillcrest took the match. [664]

Summer social activity at Hillcrest consisted of weddings. Joanne Riney and Dick Bennett's wedding was the event of the summer. On 23 July, Hillcrest had an unusual summer dance under the stars, dinner on the porch and dancing on the tennis courts that were strung with colored lights. The next week, there was a family night supper on the porch. That evening they listened to the Bartlesville-Ponca City game on the radio for entertainment. Otherwise, things were quiet. [665]

In 1948, materials were finally coming available to do needed upkeep. The kitchen had been all but closed for quite a while, but new leadership began to get things back on track. This photograph shows that some of the overgrown plantings had recently been replaced. The fancy striped awning of 1931 had been replaced with a more basic design. Still, a good round of putting practice was always available. *Courtesy Phillips Petroleum Company.*

With all the young men off to war, and later with the GI Bill, there were few caddies available. Golf carts appeared right after the war. These first models at Hillcrest were three-wheeled carts, steered with a tiller. Some privately owned ones like this were seen right in to the 1960s.

The city was shocked on the morning of 1 August to learn that Jane Phillips had died in the night. She had been in declining health for a month, and suffered a heart attack on 29 July. She seemed to improve some afterwards, her family and friends gathering and bringing her flowers. Bartlesville shut down for the funeral, as a procession slowly wound its way from the mansion to the White Rose Mausoleum where she was temporarily interred. [666]

Already, big changes were in the works for Bartlesville. At Hillcrest, Olga Foster announced her resignation in May. She was always immensely popular with many club members, but her management style was too stern for others. Dorothy Glynn Adams said that the food was always good when Mrs. Foster was manager, but that she would not allow drinking (or gambling, either) upstairs. (Its not clear whether this was actually a board policy.) In the end she was forced out by a part of the leadership that wanted more action at Hillcrest. The new manager announced on 17 June, was a man named Gordon High. He was a 30-year-old man whose wife was a Tulsa girl. He appeared to have impressive credentials: a graduate of the University of Wisconsin and the Cornell University hotel and club management program. He had been the food and beverage control supervisor for 21 hotels in the Pick chain. The couple was most recently managing the Portsmouth, Ohio country club. Among his accomplishments, he said he had been a traveling auditor for Horwath & Horwath. Notwithstanding, upon arriving in Bartlesville, he was an immediate dud with the members. At a minimum, it was hard to follow the locally popular Olga Foster. Though the membership was limited to 250 stockholders, at this juncture there were 360 total members at Hillcrest Country Club. [667]

The political season was getting interesting

despite reported voter apathy. Truman's civil rights speech, on top of the economic knots, and Red scare, made the incumbent president look vulnerable. In June, after a big tussle, the Republicans nominated Thomas Dewey for the presidential race. In Oklahoma, Bob Kerr easily won the Democrat nomination for U.S. Senate in the 6 July primary. Truman had a surly Democrat convention to deal with. It was the year of the Dixicrats and Henry Wallace's Progressives. While General Mao Tse-tsung's communists overran China, there was a manhunt and crackdown on U. S. communist leaders, amidst sensational revelations in Senate testimony of alarming numbers of communist subversives working in the government.

In Bartlesville there were some exciting summer announcements. St. Luke's Episcopal Church announced their plan to build a new parish hall in the elegant style of an English parish church. On 15 August, Frank Phillips and Boots Adams announced two major new buildings for Phillips Petroleum Company. The new 12-story office building, designed by Neville, Sharp and Simon of Kansas City, to occupy the block of Jennings, 4th Street, Keeler, and 5th Street would serve the burgeoning company needs. The 7-story apartment building, designed by Gentry and Voskamp of Kansas City, would mean razing some of the gracious old fine homes of early Bartlesville, including the former H. V. Foster home, recently vacated by the Prices. The trendy new blonde brick building would hold 206 completely furnished apartments, and alleviate some of the housing shortage in town for several years. Both buildings were examples of a more pedestrian version of the trend toward utilitarian Modern architecture. Only a week later, a bond issue was proposed to build new buildings at the airport, and the Memorial Hospital announced drawings for yet another addition to the hospital. That is a lot of new growth for Bartlesville. It was heady times.

The optimism showed in early social activity in the fall. Even before the clubhouse re-opened in September, the local Chi Omegas held an O.U. rush party at the picnic grounds. Hillcrest reopened the clubhouse on the first of September, in time to observe Labor Day with a Scotch foursome, and buffet supper on the porch at 7:00 P.M. The next week John Tyler and Ed McElvain were chairmen of a Western Night party with costumes, hayrides, games, square dancing, and a weiner roast all on the tennis courts. Events were punctuated with stunts like wild goat milking, a pie-eating contest, or catching a greased pig. It had been many years since the club had tried a September party, and never one like this. Gordon High may have been a dud, but someone was having some new ideas. [668]

The annual men's handicap championship was preceded by the Thursday night stag dinner in the dining room on 16 September. On Sunday, the championship concluded with a tie between Dr. Keiffer Davis and E. M. Kelly. Dr. Davis won the play-off on 3 October. The women hosted a Ladies Invitational golf tournament on 28 September, and the men hosted Oaks Country Club from Tulsa on 3 October. The women's handicap championship began on 19 October, and Mrs. W. F. Condrat was the victor on 26 October. The last recorded play of the season was a hole-in-one on 30 November by T. R. Cobb on number 5. [669]

Bartlesville did a good PR trick on Labor Day weekend, promoting the proposed airport bond, with an air show at the new municipal airport. 10,000 spectators attended the show – there's no telling how many watched from the backyard. Right after the annual wolf hunt and its associated festivities, the Oklahoma Federation of Music Clubs held their district meet in Bartlesville. Hillcrest hosted their luncheon

on 10 October. Despite Truman's surprise victory, the national election didn't stir much local excitement, but Bob Kerr's big majority for Senate satisfied Oklahomans that they would have effective representation. [670]

The country club held its first dance of the fall on Halloween. The clubhouse was decorated for the season, and there was a fortuneteller who was billed as "traditional," probably because people expected one at Halloween parties. Dinner-dance club held its first dance on 19 November. Doherty Girls held both their annual tea and banquet at Hillcrest. The country club held a matinee dance early in December, on Sunday afternoon. It's no wonder they had to squeeze the dance into an available afternoon – Hillcrest was back in style! The Christmas season was jammed with high profile parties and teas, and every club in town had a Christmas banquet at the country club. [671]

Dinner-Dance Club was changed from 17 December to 22 December to make way for the season's really spectacular parties. The most spectacular party in many years was given by Boots and Dorothy Glynn Adams on 17 December. For the party, the patio and porch had been enclosed, to make room for the 600 guests. The clubhouse had been festooned from top to bottom as a winter wonderland. Cotton sprinkled with glitter and silver, reflected the special blue lighting turned the clubhouse into a silver and white winter scene, foliage and flowers covered every nook. Arriving guests were served cocktails and hors d'oeuvres in the lounge. A large cake of ice presented the caviar. The patio was decorated to look like a garden, with palm trees and even a live monkey. Dancing was in the ballroom to the music of Chuck Foster, The grill downstairs was decorated like an English pub, with Telosa King playing her accordian. Buffet supper was served at 11:00 P.M. The groaning board was a U-shaped table so lavishly stocked that no decoration would have been necessary. The menu was: Smoked Turkey Forresterrain, Virginia Ham, Admiral Fickerel Gelee, Pheasant em Plumage, Galantine of turkey, Standing Prime Rib of Beef au jus, Sweet Pickled Ham, Champagne Sauce, Maine Lobster Tails, Ravigotte, Suckling Pig em Bordure, Stuffed Squab Gastraraumbe, Chicken Tetrazzine, Deviled Oyster Pan Roast, and other delights. Photographs show guests in ball gowns and tails standing around a buffet table of magnificent opulence. After such an affair, the annual Tyler bash almost paled. The clubhouse was lavishly redecorated, this time with white smilax and red poinsettias against a background of greenery, and the guests danced into the night to the music of the Bobby Meeker orchestra. Of course, the annual New Years Ball was the last grand party of the year. [672]

1949

The New Year came in much more normally than during the ice storm of last year. There were parties all over town and watch services at some of the churches. At midnight, there was the usual merrymaking and noise. The ball at Hillcrest and a dance at the Civic Center were the highlights of the holiday. Since New Years came on a Friday, the celebration stretched over the weekend. The Prices had a huge New Years Eve party, entertaining 170 guests that included the construction crew at their new home. [673]

In advance of the annual Chamber of Commerce installation, there was a great deal of review of the Chamber's accomplishments for the year. They pointed out that 1948 enjoyed the largest expansion in Bartlesville's history. Retiring President Milo Margenau cited data that the increase in bank clearings in Bartlesville was the largest of any city in the United States. The Chamber named 29 activities that they promoted, including the bonds for the hospital and

the airport. Already the American Legion was organizing a $300,000 drive to build an American Legion Community Building and Boots Adams threw his influence behind it. Besides the usual January Kiwanis and Jaycees banquets, the Chamber held a special forum at their noon meeting at the Burlingame Hotel to dedicate the new Lake Hudson opening. [674]

Western parties and square dancing had become the rage. Despite ice and snow, members turned out for a square dance on 14 January. The country club instituted a new kind of informal party that they called Dutch treat, seemingly to replace family night. On the next night, snow and all, the Dutch treat party was entertained by Happy Fenton, playing the accordion. The next weekend, Dinner-Dance Club had a Western party. More traditional entertainment did persist in a spring style show dessert-bridge. 150 women came to see their friends model the latest fashions on a runway set up in front of the fireplace in the dining room. [675]

The Hillcrest annual meeting was held on Tuesday evening, after a 6:30 P.M. stag dinner. New board members were A. F. Potter, F. B. Plank, M.J. Kirwan, C. V. Sellers, J. W. Profitt, A. K. Wilhelm, Dr. P. A. Kincade, and M. E. Foster. W. F. (Bill) Martin was elected the new president, L. S. Ambrose was re-elected secretary-treasurer. The club manager, Gordon High became the assistant secretary. [676]

Weather continued to suppress social activity at Hillcrest in February. The club had a square dance party, and Dinner-Dance Club had a George Washington's Birthday party. Otherwise, the Sigma Chi alumnae had a sweetheart dance and the K. U. alumnae meeting for the totality of February sociability. Despite the weather, there were a couple of things of interest going on in town. The city put the old city hall up for sale, hoping to use the proceeds to build a new police station. The first Continental Airlines flight into the new airport was piloted by a Bartlesville native, Richard McCoy, on 27 February. Things really took off in March, and never looked back. Luncheons, club meetings, and wedding parties filled the calendar until deep summer. An unusual event was the wedding of Emily Ann Emery to Leonard Blair at Hillcrest in the living room, before the massive stone fireplace, followed by a reception. The two social weddings of the year were Harold Price to Carolyn Propps of Tulsa in June, and Celeste Beesley to Charles Winslow in November. Mrs. Armais Artunoff gave a high profile luncheon, and Mrs. K. S. Adams entertained some New York guests in another notable luncheon. Both Dinner-Dance and the club dances grew in popularity. Dinner-Dance held a St. Patrick's party, and the last dance of their season on 15 April, while the club parties were on 27 March, April Fools, and a Beau Arts costume ball on 30 April. [677]

As the Soviets consolidated their hold on Eastern Europe and Mao's troops entered Peking, there was increasing public focus on an increasingly obvious problem of communist infiltration into American institutions. Whittaker Chambers' testimony before the House Un-American Activities Committee in August of 1948 set off alarm bells. Oklahoma legislators demanded an investigation of the University of Oklahoma in February. A resurgence of bootlegging became a public concern, along with sporadic liquor raids. Kansas went wet in July, unleashing fears of a bootlegger war on the border. At last, there was a move to rescind the federal rent control that had been in place through the war.

Frank Phillips announced that he was retiring as chairman of the board on 22 March. The board voted to create the position of honorary chairman, without the active management responsibilities. It

was another signal of the changing of the guard. K. S. "Boots" Adams would be the new head of Phillips Petroleum Company. Civic leadership was in transition. There was good news, Bartians were proud when a local son, Bill Keeler, was appointed chief of the Cherokee tribe by President Truman in June.

As summer drew near, the national polio epidemic was growing alarming. Continuing the public health measures of the last few years, some petitioners from the Chamber of Commerce, Washington County Infantile Paralysis Association, and Lions Club appeared before the city commission, "declaring that because of 'excessive filth and flies' in certain areas of the city two Bartlesville children have become stricken with polio this year." The group wanted aerial spraying of DDT to control disease-carrying insects. The city did not have the funds in its budget, but private funding was found. Though the idea was implemented, by July there were 6 cases of polio in the city. The city planning committee proposed a wide-ranging new plan for zoning changes. It was hoped that it would address growing pains in the post war city. There was a promotional play in a newspaper article about Miss Ruth Brown, the librarian, and the library's long tenure in its temporary quarters at the Civic Center. [678]

The women's golf association organized late in February, despite bad weather. The program for 1949, hoped to expand to many women who did not necessarily play golf. The feature of the year was that they offered free golf lessons. It was a month before play actually got going. The club was already anticipating the Oklahoma Men's State Amateur Golf Tournament at Hillcrest in June. The tournament committeemen were Bill Simpson, Charles Selby, and Joe Parkinson. Greenskeeper Henry Manley was already pushing to get the greens in tip-top shape for the big event. Charlie Selby conducted a caddie school for

The Oklahoma State Amateur Golf Tournament was played at Hillcrest 12 to 18 August 1949. The men in the putting contest were Bill Simpson, Jimmy Gullane, Bill Emery, and C. C. Custer. The radio station was on site, reporting the tournament. John Cronin comments to a reporter. *Courtesy Bartlesville Area History Museum.*

32 local youths in preparation for the tournament. Mike May still happily remembers his caddie duty for that tournament. The annual stag match was held on 23 April. Dr. George M. Tulloch's team defeated the Charlie Selby team. [679]

By June, the country club was in high dudgeon preparing for the big tournament. Sunset member and former Hillcrest caddie, Loddie Kempa, a national left-hand champion, played some notable warm-up rounds at Hillcrest. Tulsa amateur champion Skee Reigel followed with some even more blistering practice rounds. Don Wilkie was very high on the quality of play that was expected and the great condition of the golf course the week before the tournament. While the tournament preoccupied Bartlesville, two Hillcrest women qualified for the Oklahoma Women's Golf tournament in Muskogee. The skies clouded up as 150 crack Oklahoma golfers arrived for the State tournament. The Pro-Am on Sunday, saw Bo Winiger

of Guthrie shoot a 65, enough to usher in Labron Harris, the Stillwater pro, to his second consecutive pro-am title. The Hillcrest foursome, headed by Jimmy Gullane, attracted a sizable gallery. Junior amateur Bill Emery carded a 76, which put Gullane in 3rd place for the pro-junior amateur event. "Despite the intermittent rain and sunshine throughout the day-long play and a course that stood under water in many places," the qualifying rounds got underway. The quarter finals round saw the first day of fair skies when Bo Winiger dashed the hopes of Bartian, Loddie Kempa. Bartians Bill Simpson, Dick Booker, and Alvin Hall all lost semi-final rounds. Dee Replogle of Oklahoma City defeated young Lawrence Glosser, also of Oklahoma City, for the State championship on 17 June. [680]

Immediately, the Cities Service tournament began. A mixed Scotch Foursome and special dinner was the holiday feature for Sunday on the Fourth of July weekend, followed by a Flag tournament on Monday, the 4th. Mrs. G. R. Preston and Charles Selby won the low gross score for the foursome, and Elmer Gallery won the flag tournament. Qualifying rounds for the club championship began right after the summer holiday. The tournament was deemed wide open because Bill Simpson would not defend his title. The Tournament got off to a breath-taking start. In the first round, Dick Booker shot an ace on the 2nd hole. It turns out that Charlie Selby was the man to beat, taking the championship by defeating C. C. Custer. There were 91 ladies entered in the women's invitational tournament on 26 July. Billie Dodge of Nowata was the winner. They finished out July with the FPMC tournament, C. B. McDonald the winner. [681]

Unusual for August, there was some significant play that month, even though the dining room at the clubhouse was closed, as usual, for the month. The women hosted a Tulsa District Women's Golf Association meet early in August. Bill Simpson may have bowed out of the club championship competition, but he won the Equitable Life Insurance Company title at White Sulphur Springs, Maryland. Dr. Tom Burris won the Lions Club championship near the end of the month. [682]

Fall social activity got underway early in September. Several weddings were driving the rounds of parties. Doherty Auxiliary entertained wives of company employees, who were in town for the annual company horseshoe pitching contest, at a Hillcrest dinner on 30 September. The fall style show drew 240 members and guests to enjoy dessert and see the latest fashions for 1949. The K. U. alumni held their annual dinner with more flourish then they had in several years. The entertainment was a football movie. The first club dance for the fall was on 22 October. It was preceded by a "get -acquainted open house" in

the basement at 8:30 P.M. (probably a cocktail party), dancing starting at 10:00 P.M.. [683]

September opened with the city golf tournament. Bill Simpson won that hotly contested tourney at Sunset. Meanwhile, Hillcrest had its usual Labor Day flag tournament with C. S. Hansen the winner. Jim McColl won the Hillcrest Country Club handicap tournament on 20 September. There was a renewed fillip toward junior golf with a proposed tournament on 1 October, with C. C. Custer the sponsor. Hillcrest and Tulsa Oaks scheduled team matches in the same time space. The match was postponed because of rain and finally played 23 October with Hillcrest the victors. It is probable that the junior golf was rained out too. The women began their annual championship tournament on 11 October. The tournament quickly developed into a thriller. The final round between Mrs. C. C. Ward and Mrs. A. A. Hopper was played to a draw on 19 October. The next day, Mrs. Hopper grabbed an early lead and never relinquished it, taking the championship. [684]

The happy social activity and golf excitement happened in the context of the times. Extensive renovations were nearly complete at Douglass School, the Black school that was started in 1912. There were 121 elementary students and 82 high school students at Douglass in 1949. Renovations and a new addition, updating the building put it at the top in the state for Black students. There was worrisome local news in October after a series of raids on "booze joints" by local police. It's no wonder that the country club was more circumspect about its recent parties. The most frightening news came on 24 October, when America learned that the Soviets had tested an atomic bomb. It was thought that they were a few years away from the necessary technology, but now we faced the dual specter of a hostile atomic power and the probability of spies in our top-secret atomic program.

There is no microfilm of Bartlesville newspapers for May 1949 to October 1950. [685] Because the country club kept no records or files, there is very little that can be reported for the period. There must have been an exciting Christmas social season, as usual if the increased fall social activity is any indicator.

1950

The missing microfilm leaves a void in information about winter social activity at Hillcrest. We know that A. F. Potter was elected president of the club at the January meeting, but we have no other information. [686]

On 1 May 1950, the golf season was well underway. The weather must have been glorious on May Day weekend for 230 golfers made it around the course. Dr. George M. Tulloch carded the low score of 74. The women's golf association sponsored a Scotch foursome the next Sunday afternoon, followed by a buffet dinner. The women's spring tournament was played, after a couple of weather delays, with Mrs. C. W. Hubbell winning the three-day medal-play handicap event on 24 May. While the women's tournament progressed, Jimmy Gullane was at the state PGA in Blackwell. He returned in time to oversee the start of the Cities Service annual tournament. On 28 May, Don Anderson was in the lead of the DMF competition. The Qualifying rounds for the club championship on 9 June, were already underway. Dr. George Tulloch had his eye set on the cup. Qualifying dates were set for the FPMC tournament later in June. The winners of the various Memorial Day golf features were announced as the month drew to a close. The winners of the blind bogey were R. C. Pipes, Bob Schmidt, B. E. Witchell, Max Jennings, and S. P. Kelly; Bill Simpson won the putting contest;

and Charlie Selby was the triumphant winner of the driving contest. A four-ball tournament wound out the month with Dr. Keiffer Davis and John Pettigrove the happy winners. [687]

The 1950 political season was off to a roaring start with the announcement by Johnston Murray of his race for governor. He had the earmarks of his colorful father, and the campaign promised to be more interesting than in the past few years. Five of the local doctors held an open house at their fancy new office building on the northwest corner of Fifth and Cherokee. It was billed as "one of the finest pieces of modern architecture," reflecting the new local enthusiasm for Modernism, but not especially reflecting the quality of the design. [688] That same month, three floors of the new Phillips apartments were opened which helped some to relieve the housing pinch for Phillips employees. The city commission passed a new

The first three floors of the trendy blonde brick Phillips Apartment Hotel opened in May 1950. The Modernist style was called "functionalism." *Courtesy Bartlesville Area History Museum.*

ordinance to enforce order at public dances because of complaints about fighting and drinking at Civic Center dances. At one there was even a stabbing. The result was a raid of the Civic Center and seven arrests on 20 May. Among some, it seems, Zippity-doo-da was getting a little out of hand.

Hillcrest hosted a K.U. alumni dinner on 7 May where the dean of the School of Engineering and Architecture spoke. The Junior-Senior prom was the civic event of the month, held at Hillcrest. [689]

The spring social season's grand finale was a dance on 20 May. It was the largest crowd of the season. There was another "open house" before the dance. Evidently an official cocktail hour had become obligatory since it was instituted back in the fall. The dance began at 10:00 P.M., and Joe Linde's band played until 4:00 A.M.. John Tyler was the social chairman of Hillcrest at the time. There had been a sea change in the kind and quality of social functions at the club since the September Western party where John Tyler was the chairman. It appears that John Tyler was the front man for the change at the club as the changing of the guard began to show up in social and civic life. The social circle lead by John Tyler, John M. Kane, Scott Beesley, John Cronin, Stewart Dewer, and Chuck Doornbos were very active in the social hegemony of the city at the time, and distinct from the K. S. Adams – Phillips circle, or the H. C. Price and H. R. Straight circle. [690]

Two small parties showed up in the May reporting. Mercedi club had a bridge-luncheon as they had most months since the beginning of the club. Mrs. J. V. Wood gave a luncheon to honor three of her friends. [691]

Tyler organized the best Memorial Day celebration, probably since 1929. For only the second time in club history Hillcrest fielded a softball team to play the Bartlesville Pirates. Tom Burris was manager of HCC's "fabulous nine." The game was scheduled to "tee off" on the Hillcrest fairways at 1:00, part of a marathon of holiday activities.

Potter, Hillcrest country club president, has the unique distinction of having never won or lost a game for the roundballers of Windy Hill, however, he will be Burris' choice as a starter.

Other Hillcresters in the line-up will include Dr. E. E. Beechwood who has figured his batting average at .596, Charlie "Mouthy" Selby at second .483, S. S. Stewart, behind the plate, Doc "Hamburger" Hayes who is hitting his weight at least, a .253. The outfield will consist of Max Jennings, a guy who can find more lost golf balls than anybody and who is expected to apply his talents to good cause Tuesday; fleet-footed Don Bailey and Chuck Doornbos the hole-in-one specialist. [692]

The Bucs won the game on the improvised diamond on the driving range, 6-2. The holiday crowd of 500 even thrilled to an exhibition of stunt flying overhead by Leonard Hamilton of Dewey Hi-Way Airport. Other events included the blind bogey golf, putting and driving contests. There were toys and swings for the children and an improvised croquet court, horseshoe pitching, footraces, potato sack races, on and on, and of course, topped off with a huge picnic supper. [693]

We know of one significant retirement party at Hillcrest before the summer gap in the microfilm. It was a party given by Frank Stradley of the treasury department at Phillips, for W. I. Beavers who was retiring. Special guests were Mrs. Beavers, Mr. and Mrs. K. S. Adams, Mr. and Mrs. B. F. Stradley, and Mr. and Mrs. Paul Parker. The significance of this party is that it places Paul Parker, working in Frank Stradley's treasury department by that date. Paul and Elsie Parker came to Bartlesville in the spring of 1944, Paul working in the Phillips legal department at the time. Elsie said that shortly after Paul transferred to the treasury department, Stradley spoke to him about the country club. Membership was a financial stretch for the young couple. Nevertheless, Elsie says that the day Stradley spoke to Paul, he came home and told her they were joining the country club. Stradley was close to Boots, and it can be surmised that Boots thought it was important for executives at a certain level to join the club. [694]

There was an important civic event during the months of the microfilm gap. Beginning in February, an angry citizens group insisted that the library board dismiss Miss Ruth Brown, the Bartlesville librarian of 30 years. The outrage was that she had what appeared to be communist literature in the library, but in fact, unspoken outrage also was because of her rather sporadic efforts at civil rights activism. The library board surveyed the social science, history, political science, and economics shelves, and the periodicals; they consulted with the American Library Association, checked with the Tulsa and Oklahoma City libraries, and concluded that the material in Bartlesville Public Library was acceptable by the standards of the profession. They issued an official report to that effect on 28 May. The same day the citizens committee issued a dissenting report to the city commission with citations about specific publications from the work of the California Un-American Activities Committee. To satisfy the ruckus-makers, the city commission ended up firing the library board and appointing another, who in turn fired Miss Brown on 26 July. [695]

In 1941, the Oklahoma Tax Commission mistakenly directed the suspension of Hillcrest's right to do business because of failure to comply with the Oklahoma Corporation License Act. There is no explanation of this odd episode. It is clearly a bureau-cratic incompetence that it was ever cited, and that there was no subsequent action for most of ten years. On 29 July 1950, the Oklahoma Tax Commission reinstated Hillcrest Country Club, ruling that it was a non-profit corporation and exempt from compliance with the Oklahoma Corporation License and Franchise Act. The problem probably came to light when the board of Hillcrest Country Club made some inquiry with the Secretary of State concerning amendments to the articles of incorporation that were filed in 1951. [696]

The microfilm silence was broken for a brief period in late August. We learn that the country club had been active in the summer. There was a stag dinner on 19 August, to kick off the fall activities. A big square dance was planned for Saturday, 26 August. John Tyler had secured the "Start of the Day Gang" from KCMO in Kansas City, five top radio stars, as the feature entertainment, 4 *electric* guitars and a singer. The women's golf association was busy with guest day, and an invitation to Ponca City. If that party was held, there must have been a cloud over the festivities, for the news of the week was very sad. [697]

When Jane Phillips died in the summer of 1948, Frank Phillips was understandably in shock. She was buried at White Rose Mausoleum until construction of the mausoleum at Woolaroc was completed about a year later. Her casket was moved to the ranch and there was a brief memorial service. By then, Frank was beginning to fail, and his memory was going. He had periods of confusion and was still grieving, though he tried to keep up the old contacts. When he resigned as chairman of the board of Phillips in March 1949, he acknowledged that he was not keeping up with the young fellows. In the hot summer of 1950, he took his usual vacation on the Boardwalk at Atlantic City, New Jersey. Then, on 20 August, he was taken to the Atlantic City hospital with abdominal pain. Frank Phillips died on 23 August 1950, with his son, John G. Phillips at his side. [698]

What a towering figure he had been in the community that petroleum built. Almost from the day he arrived in Bartlesville to set up business in 1903, he had a vision for the community. He was a man who was insightful as he watched his banker father-in-law, and the oilmen he associated with, and the bigwigs he cultivated in Kansas City, Chicago, and New York. Frank Phillips understood, probably more than any man in Bartlesville, the real content and value of social capital. His years as a banker showed him the importance of the whole community in building business. His panache gave character to the little city. Not the least of all, his innate generosity benefited the community in his lifetime, and as a model to a future generation. The expressions of sympathy from Bartlesville leaders attempted to describe his meaning to the city. A. W. Ambrose, President of Cities Service, said:

> He was an outstanding example of the heights that can be reached in our American way of life. The rewards he received for his labors in the promotion and progress of the petroleum industry were plowed back to provide greater comfort and conveniences to mankind. [699]

H. C. Price expressed his gratitude:

> I will never forget the helpful advice and encouragement he gave me when I first started in business. He believed in his hometown and never let success influence him to move elsewhere. The void he has left in the community will never be filled. [700]

The funeral was held on 25 August. Again there was a day of mourning when all of the city was closed, this time in tribute to Frank Phillips. Thousand came to pay their respects, moving for hours in a line through Neekamp Funeral Home. A memorial service was held at the house, exactly where the service for Jane was held 2 years earlier. Rev. Spivey preached the funeral sermon.

> He was part of the pulsating life of the thundering oil boom days, but his was the genius that transformed that semi-chaos into a throbbing, humming, rhythmic business enterprise, who was able to catch the ear and the heart of youth and of children, of his friends the Indians, until all began to feel themselves at harmony with him… [701]

The 20 car procession wound from the house up elm-shaded Cherokee Ave., lead by a highway patrol car, then west through the town, and out to Woolaroc where Frank Phillips was buried in the mausoleum on his beloved ranch. As a sort of final act of the community builder, the family said that friends could make contributions toward the projected Jane Phillips Memorial Hospital. [702]

The post war years proved to be the end of an era. The founding leadership was rapidly passing on. The recovery after the war had not been gentle. Bartlesville had suffered somewhat less than many places because petroleum was an essential industry. Even so, Cities Service downsizing at the end of the war had tightened the local job market. Nevertheless, all the petroleum industry companies, Phillips, Cities Service, Reda Pump, and Price Pipeline experienced rapid growth and prosperity. There was an influx of new young college graduates, recruited by the companies. Housing was critical and took years to level out. The junior college at College High was faltering at a time when college education was becoming essential, and the GI Bill was paying for it. Recruitment of a small Christian college for Bartlesville looked like it would finally fill the local needs. Mostly, the old guard was becoming exhausted and maybe a little stodgy, years long past the time when they should have passed on responsibilities. The city experienced a boom in civic improvements, reminiscent of those in the early 1920s. The national economy was a tangle of government controls and regulations, high taxes, high inflation, booming business, and insatiable demand for goods and services. As the controls eased, business saw unimagined income even though much of its buying power was sapped away with high inflation.

The upsetting incident at the library is an example of social capital operating in a controversy or conflict. According to Putnam: "Social capital relies on informal sanctions and gossip and even ostracism, not just fellowship and emulation and altruism." The censure of Miss Brown may not have been just or justified, but served as a warning of the limits of public norms at the time. The city expediently dealt with the trouble at hand. But, the perpetrators of the civic embarrassment on both sides experienced some ostracism and loss of that all-important commodity, trust. In the 1950s, the town moved on to desegregate without any difficulties. [703]

Life at the country club moved through the war years, and the years immediately after with a very conservative leadership. It wasn't until W. F. Martin took up the presidency that there were signs that the young leaders in the membership were trying to take hold of the club to restore the old sparkle. The long, drawn out kitchen repairs put the clubhouse back in action and John Tyler provided the imagination to make the place really rock. Men like Charlie Selby and Bill Simpson took hold of the golf program, reactivated the excitement, and promoted it.

Once the economy was freed of its wartime controls, the rough and tumble of the free market made the 1950s a time of unprecedented prosperity. Brer Rabbit knew all about that when he managed to hornswaggle Brer Bear and Brer Fox into flinging him into the briar patch, tar and all.

But right den, Brer Fox and Brer Bear hear a scufflin' mongst de leaves, way at de other end of de briar-patch. And lo and behold, who do de see scramblin' out from de bushes, friskey ez a cricket, but Brer Rabbit hisself! Brer Rabbit, *whistlin' an singin', an combin' de last bit of tar outer his mustarshes wid a piece of de briar-bush.*

"Howdy, Brer Fox an Brer Bear!" he holler. "I told you and told you not to fling me in dat briar-patch. Dat's de place in all dis world I love de very best. Dat briar patch is de place where I was born!" [704]

12

HOLE NUMBER TWELVE.

181 Yards, Par 3. Great par 3.

Best shot left side of green since this 6,500 square foot green slopes right.

Avoid the right front bunker and remember that the historical

Delaware Indian Cemetery is out of bounds left.

If the pin placement is front, stay below the hole.

13

HOLE NUMBER THIRTEEN.

391 Yards, Par 4. This is the start of what Hillcrest members call the
Golden Triangle (three great par 4s).

If you play the Triangle in par, you will have a good back nine.

You should start this hole with the club that will place you 130 or 135 yards from the green.

The landing area on this tree-lined fairway is 256 yards off the tee.

You will find OB far right. Be sure and avoid right front bunker.

Green size: 4,500 square feet.

CHAPTER SEVEN

New Boss:
THE 1950s

Three boys darted down the stairs and loitered around while one of them slipped into the men's card room. In the room, Gary abruptly slowed his pace to a tiptoe. Mr. Price was here every afternoon, and sometimes even Mr. Adams. They for sure knew the names of all the kids, and Gary, Willie, and Bob would certainly be in trouble if their dads heard they had cut through here. Blue smoke hung low in the room and curled toward the glowing light bulbs illuminating this inner sanctum. Gary stealthily ducked into the men's restroom on the right.

Scott Beesley was dealing the last few cards of a round of gin rummy. Another table of men was similarly engrossed in a game of pitch. While they waited for their hands, John Tyler was telling a little story on Roscoe Keele, the sturdy bartender who was in charge of keeping up these quarters designated exclusively for masculine business.

"…and there were four or five of us, on our hands and knees in the dripping wet shower, feeling around the drain for his contact…"

There was the soft shuffle of cards being skillfully sorted.

"Roscoe! Bring me a screwdriver! He shouted."

Three men looked up with knowing grins just as Tyler reached the punch line.

"Right away, there came Roscoe with a screwdriver! Orange juice and vodka!"

"Ho! Ho! Ho!" Chuckled several of the men in the room.

Like a ghost, Gary silently slipped out of the room to rejoin his friends before picking up breakneck speed for the golf shop. As they passed, Roscoe, hustled by with a bourbon on the rocks for Mr. Beesley.

Just at that moment, as the conversation faded, Beesley spoke up, "Roscoe bring me a..."

Roscoe always seemed to know, even before his patrons asked. "Right here, Mr. Beesley."

The room fell silent again. "Gin!" Intoned Hal Price. There may have been $200 on the table as they slapped down their cards to shuffle for another hand.

The boys broke their pace in the neighborhood of the row of six slot machines that were lined up, arms raised, saluting sentries between the men's grill and the golf shop. Sometimes, if a boy was lucky, one of the men would make a little jackpot and then give any nearby boys a nickel. Instead, this afternoon there wasn't much activity around the machines. Cortez, the Mexican and Black man who was responsible for shining the golfer's shoes came from the locker room and saw their hopeful glances as they sauntered through. He chided the kids, "Whater you boys do'in in here? You move on outside, now."

By the summer of 1950, the United States was thoroughly mired in the Korean Conflict. As the midterm elections approached, the Truman administration struggled to hold the party line with sagging popularity in the face of an unpopular war, mounting revelations of communist infiltration at home, and persistent economic challenges. A Republican tidal wave in November ushered in the first glimmer of their new ascendancy. Across America new cars, a plethora of new appliances, new fashions, and new homes heralded the age of the consumer, and Bartlesville participated fully in its infatuation with Modern styles.

The Price Company landed a contract to build one third of the new Illinois Natural Gas Pipeline, an artery to serve the consumer demands of the central states. The first wave of the baby boom surged into the schools that fall. K. S. Adams led the local initiative to promote the local schools. Southview School was completed in time to be opened for the fall, and some more renovations were added to Douglass. St. John School was proud to open its new "functional modernistic" building just in time to enroll 200 students. New public school teachers had an orientation picnic at Woolaroc. A long-time political dream, textbooks were provided to public school students for a nominal rental for the first time. First Presbyterian and First Christian churches finished up major building projects downtown. New occupants in the Phillips apartments enjoyed the new urbanism of Bartlesville, and the "Oklahoma functional" Adams building was the pride of the skyline. The addition to Memorial Hospital was a needed stopgap until the Jane Phillips hospital could be completed. The improvements at the airport, and a high-water route for highways 75 and 60 into the city were needed improvements to transportation. With all of this, the city commission niggled away with water, light, and sewer improvements in the new parts of town. Central Christian College finally opened its doors in time for fall enrollment. They had invested $100,000 in the facilites on the old Foster estate, with $33,000 coming from the community. They had 100 students enrolled, 20 of them local kids. Meanwhile, for homecoming, College High held a new kind of dance in the field house – a sock hop. Woolaroc was closed for a month after the death of Frank Phillips, but afterwards instituted a new policy of being open for public tours on Tuesdays and Thursdays. [705]

The Hillcrest golf season wound to a slow close. Playoffs for the city golf tournament were held at Hillcrest on 30 August. The next day Mike May won the city junior golf championship, followed on 1 September, by Bill Simpson returning as city champion in play at Sunset, but Sunset ace, Hank Mattux, became the upset winner. [706]

The fall civic and social season began in October. Almost all events were being held at downtown locations, especially at the fancy new YWCA building. Oil Progress Week took up attention early that month. The Welfare Association celebrated 20 years of service to the city, proudly pointing out their position to give immediate assistance without handicap of red tape. It is notable that their budget for 1950, was just over $10,000, reflecting the vastly improved economic conditions. The Community Fund Drive was also in October, as usual endorsed by the community's leaders: W. H. Leverett of National Zinc; H. W. Trippett of Home Savings and Loan; K. S. Adams; A. W. Ambrose president of Cities Service; C. E. Burlingame; Armais Artunoff; John H. Kane; H. C. Price; J. W. Maddux representing the Business Men's Association; W. C. Smoot chairman of the board of First National Bank; John F. Cronin president of First National Bank; and D. M. Tyler chairman of the board of Union National Bank. As a sign of the times, the list of community leaders also included John G. Koster, John Marshal, and G. C. Woolery, presidents of three of the local trade unions. The wives of the Cities Service employees who were in town for the annual horseshoe pitching contest enjoyed a dinner in their honor at Hillcrest on 8 October. Otherwise, utilization of Hillcrest for civic events was almost nil. [707]

State crime bureau agents ordered 2 steaks and 2 whiskey sours at Marie's Steak House on 1 November, then raided the joint. The same night they raided the Smelter Inn and Gratt Rogers' tavern on North Johnstone. They broke up a poker game and confiscated a pistol at Rogers'. The establishments were padlocked and it was several weeks before Marie's owners opened again. [708]

On 6 December Jake Bartles' store in Dewey burned. The old landmark had been removed from its original site on the Caney River in Bartlesville to Dewey in 1898.

In the latter days of the Cherokee Nation, cattlemen were the kings and this old store was the meeting place for those engaged in this industry from the Kansas line to the banks of the Arkansas River and ranged from packing house executives, cattle barons of the West, cowboys who did not sing, and the polyglot following always in the wake of an industry. It was also the meeting place or stopping place for officers of the United States, judges and court officers en route to newly established districts in the western part of the territory, U. S. marshals, army officers, Indian police, agents and officers of the Indian department…

Politics in the Cherokee Nation was always a live-issue and the old store was a popular meeting place for most of the political leaders. [709]

Above the historic store were the family living quarters.

The old store was built and the timbers dressed and shaped entirely by hand; a large part of it from black walnut lumber from the virgin timber cut and shaped and all of the lumber sawed at the mill a short distance up the river.

The floor of the dining room was a work of art, it was laid in different kinds and colors of wood and would compare with favor to any hardwood floor of today. Some of the carpenters who were employed on this building had learned their trade in the old country and were master craftsmen.

The home was furnished in good taste and about it there was an atmosphere of real elegance. [710]

It was more than a sentimental loss to the area; it was a loss of history.

The slowness of the fall season at Hillcrest probably indicates that Gordon High was no longer at the club as manager. It is known that he moved to manage the 4,000-member Ft. Sill Officer's Club, and eventually the Wichita Country Club, but he had not been able to pull Hillcrest out of its skid. The club was in serious financial straits. [711]

The Christmas season did generate a few social notices of activity at Hillcrest. The Military Reserve ball kicked off the season. A club dance on 4 December, with an "informal social hour" preceding it, was the first official affair, with Dinner-Dance on 23 December. Dinner-Dance was again a robust organization after some non-functional years during the war, limited to 50 members and sporting a waiting list. As usual the annual New Years party was the place to be. Lee Roberts and his Stardust Eight from Oklahoma City played the dance music, beginning at 10:00 P.M., and breakfast was served at 3:00 A.M. [712]

1951

The tar baby's last gasp, late in 1950, was the reinstitution of wage and price controls by the Truman administration. The desperate move by the federal government reflected their fear of the ravages of high inflation in 1950. The same ravages were taking their toll at the country club. In the last few months, Hillcrest had clearly been limping along with few social affairs, no civic affairs, and even a lassitude in fall golf. Even with Mrs. Foster's skinflint management and Gordon High's professional skills, the desperately needed renovation in the kitchen, and probably overspending signaled by the spate of spectacular parties, were factors that built until Hillcrest was plain ol' broke. At the 16 January, annual meeting, Elmer Gallery, Price Pipeline's financial guru, was brought in to straighten out the mess. He was elected president and served for the 1951 and 1952 terms. The board members for 1951 were: E. L. Gallery, president; Scott Beesley, vice president; P. S. Ambrose, secretary and

treasurer; members F. B. Plank, C. T. Klein, C. W. Thomas, C. W. Selby, W. F. Martin, M. J. Kirwan, J. W. Profitt, and O. M. Browning. [713]

The first big business of the year was filing Article of Revival and Extension of Oklahoma Corporation on 2 March 1951. Like the curious tax exemption episode, "through inadvertence or oversight, the officers of the corporation failed to effect and extension of its period of existence before the expiration thereof, and it has been the intention of the officers of the corporation to continue the existence of such corporation." [714] Hillcrest's original certificate was filed 27 November 1925 for a period of 20 years, therefore expiring in 1945. On the same day that the revival was filed, Amended Articles of Incorporation were filed. The duration of the corporation was extended from 20 years to 50 years. The aggregate number of shares the corporation had the authority to allot was previously 250; it was increased to 400. This action was approved at the December 1950 meeting of the board, a part of the emerging effort to bring the country club back into fiscal health and civic leadership. [715]

At the time that Gordon High was hired in 1948, it was reported that there were 350 Hillcrest members. In view of the inattention to the Articles of Incorporation at the time, it is possible that the stockholding membership exceeded the by-laws limitation by 100 members. If that is the case, they were bringing membership limitations in line with practice at the time, as well as allowing for recruitment of new members to help the budget.

Less than five months after his father died, on 18 January the city was shocked to learned of the sudden death of John G. Phillips while returning from a vacation in Spain aboard the Queen Mary. Though he had been living in Dallas where he was a branch manager for Pittsburgh Steel, he had been one of the key players in the growth of the city in the 1920s and a key founder of the country club.

By now, though the Medical Society held its annual installation banquet at the country club in January, almost all civic events were held at the good old Burlingame, the new YWCA, the American Legion building, the Adams Building, College High, and occasionally Central High School or the old Civic Center. There was a city wide civic push for polio. The square dance club raised $4200 for the National Foundation for Infantile Paralysis, the March of Dimes benefited from an ugliest man contest sponsored by the farmers and stockman (J. E. "Boog" Stark was the winner). The Jane Phillips Hospital that was finally under construction boasted a state-of-the-art polio wing. On the frigid night of 30 January, the Reed Hotel at Second and Johnstone burned in a major fire that damaged some nearby buildings and threatened May Brothers, ABC Shoe Shop, the Pastime Pool Hall and the Avaneda Hotel above the pool hall. Another piece of old Bartlesville was gone.[716]

The economic straits generated a lot of activity at the Chamber of Commerce. The desperate need for expanded school facilities and expansion of the city east of the river commanded Chamber attention. They endorsed a big school bond proposal for the spring. One of their biggest efforts came from their national affairs committee and was a favorite of Boots Adams, framing a resolution to limit non-essential government spending. Otherwise, the accomplishments for the past year were reviewed with some satisfaction.

The only disappointment was from the fire prevention committee that reported 56 building fires. A Frank Phillips memorial committee was formed with K. S. Adams as president and Hal Price as chairman. They decided to petition the city commissioners to name US 60 through town, Frank Phillips Boulevard.

At the end of February, the 22nd Amendment to the United States Constitution was ratified by votes in Utah and Nevada, limiting American presidents to two terms in office. You could buy a 17" Motorola T.V. for $269.95 and watch the first T.V. station in Tulsa, KOTV, with programming from 2:00 in the afternoon to 12:00 midnight sign-off. Though the 4 radio networks competed through the day – Break the Bank, Ma Perkins, Arthur Godfrey, Young Widder Brown, House Party, Stella Dallas, Fulton Lewis, Jr. – there was only a little news programming to report the "bone dry" bill that passed the house and senate in Oklahoma City on 28 March. Likewise, everyone in the nation was shocked by the headline of 11 April that General Douglas MacArthur had been sacked in a test of wills with President Truman.

Winter social activity at Hillcrest started out predictably slowly. A few small ladies clubs had bridge parties, and some wedding showers were all that happened for almost three months. There was no regular club party in January, but Dinner-Dance Club had parties on 14 January, 25 February, 11 March, and 20 May. Probably shortly after the January annual meeting, the club persuaded Mrs. Jeanette (Stewart) Yinger to be manager. Jeanette Stewart had been the manager of Hillcrest from 1937 to 1938 when she remarried to Harry Yinger, a Phillips patent attorney. Having a good manager in place, who knew the clientele, was an immediate boost. A club dance was planned for 28 February.[718]

After all these years, bridge parties were still staple social pastime. Millie Lee Stone (left), with a group of unidentified women in 1950, plays a little bridge on the veranda before the redecoration. *Courtesy Bartlesville Area History Museum.*

In short order, there was a meeting of the activities committee. R. W. Scanlan was chairman of the committee, and sub-committees were appointed. A Chinese buffet dinner was the first event only two days later. The annual children's egg hunt was on 22 March, and a dance for teenagers was on 24 March. The Beaux Arts Ball was the biggest affair of the year on 30 March. Popcorn and pretzels were served at the "coffee bar" all evening while Joe Linde's orchestra from Tulsa played the dance music. It was one of those costume parties that were so popular then. Mr. And Mrs. Sam McBirney won first prize dressed as beggars, the Jack Madduxes won second as a Mexican couple, Mr. And Mrs. Charles Seanion were dressed in black face for third prize. A month later, the Richard Kanes were hosts for a Western party with R. R. Lindsly as the square dance caller. The last dance on 19 May featured Jim Parks and his swingsters, followed by a midnight breakfast. It was good to see the club normalizing. [719]

In the middle of February, Don Wilkie reported that the Sunset golfers were already out practicing their strokes and putts. They had been able to play through a warm January, so it is supposed that the Hillcrest devotees were similarly active. About the time Mrs. Yinger came, Hillcrest women began to make noises about getting organized. The women met on the last day of February, and the season was off with play every Wednesday, followed by luncheon and cards. The routine was forced indoors on 11 April by rain, snow, and sleet. [720]

The men opened their season 10 days later with their annual stag golf match. The team captains were Charles Selby and Dr. George M. Tulloch. Selby's team won the match and the steak dinner. Keiffer Davis and John Pettigrove again won the annual four-ball tournament on 13 May. Norman Millis won the annual Reda tournament, and qualifying rounds for the annual Hillcrest men's championship began. [721]

Jeanette Yinger was a very successful manager during her career, and the spring turn-around at Hillcrest was the achievement of a gifted and experienced professional. Surely, the board and the club members could not have been more pleased. There were big plans afoot. Then suddenly, disaster struck. Mrs. Yinger made a trip to the post office downtown one evening in May, after the club closed. On the return trip, she fell asleep at the wheel, ran into the Caney River bridge, and was killed. [722]

On 27 May, it was announced that Olga Foster had graciously agreed to manage the club through June. The accompanying news was that the clubhouse would be closed through July and August for extensive improvements. In fact, work was already underway. On the day Mrs. Foster took the helm, the Dinner-Dance closed their season. Besides June weddings, at the social committee's instruction Mrs. Yinger had arranged an active schedule for season's end. Mrs. Jack Maddux was chairman of the family affairs [sub]committee that was in charge of the family night parties. The first, on Memorial Day, included pole bending, horseshoe pitching, driving and putting contests, a softball game, and cards inside. On 22 June, Mary and Dick Kane were the committee hosts for a family night smörgasbord and an old fashioned community sing with Lois Lynd playing the piano and Bob Durant leading the singing. Dorothy Glynn Adams was in charge of the Fourth of July family extravaganza, which was organized to the teeth. James McColl was responsible for men's golf contests. Mrs. Gerald Preston was responsible for women's golf activities, Mrs. Joe Bower arranged the peanut hunt and the story hour for children, the Richard Powells organized the teen's putting contest and bingo games. There was a fried chicken buffet from 6:00 to 8:00. After supper there was a Western band, and fireworks after dark. All of this squeezed in on the heels of the first big flood since the Hulah Dam and the high-water highway. [723]

Of course, an active summer golf season was planned despite the renovations in the clubhouse.

While the club championship eliminations were progressing, Hillcrest women hosted Tulsa District Women's Golf Association on 1 June, and started a medal play handicap tournament on 3 June. Some of the men took a few days to play in the Oklahoma Amateur in Tulsa. In the first day's play the tournament was interrupted for 3 hours by a cloudburst, but Bartlesville was made proud by Charles Selby's performance, sinking a 25-foot putt for a birdie that eliminated Oklahoma City's Dean Wood that day. The next day was even more thrilling with Selby paired against Bill Simpson. This time Selby upset his Hillcrest fellow 3 and 2, but he faltered on the third day. The Doherty Men's Fraternity started its annual tournament at Hillcrest on 9 June, won by Don Anderson the next day, before the final round of the club championship. A week later the Cities Service inter-company championship was played at Hillcrest. In between, Bill Simpson took vengeance on Selby, winning the Hillcrest title again. The crowd was entertained on 12 June, with a famous trick shot act by Hilo, Hawaii pro, Paul Hahn. The highlight of the performance was a William Tell shot where a volunteer, lying on his back, held a golf tee between his teeth while Hahn teed off. [724]

Mike May won, for a second year, the Junior Golf Championship that was played at Sunset. The Seniors of the Chamber of Commerce defeated the Jaycees at their annual tourney, played at Hillcrest. After being rained out on the last day of June the FPMC tournament was delayed by flooding so it was played right after the 4th of July. The American Legion, Boots Adams' favorite civic group, held a golf tournament at Hillcrest in connection with their First District convention at the end of July. That weekend, the Hillcrest aces traveled to Twin Oaks in team play in a tie match; then the following week Twin

Oaks came to Bartlesville. The summer closed with a crescendo, 106° for the city championship. Sunseter Hank Mattux won the title for the second year. Albert Roth won the Men's Handicap tournament on 25 September, and Mrs. C. W. Hubbell won the Ladies Handicap Championship on 5 October. [725]

With the advent of air conditioning, some civic activity had shifted to summertime. The Chamber of Commerce held its new board nominations with the end of the fiscal year. In a show of civic unity, the Chamber elected 34 new men to the board, and all 20 past presidents who were living in Bartlesville also agreed to serve on the 1951-52 board. By the first of August, a "get acquainted" issue of the newspaper touted all of the major civic organizations in town. The new Negro Community Center was proudly opened. According to the Examiner, the project was started in 1950 when a group of businessmen met with Negro community leaders. It was an outgrowth of the heads-up that came from the embarrassing Miss Ruth Brown episode. The YWCA was receiving some of the attentions of the same "citizens com-mittee," so that another outgrowth was the proactive strengthening of the YWCA. This was signaled by an unusually long article in the "get acquainted" issue of the newspaper, and by the return of Miss Martha Good, who led the local YW in the 1930s, a well-es-tablished personage and professional, to manage the YW again.

On 10 July, the clubhouse closed for the much-anticipated remodeling. It was announced that it would open for Labor Day with George M. Latham, who had opened the Phillips cafeteria a couple of years earlier, as the new manager. Stanley Learned had the clout to get the clubhouse for his daughter's wedding reception on 26 August, otherwise it was a summer of expectancy. [726]

It was the threshold of a new era for Hillcrest, and a changing social hegemony for the town. It showed up immediately. Don Tyler hosted a "bathing beauty revue," a burlesque of a beauty contest, at the new swimming pool on the Tyler Farm south of town, for a party for Rotarians. The event drew a full-page spread of party-pics in the society page. Gone were the days of guest lists and elaborate flowers as the markers of high society parties. The new paradigm was a full-page spread of party pics if the party was a really – really important one. [727]

The Modernization of Bartlesville

The Frank Phillips Men's Club finished the summer with a birthday bash for the new boss, K. S. Adams, at the Adams Building Auditorium on Friday, 31 August. Claude Thornhill's fifteen-piece orchestra played for the dance that was broadcast on KWON. It was a more sophisticated take-off on the old birth-day parties they always held for Frank Phillips. At Hillcrest, finishing touches occupied the last few days before the Labor Day opening of the redecorated clubhouse.

During the summer, Dorothy Glynn Adams headed up the decorating committee comprised of Mrs. A. W. Ambrose, Mrs. H. C. Price, Mrs. J. F. Cronin, Mrs. Carl Barrett, Mrs. William R. Lund, Mrs. Scott Beesley, Jr., and Mrs. M. J. Kirwin. The clubhouse had not been redecorated since it was built in 1926, and was unquestionably becoming a little frayed at the elbows. Mrs. Adams brought in Mildred English, Inc. of San Antonio who had been her own decorator in Texas. Some furniture was replaced and some new furniture was needed, while most was sim-ply recovered with updated fabrics, and new draperies were made. Special attention was focused on redecoration around the huge fireplace in the ballroom, with new white chandeliers, and smoked glass mirror that Dorothy Glynn remembered as "stunning." During the summer, the screened-in west porch had been glassed in to make an upstairs lounge. The new space was decorated with bamboo easy chairs with floral upholstery and glass top tables all on a bright green rug. It's not clear when the clubhouse was air conditioned, but it makes sense that at least the new lounge must have been at this time. Otherwise, this newly hermetically sealed space would have been too hot for human life on a Labor Day weekend that was over 100°. Throughout the club the old Spanish motif and original antiques had given way to trendy oriental themes: new lamps, Lawson sofas, shiny silks, and chinoiserie valances. Boots Adams prevailed on Phillips to pick up the bill. [728]

On Labor Day, the club was finally ready for the open house celebration. A fried chicken buffet supper preceded a dance with the Tubby Young orchestra from Tulsa furnishing the music. Of course, the open house was properly reported with a full-page spread of pictures in the Sunday paper. [729]

Social activity was immediately off and running. The first club event was a Mexican supper on 23 September. The Women's Golf Association held a flashy style show on 22 September. The Doherty Girls Club added a Hillcrest dinner and card party to the horseshoe pitching contest activities on 16 September. The Chamber of Commerce planned an annual banquet at Hillcrest to honor the retiring president Boots Adams, and welcome the new president, W. D. McGinley. Homage was paid to the successful year by the new board of 20 past presidents and 34 board members. The speaker for the evening, Stewart Harral, the director of public relations studies at the University of Oklahoma, addressed a crowd of 275 Chamber members. Small clubs kept up a lively meeting activity routine at the club, while it remained the site of choice for wedding parties and showers. Family night remained popular. The Women's Golf Association finished out the season with a lively buffet supper. Dinner-Dance Club began on 26 October, and again on 14 December, with Jackson's Orchestra furnishing the season's music as it had for several years. The Christmas party was decorated with cedar and spruce,

After enclosing the veranda, redecorating, and air conditioning the new lounge was considered very elegant. The bamboo furniture is remembered as especially stylish. New draperies and cornice boards brought the window treatments right up to date. The woman turning around is Mrs. Singer Irelan, just behind her is W. H. Shipman, the woman with a wrap over her shoulders is Amelia Cronin, 8 October 1954.

red candles, Christmas balls, and a snow sprinkler, the first party decorations described in many months. Winter began early with the first snow on 6 November and frigid weather defying the Santa Claus fly-in at the airport on 16 December. A club dance was announced for 11 November. A cluster of luncheons and a major tea at Hillcrest for Thanksgiving warranted one of those full-page spreads party pics. The club served Thanksgiving dinner for the first time in many years. The annual News Years ball, with the Horace Puckett orchestra from Dallas playing before a 2:00 A.M. breakfast finished off the season. [730]

After the opening of the redecorated clubhouse, social life normalized after lagging for a very long time. Some things are notable. Except for the Chamber of Commerce fete honoring Boots Adams, large civic club events were not held at Hillcrest. Though there was a constant patter of small club meetings, lady parties, and club parties, large private parties were not reported. This was especially notable at the Christmas season when there was almost nothing reported between the big Thanksgiving teas and the New Years Ball. Yet, when old club members are queried, they affirm that the social whirl was definitely active in those years. It appears that along with the Texas orientation of the club redecoration and the New Years orchestra, the club was coming to a new way of self-understanding. At the same time, *Examiner-Enterprise* editor, Joe Edwards, was of the opinion that the change in social reporting was the result of a policy change at the newspaper, stemming from the time that Donray bought the local paper.

1952

As 1951 wound down, Congress took the opportunity of an off-election year to raise taxes, the average tax bill going up 11 to 12% in order to pay for the war and foreign aid. The year ended with test flights for the new Air Force stratofortress B-52, a bomber that remained a workhorse through the Cold War and into the War on Terror era. While ordinary Americans enjoyed a religious revival in the early 1950s, theologian Rheinhold Niebuhur complained that the ecumenical movement was on the ropes with relations between denominations deteriorating.

Britain's King George died early in February, and England's monarchy smoothly passed to his daughter Elizabeth, sadness and celebration in an ancient ceremony, seen on television by millions of Americans. Meanwhile, American political life came alive early in January when Dwight Eisenhower announced he would be willing to take the nomination for president. Weeks later, President Truman announced he would not run again. By summer, the Republicans had nominated General Ike for their ticket. Excited Oklahoma Democrats decided to take Senator Robert S. Kerr to the convention as their favorite son. In a free-for-all wrangle, the Democrats nominated Adlai Stevenson on the third ballot. The convention riveted American's attention with televised broadcasts. Of course, Eisenhower was elected in November.

Bartlesville enjoyed a few civic landmarks in 1952. Local employment numbers looked very good, with over 10,500 people working in the city. A civic orchestra was organized. Though there were 25 conventions in Bartlesville in 1951, and the Chamber of Commerce was actively promoting the city as a convention center. Hillcrest was no longer a part of that type of civic activity as it had been in the past. The Adams Building received an award from the Kansas City Chapter of the American Institute of Architects for the best design in the commercial classification. Amazingly, it was dubbed "Oklahoma Functional."

The Adams Building in the new minimalist Functional Modern style was finished in 1950. In 1951 the Kansas City Chapter of AIA gave an architectural award for the work, and dubbed it "Oklahoma Functional." *Courtesy Bartlesville Area History Museum.*

There were several liquor-gambling enforcement raids in Washington County during the year. The American Legion's competitor for the hearts and minds of local veterans was the Amvets, who were raided on 7 June. A few weeks later, K. S. Adams was voted the state's outstanding Legionnaire. The old Crystal Ice Cream plant burned on 14 November. The new Jane Phillips hospital was dedicated the next day.

Meanwhile, the climate of the Great Plains took the upper hand with a spring season of dust storms. Things were bone dry by summer, drier than 1936. Still, there was a 1.8-inch rain on the Fourth of July, and hopes were high that the drought was broken, but hope petered out soon enough. Oklahoma farmers and ranchers braced for disaster. It was the first year that air conditioning became commonplace. Fire was on people's minds, and people living in the neighborhood of Hillcrest Country Club self-organized into a fire-prevention team. It was none

too soon for a range fire burned off 5,100 acres near Hulah that same day. [731]

The Hillcrest Women's Golf Association organized for 1952, on 1 March. Lillian Swatzel was in charge of junior golf, the first sign of renewed interest in golf for girls since before the war. The women had weekly pairings, features, and frequent guest days throughout the year. On 1 June, the featured a driving contest. Mrs. E. M. Wolters was the winner of a three-day medal handicap tournament on 22 June. Mrs. Bill Hughes won the handicap championship in October. [732]

There was a fire in a workshop on 5 April. A driver drove a pickup into the building and knocked over a pan of gasoline. The fumes from the gasoline were ignited by a gas stove. The metal building and its contents, valued at $7,000, were destroyed. They rescued a tractor and 2 mowers out of the burning building. [733]

Hillcrest Women's Golf Association, four ball tournament, August 1952. Women in the lounge white shirts and rolled jeans are Virginia Hubbard and Treva Burlingame. *Courtesy Virginia Hubbell Collection.*

The annual stag team play was scheduled for 15 April. Don Gordon and Walter Englebrecht were team captains, with 70 eager golfers signed up. The match was rained out, but Gordon's team won on 20 April. Meanwhile, the welcome rain did not dampen the stag party on Saturday night. The highlight of the evening was golf movies of Sam Snead, Ben Hogan, Gary Middlecoff, Charles Selby, and Bill Simpson. A mixed Scotch Foursome was played on 27 April, and the annual four ball began on 10 May, followed by a buffet supper. Keifer Davis and John Pettigrove won the four ball. [734]

Dick Booker won the district championship for the Cities Service tournament on 15 June. Later in the evening, the wives of the contestants joined their husbands for a dinner party, followed by bridge. Dick Brooks, of local tennis fame, won the FPMC

championship. Bill Simpson captured the Hillcrest club championship for yet another year on 8 July. He also returned to the city championship on Labor Day weekend. After the Labor Day golf activities on Saturday and Monday of the holiday weekend there were buffet suppers. C. C. Custer won the handicap championship at the end of September. [735]

January of 1952, was frigid which may be partly why there was not much social activity evident at the club. It is known that Elmer Gallery was elected for a second term as president of the board at the January meeting. The club was in improving financial condition by then, and there was an active membership recruitment campaign that year. Many of the old members date their membership to this time frame, saying, "Oh, John Tyler got us to join," or something similar.

At the end of January, there was a folk dance with Bob Lindsly the caller, and another at the end of February. The folk dances were free and popular with more such dances regularly. Of course Dinner-Dance Club was regular, as was Family Night. A new series of Dinner-Bridge parties began in March. The year closed out with a teenage dance on 7 May. The final dance of the season was a "sports shirt" informal, with the VanSant Orchestra, the same as the teenage dance the week before, playing the dance music. [736]

Mr. and Mrs. A. W. Ambrose, the president of Cities Service, hosted a very large reception and dinner party for Mr. And Mrs. S. B. Irelan, the incoming president of the company, on 17 February. The black tie affair filled the ballroom to capacity with a long hosts table along the south side of the room and 7 long tables of guests from east to west, each seating 40 guests. The tables were set with white tablecloths, candles and flowers, and fine china. Of course, all of this was recorded in a newspaper page of pictures. The second big party of the spring was the Beaux Arts Ball on 19 April. The theme was "All the world's a stage," and guests arrived in full costume. Many were unrecognizable, outlandish, and imaginative. Awards were given in several categories. Pete Bertie and his orchestra played the dance music. Once again, the newspaper ran a full page of party pics. [737]

The Fourth of July was celebrated with the usual golf activities, and a buffet supper, followed by fireworks. They expected a crowd of 500 for the celebration. It isn't clear if rain that day put a damper on things. Family Night continued through the year, even in August. The air conditioning of at least some of the clubhouse evidently enabled the club to stay open through the hot months. [738]

Accordingly, the fall season opened early. Joe Linde was caller for a square dance on 4 October and 1 November. There was a regular club dance on

Scotch Foursome was often a popular season opener. Outrageous play and outrageous costume were common with a lot of cutting up and joshing. In this 1952 game Harry Burlingame hamed it up, shooting pool, while Paddy Hughes Gaddis, Margie Ward, and Charlie Hubble watched. The same day, Fred Wallingford played in his nightshirt.

23 October, with Pete Bertie's orchestra playing. The dance committee was Mrs. And Mrs. Ralph Mayo, Mr. And Mrs. Carsten Slack, and Mr. And Mrs. Frank Tallman, and Dick Kane was square dance chairman. There was a children's Halloween party with stories and games. [739]

All of November's club activities were conveniently announced ahead, so that a typical month at Hillcrest becomes evident. The month began with a square dance on 1 November, hosted by the Dick Kanes; a junior (record) dance on 28 November, hosted by the Truman Wadlows; Family Night, hosted by C. R. Dougherty on 15 November; Dinner-Dance Club chairman for 21 November was Mrs. Bessie Smysor; club, dinner-bridge chairmen were Mr. and Mrs. Charles Davidson on 25 November; and ending the month with another informal dance on 29 November, hosted by the John Freibergers and John Tylers. Doherty Girls Club also held their annual banquet at Hillcrest on 21 November. [740]

Once again, the Christmas season reported very few parties. There was another square dance and Family Night early in the month. Dinner-Dance club was on 20 December. H. C. Price Company entertained 75 company employees at a dinner-dance on 24 December. Though it is certain that there was an annual New Years ball, there was nothing reported. [741]

1953

By 1953, it had been five years since the newspaper reported the annual stockholders meeting at Hillcrest in January. We know that C. W. Thomas was elected president at the subsequent board meeting. C. T. Klein was vice president and P. S. Ambrose was secretary-treasurer. [742]

Nevertheless, January was a fairly active month for the club. The Women's Golf Association was already active, with a board meeting on 4 January, and weekly luncheons continuing through the winter. The monthly square dance in January featured coffee and doughnuts with a record player providing the music. Family Night braved the winter weather and the flu epidemic that month, but Dinner-Dance was canceled. Dinner-Bridge wound up the month. "Informal" parties were becoming more characteristic, in fact, every occasion in February was "informal": Square Dance, Dinner-Dance Club, and informal club dance, and an informal Sewing Club luncheon. [743]

By April, the mood had changed. Doherty Auxiliary held a spring tea, dessert and card party to end its social season. The Women's Golf Association held the last of its series of benefit bridge luncheons to raise money for the state tournament they would be hosting in June. Forty tables played bridge that afternoon, and one hundred ladies attended the luncheon. Flowers and decorations for the last two Dinner-Dance Club parties were the markers of more formal parties. The last, in May, was converted into a farewell party for the R. L. Kidds, with 200 in attendance. [744]

The nation began to settle in to the rhythm we fondly remember as typical of the 1950s. The Cold War was on everybody's mind. The new president, Eisenhower, quickly fulfilled his campaign pledge to extricate us from the Korean War. By summer, POWs were arriving home. In March, Stalin died, but it did not curtail Soviet expansionism. A coup in Iran freed that country from the rule of a Soviet puppet. There was ominous saber rattling over Formosa. At home, as Eisenhower moved to undercut McCarthy's excesses. The Rosenberg's were executed for treason, and in Oklahoma a communist zoology professor was purged at OU. The struggle against communism was the political news of the era, but one of the most significant milestones of modern medicine came to fruition that year. The Salk vaccine for polio successfully passed through the first human trials that spring. All of those Roosevelt birthday parties, all of those infantile paralysis fund drives and March of Dimes drives, were finally paying off.

A black duster roared through western Oklahoma on 17 February. It was the spectacular beginning of the drought and heat wave of the middle 1950s, a staggering agricultural disaster and a worse drought than the 1930s. A month later, Washington and Osage County cattlemen took a belly blow when a late sleet storm and frigid blizzard winds visited huge losses of new steers recently brought into the bluestem country for spring grazing. Despite the spectre of drought, the city's Easter egg hunt was rained out on 7 April.

The city was really growing. The Chamber of Commerce was struggling with prospects of adding almost 20,000 residents in the new areas east of the river. Boots Adams took the helm again as president of the Chamber. Burlingame Heights, just northeast of the country club pushed the new development into the environs of the big estates surrounding Hillcrest. [745]

A new frontier in the contest for local Modernist architectural hegemony was announced in May. In the wake of two major buildings built by Phillips who used Kansas City architects, with the encouragement of Harold Price, Hal Price decided to cut out a real legacy for himself. H. C. Price Company would build an 18-story skyscraper, designed by Frank Lloyd Wright. A model of the proposed new building was displayed at the International Petroleum Exposition in May. The Price tower would put Bartlesville on the map for architectural cognoscenti. At the same time, Harold and Carolyn Price had the pleasure of working with the famous architect to build their new home in the Price compound, directly across from the country club.

With the new growth in town, the old practice of "the country club being a part of every civic event" passed out of currency. There were plenty of other places to hold big events. In 1953, the state Jaycees convention and the state Lions convention were held in Bartlesville, but no events associated with either of these were held at Hillcrest.

The Women's Golf Association got an early start with a series of benefit bridge luncheons, even before the weather permitted golf play, preparing for the big state tournament in June. The annual stag team golf match opened the season for Hillcrest men on 25 April. H. A. Gardner's Divot Diggers "whipped" R. H. Tucker's Sweet Swingers that day. Al Holt became the DMF champion on 12 May. Frank Riney won the Memorial Day flag tournament [746]

Bartlesville civic clubs may not have been using the country club for major events, but Hillcrest Women really put the city on the map in classic style. They began to build the drama in preparation for the big state tournament early in the playing season. Bartlesville's women stars got plenty of publicity in the build-up. The 36th annual Women's Oklahoma Golf Association Amateur tournament was held at Hillcrest 8 through 12 June. Jimmy Gullane pointed out that the course was in good shape for the grueling test. "The greens are in tip-top shape and the fairways except for shorter holes are good." There was a swimming pool (at long last) under construction, at the former site of the putting greens, but the new greens would be ready for the tournament. In true Bartlesville style the women put together a very effective tournament committee. The chairman was Mrs. J. E. Kendall, the publicity chairman was Mrs. J. R. Hatfield, and the Women's Golf Association chairman was Mrs. Earl Walters. Mrs. W. H. Wallace was in charge of the entertainment, and she put together a full agenda. A Western picnic on the tennis courts where 300 danced to Western music preceding the tournament on 7 June. Mary Lou Price had the open house for the women on Monday at Star View Farm, followed by the buffet dinner at Hillcrest, the banquet tables decorated with magnolias floating in low bowls. There was a Tuesday banquet, and on Wednesday there was a swimming party for the juniors and a costume party for the others, concluding the week with an awards banquet. [747]

Actual tournament play got off with the favorites all coming up to expectations. Bartlesville's Virginia Hubbell successfully carried the HCC banner through the first round. In the end Mrs. Hack Williford of Ponca City emerged the state amateur champion as a gallery of 500 followed the contenders. [748]

The $80,000 swimming pool [749] that was under construction in the late spring and early summer quickly became an important focal point of club life. A swimming pool was always a part of the original master plan of the club fathers back in 1925. A pool was not built then because of several problems at the time. Those first Hillcrest leaders had ample experience with the chronic and severe problems of swimming pool maintenance from the old Oak Hill pool. For one thing, in 1926 the art of water cleaning and filtration for pools was fairly new and expensive. One immediate obstacle for the new club was simply the expense, followed quickly by the Depression and then wartime construction constraints. But, the biggest problem for Hillcrest, right up to the time of the 1953 pool construction, was water. Water for general purposes other than drinking was obtained from holding

After many years without a swimming pool, in 1953, Hillcrest constructed an Olympic size pool on the south side of the clubhouse, overlooked by the veranda lounge. After the old clubhouse was torn down, the old pro shop and locker room area was still being used for the pool showers and lockers and snack bar. Te first pool manager was Julian Dyason, here with one of the lifeguards, Gregg Walls.

tanks or ponds, cisterns, or from the river. There were no useful wells. The large houses in the neighborhood used similar water sources. It wasn't until the city water line came that far south of town that good quality water became available. Hillcrest greenskeeper Eddie Brookshire speaks of the infections that were endemic with the golf course greens that were watered from the river. In drought conditions of 1953, for the big tournament, Jimmy Gullane gave only faint praise to the acceptable condition of the fairways where they had no reliable way to water the grass.

In Delk's 1926 plan for the clubhouse, there was deliberate consideration for future expansion. The area of the old club house then sited for expansion was on the south side, where the 1953 pool was built, and on the north wing, where the employee's parking lot was situated. The original Hillcrest putting green was in the circle in front of the clubhouse. It had been moved to the south side during the 1950 redecoration only a few years earlier to provide a more formal entry. Doing so had required some re-engineering of the Perry Maxwell-designed golf course. The decision to again move the putting green, and put the new swimming pool right next to the clubhouse on the south was fateful. It cut off half – the most likely half - of the possibility of needed expansion of the clubhouse.

In the lower level of the clubhouse, a part of the men's locker room was requisitioned to build bathhouse dressing rooms and showers for the swimmers. In turn, the golf shop was moved and enlarged to accommodate a more fully modern operation. Boots Adams and Phillips Petroleum Company had an interest in competitive swimming, so that they saw that the club immediately had a very fine pool manager from Pretoria, South Africa. [750]

Julian Dyason was a geology student at O.U., on a swimming scholarship, when Ken Tredway, Phillips Petroleum Company's athletic coordinator, hired him for Hillcrest's first pool manager. He worked at Hillcrest for 3 summers. Dyason was an impressive attraction at the HCC pool. He was a breaststroke champion at several levels, including the NCAA gold medal. It may also have been appealing to Hillcrest that his father was a pool manager in South Africa. A long-term swimming program and well-managed staff was developed over the next few years when former HCC lifeguard Carlyn Cruzan became pool manager. Cruzan had been an intercollegiate swimmer and was the manager of the Phillips Splash Club during the competitive season. He was immensely popular with the Hillcrest young people.

The new lounge that was enclosed from the porch in 1951 overlooked the swimming pool, making a pleasant and attractive environ to linger over a cocktail and visit with friends.

Very quietly in 1953, the club acquired a very important new employee. Billy Joe LeFlore was born in Carlsbad, New Mexico in 1938. He moved to Bartlesville when he was 8 years old and his mother worked for Mary Lou Price. He was 11 1/2 years old when he landed a job, working for Jimmy Gullane, shagging balls. Gullane allowed the plucky little Black kid to play a little golf on Mondays, along with the caddies, when the golf course was closed, using member's old discarded clubs. In time he moved up in the ranks at the clubhouse, first washing pots, then a busboy, waiter, and maitre d'. In better than 50 years at Hillcrest, B.J. became a discrete and beloved landmark at Hillcrest, and active in the Bartlesville civic life. He was an employee for more than 50 years.

Immediately after the Hillcrest women finished their state tournament extravaganza, the men began play for the club championship. For the first time in several years Bill Simpson was not defending his championship, but the field was not wide open. Charles Shelby immediately set the pace only to be surprised by Howard Lambdin in the semi-finals. Lambdin became champion. [751]

Women's golf remained active through the summer and more visible than in several years. Jimmy Gullane had always been a great encourager for the young golfers at Hillcrest, whether member's children or caddies. There had been some effort in the 1930s to get junior golf going at Hillcrest, but it petered out before the war. By the middle 1950s, organized junior golf was finally getting support and it was the women's association that fostered the effort. The

Bartlesville's high school hero, Dee Ketchum, won the Jaycee's 4th Annual Junior Golf Tournament, 1 July 1953. Here shaking hands with 2nd place Walter Sturek, son of the Oklahoma A&M golf coach. *Courtesy Dee Ketchum.*

assistant pro after 1952 was Rookie Smith, who well remembered the encouragement of Jimmy Gullane years before when he was just a caddie, and was very helpful to the program. Elsie Parker and Martha Mae Beard were the devoted sponsors of the effort. In the summer, junior golf was in the mornings: a day for boys and a day for girls, playing 9 holes. The minimum age was 9 years old. Elsie Parker said, "No one had more fun than we did." One manifestation of the new interest was the Jaycee's junior golf tournament. Dee Ketchum won the fourth annual Jaycees junior golf tournament at Hillcrest on 1 July. [752]

Hillcrest held its usual celebration for the Fourth of July. Bob Neumann won the tournament that day. There was a box supper and fireworks in the evening. [753]

Bill Ware won the Frank Phillips Men's Club tournament on 28 July. Lewis Ketchum became the Reda Pump championship on 9 August. In August, there were 3 inter-club matches, followed by the city championship at the end of the month. At the end of September, Mrs. W. H. Satzel became the new women's handicap champion. A week later, E. D. Hollingsworth tied with Bill Simpson for the men's handicap champion. [754]

Beginning in September, Fiskie Robertson took it on herself to edit a club monthly newsletter, Hillcrest Happenings. It was thought to be a new innovation, nobody remembering the short-lived newsletter started by the popular manager, Tom Moore, before the Depression. Unfortunately, the corpus of Fiskie's work was not saved, but a number of clippings and an occasional whole edition have survived. [755]

The fall social season became active early in 1953. On 10 September, the Ted Weems orchestra played for a dance and program that was a reminder of the good ol' days. There was a singer, a novelty

Fiskie Robertson took on the job or writing the monthly Hillcrest Happenings in September 1953. Though the corpus of her work is lost, random issues that happened to be saved by members are a principle source of club activities during the 1950s, 60s, and 70s. Hillcrest Happenings, January 1956.

vocalist, a whistler, dancer, a balladeer and a comedian. Of course, the new pool provided a focus for some swimming parties. There was a pre-football buffet before the College High-Tulsa Central game, with buses chartered to take the crowd to the game. The junior high crowd had a costume record (probably 45 rpm) dance on 11 October, and the next night was Western night for the opening of another square dance season. Dinner-Dance Club had its first dance near the end of October, and again in the middle of November. They were using a new orchestra, the Bates Hunt Orchestra, at most of the fall dances. The teenagers held a Halloween costume party. [756]

Again, after reporting an active fall social season, there were no Holiday season parties reported.

1954

At the annual stockholders meeting on 19 January there was the usual stag dinner for $2.25 a plate. Member in good standing who were present elected C. T. Klein, J. W. McColl, C. W. Selby, and C. W. Thomas to the board. The annual balance sheet showed the club closed 1953 in the black with about $9,000 in the bank and a hefty $15,000 in accounts receivable. Subsequently, at the January meeting of the Hillcrest board, C. T. Klein was elected president for 1954. Otherwise, there was precious little society news reported in the whole spring season. The usual wedding parties appeared, and Dinner-Dance Club was always listed on the "social calendar." [757]

H. C. Price brought Frank Lloyd Wright to speak for the January Town Talks at the Civic Center. Architectural students and faculty from the universities of Oklahoma, Oklahoma A&M, Kansas, Arkansas, Northeastern A&M, and a busload of high school students from Duncan arrived for the lecture. Wright opined about "organic architecture, designed from the inside out to fulfill human needs with the optimum understanding and appropriate use of the materials at the builders command." (One wonders if he was talking about the Price Tower?) He offered some cranky social commentary: that most universities had deteriorated into glorified trade schools; monocracy by the common man will destroy democracy by crushing the uncommon man; the United States must decentralize its great cities. The talk was a major cultural coup for Bartlesville. [758]

Civic life in Bartlesville continued apace. H. C. Price spearheaded plans for the new Bartlesville Boy's Club. A few weeks later, Jo Allen Lowe was appointed director of the new organization. There was another polio drive, the Chamber of Commerce held its annual awards dinner, Tuesday Club celebrated 50 years, a $1.125 million bond to improve schools and for an improved water facility passed. The state DAR held its convention in Bartlesville in February. The convention opened at the Colonial Chapel of the funeral home. (That is real determination not to use the country club!) Their banquet was at the Burlingame Hotel with the national President-General speaking. There were concerns that a bootlegging syndicate was getting established in the area. On a tip, the Washington County sheriff raided Kelly's Tavern at the intersection of old highways 75 and 60, scooping up some pretty big crime figure gamblers and a good deal of gambling equipment. But, there were no more incidents over the next few months. Meanwhile, Bartians poured into the 6th annual appliance show at the Civic Center.

The winter temperatures were by and large quite mild, anticipating the drought pattern that had its grip already set. On 20 February, the first big dust storm swept across the Plains, the worst since the Dust Bowl. By the next storm two weeks later, fear gripped the country with memories of only 20 years back.

The golf season opened with the normal pattern. R. O. Dunbar's team defeated Mike Nelson's team for the annual stag dinner team match at Hillcrest. Yet, beneath the veneer of routine, an era had already come to an end. With the fine new golf shop languishing, John Cronin was fed up with Jimmy's Gullane's old-fashioned ways, and got a burr under his saddle to move him out. The rest of the golf course heavy-weights seem to have agreed, and it was decreed that Jimmy Gullane must go. In fact, the deed had already been done. He was unceremoniously fired without benefit of any of the modern niceties. There was no severance package, no retirement package, no

golf pro-emeritus status, nothing to soften the blow. The news generated quite a bit of indignation among the membership, and quickly the board produced a package.

It provides that Jimmy will not be required to continue his duties and responsibilities until his retirement date; that he will be given the title of Honorary Pro with all the privileges of of a Member of the Club without payment of dues; that he will continue to receive a salary until he is 65 years of age and retirement benefits thereafter which, together with income from other duties at the Club which he may take on, will not substantially reduce his current income. [759]

This may have been negotiated in exchange for a conciliatory public announcement from Jimmy, published in the *Happenings*:

I have been your pro at Hillcrest since the club was built, which is a long time. I have been wondering what would happen when it came time for my retirement. Last Saturday evening members of the Board of Directors presented for my approval a plan for my retirement. It is very generous and will permit me to give up my duties and responsibilities around the club and give me more time to play golf. Also, and most important, it will provide an adequate income for life with no worries for the future.

I want each of you to know that I am very grateful to the board of directors for this plan. It is the finest thing that could ever happen to me. I also want to thank you for your many courtesies all these years and express my appreciation for all the kindness you have shown me. [760]

A Jimmy Gullane testimonial dinner honored the old pro in June and the board presented an appreciation check to him.

Jimmy Gullane wags the check presented by the board at his retirement banquet in May 1954. Check presentation in the inset, Charles Klein and Gullane. Dwight Travis sits at the table. Klein is partly behind Gullane at center, Charles Selby is on the right. *Hillcrest Happenings*

The club had already found a replacement for the beloved first and only Hillcrest golf professional. He was Dwight Travis, an assistant pro at Wichita Country Club. Travis was born at Newkirk, Oklahoma, on 1 December 1922. As a child, his family moved to Arkansas City, Kansas, where the boy lived within sight of the Arkansas City Country Club. It is not known whether Dwight might have been introduced to the game as a caddy at that club's rolling golf course, overlooking a picturesque bend in the Walnut River.

However, in 1934, the family moved to Wichita, where he graduated from North High School in 1938. He did not play golf in high school, but after high school graduation, he organized a dance band that played around the Wichita area, and he took up golf. Travis played trumpet. During the World War II years, he traveled throughout the nation, playing in the Army-Navy Band. In 1947, he began work at

Wichita Country Club. In 1949, he married Betty Long, a singer in his band, and that same year he began working as an assistant pro at WCC, training as a golf professional under their great pro, Mike Murra.

Travis was probably Stewart Dewer's discovery, possibly the recommendation of Murra to Dewer. Lee Phillips says he remembers Travis as an assistant pro: nice, soft-spoken, and even-tempered. He was a trendy guy and may have proven himself as a successful merchandiser in the WCC golf shop - which was the stated problem when Hillcrest let Jimmy Gullane go. At HCC the golf shop merchandise was Travis' business, and he pushed it pretty hard.

Travis was never well liked by the general membership at Hillcrest: the women said he was a masher, he was gruff to the kids, he was rude to the old duffers, but he sure knew whom to butter up. He was a capable golfer and was a lifetime PGA class-A golf pro. One of the highlights of his golf career was that he once gave a golf lesson to President Dwight D. Eisenhower. Ike was a friend of Boots Adams and was in town for Boots' birthday, playing at Hillcrest in 1965. Yet, over the years, Travis' game proved very unreliable because he had a hair trigger temper, with a habit of blowing up over a missed shot.

After Boots and Dorothy Glynn Adams took up an interest in golf about 1960, Travis worked overtime, currying favor with the chairman and his wife. During this period, Travis enjoyed excursions to some of the nation's great golf spots, such as Palm Springs, California, with Boots and Ted Lyon, and some of the other top Phillips executives. Boots once told Jerry Cozby that he had believed Travis was underpaid and was in the habit of sending him $100 a month. Travis evidently understood this to be a tip for special treatment and responded with obsequious favoritism. In time, the toadying became so distasteful that Boots began to not like the man. Yet, Travis persisted at favoring some of the other more prominent members.

In the last two years that he was at Hillcrest he became a very serious diabetic, which is doubtless the explanation for what was probably a change in his temperament. His wife was also chronically ill, so that some of his erratic behavior might be credited to his own illness and home life. Other club employees who remember him, liked him, but concede that he had a problem with authority. In the end, the board decided the situation had to be rectified. Club President Harry Woods and Pop Freiberger were given the job of terminating his employment in September of 1969. When they talked to him, he said, "Why, you can't do that, I'll tell Boots Adams." Of course, Boots knew and Travis had no such recourse.

When Jerry Cozby was considering coming to Bartlesville, he interviewed Travis, who confided to Cozby that he had not done a good job at Hillcrest the last two years. Still, Jerry points out signs of some fine contributions that the second pro made when he was at HCC. Most notable is the large plaque-trophy that hangs on the south wall just outside the golf shop where it adjoins the mixed grill, recording all the Hillcrest golf club champions after Travis came in 1954. Travis and John Cronin were the principle donors for the $1,000 plaque. B. J. LeFlore gratefully remembers the generous support that Travis gave the Bartlesville Boy's Club, including old clubs, bags, and balls for the kids to play with. He was clearly very aggressive

Dwight Travis and Rookie Smith point to the plaque (which now hangs just outside the golf shop adjacent to the mixed grill) listing all of the Hillcrest men's golf champions after 1954. John Cronin and Travis purchased the plaque for $1,000. *Hillcrest Happenings.*

in getting important state tournaments to Hillcrest at least up until the last years.

Having observed Jimmy Gullane's termination, from the beginning he insisted on an excellent contract and good severance. After leaving Hillcrest, he remained in town for a couple of years, taking time to consider his options. In the middle 1970s, he opened the House of Golf in Tulsa, a retail shop that sold golfing clothes and equipment. He is remembered by Tulsans who knew him through the golf shop as an estimable fellow. He did guest teaching at Meadowbrook and at some other places in the Tulsa area. He died in Tulsa on 24 May 1986, and was buried at Newkirk, Oklahoma. [761]

The 1954 spring schedule, set up by Jimmy Gullane, continued amidst the hubbub. The annual four-ball tournament began immediately, and the women's annual spring handicap began two weeks later. Hillcrest president, Charles T. Klein won the Cities Service tournament on 25 May, and on 15 June he won the national Cities Service tournament. Ignoring the civic chill, during the tournament, Cities Service entertained the golfer's wives at a dinner at Hillcrest and provided a social notice to the newspaper. Charles Selby and George Tulloch won the four-ball on Memorial Day weekend. Warren Skaggs won the Reda tournament the next week. [762]

With school out, Elsie Parker and Martha Mae Beard again shepherded the junior golf program. Girl's classes were at 1:00 P.M. on Tuesdays and play was either before or after the lesson. Women's golf was very active in the summer. Mrs. Kenneth Grigsby won the annual spring medal tournament. Mrs. Hack Williford, the state women's champion, from Ponca City, won a field day on 12 June. Nine women from Hillcrest entered the State Women's Amateur Championship Tournament at Indian Hills Country Club in Tulsa. [763]

The state Junior AAU Golf Tournament was held at Hillcrest on 25 June. Forty-four boys from all over the state entered the tournament. Bartlesville's Dee Ketchum made a proud showing, but Ponca City's Jack Baldwin won the championship. [764]

While the boys were playing golf, the Chamber of Commerce held an anniversary celebration for 50 years with an open house at their downtown offices. After the annual meeting, the city began work on a face-lift for the old Civic Center. Meanwhile, the Chamber of Commerce expressed interest in a new all-purpose public auditorium or community center for the city. At the time they were looking toward the fair grounds for the project. [765]

Hillcrest had the usual Fourth of July festivities. Box suppers were served to 600 members and their families. Chris Criswell was in charge of the fireworks display. The finale was a cross and "Lest We Forget" blazoned in the night sky. [766]

By the end of June, the golf course was so dry there was danger of fire. There were only 54 entries for the 104° Flag Day tournament which was carried by Don Leisure. Right after the holiday, temperature began to really soar as qualifying rounds for the club championship began. In the mean time, Hillcrest was the host of the state Jaycees Junior Golf Tournament. It was 114° on the day the tournament began, and 117° (unofficial at HCC) on the afternoon Bob McAfee of Chickasha came in first place. The top 4 players went on to the national championship tournament in Albuquerque. While the boys played, on the other side of town, Don Wilkie staged a 114° match at Sunset between himself and Jimmy Gullane against Hank Maddix and Indian Hills pro, Jack Shields. Wilkie had already hired Jimmy Gullane for Sunset, and the match may have tweaked a few guilty souls at Hillcrest. While qualifying rounds for the FPMC tournament began in the now record heat, Bill Simpson reclaimed the title, to be Hillcrest club champion for 1954. Ken Pryor won the FPMC tournament in a sudden death play-off on 5 August. [767]

By August, the *Happenings* suggested that there was some discussion of air conditioning the ballroom. It is hard to imagine that the club had delayed this long in modernizing in this way. But, it is also understandable that the thick concrete construction would have made central air conditioning very difficult and expensive, and that the window unit alternative would have been noisy and unattractive. You can bet that after that hot summer, the membership developed a new enthusiasm for modernization. [768]

August golf play seemed only fit for women and girls. Junior girls continued their active schedule with weekly pairings and feature play. Hillcrest women hosted the Women's Tri-State Golf Association annual medal play tournament in the middle of August. Jean Ashley of Chanute was the tournament winner, but Hillcrest's Virginia Hubbell came in second. The men's city tournament qualifying rounds began before Labor Day, and Kay Browning ended the summer with the Junior Girls Golf title at Hillcrest. As the heat rolled on, Bill Simpson took the Labor Day city championship for the third time. [769]

The spring social season wound to a close at Hillcrest with the annual Doherty Auxiliary tea on 30 April, and the last Dinner-Dance Club on 21 May. But, once again, the Beaux Arts Ball was the social extravaganza of the year. Members came in costumes to suggest song titles. The deep summer saw only a few weddings brave the heat. [770]

On 19 September, Russell Blachley came from in the pack to win the handicap championship for 1954. It was finally the end of a sweltering summer.

Hillcrest hosted the Tri-State Women's Golf Association 36-hole medal play tournament, 17 to 18 August 1954. (left to right) Jean Ashley, a high school senior from Chanute, winner, Virginia Hubbell, 2nd place, and Evelyn Grigsby, 3rd place. *Courtesy Virginia Hubbell Collection.*

A break in the temperatures came very late, on 21 September dropping to 72° following a 102° day. The annual women's handicap began that week. Mrs. A. B. Cook became the handicap champion. The Chamber of Commerce defeated the Jaycees team for their annual championship on 6 October. The annual women's awards luncheon was held on 31 October. The last golf event of the year was a women's exhibition and clinic on 10 November, featuring Marilyn Smith, a pro from Wichita. [771]

H. R. Straight's 80th birthday party, 8 October 1954, is an example of one of the very elegant private parties of the era. Society turned out in black ties and evening dresses for a reception, banquet and dance. Receiving guests at the front door, Katherine Straight, Lois Straight, and Harriet Straight Stevens, background between Katherine and Lois are H. R. Straight and Nodie Phillips. Later, the guests are seated in the ball room. The first course on the table is shrimp cocktail. The new chandeliers, window treatments, and the smoked glass mirrors around the mantel were the fruit of the 1951 redecoration by San Antonio decorator, Mildred English.

The reporting of the fall social season was flat, with only monthly square dance parties and Dinner-Dance Club showing up. The Doherty Auxiliary produced an annual banquet that rated a full-page spread on 21 November. But there was lots of exciting progress on the civic front. The Chamber of Commerce Modernization Committee had been at work, trying to get merchants to spiff up their downtown storefronts. Another full-page spread showed some of the 15 stores and businesses that had added new facades in order to look more up to date. Civic initiatives promoted after the annual Chamber of

Commerce banquet on 26 September included an industrial expansion drive, more demand for water in the suburban developments, and new Central Airlines schedules. There was an exciting announcement that Cities Service was adding an up-to-date-looking annex adjoining to the south of their 1919 office building. With water available south of town, homes in Country Club Terrace sprang up like mushrooms on the old Dahlgren estate. By fall, 12 houses were already built in this trendy new neighborhood across from the country club, and 2 more houses were planned. Just before Christmas, St. Luke's Episcopal Church announced the construction of their elegant – and decidedly not Modern - English Gothic style church building, adjoining the newly erected parish house. [772]

That a great deal of the problem with social reporting can be credited to new policy at the newspaper, growing since the 1947 purchase of the *Examiner-Enterprise* by Reynolds, finally becomes documentable in October. Cities Service press release dated 7 October 1954, announcing H. R. Straight's 80th birthday party on 8 October, generated articles in the *Tulsa World* and *The Bradford Era* (Bradford, Pennsylvania), but not a word in the Bartlesville newspaper.

The gala was a classic Bartlesville command social performance. There were 128 guests at the event, with numerous congratulatory letters and telegrams from out-of-town friends. The men wore black tuxedos and the wives wore the most elegant ball gowns of the era. Smiling, laughing friends wound through the long receiving line. Herbert and Katherine Straight took seats at the head table that was piled high with elegant chrysanthemum arrangements, immediately in front of the huge fireplace. Others sat at long tables of 20, each table with smaller centerpieces. Speeches, toasts, and testimonials punctuated the dinner. Photos show they enjoyed a soup course, salad, shrimp cocktail, a main course, ice tea, pie for dessert and coffee after dinner. The crowd lingered in the lounge afterwards, and danced to the music of a small combo. It was a huge, very important party, and nary a word reported in the local paper. It can be surmised that very many important events similarly escape our memory. [773]

The reporting on the Christmas social season was once again sparse. The clubhouse was beautifully decorated for the season with many Christmas trees of different sizes, and with ropes of greenery over the doors and windows, colored lights, ornaments, and wreaths. Yet, the only two parties reported were a junior high dance on 5 December, and the annual sons and daughters Christmas dance, held 30 December. Of course, there was the usual monthly square dance, and Dinner-Dance Club. Phillips held its annual Christmas Show in the Adams Building. An eager crowd of 5,000 Bartians gathered for opening night on 16 December. The K. S. Adamses had the flashiest social event of the season, an open house at their home on Christmas Day. A good soaking one-inch rain appeared to break the long drought on 27 December. Winter set in the next day with frigid rain, then sleet and snow, reaching 10 1/2 inches by the next day. [774]

Slick roads didn't hinder the Phillips New Years dance at the Adams building, or the annual New Years Ball at Hillcrest.

It had been quite a year. The first trouble in Vietnam flared up. But, who would guess the significance? The Supreme Court finally decreed desegregation of the public schools. Who would guess that significance, either? Another election year saw Bob Kerr re-elected to the U. S. Senate and Raymond Gary elected governor. Locally there had been prosperity and growth, with the addition of several new landmarks to the city skyline.

1955

In January 1955, the club saw the now familiar utilization by Dinner-Dance club, the monthly square dance, and Mercredi Club returned for its monthly luncheons. The Annual Meeting on 19 January 1955 elected new Hillcrest board members. The new board was John Houchin, Gerald Preston, J. A. Young, Mac Wallace, Jim McColl, Don Gordon, Charles Selby, Chuck Klein, and John Tyler. John Houchin was elected president. It was not a happy meeting. The year-end balance sheet for 1954 found the club with a $12,000 deficit. On 2 February a committee appointed by the board met to consider proposals from the meeting concerning memberships. On 17 February, there was a special stockholders meeting. It appears there was discussion of increasing the number of members in order to meet budgetary shortfalls. The membership unanimously favored raising fees. Initiation was raised from $100 to $250, monthly dues were raised from $15 to $20, and all other classes of memberships were raised $2 a month. The board further recommended that any future proposals to increase the number of memberships should be accompanied with a plan, including costs of expansion. It is clear that in 1955, the membership was not prepared to shoulder the expense of expansion of the facilities, and that leadership had thrown a wet blanket on the idea. The other problem discussed at the meeting evolved from the cap on the number of memberships. Though the stock officially sold for $100, individuals had fallen into the habit of selling their shares for many times the posted price. It is said that at the height of the frenzy, Foster Doornbos had the dubious distinction of paying the highest price of $900 for his stock. Of course, these unseemly profits were not coming to the club, but being pocketed by the sellers. The board put an end to the practice, requiring former members to sell their shares to the club. Despite the fiscal conservatism of the board, the new fees may have provided funds to finally air condition the clubhouse during the summer. [775]

The Beaux Arts Ball returned as the feature of the winter season. The Joe Linde orchestra from Tulsa played the dance music. The costume theme was book titles. Yet, there was no full-page spread of society reporting this year, instead only a small photo in the *Happenings*. March featured a dance with the Henry Busse orchestra from Chicago. The meetings of Mercredi Club, and Dinner-Dance Club continued in the spring. Doherty Auxiliary's spring tea warranted the only major social notice. There were signs that some of the alternative sights around town were losing luster for civic events. The Bar Association entertained their wives at a Hillcrest spring banquet. For the first time in several years, the high school prom abandoned the College High gym in favor of the Hillcrest ballroom. [776]

The Beaux Arts Ball, an annual early spring costume party, was usually the party of the year during the 1950s. In 1955, Elmer and Vivian Gallery went dressed as hillbillies. *Hillcrest Happenings, March 1955.*

Indoor golf lessons (in the ballroom) commenced on 26 January for 55 enthusiastic ladies. The Women's Golf Association got organized for the season early in February. Margye Ward was the new president. It was decided to continue sponsoring junior golf, and Dwight Travis and his assistant, Rookie Smith, agreed to continue indoors golf instructions until the weather permitted regular play. It was just as well, the extreme weather pattern of the last few years continued. A big dust storm roared through on 11 March, and temperatures set new records, grazing 90°. A week later, 2 inches of snow blanketed the city. College High Wildcat golf began practices at Hillcrest early in April. The high school team consistently used Hillcrest for their home course for several years. Their first 1955 tournament was on 12 April. [777]

Bartlesville inaugurated a long and significant tradition in mid-April. The first science fair was held at College High. Students from Bartlesville elementary, junior high, and high schools, including Douglass, and St. John's brought entries, and winners planned to

Dwight Travis and Rookie Smith gave the Women's Golf Association indoor golf lessons during the winter, until the weather permitted outside play. Betty Sneed (McCullough), Ruth Selby, Marge Maltby, and Helen Wheatly line up for lessons. *Hillcrest Happenings, February 1955.*

attend the state science fair. Science was on everyone's mind as the community organized one of the first mass vaccination drives in the country, vaccinating 1600 school children in only 2 hours with the new Salk vaccine for polio. Supply problems subsequently developed and consequently for many months Washington County was the only area of the state that was vaccinated. [778]

John Cronin and Stewart Dewer were captains of the annual stag team match on 30 April. There was a robust turnout for the opening event. Johnnie Welty, the women's association publicity chairman, was doing the best job in years of reporting their weekly activities. Alf Holl won the Cities Service district tournament on 24 May. But, Calgary golfer, Don Anderson won the company tournament on 14 June. Heavy weather that blew in on the weekend of deadly tornados at Blackwell, Oklahoma, and Udall, Kansas, and rained out the Reda Pump tournament that was won by Pete Livingston in Monday play, 30 May [779].

Jim Conaster was selected to be chairman of the annual Jaycees junior golf tournament. A good time was anticipated by all, so that his friends even volunteered that "he hits more balls on Starview Farms than he does on Number 8 at Hillcrest." Notwithstanding the leadership, Dee Ketchum was the one who took top honors at the tournament on 10 June. Charles Selby and Bill Simpson represented Hillcrest at the Oklahoma Amateur golf tournament at Muskogee, while Hillcrest girls participated in the first AAU Junior Olympic Golf Tournament, played at Hillcrest. Once again, Bill Simpson was not defending his club championship, when the 1955 tournament got underway on 18 June. Ken Pryor emerged with the title. Summertime Hillcrest social activity decided to feature golf with a buffet following golf and Spey Fields and his "Rippling Rhythm" for

Women's Oklahoma Go f Association, 6th Annual Junior Girls Championship Tournament, 28 June 1955. (left to right) Nancy Stone, Virginia Hubbell, Marianne Looney (Ponca City, Pres. OkWGA), Patty Davis, Martha Painter, Mrs. W. A. Hughes, Ginger Emerson. *Courtesy Virginia Hubbell Collection.*

entertainment on the last weekend of June, after the championship tournament. [780]

After the Fourth of July, the annual four-ball tournament was played, followed by the FPMC Championship, finished on 2 August with Tom Holl the 1955 champion. The City Championship tournament started on Labor Day weekend, and Bill Simpson wrapped up another championship in play at Sunset on 6 September. The men's handicap championship was played in September. [781]

Phillips Petroleum Company announced that a contract had been awarded to build the new Research Center west of town. The growth of the research facilities became a great boon to many aspects of the Bartlesville community.

Dwight Travis led the Bartlesville contingency in the Oklahoma Open Golf Tournament at Southern Hills in September. His visibility at the tournament was a public relations success for the new Hillcrest pro. The Chamber of Commerce did it again in No-

vember, trouncing the Jaycees in their annual tournament. [782]

Fall social activities continued with the usual Western parties and Dinner-Dance Club, sprinkled with occasional small luncheons. Once again, Doherty Girls held their anniversary banquet in November. The Board of Directors issued new house rules for the clubhouse, pool, and golf course. With special exceptions, men were to always wear jackets. That it was stressed probably indicates that over the summer, some were taking off their coats and that with the new air conditioning they were re-establishing standards. [783]

The December Dinner-Dance Club took advantage of the beautiful clubhouse Christmas decorations on 18 December. The dining room was decorated with holiday greens, Christmas candles, and assorted Christmas balls. The 104 Dance Club members danced to the Bates Hunt orchestra A spectacular life-sized Santa Claus graced the alcove off the living room, and pink was the theme color. The junior high crowd had a formal Christmas dance with the Don Elkins orchestra playing the music. Of course, the annual New Years ball was planned to ring in 1956. [784]

The Rest of the Fifties

The remaining years of the 1950s at Hillcrest followed the familiar established patterns of long standing. In 1956, Charles Selby was elected president of the club; J. W. McColl in 1957, and Tom Cubbage in 1958. Charles Selby says that there was no talk of plans for a new clubhouse during his time as president. The year-end statement for 1955 showed improved financial status, but by December 1956 things had sagged back into trouble. There was quite a bit of red ink in the clubhouse expenses, but the main difficulty was a loan to install a new golf course watering system (it is essentially the same system in operation today). At the February board meeting monthly

dues were raised $5.00. It was the first raise in 6 years. In those inflationary years it is no wonder they got behind. By the spring of 1957, there was a club improvement committee active and Club President J. W. McColl announced,

You will receive plans soon for a clubhouse improvement. This has been sorely needed for a long time. Plans are now in shape to submit for your approval. This will be done as soon as possible. [786]

The Price Tower was dedicated 10 February 1956. The crowd stands outside at the dedication. Across Dewey Street, the friendly old neighborhood houses were still standing next to the beautiful new Presbyterian Kirk, a monument to traditional architecture, all soon to be swept away by the tidal wave of Modernism. *Courtesy Bartlesville Area History Museum.*

After the grim January financial report the 28 March membership letter about the new ideas was decidedly upbeat. A formal letter to stockholders, seeking to raise $150,000 to remodel the club house went out on 28 June, and had already received significant support. The board decided that a minimum of 300 members must contribute. On 6 December President McColl sent out a disappointing letter that the necessary funds had not become available. [787] Though nothing finally seems to have come of the initiative, because of the newspaper article, we have a rare complete listing of the board at the time of the seminal thinking about clubhouse changes. Tom Cubbage was vice president and Bob Durand secretary-treasurer. Directors were John Houchin, J. A. Young, Gerald Preston, Harris Bateman, Clint Beard, Mac Wallace, Doyle Matberry, Gene Wilson, and Hal Price. Bateman chaired the greens committee, Mayberry tournaments, Beard house, Preston finance, and Jim Akright social activity. Pat Johnson, formerly from Oklahoma City Golf and Country Club, was hired as the new club manager.

There was good newspaper coverage of the golf events. After ceding the 1955 championship to Ken Pryor, Bill Simpson entered the 1956 championship at the end of May, loaded for bear. The final round with Tom Preston 4 June, was very close, but on the back nine, "Simpson's putter got hot…" and again he won the club championship. The women's golf association began match play in June. They also supervised the junior golf program that had its first meeting on 27 May. Paddy Hughes, Virginia Hubbell, Agnes Foster, and Iris Knight were the sponsors. Many of today's most enthusiastic golfers at Hillcrest got their start in the fine youth program that was fostered by the women's association in the 1950s. Iris Knight won the Women's Flag Day Tournament on 17 June. Lynn Gray won the Jaycees tournament, and Pete Livings-

ton won the Reda tournament.

Tucked amidst the summer golf, two high profile social events popped up. A high school social club, the Les Des, had a tea that garnered a full page of photos and among the many weddings. Naturally, the parties for the Foster Doornbos wedding drew special attention. [789]

Reese Tucker won the Cities Service District golf tournament. Early in August, the women hosted 6 visiting clubs. The boys held a tournament at midmonth. Bill Davis was the winner. Immediately the girls started a tournament. Kay Browning won for the second year. Bill Emerson won the FPMC tournament. After two months delay, the four ball winners were Tom Cubbage, Reese Tucker, Jim McColl and Larry Wright. The handicap championship began on 22 September, with Bill Emerson winning on 25 September; the women began their handicap tournament on 23 September, with Joan Simpson claiming the championship just before the Oklahoma Open began. [790]

It was a fairly quiet election year, with Dwight Eisenhower running for a second term, but it was the summer of the Suez crisis, and the beginnings of the school integration confrontations that would rock the country the next year. Governor Gary's administrative assistant and State Senator Russell were indicted for voting fraud in Wagoner County during the primary election, a scandal that grew during the year and probably influenced the election of J. Howard Edmonson as governor. In Bartlesville, middle-America normalcy kept the focus on golf and weddings and a new city bond election.

In 1956, Hillcrest spent about $60,000 installing a fairway watering system, but poor quality water from the Caney River, especially in the ongoing drought retarded the club's ability to keep the grass in prime condition even though the Oklahoma Open was scheduled for play at Hillcrest in October. In August, Sunset Country Club announced they would be building a new larger, modern clubhouse, expanding their membership programs to include a social membership, and adding a swimming pool. This was new pressure for Hillcrest Club Improvement Committee. [791]

The first round of the 1956 Oklahoma Open was played on Wednesday, 2 October, and the club welcomed the guests with a social hour in the cocktail lounge and ballroom after the rounds were finished. At the end of the week, Jimmy Gauntt claimed the title for the third year in a row. We know from the published program for the 1956 Oklahoma Open some membership statistics for Hillcrest at the time: 350 members, 22 non-resident, 35 lady members, 71 associate members, 8 special members, and 1 junior member. This was a much healthier membership than that of only seven years earlier. [792]

Least the lack of society reporting give the impression that Hillcrest parties had taken a more staid turn since the good old days, we have some references to heavy partying at Hillcrest during those years from *The Mullendore Murder*. Interviewed by the author, Mullendore Ranch manager, Chub Anderson said of E. C. Mullendore, "he might be a little tight or something, but this was at parties or at the Bartlesville country club." Some even said that in the middle 1960s, the couple bought a house in the fancy new Kenilworth Addition, along the south edge of the country club where the stables once stood, in order to be closer to the club. [793]

With The State Amateur Tournament scheduled at Hillcrest in June of 1957, after years of severe drought, greenskeeper Henry Manley had his work cut out for him in the spring. Manley had been in charge of the greens since 1943, and knew the whole history of this classic Perry Maxwell course. The new watering system was a big help, but as luck would have it, they had a wet spring. To get ready, the greens were being airified and fertilized.

Present work on the club includes deep drilling and the replacing of the soil with a mixture of soil peat moss and sand that will drain off any salt from the river water. The greens are to be verticut and get fertilization plus seeding in the weak portions of the turf.

The course has a total of 38 traps, 20 in the front nine and 18 in the back. All of these are to be resanded and trimmed. Routine treatment is due the big trees.

In reserve for use on greens should it be needed is a huge new 24,000 square foot nursery which is half Seaside bent and half C-7. Present greens are in Seaside. Eventually the club hopes to have all 18 greens in C-7. Two of these may be sodded in late this year.

Hampering work on the greens has been a shortage of suitable soil. Nine samples were rejected from the course property and nine others from Bartlesville area before a usable one was discovered east of Dewey. [794]

Spring play was normal in 1957, with the spring women's handicap, the start of junior golf, and the first rounds of the club championship running right up to the beginning of play for the State Amateur Golf Tournament. Late in May, they were still short on caddies, but Dwight Travis was holding a caddie clinic at the Boys Club. Despite the effort there was a shortage of caddies at the tournament. [795]

On Monday, 9 June, the state amateur tournament opened with the Pro-Am. The next morning, rain threatened to scratch the tournament, but the skies cleared just in time to bake up a steam bath.

Hillcrest members Charles Selby, Howard Lambdin, Art Gorman, and Harris Bateman qualified for the championship flight on Wednesday. Still, the rains continued all week, with 5 inches on Thursday delaying the game 3 hours, and gray skies and rain marking even the the finals. OSU golfer, Bobby Goetz, skimmed "through the opposition like water skiers over the soggy Hillcrest Country Club course." [796]

No more did the tournament end, than the high school crowd held a dance at the clubhouse and junior golf held its organizational meeting with Elsie Parker and Martha May Beard again acting as sponsors from the women's golf association. The annual Reda tournament kicked off. [797]

Hillcrest Country Club held its first reported swim meet on 7 July. Besides the 5 competitive events, there were exhibitions by some visiting high school and college champions, and some fun events. [798]

Bill Simpson again claimed the club championship on 13 July. Phil Rippy won the local Cities Service golf tournament and looked forward to representing Bartlesville at the company-wide tournament in August. The DMF golf tournament began on 18 August. Kay Browning and Mark Mayberry won their respective junior girls and boys championships. Ransome Wiggins won the city championship, played at Hillcrest in 1957, after a closely fought final round that required 4 extra holes. Earl Schultz won the FPMC championship in another close contest that was played at both HCC and Sunset for the first time. [799]

As the schools opened in September, to everyone's relief, Bartlesville schools integrated smoothly, but the nation watched the desegregation crisis unfold in Little Rock that fall. Meanwhile, Washington County stockmen were quarantined by an Anthrax epidemic that crept in from Rogers County during the summer. It took most of the fall to resolve the hazard to local agriculture. Still, there was good local news. It was announced that a dial telephone system was planned for Bartlesville (and finally implemented in 1959).

With the dearth of newspaper reporting, by this time *Hillcrest Happenings* had absorbed virtually all of the social reporting that members deemed necessary. The October 1957, *Happenings* reported all of the month's activities, showing a busy regular schedule: 5 October Scotch Foursome, 12 October Western Night, 19 October Central High Dance, 26 October Halloween Party, 26 October Club Dance, along with dances already planned for November and December. Regular club business proceeded as usual. [800]

On 21 January 1958, Jack Straight, Bob Durand, Tom Cubbage, and Larry Wright were elected to the board at the annual meeting. Tom Cubbage was elected president. The year-end financial statement show considerable improvement "due largely to increased dues and decreased cost of operating the golf course, which was partially offset by increased administration cost and reduced revenues from the dining room, grill, and lounge." [801]

Even though there is thin evidence of social events, it does not mean that there was any change from the long-established patterns at Hillcrest. The Beaux Arts Ball was held on 14 March 1958, as it had been for several years, and would be for years into the future. As in the past, it was the biggest event of the spring season and everyone turned out in outlandish costume. The Western night parties had expanded beyond the core of square dance enthusiasts to include a large number of "watchers and card players." Monthly juke box parties were being held for the College High kids, and another party for the Central Junior High kids too. The last dinner dance of the season was held on 16 May. At that party, George Downs added a new note of humor by posting a spreadsheet of sorts, listing the women in columns of tall, medium, and short by blonde, brunette, and miscellaneous for purposes of assigning dance partners. By June, the youth parties had moved to poolside with a charge of $1.50. A change was made in the Fourth of July routine when the annual fried chicken box supper was changed to a buffet, and of course the evening was crowned with the best fireworks on town. There was a buffet dinner and dance on Labor Day weekend. The children's Halloween party was especially well done with spider webs on the ceilings and in the corners, and "bodies" in the lobby, and a scary witch in the TV room. Dinner-Dance Club season resumed on 21 November. The Central High semi-formal dance was scheduled for 5 December, and the College High Christmas dance was 27 December.

The 1958 golf season began with the annual organizational luncheon meeting for the Hillcrest Women's Golf Association on 5 February. Iris Knight won the annual ladies spring tournament in May. Bill Simpson took the annual men's spring four ball. Jack Maddux, Jr. won the annual club championship on 9 June. Meanwhile, Elsie Parker and Martha Mae Beard again sponsored the junior golf programs that began on 27 May. Hillcrest youth also enjoyed special swimming events and a swim meet that were scheduled as part of the 4th of July celebrations. [803]

J. C. Net won the annual Reda Pump golf tournament on 2 July. Jim McColl narrowly won the Cities Service DMF championship. The junior golf tournaments were held on 10 through 16 August. Bill Davis and Susan McDonald were the boys and girls champions, receiving trophies at the awards banquet afterwards. The Cities Service national championship was played at the end of August and Bob Crabtree of Kansas City walked away with the honors. Frank

Pierce won the FPMC championship that was played at both Hillcrest and Sunset in September. Two weeks later the men's Calcutta ended in a tie between Virgil Daniel, Jack Leonard, and Larry Wright. It was tie week - the fall women's handicap championship ended in a tie between Iris Knight and Lois Mayo. The women ended the season with the annual awards luncheon, a tacky party. But the 1958 season was not finished until the very end. Three holes-in-one were reported in the last week of December. Harry Woods scored his very first ace on 27 December, then, on a foggy 31 December morning, Cotton Fry and Ty Cobb both landed aces. [804]

The year 1958 was a landmark year for other reasons. Central Christian College closed its doors in Bartlesville after the spring semester, and moved to Oklahoma City. It was a blow to Bartlesville. Higher education had long been a felt need in the community and the city had worked hard to support this local college. The old H. V. Foster La Quinta estate was put up for sale, a sad realtors sign along the old Tulsa Road in the country club neighborhood. As coincidence would have it, at that very time the Pilgrim Holiness Church had decided to relocate their Colorado Springs, Colorado, Bible college. They were looking for a good place to move. It just happened, on a hot summer day, one of the denomination's leaders, C. B. Colaw, was driving through Bartlesville and had a flat tire. While at the service station, getting the tire fixed, he heard about the local college site that was for sale. In November, the Pilgrim Holiness Board of General Superintendents voted to purchase the Bartlesville property. A year later, they voted to also merge their El Monte, California college with the Bartlesville school that would become Central Pilgrim College. At first, before the 1968 denominational merger with The Wesleyan Church, it was a secondary boarding school and Bible college. It has grown into a well-respected Christian liberal arts college, now university, the answer to Bartlesville's long-held educational aspirations. [805]

That same year, a friend of Dorothy Glynn Adams came to visit from San Antonio. Sue Rugh held a small ladies luncheon at her house, inviting Betty Pettigrove, Louise Houchin, and Keitha Davis to meet Carlotta Hartman, Dorothy Glynn's friend. The luncheon conversation drifted toward Carlotta's Junior League activities in San Antonio. The Bartlesville women wished they had an organization like that. But, Bartlesville was too small to qualify for Junior League membership. Before the afternoon was out, the women resolved to organize a women's club in Bartlesville, modeled on the San Antonio Junior League. A short time later they had an organizational luncheon at the home of Jane Rowland, inviting the 19 women who became the charter members of Bartlesville Service League. Never anticipating the importance of their actions, in one fell swoop this group of leading women asserted total dominance of the social hegemony of Bartlesville, totally changing the hierarchy of women's activities. The importance of Service League in the long-term civic success of Bartlesville cannot be overstated. The Service League projects of the Bargain Box and the Youth Canteen are social service fixtures in the city. Their first fundraiser was a "Night on the Town" review held at the Adams Building. It was so much fun that the people who participated are still animated when they talk about it. The social capital generated through this women's organization has driven civic initiatives such as the Bartlesville Civic Ballet, the Bartlesville Symphony, the Bartlesville Choral Society, and OKMozart, building the new Community Center and the new Bartlesville Public Library, among countless

others. [806]

1959 would be a landmark year too. 1 January headlines sobered the New Year with Fidel Castro moving his rebel forces into Havana, and a Russian rocket making a New Years pass by the moon. Heavy snow blanketed Bartlesville that day. The evening news dithered about whether Castro was a communist, as the new dictator wasted no time in beginning a bloodbath of political executions that very week. Even though times were scary, business was pretty good even with chronic inflation pressures and high taxes.

According to the annual reports, presented at the annual stockholders meeting in January 1959, 1958 was a banner year for Hillcrest. The years of hard work, and the national prosperity were paying off. The membership elected three new boards members: Harry Burlingame, Ken Rugh, and F. E. McLeod. Harris Bateman was elected president, Larry Wright became vice president, and Bob Durand became secretary-treasurer at the subsequent board meeting. In 1958, the board established a reserve fund. The year would be one in which the club leadership would wrestle with the growing needs of the country club, and a growing idea that some improvement of the clubhouse, or even a new clubhouse, was needed.

Regular winter social activity continued to be the monthly Dinner-Dance Club, and the Western night party. Bingo had became a very popular new weekly activity that year. The Women's Golf Association held the first meeting of the year on 4 February, but weekly icy weather systems suppressed any urge to hit the links well into April.

Washington County turned out in big numbers to vote in the 7 April election to repeal prohibition. Still, the liquor stores didn't open until Labor Day. At last members could eliminate the silly practice of hiding bottles in their golf lockers. The new law required people to bring their own bottles of liquor to bars or restaurants. At first Hillcrest members brought their own bottles to the club when they came, but quickly enough, a more sophisticated practice evolved. They made a deposit of $7.00 for a beverage locker that they maintained themselves. A September letter outlined a new further improvement. The House Committee called it the "HCC Unit Syndicate." The purpose of the Syndicate was "to purchase, care for, and dispense beverages." There was a $10.00 deposit and the member was billed for replacement costs. Eventually each member submitted a list of the liquor stock he wished to maintain, then HCC collected a liquor fee from members that, in theory, was to buy their personal supply of liquor that was then kept in the bar for their use. This was the practice until "liquor by the drink" was eventually passed in a similar referendum.

There was new external pressure on the improvement committee to assess needs at Hillcrest and come up with a proposal. In March 1959, Sunset announced improvements to the clubhouse, a big new putting clock, and improvements on the golf course would be ready to open the spring season. Meanwhile, the Elks Club was putting finishing touches on its elegant new modern lodge at a new site southeast of the city. Their splashy open house was in May.

The Hillcrest men opened their golf season with their annual stag. On 26 April, Art Gorman's team of "wets" soundly defeated John Hoyt's "drys." Wet, cool weather, punctuated with floods and alternating with steamy heat, continued to plague the golf season until late summer, quite a change from the drought of only a year ago. Junior golf organized right after school was out in May. The city junior golf championship was played at Sunset right before Memorial Day with the HCC boys taking the day. Right

Hillcrest Women's Golf Association 1 June 1959: (left to right) Betty (Sneed) McCullough, Lynn Leisure, unknown , Virginia Hubbell, Isobel Beechwood, Betty Kistner, Iris Knight, Betty Burris, Lorraine Disney. *Courtesy Virginia Hubbell Collection.*

after the holiday Lynn Leisure won the John Cronin Women's Handicap Championship. The next day, the men's club championship began. Bill Simpson again emerged with the club championship on 15 June. [809]

Charles Klein won the Cities Service championship on 20 July, and the company's national championship on 24 August. Sunseter Hank Mattix won the city golf championship on Labor Day weekend at Hillcrest. Glen Patterson won the Frank Phillips Men's Club championship. Men's play wound up the season on 21 September with a tie between George Wash and W. D. Engelbrecht for the handicap championship. [810]

At the beginning of the fall season, Hillcrest women were delighted to have new tee markers. The HWGA finished the season in October, with Evelyn Grigsby taking women's handicap championship. They celebrated the end of the season on 29 October with a tacky party picnic, and Lynn Leisure celebrated the end of her successful year with a hole in one. [811]

Club manager Pat Johnson left in September. He took a position in San Antonio, Dorothy Glynn Adams old stomping grounds. He had been a very successful and popular manager. The new manager, Earl Hedges, was on board fairly quickly. He was an Oklahman from Enid where he attended Phillips University. After World War II service where he was a commissary officer, he spent his career in food service management, most recently from the Ramada Inn in Tulsa. He is probably the one who initiated the bingo parties on Thursday nights about this time. Bingo night consisted of a "happy hour," a buffet, and bingo. It was considered family entertainment and was very popular with the membership. The year-end balance sheet had the usual losses in the clubhouse operation and new expenditures on the golf course, but the finance committee seems to have been quite pleased

with Mr. Hedges' management. [812]

1960 saw a development of thinking about club improvement turn toward interest in a new clubhouse. The new board members were Fred Wallingford, Jim McColl, Charles Musgrave, and Gerald McGrew, Larry Wright was elected president. Other members were assigned committees: Vice President, Harry Burlingame, had the House Committee, with Bob Musgrave his assistant, Jack Straight was membership chairman, Tom Cubbage was greens committee, Jim McColl had the Long Range Planning Committee, and F. E. McLeod. The organization of the board showed no special signs of early movement toward the new clubhouse. [813]

However, there were signs of a push to keep the membership full and active. For example, the Women's Golf Association was already planning for the 1961 Women's State Golf Tournament, in addition they continued their sponsorship of junior golf, and they additionally decided to sponsor junior bridge lessons in the summer. Dwight Travis gave 4 free golf lessons in the spring. The women planned a series of fundraisers, including a modeling lessons luncheon, hoping to generate $1500 for the 1961 golf tournament. After a series of parties, charm schools, and similar efforts, HWGA resorted to a raffle. The women's association bought a Ford Valiant for $2,145 and raffled tickets to raise the final $1,000. It was posed as the patriotic duty to Hillcrest for members to pick up a book of tickets to sell for the ladies. Meanwhile, the pressure was on, with the Class of '35 holding its 25th reunion at the fancy new Elks Club. [814]

The golf season took a normal pattern. The men's four-ball opened the season as usual. Earl Porter and W. B. Engelbrecht took the honors. The Jaycees Junior Golf Tournament was played at Hillcrest that year. The summer held its usual full compliment of company tournaments: DMF, Reda, and FPMC. The club championship began on 12 June. Jack Maddux took that coveted title on 20 June. Hillcrest girls and boys each held tournaments in August. HWGA held its complete panoply of women's weekly pairings, feature play, Scotch Foursomes, and guest days. They held their spring John Cronin medal tournament in May. Mary Dunn was the victor. They hosted the Tulsa District ladies, and 18 women played in the Tri-State tournament at Sunset in July. In the summer heat someone must have indulged the unthinkable, for the August meeting of the board passed a new ruling that shirts must be worn on the golf course at all times. [815]

The annual E-E city golf tournament, to be held at Sunset over Labor Day weekend, was canceled because Don Wilkie said the new sprinkler system wasn't working right, but Hillcrest filled the void with a lot of hoopla around their bind bogey golf tournament the last weekend in August. On the fifth green, players shot at targets for prizes. There was a dinner after the contest, and everyone got a green and white Hillcrest golf cap. The men finished the season in September with Tom Huffman taking the annual handicap championship. The WGA handicap champion turned out to be Mary Dolman. [816]

In September a Hillcrest Modernization Planning Committee was formed. K. S. Adams (the chairman of Phillips Petroleum Company) agreed to serve as chairman. Other members were: Armais Artunoff (chairman of Reda Pump), Scott Beesley (president of Union National Bank), H. W. Burlingame (developer), B. F. Buff (National Zinc), John F. Cronin (First National Bank), J. S. Dewer (Phillips Petroleum Company), R. L. Kidd (president of Cities Service), H. C. Price (Chairman, H.C. Price Company), and L. H. Wright (Phillips Petroleum Company and chairman of the board of Hillcrest Country Club). "The committee has agreed to study, recommend, and implement a program for the replacement or modernization of our Clubhouse." The members of this committee and their charge indicate that the decision had finally been made to move on the long-discussed changes at the clubhouse. [817]

The 1950s was an era of many texts and subtexts. At the end of World War I, F. Scott Fitzgerald observed that his contemporaries were "a new generation dedicated more than the last to the fear of poverty and the worship of success; grown up to find all Gods (sic) dead, all wars fought, all faiths in man shaken." If that was so of the generation after the Great War, it was true in spades of the generation who survived the Great Depression and World War II. Their generation lived at the apotheosis of the age of psychology; the age of the expert; the age of bigger is better and old is quaint; the full expression of Modernism. And yet, the young Turks who took the reins after the war also partook in one of the great religious revivals in American history, modeling idealistic family values, deep patriotism, and civic duty. They were Americans, not cynical Europeans, and they had that sense of optimism that is characteristically American. They were Cold Warriors and capitalists.

In those years, Bartlesville saw the passing of the older generation that had built the community to put it on the national map. One of the casualties, along with many of the charming old-fashioned landmarks, was the overt understanding of the purpose of the country club. Hillcrest seemed to see itself and the community seemed to feel that Hillcrest Country Club existed as an exclusive social organization. The original overt purpose, that the country club primarily had civic function, to build Bartlesville, seemed to have passed from consciousness. Yet, despite the amnesia, Hillcrest still functioned as an engine, essential to the community, for the generation of social capital.

14

HOLE NUMBER FOURTEEN.
391 Yards, Par 4. Strictly a placement shot from the tee –
slight dogleg right with a fairway that slopes left.
Landing area is only another 230 yards off the tee. Stay away from driver.
Second shot usually downwind and will play one club less.
Small green: 4,000 square feet.

15

HOLE NUMBER FIFTEEN.
408 Yards, Par 4. You are on the last leg of the Golden Triangle.
I hope you are even par. This hole is a dogleg left at 270 yards off the tee.
Stay down the right side – left side of fairway will block shot to green.
This green is 5,000 square feet and split level.

CHAPTER EIGHT

Camelot:
THE *New* CLUBHOUSE

A faint, "beeeep, beep, beep, beep," (_... ..._ ___, Morse code for BVO, the call letters of the Bartlesville VOR), then a male voice, "Bartlesville (pause) omni," over and over again, blended with the drone of the twin Rolls Royce Dart turbo-props. On a vector of 067°, Clarence Clark slightly backed off the throttle of the G–1. The new Gulfstream aircraft, painted with the jaunty Phillips Petroleum Company colors and the bright new logo, slowly descending into the bumpy lower altitude, looking for the Bartlesville airfield just beyond the Osage Hills. The tall buildings of Bartlesville's modern skyscrapers were already in sight. Back in the cabin, Boots Adams sat comfortably, intently visiting with Saudi Prince Izzatt Gaafer, both men relieved to be near the end of their flight from Palm Springs. Even at 300 mph, the flight still took a chunk out of a day.

On a family vacation that went around the world in the summer of 1958, Boots Adams had caught a grand vision for Phillips Petroleum Company. [819] Since then, he had intently focused on the company's worldwide operations and cultivated international contacts to build the company into a major player in international oil operations, chemicals, and refining. At this airport, as the two men alighted the sleek Gulfstream, they repeated a scene reminiscent of one that was played out many times at that airport over the years – Will Rogers, Alf Landon, Amon Carter, Felix DuPont, Herbert Hoover, Cardinal Spellman, J. M. Davis, John Markle, Harry Truman, Henry Ford – the powerful and influential people of an earlier generation arrived right here. This day, as the ground crew opened the Gulfstream cabin, another guest, one of the new leaders of the mid century, alighted from a company aircraft to be feted at the Adams Ranch, Woolaroc, and the country club, and do big business in Bartlesville.

Phillips was not the only Bartlesville company in the global market. Cities Service had long been a much larger company than Phillips, even though, in the old days, their offices were in New York. By the 1960s, H. C. Price Company and Reda Pump had become international players in the oil industry too. As the old saying goes, "the more things change, the more they stay the same." A lot had gone into modernizing Bartlesville since the end of the war. Still, the gracious old Delk-designed Hillcrest Country Club remained at the center of the civic institutions needed by the business community. But, to 1960s eyes, the club was looking old fashioned and dowdy. It had been gussied up sufficiently in 1951, but it was just not up to to the likes of Prince Izzatt Gaafer. Just as H. V. Foster, Frank Phillips, and H. R. Straight did in an earlier generation, now at the initiative of Boots Adams, H. C. Price, R. L. Kidd, and Armais Artunoff collaborated in 1960 to see a new, modern clubhouse replace the old one in order to build Bartlesville, in order to build their companies.

In the fall of 1960, Americans gathered round their TV sets to watch the first televised presidential debates. It wasn't like standing in a crowd watching Lincoln and Douglas, or gathering around a radio to listen to a fireside chat. The camera zoomed in close on the sweaty vice president who appeared to have a five o'clock shadow, and on his handsome opponent with perfect camera make-up, looking cool and collected. America seemingly didn't hear the content of the exchange; they only responded existentially to the images on the living room television. Whether America changed that evening, or a few weeks later when they went to the polls, the election of 1960 issued in a new age, and the storied Kennedy administration, often styled as Camelot. [820]

That once there was a fleeting wisp of glory
Called Camelot.

Maybe the same sprites brought a similar interlude to Bartlesville.

In short, there's simply not
A more congenial spot…

While Camelot unfolded, the Hillcrest Modernization Planning Committee sent George Downs and W. Glenn Palmer, Phillips engineers, and John M. Leisure, a Cities Service engineer, for a tour of some of the most elegant Modern architecture country clubs in America on a fact-finding mission. At a request, probably coming from Boots Adams, Palmer and Leisure first went to Pier 66, from which they examined some south Florida clubhouses. Afterwards they traveled to Shreveport Country Club in Louisiana at the request of Bob Kidd. Hal Price invited them to his home in Scottsdale and they examined Price's recommendations there, Camelback Inn and Paradise Valley Country Club. Then they journeyed on to see Phoenix Country Club. Phoenix was the first club that they felt was really informative. Their last stop was in Palm Springs and Palm Desert. George Downs joined them there and they investigated several clubs in the area. Downs also looked at the golf courses, which was a joyful duty to him. In all, the investigations trips took about 6 months. When they returned home, they had 5 boxes of photographs mostly taken at Thunderbird Country Club, and El Dorado Country Club in Palm Springs, principally of the outside of the buildings and emphasizing an engineerly interest in features like loading docks.

There were very few interior photographs. The engineers maintained that their eventual drawings were a composite of elements from many of the clubs they visited. In appearance, the model for the sophisticated new Bartlesville clubhouse was principally El Dorado Country Club in Palm Springs, California, where the Adamses were members. [821]

By the 17 January 1961, stockholder's meeting, the decision was made. The board was not really consulted, even though Larry Wright was on the Modernization Planning Committee. A new Modern clubhouse would be built, using the Phillips architectural design group whose head was Millard Dornblaser, a Phillips architectural engineer. W. Q. "Smitty" Smith was the actual architect of the clubhouse. Mildred English, Dorothy Glynn Adams' San Antonio interior decorator, was given the task of designing the floor plan of the public rooms in the interior. Alterations would be necessary to the Perry Maxwell golf course, using Floyd Farley as architect, and the old Delk clubhouse would be razed. [822]

The new Hillcrest directors for 1961 were E. H. Dissler, George F. Downs, John C. Hoyt, and W. H. Swatzel. Harry Burlingame was installed as the new president who would lead the board through the planning of the new facility. Gerald McGrew was vice president and Bob Durand was secretary-treasurer. [823]

The committee appointments were made in February: Fred Wallingford, membership, Bob Musgrave, house, John Hoyt, greens, Ernie Dissler, men's golf, Gerald McGrew, finance, and Ken Rugh, entertainment. At the February meeting, the board moved to amend the Articles of Incorporation for Hillcrest Country Club to increase the membership limit from 400 members to 500 members. The meeting notice was mailed to the stockholders on 11 March and the board called a special stockholders meeting for 14

April. There were 116 members in attendance, and 266 shares were voted unanimously to amend. An increase in membership would be needed to help finance the new clubhouse and to liven up club activity. By summer the roster had added many new families, especially Phillips employees. Evidently the word was out in the company that this was a good idea. [824]

While this was transpiring, on 29 March, the board heard a report from the Architectural-Engineering Committee, John Leisure, Glenn Palmer, and George Downs.

We were asked to present a club design which in our opinion would adequately fill the needs of the Club with a membership of 500. We were instructed to set up the necessary premises and make whatever decisions were required without further reference to standing committees of the Club, the Club Manager, or the Pro. [825]

At that meeting, they estimated the cost to be $750,000.

Meanwhile, the normal life of the club continued. The New Year's party had been a real bash, with streamers ankle deep in the ballroom, so that it was impossible to dance. The Beaux Arts Ball was 11 February. There were regular teen dances, Dinner-Dance Club, Bingo, club dances, and Sunday buffet. The Women's Golf Association activated early, looking toward the State Women's Open in June. HWGA sponsored junior golf, as usual, and several special events, such as modeling lessons and a white elephant sale. [826]

Iris Knight won the John Cronin Championship tournament in May, before the State tournament. Of course, the women hosted the tournament in grand Bartlesville style. There was a cocktail party reception, buffet and dance for openers, later a chuck wagon party, and a banquet to wind up the week.

After lots of exciting headlines, and a tightly played contest, Betsy Cullen of Tulsa won the State title on 25 June. The men's championship was played with Ted Cobb the 1961 winner.

The progress on the new clubhouse continued amidst the tournament excitement. On 8 June, a formal proposal was received by the board from the Architectural Engineering Committee. The estimated cost for their optimal plan had firmed-up at $864,000. Drawings of the proposed new building were presented by Millard Dornblaser. The board had a number of questions and changes were made to the document before its presentation to the membership on 15 June. There were 500 members and their wives on hand for the stockholder's meeting. Afterwards, a model, produced by the Phillips Engineering Department, was on display in the clubhouse for all to see. [827]

Hillcrest made its final land purchase in August 1961. Corinne Gray Kane and Clifford Peck, executors of the estate of Ida May Gray, sold 5.5 acres in the extreme southeast corner of the club to Hillcrest. It is property that always had been leased by the club. [828]

It was hoped that plans for the clubhouse could be completed by 31 August so that construction bids could be obtained in September, and break ground in October.

Financing was another problem. The finance committee members were the sort of men who could get it done: Bob Kidd, chairman, Scott Beesley, Harry Burlingame, John Cronin, Stewart Dewer, and Stanley Learned. The board members all received post cards asking for a $200 special contribution. It was noted that, "…income for the past few years varied from $145,000 to $148,000 annually. The operating expenses varied…from $143,000 to $153,000." It was projected that the new clubhouse would generate considerably higher expenses and income. To finance the building program new members were asked to contribute $1000, while the original 350 members, who had financed repeated improvement programs,

The winter was wet so that concrete work was often delayed. It was March before real progress was made. The old clubhouse can be seen in its last days, standing behind the concrete forms for the foundation of the new construction.

A photograph taken from the second story of the old clubhouse, over a gable, show the orientation of the new construction as the steel goes up.

Dwight Travis and Rookie Smith in one of the last photographs from the golf shop of the old clubhouse. *Hillcrest Happenings, January 1961*.

were asked for $650. As of old, the major corporations were kicking in a good half of the costs: Phillips $300,000, Cities Service $100,500, others $67,500, and special solicitations $18,500. [829]

The new Phillips Building and First National Bank Building were under construction downtown, and Boots insisted that Hillcrest use the same contractor, George A. Fuller of Dallas, Texas. By doing so, Adams asserted, the club could be built for direct cost.

Art Gorman remembers that there was some stiff argument in the architectural committee about the space allotted to a lounge, since state liquor laws at the time theoretically severely restricted the club. That is why the original floor plan had only a small interior space devoted to a bar. It was a design problem from the very beginning until it was corrected by adding on a lounge on the west side in 1981.

Still, in the fall of 1961, all was excitement. The women's handicap tournament was postponed because of rain in September. Mary Dolman finally won in October. The same rain hampered the ground breaking for the new clubhouse, which was finally started on 7 November.

While all of this was going on the Club Modernization Committee was simultaneously at work on new plans for the golf course. Boots Adams' candidate for the architect's job was a man already familiar with Hillcrest, Floyd Farley. Bids were submitted by other men, but Farley had the nod. Farley's redo was necessitated by the relocation of the clubhouse building. The old clubhouse remained standing until the new building was complete. As it might be imagined, that caused a tremendous discombobulation on the golf course, starting in October.

The regular golfers saw lots of changes every time they played. In fact they never knew where the temporary greens and tees might be. [830]

Working in the wet fall weather, the topsoil was scraped clear and piled up on the practice tee. By December, the prospective new greens looked like wading pools.

The club held a surprise banquet to honor Rookie Smith on 19 November. An employee until 1969, over more than 44 years (he caddied at Oak Hill, too), he had been caddie, caddie master, and assistant pro. He was the patient and ever-willing tutor that helped many a Hillcrest junior to learn the game. The club gave Rookie a new Chevy Corvair and a hefty $600 check at the breakfast banquet.

By the 1960s, Night on the Town, a dance review and blow-out party, replaced the Beaux Arts Ball as the most important social event in town. The party was a fundraiser or Service League. In 1965, Mary Kane and Dorothy Glynn Adams bought their designer dresses especially for the event. Mary's dress was from New York, and Dorothy Glynn's from Los Angeles. Imagine their surprise when they had the same knockout dresses.

The trendy gold anodized aluminum façade was the subject of considerable excitement as it began to go up around Labor Day.

Regular club life in the old clubhouse proceeded with a Halloween party for the children, junior high and high school sock hops, and Dinner-Dance Club, bingo, Sunday buffet, and club dances. College students, home over Thanksgiving vacation, introduced a new dance that was all the rage, the "Twist." School formals were held at the country club in December. Of course, the New Year's party was an annual landmark.

New members were elected to the board at the 16 January stockholder's meeting. They were Scott Beesley, Harold Price, Jr., and Bill Hewitt, replacing Harry Burlingame, Ken Rugh, and F. E. McLeod. Gerald McGrew became the 1962 president of the Hillcrest board, Bill Hewitt, vice president, and Bill Durand continued as secretary-treasurer. George Downs reported that it was hoped that the new greens would be ready for play late in July. The club had operated at a $27,000 profit in 1961. [831]

The membership was full, so that in January, only the resignation of W. C. Smoot enabled D. E. Shepherd to join. Another sign of returned health was a notice in the *Happenings* that try-outs for the Service League's second "Night on the Town" review would be taking place at the Adams Building. It was a return to the overt coordination of country club resources with other important civic events, a pattern that had been lacking for almost 20 years. [832]

Cold weather slowed progress on the new building because the contractor was not able to pour concrete. In March, the caddy cart house was finished and in use, and foundation walls were poured. By May, the steel was up and concrete was being poured for the second floor. In June some of the brickwork was up. [833]

Golf gamely kept up its usual routine even with the golf course renovation going on around

them. The women were as active as ever. Jo Ann Simpson won the John Cronin Tournament in the spring, and Marjorie Kidd won the fall handicap. Charlie Selby won the men's championship for 1962.

After Labor Day, the goldtone anodized aluminum facade was installed. People were anxious to begin work on the interior as soon as the air conditioning could be installed. Mildred English had been given free reign. Mary Kane, a member of the decorating committee, said the committee was never consulted on decorating choices, though she did agree with Mildred's tasteful decisions.

Planning was already underway for the grand opening gala. Open House for the new clubhouse was held on 7 December 1962. It was the height of fashion, exactly the kind of toney glitz to impress the out-of-town big wigs, a clubhouse to be envied. Of course, the party to show off the new building was an extravaganza. There were dance bands both upstairs and downstairs, a sumptuous buffet, with flowers and extravagant decorations, plenty of cocktails, and the arms of the slot machines in the men's, and the women's locker rooms were busy all night. Many of the women wore elegant evening ensembles that they bought for the occasion in New York, and Dallas, and Los Angeles, and the men wore tuxes with the narrow ties and cumber buns that were stylish then. Only a few years later, writer Jonathan Kwitny included his impression of the new clubhouse in his book, viewing it with contemporary eyes:

> … *a lavish country club in Bartlesville, replete with an indoor garden and river that follows the main staircase down a cascade of waterfalls.* [834]

As Hillcrest celebrated, the city had already let a contract for the construction of the new Sooner Park Golf Course, with Floyd Farley as its architect. Another "grand plan" for the development of Bartlesville was already underway. Those old time found-ers would have been satisfied to learn the news that Henry Bellmon, the state's first Republican governor, was elected that fall. Other new faces appeared in the nation's political scene – Ted Kennedy, John Connelly – and the chilling events of the Cuban missile crisis unfolded. But, Bartlesville was prospering. The new Phillips Building, and its north door neighbor, the new First National Bank Building were rising on the skyline.

The Adams era grand plan principally focused on the new development of Bartlesville east of the river. Madison Middle School (then junior high) and Sooner High (now Bartlesville Mid-High) were planned to draw population east. Hoover Elementary School was drawn by a Cal-ifornia architect. It has had chronic problems, mostly drainage, from unsuitable design. Sooner Park and Sooner Park Golf Course were part of the plan. Along the way, the relatively new Kirk-style First Presbyterian Church was razed and replaced by a Modernist church building. A late addition to the plan was the razing of the Tudor-style Burlingame mansion across from the country club, in favor of the Palm Springs style gated community of Glynnwood. (The gate concept was a flop.)

By Memorial Day in 1963, the old clubhouse was down, and the hole was filled with the dirt that had been piled on the old practice tee in 1961. Work was being done around the swimming pool, turn-ing the old pro shop into a snack shop, and so forth. Landscaping was in progress. A parking lot was built where the old clubhouse once stood.

Afterwards

It has been more than 40 years since the Delk clubhouse was razed. There have been a number of notable landmarks in the story of Hillcrest in those years. The renewed club strutted its stuff for several years. Dignitaries like Former President Dwight D. Eisenhower, movie star Pat Robertson, and golf leg-end Ben Hogan came to Bartlesville and played golf at Hillcrest.

The city was shocked in 1970 when Cit-ies Service decided to move its corporate offices to Tulsa. It was whispered that it was the many slights of corporate wives and the ascendant social dominance of Phillips doyans that influenced the move. Phillips was prospering mightily and growing like Topsy. The town seemingly hardly missed a beat. Hillcrest went through a predictable series of changes of manage-ment.

In 1969, Jerry Cozby was hired as the new golf pro. He was a particularly salubrious choice for Hillcrest. Over 36 years, the growth and reputation of Hillcrest golf has been ably husbanded by Jerry, only the third head pro to work at the country club.

Jerry Cozby was born in 1941 at Breckenridge, Texas. At the time, his dad owned a Phillips 66 gaso-line station. Soon his father took a new job working for Gulf Pipeline at Goldsmith, Texas. The location was a company camp of only 600 residents. There wasn't much recreation in that West Texas location, but there was plenty of space, so the men improvised by building a 9-hole golf course there. That was Jerry's early exposure to the game of golf. When Jerry was in the eighth grade, the company sold the camp, and Jerry's family moved to town at Odessa, Texas. In high school, Jerry was active in all sports, but by his sophomore year he focused only on golf. He gradu-ated in 1959 and started junior college at Odessa on a

The Hillblast was an annual celebrity golf tournament at Hillcrest for a few years in the 1960s. Golf pro, Don Massengale (left), Phillips Chairman, Boots Adams (seeond, left) stands next to actor, Dale Robertson (third left) at the 1968 Hillblast. Afterwards the Micky Finn Band was the entertainment, with Dale Robertson and George Goble.

full golf scholarship. In those days freshmen were not eligible for varsity play, so the junior college route was preferable. He transferred as an upperclassman to Beaumont-Lamar Tech which had a superior golf program at the time, graduating in 1964 with a degree in business and marketing. During his junior year Jerry's team took the NCAA National Championship. After graduation, Jerry became an assistant pro at Oak Hills Country Club in San Antonio.

By then, Jerry was married to Karole Stanley, a Houston girl, and his college sweetheart. The manager of Oak Hills at the time was none other than Bartlesville's old favorite, Pat Johnson. Jerry remembers that one day in 1968, Pat Johnson came into the pro shop to twist Jerry's arm to apply for the pro job at Hillcrest. Jerry quipped facetiously, "I'm going to Westchester." Bartlesville certainly wasn't a place in his sites. In fact, he really didn't know anything about it. But, he did go for an interview. When he returned, he suggested to Karole, "the clubhouse is perfect; the golf is rough – we'll stay five years."

When he was hired, the board especially wanted Jerry and Karole to take part in club social functions, and they wanted him to promote the game of golf. The club had really never had a golf pro who was able take part in the social life of the club. Jerry, with his gentlemanly respect for his game, his professional demeanor, and his pretty, spunky wife was exactly cut out for the job. The members enthusiastically embraced them, and the town welcomed them into the many civic and social activities of the community. The Cozbys were an interesting and exciting addition to young Bartlesville society. Meanwhile, their family of three boys began to arrive. It just didn't take the young couple long to realize that Bartlesville was a terrific place to bring up a family. The five years came and went.

At Jerry's first Hillcrest board meeting in January 1969, management was in a turnover. The board fired the restaurant management company that was provided through Phillips Petroleum Company. In the years since the new clubhouse was built, that company had been in charge of the kitchen. The manager, Gene Barrow had been hired from Phillips cafeteria in 1965. But by 1969 the arrangement had become unsatisfactory. At the February board meeting, Pat Johnson had already been offered the job. He liked Bartlesville and seriously considered taking the offer, but the board's secretary, Gene Durand, was in his cups, reading minutes when Johnson slipped into the room. Durand didn't notice him and read that the club intended to offer Johnson $18,000

Jerry Cozby was the new pro in 1969, shaking hands with his first staff, Kent Carter and John Darling.

salary, but would go to $22,000. That was the offer, and Johnson returned to Texas fairly shaken. In San Antonio meanwhile, they did not intend to lose their good manager and offered him a substantial raise, so he stayed there. It was a disappointing fiasco for Hillcrest. They quickly hired Kirby McLain, remembered for his maxim, "don't talk to my employees." His tenure was quite short. The well-remembered manager who was eventually hired later that year, in 1969, was John Sullivan, one of the best and most popular men to serve at Hillcrest.

As the board had hoped, Jerry Cozby did promote the game of golf. When he was hired, with 422 members, 15,000-18,000 rounds of golf were played each year at HCC. During his tenure the high was 39,000 rounds played one year, and many years with 32,000-35,000 rounds. Presently with a much smaller membership, there are 25,000 rounds a year. He has also been a strong promoter of junior golf, the first time that that initiative originated as an on-going program with the pro. Jerry has personally been the mentor to many a golfer of the upcoming generation, and has encouraged many a budding young pro. Not long after Jerry Cozby came to Hillcrest there was another significant change in the management of the golf program. In May 1970, Henry Manley, the golf course superintentant for many years retired because of illness.

Manley was born at Sabala, Missouri in 1905. He married in St. Louis in 1926. The young couple moved to Bartlesville to take a job at the new Hillcrest Country Club in 1927. It is not clear if Henry was working as a greenskeeper in the St. Louis area. The move to Bartlesville seems to have been very purposeful, thus it seems likely that he was hired by someone who knew of him already. If so, he was the first greenskeeper at HCC. In 1929, he started his own business as an independent landscape gardener. It may be that he left Hillcrest at that time after an accident in which he lost an eye. It appears that the golf course was maintained by a skeleton grounds crew for a few years in the 1930s. When the state championship tournament was held at Hillcrest in 1931, and again in 1933, Hillcrest consulted Oscar Bowman of Tulsa Country Club and the Grass Greens Experimental Station in Tulsa. It appears that Bowman served for special occasions in lieu of a real Hillcrest greenskeeper. By 1940, a man by the name of Ted McCaslin was mentioned as greenskeeper. [835]

The old fashioned reference to men who were responsible for the care and nurture of a golf course was "greenskeeper." In 1926, the National Association of Greenskeepers was formed at Toledo, Ohio. After that time the field developed as professionalization went forward. By 1951, the professional greenskeeper had morphed into golf course superintendant. Ted McCaslin must have been drafted into military service, so that Henry Manley was hired back as greenskeeper in 1942. Henry was blind in one eye, so in no danger of the draft. He immediately became very active in Oklahoma professional greenskeeping organizations. He joined the Oklahoma Turf Grass Research Foundation, by this time at Oklahoma A&M. He was one of the founders of the Oklahoma Greens Superintendent's Association in 1955, and a president of that organization. Older members of the club remember Henry Manley as the old man that mowed on the tractor, but in fact, he was a man who brought a professional interest to the quality of care of the Hillcrest golf course. [836]

A young man who came to work for Henry during his high school years, in 1958, was Eddy Brookshire. Eddy had been working at Hillcrest as a caddy since he was 13 years old. He showed particular aptitude at the greenskeeper work, and old Henry encouraged him in the job.

Louis Ed Brookshire is a Bartlesville boy, born in 1943, and raised next door to the old Haines greenhouse. From childhood he was exposed to the wonder of growing things. He is one of those lucky men who has been able to follow a calling. After school and on weekends he also picked up some yard work for Margaret Riney, and it was she who took an interest in the promising young man, encouraging him to pursue his education. When Eddy decided to go to turf school, she helped him find out the best two or three programs in the United States. Eddy applied to all of them, and was accepted at all, but chose Rutgers University in New Jersey because he liked the idea that it is close to New York City. Henry Manley precipitously retired at that very time, so Eddy applied for the job and was hired, with the understanding that he would be away in school during 1970 and 71. Even so, Eddy oversaw the installation of a new irrigation system on the front 9 in 1970. He is proud that it

Henry Manley (second, right), the long-time greenskeeper, retired in 1969. In a 1958 *Hillcrest Happenings* photo, Eddie Brookshire (first left) stands next to his father Virgil. Eddie succeeded Manley as greenskeeper, serving a full fifty years.

was an in-house job. In 1977 the club razed the old greenskeeper's cottage, an old farmhouse that preexisted Hillcrest, and built the present house. Extensive remodeling of the golf course was done in 1981, 82, and 83, using architect Ed Seay . The old wooden maintainence barn was torn down and replaced by a modern metal building in 1981. Jerry Cozby carefully guarded the classic Perry Maxwell design, while Eddy rebuilt the greens to modern standards. Eddy has also been active in the Oklahoma Greens Superintendent's Association, serving 2 three-year terms on that board.

Since Jerry Cozby came to Hillcrest in 1969, the club has remained very active, keeping Hillcrest on the short-list of fine Oklahoma golf clubs. Amidst a growing count of glitzy new stars, built in the totally artificial postmodern model, the classic Perry Maxwell

course remains a challenging and intellectual play. The Oklahoma Women's Amateur Champioinship was played at Hillcrest the same year that Jerry was hired, 1969. In 1970 the Men's Amateur was at Hillcrest. It was an ambitious start for a young professional. Since then there have been several USGA U.S. Amateur qualifying rounds hosted at Hillcrest, U.S. Open qualifying rounds, Oklahoma Mid-America Championship, South-Central PGA Section Championships, Oklahoma State Junior Championships, and Oklahoma State 6A High School Championships. For the 1991 NCAA Regional Qualifying rounds, at which Jack Nicklaus' son Gary played for Ohio State, 250 members volunteered in various capacities. Bartlesville always loves boosterism. In 2004, the qualifying rounds for the Women's Mid-Amateur Champion-

ABOVE: In 1985, Jerry Cozby was selected National Golf Pro of the Year, shaking hands with Jack Nicklaus at West Palm Beach, Florida.

Jerry Cozby was elected to the National PGA Hall of Fame in 2005, here with PGA President, Royal Warren at Port St. Lucie, Florida. These are wonderful honors for Jerry and a point of pride for Hillcrest.

Pat Ritchie has taught a generation of young Hillcresters the game of tennis.

ship were at HCC, and in 2005, there were qualifying rounds for the National USGA Mid-Amateur Championship. In 2005 Jerry became a member of the USGA Hall of Fame, a tremendous honor for Jerry and our club. Jerry has ably served in the hallowed tradition of Jimmy Gullane to boost Bartlesville, and set his own standard for the promotion of his beloved sport with junior players.

There have been a few other milestones for Hillcrest along the way. The old tennis courts disappeared in the golf course renovations of 1961. The other disappearance of the era was the slot machines. Bob Musgrave was the house and grounds chairman on the board in 1966, and at the same time serving as president of the American Legion. The Legion was being repeatedly raided for gambling, and the club was getting lots of tips that a raid was going to happen. As always, someone hustled out the one armed bandits and hid them before the swoop. Musgrave said, "I just thought it was undignified." Thus the hoary institution came to an abrupt end.

In the middle 1970s there was a national tennis boom, generated by the great era of John McEnrow and Jimmy Connors. It resussitated interest in tennis in Bartlesville and the club decided the time was right to build some new tennis courts. In 1978 the new tennis courts were built just east of the clubhouse parking lot. While they were under construction, Hillcrest took the step of hiring its first tennis pro, a young man named Terry Bobbit. He was only at Hillcrest a few months. It was Jim Connors who broached the Bartlesville job to a University of Tulsa senior, Pat Ritchie. Meanwhile, there was an expectant flurry of new interest in the game in Bartlesville. Ritchie came on as tennis pro in June.

Pat Ritchie is the oldest son in a large family of 10 children from Sapulpa, Oklahoma, born in 1955. His father was the local veternarian and his mother was a schoolteacher. With a growing family, Pat's father started the tennis program in Sapulpa when Pat was 10. Pat went on to be the state high school champ for 2 years. He went to the University of Tulsa on tennis and basketball scholarship, graduating in 1978 with an education degree. In Bartlesville, the young man ably shouldered building a whole new program, and an assessment of his goals. He says he felt the burden of being oldest son, and the need to do well in the adult world beyond athletics. He married Linda Floyd in 1983, a young woman from Wilmington, Delaware, who he met when her father was working on a Phillips contract in Bartlesvillle. They have 2 children, both of whom are nationally rated tennis players.

The new courts were followed a few months later by a fine tennis shop and patio at the edge of the parking lot. A number of new tennis members joined Hillcrest. As the tennis program grew at HCC there was a call for an indoor facility to augment the outdoor courts. The board had okayed the indoor courts and plans were under way when the corporate raiders struck Bartlesville in 1984. The board told Pat that they thought the new building would no longer be feasible. But, Pat found a used "bubble" through a friend in Wichita. The bubble served for 9 years. In the end, climbing the bubble became a local adolescent rite until, predictably, a girl fell through and broke her leg. A metal building replaced the temporary bubble in 2000.

Pat has husbanded Hillcrest tennis to a successful family oriented program. Men's tennis, women's tennis, mixed doubles, tournament play, and outreach to the city, especially through the schools are year in-year out events. He has become a veteran manager, handling everything from the teenage repellers, to deer on the tennis courts. He is an excellent teacher and coach of young tennis players, but also has an eye to the character development of Hillcrest youth. The lessons of proper behavior, the value of a good work out, learning to focus, and maintaining a good attitude are lessons that transcend hitting the ball.

The change in liquor laws in the 1970s engendered a series of renovations, seeking a better situation for the bar. In 1981, the bar was added, all floor to ceiling windows along the west side of the clubhouse with a beautiful view of the golf course. At the time Pete Morrison was president, with Art Gorman serving on the board to help shepherd the vision. It was a huge improvement. The scrunched-feeling old inner sanctum bar area was turned into a "board room" and extra dining area.

In 1984 a committee was formed with Bill Thompson as chairman to build a new swimming pool. The last vestiges of the old Hillcrest clubhouse were removed along with the old pool. The new swimming pool was situated a little closer to the clubhouse on the northwest, and appropriate work was done to the adjacent golf course. The new pool was opened in 1985. There were kitchen fires in 1989 and 2004, both initiating major redecorations of the clubhouse.

In a 1970s photo, the awkward, cramped old interior bar area served social events in the days when members theoretically owned their own stock.

The social life of the club has waxed and waned with the fortunes of the city and the quality of the management. The era of good management during John Sullivan's first tenure, from 1969 to 1974, saw active social and civic utilization of the clubhouse and membership growth in spite of the Cities Service move. John moved on to advance his career, and was followed by Carol Rodman, then George Upshaw who brought along Chef Pocone. Pocone's tenure was not long, but his French menu, and the best desserts in the history of the club are of fond memory. John Sullivan was lured back to Bartlesville from Quail Creek Country Club in Oklahoma City, from 1979 to 1986, years that saw more progress. During that time he hired Charles Downing as chef. Downing remained until 2005. Following manager John Sullivan, came Nick Klisares who remained for several years. Don Carter, a former assistant manager, returned as manager in 1999. Billy Johnson, another former assistant manager, replaced the ailing Carter in 2004, followed by a local man, Gary Wise, in 2005. In 2006 the board hired Grant Raybourn as the new manager. Grant brought along Jeff Stark as assistant manager and Victor Melgozas as the new chef. Finally, in 2007 Gordon Brown came the manager.

Along the way, the oil crash, followed by the corporate raiders in the middle 1980s issued in a new era to Bartlesville. Phillips Petroleum Company changed its long-standing policy of subsidizing club memberships for some of its executives, and became skittish about twisting arms to join the country club. The H. C. Price Company sold out and left town. Of course, oil and gas prices were exceedingly low the whole time. Finally, in 2002, Phillips merged with Conoco to form Conoco-Phillips, and moved its corporate headquarters to Houston, taking 300 executives with them. These were blows to community leadership and to club membership. For a time, city and club demographics were decidedly aging. Donny Storey, the president of Arvest (heir to First National Bank), stepped up with his "Bartlesville Unstoppable" campaign. Soon the gap was filling with some new businesses in town, and especially by startup local business entrepreneurs. After 1980, the new Community Center, like the Hotel Maire and the Civic Center of old, cut deeply into activity and revenues at Hillcrest. Quaint old policies – never exactly followed – of race and gender exclusion fell by the wayside along the way. The demise of dancing after the rock revolution of the 1960s has changed the character of parties, but old institutions like Dinner-Dance Club persist, as popular as ever with all age groups. Dress standards are a casualty of the corporate casual revolution of the '90s. Interestingly, it is the club employees who disapprove, thinking that the proletarian dress standards reflect on the status of their jobs.

Bartlesville really is unstoppable. There is a sense that the giant ghosts of H. V. Foster, Frank Phillips, Don Tyler, H. R. Straight, H. C. Price, Armais Artunoff, … Boots Adams are hovering in the place. It is their legacy, and their tutelage that is inherited by a modern generation of "dwarfs, standing on the shoulders of giants." The culture of social capital that they fostered in Bartlesville is one of the great stories of Oklahoma. Hillcrest Country Club remains at the center of the Bartlesville story.

16

HOLE NUMBER SIXTEEN.
142 Yards, Par 3. This is Hillcrest's only water hole. Beautiful!
Not a difficult shot to this 6,000 square foot green with the out of
bounds far left and a pot bunker right.

17

HOLE NUMBER SEVENTEEN.
357 Yards, Par 4. Dogleg left at 230 yards off tee.
Fairway wood or driving iron that will leave you
with a 125 yard shot to an elevated green.
Be sure to check pin placement on this hole after playing Hole No. 10.

CONCLUSION

DWARFS ON THE SHOULDERS OF GIANTS

On 5, 6, and 7 May of 2002, Hillcrest hosted the annual state high school 6A golf tournament. As usual, intensive planning went into all of the preparations and invitations. The grounds crew had the golf course in tip-top shape. There was nary a stray dandelion poking up its head when everyone went home the evening after the practice rounds on 5 May. Rain was forecast. In the night, a thunderstorm with heavy winds moved over south Bartlesville, wrecking havoc on the pristine golf course. Worst of all, some big trees were down across the fairways and the greens were littered with huge limbs. Eddy Brookshire's crew was there at dawn and the cleanup commenced, though there was little hope of removing the prostrate hulks in time for the tournament. But, the high school coaches had willing manpower on hand. Quickly, Jerry Cozby mustered the coaches to organize their athletes, and even some of the local scout troops, into work crews that removed the impromptu obstacles from the fairways in time for the tournment to go on at noon, only a little late.

This small incident is a snapshot in the ongoing civic function of Hillcrest. The country club was hosting a state golf tournament that was slated to give a lot of young men, their coaches, and families a favorable impression of the city – Boost Bartlesville. Most towns would have postponed the event, but Bartlesville's habits of civic initiative and self-organization manisfested this time to get the course cleared in time to play golf. You can bet that the boys all had much more fun than any ordinary tournament, and learned some civic skills to take home.

The present clubhouse, taken from the patio, across the putting green; the ballroom is upstairs and the mixed grill is downstairs; on the left, the new lounge addition is upstairs, the golf shop is at the end right downstairs, obscured by bushes.

Jerry Cozby is only the third man to serve as golf pro at Hillcrest, a record that Jerry proudly cites often.

As FEMA (Federal Emergency Management Agency) has taught us, government is no substitute for social capital: the habits of self-organization, and initiative. Elected officials and their bureaucratic creations are not leadership, they are public servants. They are seldom the engine that runs the ship. Real leadership may be inate, but it is also earned. Bartlesville has been unusually blessed by a history of remarkably effective and visionary leaders, who have understood the value of working within a civic structure of social capital generation, and earned trust. It is this civic life that is the sieve of leadership.

Modern Hillcrest is hardly aware of its function within the civic structure of Bartlesville. It was not always that way. In 1910, Judge Shea told the newspaper that they were building The Bartlesville County Club to boost Bartlesville. Likewise, in 1925, the new Hillcrest board opined that the new country club would be part of every civic event. Indeed, it is hard to imagine the remarkable development of Bartlesville without Hillcrest Country Club and its antecedants as a part of the civic structure of the city.

These habits of self-organization and initiative, building trust and familiarity, are not a univer-

Dawrfs on the shoulders of giants is a reference to *Metalogicon* by John of Salisbury in 1159, who was quoting, "Bernard of Chartes used to say we are like dwarfs on the shoulders of giants, so that we can see more than they, and things at a greater distance, not by any virtue of any sharpness of sight on our part, or any physical distinction, but because we are carried high and raised up by their giant size."

sal pattern of civic development, and may be a key explanation of success and failure in the development of many communities. Francis Fukuyama refers to this as *social capital*, and thinks it is probably also tied to cultural patterns of the local populations. Indeed, I observed this serendipitously in my own research. One of the remarkable things about reading all of those old Bartlesville newspapers was reading the reports of *all of those quaint old clubs*. Bartlesville was *club city* right from the beginning: Odd Fellows, Woodsmen of America, Commerical Club, Musical Research Society, Tuesday Club, church missionary societies, Elks, and so on, including about 20 ladies bridge clubs. They seem almost humorous. One might assume that this was a norm for the era. I found that is not the case. At the State Historical Society in Oklahoma City with some free time on my hands, I took the opportunity to do some genealogy research, reading a newspaper from a southern Oklahoma town that was then about the same size as Bartlesville, in the time frame circa 1910. The little newspaper recorded no social notices, and only three church missionary societies, meeting once a month. No bridge clubs, no garden club, no Odd Fellows. There was only an occasional report when someone took his wagon over to Ada for the day. In 1910, there was a national Chamber of Commerce program called boosterism. *Washington County: A Century of History* has a wonderful photo of some of the city leaders on the back of a caboose draped with buntings, waving little flags, with huge smiles, going to Independence, Kansas, to boost Bartlesville. About that time, the town in southern Oklahoma got a letter from Oklahoma City, saying OKC would like to come to their town to boost Oklahoma City. With narrowed eyes and furrowed brow, the local response was, "wa fer?" That town has not grown. It is still there, one of the hide-bound places that a lot of people's families

came from when they moved to Oklahoma City and Bartlesville.

It was a stroke of luck for me that Hillcrest had not saved any old records. As I started this project when Hillcrest was 75 years-old, I simply envisioned a pamphlet with a little thumbnail sketch of the old golf pros and tournaments, and a few parties. With no records to work from, I was forced to go to the library to read microfilm. It did not take long, reading the old events of the country club in the total context of the city's life, to realize that the country club was not what I had thought. It is not a selective social club: it is a broad-based *civic* organization. It fitted/fits into the whole story of building Bartlesville.

The earlier two country clubs in Bartlesville followed a pattern that was very similar to many of the small town country clubs that they competed with in those old golf tournaments. Independence, Kansas, Tulsa Country Club, Ponca City, Muskogee, Pawhuska, even Burbank and Shidler were established in the enthusiasm of the era for the trendy new game of golf, and incidentally, a social center for the town. A few, like Bartlesville, intentionally envisioned and used their clubs as instruments in building their cities. Those clubs that lasted, such as Tulsa, Muskogee, Okmulgee, and Independence, were a part of that vision for growth. From the beginning, Bartlesville looked toward Tulsa, but it was the vision for building Hillcrest that put Bartlesville into a class that was not overshadowed by the big, glitzy, clubs in Tulsa and Oklahoma City. It was Frank Phillips' vision in the 1920s for a total community improvement project, which included a first class country club, with the goal of promoting Bartlesville business with Eastern investors, which resulted, among other things, in Hillcrest Country Club in 1926. The beauty of the clubhouse and golf course were unexcelled in Oklahoma at the time. Hillcrest has persisted, when many of the others have languished and/or failed. One reason may be because of the club's relationship with the city's business base has mostly remained vital in the town, and especially because of the town's unusually robust culture of voluntary associations of which the club is one. Indeed, in Bartlesville, social capital has been found to be real capital, just as Francis Fukayama suggests.

The all-important Bartlesville civic events of those long- ago years: the grand opening at The Bartlesville Country Club, building the road to Tulsa, the response to the Flood of '26, the opening of Hillcrest, the Bartlesville Welfare Association, the Bartlesville International Horse Show, the Beaux Arts Balls, Night On the Town, and so many others, have faded from memory as new families move to town. Newer projects like OKMozart and Elder Care continue to fulfill Bartlesville's volunteering inclination. Bartlesville is long accustomed to its mobile population that brings the town new life and ideas. Yet, the long established habits of civic responsibility, participation, and initiative persist and by example are passed to the new citizens. These continue to be fostered through an accessible social structure of clubs and organizations in which Hillcrest Country Club has always had a key role.

18

HOLE NUMBER 18.

575 Yards, Par 5. Be careful.

Play for par on this hole until you get a chance for a birdie on the green.

Stay right of the tennis light pole for this blind tee shot with the fairway sloping left.

The second shot should stay on the left side of the fairway sloping right into lateral hazard.

The smart player will hit an iron for the second shot

leaving himself a third shot of 130 yards.

Green size: 5,000 square feet.

$\mathcal{B}$IBLIOGRAPHY

Clouser, Christopher, *The Midwest Associate: The Life and Work of Perry Duke Maxwell*, Victoria, BC, Canada: Trafford, 2006.

Ellis, William Donohue, *Out of the Osage: The Foster Story*, Oklahoma City: Oklahoma Heritage Association, 1993.

Fukuyama, Francis, "Culture and the Future of the English-Speaking Peoples," *American Outlook*, March/April 2001, p.23-25.

---, *Trust: The Social Virtues and the Creation of Prosperity*, New York: Simon & Schuster, 1995.

Haines, Lee M. and Paul William Thomas, *An Outline History of the Wesleyan Church*, Indianapolis, Indiana: Wesleyan Publishing House, 2000.

Harris, Joel Chandler, *Walt Disney's Uncle Remus Stories*, retold by Marion Palmer, New York: Simon and Schuster, 1946, p.11.

Hayek, F. A., *The Road To Serfdom*, Chicago: University of Chicago Press, 1944.

Herman, Arthur, *Joseph McCarthy*, New York: The Free Press, 2000.

Johnson, Paul, *A History of the American People*, New York: HarperCollins, 1997.

Jones, Billy M., *L. E. Phillips: Banker, Oil Man, Civic Leader*, Oklahoma City: Oklahoma Heritage Association, 1981.

Kane, Gale Morgan, *Frank's Fancy: Frank Phillips' Woolaroc*, Oklahoma City: Oklahoma Heritage Association, 2001.

Kwitney, Jonathan, *The Mullendore Murder*, New York: Farrar, Straus and Giroux, 1974.

Lambert, Paul F., et. al., *Washington County: A Centennial History*, Oklahoma City: Oklahoma Heritage Association, 1999.

Lemon, Del, *The Story of Golf in Oklahoma*, Norman: University of Oklahoma, 2001.

Lobenz, Norman M., *The Boots Adams Story*, Bartlesville, Ok: Phillips Petroleum Company, 1965.

Mayo, James M., *The American Country Club: Its Origins and Development*, New Brunswick, N.J.: Rutgers University Press, 1998.

MacLeod, Ken, "Hillcrest CC Celebrates 75 Years," *South Central Golf*, October-December 2001, p.28-29.

McMillan, Robin, ed., 2001 U.S. *Open Championship Magazine*, New York: Golf Magazine, 2001.

Miner, H. Craig, *A History of the Wichita Country Club 1900-1975*, Wichita: Wichita Country Club, 1975.

Moss, Richard J., *Golf and the American Country Club*, Urbana: University of Illinois, 2001.

Murray, William H., *Memoirs of Governor Murray and True History of Oklahoma, Vol. II*, Boston: Meador Publishing, 1945.

Pearson, Robert and Brad Pearson, *The J. C. Nichols Chronicle*, Kansas City: Country Club Plaza Press, 1994.

Pretty, Jules, "Social Capital and the Collective Management of Resources," *Science*, 12 December 2003, p.1912-1914.

Putnam, Robert D. and Lewis M. Feldstein, *Better Together*, New York: Simon & Schuster, 2003.

Putnam. Robert D., *Bowling Alone*, New York: Simon & Schuster, 2000.

Robbins, Louise S., *The Dismissal of Miss Ruth Brown*, Norman: University of Oklahoma Press, 2000.

Ryan, Mary P., *Cradle of the Middle Class: The Family in Oneida County, New York, 1790-1856*, New York: Cambridge University Press, 1981.

Sapp, Jane, booklet ed., *The Smithsonian Collection of Classic Jazz. revised ed.*, Washington, D.C.: Smithsonian Institution Press, 1987.

Shlaes, Amity, *The Forgotten Man: A New History of the Great Depression*, New York: HarperCollins, 2007.

Upchurch, Jay C., "The South African Contingent," *Sooner Magazine*, Fall 2005.

Wade, Don, *Talking on Tour*, New York: McGraw-Hill, 2003.

Wallis, Michael, *Oil Man*, New York: Doubleday, 1988.

Walton, John Brooks, *The Architecture of Charles Stevens Dilbeck*, Tulsa: JBW Publications, 2006.

---, *The Architecture of John Duncan Forsyth*, Tulsa: JBW Publications, 2007.

Wertz, William, ed., *Phillips: The First 66 Years*, Bartlesville, Ok: Phillips Petroleum Company, 1983.

Williams, Joe, *Bartlesville: Remembrances of Times Past, Reflections of Today*, Bartlesville, Ok. : TRW, 1978.

Williams, Michael, *History of Golf*, Secaucus, N.J.: Chartwell Books, 1987.

Young, Thomas E., *Edward Beuhler Delk, Architect*, Tulsa, Ok.: The Philbrook Art Museum, 1993.

Notes

1 James M. Mayo, *The American Country Cub*, New Brunswick, NJ: Rutgers University Press, 1998.

2 Mary P. Ryan, *Cradle of the Middle Class: The Family in Oneida County, New York, 1790-1865*, New York: Cambridge University Press, 1981; Richard J. Moss, *Golf and the American Country Club*, Urbana: University of Illinois Press, 2001; Robert D. Putnam, *Bowling Alone*, New York: Touchstone, 2000.

3 Mayo, chapter 1.

4 Crane Brinton, *Ideas and Men: the Story of Western Thought, 2 ed.*, Englewood Cliffs, NJ: Prentice-Hall, 1963.

5 Moss, p.80, from C. O. Morris, "Country Clubs For Everyone," *Country Life*, July 1909, p.295.

6 H. Craig Miner, *A History of the Wichita Country Club*, 1900-1975, Wichita: Wichita Country Club, 1975, p.15.

7 Mayo, 120-124; Robert Pearson and Brad Pearson, *The J. C. Nichols Chronicle: The Authorized Story of the Man, His Company, and His Legacy*, 1880-1994, Kansas City: Country Club Plaza Press, 1994.

8 Harve Pemberton was the son in law of William Johnstone. Johnstone was a Delaware Indian and partner in the Johnstone & Keeler general store. He was patriarch of one of Bartlesville's founding families.

9 Advertisement, *Bartlesville Weekly Examiner*, 27 November 1908, p.1.

10 "Country Club Incorporated," *Bartlesville Weekly Examiner*, 11 December 1908, p.1.

11 Del Lemon, *The Story of Golf in Oklahoma*, Norman: University of Oklahoma Press, 2001, p.14; *The American Annual Golf Guide*, New York: Golf Guide Company, Inc., 1925, p. 335.

12 State of Oklahoma, Secretary of State, Articles of Incorporation, 629, The Bartlesville Country Club.

13 *Prewitt's Bartlesville Indian Territory Directory for 1907-1908*, Springfield, Mo: Prewitt's Directory.

14 *IBID.*

15 "Interurban Will Enter Commercial Field Soor," *Bartlesville Weekly Examiner*, 11 December 1908, p.1.

16 Paul F. Lambert, Kenny A. Franks, and Margaret Wither Teague, *Washington County: A Centennial History*, Oklahoma City: Oklahoma Heritage Association, 1999; "Joseph J. Curl Dies at Cleveland, Ohio," *The Morning Examiner*, 23 March 1934.

17 "Country Club Opening Is A Dream Come True," *The Morning Examiner*, 30 November 1911, p. 1. The article says the club was the idea of one half dozen men, probably these seven signers of the articles of incorporation.

18 File Bartlesville Public Library, citing Hill, Luther B., *State of Oklahoma, Vol. II*, 1909, p.393.

19 State of Oklahoma, Secretary of State, Articles of Incorporation, 629, The Bartlesville Country Club.

20 Margaret Withers Teague, *History of Washington County and Its Surrounding Areas, Vol. II*, Bartlesville Historical Commission, 1968, p.270.

21 Osage County Clerk, Misc. 15, p. 459, Paul B. Mason, C. W. Mason, B. F. Mason, lease to Bartlesville Country Club, $200 and taxes, 14 Apr. 1911, NE 1/4, NE 1/4, SW 1/4 4-26-12.

22 Osage County Clerk, WD 10, p 194, Paul B. Mason, et. al, to Bartlesville Country Club, $500, 20 ac., 11 May 1911, S 1/2 NW 1/4 SW 1/4 4-26-12.

23 "Twenty-five Thousand Club Was Organized," *The Morning Examiner*, 17 March 1910. p.1.

24 "Johnstone Heights Will Receive First Attention," *The Morning Examiner*, 8 January 1910, p.1.

25 "Country Club Will Get Healthy Boost," *The Morning Examiner*, 31 March 1910, p.1.

26 "Country Club Opening Is a Dream Come True."

27 "Old Robbery Recalled," *The Morning Examiner*, 30 January 1921, p. 7.

28 A familiar geological feature near the Bartlesville airport. It is a lone hillock with a hard caprock and formed by erosion around it.

29 Telephone conversation with Harry Herzig, 6/7/04. As a young man Herzig worked for Walton Everman, but he has no knowledge of whether Everman was the clubhouse architect. Everman did design a number of early Bartlesville homes and buildings, including the Frank Phillips home. He is the most logical local person to have done the job. But, he was not on the roster of early club members.

30 *Bartlesville Enterprise*, 6 October 1911, p.8. It is possible that there was an even earlier man named Fernie, possibly the person who laid out the golf course. "dateline Muskogee," *Daily Oklahoman*, 5 June 1911, p.3. "The Tri-State professional golf match for which the Oklahoma State Golf Association offered a purse of $100 was won today by Nichols of the Muskogee Town and Country Club in 153 strokes for 36 holes. Fernie of Bartlesville was second with 154." William Fernie was an early golf course architect and pro in Scotland during the 1830s. Perhaps this man was a relative, capitalizing on his respected kinsman.

31 "Entertained At Country Club," *The Morning Examiner*, 29 January 1912, p. 3; "English Golfer To Leave Country Club," 12 January 1912, p.1.

32 "Country Club Opening," *The Morning Examiner*, 28 November 1911, p.3.

33 "Country Club Opening Is a Dream Come True." The other contestants and scores were: Robert King 45, H. B. Henry 40, Clyde Fowler 43, A. C. Moore 41, John Bell 39, H. D. Foster 46, J. E. Johnson 43, Paul Dahlgren 46, G. S. Coburn 45, Roswell Johnson 51, John H. Kane 47, Paul Johnson 46, L. E. Phillips 46, John Taylor 45, M. E. Michaelson 43, A. D. Morton 53, Frank Breene 39. The golf balls were very fine prizes in those days. It had only been a few years since the game was played with gutta-percha balls. The Haskell rubber core ball that must have been used for the prizes at the tournament were an invaluable, and expensive, enhancement to the game. According to the dialog in *Bobby Jones: Stroke of Genius (BJ Films LLC, 2004)*, about this time a golf ball was worth 20¢ ($3.71 in 2002 dollars).

34 IBID.

35 IBID. Several of the ladies' evening dresses were described in this manner.

36 "Society and Social Events," *The Morning Examiner*, 4 December 1911. It can probably be inferred that Nichols was an important consultant in the organization of the country club. "Society and Social Events," 7 December 1911, 9 December 1911, 11 December 1911, 27 December 1911, 29 December 1911, 31 December 1911, 6 January 1912. Since the Shea party ate dinner at home, it might be surmised that there was no cook at the club at this time.

37 "Country Club Opening Is a Dream Come True."

38 "Country Club," *The Morning Examiner*, 17 March 1912, p. 1.

39 "Country Club House Party," *The Morning Examiner*, 29 March 1912, p. 3.

40 American Annual Golf Guide.

41 "Country Club To Have $20,000 Improvements," *The Morning Examiner*, 29 May 1912, p.1. The furnishings they asked for were not furniture, like we would think of. They asked for sideboard covers, dresser covers, toilet articles for dressing table, jardinières, sofa pillows, porch pillows, pictures, clock, candle sticks, smoking sets, magazine subscriptions, vases, bookracks, leather pelt for the library table, jerneries for the dining table, porch swings, hammocks, etc.

42 "Bartlesville Country Club," *Morning Examiner*, **Special Industrial Edition, supplemental,** 7 December 1912. The names of the membership at the end of 1912 are within a half-dozen names of the charter membership one year earlier. Miss Jeanne Kirwan appears repeatedly on lists that give the impression she was a club member. She was, in fact, probably the first "lady" member. She was a "bachelor" lady school teacher, living on South Johnstone. She was the sister of Mrs. Rood and very socially active.

43 "Country Club Members Enjoy Grounds," *The Morning Examiner*, 29 September 1912.

44 "Nelson Defends His Professional Title," *The Daily Oklahoman*, 2 June 1913, p.3.

45 "Medal Tournament On Country Club Golf Links Today," *The Morning Examiner*, 22 September 1912.

46 "Winners In Sunday's Handicap Tournament," 42, 24 September 1912.

47 "Country Club Members Entertain Kansans Sunday," *The Morning Examiner*, 5 October 1912; "Tulsa Golf Players Invade Bartlesville," 27 October 1912; "Tulsa Golf-Players Lose To Bartlesville Score Of 17 To 2," 29 October 1912; "The Local Golf Enthusiasts Will Invade Tulsa Today," 10 November 1912; "Bartlesville Country Club Loses To Tulsa 22 To 11," 12 November 1912.

48 "Bartlesville Country Club," 7 December 1912.

49 "H. G. Durnell Badly Hurt By Automobile At The Country Club," *The Morning Examiner*, 19 November 1912, p. 2. Since 1906 Bartlesville had a hospital, located at Keeler and 12th Street, but treatment available at the time made it more of a last resort.

50 "Bartlesville Country Club," 7 December 1912.

51 "Kid Party A Success As Social Function," *The Morning Examiner*, 1 January 1913.

52 "A Scotch Dinner," *The Morning Examiner*, 27 January 1913.

53 Del Lemon dlemon@sprintmail.com, "question," Private e-mail message to Gale Kane, 6/26/01.

54 "At Country Club, " *The Morning Examiner*, 26 March 1913; "Country Club Program," *The Morning Examiner*, 12 April 1913; "Country Club Affairs," *The Morning Examiner*, 13 April 1913; "At The Country Club," *The Morning Examiner*, 15 April 1913; "Oklahoma Editors Here For Convention," *The Morning Examiner*, 9 May 1913; "At The Country Club," *The Morning Examiner*, 1 June 1913.

55 The Bartlesville Country Club stock certificate (Hillcrest Country Club files). John O. Taylor was one of the original organizers of The Bartlesville Country Club. He appears in the early city directories as a bachelor. His business was real estate and investments, and he had a Cherokee allotment. He disappeared from the city in 1918. Possibly he went to war. There was a T. C. Davis in the 1912 city directory who was a smelter laborer. Possibly Taylor brought the certificate to Kayser's office and they just collared a man to witness the document. The $100 spent for the 1912 stock would be $1854 in 2002 dollars (The Inflation Calculator, http://www.westegg.com.)

56 *Prewitt's Bartlesville City Directory for 1913*, Springfield, Mo: Prewitt's Directory.

57 Telephone conversation with Brooks Spies, 14 September 2001.

58 Hal Price was from a Washington, D. C. family of cultural and financial means. He was especially interested in opera as a young man, and even got a job ushering so he would be sure to be able to see all the performances. He graduated from Colorado School of Mines in 1913, and that summer moved to Bartlesville with a very promising first job as a chemist for National Zinc. He was a dedicated tennis enthusiast all his life, and very proud of his numerous championship trophies from Hillcrest tournaments over the years. It is not surprising that he would join the country club shortly after moving to town. (Telephone conversation with Carolyn Price, 18 September 2001.)

59 "Dry As A Desert In Bartlesville" *The Morning Examiner*, 19 July 1913, p.8.

60 "Large Number Have Accepted Invitation For Tomorrow Evening," *The Morning Examiner*, 20 July 1913, p.6; "Hotel Maire," 27 July 1913; "Hotel Maire Dinner," 21 September 1913; S. Morgan Friedman, The Inflation Calculator, http://www.westegg.com/inflation/infl.cgi, $125,000 in 1913 dollars calculates to $2,150,974.06 in year 2000 dollars.

61 "Many Entries In Golf Meet," *The Morning Examiner*, 12 June 1914, p.1; "Tournament Has Started," 16 June 1914, p.5; "Final Play Today," 17 June 1914, p.5.

62 "Handicap Event," *The Morning Examiner*, 18 October 1914, p.7; "Foster Cup Game Ended In A Tie," 18 October 1914, p.5. Frank Rollins and Dr. F. N. Buck are new names for the membership list.

63 Minutes of the Chamber of Commerce Board of Directors Meetings from May 21, 1913 to August 21, 1915, 29 September 1914 (Bartlesville Chamber of Commerce).

64 "Loss of Club May Result," The Morning Examiner, 1 November 1914.

65 *IBID*; "Going To Raise That Club Debt," *The Morning Examiner*, 3 November 1914, p.8. These property valuations are probably much closer to correct than the grand opening hype of November 1912. 111 members would have generated $11,000 to build the club, then they must have borrowed $8,000 for improvements the next summer. H. R. Straight is another new name for the membership list.

66 "Permanent Fair Ground," *The Morning Examiner*," 30 June 1915, p.6.

67 "Country Club Active Again," *The Morning Examiner*, 17 July 1915, p.6; Abraham and Cora Bell Quackenbush moved to Bartlesville in 1915 from New York.

68 "Country Club Dance," *The Morning Examiner*, 2 January 1916. The guest list was: Esther Rood, Blanche Shonaerts, Margaret Walsh, Leah Eastburn, Mary Stevens, Ruth Snyder, Murdeen Breene, Mildred Beattie, Harold Bucher, Minn (?) Duke, Carl Rhen, Ed Walsh, Harold Breene, Ed Butts, Ralph Connelly, Tom Shea, John Phillips, Ralph Turner, Everett Holm, Ivan Irwin, Milo Overlees, Hal Price, Sol Madansky, and out of town guests Margaret Gavin of Tulsa, Esther Lockard of Muskogee, and Helen Shaw of Chicago.

69 *Daily Oklahoman*.

70 "Tennis Play To Begin Friday," *The Morning Examiner*, 31 August 1916, p.6; "Fred J. Spies Tennis Champ," 16 September 1916, p.6.

71 "Committee Report On Country Club Situation," (Bartlesville Engineer's Club).

72 Michael Wallis, *Oil Man*, New York: St. Martin's Griffin, 1988.

73 State of Oklahoma, Secretary of State, Index to Corporations, 18674.

74 Osage County Clerk, WD 22, p. 354, Bartlesville Country Club to Otto C. Massey, 10 May 1917, $1.00, S 1/2 NE 1/4 SW 1/4 4-26-12; WD22, p.355, Otto C. Massey to Oak Hill Club, 14 May 1917, $1.00, S 1/2 NE 1/4 SW 1/4 4-26-12.

75 State of Oklahoma, Secretary of State, Articles of Incorporation, 15614, Oak Hill Club.

76 *Prewitt's Bartlesville City Directory for 1916-1917*, Springfield, Mo: Prewitt's Directory.

77 "Committee Report On Country Club Situation"(Bartlesville Engineer's Club).

78 "To Revive Interest In The Country Club," *The Morning Examiner*, 28 June 1917, p.1.

79 *The Tulsa World*, 17 June 1917.

80 "At Oak Hill's Club," *Morning Examiner*, 30 June 1917, p.6. The committee for the tournament was H. L. Bullock, H. E. Bonnette, G. W. Allen, chairman.

81 "The Gist Of It," *Morning Examiner*, p.6. "The following are the players with their scores: Nash, 64-64; Allison, 49-56; Durnell, 45-50-53; Govreau, 62; Gratton, 63; Graham, 60; Bocock, 55; Drath, 51; Nelson, 64; Moore, 48; Hockensmith, 52-54; Clark, 58-60; Myers, 58-62; Sellers, 65; Brodnax, 55; Ballard, 42; Dewer, 56; Johnson, 55; Dial, 60; Koopman, 59; Buck, 56-54; Smheimer, 55; Diescher, 60; Stubbs club house bogie." This is a very different list of golfers than those playing in 1914.

82 "The Gist Of It," *Morning Examiner*, 22 July 1917, p.5.

83 IBID, 26 September 1917.

84 Personal interview with Russell Davis, 1110 Cherokee, on 9 January 2002. Russell, born 1908, was a young teenager in those years.

85 "The Gist Of It," *Morning Examiner*, 2 December 1917, p.6.

86 *The Tulsa World*, 17 June 1917; "Oak Hill Club Plans A Gay Social Season," *The Morning Examiner*, 26 September 1918, p.1; *The Daily Oklahoman*, 23 September 1918.

87 IBID.

88 "Henry L. Doherty Pays His First Visit To City," *The Morning Examiner*, 19 April 1919, p.1.

89 "Will Give Dinner At The Maire," *The Morning Examiner*, 30 October 1919, p.8.

90 "Empire Company Personal Items," *The Morning Examiner*, 13 March 1919, p.5.

91 "Country Club Plans To Extend Its Membership." *The Morning Examiner*, 13 March 1919, p.5.

92 "Gist," *The Morning Examiner*, 4 May 1919, p.4.

93 "No Meals At Country Club," 42, 2 October 1919, p.5.

94 "Country Club Plans To Extend Its Membership," *The Morning Examiner*, 22 April 1919, p.1.

95 "Gist," *The Morning Examiner*, 5 July 1919, p.6.

96 "City Water For Country Club," *The Morning Examiner*, 3 April 1920, p.3.

97 "Washington County-Seat Has Developed In 20 Years Into A Modern City," *The Morning Examiner*, 12 October 1919, p.1A.

98 Moss, p. 103, citing Benjamin G. Radar, "Quest for Sub-Communities," *American Sports From the Age of Folk Games to the Age of Televised Sports*, Upper Saddle River, NJ, 1999, p. 355-60.

99 "Get Fine Taft Pictures," *The Morning Examiner*, 27 February 1920, p.3. None of the movie footage has been found.

100 For more detailed accounts see the following articles: "Dr. Buck Wins Trophy," *The Morning Examiner*, 15 July 1920, p.8; "Pro Golfers Play Sunday," 17 July 1920, p.4; "Oak Hill Beats Empires," 31 August 1919, p.3; "Tennis Meets Near Finals," 7 October 1919, p.5; "To Play For Golf Trophy," 27 August 1920, p.4; "Eight Golfers Qualify," 7 September 1920. p.4; "Michaelson Wins Golf Cup," 14 September 1920, p.6; "Keewan Golfers Confident," 21 September 1920, p.4; "Rote Golfers Beat Keewans," 28 September 1920, p.4; "Play Golf today," 3 October 1920, p.4; "Play For McMorrow Cup," 1 June 1921, p.5; "Local Golfers Win," 28 Jun 1921, p.5. "Will Play Independence Golfers," 15 July 1921, p.8; "Will Play At Parsons," 24 July 1921, p.9A; "To Meet Independence Golfers," 5 August 1921, p.5; "Golfers Won Sunday," 25 August 1921, p.4; "Bartlesville Golfers Clean Up On Kansas," 6 September 1921, p.6; "Oak Hill Golfers Win Championship," 20 September 1921, p.4; "Hockensmith Victor," 28 September 1921, p.5; "Display Golf Trophies," 28 September 1921, p.5.

101 "Ed Dudley," FAX, 6 November 2001, PGA foundation; FAX, 6 November 2001, Augusta National containing pages from David Owen, Making of the Masters, 1999, p.220-221; Clifford Roberts, *The Story of the Augusta National Golf Club,* 1976, p.18; newspaper article 10 January 1933, "Ed Dudley, New Pro At National Course, Arrives. Telephone conversation with his niece, Susie Hurst, 1/24/02; "Dudley Goes To Hollywood," *The Morning Examiner,* 26 January 1927, p.4.

102 "Many Can Enjoy Use Of The Country Club," *The Morning Examiner,* 3 February 1921, p.6.

103 Committee Report On Country Club Situation (Bartlesville Engineer's Club).

104 Gave Stag Party for Koopman," *The Morning Examiner,* 15 June 1919, p.5.

105 O. P. Warlick to Smelter Gas Company, attn: Mr. James Surdoval, letter, 23 April 1929. (HCC files)

106 State of Oklahoma, Secretary of State, 1 July 1921, Amended articles of incorporation, No. 36513; Certificate of increase, 36522.

107 Minutes of the Meeting of the Board of directors of the Chamber of Commerce, 8 November 1921 (Bartlesville Chamber of Commerce).

108 O. P. Warlick to Smelter Gas Company, attn: Mr. James Surdoval, letter, 23 April 1929. (HCC files); Bartlesville Engineer's Club report.

109 "Will Increase Club Membership," *The Morning Examiner,* 12 January 1921, p.3.

110 Bartlesville Engineers Club.

111 State of Oklahoma, Secretary of State, Index to Corporations, 629. *American Annual Golf Guide.* In 1925 H. V. Foster was listed as president and Paul F. M. McBride of Empire Companies was secretary-treasurer. McBride must have submitted the information. It stated that the club was organized 1900. Oak Hill Club officers were the same as above, with O. P. Warlick, vice president. Their annual meeting was in December and the informant said they were organized 1908. There are other small differences in the accuracy of the data, probably McBride was not very interested in his responses to the *Guide.*

112 Osage County Clerk, WD 37, p.51, B. F. Mason to Oak Hill, 11 May 1920, $1.00, N 1/2 NE 1/4 SW 1/4 4-26-12.

113 Bartlesville Engineers Club.

114 "Will Pave To Osage Line," *The Morning Examiner,* 21 September 1920, p.4.

115 Minutes of the Board of Directors of the Chamber of Commerce, 8, 9, 15 March 1921 (Bartlesville Chamber of Commerce).

116 "Country Club Golf Players Celebrate," *The Morning Examiner,* 25 November 1921, p.6. The scores for the all club handicap tournament were reported. They are an extensive, though partial list of the members at the time, and an indication of their golf expertise: J. H. Kane, 55, 8, 47; H. R. Straight, 48, 4, 44; William Raymond, 48, 4, 44; C. J. Allsworth, 46, 3, 43; R. A. Brown, 48, 5, 43; J. S. Leach 48, 8, 40; Harold Price, 68, 9, 59; S. C. Blair, 57, 9, 48; Jim Zofness, 67, 9, 58; Dr. Van Duzer, 54, 6, 48; Bob Van Duzer, 53, 5, 48; Leike, 58, 8, 50; O. K. Wing, 46, 1, 45; George Van Dall, 51, 7, 44; H. C. Charles, 55, 8, 47; C. W. Harrison, 50, 7, 43; Dr. F. B. Corlin, 55, 9, 46; Carl Wood, 72, 9, 63; G. E. Smith, 52, 5, 47; Don Allison, 51, 2, 49; H. E. Hulen, 49, 7, 42; Cushman, 61, 9, 52; H. V. Foster 49, 1, 49; Paul Dahlgren, 47, 4, 43; C. H. Caldwell, 49, 5, 44; L. D. Messner, 47, 0, 47; Chamberlain, 54, 7, 47; T. K. Stout, 54, 9, 45; Hockkensmith, 50, 0, 50; Jim Collins, 47, 2, 45; F. N. Buck, 48, 2, 46; F. A. Roney, 47, 1, 46; J. H. McMorrow, 54, 5, 49; O. P. Warlick, 47, 0, 47; E. C. Jacobson, 55, 7, 48; W. A. Lynott, 49, 2, 47; Ralph Cormen, 56, 9, 47; Glen Skinner, 62, 8, 54; L. M. Pendy, 47, 5, 42; Nesbit, 58, 7, 51; Sands 59, 8, 51; Hines 47, 4, 43. Women's scores: Mrs. H. R. Straight, 88, 12, 76; Mrs. J. H. Kane, 71, 9, 62; Rosemary McMorrow, 67, 11, 56; Virginia McMorrow, 67, 11, 56; Mrs. T. K. Stout, 59, 2, 57; Mrs. Carl Wood, 67, 1, 66; Mrs. O. K. Wing, 99, 12, 87; Mrs. Sam Blair, 68, 3, 65; Mrs. M. A. Kirkpatrick, 68, 9, 59.

117 "Country Club Will Celebrate Victory," *The Morning Examiner,* 20 November 1921, p.12.

118 "When the Klansmen Gathered," *The Morning Examiner,* 9 July 1922, p. 1; "Entertains At Oak Hill Club," 2 July 1922, p.6; Charles Alexander, *The Ku Klux Klan in the Southwest,* Norman: University of Oklahoma Press, 1995, p.xv-xix.

119 "Dudley Sets Record For Driving At Club," *The Morning Examiner,* 23 August 1922, p. 6.

120 Myron Messner Winner Of McMorrow Golf Trophy," *The Morning Examiner,* 6 October 1922, p.6.

121 "Messner Lowers Record At Oak Hill Saturday," *The Morning Examiner,* 22 October 1922, p.4.

122 Bartlesville Engineers Club. It is possible that these salaries represent the budget for the pro and greenskeeper and their employees.

123 "Halloween Dance At Oak Hill Club," *The Morning Examiner,* 27 October 1922, p.3

124 "Forty and Eight Are Hosts," *The Morning Examiner,* 2 January 1923, p.3.

125 Wallis, p.223.

126 Frank Phillips appointment diaries (Woolaroc Archive).

127 "Learn Golf In Door," *The Morning Examiner,* 23 February 1923, p.5.

128 Minutes of the Meeting of the Board of Directors of the Chamber of Commerce, 30 January 1923 (Bartlesville Chamber of Commerce).

129 "Country Club Members Are Called For A Meeting Tonight," *The Morning Examiner,* 9 February 1923, p.1.

130 "Independence Team in Debt," *The Morning Examiner,* 8 October 1922, p.3.

131 "Larger Country Club Advocated At Big Meeting," *The Morning Examiner,* 10 February 1923, p.1; "Plan $100,000 Country Club For This City," *Bartlesville Daily Enterprise,* 10 February 1923, p.1.

132 "Local Golfists To Be Tutored By Professional," *The Morning Examiner,* 15 August 1923, p. 4.

133 "Sunrise Dance on the Fourth," *The Morning Examiner,* 1 July 1923, p.2.

134 Country Club To Have House Warming," *The Morning Examiner,* 11 November 1923, p. 10.

135 *American Annual Golf Guide.*

136 Telephone interview with Brooks Spies, 10 September 2001; *American Annual Golf Guide*; Telephone interview with Joe Bowden, 19 September 2001.

137 "Good Time For Caddies," *The Morning Examiner*, 24 July 1924, p.8.

138 Telephone interview with Joe Bowden, 9/19/2001; "Inflation Calculator"; Bartlesville Engineers Club report.

139 Gale Morgan Kane, *Frank's Fancy*, Oklahoma City: Oklahoma Heritage Association, 2001, p.61.

140 "Country Club To Have House Warming," *The Morning Examiner*, 11 November 1923, p.10; "Winter Club Gives Formal Dance," 25 November 1923, p.4; "Society," 2 December 1923, p.2; "Country Club Party," 21 December 1923, p.5; "Phillips Sign 5 Year Lease Offices Here," 28 December 1923, p.1; "Winter Club's New Years Dance," 30 December 1923, p.4; "Winter Club Dance," 2 January 1924, p.2.

141 William Donohue Ellis, *Out Of The Osage The Foster Story*, Oklahoma City: Oklahoma Heritage Association, 1993, p. 103-104. It mentions the song, "Last Night On The Back Porch (I Loved You Best Of All), Green Brothers Novelty Band," http://turtleservices.com/lastnite.htm, 28 July 2000. The song can be dated to 1923.

142 Frank Phillips appointment diaries (Woolaroc Archive); "Country Club Prospers," *The Morning Examiner*, 1 February 1924, p.6; Annual Report of Oak Hill Country Club, December 31, 1923. (Bartlesville Engineers Club). The engineer's report states that by 1925 all records from The Bartlesville Country Club were lost.

143 "Cold Is Causing Suffering In City," *The Morning Examiner*, 6 January 1924, p.1. It was -9°, but no precipitation; "Informal Dinner Dance," 26 January 1924, p.3; "County Club Dinner Dance," 27 January 1924, p.6; "Winter Club Dance," 10 February 1924, p.4; "Winter Club Dance At Oak Hill," 17 February 1924, p.4; "Dinner and Dance At Oak Hill," 22 February 1924, p.3; "To Give Masquerade Dance," 2 March 1924, p.4; "Empire Bids In One Tract For Over A Million," 19 March 1924, p.1; "Oil Companies Bartlesville Purchases Big," 20 March 1924, p.1; "Club Meeting In Maire Hotel," 15 March 1924, p.3; "Business Women To Lunch At Maire," 20 March 1924, p.3.

144 "Golf Matches Are Planned," *The Morning Examiner*, 19 May 1925, p.4; "Teams Picked For Golf Tournament," 22 May 1925, p.8; "Broaddus Golfers Win," 2 June 1925, p.7.

145 "City Golfist In Title Play," *The Morning Examiner*, 16 June 1925, p.6; "Dudley Captures Open Golf Title," 14 June 1925, p.4; "Youth Turns In Low Golf Score," 16 June 1925, p.4; "Bartlesville Golfer Among Eight Tournament Survivors," 17 June 1925, p.4; "Tennis Tournament Here in September," *Bartlesville Daily Enterprise*, 23 July 1925, p.7.

146 "Talk Moving of Country Club," *The Morning Examiner*, 1 July 1925, p.1.

147 "Most Members Of Local Country Club Golfers," *The Morning Examiner*, 30 August 1925, p.1; *Polks Bartlesville City and Washington County Farmers Directory*, Kansas City, Mo: R. L. Polk Co., 1925, p. 16.

148 Hosts At Dinner In Club House," *The Morning Examiner*, 6 July 1924, p.3; "Pawhuska Guests Spend Holiday Here," IBID; "Improve Swimming Pool," 15 July 1924, p.3; "Postpones Dinner Dance," 16 November 1924, p.4; "Winter Club Formal Dance," IBID; "Winter Club Formal," 23 November 1924, p.4.

149 Kane, p. 27; "Frank Phillips Denies Merger With Texas Company," *The Morning Examiner*, 7 November 1925, p.1; "City's Future As Foreseen By J. C. Nichols," *Bartlesvile Daily Enterprise*, 4 November 1925, p.1; "Bartlesville's New Country Club Assured," 16 November 1925, p.1.

150 "Dawn Of New Year Is Quiet In City," *The Morning Examiner*, 1 January 1926, p.1 and p.5.

151 "Hockensmith Victor In First Net Play," *The Morning Examiner*, 31 August 1926. p. 4; "Beall, Price Tied in Net Tournament," 16 September 1926, p.6.

152 "Last Day Of Play For Oak Hill Members," *The Morning Examiner*, 3 October 1926, p.1; "Lafayette Club Meets," 6 October 1926, p.3. The Lafayette Club met regularly at Oak Hill. It was an organization of the most dashing young bachelors in town.

153 "Wilkie's Nine-Hole Golf Course Open to Public Today," *The Morning Examiner*, 27 February 1927, p.6.

154 "Oakhill Club To Be Opened." *The Morning Examiner*, 10 March 1929, p.1; "Rain Delays Opening of Oak Hill Another Week," 30 March 1929, p.12; Osage County Clerk, Mortgage 56, p.329 Oak Hill Club to O. P. Warlick, NW 1/4 SE 1/4 4-26-12, SW 1/4 SE 1/4 4-26-12, NE 1/4 SW 1/4 4-26-12.

155 Osage County Clerk, WD 71, p. 59, Oak Hill Club to O. P. Warlick. 15 Oct. 1930, $1.00 and cancellation of certain mortgage notes by first party to second party in the total amount of his $3800, NE 1/4 SW 1/4 4-26-12; WD 71, p. 73, Quit Claim, 2 October 1930, R. W. Buzan and Ethel to Oak Hill Club, $1.00, NE 1/4 SW 1/4 4-26-12.

156 O. P. Warlick to Smelter Gas Company, attn: Mr. James Surdoval, letter, 14 March 1929 (HCC files)

157 O. P. Warlick to Smelter Gas Company, attn: Mr. James Surdoval, letter, 23 April 1929. (HCC files)

158 "Members of Oak Hill Country Club in Meet," *The Morning Examiner*, 5 October 1929, p.1; "Oakhill Hires Professional," 10 November 1929, p.8; "Oakhill Club's Beautifying and Improvement Plan Well Underway," 15 December 1929, p.11.

159 "Osage Lease Sale Poorest In Years," *Bartlesville Enterprise*, 2 March 1922, p.1.

160 William Wertz, ed., *Phillips: The First 66 Years*, Bartlesville, Ok: Phillips Petroleum Company, 1983, p.21.

161 "Phillips Pays Record Price At Osage Sale," *The Morning Examiner*, 3 March 1922, p.1.

162 IBID.

163 "Town Has Moral Atmosphere," *The Morning Examiner*, 20 May 1922, p.3.

164 Pat Doyle, "Bartlesville, Biggest Little City in Oklahoma," *The Morning Examiner*, 14 June 1923, p.4.

165 *Bartlesville Enterprise*, 9 June 1908; Minutes of the Regular Meeting of the Board of Directors of the Chamber of Commerce, 1921, 1922, 1923; "Archer's Old Survey Favored Butler Creek As City Water Source," *The Morning Examiner*, 8 February 1926, p.1; "Water Company To

Begin Work Soon, 23 December 1926, p.1; Oklahoma Inspection Bureau, "Report On Bartlesville, Washington County, Oklahoma, January 1921(Bartlesville Public Library).

166 Frank Phillips Appointment Calendar, 1921 (Woolaroc Archive). Murray Doan was an early vice president of Phillips Petroleum Company.

167 *Fifty Years of Apawamis*, Rye, N.Y., 1940.

168 Frank Phillips Appointment Calendar, 1921 (Woolaroc Archive).

169 IBID.

170 IBID, 1922.

171 IBID.

172 IBID.

173 IBID, 1923.

174 "Larger Country Club Advocated At Big Meeting," *The Morning Examiner,* 10 February 1923, p.1.

175 Frank Phillips Appointment Calendar, 1923 (Woolaroc Archive). The architect was not named.

176 Chamber of Commerce, 1921.

177 *Minutes of the C of C Board of Directors Meetings from May 21, 1913 to August 24, 1915,* 22 September 1913 (Bartlesville Chamber of Commerce).

178 *Minutes Of The Meeting Of A Committee Called In The Interest Of Good Roads In Washington County; Minutes of Special Meeting of the Board of Directors, 7 February 1923* (Bartlesville Chamber of Commerce); "Inflation Calculator."

179 "7th Street Bridge Plans Are Accepted," *The Morning Examiner,* 20 June 1923; "Dedication Of Memorial Bridge Today; Patriotic Services For Occasion," 24 May 1925, p.1; Chamber of Commerce, 1922; "Washington County To Dedicate Enduring Memorial To Heroes Who Served In World War," *The Bartlesville Enterprise,* 23 May 1925, p.1. The bronze plaques have been moved to the grounds of James H. Teel American Legion Post #105 where they are respectfully preserved and displayed.

180 Chamber of Commerce, 1921, 1922; "Convention Hall Balcony Tested," *The Morning Examiner,* 23 August 1923, p.4; "How Bartlesville Came To Build Civic Center," 12 November 1923, p.1.

181 Kathy Jones's 2nd and 5th hours 8th grade English classes, *This We Remember,* May 1981 (pamphlet, Central Junior High School file, Bartlesville Public Library); "Read Carefully," June 1926 (flier, Central Junior High School file, Bartlesville Public Library); "Men Behind The Scenes," The Morning Examiner, 11 June 1926, p.10; "Junior College To Open Here In Fall," *The Morning Examiner,* 22 December 1926, p.1.
182 "Mass Meeting Talked New Plan," *Bartlesville Enterprise,* 30 January 1920, p.1; Editorial, The Morning Examiner, 1 April 1925; "Manager Form Is Extolled," *The Morning Examiner,* 3 April 1925.

183 Tourist court was the term used at the time, basically for a motel.

184 Meda Smith, "City Park History Told Historical Society," *The Examiner-Enterprise;* Chamber of Commerce, 18 July 1922; "City's Future As Foreseen By J. C. Nichols," *Bartlesville Daily Enterprise,* 4 November 1925, p.1.

185 Chamber of Commerce, 1922, 1923, 1924, 1925.

186 Richard Kane, "A Brief Background and History of Hillcrest Country Club," July 2001, (personal essay in possession of the author); "Caney River Crossings," a typed essay, dated 8/8/1965, but unattributed, Roads and Bridges file (Bartlesville Public Library).

187 Washington Country Clerk, Miscellaneous Book 58, p.99.

188 Washington County, Deed Book 57, p.150, 189, 190; D.B. 58, p. 123; Misc. Book 58, p.101; Plat Envelope 140; "Landscaping Plans For New Addition," *The Morning Examiner,* 18 February 1926, p.8.

189 Frank Phillips Appointment Calendar, 1924, 1925 (Woolaroc) Executive Committee minutes of Phillips Petroleum Company do not mention the country club action at that meeting.

190 Chamber of Commerce, 13 February 1925.

191 Tillinghast had recently completed the redesign and nine-hole expansion at Tulsa Country Club, so his work was probably known by several men. Travis is more of a mystery. He may have been suggested by Frank Phillips, or possibly H. V. Foster or H. R. Straight who probably had played on golf courses he had designed in the East.

192 "Question Still Hanging Fire," *Bartlesville Daily Enterprise,* 18 June 1925, p.5; "Discuss Plan For Moving Country Club," 27 June 1925, p.3, "Talk of Moving Country Club," The Morning Enterprise, 1 July 1925, p.1.

193 "Frank Phillips To Return Tuesday," *The Morning Examiner,* 5 July 1925, p.1.

194 Committee Report on Country Club Situation; Annual Report of Oak Hill Country Club, 1924, 1925; E. L. George to A. H. Riney, letter, 10 July 1925 (Bartlesville Engineer's Club).

195 "New Country Club Will Be Built," *The Morning Examiner,* 18 July 1925, p.1.

196 Opinion of Russell Davis, an old Bartlesville resident who knew these people.

197 Washington County, Warranty Deed, No. 56, p.318, W1/2 NE1/4 NE1/4 & E1/2 NW1/4 NE1/4 & N1/2 SW1/4 NE1/4 of 30-26-13; Warranty Deed, No. 56, p.400, 1/2 interest W1/2 NW1/4 NE1/4 NE1/4 NW1/4 N1/2 SE1/4 NW1/4, 30-26-13, less 3 acres for cemetery; Warranty Deed, No. 54, p.597, NE1/4 NE1/4 NE 1/4, 30-26-13, Deed Book Index, 56-607. For an interesting article on the Delaware Cemetery, just west of the sixteenth green, see: Peggy Carman, "Peggy Visits Old Delaware Burial Ground," The Morning Examiner, 24 October 1926, p.1.

198 Frank Phillips Appointment Calendar, 1925 (Woolaroc Archive).

199 "Architects For C. C. Coming," *The Morning Examiner,* 29 October 1925, p.1; "Begins Survey For 18 Hole Golf Course," 30 October 1925, p.1; "Business Men At Meeting Last Night Decide Upon South Side," *Bartlesville Daily Enterprise,* 30 October 1925, p.1.

200 Richard Kane essay.

201 "Bartlesville Fast Losing Its Pioneer Habiliments; Dolling up For Better Day," *The Morning Examiner,* 11 October 1925, p.1.

202 "Maps of Hillcrest Now On Display," *The Morning Examiner*, 7 November 1925, p.1.

203 "Business Men At Meeting Last Night Decide Upon South Side," *Bartlesville Daily Enterprise*, 30 October 1925, p.1, "City's Future Foreseen By J. C. Nichols," 4 November 1925, p.1; "Brilliant Affair At Oak Hill," *The Morning Examiner*, 5 November 1925, p.3; Frank Phillips Appointment Calendar, 1925 (Woolaroc Archives).

204 "Will Speed Up Country Club," *The Morning Examiner*, 5 November 1925, p.1.

205 "New Members For Hillcrest," *The Morning Examiner*, 10 November 1925, p.1; "Submits Plan For Hillcrest," 12 November 1925, p.1; "Bartlesville's New Country Club Assured," *Bartlesville Daily Enterprise*, 16 November 1925, p.1; "Country Club Meeting Called November 20th," *The Morning Examiner*, 19 November 1925, p.4; "Country Club List Closed Saturday Night," 22 November 1925, p.1; "177 Members Enrolled For Hillcrest Club," 18 November 1925, p.1. The 177 members listed in the 18 November Enterprise article did not all eventually appear on the membership roster. W. C. Dickey, Glen Skinner, W. C. Martin, Warren Stowe, D. C. Phillips, J. M. Leonard, William L. Clark, H. E. Norton, S. J. Montgomery, S. J. Bradfield, Guy W. Shanks, and Joseph S. Butler, listed in the November article, for whatever reasons, did not end up charter members of the club. Also, Walsh Motor Company, Southwest Supply Company, Leamon Motor Company, Bateman's Modern Cleaners, and Black, Sivalls and Bryson were companies on the first list. When the official roster came out there were no more company memberships (With the exception of India Tire and Rubber Company of Akron, Ohio. This was one of Frank Phillips' important contacts and he probably said to accept the company membership). Instead, both E. F. Walsh and E. F. Walsh, Jr. were members, W. J. Leamon, B. O. Bateman, and both Charles Sivalls and J. A. Sivalls were individual members.

206 "New Country Club Gets Off To Good Start," *Bartlesville Daily Enterprise*, 5 December 1925, p.1; "Holm Chosen As Hillcrest Building Head," 16 December 1925, p.1; "Hillcrest Committee Meeting To Be Tuesday," 3 January 1926, p.1.

207 *By Laws, Rules, Roster Of Members, Committees*, 1926 pamphlet published by Hillcrest Country Club (Hillcrest Country Club).

208 "Delk Is Chosen For Hillcrest," *The Morning Examiner*, 7 January 1926, p.1; "E. B. Delk To Draw Country Club Plans," *Bartlesville Daily Enterprise*, 7 January 1926, p.1

209 Thomas E. Young, *Edward Beuhler Delk Architect*, Tulsa: The Philbrook Museum of Art, 1993; Sandra L. Tatman, Roger W. Moss, *Biographical Dictionary of Philadelphia Architects, 1700-1930*, Boston: G. K. Hall, 1985; Susan Jazak Ford, "Edward Beuhler Delk," Kansas City Public Library, http://www.kclibrary.org/sc/bio/delk.htm, n.d; Thomas E. Young, reference to James S. Jackson, "It Happened In Kansas City," *Kansas City Star*, 4 September 1956.

210 "Golf Engineer Employed For Hillcrest Club," *Bartlesville Daily Enterprise*, 12 January 1926, p.1.

211 James W. Finegan, "The House of Maxwell," *2001 U. S. Open Championship Magazine*, p. 96-103; Lemon, p.28-32; Charles Evans, "Perry Duke Maxwell," *The Chronicles Of Oklahoma*, Oklahoma Historical Society, vol. 31, no.2 (summer 1953), p.133.

212 IBID.

213 IBID.

214 Lemon, p.30.

215 Bob Davis, "Photo-Biographies – No. 33," *The American Golfer*, undated article from the spring of 1935.

216 Finegan, p. 96-103; Lemon, p.28-32. Maxwell collaborated with MacKenzie on golf courses at the University of Michigan, Ohio State Universtiy, Iowa State University, Crystal Downs. He did remodeling at Pine Valley in Clementon, N.J., work at Augusta National, Vencker Memorial, designed Southern Hills in Tulsa, Prairie Dunes, Ohio State, remodeling at Merion Golf Club in Ardmore, Pa., and Colonial Country Club in Ft. Worth. In all he built 70 golf courses and redesigned 40.

217 Lemon, p.32.

218 *American Golfer*.

219 "Architect Delk To Be Here Saturday," *The Morning Examiner*, 30 January 1926, p.1; "Construction Work On Hillcrest Is Started," 3 February 1926, p.8; "Clear Ground At Hillcrest," 11 February 1926, p.1.

220 "Contract Let For Hillcrest Country Club," *The Morning Examiner*, 25 May 1926, p.1.

221 "Hillcrest To Be Open Soon," *The Morning Examiner*, 14 September 1926, p.3; By Laws, Rules, Roster Of Members, Committees.

222 IBID; "Colorado Pro Secured For Hillcrest Job," *The Morning Examiner*, 26 September 1926, p.1; Telephone conversation, Jerry Cozby with Floyd Farley, 6 February 2002: In 1924 Blue Hills Country Club in Kansas City hosted the Heart of America Open with a prize of $1,000. Leo Digel was 1st, Walter Hogan was 2nd, Bobby Cruickshank was 3rd. Cruickshank was from Congressional Country Club in Washington, D. C. at the time, but later moved to Twin Hills in Oklahoma City. In the 1926 Tri-State tournament, Wild Bill Mehlhorn placed 1st, and Floyd Farley was 2nd.

223 Davy Hoffman, *America's Greatest Golf Courses*, New York: Image Books, 1987, p.77.

224 "James Gullane Sr.," *Bartlesville Examiner-Enterprise*, 27 July 1986, p.3; Interview with Jerry Cozby 5 February 2002; Telephone conversation with Art Gorman 5 February 2002; telephone conversation with James Gullane, Jr., 13 February 2002; Hillcrest Men Pay Tribute To Gullane On His 20th Year," *The Morning Examiner*, 22 September 1945, p.6.

225 "Gullane Plays Sarazen Today," *The Morning Examiner*, 15 October 1932, p.10.

226 Frank Phillips Appointment Calendar, 1926 (Woolaroc Archive).

227 Interview with Jerry Cozby, 5 February 2002; Lemon, p.42, 43; "Gullane and Broaddus in Trans-Mississippi." *The Morning Examiner*, 29 May 1932, p.6.

228 Farley conversation, 5 February 2002; Gorman conversation, 5 February 2002; "James Gullane Sr.," *The Examiner Enterprise*, 27 July 1986. p.3.

229 "Inoculations For Typhoid To Start Today," *The Morning Examiner*, 6 October 1926, p.1.

230 IBID.

231 "Hillcrest's Total Cost To Be $165,500," *The Morning Examiner*, 9 December 1926, p.3.

232 "Local Oil Barons Laud New Hillcrest Country Club As Great Community Achievement," *The Morning Examiner*, 11 December 1926, p.1.

233 IBID. Besides the above men, there were F. E. Dunn, Dana Reynolds, E. F. Walsh, Don Tyler, H. E. Hulen, M. E. Michaelson, John G. Phillips, Stewart Dewer, F. K. Haskell, E. F. Walsh, Jr. and Sr., O. P. Warlick, Clay Briggs, Paul McIntyre, Floyd Brown, Hal Price, Harry Hewitt, O. K. Wing, J. H. Collins, J. F. Sanderson, Forest Plank, Newton Holman, C. B. Fowler, Fred Spies, Marshal Hockensmith, D. W. Harris, Clay Smoot, N. D. Welty, Jess Leach, H. J. Holm, Glen Skinner, and A. H. Riney.

234 "Club Opening Is Brilliant Social Event," *The Morning Examiner*, 12 December 1926, p.1

235 "New Country Club Is Open Saturday," *The Morning Examiner*, 5 December 1926, p.6.

236 IBID.

237 "Halcyon Party At Hillcrest," *The Morning Examiner*, 19 December 1926, p.6; "Halcyon Set Has Party"; "Mr. and Mrs. Musgrave Hosts At Club," 19 December 1926, p.3; "The Misses Straight Give Christmas Dance," 21 December 1926, p.3; "John M. Kane Host at Hillcrest," 22 December 1926, p.3; "Buffet Supper Party," 22 December 1926, p.3; "Holiday Dance At Hillcrest Club," 23 December 1926, p.3 "Miss Martha Jane and L. E. Phillips, Jr., Entertain," *The Morning Examiner*, 30 December 1926, p.3; "Messrs. And Mesdames Rood Hosts At Hillcrest," 31 December 1926, p.3.

238 "Empire To Bring Oil Finance Forces Here," *The Morning Examiner*, 21 December 1926, p.1; "Water Company To Begin Work Soon," 23 December 1926, p.1.

239 "Businessmen Are Jubilant," *The Morning Examiner*, 1 January 1927, p.1; "Frank Phillips Host at Hillcrest," 16 January 1927, p.3.

240 "Hillcrest Directors Offer Camping Site," *The Morning Examiner*, 10 March 1927, p.1.

241 "Treat In Store For Golf Fans," *The Morning Examiner*, 8 May 1927, p.6; "Tulsa Golfers Here Sunday," 18 May 1927, p.2; "Hillcrest Meet to Bring Long Driving Golfers Together," 19 May 1927, p.4; "Broaddus Downs Tucker nineteenth Hole; Hillcrest Men Defeat Oakhurst," 24 May 1927, p.4; "Professionals Tie For first at Tulsa," 29 May 1927, p.3; "Hillcrest To Have Flag Tournament," 29 May 1927, p.9.

242 "Roods Give Tea In Governor's Honor," *The Morning Examiner*, 5 May 1927, p.1.

243 "Hillcrest Golfers Start On First Round Matches To Determine Champ," *The Morning Examiner*, 14 June 1927, p.8; "Hillcrest Golfer Lose at Oakhurst," 21 June 1927, p.4; "Johnstone Is New Champion," 19 July 1927, p.4; "State Qualifying Pro Rounds Will Be Here," 7 August 1927, p.1; "Golf Tourney Will Be Here," 21 August 1927, p.4; "Golf Tourney Begins Today At Hillcrest," 27 August 1927, p.1; "Gullane And Feist Take Top Honors," 28 August 1927, p.1; "Gullane Wins Pro Gold Title," 29 August 1927, p.8.

244 "Three Tie For Handicap Event, " *The Morning Examiner*, 6 September 1927, p.4; "Play For H. V. Foster Handicap Cup Starts At Hillcrest On Saturday," 16 September 1927, p.9; "Broaddus Wins In Tulsa Meet," 29 September 1927, p.8; "Kiwanis-Rotary TLT Slated For Saturday," 2 October 1927, p.8; "Two In Semi-Finals Of Foster Turney," 25 October 1927, p.4; "Ed Dudley, Noted Golf Player, Visiting Here," 25 October 1927, p.4; "Gullane Loses To Dudley,: 2 November 1927, p.4; "Joe Kirkwood Lauds Local Country Club," 11 November 1927, p.8.

245 "Hillcrest Women To Decide Golfing Title This Month," *The Morning Examiner*, 1 September 1927, p.4; "Four Survive First Round in Women's Golf Tourney Here," 5 October 1927, p.9; "Mrs. Plank To Oppose Mrs. Wood In Finals," 7 October 1927, p.7; "Mrs. Wood Hillcrest Golf Tourney Winner," 15 October 1927, p.2; "Women's Handicap Tournament Begins," 25 October 1927, p.4; "Second Lap Begins In Women's Tourney," 27 October 1927, p.5; "3 Extra Tilts In Golf Meet," 30 October 1927, p.9; "Mrs. Leike Is Victor In Hillcrest Tourney." 1 November 1927, p.4.

246 "Annual Hillcrest Tennis Tournament Will Begin Today," *The Morning Examiner*, 8 October 1927, p.2; "Hockensmith, Spies In Net Meet Finals," 25 October 1927, p.4; "Finals in Hillcrest Tennis Tourney Today," 29 October 1927, p.8.

247 "Hillcrest Progressing Under New Management," *The Morning Examiner*, 29 October 1927, p.8.

248 "Rotary Club Host To City's Teachers," *The Morning Examiner*, 24 September 1927, p.1; "Novel Feature Dance For Mr. and Mrs. Durham," 16 October 1927, p.7; "Armistice Entertainment At Hillcrest," 12 November 1927, p.3. "Empire Entertains Newspapermen With Dinner-Dance At Hillcrest," 17 November 1927, p.1.

249 "Holiday Calendar Takes On Numerous Events," *The Morning Examiner*, 11 December 1927, p.11.

250 "Bartlesville Greets 1928 Advent Quietly," *The Morning Examiner*, 2 January 1928, p.1; Festive Cabaret Party Rings In '28 at Hillcrest," 1 January 1928, p.3.

251 "Country Club Members Have Dinty Moore Supper," *The Morning Examiner*, 19 February 1928, p.4; "University Man Guest At Hillcrest," 21 February 1928, p.3; "Musical Entertainment At Hillcrest," 4 February 1928, p.3; "Hillcrest Club To Have Interesting Dinner Parties," 21 March 1928, p.5; "Wichita Boosters To Be Here Tonight," 3 May 1928, p.1.

252 "Golf Tourney Planned Here," *The Morning Examiner*, 6 May 1928, p.4; "Out-of-Town Visitors At Hillcrest," 4 May 1928, p.5; "Three Local Golfers Win," 6 October 1928, p.2; "Mrs. Carl Wood Retains Championship," 26 October 1928, p.8.

253 "Bartlesville Golfer Wins," *The Morning Examiner*, 6 June 1928, p.9; "Golf Trophies Are On Display," 31 August 1928, p.2; J. H. Collins Breaks Links Record Here," 18 September 1928, p.4; "Hillcrest Course Record Is Broken By Collins Again," 26 September 1928, p.6; "Broaddus Beats Collins For Title," 2 October 1928, p.4; "Hillcrest Golfer Keeps State Title," 4 September 1928, p.4; "Gullane, Collins Win Exhibition Tilt," 8 September 1928, p.4.

254 "Descendant of Indian Chiefs May Become President U.S.," *The Morning Examiner*, 27 November 1927, p.5; "Mrs. Rood Wins Re-Nomination," 12 June 1928, p.1; "Malaria War On In Earnest," 27 June 1928, p.2.

255 "Big Program For Kiwanis," *The Morning Examiner*, 28 May 1928, p.1; "1,000 Attend Empire Picnic," 7 June 1928, p.1; "Empire Host To Big Army Of Salesman," 8 September 1928, p.1; "Hillcrest Entertains Bureau," 24 June 1928, p.4; "Dances Climax Observance Of Armistice Day," 13 November 1928, p.1; "Rotary Inter-City Meeting Tuesday," 25 November 1928, p.1.

256 "Hostesses Choose Dates For Christmas Parties," 2 December 1928, p.4; "Night Club Party Rings in New Year at Hillcrest Dance," 1 January 1929, p.5; "Cold Weather Accompanies 1929's Advent," 1 January 1929, p.1.

257 "Hillcrest Will Hold Annual Meet on Feb. 12," *The Morning Examiner*, 10 January 1929, p.1; "Hillcrest Directors Are Named: Stock Increased," 13 February, p.1; "Reynolds is Elected President of Hillcrest," 21 February 1929, p.6; "Women Arrange for N. E. Golf Play," 7 March 1929, p.5; "Arrange for Hillcrest Dance," 7 March 1929, p.5; "Hillcrest Bridge Tea Party," 9 March 1929, p.6.

258 Osage County Clerk, Mortgage 56, p.329. "Oakhill Club To Be Opened," *The Morning Examiner*, 10 March 1929, p.1; "Clicoquot Club Proves Popular," 9 March 1929, p.6; "Unit of Cliqut Players to Play Here," 10 March 1929, p.11; "Cliquot Club Eskimos Entertain at Hillcrest," 18 March 1929, p.5.

259 "To Have Easter Egg Hunt at Hillcrest,' *The Morning Examiner*, 30 March 1929, p.5; "Hillcrest to Have Easter Program," 31 March 1929, p.6; "Rain Delays Opening of Oak Hill Another Week," 30 March 1929, p.12; "Hillcrest Country Club Dance," 14 April 1929, p.12; "Dining Room Remains Open, "26 October 1929, p.4.

260 "Mrs. Wood Wins," *The Morning Examiner*, 27 September 1929, p.6; "Mrs. Ball Garners Title On 18th Hole," 2 November 1929, p.7; "Hillcrest Ladies Club Meet For Last Day of Season," 29 November 1929, p.5.

261 "Empire Team, With 66, Wins Golf Tournament," *The Morning Examiner*, 30 April 1929, p.6; "Club To Hold City Tourney," 14 July 1929, p.7; "Golf Finals Today," 11 August 1929, p.4; "Caddies At Hillcrest Start Tourney Play," 21 August 1929, p.7. The caddies in 1929 were: Clarence LaPrade, Julias Sas, Dale Storie, Claude Rinker, John LaPrade, Teddy Synos, LeRoy Johnson, Alton LaPrade, William Waller, William Tuttle, Marion Sears, Stanley Orioski, Alfred Vanley, Roy Lee, Harley Hicks, Vernie Vaughn, Clarence Hoening, Gus Resrick, Sherman Elliott, Casinos Sas, Laddie Pietras, Henry Waller, Glen Brantley, Alfred Lehman, John Myers, Victor Easton, Roscoe Stahl, Laddie Macula, Lewis Teeters, Joe Ball, Otis Ramsey, Stanley Mekno, Raymond Resnick, Delbert Hamlin, Clem Sears, George Sas, Leo Sas, Virgil Brantley, Marvin Butcher, T. D. Storie. "Good, Bad, Worse and Usual Golf Seen; Kiwanis Wins 30-23," 20 September 1929, p.6; "Broaddus Keeps Title Beating Neumann, 5-4," 24 October 1929, p.4.

262 "Goodfellows Welcomed By John H. Kane," *The Morning Examiner*, 16 May 1929, p.1; "41 Attend Lions Club Ladies Night Program," 23 October 1929, p.1; "Public Opinion and Peace Are A.A.U.W. Topic," 9 November 1929, p.1; "Miss Shertz Heads A.A.U.W.," 10 November 1929, p.1.

263 "C. Cf C. Holds First Meeting," *The Morning Examiner*, 7 September 1929, p.1; "New Maire Hotel to Open Main Dining Room Today," 22 September 1929, p.1; "City Beautiful Campaign Is On, " 29 October 1929, p.3; "Hillcrest Road, Bridge Locations Are Approved," 30 October 1929, p.1; "Maire Opening Among Leading Social Events," 30 November 1929, p.1; "Dana Reynolds Wins Contest," 25 December 1929, p.1.

264 "Doombos-Foster Dance Last of Parties of a Busy Social Week," *The Morning Examiner*, 30 December 1929, p.5.

265 "Three Dances Will Be Held on Monday Night," *The Morning Examiner*, 6 November 1929, p.10; "Society," 12 November 1929, p.5; "Hillcrest Secures Famous Dancing Trio for Friday," 29 November 1929, p.5; Advertisement, 27 December 1929, p.10; "Annual Frolic at Hillcrest Ushers in The New Year," 1 January 1930; Paul Johnson, *A History of the American People*, New York: HarperCollins, 1997, .p 707.

266 Paul Johnson, p.719.

267 Club of '35 was a social club of high school boys who would graduate in the spring of 1935. There were 10 members: Frank Heller, Frank Finney, Dick Kane, Lloyd Rowland, George Bunn, David Burch, Lucius Hubbell, Leo Johnstone, Alex Nagel, Bob Trippett, and Eddy Watkins.

268 "Riots, Strikes Here Financed By Communist," *The Morning Examiner*, 3 May 1930, p.1.

269 Bartlesville, p. 140; "Subscription To $100,000," *The Morning Examiner*, 21 January 1930, p.1; "Bartlesville Is Picked By Big Industry," 16 January 1930, p.1: Conversation with Mike May, 10 May 2002.

270 "Unique Party at Hillcrest," *The Morning Examiner*, 22 March 1930, p.5. The acronyms here may be a good case in point for the absurdity of our contemporary obsession for impenetrable acronyms.

271 "Guests For Straight-Stevens Wedding Entertained At Four Affairs Today," *The Morning Examiner*, 3 May 1930, p.5; "Straight-Stevens Marriage Consummated In Beautiful Service Saturday," 4 May 1930. p.12.

272 "Moore Wants Name For Hillcrest's Bulletin," *The Morning Examiner*, 20 March 1930, p.1.

273 Walter Wallis, "Golf Report," newspaper clipping probably from 1957 *Examiner-Enterprise*, n.d. in HWGA #1 scrapbook.

274 "Plan For Tennis," *The Morning Examiner*, 6 May 1930, p.7; "Tennis Stars Here Sunday," 30 May 1930, p.1; "400 Are Expected To See Tennis Exhibitions, 1 June 1930.

275 "Empire Picnic At Hillcrest," *The Morning Examiner*, 7 June 1930 p.1; "Over 2,000 At Empire Picnic," 8 June 1930, p.1; "200 Attend Jr. C. Of C. Picnic," 20 June 1930, p.1; "To Hold All Kiwanis Night," 29 June 1930, p.1; "Food Service At Hillcrest," 4 July 1930, p.3; "Miss Ella Roach Named Manager Hillcrest Club," 30 July 1930, p.3.

276 "Work On Bridge Is Progressing," *The Morning Examiner*, 13 July 1930, p.1.

277 "Mrs. Carl Wood Takes Part in Tulsa Tournament," *The Morning Examiner*, 6 June 1930, p.5; "Intercity Golf Tourney Today," 27 July 1930, p.10; "Golfers Gird For City Open," 2 August 1930, p.4; "Finish First Tourney Play," 13 August 1930, p.4; "Bartlesville Ranks Among Heat Leaders," 5 August 1930, p.1; "Hillcrest to Hold Junior Golf Event," 13 August, p.4; "Broaddus To Take Lott Today In open," 17 August 1930, p.6; "Golfers Begin Flights Today," 31 August 1930, p.6; "Caddy (page torn) This Morning," 31 August 1930, p.6; "Sports 25 Years Ago," 12 October 1955, p.9.

278 "Two Favorites In Tournament To Battle Today," The Morning Examiner, 1 October 1930, p.9; "Beats Titlist In Last Match," 15 October 1930, p.6; "Mrs. Phillips Title Winner," 5 November 1930, p.7.

279 "Vagabonds Picnic At Hillcrest," The Morning Examiner, 2 August 1930, p.5; "T. B. Hudson Honored At Birthday Party," 17 September 1930, p.5; "John Kane On Relief Board," 11 December 1930, p.3; "100 Families Need Baskets," 21 December 1930, p.1.

280 "Hillcrest Elects Directors," The Morning Examiner, 21 January 1931, p.2; Wallis.

281 Ellis.

282 "Reynolds Re-Elected Hillcrest President," 3 February 1930, p.1; Washington County Clerk, Mortgage Book 101, 125512, 7 February 1931 (microfische).

283 "Murray's 'Supper' Consists of Biled Turnips, Hog Jowl," The Morning Examiner, 15 January 1931, p.2; "6 More Caught In Liquor Drive," 16 January 1931, p.1; "State Tourney Brought Here," 25 January 1931, p.8;

284 "41 Men Put to Work on Second District's Roads," 27 January 1931, p.1. 25¢ in 1930 is equal to $3.00 in 2007.

285 "Bartlesville Laughs Today To Aid Needy," The Morning Examiner, 6 February 1931, p.1; "One Day's Pay Will Be Asked in 3-Day Drive," 15 February, p.1; "Welfare Drive Total $16,508," 10 April 1931, p.1.

286 "Country Club Women Annex Golf Laurels," The Morning Examiner, 16 May 1931, p.7; "Country Club Reds and Blues Play Saturday," 15 May 1931, p.12. It is interesting to note the pairings since these are men who we consequently know were still members at this low point: Broaddus vs. Gullane, Kincade vs. Fowler, Newman vs. Lott, Hockensmith vs. Fitch, Johnson vs. Feist, McIntyre vs. Sherman, Matkin vs. Cronin, Dewer vs. Wing, Heine vs. Charles, Phillips vs. Stone, Caldwell vs. Blank, Haskell vs. Alexander, Holm vs. Michaelson, Reudy vs. Ringo, Fowler vs. Durnell, Nesbit vs. Crooks, Lernertz vs. Holm, Howell vs. Shaffer, Kaiser vs. Hubbell, Dahlgren vs. Adams, Dahlgren vs. Murray, Gratton vs. Crawford, Julian vs. Wood, Wells vs. Sands, Connelly vs. Harris, Morton vs. Doornbos, Hudson vs. Peyton, Edgerton vs. White, Reed vs. Westby, Gardner vs. Emenheiser.

287 "Laffoon And Thompson In Match Today," The Morning Examiner, 31 May 1931, p.12; Don Wade, Talking on Tour, New York: McGraw Hill, 2003, p.197; Wallis, p.224-227.

288 Wallis, p.226.

289 "Course Here Wins Praise," The Morning Examiner, 31 May 1931, p.12; "Country Club Road Complete, 12 June 1931, p.3.

290 "Amateurs To Take Course As Play Nears," The Morning Examiner, 3 June 1931, p.3; "Golfing Field Flocks Here As tourney Nears," 6 June 1931, p,8; Alva Dopking, "Hillcrest Where Amateur Golfers Campaign for Championship This Week," 7 June 1931, p.10; "Young Golfers Play Veterans In Semi-Finals," 11 June 1931, p.1.

291 "Home Golfers Take Share of Meet Trophies," The Morning Examiner, 13 June 1931, p.6; "Tourney Host Club Popular With Golfers," 13 June 1931, p.6.

292 "Lawyers Hold Annual Dinner," The Morning Examiner, 21 June 1931, p.1.

293 Ellis, p.252-3.

294 "Lott New City Golf Champion," The Morning Examiner, 4 August 1931, p.6; "57 Qualify in Caddy Tourney," 26 August 1931, p.8; "Caddies Play Near Par Golf," 29 August 1931, p.4; Lemon, p.340, 10.

295 "Final Match Slated Today," The Morning Examiner, 27 September 1931, p.6; "Mrs. Wood To Keep Dunn Cup," 4 October 1931, p.6; "Hillcrest Tournament Play Delayed By Rain," 13 October 1931, p.6; "Tulsa Players Win Golf Meet," 27 October 1931, p.4; "Gullane Sinks 90-yard Shot," 19 November 1931, p.4.

296 "350 Baskets Distributed," The Morning Examiner, 25 December 1931, p.1; "Woman Provides Dinners For 500 Needy Persons," 25 December 1931, p.1.

297 "Large Tea Honoring Mrs. Kirk," The Morning Examiner, 27 December 1931, p.5.

298 "Hillcrest New Years Dance of Interest," The Morning Examiner, 27 December 1931, p.5; "Many Celebrate Coming of New Year," 1 January 1931, p.5.

299 "Junior Dance Club To Begin," The Morning Examiner, 14 February 1932, p.5. $35 is $430 in 2007 dollars – pretty pricey.

300 "Hillcrest Re-elects Members of board," The Morning Examiner, 20 January 1932, p.1.

301 "Broaddus and Orloski Meet," The Morning Examiner, 1 May 1932, p.7; "(illegible)," 3 May 1932, p.7; "Mrs. Wood In Championship," 24 May 1932, p.4; "Gullane and Broaddus In Trans-Mississippi," 29 May 1932, p.6.

302 "Mrs. Wallace Wins With 86," The Morning Examiner, 18 June 1932, p.10.

303 "Orloski Triumphs On 27th Green 10 Up," The Morning Examiner, 2 September 1932, p.7; "Broaddus Wins Meet With 231," 6 September 1932, p.4; "Feist Defeats Club Champion," 20 September 1932, p.4; "Gullane Wins State Crown," 11 October 1932, p.4; "Heine and Cronin Tie Twice, to Play Again," 11 October 1932, p.4; "Mrs. James Phillips Wins Another Title," 28 October 1932, p.6; "Mrs. Phillips New Champion," 21 October 1932, p.6.

304 "Gullane Plays Sarazen Today," The Morning Examiner, 15 October 1932, p.10; "Gullane To Play Today In Okmulgee Exhibition," 26 October 1932, p.5; "Gullane Heads State's Pros," 15 December 1932, p.6.

305 "Plans Made for Starting Garden for City's Needy," The Morning Examiner, 25 March 1932, p.1; "Party of City Young People Fired Upon," 2 September 1932, p.1; "Welfare Drive For $40,000 To Start Today," 21 September 1932, p.1.

306 "Hillcrest Gets Well-Known Band," The Morning Examiner, 13 November 1932, p.5; "Series Of Dances Planned," 16 December 1932, p.5; "Society News," 20 December 1932, p.5; "Miss Foster Entertains With Dance," 29 December 1932, p.5; "New Year Will Find Jolly Welcome," 31 December 1932, p.5.

307 "Holm Heads Hillcrest," The Morning Examiner, 22 January 1933, p.3; "Reynolds Services Recognized," 24 January 1933, p.3.

308 "Musicale at Hillcrest at Four," The Morning Examiner, 19 February 1933, p.5; "Phillips To Broadcast Tonight," 2 March 1933, p.5; "Foster-Kane Engagement Is Announced; Friends Hear News At Dinner Party," 19 March 1933, p.5.

309 "Were Hosts at Dinner Party," *The Morning Examiner*, 2 April 1933, p.2; "Dance at Hillcrest," 16 April 1933, p.5; "Saddle Club Will Stage Horse Show On May 20," 1 May 1933, p.4.

310 "Golfers Are Active," *The Morning Examiner*, 24 January 1933, p.3; "Elephant Hunt Is Feature At Hillcrest," 2 March 1933, p.4.

311 "Guest Players Defeat Locals," *The Morning Examiner*, 22 April 1933, p.5; "Jackson and Cronin Beat Gullane, Smoot," 10 June 1933, p.7; "Fowler Wins Golf Tourney," 30 May 1933, p.4; "Blind Bogey Tourney Will Continue Today," 30 May 1933, p.4.

312 "Saddle Club Will Stage Horse Show Here On May 20," *The Morning Examiner*, 1 May 1933, p.4.

313 "Local horses After Honors," *The Morning Examiner*, 17 March 1933, p.4. The complete listing of horses besides Kane and Morton were: Phil Phillips' black mare, Black Beauty; Mrs. Carl Minnig's bay mare, Bay Beauty; C. E. Murray's bay gelding, Bill; R. M. Riggins' black gelding, Midnite; Mrs. R. M. Riggins' bay mare, My Louise; F. K. Haskell's sorrel gelding, Prince Adair, and dapple gray gelding, Silver; Mrs. H. J. Sherman's bay mare, Lady Great; H. L. Montgomery's sorrel gelding, Dan; J. S. Dewer's sorrel gelding, Flash; C. E. Burlingame's sorrel gelding, Sport; Mrs. Clyde Fowler's bay mare, Princess; Marie Foster's black mare, Dixiana.

314 "Horse Show to be Sporting and Social Interest," *The Morning Examiner*, 14 May 1933, p.4; Wallis, p.334.

315 "Women Stage Fashion Show At Hillcrest," *The Morning Examiner*, 21 May 1933, p.1; "Horse Show Entertainment Complete," 19 May 1933, p.3.

316 "Gullane, Broaddus To Be Paired In O.C. Event," *The Morning Examiner*, 11 June 1933, p.5; "Wing and Edgerton Turn In Low Medal Scores," 11 June 1933, p.5; Johnson Shots 74, One Under Jackson In Hillcrest March," 11 June 1933, p.5; "Fowler Wins Medal Score," 18 June 1933, p.4; "Broaddus and Gullane Win at Coffeyville," 20 June 1933, p.4; "Johnson Makes Best Local Amateur Score," 22 June 1933, p.4; "Fowler Wins Title," 28 June 1933, p.4.

317 "Gullane Wins State P.G.A.," *The Morning Examiner*, 14 July 1933, p.6; "Hillcrest Men Enter Tourney," 1 August 1933, p.4; "Golf Greens Are Problem," 30 July 1933, p.6; "21 Entrants Play Rounds," 2 August 1933, p.4; "Johnson Makes Best Local Amateur Score," 22 June 1933, p.4; "Fowler Wins Title," 28 June 1933, p.4. 35¢ is %5.27, and. 75¢ is $11.29 in 2007 dollars.

318 "A- The State Open," *The Morning Examiner*, 4 August 1933, p.8.

319 "A- The State Open," *The Morning Examiner*, 5 August 1933, p.8.

320 "A- The State Open," *The Morning Examiner*, 6 August 1933, p.4.

321 "R ney Reports Hulah Project Most Feasible," *The Morning Examiner*, 13 June 1933, p 1; "Hulah Dam Goes To Ickes With Six-State Okay," 27 December 1933, p.1; "Sewage Bonds Are Approved By 2 To 1 Vote," 13 December 1933, p.1; "City Gets On Tulsa-K.C. Air Route," 27 December 1933, p 1.

322 "Caddy Tourney Starts Today," *The Morning Examiner*, 24 August 1933, p.4; "Mrs. G. S. Coburn Wins Consolidation Flight,' 22 September 1933, p.4; "Mrs. Phillips Retains Hillcrest Championship," 7 October 1933, p.8; "Broaddus Wins Medal Honors," 24 September 1933, p.4

323 "Social Interest To Focus On Horse Show," *The Morning Examiner*, 1 October 1933, p 7; "Horse Show Postponed Until Saturday, Oct. 14," 5 October 1933, p.3.

324 "Gullane Sets Course Record," *The Morning Examiner*, 11 November 1933, p.6.

325 "Annual Thanksgiving Dance At Hillcrest," *The Morning Examiner*, 30 November 1933, p.5.

326 "Road Being Improved," *The Morning Examiner*, 3 January 1934, p.3; "Only 352 Families On Welfare Agency," 7 February 1934, p 1; "Governor Opens Campaign," 25 January 1934, p.1; "Bartlesville Undergoing Protracted Dry Spell," 21 January 1934, p.4; "R. Cantwell Is Awarded JCC Service Medal," 20 January 1934, p.1.

327 "Kiwanis Induction Attended By 150," *The Morning Examiner*, 6 January 1934, p.1; "Here's How And Why Of Tuesday's Dance," 28 January 1934, p.7; "Mr. and Mrs. R. C. Jopling Entertain At Large Dinner, 28 January 1934, p.4.

328 "Hillcrest Re-elects 3 Directors, Add One," *The Morning Examiner*, 17 January 1934, p.1; "Club Of '30 Had Second Meeting," The Bartlesville Enterprise, 5 July 1934, p.7.

329 "Ladies Day At Hillcrest Is Enjoyed By Forty Guests." *The Morning Examiner*, 15 March 1934, p.5.

330 "Gullane Stays At Or Near Par Consistently," *The Morning Examiner*, 8 April 1934, p.6; "K. C. Golf Aces Will Play Here," 3 May 1934, p.6; "Trower Three Up On Broaddy," 9 May 1934, p.4; "Broaddus Sets Record With 71," 13 May 1934, p.8; "187 Women Participate In Hillcrest Golf Meet," 17 May 1934, p.4; "Johnson Captures Hillcrest Flag Tournament, " 31 May 1934, p.4.

331 "Saddle Club To Be Guests At Kanes," *The Morning Examiner*, 7 April 1934, p.7; "The Saddle Club Elects Officers For 1934," 8 April 1934, p.1, The new club officers for 1934 were C. E. Burlingame, president, R. M. Riggins, vice president, Phil Phillips, secretary-treasurer. The trustees were C. E. Burlingame, John H. Kane, H. A. Trower, F. K. Haskell, A. M. Hughes, C. E. Murray, and C. W. Doerndos. The committees were, chairmen named first: House, R. L. Morton, K. S. Adams, H. E. Holm; bridle path, Mrs. R. L. Morton, Mrs. R. M. Riggins, John H. Kane, P. F. Dahlgren, R. C. Jopling; Horse show, R. M. Riggins, Rigby Slight, H. A. Trower; Membership, Mrs. Carl Minnig, Mrs. Don Friday, Mrs. H. C. Price; supervise management of stables, F. K. Haskell. "Riggins Names Committee To Help Conduct Horse Show," 8 April 1934, p.1; The next day Russell Riggins, chairman of the show committee, appointed sub-committees: local classes, K. S. Adams; grounds, H. E. Hewitt; railway traffic, E. C. Kitching; tickets, R. L. Morton; prizes, J. F. May; hotels, Rigby Slight; publicity, H. A. Trower; reception and entertainment, O. K. Wing; show superintendent, F. K. Haskell; stakes, P. F. Dahlgren. The Chamber of Commerce appointed a citizens advisory committee: Clyde Alexander, C. E. Burlingame, H. F. Cameron, H. G. Ellis, R. J. Daugherty, H. V. Foster, Bert Gaddis, W. H. Gill, H. E. Hulen J. H. Kane, J. S. Leach, H. H. McClintock, J. L. Overlees, Frank Phillips, L. E. Phillips, C. E. Perkins, M. E. Perser, A. F. Potter, H. R. Straight, D. M. Tyler, H. C. Webber, N. D. Welty, M. L Zofness, W. C. Smoot, and Ralph Taylor. The publicity committee was Ralph Taylor, A. F. Potter, and C. E. Perkins.

332 "55 Show Sponsers Already Obtained," *The Morning Examiner*, 22 April 1934, p.3; "Horse Show Prize Total Passes $4,000," 28 April 1934, p.7; "Gene Cawley Engaged By The Hillcrest Saddle Club," 21 April 1934, p.4; "Horse Show Prize List Made Public," 29 April 1934, p.1; "Judge and ringmaster Chosen For Horse Show," 1 May 1934, p.5.

333 "Editor Urges Horse Men To Make Show," *The Morning Examiner*, 20 May 1934, p.1; "Many Local Horses Entered In Second Annual Horse Show," *The Bartlesville Enterprise*, 29 April 1934, p.3. It is interesting to see who the local horses and exhibitors were: In Western Class R. L. Morton brought Pippin's Choice; Sally Wallace brought Wallace Brown; Stewart Dewer entered Flash, Fred Haskell entered Prince Dare; Mrs. Van H. Montgomery entered Lady Ghost; Bill Hale Montgomery brought Pinto; R. C. Jopling brought Pecos; Mrs. Clyde Fowler rode Lassie McDonald, Mrs. R. M. Riggins brought Blue Heaven and Aletha Highland; Al Gililand entered Zed; L. E. Sheridan entered High Hat Jimmy, My Pal, and Tony Boy; Billy Dancer rode Tony; Grace Koster rode Button; Belle Meade Academy entered Blackie; S. N. Van Wort entered Pin Toy; Vicki Kerr entered Tony, Wallace Brown rode Sally; Loren Nye rode Silver; Oren Mair entered Pal; Morton Murray entered Blue Bell and Spot; Jimmie Potts rode Major Kickapoo; Mrs. H. V. Foster entered Jean Bourbon; Mrs. H. C. Weber entered Rex; G. C. Clark entered Duke Macdonald; Wilbur Barr entered Margaret Marie. "Society Notice," *The Morning Examiner*, 19 May 1934, p.9; "Entry List is Closed," 2 June 1934, p.1; "Million Dollars in horse Flesh To be Housed in Tented City," *The Bartlesville Enterprise*, 2 June 1934, p.1.

334 "Out-of-Town Guests To Attend Horse Show," *The Morning Examiner*, 5 June 1934, p.5; "Saddle Club Entertains Horse Show Visitors," The Bartlesville Enterprise, 8 June 1934, p.5; "Visitors Being Extended Social Courtesies," 9 June 1934, p.3; "Affairs Given Yesterday For Horse Show Visitors," *The Morning Examiner*, 10 June 1934, p.5; "Horse Show Costumes," 10 June 1934, p.5.

335 "109 Exhibitors To Be Here For The Horse Show," *The Bartlesville Enterprise*, 4 June 1934, p.1. 25¢ is $4.00 and 55¢ is $8.75 in 2007 dollars "Tulsa To Broadcast City's Horse Show," *The Morning Examiner*,

5 June 1934, p.1; "10,000 People Expected Here For Horse Show," The Bartlesville Enterprise, 7 June 1934, p.10; "Thousands To Attend Horse Show Tonight," *The Morning Examiner*, 8 June 1934, p.1; "Oklahoma Editors To Visit Here Today," 9 June 1934, p.1; "Bartlesville Today," 10 June 1934, p.1; "Overflow Crowd Of 3,600 Sees The opening Of Horse Show," *The Bartlesville Enterprise*, 9 June 1934, p.1; "Plans Bigger Show," *The Morning Examiner*, 17 June 1934, p.1.

336 "New Champion," *The Bartlesville Enterprise*, 9 July 1934, p.7

337 "Cattle From Drought Areas Shipped Here," *The Morning Examiner*, 29 June 1934, p.3; "Plenty Of Water For City, Report Shows," *The Bartlesville Enterprise*, 20 July 1934, p.1; "Welfare Out Of Funds," 5 July 1934, p.6; "FERA Office Hours Schedule," 25 July 1934, p.1; Secretary to Edith Williams, letter, 21 June 1934 (Woolaroc Archive).

338 "Nudists Plead Guilty," *The Bartlesville Enterprise*, 12 July 1934, p.8; Edwin L. Queen, et. al, *The Encyclopedia of American Religious History*, New York: Facts On File, p.394-395; "Sister Aimee Here Today For Five Meetings," *The Bartlesville Enterprise*, 30 July 1934, p.1.

339 "318 Families Given Beef Through W.A.," *The Morning Examiner*, 1 August 1934, p.2; "Entire State Is Placed In Primary Drought Class, 100,000 Families Suffering,"5 August 1934, p.1; "Cattle Buying To Start Here," 10 August 1934, p.1.

340 "Borers Hurt Trees," *The Morning Examiner*, 10 August 1934, p.1; Frank Phillips appointment book, 1934 (Woolaroc); "Bartians Searching For Stray Breezes," 12 August 1934, p.1; "Reports Of Water Shortage Denied," 12 August 1934, p.1; "Soundings Made For City Sewage Plant," 8 September 1934, p.1.

341 Tournament Into Semi-Final," *The Morning Examiner*, 1 August 1934, p.4; 6/30/02 telephone interview with Walter Szalla, Chicago.

342 "Dance Is Included," *The Morning Examiner,* 16 September 1934, p.1; "St. Luke's Host To Church Dignitaries," 16 September 1934, p.2; "150 Are Expected At Business Men's Dinner," 27 September 1934, p.1; "350 Traffic Men To Attend Meet Today," 27 September 1934, p.1.

343 "Trower Captures Club Handicap," *The Morning Examiner*, 14 October 1934, p.4; "Mrs. Phillips Beats Mrs. Hopper 3 and 2," 26 September 1934, p.4; "Mrs. Phillips Is Victor Again," 26 October 1934, p.6.

344 "To Oil Hillcrest Road," *The Morning Examiner*, 18 September 1934, p.1; "Old Order Must Go," 28 September 1934, p.1; "500 hounds To Compete In Annual Meet Next Week," 6 October, 1934, p.1; "200 Dogs Hit Trail After Wily Coyotes," 9 October 1934, p.1; "1500 Attend Night Program Held At Wolf Hunters' Camp," 10 October 1934, p.1.

345 "New Social Club Is Organized," *The Morning Examiner*, 5 October 1934, p.7.

346 "Bankers Impressed With Bartlesville," *The Morning Examiner*, 3 November 1934, p.1; "Welfare Drive Nets $800 Above Goal Set," 15 December 1934, p.1; "Dinners To Precede Country Club Dance," 27 October 1934, p.4.

347 "Dance Given By Senior Club," T*he Morning Examiner*, 1 December 1934, p.6; "Thanksgiving Dance At Hillcrest Club," 2 December 1934, p.6; "Dance Planned For Next Week," 23 December 1934, p.6; "Breakfast-Bridge To Be Held On Saturday," 25 December 1934, p.5; "Open Houses Planned For New Years Day," 30 December 1934, p.6; "Open Houses Precede New Years Club Dance," 30 December 1934, p.6; "Supper-Dance Planned For Monday," 30 December 1934, p.6; "New Years Arrival Celebrated At Affairs," 1 January 1935, p.3.

348 "Hillcrest Stockholders Will Meet Tuesday Night," *The Morning Examiner,* 12 January 1935, p.1; "Three New Directors Named By Hillcrest," 16 January 1935, p.1; "Hillcrest Directors Re-Name All Officers," 1 February 1935, p.1.

349 "Moore Terms J.C.C. Best In State," *The Morning Examiner*, 19 January 1935, p.1; "Rotes To Dine Tonight," 22 January 1935, p.1; "Joint Luncheon To Observe Founders Day," 30 January 1935, p.5. "Mrs. Feist Names Two Committees," 20 January 1935, p.1.

350 "Dance Tonight To Be Interesting Affair," *The Morning Examiner*, 22 February 1935, p.3; "Unity Chapter To Have Dance," 8 March 1935, p.7; "KU Alumnae Association Meets At Hillcrest," 19 May 1935, p.1.

351 "Dance Planned For Club Saturday," *The Morning Examiner*, 1 March 1935, p.7; "Large Dance at Hillcrest Saturday," 7 April 1935, p.4; "Dance Given By School Friends," 21 April 1935, p.5; "Spring Dance At Hillcrest," 5 May 1935, p.5.

352 "Dust Settles Over The City On Trail of Winds," *The Morning Examiner*, 22 February 1935, p.1; "Stifling Dust Moves Eastward After Paralyzing Southwest," 21 March 1935, p.1.

353 "Rube Party Given At Hillcrest Club," *The Morning Examiner*, 10 March 1935, p.5; "Horse Show Planned," 16 March 1935, p.1; "Saddle Club Members Schedule Weekly Rides," 28 March 1935, p.3; "Dinner At Maire For Saddle Club," 7 April 1935, p.4; "Saddle Club To Stage Monthly Horse Show," 2 May 1935, p. 7.

354 "Saddle Club To Stage Monthly Horse Show," *The Morning Examiner*, 2 May 1935, p. 7; "Horse Show Planned," 16 March 1935, p.1; "Maryin Couch To Become Hillcrest Saddle Trainer," 9 May 1935, p.4.

355 "Show Date Advanced," *The Morning Examiner*, 12 May 1935, p.1; "Horse Show Postponed Until Sunday, May, 26," 19 May 1935, p.1; "Horse Show Will Be One Of The Best In U. S.", 1 June 1935, p.1.

356 "Hillcrest Women Elect Officers," *The Morning Examiner*, 16 January 1935, p.5; "Today Officially Ushers In Golf Activities Here," 21 April 1935, p.6; "Broaddus Captures Phillips Tournament," 14 May 1935, p.4.

357 "Smoot Wins Jaysee," *The Morning Examiner*, 30 April 1935, p.6; "216 Take Part in Junior C. of C. Qualifying Round," 30 April 1935, p.6; "Dance Tonight For Golf Association," 11 May 1935, p.5.

358 "Hostesses To Women Golfers," *The Morning Examiner*, 2 June 1935, p.2; "Women to Begin Play With Scotch Foursomes Sunday," 2 June 1935, p.6.

359 "56 Players Enter City Golf Tourney," *The Morning Examiner*, 11 June 1935, p.4; "Johnson Takes the City Golf Crown," 25 June 1935, p.4; "Hillcrest Open Will Attract 150 players," 30 June 1935, p.4.

360 "Hillcrest Members Play Golf, Eat Barbecue," *The Morning Examiner*, 4 July 1935, p.4; "Expect Big Crowd," 4 July 1935, p.5; "Gullane Establishes A New Course

Record," 5 July 1935, p.6.; "Wilson Shoots A 76 At Hillcrest Club Course, 28 July 1935, p.4.

361 "Special Exhibition Golf Match For Hillcrest," *The Morning Examiner*, 4 August 1935, p.6; "Ministers To Seek Vote On Slot Machines," 3 July 1935, p.1; "Visiting Golfers Win Exhibition Match 1 Up," 29 October 1935, p.4.

362 The city's official thermometer had been on top of the tar roof of the Empire Building at one time. The Chamber of Commerce thought the astronomical summer temperatures that were often reported were bad publicity, and so the thermometer was moved to the airport. The date of this move is not known, but newspaper reports from the 1930s heat waves specifically mention that the thermometer was at the airport by that time.

363 "Bad Weather Causes Scores To Skyrocket," *The Morning Examiner*, 24 August 1935, p.10; "First Round Finished In The Caddy Tournament," 29 August 1935, p.4; "Hillcrest Plays Labor Day Golfing Feature," 1 September 1935, p.6; "Even When Match Ends," 3 September 1935, p.4.

364 "Horse Show Offices Will Open At Hotel," *The Morning Examiner*, 18 June 1935, p.1; "Schilling To Be Ringmaster," 23 June 1935, p.7; "Long To Head Horse Show Judging Here," 28 July 1935, p.4.

365 "Show Committees Doing Great Work," *The Morning Examiner*, 4 July 1935, p.5.

366 "Horse Show Group To Spend $10,000 Here," *The Morning Examiner*, 21 July 1935, p.4; "Box Seats For Horse Show Are Going Fast," 16 August 1935, p.1.

367 V. T. Broaddus Takes The Hillcrest Title," *The Morning Examiner*, 24 September 1935, p.4; "100 Sign Membership Cards In New Golf Club," 15 September 1935, p.1; "Doornbos, Allen Win," 24 September 1935, p.4; "Mrs. Phillips Wins Women's Tourney," 3 October 1935, p.4; "Smoot Wins Junior Chamber Golf Meet," 1 October 1935, p.4; "Willet goes To Final Round Men's Handicap," 6 October 1935, p.6; "Hillcrest Women Are Awarded Prizes," 21 November 1935, p.4.

368 "Transportation Men Assemble For Outing," *The Morning Examiner*, 25 September 1935, p.1; "Lions Go On Air," 25

September 1935, p.1; "Charter Presented To Bartlesville BMA," 28 September 1935, p.1.

369 "Horse Show To Mobilize Society's Elite Here," *The Morning Examiner*, 8 September 1935, p.4. $4.44 is $68 and $26 in 2007 dollars. "Senator Crawford's Trainer Is Injured," 11 September 1935, p.3; "Nation's Best Horses Arrive For The Show," 29 September 1935, p.1; "City Hostesses To Entertain Out-Of-Town Show Guests," 29 September 1935, p,6; advertisement, 29 September 1935, p.7; "Large Affairs Are Planned This Week For Show Guests," 1 October 1935, p.5; "Daily Broadcasts Planned For Show," 2 October 1935, p.1.

370 "Marland Will Arrive At 5:15," *The Morning Examiner*, 2 October 1935, p.1.

371 "Governor Knows Horses," *The Morning Examiner*, 3 October 1935, p.1; "1,000 Meet Marland," 3 October 1936, p.1; "Records," 4 October 1935, p.1.

372 "Marland Will Arrive At 5:15," *The Morning Examiner*, 2 October 1935, p.7; "Landon Will Arrive At 11:45 This Morning," 3 October 1935, p.1; "Exhibitors Sample Delights Of FP Ranch," 4 October 1935, p.1; "The Senator, Belle Sarita Still Supreme," 4 October 1935, p.1.

373 "Extend Horse Show Thu Sunday Night," *The Morning Examiner*, 5 October 1935, p.1; "Horse Show's Activities Take Society Spotlight," 5 October 1935, p.6; "Dance Last Night Climaxed Horse Show Activities," 6 October 1935, p.7; "Horsemen Hail Show As Greatest Of 1935," 8 October 1935, p.1.

374 "City Goes For Polo," *The Morning Examiner*, 30 October 1935, p.1; "Tulsa Poloists Win Sunday Game, 11-8," 26 November 1935, p.4.

375 "Hal Price Company Gets Many Big Jobs," *The Morning Examiner*, 9 October 1935, p.1; "Phillips Raps Share The Wealth Program," 16 October 1935, p.1; "Educator Raps Legion, D.A.R. As Intolerants," 16 November 1935, p.1.

376 "Welfare Fund Drive Is Over-Subscribed," *The Morning Examiner*, 23 November 1935, p.1.

377 "Christmas Party Planned For Children," *The Morning Examiner*, 20 December 1935, p.4; "Serenaders Acquire Singer,"

24 December 1935, p.2; "Holiday Dance Gay Affair At Hillcrest Country Club," 28 December 1935, p.4; Holiday Dance At Hillcrest Club," 29 December 1935, p.4; "Western Oklahoma Buried Under Six Inch Covering; 3 Persons Die On Highways," 29 December 1935, p.1.

378 "New Years Dance At Hillcrest Club," *The Morning Examiner*, 29 December 1935, p.4; "Pre-Dance Affairs Planned For Tonight," 31 December 1935, p.5; "Hillcrest Country Club Setting For Gala Dance," 1 January 1936, p.5; "Open House At Burlingame Place." 2 January 1936, p.5.

379 "New Building To Reach High Mark," *The Morning Examiner*, 2 January 1936, p.5; "Medical Association To Have Dinner Meeting," 1 January 1936, p.5; "Saddle Club To Have Rube Party Saturday, 14 January 1936, p.3; "Rube Party To Be Gala Affair," 18 January 1936, p.4; "Musical Tea Planned At Hillcrest Club," 16 January 1936, p.3.

380 "Hillcrest CC Elects Ambrose, Owen, Holm," *The Morning Examiner*, 22 January 1936, p.1; "Hillcrest To Elect Directors Tonight," 19 January 1937, p.4.

381 "Leap Year Party At Hillcrest Club," *The Morning Examiner*, 15 February 1936, p.4; "Dance Planned At Hillcrest," 5 March 1936, p.5; "Dance Last Night At Hillcrest Club," 22 March 1936, p.5; "Dance Planned At Hillcrest,' 11 April 1936, p.7; "Novelty Dance Planned At Club," 14 April 1936, p.5; "Concluding Dance For Hillcrest Club," 1 May 1936, p.6.

382 "Mr. and Mrs. Riggins To Have Dinner At Club," 2 April 1936, p.3' "Hillcrest Saddle Club Luncheon At Freiday's," 2 April 1936, p.3; "Morton Heads Club," 25 April 1936, p.1.

383 "Spring Horse Show Will Be Staged Under Auspices Of Newly Formed Association," *The Morning Examiner*, 5 May 1936, p.1.

384 "Prices Are Fixed For Spring Horse Show," *The Morning Examiner*, 6 May 1936, p.1; "Entries Pouring In For The Horse Show," 10 May 1936, p.1; "Classy Spring Show to Open Tonight," 29 May 1936, p.1; "Nichols Horse Wins 5 Gaited Saddle Stake," 31 May 1936, p.1; "Dance Last Night For Show Guests," 31 May 1936, p.4.; "No Fall horse Show," 3 July 1936, p.1.

385 "To Banquet Tonight," *The Morning Examiner*, 17 January 1936, p.1; "Meningitis At Newkirk," 6 March 1936, p.7; "250 Visitors Will Attend Conference," 28 February 1936, p.1; "Hundreds Will Hear Admiral Byrd Today," 28 February 1936, p.1.

386 "City Gets First Taste of Dust This 'Season'," *The Morning Examiner*, 12 March 1936, p.1; "Business Women Banquet," 17 March 1936, p.5; "Lions Will Entertain Their Ladies Tonight," 24 March 1936, p.1; "A.B.C. Charter Dinner On Tomorrow Night," 16 April 1936, p.1; "Sizzling Heat Parches State," 14 April 1936, p.1; "Dance Last Night At Hillcrest Club," 26 April 1936, p.2, "Selling Stampede Causes Stocks To Fall $1 to $10; Wheat Loses 5¢ A Bushel," 28 April 1936, p.1.

387 "Mrs. Hudson New Head of Hillcrest Women," *The Morning Examiner*, 16 January 1936, p.4; "Gullane Vice President of State Pro Golfers," 12 February 1936, p.4; "Broaddus and Fowler Tie For Low With 76," 22 March 1936, p.9; "Broaddus Sets A New Low For Amareurs," 24 April 1936, p.6; "Trower Shoots Medal Score At Tulsa Meet," 24 pril 1936, p.6; "Trower Takes Oil Exposition Golfing Crown," 22 May 1936, p.1; "Trower Beat Storie 7 And 6," 31 May 1936, p.6.

388 "Mrs. Phillips Wins City Title Again," *The Morning Examiner*, 23 May 1936, p.10; "Mrs. Phillips Plays A Champ," 2 June 1936, p.4; "Keith Fowler Wins Flag Tournament At Hillcrest," 31 May 1936, p.6.

389 "Junior-Senior Prom Next Friday Night," *The Morning Examiner*, 2 May 1936, p.1; "Miss Fischer Honoree At Scholarship Luncheon," 3 May 1936, p.5; "100 Attend Kiwanis Party," 13 May 1936, p.1; "Doherty Girls Had Annual Banquet," 11 June 1936, p.3; "Fifty Attend Rotary Club Father-Daughter Dinner," 23 June 1936, p.1; "B.P.W. Club To Install Officers Monday Night,' 28 June 1936, p.1; "Lions Club Observes Ladies Night Tonight," 7 July 1936, p.1.

390 E. P. Earle to Frank Phillips, letter, 28 October 1936. Woolaroc Archive.

391 "Bartlesville, Nowata 'First' In The Nation," *The Morning Examiner*, 16 July 1936, p.1.

392 "Trower and Gullane To Pair in Pro-Amateur," *The Morning Examiner*, 7 June 1936, p.6; "Amateurs Pouring In For Practice Rounds," 11 June 1936, p.6.

393 "I Broke 200," *The Morning Examiner*, 16 June 1936, p.1.

394 "Trower-Less Field Narrows To 8 Amateurs," *The Morning Examiner*, 18 June 1936, p.6.

395 "Flashes Par Golf To Win," *The Morning Examiner*, 21 June 1936, p.8.

396 "Women To Hold District Meeting Here On Friday," *The Morning Examiner*, 25 June 1936, p.4; "Jaysee, ABC, And Oil Firm Slated," 27 June 1936, p.6; "Skelly Golfers Beat Phillips Team By 1 Point," 29 June 1936, p.10; "Hofstrom Wins D.M.F. Tournament With 254," 14 July 1936, p.4; "Plenty Of Water In The Caney River Here," 12 August 1936, p.1; "River Is Lower Than It Was In 1934 Drought," 19 August 1936, p.1; "Water Wells To Be Put Down In This County," 25 August 1936, p.1; "Rookie Smith Defeats Brother John For Title," 2 September 1936, p.5.

397 "Traffic Club Outing Sets New Record," *The Morning Examiner*, 24 September 1936, p.1; "Hillcrest Women Present Golf Trophies," 5 November 1936, p.5; "Alexander and Kinkaide," 12 November 1936, p..

398 "Horsemanship School In Debut Here Sunday," *The Morning Examiner*, 21 November 1936, p.10.

399 "Dates Picked For Welfare Money Drive," *The Morning Examiner*, 15 November 1936, p.1; "Turkeys For Needy," 17 December 1936, p.1; "Rineys Win First Prize In Decoration Contest," 23 December 1936, p.1; "Hitler Tones Down Attacks By His Pagans," 22 December 1936, p.1; "Oil Chiefs Are Indicted Again," 23 December 1936, p.4.

400 "Musical Tea At Hillcrest," *The Morning Examiner*, 14 October 1936, p.3; "Annual Halloween Dance, 15 October 1936, p.5.

401 "Hillcrest Dinner-Dance Club Reorganized," *The Morning Examiner*, 17 November 1936, p.3.

402 "Hillcrest Saddle Club To Have Steak Fry," *The Morning Examiner*, 4 December 1936, p.4; "Musical Research Luncheon," 13 December 1935, p.5; "Children's Program At Hillcrest," 18 December 1936, p.7; "Young People's Dance At Hillcrest," 13 December 1936, p.9.

403 "Tyler-Beasley Wedding Last Night," *The Morning Examiner*, 19 December 1936, p.7.

404 "Gordons To Give Dance At Hillcrest," *The Morning Examiner*, 15 December 1936, p.7; "Dance At Hillcrest Last Night," 23 December 1936, p.4; "Christmas Dace At Hillcrest," 24 December 1936, p.2; "Dance At Hillcrest Last Night," 27 December 1926, p.5; "Holiday Dance At Hillcrest," 30 December 1936, p.5; "Dance At Hillcrest Last Night," 1 January 1937, p.5; "New Yorkers Are Guests At Phillips Home," 1 January 1937, p.5. The Frank Bucks were Hollywood celebrities and African big game hunters, Pearl Mesta was the Oklahoma City native who was the Washington, D.C. social arbiteur of the era, and George Vierheller was the director of the St. Louis Zoo.

405 Washington County, Deed Book 126, 141461 general warranty deed, 12 November 1936, p.493; 141698 general warranty deed, 12 November 1936, p.540; Deed Book 129, 141460 release of real estate mortgage, 12 November 1936, p. 214.

406 "Hillcrest To Elect Directors Tonight," *The Morning Examiner*, 19 January 1937, p.4; "Eight New Directors Named At Hillcrest," 20 January 1937, p,1; "Doornbos Is Elected Hillcrest President," 22 January 1937, p.1.

407 "Phillips Highest Paid Oklahoman," *The Morning Examiner*, 7 January 1937, p.1. $91,000 translates to a little more than $1.3 in 2007 dollars; "City Office Buildings To Be Air-Conditioned," 7 January 1937, p.1.

408 "State Leaders To Attend C. C. Banquet Friday," *The Morning Examiner*, 26 January 1937, p.1; "Medical Association To Install Officers," 17 January 1937, p.1; "Jaycees Will Install New Officers Tonight," 22 January 1937, p.1; "Horse Show Is Up To Bartians," 1 January 1937, p.1; "Polo Club Is Formed," 6 February 1937, p.7; "Three Day Rodeo Is Planned," 15 May 1937, p.1.

409 "Luncheon At Hillcrest For Miss Phillips," *The Morning Examiner*, 15 January 1937, p.7; "Mrs. Foster Resigns; Mrs. Stewart Succeeds," 11 March 1937, p.3.

410 Telephone conversation, 5/14/2004, with Bill Yinger, son of Jeanette Hawks Stewart Yinger.

411 "Women Lawyers Will Attend Tulsa Meeting," *The Morning Examiner*, 10 April 1937, p.1.

412 "Country Club Raided," *The Morning Examiner*, 5 May 1937, p.1; "Masters Starts On Machines On Monday," 30 May 1937, p.1; "City Youngster To Be Barred From Dance Halls," 14 May 1937, p.1.

413 "Mrs. Coburn Named Head Hillcrest Women's G. A.," *The Morning Examiner*, 14 January 1937, p.4; "Hillcrest To Be Host To Over 100 Golfers," 5 May 1937, p.9; "Around The Fairways," 1 June 1937, p.5.

414 "New Tennis Group Is Formed," *The Morning Examiner*, 11 May 1937, p.4; "Polo Game Scheduled For Dewey Saturday," 20 May 1937, p.4; advertisement, 8 June 1937, p.4. $38.95 would be $577, $23.45 would be $347, and 75¢ is $11.11 in 2007 dollars.

415 "40 To Participate In Foursome Event," *The Morning Examiner*, 6 June 1936, p.9; "Foursome Winners," 8 June 1936, p.4.

"50 Caddies Strike for More Pay; They're Fired," The Morning Examiner, 13 June 1937, p.9; "O. C. Caddies Strike," 13 June 1937, p.9. In a world where grown men were making 25¢ and hour only a few years earlier, this notion was quite outrageous. 60¢, 70¢, and 80¢ translate to $8.89, $10.37, and $11.85 for adolescent boys working a 4-hour round of golf. 20¢ raise is $2.96 in 2007 dollars.

416 "Trower Breaks Record," *The Morning Examiner*, 17 June 1937, p.5; "George Roach DMF Medalist," 20 June 1937, p.8; "Lund Wins O. K. Wing Handicap Trophy," 29 June 1937, p.4; "Will Enter Tourney," 27 August 1937, p.6.

417 "Shoots Her Lowest Score," *The Morning Examiner*, 3 July 1937, p.8; "Wins First Prize," 6 July 1937, p.2.

418 "Caddie Tourney Into Finals," *Bartlesville Daily Enterprise*, 4 September 1936, p.6; "Special Events Labor Day," 7 September 1936, p.7; "Fore!" 23 September 1937, p.6; "C. V. Johnson Wins Golf Title at Hillcrest," 4 October 1937, p.6; "Fore!," 5 October 1937, p.8; Mrs. G. B. Hubbell Is Hillcrest Champion," 15 October 1937, p.10; "Fore!," 1 November 1937, p.5.

420 "ITIO Co. Employees Will Be Guests Of Company," *The Bartlesville Enterprise*, 23 September 1937, p.1; "Traffic Men Here Wednesday," 4 October 1937, p.1; "Golf tourney One of JCC Convention Features," 13 October 1937, p.6; "Rotarians To Entertain Visitors Monday Night," 22 October 1937, p.1; "Many Social Affairs Planned For Visitors," 13 October 1937, p.5.

421 "C. E. Burlingame To Build Fine New Home," *Bartlesville Daily Enterprise*, 18 September 1937, p.1.

422 "H. V. Foster's Condition Improved," *Bartlesville Daily Enterprise*, 6 October 1937, p.3.

423 "Frank Phillips Reviews Oil Industry's Activities Before Tulsa C. of C.," *Bartlesville Daily Enterprise*, 31 December 1937, p.1.

424 "Halloween Festivities In Full Sway Tonight," *Bartlesville Daily Enterprise*, 30 October 1937, p.3; "Young Folks Celebrate At Hillcrest," 1 November 1937, p.8; "Interesting Party For Dinner-Dance Club," 10 November 1937, p.2; "Holiday Dance Tonight At Hillcrest," 27 November 1937, p.3.

425 Meda Smith, "Gay Holiday Season is Being Planned In Bartlesville," *Bartlesville Daily Enterprise*, 11 December 1937, p.6.

426 "Annual Christmas Party For Hillcrest Children," *Bartlesville Daily Enterprise*, 16 December 1937, p.6; "Society," 28 December 1937, p.2.

427 "Interest Centers At Hillcrest," *Bartlesville Daily Enterprise*, 29 December 1937, p.3.

428 "Many New Years Eve Affairs Planned," *Bartlesville Daily Enterprise*, 31 December 1937, p.6; "Three Large Open Houses Mark Holiday Observance," 1 January 1938, p.2.

429 "Guests Arrive For Artunoff Dance," *The Morning Examiner*, 8 January 1938, p.3.

430 "Large Dance Given By Mr. and Mrs. Artunoff," *The Morning Examiner*, 9 January 1938, p.4.

431 "Children's Party At Hillcrest Saturday," *The Morning Examiner*, 15 February 1938. p.5.

432 "Hillcrest Elects Two New Board Members," *The Morning Examiner*, 19 January 1938, p.1.

433 "Wolf Roping Contest Here Next Sunday," *The Morning Examiner*, 27 February 1938, p.9.

434 "Around The Fairways," *The Morning Examiner*, 6 May 1938, p.6; "Simpson Is New DMF Champ," 10 May 1938, p.4; "Around the Fairways," 20 May 1938, p.4; "Hillcrest Teams Will Battle For Dinner," 21 May 1938, p.8; "100 Per Cent Handicap," 24 May 1938, p.4.

435 "Phillips Annual Meeting Tuesday At Office Here," *The Morning Examiner*, 24 April 1938, p.1; "Summary of Phillips Meetings," 27 April 1938, p.3.

436 "Oil Companies Offer To Pay $400,000 Fines," *The Morning Examiner*, 26 May 1938, p.1.

437 "Phillips Still Believes Firm Was Right," *The Morning Examiner*, 3 June 1938, p.1.

438 "Frank Phillips Is Acquitted By Court," *The Morning Examiner*, 20 July 1938, p.1.

439 "Hillcrest Easter Egg Hunt Will Be Sunday," *The Morning Examiner*, 15 April 1938, p.2; "Mrs. David Phillips is Honor guest at Tea," 3 May 1938, p.6; "Junior-Senior Prom at Hillcrest Tonight," 13 May 1938, p.3.

440 "Dancing Party For Class Is Wednesday," *The Morning Examiner*, 1 June 1938, p.5; "Hillcrest Celebration Of July 4 Planned," 2 July 1938, p.3; "Noted Dance Band Plays At Hillcrest Saturday," 10 July 1938, p.3.

441 "Big Attendance Is Expected At Lions Convention," *The Morning Examiner*, 27 May 1938, p.1; "Caddies Are Needed For Lions Golf Tournament," 4 June 1938, p.7; "Full Program For Delegates Starts Today," 5 June 1938, p.1; "Lions Told To Look For The Sunny Side," 8 June 1938, p.1; "12,000 Attend Dewey's Rodeo," 5 July 1938, p.1.

442 "Text Of President Roosevelt's Speech," *The Morning Examiner*, 10 July 1938, p.4.

443 "Children To Be Circus Guests Of Phillips," *The Morning Examiner*, 30 August 1938, p.1; Washington County Deed Book, 136, quit claim deed 147757, p.413, 30 September 1938; Washington County Deed Book 145, lease 150233, p.235, 15 October 1938.

444 "Phillips Golfers Beat Skellys, 52 to 26," *The Morning Examiner*, 5 June 1938, p.6; "Mrs. Phillips and Mrs. Wood In Golf Final," 16 June 1938, p.2; "Keith Fowler Wins Title," 28 June 1938, p.4; "Boggs Wins Tourney," 12 July 1938, p.5; "Mrs. Wallace and Mrs. Wood Tie For Low Gross," 14 July 1938, p.7; "Around The Fairways," 24 July 1938, p.6.

445 "Fore!" *The Daily Enterprise*, 7 September 1938, p.5; "Fore!" 10 September 1938, p.5; "Fred Smith Is King Of City's Golf Players," 12 September 1938, p.3; "Fore!" 2 October 1938, p.5; John H. Kane Ladies Championship trophy, trophy case, women's locker room, Hillcrest Country Club; "Mrs. Opal Hill To Play Exhibition Golf Game," 1 December 1938, p.6.

446 "300 Will Go Back To Work On Reopening," *The Morning Examiner*, 5 August 1938, p.1; "H. E. Wilkins To Open South View Addition," The Daily Enterprise, 3 September 1938, p.1.

447 Kane, p. 90; "Traffic Club To Entertain 500 Visitors," *The Daily Enterprise*, 29 September 1938, p.1; "Fore!" 6 October 1938, p.7.

448 John Brooks Walton, *The Architecture of John Duncan Forsyth*, Tulsa: JBW Publications, 2007; "Frank Phillips Foundation Aids City Schools," *The Daily Enterprise*, 15 October 1938, p.1; "Teachers Plan For A Banquet," 30 November 1938, p.2; "Welfare Drive Gets Underway," 7 December 1938, p.1.

449 An interesting social notice, and the listing of fund drive assignments in the newspaper shed direct light on which organizations were considered the workhorses of the community. "Welfare Drive Gets Underway," *The Daily Enterprise*, 7 December 1938, p.1; "Clubs Preparing For Coming Season," 17 September 1938, p.6.

450 "Change At Hillcrest Country Club," *The Daily Enterprise*, 31 October 1938, p.2; Telephone conversation with Bill Yinger, 5/14/04, Mrs. Stewart married Harry Yinger, a Phillips patent attorney, in 1938, and young Bill was adopted by his stepfather; "Opening Party For Dinner-Dance Club," 12 November 1938, p.3; "Opening Club Dance At Hillcrest," 19 November 1938, p.6.

451 "Program Arranged For Children's Party," *The Daily Enterprise*, 14 December 1938, p.6.

452 "Large Holiday Parties At Hillcrest," *The Daily Enterprise*, 17 December 1938, p.6.

453 ""Many Shared Saturday Night In Gay Dancing Party," *The Daily Enterprise*, 19 December 1938, p.6; "Large and Lovely Affair At Hillcrest,"; "Young Folks Gathered At Hillcrest," 26 December 1938, p.2; "Tea Dansant Toady At Hillcrest "; "Younger Social Set Takes Over Hillcrest For Tonight," 27 December 1938, p.2; "Dancing Party Tonight At Hillcrest," 30 December 1938, p.3.

454 "New Years To Receive Festive Welcome Tonight," *The Daily Enterprise*, 31 December 1938, p.8.

455 "3 New Directors At Hillcrest," *The Morning Examiner*, 18 January 1939, p.1; "Luncheon Wednesday For Hillcrest Women Golfers," 17 January 1939, p.3; "Mrs. Wood Is Hillcrest Golf Association Head, " 19 January 1939, p.4.

456 "Dance Club Party Monday Evening," *The Morning Examiner*, 19 January 1939, p.4; "Informal Dance At Hillcrest Saturday," 27 January 1939, p.3; "Supper Dance At Hillcrest Tonight," 28 January 1939, p.3. The racial references "colored" or "Negro" may strike us as offensive these days, but at the time they were thought of as solicitous language. The significance of a "colored" band here is that only a few years earlier, they would not have thought of employing a Black group. The times were changing. It is an early sign of a modern social conscience; "Housewarming For Burlingame Place, 29 January 1939, p.3.

457 "Military Ball Tonight Will Be Colorful Event," *The Morning Examiner*, 18 February 1939, p.3; "George Washington Dance At Hillcrest Saturday," 19 February 1939, p.6; "George Washington Party For Dinner-Dance Club," 21 February 1939, p.3.

458 "Beatty Favors Modified Federal Control Of Oil," *The Morning Examiner*, 2 March 1939, p.1.

459 "Phillips Petroleum Earned $2.32 Per Share Last Year," 15 March 1939, p.1; "Reda Pump Earned $1.12 Per Share Last Year," 10 March 1939, p.1; "Needy Persons Not Getting Full Amount," 17 March 1939, p.1; "Cities Service Reports Strengthened Position," 18 M<arch 1939, p.1.

460 "Breakfast Will Conclude Events of House Party," *The Morning Examiner*, 2 March 1939. p.2; "Doherty Girls Will Be Dance Hostesses Tonight," 17 March 1939, p.3; "Dinner-Bridge Monday For Geologists' Wives," 19 March 1939, p.7; "Hillcrest Dinner-Dance Club Has Annual Guest Night," 22 March 1939, p.3: "Golf Association Dance At Hillcrest Tonight," 25 March 1939, p.3; "Lindenwood College Has Dinner at Hillcrest," 25 March 1939, p.4.

461 "Breakfast Party At Hillcrest," *The Morning Examiner*, 15 April 1939, p.3; "Buffet Dinner Party At Hillcrest," 16 April 1939, p.6; "Informal Dance to Close Season For Members Of Dinner-Dance Club, " 16 April 1939, p.6; "Sigma Chi Dancing Party A Successful Affair," 23 April 1939, p5; "Season's Last Formal At Hillcrest," 23 April 1939, p.5; "600 Couples At Sorority Dance," 2 May 1939, p.1.

462 "Phillips Tourney Starts," *The Morning Examiner*, 6 May 1939, p.8; "Keith Fowler Wins Trophy," 4 July 1939, p.4.

463 "Liquor Harder To Get: Price Going Up," *The Morning Examiner*, 6 May 1939, p.1. ($21.86 in 2007 dollars for cheap hooch.)

464 "Hillcrest Was Setting For Sorority Party," *The Morning Examiner*, 2 May 1939, p.5; "B.P.W. Club Holds Mothers Day Banquet," 11 May 1939, p.5; "Kiwanis Honor Mothers At Banquet," 12 May 1939, p.8; "John Kane To Be Bar Speaker," 23 May 1939, p.3; "Lions Club Officers Installed By Clements," 1 July 1939, p.1; "Wilson Recital At Hillcrest," 21 May 1939, p.4.

465 "Reservations Requested For Wednesday Picnic," *The Morning Examiner*, 21 May 1939, p.7; "Wednesday's Pairings," 23 May 1939, p.8; "Heine Wins Flag Tourney," 31 May 1939, p.7.

466 "New Champ To Be Crowned At Hillcrest," *The Morning Examiner*, 4 June 1939, p.1: "Country Club Taken Over By Golfers," 4 June 1939, p.8; "Strong Comeback Gives Her 2 Up Win Over Wood," 10 June 1939, p.8.

467 "Around The Fairways," *The Morning Examiner*, 11 June 1939, p.6; "Around The Fairways," 20 June 1939, p.5; "Simpson Beats Hyatt For Hillcrest Crown," 27 June 1939, p.5.

468 "Bob Wills and Gang At Dewey, July 3," *The Morning Examiner*, 28 June 1939, p.3; "Dewey Rodeo Draws Crowd," 4 July 1939, p.1; "Keith Fowler Wins Trophy," 4 July 1939, p.4; "Tippit Get Hole-in-One On Hillcrest Number 12," 20 July 1939, p.3.

469 "Court Dismisses Jury Hearing Gasoline Case," *The Morning Examiner*, 2 September 1939, p.1.

470 "School Days Are Just Around The Corner In City," *The Morning Examiner*, 27 August 1939, p.11.

471 "Phillips Says We Know As Much As Europe Does," *The Morning Examiner*, 1 September 1939, p.1; "Court Dismisses Jury Hearing Gasoline Case," 2 September 1939, p.1.

472 "Smith Wins Tourney," *The Morning Examiner*, 10 September 1939, p.8; "Mrs. Phillips Wins Tulsa District Title," 30 September 1939, p.7; "Mrs. Phillips Retains Title," 17 October 1939, p.2; "35 At Banquet," 9 November 1939, p.8.

473 "Social Calendar," *The Morning Examiner*, 15 October 1939, p.7; "Hillcrest Is Setting For Autumn Tea," 19 October 1939, p.7; "Lindenwood College Club Announces Luncheon," 2 November 1939, p.2; "Hill Billy Dance Draws Large Crowd," 29 October 1939, p.4; "Buffet Supper At Hillcrest," 2 November 1939, p.2; "First Thanksgiving Featured At Club Banquet," 23 November 1939, p.3.

474 "Traffic Club Shown Royal Good Time," *The Morning Examiner*, 5 October 1939, p.1; "Hounds Turned Loose On Wolves," 10 October 1939, p.5; "4,500 Attend Hallowe'en Celebration," 1 November 1939, p.1; "K.U. Alumni To Hold Meeting," *The Morning Examiner*, 19 October 1939, p.7; "Welfare Drive Opens Tonight," 7 November 1939, p.1.

475 "Old Friends Pay Tribute To Phillips," *The Morning Examiner*, 26 November 1939, p.1; "Mr. Phillips Birthday Party Takes Precedence This Weeks," 26 November 1939, p.4; "Dismissal Of Phillips, Other Oil Men Upheld," 23 November 1939, p.6; "Dinner-Dance Club To Meet At Hillcrest," 17 December 1939, p.9; "Annual Holiday Party Held At Hillcrest," 20 December 1939, p.5; "Tea Dance Initiates Holiday Festivities," 24 December 1939, p.3; "Second Annual A.K.A. Dancing Party At Hillcrest," 28 December 1939, p.2; "Hillcrest Dance At-

tracts Many young People," 30 December 1939, p.3.

476 "Dinner-Dance Club To Meet At Hillcrest," 17 December 1939, p.9; "Annual Holiday Party Held At Hillcrest," 20 December 1939, p.5; "Tea Dance Initiates Holiday Festivities," 24 December 1939, p.3; "Second Annual A.K.A. Dancing Party At Hillcrest," 28 December 1939, p.2; "Hillcrest Dance Attracts Many young People," 30 December 1939, p.3; "Tylers Are Hosts At Dancing Party At Hillcrest," 31 December 1939, p.6.

477 "New Year Will Be Welcome By Many Parties In City," *The Morning Examiner*, 31 December 1939, p.7.

478 "23 Kiwanians Have Perfect Attendance," *The Morning Examiner*, 5 January 1940, p.1; "Tulsa Rabbi Will Address Medical Society Meeting," 7 January 1940, p.6; "Jaycee Inaugural Ball Will Be Held January 14," 13 January 1940, p.1; "New C. of C. Chief Outlines Policy For Coming Year," 6 January 1940, p.6; "Welfare-Salvation Army Make Report," 10 January 1940, p.2.

479 "Another Interesting Affair For Dinner-Dance Club," *The Morning Examiner*, 17 January 1940, p.3; "Around The Fairways," 18 January 1940, p.7; "Social Affairs At Hillcrest Are Highlights," 28 January 1940, p.3; "Everybody Urged To Turn Out For Dance," 27 January 1940, p.1

480 "That Salty Taste Won't Last Long," *The Morning Examiner*, 18 January 1940, p.1; "U.S. Drops Its Request For Oil Rehearing," 30 January 1940, p.1; "Complete Control of Oil Demanded By Federal Bureau," 8 February 1940, p.1.

481 "Next Hillcrest Club Dance Will Be Held Feb. 10," *The Morning Examiner*, 30 January 1940, p.5; "Hillcrest Entertains With Dance," 11 February 1940, p.10; "A Second Group Of Guests To Be Entertained At Hillcrest," 2 February 1940, p.3; "Military Ball To Culminate Defense Week," 11 February 1940, p.3; "Patriotic Colors Decorate Hillcrest Dinner Table," 22 February 1940, p.3; "Dinner-Bridge For Club At Hillcrest," 10 March 1940, p.7; "Guest Party Planned for Hillcrest Dinner-Dance Club," 10 March 1940, p.7; "Easter Egg Hunt At Hillcrest Announced," 21 March 1940, p.2; "Spring Dance Is Held At Hillcrest," 31 March 1940, p.4; "Largest Dinner-Dance Club Held At Hillcrest,"

18 April 1940, p.3; "Informal Dancing Party To Close Season At Hillcrest," 4 May 1940, p.8; "Phil Phillips Entertains For 66 Players," 5 May 1940, p.7; "Concert At Hillcrest On Next Sunday," 28 April 1940, p.8; "Public Invited To Hillcrest Concert," 5 May 1940, p.8; "Lions Ladies Night," 14 May 1940, p.5; "Hillcrest Is Setting For Attractive Luncheon," 16 May 1940, p.3.

482 "Hillcrest Benefit Draws Large Attendance," 29 February 1940, p.2; "Women Golfers Play Outdoor Competition," 3 March 1940, p.6; "Hillcrest Golf Schedule Is Completed," 31 March 1940, p.10; "Tourneys Postponed," 9 April 1940, p.5; "Doornbos Squad Noses Out Cronin 85 1/2 to 82 1/2," 14 April 1940, p.11; "Women To Meet," 16 April 1940, p.7.

483 "Women To Meet," *The Morning Examiner*, 16 April 1940, p.7.

484 "Bill Simpson Is Medalist With a 74," *The Morning Examiner*, 5 May 1940, p.10; "Mrs. Phillips Set Pace," 4 May 1940, p.11; "Archer Beats Golfer, 67 to 71," 21 May 1940, p.5.

485 Union National Bank advertisement, *The Morning Examiner*, 31 March 1940, Sec. A.

486 "Governor Here Tonight For Trade Address," *The Morning Examiner*, 7 May 1940, p.1; "C. of C. To Help Census Takers Closing Drive," 17 May 1940, p.1.

487 "Junior-Senior Prom to Be Held Tonight," *The Morning Examiner*, 10 May 1940, p.4; "Traffic Men At Woolaroc Between Busy Sessions," 12 May 1940, p.9.

488 "Soldiers Return To Camp," *The Morning Examiner*, 4 May 1941, p.13. Brady and Fitch filed their discharge papers at the Washington County courthouse after the war, but the other two men evidently did not return to Bartlesville.

489 "Neptune, Leonard And Simpson Called By Army," *The Morning Examiner*, 15 April 1941, p.1.

490 "Bar-Dew Opening Is Postponed," *The Morning Examiner*, 28 May 1940, p.7; "Matthews Takes D.M.F. Tourney," 31 May 1940, p.4; "49 Qualify for Hillcrest Meet," 31 May 1940, p.4; "Hurst To Address Lawyers' Banquet," 29 May 1940, p.1; "Wilkie Comes to Kansas; Calls FDR a Piker," 31 May 1940, p.1; Kane, p. 97.

491 "American Business Rises On Strength Of Home Front," *The Morning Examiner*, 16 June 1940, p.1; "Oil Industry Is Asked to Go on 24-Hour Basis," 19 June 1940, p.1.

492 "Four Local Golfers Enter State Amateur," *The Morning Examiner*, 8 June 1940, p.10; "Mrs. Wood Second: Mrs. Phillips Third," 15 June 1940, p.7; "Simpson Retains Hillcrest Title," 18 June 1940, p.3; "Miller Takes ITIO Tourney With 145 Net," 25 June 1940, p.2; "Alexander Scores Eagle at Hillcrest," 28 June 1940, p.8; "Defeats Phillips In Finals By a Score of 6 and 5," 30 June 1940, p.9.

493 "Dancing Party As Farewell Courtesy," *The Morning Examiner*, 6 June 1940, p.8; "Doherty Girls hold breakfast Party at Hillcrest," 11 June 1940, p.3.

494 "Hillcrest Members To Gather at Club House," *The Morning Examiner*, 4 July 1940, p.3; "$300,000 Cash Sent Engineers For Hulah Dam," 30 June 1940, p.8; "184 Welfare Cases in June," 10 July 1940, p.5.

495 "Alfalfa Bill Has No Fear of Hitler," *The Morning Examiner*, 18 June 1940, p.3; "Klan Holds Rally at Bund Camp," 21 August 1940, p.3; "Huge Crowd Turns Out For Defense Day," 19 July 1940, p.1.

496 "Simpson Wins," *The Morning Examiner*, 9 July 1940, p.5; "Golfers To Picnic," 23 July 1940, p.5; "Fowler Meets Finney Today," 7 August 1940, p.5; Gets Hole-in-One," 23 August 1940, p.12.

497 "Unity Council Co-ordinates Day's Events," *The Morning Examiner*, 1 September 1940, p.7.

498 "Dinner At Hillcrest Honors Birthday," *The Morning Examiner*, 1 September 1940, p.4; "Miss Grennan, Mr. Dimit Are Honor Guests," 1 September 1940, p.4.

499 "4,000 Attend Martin's Opening," *The Morning Examiner*, 6 September 1940, p.1; "Koppels to Hold Formal Opening This Evening," 12 September 1940, p.1.

500 "Typhoid Outbreak Is Well In Hand," *The Morning Examiner*, 11 September 1940, p.1; "2 More Cases of Typhoid Diagnosed in City," 18 September 1940, p.1.

501 "Defense Board Says Oil Suit Hurts Program," *The Morning Examiner*, 18 September 1940, p.1.

502 "Mixed Foursomes Sunday," *The Morning Examiner*, 7 September 1940, p.7; "Intra-Club Match At Hillcrest Today," 7 September 1940, p.10; "Gullane Sets Course Record," 22 September 1940, p.2; "Mrs. Phillips Retains Title as Hillcrest Champ," 19 September 1940, p.7; "55 Women Play In Invitational," 26 September 1940, p.7.

503 "Open House At Hillcrest Friday For Open Entries," *The Morning Examiner*, 26 September 1940, p.7; "High Class Golf Assured in State Open Tournament," 27 September 1940, p.11; "Emery Is State Champion," 1 October 1940, p.2.

504 "Mrs. Phillips Retains Title," *The Morning Examiner*, 8 October 1940, p.2; "Noted Golf Pro Will Play Here Next Wednesday," *The Morning Examiner*, 10 November 1940, p.8; "Shute's Shooting Will Depend Upon Weather," 13 November 1940, p.2; "Shute Tells FPMC All About Golf," 14 November 1940, p.4.

505 "Hillcrest Dinner-Dance Club Ready for Opening Party," *The Morning Examiner*, 13 October 1940, p.7; "Hillcrest Club Announces First Dance," 20 October 1940, p.8; "Costume Dance At Hillcrest Opens Season," 27 October 1940, p.4; "Beta Sigma Phi Has Dinner at Hillcrest," 26 October 1940, p.8; "Birthday Theme Is Used At Clever Banquet," 16 November, p.3; "Thanksgiving Dinner Party For Hillcrest Dance Group," 21 November 1940, p.3; "Large Crowd Expected At Hillcrest Tonight," 23 November 1940, p.2; "First Formal Dance Held At Hillcrest," 24 November 1940, p.3; "Young Guests Are Entertained At Hillcrest Saturday," 17 November 1940, p.6.

506 "Welfare Drive Opens With Tuesday Night Dinner," *The Morning Examiner*, 2 November 1940, p.2; "60 Men Will Distribute Xmas Baskets to Needy," 19 December 1940, p.16.

507 "Disney Says Oil Control Up To R'velt," *The Morning Examiner*, 9 November 1940, p.1; "Ickes Wants To Control Oil Industry," 29 November 1940, p.1.

508 "Service Awards Presented to 213 I.T.I.O. Employees," *The Morning Examiner*, 4 December 1940, p.1; "Sweetheart Dance of Sigma Chi," 8 December 1940, p.12; "Shower At Hillcrest For Miss Easter," 13 December 1940, p.10; "Mrs. Fowler, Mrs. Coburn Entertain Large Group At Pre-Holiday Luncheon," 14 December 1940, p.4.

509 "Dance Club Members Have Holiday Party," *The Morning Examiner*, 19 December 1940, p.3.

510 "Hillcrest Is Setting For Holiday Tea," *The Morning Examiner*, 20 December 1940, p.9; "Hillcrest Children To Be Entertained," 15 December 1940, p.6; "Musical Research Society Has Christmas Luncheon," 25 December 1940, p.6; "A.K.A. Members Entertaining Tonight," 28 December 1940, p.3, the members of A.K.A. club were Mary Louise Adams, Anait Artunoff, Beverly Ann Duston, Peggy Pierce, Martha Fitzjarrald, Mercedes Freiday, Helen Gardner, Dorothy Jean Gleason, Ginger Hoffman, Ruth Ann Hummer, Jo Ann Johnson, Marie Pinkerton, Louise Rodgers, and Jane Stites; "Younger Set Will Gather At Freiday Home," 28 December 1940, p.3.

511 "AKA Members Guests Dance At Hillcrest," *The Morning Examiner*, 29 December 1940, p.2.

512 "Holiday Dancing Party Planned For Monday," *The Morning Examiner*, 29 December 1940, p.3; "Brilliant Dancing Party a Holiday Affair At Hillcrest," 1 January 1941, p.3.

513 "New Year Dance At Hillcrest On Tuesday," 29 November 1940, p.3; "Large Dinner Party Is Outstanding Affair," 2 January 1941, p.4.

514 "Kiwanis Club Officers Installed," *The Morning Examiner*, 7 January 1941, p.1; "200 Will Attend Junior Chamber Dinner Tonight," 17 January 1941, p.3; "Dance Club Holds January Party at Hillcrest," 22 January 1941, p.3; "Three Directors Re-elected," 22 January 1941, p.2; "Plank Will Head Directors At HCC," 31 January 1941, p.1.

515 "Round-up Club Is Organized," *The Morning Examiner*, 21 January 1941, p.1; "Birthday Ball At 9 Tonight," 31 January 1941, p.2.

516 "Hal Brown Orchestra To Play for Doherty Dance," *The Morning Examiner*, 5 February 1941, p.5; "Mrs. Smythe Is hostess At Hillcrest Luncheon," 6 February 1941, p.5; "Sunday Musical To Be Held At Hillcrest," 6 February 1941, p.5; "Dinner Dance Planned At Hillcrest," 2 February 1941, p.4; "Hillcrest Dinner-Dance Club Holds February Party," 20 February 1941, p.5; "Military Ball Tonight," 22 February 1941, p.5; "Reserve Group Planning for Annual Dance," 2 February 1941, p.9.

517 Telephone conversation, 5/14/04, with Bill Yinger.

518 "Family Night Affair At Hillcrest," *The Morning Examiner*, 5 March 1941, p.5.

519 "Foster Estate Pays $1,954,850 In Federal Tax," *The Morning Examiner*, 11 February 1941, p.1.

520 "Will Not Seek Big Conventions," *The Morning Examiner*, 19 February 1941, p.2; "C. of C. Endorses Group Hospital," 5 February 1941, p.1.

521 "Noted Speaker on Program of Two Day Meet " *The Morning Examiner*, 2 March 1941, p.2; "DAR Leader Urges Congess To 'Think Of America First," 6 March 1941, p.1; "Two of Five U. S. Workers Are Women," 27 April 1941, p.16B.

522 "Phi Delta Theta Dinner Is Announced," *The Morning Examiner*, 7 March 1941, p.2; "Sorority Members And Guests Share In St. Patrick's Dance," 16 March 1941, p.4; "Social Calendar," 16 March 1941, p.3; "Easter Decorations Used For Dinner-Dance," 20 March 1941, p.13; "Toastmasters Are Installed," 30 March 1941, p.11 "Club Dance Planned At Hillcrest," 6 April 1941, p.10; "Easter Egg Hunt Set For Sunday," 8 April 1941, p.5; "Spring Auto Show For Dinner Dance Club," 17 April 1941, p.8; "Sigma Chi's Hold Annual Spring Dance," 20 April 1941, p.5; "River Rising Here Again," 19 April 1941, p.1; "Oil Accountants Hold Annual Outing Here," 26 April 1941, p.4.

523 "BPW Members Honor Mothers," *The Morning Examiner*, 2 May 1941, p.6; "Junior-Senior Prom At Hillcrest Friday," 4 May 1941, p.11; "OPA Calendar," 17 May 1941, p.1; "Sorosis Club Announces Guest Tea," 11 May 1941, p.12.

524 "Many Guests Share In Hillcrest Luncheon," *The Morning Examiner*, 20 April 1941, p.5; "Mrs. Riney, Mrs. Learned To Be Luncheon Hostesses," 20 April 1941, p.4; "Two Entertain At Hillcrest Party," 26 April 1941, p.3; "Three To Give Hillcrest Tea On Wednesday," 27 April 1941, p.7; "Pre-Wedding courtesy At Hillcrest," 11 May 1941, p.11;"Two Parties At Hillcrest," 28 May 1941, p.4; "Entertain at Hillcrest Luncheon Party," 5 June 1941, p.3.

525 "Breakfast At Hillcrest For Two June Brides," *The Morning Examiner*, 18 June 1941, p.3; "Dinner Party At Hillcrest Compliments Visitors,"3 June 1941, p.3;

"Doherty Girls Holding Annual Breakfast At Hillcrest," 8 June 1941, p.11; "Nowatans Entertain At Hillcrest," 15 June 1941, p.11; "Miss Swain Is Honored With Hillcrest Dinner Party," 29 June 1941, p.7.

526 "CC Men Tackle Defense Task," *The Morning Examiner*, 10 May 1941, p.1; "Country Club Men Arraigned on Slot Machine Charges," 2 May 1941, p.3; "Police Kill Snake In Business District," 23 May 1941, p.1; "Senate Passes Measure For Hulah Construction," 24 May 1941, p.1; "Foster Town Home Sold," 25 May 1941, p.10.

527 "Special Demonstration," *The Morning Examiner*, 16 March 1941, p.10; "Osage Hills Golf Course Rejoins In Sekanokla," 26 March 1941, p.9; "Golfers Warm Up," 18 March 1941, p.2; "Three Tulsa Golf Teams Here for Match Thursday," 9 April 1941, p.5.

528 "Hillcrest to Hold Annual Match Next Saturday," *The Morning Examiner*, 13 April 1941, p.8; "Calvert Captures O. K. Wing Trophy," 6 May 1941, p.5; "Sports Gossip," 7 May 1941, p.5; "100 in DMF Golf Meet," 6 May 1941, p.5; "Matthews Retains Title," 20 May 1941, p.8; "Busy Week of Play Planned By All Three Golf Courses," 27 May 1941, p.5; "Annual Bankers Match Today At Hillcrest C. C.," 22 April 1941, p.2; "Gullane-Fowler To Practice For Open Qualifying," 25 May 1941, p.9.

529 "I. T. I. O. To Merge With Cities Service," *The Morning Examiner*, 10 June 1941, p. 1.

530 "I.T.I.O. Merges With Cities Service," *The Morning Examiner*, 2 August 1941, p.1.

531 "Booker Wins I. T. Title," *The Morning Examiner*, 3 June 1941, p.8.

532 "Qualifying Rounds For HCC-Sunset Titles Start Today," *The Morning Examiner*, 1 June 1941, p.9; "Women Win At Coffeyville," 4 June 1941, p.2; "All Sport Events Here Rained Out," 7 June 1941, p.7; "Hillcrest," 8 June 1941, p.12; "Mrs. Phillips One Stroke Behind Medalist at Tulsa," 17 June 1941, p.5;"58 Qualify for FPMC Tourney," 22 June 1941, p.6.

533 "Golf to Occupy Spotlight Today," *The Morning Examiner*, 4 July 1941, p.7; "Hillcrest Country Club," 5 July 1941, p.10; "Hillcrest Will Hold Usual Box Supper," 1 July 1941, p.3; "Liquor Hard to Get For Holiday Thirst," 5 July 1941, p.1; "Best Roundup In 15 Years Draws 27,000," 6 July 1941, p.1.

534 "Huffman-Timmons Tie," 8 July 1941. p.2; "Timmons Wins FPMC Title," 20 July 1941, p.7; "Hillcrest Pairings," 8 July 1941, p.2; "Phillips, Thompson Tie," 13 July 1941, p.9; "Exhibition at Hillcrest," 13 July 1941, p.9; "Civic Club Match At HCC Sunday," 26 July 1941, p.10; "Kiwanis Beats Lions, Rotarians," 29 July 1941, p.10; "Fowler Captures Junior Open Cup," 29 July 1941, p.10; "Reda Pump Opens Annual Golf Meet At Hillcrest Today," 19 July 1941, p.7; "Ladder Tourney Today at Sunset For Sunday Meet," 9 August 1941, p.7; "Seven Bartians In State Open Tourney Today," 17 August 1941, p.12; "Special Match Monday," 31 August 1941, p.6.

535 "Mrs. Straight and Mrs. Walsh Honor Departing Secretary," *The Morning Examiner*, 13 July 1941, p.2; "Hillcrest Closed Its Dining Room," 13 July 1942, p.3.

536 "Modernized Hotel Takes a New Name," *The Morning Examiner*, 14 September 1941, hotel section p. 5.

537 "The Nation's Traffic Chiefs Assemble Here," *The Morning Examiner*, 8 October 1941, p.1; "Wolf Hunt Moved To Sunset Lake," 17 October 1941, p.7.

538 "Will Hold Family Night," *The Morning Examiner*, 30 September 1941, p.5; "Dinner-Dance Club Is Reorganized," 5 October 1941, p.5; "Season's First Dance Party at Hillcrest," 12 October 1941, p.3; "Western Banquet at Hillcrest For Beta Sigma Phi," 19 October 1941, p.7; "Luncheon At Hillcrest Honors Miss Mancill," 26 October 1941, p.6.

539 "Hillcrest," *The Morning Examiner*, 2 September 1941, p.2. Evidently they kept playing to a tie-breaker. "Keith Triumphs 3 and 1 as James Eases in 7 and 6," 6 September 1941, p.4; "Bennett Is Champ Hillcrest Caddy," 5 September 1941, p.8; "Hillcrest Beats Tulsans," 9 September 1941, p.2; "Rice Wins Tourney," 30 September 1941, p.2; "Mrs. Phillips Wins Tourney," 2 October 1941, p.6; "Fowler Is City Champion," 14 October 1941, p.5; "Mrs. Plank Wins," 29 October 1941, p.5; A.S. Eby, Ladies Championship trophy, trophy case, women's locker room, Hillcrest Country Club.

540 Oklahoma Secretary of State, Reinstatement of Hillcrest Country Club, Bartlesville, Oklahoma, 132087, 1 August 1950.

541 "Dinner-Dance Is Held at Hillcrest," *The Morning Examiner*, 23 November 1941, p.16; "Tylers Give Dinner Party at Hillcrest," 22 November 1941, p.3; "Hillcrest Luncheon Honors Miss Simpson, " 2 December 1941, p.4; "Mrs. Horne, Mrs. Fisher Are Luncheon Hostesses," 7 December 1941, p.9; "Three Hostesses Entertain At Tea At Hillcrest," 14 December 1941, p.10.

542 "Dinner Dance Club To Have December Party," *The Morning Examiner*, 14 December 1941, p.11; "Will hold Open House At Hillcrest," 21 December 1941, p.5; "Young Guests Invited For Dancing Party," 21 December 1941, p.5; "Hillcrest Party Given For Young Folks Today," 21 December 1941, p.5; "Large Crowd Attends Musical Research," 23 December 1941, p.3.

543 "Big Dinners Are Presented to 250 Needy Families," *The Morning Examiner*, 25 December 1941, p.8; Cronin Elected 1942 President," 13 December 1941, p.5; "Tires Limited To 7 Sharply Defined Classes of Users," 26 December 1941, p.1.

544 "New Years Eve Ball at Hillcrest," *The Morning Examiner*, 28 December 1941, p.5; "City Gives 1942 A War Welcome," 1 January 1942, p.1.

545 "25 Per Cent Tax On Income Being Talked," *The Morning Examiner*, 8 January 1942, p.1; "New Restrictions Are Slapped Upon The Oil Industry," 14 January 1942, p.1; "90 Per Cent Excess Levy Agreed Upon," 1 May 1942, p.1. Excess was "defined as profits exceeding 95% of average earning during 1936-39 or exceeding 8 per cent return on the first $5 million dollars of invested capital and 7 per cent of capital above $5 million." That's pretty stiff in an "improving" economy.

546 "Hill Billy Party At Hillcrest," 18 January 1942, p.4; "Hillcrest Dinner Club To Have Monday Night Party," *The Morning Examiner*, 18 January 1942, p.4; "Dinner-Dance Club Has Patriotic Party," 21 January 1942, p.2: "Young Folks Dance At Hillcrest," 25 January 1942, p.2; "Dinners Cancelled," 16 January 1942, p.12.

547 "Hillcrest Elects Directors," *The Morning Examiner*, 21 January 1942, p.5; "Hillcrest Dances Cancelled," 25 January 1942, p.2; "Hillcrest Club Dance," 19 February 1942, p.8.

548 "Hillcrest Re-Elects Officers For A Year," *The Morning Examiner*, 18 February 1942, p.8.

549 "Benefit Party To Be Held For Red Cross," *The Morning Examiner*, 28 January 1942, p.3; "Mrs. L. E. Phillips' Red Cross Attended By 300," 5 February 1942, p.3. That is nearly $6,000 in 2007 dollars.

550 "Hillcrest To Elect," *The Morning Examiner*, 21 January 1942, p.5; "Country Clubs, Spencers And Barlow Leading, 8 February 1942, p.8. It is interesting to note that women used their married names in reference to Hillcrest events (eg. Mrs. James Phillips), but often used their given names in other contexts (eg. Leora Phillips).

551 "Ladies Night Tonight," *The Morning Examiner*, 3 January 1942, p.3; "JCC Banquet Jan. 16," 6 January 1942, p.3; "Chamber Pledges Assistance in Civilian Defense," 7 January 1942, p.1; "102 Kiwanis Meet," 7 January 1942, p.1; "Rowland Is Speaker At Medic's Banquet," 15 January 1942, p.1; "Doherty Girls Entertain At Dance," 13 February 1942, p.3.

552 "Bread Man Uses Horse and Wagon," *The Morning Examiner*, 15 February 1942, p.1; "Phillips Pete Occupies Three More Buildings," 1 March 1942, p.1; "F. B. I. Nipps Japanese Fifth Column Plot In Coast Navy Yard," 6 February 1942, p.1; "Roosevelt Warns Of Likely Attacks On Cities of U.S.," 18 February, p.1.

553 "Hillcrest Dance Club Holds March Party," *The Morning Examiner*, 19 March 1942, p.8; "Dance Club Closes Year," 23 April 1942, p.5; "Newcomers Meet At Hillcrest," 26 March 1942, p.6; "Plan Informal Dance," 10 april 1942, p.4A.

554 "Over 120 Attend Rotary Club Party," *The Morning Examiner*, 31 March 1942, p.5; "Kenneth Adams Entertains Kansas U. Students," 12 April 1942, p.6; "Sigma Chi Holds Annual Dance At Hillcrest Club," 12 April 1942, p.6; "Choir Is Entertained At Hillcrest," 14 April 1942, p.3; "Morning Musical Attracts Big Crowd," 21 April 1942, p.2; "Many Reservations Made For Luncheon," 7 May 1942, p.2; "Large Crowd Attends Dance At Hillcrest," 26 April 1942, p.4. The C.D.G. club members were Bonnie Bandy, Marybelle Beecher, Margaret Camp, Ernestine Eddelman, Emily Ann Emery, Edith Morton, Dorothy Mills, Jane Rippel, Christan Taylor, Mildred Turner, Jo Ann Whitcomb, and Margaret Ann Witchell.

555 "60 Out at Hillcrest," *The Morning Examiner*, 14 April 1942, p.9; "Match At Hillcrest," 2 May 1942, p.7;"Kiwanis Golfers Win 3-Way Meet," 5 May 1942, p.5; "Blues Beat Reds In Hillcrest Meet," 3 May 1942, p.9.

556 "75 Attend BPW Mothers Banquet," *The Morning Examiner*, 8 May 1942, p.10; "'Bridge Of Sighs' Is Gone," 6 May 1942, p.8; "Prom Opens Final Weeks In City Schools," 15 May 1942, p.9; "500 horsemen Take Part In Roundup Club Festival," 17 May 1942, p.1; ; "Tuesday's Heads-up Banquet The Biggest Civic 'Bargain'," 24 May 1942, p.2; "City Clubwomen Meet Monday Afternoon at Hillcrest C. C.," 24 May 1942, p.5; "1000 See Runyon Show," 30 May 1942, p.1.

557 "Hillcrest Party Honors Miss Bonnie Berger," *The Morning Examiner*, 14 June 1942, p.6; "Miss Fitzjerrald Is Honored At Hillcrest Luncheon," 12 July 1942, p.7; Fitzjarrald-Haberlein Wedding This Morning," 11 August 1942, p.3.

558 "Collins' 249 Wins DMF Meet," *The Morning Examiner*, 19 May 1942, p.5; "Father and Son Match Features Today's round," 31 May 1942, p.8; "Most Favorites Survive," 9 June 1942, p.6; "Golf Links Undamaged," 13 June 1942, p.5; "Hillcrest," 23 June 1942, p.2; "Army, Victory Gardens And Tires Hit Golf Links," 14 July 1942, p.4; "Cards 87; Grant Is Medalist With A Score of 79," 16 June 1942, p.6; "Large Field In Women's Play," 29 July 1942, p.2.

559 "Five Local Golfers In Muskogee Meet," *The Morning Examiner*, 21 June 1942, p.8: "Blasts Former Champion 3 and 2 Meets Panner," 24 June 1942, p.6; "Fowler Sets New Course Record At Hillcrest," 1 July 1942, p.8.

560 "Local Courses Will Get Heavy Play on Fourth," *The Morning Examiner*, 3 July 1942, p.8; "Hillcrest Country Club," 5 July 1942, p.5; "Smith Wins Reda Event," 14 July 1942, p.6; "Fowler Headed For Two Chicago Tournaments," 17 July 1942, p.10; "Bailey Defeats Smith 5 and 3 For Junior Title," 13 August 1942, p.6.

561 "Bill Martin Wins Labor Day At Hillcrest C.C.," *The Morning Examiner*, 8 September 1942, p.2; "McElvain Is Phillips Medalist At Hillcrest,"; "Women Facing Caddy Problems," 22 September 1942, p.6; "Wickersham Wins Grand Prize," 29 September 1942, p.6; "Around The Fairways," 4 October 1942, p.9; "Golf Event Is Planned For Red Cross Benefit," 6 October 1942, p.3; "Mrs. Feist Takes Lead," 14 October 1942, p.2; "Around The Fairways," 10 November 1942, p.5.

562 "Fulton Lewis, Jr. Signs For Town Hall Engagement," *The Morning Examiner*, 9 August 1942, p.12; "Annual Banquet Held By BMA," 7 October 1942, p.1; "Officials Ask Cooperation in Needed Effort," 1 November 1942, p.3; "Bartians Asked To Get Behind Swap-Ride Plan," 29 November 1942, p.1; "To Supply Transportation To Hillcrest," 1 September 1942, p.3; Photo, 16 January 1943, p.1.

563 "Mrs. H. C. Claudy of Hillcrest," *The Morning Examiner*, 20 August 1942, p.12; "Gist of Local News," 17 September 1942, p.5; "Initiate Informal Suppers At Hillcrest," 20 September 19452, p.5; "Hillcrest Club Dinner Tonight," 3 October 1942, p.3; "Glider Class Party Tonight," 23 September 1942, p.6. The glider training school was a program in which Bartlesville students took ground school and glider training as the first part of the flight training for the Army Air Corps at the Bartlesville commercial airport in Tuxedo. "Many Share In Dinner And Dance At Hillcrest," 19 November 1942, p.3.

564 "Hillcrest Club Opens New Season," *The Morning Examiner*, 22 October 1942, p.7; "Many Share In Dinner And Dance At Hillcrest," 19 November 1942, p.3; "Hillcrest Dinner and Dance Draw Large Crowd," 29 November 1942, p.5; "Hillcrest Dinner-Dance Club Plans Next Party," 6 December 1942, p.7.

565 "Dancing Party Honors Miss Beesley," *The Morning Examiner*, 15 November 1942, p.5; "Dahlgrens Host At Dinner Party," 21 November 1942, p.5; "Over 350 Couples Attend Phillips Birthday Dance," 27 November 1942, p.1; "Colorado Mines Alumnae Take Over Hillcrest," 8 December 1942, p.5; "Hillcrest Party Honors Lt. Rice and Mrs. Rice," 25 December 1942, p.14; "Entertains with Dance At Hillcrest," 29 December 1942, p.6; "Entertains At Hillcrest," 29 December 1942, p.6; "Vows Read For Miss Trower and Dean Walker," 30 December 1942, p.2.

566 "New Year's Dance At Country Club," *The Morning Examiner*, 31 December 1942, p.3.

567 "Hillcrest Club Names Directors," *The Morning Examiner*, 20 January 1943, p.1; "Reid Heads Hillcrest," 26 January 1943, p.1.

568 "100 at Kiwanis Program," *The Morning Examiner*, 8 January 1943, p.1; "Sweetheart Dance Is Held At Hillcrest Club Room," 13 January 1943, p.6; "Many Parties At Hillcrest For Family Night," 7 February 1943, p.7; "Young Folks Dance At Hillcrest," 6 February 1943, p.7; "Many Share in Family Night at Hillcrest," 21 February 1943, p.4; "Dance Club Has Ration Party At Hillcrest," 18 February 1943, p.3; "United Community Fund Elects Kane President," 31 March 1943, p.1.

569 "Golf Tournaments Are Cancelled," *The Morning Examiner*, 14 March 1943, p.9; "Servicemen Dance Tonight as Guests of the Legion," 27 March 1943, p.1; "Junior College Will Be Dropped," 7 April 1943, p.1.

570 "Musical Research Morning Musical On Monday," *The Morning Examiner*, 18 April 1943, p.6; "To Elect Officers," 5 May 1943, p.5; "Retain Present Officers." 6 May 1943, p.8.

571 "Julian's Team Beats Kinderman's 56 1/2 to 39 1/2 Points," *The Morning Examiner*, 16 May 1943, p.7; "Defending Champ Is DMF Medalist With 35-44---79," 25 May 1943, p.9; "Johnson Takes Hillcrest Flag Day Tournament," 1 June 1943, p.6; "Johnson Shoots 75 as a Medalist In Hillcrest Play," 5 June 1942, p.3; "Hillcrest Golf Title Play Today," 13 June 1943, p.9; "Keith Fowler Qualifies in O. C. Golf Meet," 9 June 1943, p.6; "Wins 4 and 3 Sunday Over Engelbrecht," 15 June 1943, p.5; "Neumann Is Low With 78 At Hillcrest," 27 June 1943, p.7;"Hillcrest Women Plan Foursomes," 27 June 1943, p.7.

572 "Lions Club Governor To Attend Meeting Here," *The Morning Examiner*, 4 May 1943, p.1; "Enlarged Hospital Inviting Inspection Here Wednesday," 9 May 1943, p.2; "Lowlands Here Move Out As Caney Rises 15 Feet," 12 May 1943, p.1; "Concert Will Follow AAUW Dinner Meeting," 13 May 1943, p.2; "Tea at Hillcrest Club Is Postponed," 19 May 1943, p.3; "Dinner At Hillcrest Is Cancelled," 22 May 1943, p.3; "Welfare Association Handles All Needy Victims of Flood," 20 May 1943, p.1; "Hundreds Cared For By Citizens, Relief Agencies," 20 May 1943, p.1.

573 "Roundup, Golf, Fishing Only Feature Today," *The Morning Examiner*, 4 July 1943, p.9.

574 "Judson Wins Annual Reda Golf tournament," The Morning Examiner, 13 July 1943, p.6; "Donaldson Is FPMC Champ," 11 August 1943, p.6; "Simpson Ties Course Record Over Hillcrest," 14 August 1943, p.6; "Simpson Is Low," 15 August 1943, p.6.

575 "Around The Fairways," The Morning Examiner, 5 September 1943, p.9; "Doornbos Wind Handicap Play," 7 September 1943, p.8; "130 Tour Hillcrest," 12 October 1943, p.5. Bad microfilm obscures information of the winners of both tournaments.

576 "Annual Osage Hills Wolf Hunt Planned," The Morning Examiner, 6 October 1943, p.1; "One-Day $85,000 Drive For War Amd Local Relief," 17 October 1943, p.1; "Tommy Novak Reported Killed In Italy," 12 November 1943, p.1.

577 "Another Large Crowd Attends Family Dinner," The Morning Examiner, 7 September 1943, p.2; "Hillcrest Club And Course To Hold Red Cross Benefit," 5 October 1943, p.6; "Hillcrest Dessert Party Compliments Miss Adams," 10 October 1943, p.5; "Wedding Rehersal Dinner Tonight," 29 October 1943, p.9; "Brides Parents Hosts At Dinner," 30 October 1943, p.3; "Jaycees to Hold Members' Dance Next Saturday," 14 November 1943, p.2.

578 "Research Department To Have Annual Party," The Morning Examiner, 17 December 1943, p.5; "Celebrate Holiday Season at Hillcrest," 19 December 1943, p.7; "Dinner Dance At Hillcrest Tonight," 29 December 1943, p.2.

579 "Many Will Dance Tonight At Hillcrest," The Morning Examiner, 31 December 1943, p.3; Mr. And Mrs. Kane To Entertain Friends," 31 December 1943, p.3; "Quiet Affairs Mark Society's New Year Holiday," 2 January 1944, p.2.

580 "Chamber Lists Accomplishments, Its Future Plans," The Morning Examiner, 5 January 1944, p.6; ""New C.C. Chief Gives Points To The Cussers," 8 January 1944, p.1; "Local Post-War Planning Help Asked Of citizenry," 16 January 1944, p.2.

581 Photograph of W. R. Lund, photograph gallery of former presidents, Hillcrest Country Club. The newspaper did not report either the stockholder's meeting or the election of the new president in January 1944. "Olga Foster Returns To the Country Club," The Morning Examiner, 25 June 1944, p.5.

582 "Family Night Dinner Planned Saturday Night," The Morning Examiner, 27 February 1944, p.4; "Leap Year Dance To Be Sponsored By Phillips Club," 25 February 1944. p.2; "Frank Phillips To Be Caller At Square Dance," 3 March 1944, p.4; "Young Folks Dance At Hillcrest," 12 May 1944, p.5.

583 "Red Cross Fund Goes Over By Scant Margin." The Morning Examiner, 2 April 1944, p.1; "Irelan Is Named President Of Cities Service Gas Co.," 18 April 1944, p.1.

584 "Hillcrest Egg Hunt," The Morning Examiner, 9 April 1944, p.9; "Wedding Party At Hillcrest Tonight," 28 April 1944, p.4; "Koopman-Armstrong Wedding Vows Exchanged Here Saturday," 30 April 1944, p.6.

585 "Reda Meet Starts Today," The Morning Examiner, 30 April 1944, p.9; "Tourney Washed Out," 2 May 1944, p.6; "34 Are Paired in Reda's Two-Day Golf Tournament," 23 May 1945, p.5.

586 "Notice Golfers," The Morning Examiner, advertisement, 30 April 1944, p.9.

587 Telephone interview with Frances Emerson, 9/16/03.

588 "BHS Golfers Beat Kansans," The Morning Examiner, 5 May 1944, p.10; "Daniel Team Wins tourney," 14 May 1944, p.9; "DMF Tourney Is Rained Out," 21 May 1944, p.9; "Collins Is Winner," 30 May 1944, p.6; "Emerson Wins Flag Event," 31 May 1944, p.6.

589 "Lawyers Banquet On Friday Night," The Morning Examiner, 1 June 1944, p.3; "Olga Foster To the Country Club," 25 June 1944, p.5.

590 "Hillcrest Club Golf Tournament Opens Today," The Morning Examiner, 3 June 1944, p.6; "Emerson Beaten By Lyon, 1 Up On The 19th Green," 4 June 1944, p.13; "Kincaid Wins Hillcrest Country Club Golf Title," 11 June 1944, p.9; "Around The Fairways," 4 July 1944, p.6; "Pairings Made For Phillips Golf Meet," 9 July 1944, p.11; JCC-C. of C. Golf Match To Be Played Today," 16 July 1944. p.9. Bad microfilm prevents learning the winners of these contests.

591 "Church Finances Improve In Spite Of War And Tax," The Morning Examiner, 9 July 1944, p.2.

592 "Johnson and Holt Win Flag Tournament," The Morning Examiner, 5 September 1944, p.8; "Arnold Wins Tourney," 26 September 1944, p.6; "Hayes and Custer Win," 10 October 1944, p.6; "Open Affair," 6 October 1944, p.6; ""Leathers Shoots An Ace," 12 November 1944, p.10.

593 "Tea Is Farewell Courtesy to Big Group of Matrons," The Morning Examiner, 15 October 1944, p.4; "Doherty Girls Have Hillcrest Banquet." 25 October 1944, p.5.

594 "Hillcrest Party To Honor Uncle Frank's Birthday," The Morning Examiner, 16 November 1944, p.2; "Phillips Birthday Party Tonight," 22 November 1944, p.5.

595 Telephone Interview with Elsie Parker, 9/16/03, to follow up on earlier conversation about this Frank Phillips episode.

596 "OU President To Deliver Three Talks Here Today," The Morning Examiner, 15 December 1944, p.12; "Dinner Club Announces Holiday Dancing Party," 10 December 1944, p.6; "Interesting Plans being made for Dinner-Dance," 17 December 1944, p.9; "Holiday Dance At Hillcrest," 29 December 1944, p.5; "Breakfast and Slumber Party Follows Holiday Dance," 31 December 1944, p.7; "Phillips Minstrel Rollick Full House at Civic Center," 22 December 1944, p.1.

597 "74 Golfers Turn Out," The Morning Examiner, 14 January 1945, p.11.

598 "Many Attend Family Night Dinner At Hillcrest," The Morning Examiner, 14 January 1945, p.7; "Dinner-Dance Club Plans Another Party," 14 January 1945, p.7; "Dinner-Dance Is Cancelled," 23 January 1945, p.5; "Hillcrest Elects Five New Directors," 17 January 1945, p.1; "Good Ticket Sale For Polio Dance," 25 January 1945, p.2.

599 "To Have Dinner-Dance At Hillcrest," The Morning Examiner, 10 March 1945, p.5.

600 "Shortages Bring Funny Incidents To Many Bartians," The Morning Examiner, 25 March 1945, p.11.

601 "Congress Investigation Of Food Mess Demanded," The Morning Examiner, 15 March 1945, p.1.

602 "A Different House," Examiner-Enterprise, 17 October 1954.

603 "Prewar Golf Ball Worth Nine Times Weight In Silver," *The Morning Examiner,* 1 May 1945, p.6; "Leathers' Golfers Win Hillcrest Stag Match," 13 May 1945, p.11.

604 Though this sounds jolting, it is actually a sign of the immense progress of medical care in these years. New technology and drug therapy meant that for the first time there was actually something a doctor could do for acutely sick patients.

605 "Odis Everett Wins DMF Title," *The Morning Examiner,* 12 June 1945, p.11. ($107 is almost $1250 in 2007 dollars); "Rain Knocks Out Several Matches In Hillcrest Meet," 17 June 1945, p.9; "Everett-Daniel Will Meet for Class A Title," 24 June 1945, p.9; "Women Revive Golf Day For Hillcrest," 24 June 1945, p.9.

606 "Flag Tourney," *The Morning Examiner,* 1 July 1945, p.5; "Hotel, Café Food Rations Will Be Cut," 6 June 1945, p.1; "J. V. Wood Wins Hillcrest Flag Day Tournament," 5 July 1945, p.5; "Holiday Picnic Is Planned At Hillcrest Club," 1 July 1945, p.6; "Hicks Is Winner Of FPMC Crown," *The Morning Examiner,* 10 July 1945, p.6.

607 "Unlike Any Force Ever Before Released On Earth," *The Morning Examiner,* 7 August, p.1; "Hillcrest Open Today," 16 August 1945, p.2.

608 "Lyon Sets Season Low," *The Morning Examiner,* 12 August 1945, p.9; "Junior, Senior Chambers Meet Today On Links," 26 August 1945, p.9; "Seniors Win Again," 28 August 1945, p.8; "204 Players Turn Out," 4 September 1945, p.6; "Golf Tournament At Osage Hills," 6 September 1945, p.4.

609 "Hillcrest Men Pay Tribute To Gullane On His 20th Year," *The Morning Examiner,* 22 September 1945, p.6; "Cobb Is Medalist With A Net 65 At Hillcrest; "River Nears Flood Stage Here," 25 September 1945, p.1.

610 "Adams Suitcase Thief Is Given Two-Year Term," *The Morning Examiner,* 14 October 1945, p.2; "Thousands Turn Out For City's Halloween Parade As Pranksters Cut Loose," 1 November 1945, p.1; "Jaycees Sponsor Drive To Boost Church Attending," 10 November 1945, p.2.

611 "Lions Here For Zone Meeting," *The Morning Examiner,* 27 November 1945, p.1; "Seven New Homes Are Being Started," 4 December 1945, p.1.

612 "Newcomers Have Meet," *The Morning Examiner,* 22 September 1945, p.5; "Opens Club Year At Hillcrest," 29 September 1945, p.3; "Luncheon At Hillcrest For PEO Chapter," 11 October 1945, p.7; "Hillcrest Party Honors Birthday," 14 October 1945, p.6; "Mrs. Guardiola Will Honor Houseguest," 19 October 1945, p.9; "Hallowe'en Party Opens Season At Hillcrest," 28 October 1945, p.6; "Doherty Tea Planned At Hillcrest," 11 November 1945, p.10; "Doherty Girls Club To Hold Banquet," 28 November 1945, p.10; "Luncheon Honors Visitor Before Departure," 1 December 1945, p.13.

613 "Jaycees To Aid Christmas Fund," *The Morning Examiner,* 5 December 1945, p.3; "Reception At Hillcrest Welcomes Young Matron," 16 December 1945, p.15; "Wintry Weather Enhances A Tea," 21 December 1945, p.10; "Two Parties Planned For Hillcrest," 20 December 1945, p.2; "Dancing Party At Hillcrest," 29 December 1945, p.3; "Many To Welcome New Years At Holiday Parties," 30 December 1945, p.6.

614 Joel Chandler Harris, *Walt Disney's Uncle Remus Stories,* retold by Marion Palmer, New York: Simon and Schuster, 1946, p.11.

615 "Chamber Names Committees And Sets Programs," *The Morning Examiner,* 10 January 1946, p.6. "OC Man To Address JCC Annual Banquet," 29 January 1946, p.5.

616 "Hillcrest Names Five Directors," *The Morning Examiner,* 16 January 1946, p.1; "All Hillcrest Women Invited To Wednesday Luncheon," 31 March 1946, p.11; "Hillcrest Club is Setting For Spring Luncheon," 26 April 1946, p.3; "Hillcrest Club Dining Room Will Be Closed This Week," 5 May 1946, p.12; "Tight Ban Goes On Every Type Of Construction," 27 March 1946, p.5.

617 "Hostesses Entertain Guests At Hillcrest," *The Morning Examiner,* 23 May 1946, p.5; "College Misses Hold Spotlight Over Weekend," 30 June 1946, p.12; "Many Share in Family Program at Hillcrest," 8 August 1946, p.11; "Scotch Foursome Precedes Family Night Dinner," 2 August 1946, p.10; "Around The Fairways," 3 August 1946, p.6.

618 "Stephens-Adams Vows Exchanged At San Antonio," *The Morning Examiner,* 10 November 1946, p.10; "Dahlgrens, Webers Are Dinner Guests at Country Club," 11 November 1946, p.10; "Doherty Auxiliary Plans A Special Social Affair," 10 November 1946, p.11; "Successful Holiday Party at Hillcrest," 25 December 1946, p.6; "Many Informal Parties Are Scheduled For Week Here," 29 December 1946, p.5; "Holiday Dance Is Held At Hillcrest," 1 January 1947, p.2.

619 "Clover Club Raided," *The Morning Examiner,* 14 February 1946, p.1.

620 Louise S. Robbins, *The Dismissal of Miss Ruth Brown,* Norman: University of Oklahoma, 2000, p.35; "Survey Finds 845 Negroes In the City," 11 May 1947, p.3. The survey found 845 Black residents and reported age grouping, years in residence, education, place of employment, and homes.

621 "Here Is The New Station You're Invited To Inspect," *The Morning Examiner,* 12 April 1946, p.1; "New St. John's Parochial School Plans Announced," 14 April 1946, p.1; "Open house At Hospital," 12 May 1946, p.1.

622 "They Eat Crow And Like It," *The Morning Examiner,* 4 May 1946, p.1.

623 "About The Hulah Dam," *The Morning Examiner,* 31 October 1945, p.1; "First Blow Struck In Hulah Crow Dinner," 21 April 1946, p.12; "Jaycees Appoint Committee To Fatten Crows," 24 April 1946, p.5.

624 "JCC's Adopt 6-Point Plan In Polio Fight," *The Morning Examiner,* 1 August 1946, p.1.

625 "Hillcrest Women To Start Play March 27," *The Morning Examiner,* 21 March 1946, p.8; "Sunset To Open Back Nine Sand Greens Sunday," 23 March 1946, p.6; "Notice To Golfers," advertisement, 23 March 1946, p.6; "Gullane Shoots A 65," 14 April 1946, p.7.

626 "Kincade Team Wins Hillcrest Event 199-86." *The Morning Examiner,* 28 April 1946, p.7; "Nelson Wins Reda," 21 May 1946, p.4; "Lhuiller Wins D.M.F.," 11 June 1946, p.6; "Wood Gets An Ace," 21 June 46, p.9; "Gullane To Meet Guild In Opener Gauntt Gets A 66," 27 June 1946, p.7; "72 Low At Hillcrest," 9 July 1946, p.4.

627 "Bank Teams Tie," *The Morning Examiner,* p.4; "Conn Wins Tournament," 5 July

1946, p.9; "Kinslow Wins FPMC Tourney," 16 July, p.8; "Martin is Medalist," 21 July 1946, p.8.

628 "Golf Dinner Tonight," *The Morning Examiner*, 13 September 1946, p.5; "Maddox, Mayo In Playoff," 17 September 1946, p.4; "Handicap Tourney," 16 September 1947, p.5; "DMF Beats Ponca," 1 October 1946, p.2; "Senior Chamber Wins," 1 October 1946, p.2; "Hillcrest Women's Finals," 20 October 1946, p.7.

629 "Hillcrest Women's Finals," *The Morning Examiner*, 20 October 1946, p.7; "Mrs. Hubbell Wins Hillcrest Tourney," 30 October 1946, p.4; "Gullane Wins Twice," 22 October 1946, p.8.

630 "Holiday Dancers Welcome the New Year At Hillcrest Club," *The Morning Examiner*, 1 January 1947, p.2; "No Horns Blow, Not a Shot Fired to Welcome 1947 Here," 1 January 1947, p.1; "251 Houses Completed During Year," 10 January 1947, p.8.

631 "Scott Given Honor Award Of Jaycees," *The Morning Examiner*, 1 February, p.1; "Hillcrest Club Members Attend Valentine Dance," 16 February 1947, p.15; "Dinner-Dance Held At Hillcrest Club," 27 February 1947, p.4; "Completing Plans For Next Dinner-Dance," *The Morning Examiner*, 21 March 1947, p.2.

632 "Years Rolled Back in Ceremony for Mr. And Mrs. Phillips." *The Morning Examiner*, 19 February 1947, p.1.

633 "40,000 People View Colorful Fiftieth Anniversary Parade," *The Morning Examiner*, 2 April 1947, p.1.

634 "Chamber Takes a Bow This Week For Its Continuing Civic Work," *The Morning Examiner*, 13 April 1947, p.11; "City Has Many New Businesses," 13 April 1947, p.11; "Forum Program Will Describe Scope of the Chamber's Work," 18 April 1947, p.9.

635 "FPMC Announces Easter Egg Hunt For City's Kids," *The Morning Examiner*, 16 March 1947, p.14; "Easter Dancing Party At Hillcrest," 6 April 1947, p.21.

636 advertisement, *The Morning Examiner*, 29 April 1947, p.8.

637 "Famed Woolaroc Museum To Open Again On Sunday," *The Morning Examiner*, 2 May 1947, p.1.

638 "Hillcrest Annual Club Tournament April 26," *The Morning Examiner*, 20 April 1947, p.6; "Doornbos King of the Central Golfers," 7 May 1947, p.4; "Kincade Scores 76," 27 April 1947, p.8; "306 Tour Hillcrest," 6 May 1947, p.4; "S.A.E. Holds Spring Meeting Here Today," 8 May 1947, p.5; "Simpson Cops Hillcrest Cup O'er Chapman," 3 June 1947, p.4.

639 "Two Social Affairs For Senior Class," *The Morning Examiner*, 9 May 1947, p.14; "Holiday Party Planned At Hillcrest," 29 July 1947, p.10; "Country Club Dining Room To Close," 27 July 1947, p.5.

640 "Dick Booker Shoots Way to Two Victories at Hillcrest," *The Morning Examiner*, 10 June 1947, p.4; "Around The Fairways," 15 June 1947, p.9; "Tulsa District To Play At Hillcrest Course On Friday," 19 June 1947, p.6; "Around The Fairways," 5 July 1947, p.5; "Around The Fairways," 27 July 1947, p.11; "Keith Fowler Second To Coe At Broadmoor, 30 July 1947, p.5; "Sunset Country Club Organized; Officers Elected," 13 August, p.3.

641 "Carle Wins Feature," *The Morning Examiner*, 2 September 1947, p.8; "Proffitt's 69 Leads Field At Hillcrest," 23 September 1947, p.4. "250 Tour Hillcrest," 7 October 1947, p.5; "Around The Fairways," 23 October 1947, p.4; the Women's Golf Association trophy records that Mrs. H.A. Gardner was the women's club champion for 1947, trophy case in Women's locker room; "Around the Fairways," 26 October 1947, p.4; "Hillcrest." 28 October 1947, p.3; "Tacky Costume Prizes Given At Hillcrest," 31 October 1947, p.9; "Hillcrest," 2 November 1947, p.4; "Golf," 23 December 1947, p.7.

642 "Truman Spokesmen Hear Shouts Of Socialism," *The Morning Examiner*, 24 November 1947, p.1; "Says Racial Discrimination Is The Basic Issue In Case," 13 November 1947, p.1.

643 "CAA Says Bartlesville first In State For Federal Aid Funds," *The Morning Examiner*, 17 October 1947, p.1; "Phillips Gives Airport," 2 December 1947, p.1, this is about $2.1M in 2007 dollars; "Mayor Appoints Bartlesville Community Planning Group," 9 November 1947, p.1; "Complete Formation Of New City-Wide Planning Groups," 27 November 1947, p.1.

644 "Have first Dance Of The Season," *The Morning Examiner*, 2 November 1947, p.11; "Hold Annual B.M.A. Banquet Wednesday," 2 November 1947, p.1; "Dinner-Dance Club Resumes No. 25th," 16 November 1947, p.14; "More Than A hundred Attend Opening Dinner At Hillcrest," 27 November 1947, p.2; "Hillcrest Club To Hold Dance," 23 November 1947, p.11.

645 "Overlees Observe Golden Wedding Anniversary Here," *The Morning Examiner*, 4 November 1947, p.2.

646 "Phillips Men Hold A Holiday Dance," *The Morning Examiner*, 29 November 1947, p.3; "Entertains With Dinner Party At The Hillcrest Club," 30 November 1947, p.18.

647 "Hundreds Attend Burlingame-Phillips Party," *The Morning Examiner*," 4 December 1947, p.4.

648 "Pre-Yule Dance Planned At Club," *The Morning Examiner*, 7 December 1947, p.14; "Dinner-Dance Club Holds A Christmas Dance," 21 December 1947, p.13; "Rowlands Entertain Tonight At Hillcrest," 28 December 1947, p.6; "Hillcrest Country Club Is The Scene of Tyler-Beesley Party," 31 December 1947, p.3; "Ball At Hillcrest Will Start At 11:00," 31 December 1947, p.3.

649 "City Damaged By Rain And Sleet Storm," *The Morning Examiner*, 1 January 1948, p.1: "City Covered By Eight-Inch Snow," 2 January 1948, p.1.

650 IBID.

651 IBID.

652 "Around The Fairways," *The Morning Examiner*," 13 January 1948, p.4; "Around The Fairways," 22 January 1948, p.8.

653 "Kiwanis Install New Officers At Hillcrest Banquet," 10 January 1948, p.1; "It Happened Yesterday," 16 January 1948, p.3; "Chamber Accomplishments Out Lined By Secretary,' 18 January 1948, p.7; "Work Program Is Arranged By C.C. For Coming Year," 19 January 1948, p.9.

654 "Pick Four Directors For Hillcrest Club," *The Morning Examiner*, 21 January 1948, p.1.

655 "Dinner-Dance Club Party At Hillcrest," *The Morning Examiner*, 29 January 1948, p.4; "Hillcrest Country Club Couples Hold Regular Party For February," 15 February 1948, p.11; "Hillcrest Members To Hold Dance," 21 February 1948, p.3;

"Dinner-Dance Club Uses Easter Theme," 14 March 1948, p.12; "Dinner-Dance Club Closes Its Season," 4 April 1948, p.11; "Spring Dance At Hillcrest Tonight," 15 May 1948, p.3.

656 "Douglass School Recommended For Approval By NCA," *The Morning Examiner*, 12 March 1948, p.1; Robbins, p.37-38.

657 "H. R. Straight, Cities Service Head, Retires," *The Morning Examiner*, 1 February 1948, p.1.

658 "Custer Resigns Post As Athletic Director," *The Morning Examiner*, 14 March 1948, p.16.

659 "Large Crowd Attends Hillcrest Luncheon," *The Morning Examiner*, 12 March 1948, p.3.

660 "Around The Fairways," *The Morning Examiner*, 2 May 1948, p.6; "Criswell Hits Ace At Hillcrest," 4 April 1948, p.8; "Kincade Gets Ace," 25 May 1948, p.4.

661 "Jane Phillips Sorority Members Hold Spring Social At Hillcrest," *The Morning Examiner*, 17 April 1948, p.2; "To Hold Annual CAR Meeting At Hillcrest Today," 17 April 1948, p.2; "Will Entertain At Hillcrest Luncheon," 25 May 1948, p.3; "Lawyers To Hold Banquet Thursday Night At Hillcrest," 23 May 1948, p.1; "Plan Buffet Supper," 28 May 1948, p.3.

662 "Announce Plans For Establishing Central Christian College Here," *The Morning Examiner*, 17 April 1948, p.1; Benson was at the center of a growing conservative movement in the United States that included such well know personages as William F. Buckley, Brent Bozell, Taylor Caldwell, H. L. Hunt, and Ayn Rand. See schematic: Forster, Arnold and Epstein, Benjamin R., Danger on the Right, New York: Random House, 1964, http://www.namebase.org/sources/BG.html.

663 H. C. Prices Move To Country Home," *The Morning Examiner*, 23 April 1948, p.14.

664 "Hillcrest Country Club," *The Morning Examiner*, 2 June 1948, p.4; "Simpson Defeats Custer in Tourney At Hillcrest Club," 22 June 1948, p.4; "Mrs. Hubbell Wins First Round Match," 9 June 1948, p.4; "Five Local Golfers Qualify In State Tourney," 15 June 1948, p.4; "Dick Booker Wins Playoff In Cities Service Tourney," 20 June 1948, p.6; "July 4 Celebration," 4 July

1948, p.11. "Charles Keller, " 25 July 1948, p.6; "Fowler Captures Pikes Peak Meet," 9 August 1948, p.6; "Hillcrest Wins,: 24 August 1948, p.4.

665 "Invitations Sent Out For Hillcrest Dance," *The Morning Examiner*, 21 July 1948, p.3; Hold Family Supper," 31 July 1948, p.3.

666 "Mrs. Phillips Dies at Home Early Today," *The Morning Examiner*, 1 August 1948, p.1; Oil Man, p.450-454.

667 Telephone interview with Dan Gallery, 2/20/04. Dan was the son of E. L. Gallery who was club president in 1951 and 52. Telephone interview with Dorothy Glynn Adams, 1/20/04. "Gordon High New HCC Manager," *The Morning Examiner*, 17 June 1948, p.1; Miner, p.75; interview with Duke Evans, Wichita Country Club historian, 21 May 2004. Inquiry on 20 May 2004 with University of Wisconsin Alumnae Association and Cornell University Alumnae Association find no Gordon High as either a graduate or person who had attended those universities. High was fired at WCC after the board discovered he had "bugged" the board room. He is remembered as a big talker.

668 "Served As hostess At A Picnic Supper," *The Morning Examiner*, 25 August 1948, p.3; "HCC Buffet Supper," 6 September 1948, p.10; "Western Night Party," 15 September 1948, p.9; "Western Party Held At Hillcrest," 28 September 1948, p.3; "Hole-In-One," 30 November 1948, p.4.

669 "Tie For Title," *The Morning Examiner*, 21 September 1948, p.4; "Visiting Golfers Take Top Honors In Tourney Here," 30 September 1948, p.16; "Team Matches," 3 October 1948, p.7.

670 "City Will Be Host To District Music Meet," *The Morning Examiner*, 10 October 1948, p.9.

671 "Party At Hillcrest," *The Morning Examiner*, 2 November 1948, p.3; "Hillcrest Dinner-Dance Club To open Soon," 7 November 1948, p.9; "Doherty Auxiliary Holds Guest Day Tea," 11 November 1948, p.3; "Doherty Girls Use Winter As Banquet Scene," 3 December 1948, p.5; "Early Holiday Party," 5 December 1948, p.13.

672 "Hillcrest Dinner-Dance," *The Morning Examiner*, 12 December 1948, p.14; "Hillcrest Supper-Dance of K. S. Adams

Brilliant Affair," 19 December 1948, p.12; "Adams Party Highlight of Season," 21 December 1948, p.9; "Dancing Party In D. M. Tyler Home Is Holiday Highlight," 29 December 1948, p.4; "Hillcrest Country," 26 December 1948, p.6.

673 "New Price Home Is Opened With A Party," *The Morning Examiner*, 9 January 1949, p.9.

674 "City Made Rapid Strides In All Activities During 1948," *The Morning Examiner*, 2 January 1949, p.1; "C.C. Reviews Year's Work And Installs New Officers," 15 January 1949, p.5; "Adams Outlines Need For New Community Building At Legion Kickoff Dinner," 14 January 1949, p.1; "C.C. forum Will Dedicate Lake Opening," 21 January 1949, p.9.

675 "Hillcrest Club Parties Planned For Weekend," *The Morning Examiner*, 14 January 1949, p.3; "Hillcrest Dancers To Go Western," 16 January 1949, p.9; "150 See display At Hillcrest Style Show," 23 January 1949, p.10.

676 "Hillcrest Elects Officers," *The Morning Examiner*, 27 January 1949, p.2.

677 "Hillcrest Set For Square Dance Tonight," *The Morning Examiner*, 5 February 1949, p.3; "Plan Washington Party," 15 February 1949, p.5; "Alumni To Hold Party," 10 February 1949, p.5; "Emery-Blair Vows Are Read In Hillcrest Club Setting," 13 March 1949, p.11.

678 "Action Started In DDT Spray City Against Polio," *The Morning Examiner*, 28 June 1949, p.1; "Provision Is Included For Expansion," 7 July 1949, p.1; City Library Serves 10,000," 28 August 1949, p.8.

679 "Hillcrest Ladies' Golf Association To Start Play Wednesday Morning," *The Morning Examiner*, 27 February 1949, p.6; "32 City Youths To Help Caddie For State Golf Tournament," 1 June 1949, p 6; Don Wilkie, "Around The Fairways," 27 March 1949, p.6; "Washington Over Hillcrest Green With Low Of 77," 24 April 1949, p.9.

680 Don Wilkie, "Around The Fairways," *The Morning Examiner*, 24 April 1949, p.9; "Skee Reigel Sets Pace Among Weekend Golfers At Hillcrest," 5 June 1949, p.8; Don Wilkie, "Around The Fairways," 5 June 1949, p.9; "Bartians Qualify For Golf Tourney," 7 June 1949, p.5; "Six Bartians Land Berths In 2nd Round Qualifying Today,"

14 June 1949, p.8; "Wininger's 65 Tops In Pro-Amateur," 14 June 1949, p.8; "Defending Links Monarch Beats Lefthanded King In Thrill Match," 17 June 1949, p.5; Don Wilkie, "Around The Fairways," 19 June 1949, p.6; "Consistency Pays Off As Loser Concedes On 34th," 19 June 1949, p.6.

681 "40 Hillcrest Golfers Play In Holiday Feature," *The Morning Examiner*, 6 July 1949, p.8; "Booker Fires Ace To Set Pace In HCC Golf Meet," 10 July 1949, p.8; "Selby Grabs HCC Golf Title Sunday," 18 July 1949, p.7; "Nowatan Is Ladies Low At Hillcrest," 28 July 1949, p.7; "2-day FPMC Golf Meet Starts Today," 30 July 1949, p.7; "McDonald Wins FPMC Tourney," 2 August 1949, p.7.

682 "Mrs. L. G. Sutter wins Low Gross In Hillcrest Play," *The Morning Examiner*, 6 August 1949, p.3; "Bill Simpson Wins Company Golf Tournament," 7 August 1949, p.10; "Dr. Burris Wins Lions Golf Tourney Sunday," 23 August 1949, p.7.

683 "Dinner Is Planned for City Guests," *The Morning Examiner*, 30 September 1949, p.4; "Style Show Draws Large Attendance," 9 October 1949, p.15; "Annual K.U. Dinner Set For Tonight At Hillcrest," 20 October, 1949, p.7; "Hillcrest Announces First Dance," 11 October 1949, p.4.

684 "Simpson Defeats Bob Neumann For City Title," *The Morning Examiner*, 6 September 1949, p.8; "C. S. Hansen Wins Hillcrest Flag Tournament," 6 September 1949, p.8; "McColl Wins Club Tournament," 20 September 1949, p.7; "Hillcrest Club Defeats Tulsa Team, 34 to 26," 25 October 1949, p.7; "Mrs. Hopper Wins Hillcrest Women's Gold Championship," 20 October 1949, p.11.

685 The Examiner-Enterprise microfilm for May 1950 is filed on the second quarter of 1949 and May 1949 is missing; microfilm from 1 November 1949 to 30 April 1959 is missing; microfilm from 1 June 1950 to 19 August 1950 is missing; microfilm for 20 August 1950 to 31 August 1950, the period covering the death and funeral of Frank Phillips, is extant; microfilm from 1 September 1950 to 1 October 1950 is missing.

686 Membership handbook for Hillcrest Country Club has an unattributed list of past presidents.

687 "Tulloch Cards Best HCC Round," *The Morning Examiner*, 2 May 1950, p.7; "Scotch Foursome Feature Today," 7 May 1950, p.11; "Mrs. Hubbell Wins Hillcrest Spring Event," 25 May 1950, p.9; "Gullane Loses To Metz In State PGA," 24 May 1950, p.7; "Cities Service Golf Meet Set Saturday," 26 May 1950, p.9; "Anderson Leads DMF tourney," 28 May 1950, p.13; "Annual HCC Golf Tourney Set Saturday," 28 May 1950, p.13; "Qualifying Dates For FPMC Golf Tourney Set," 31 May 1950, p.7; "Hillcrest Bogey, Putting, Driving Winners Slated," 31 May 1950, p.7; "Dr. Davis-Pettigrove Win Hillcrest Four-Ball Crown," 31 May 1950, p.7.

688 "Five Doctors To Practice At Building," *The Morning Examiner*, 7 May 1950, p.20. The building is now a First Baptist Church annex.

689 "K.U. Dean To Address Alumni," *The Morning Examiner*, 7 May 1950, p.5; "Jr. Sr. Prom, Party Set For Friday," 9 May 1950, p.4.

690 "Large Crowd Is Present At Dance," *The Morning Examiner*, 24 May 1950, p.4.

691 "Entertains Mercredi At Hillcrest," *The Morning Examiner*, 11 May 1950, p.4; "Hillcrest Party Honors Trio," 27 May 1950, p.4.

692 "HCC Frolics Tuesday! Bucs To Be Guests," *The Morning Examiner*, 30 May 1950, p.7.

693 "Fun, Frolic Enjoyed At Club Parties," The Morning Examiner, 31 May 1950, p.1.

694 "W. I. Beavers Honored At Dinner Party," *The Morning Examiner*, 31 May 1950, p.7; telephone interview with Elsie Parker, 16 September 2003. Elsie couldn't remember the year that Paul changed departments, but thought it was 1950.

695 "Library Board Makes Its Report To Commissioners," *The Morning Examiner*, 28 May 1950, p.24; "Report On City Library Is Made By Citizens Group," 28 May 1950, p.24; Robbins.

696 Oklahoma Secretary of State, 132087, Reinstatement of Hillcrest Country Club, 1 August 1950.

697 "Radio Stars To Entertain Hillcresters," *The Morning Examiner*, 23 August 1950, p.13.

698 "Uncle Frank Phillips Dies Today," *The Morning Examiner*, 23 August 1950, p.1. Microfilm for 20 August through 31 August 1950 conveniently survived, the period of Frank Phillips death and funeral. Wallis.

699 "Civic Leaders and Governor Express Sorrow in Death," *The Morning Examiner*, 24 August 1950, p.1.

700 IBID.

701 Wallis, p.465. Quotation form the funeral sermon, delivered by Rev. James E. Spivey of First Presbyterian Church.

702 "Frank Phillips Is Paid Final Visits By Friends, Employes," *The Morning Examiner*, 25 August 1950, p.1; "Final Phillips Rites Held," 27 August 1950, p.1.

703 Putnam, p.3.

704 Harris, p.13.

705 $33,000 is a little more than $284,000, and $100,000 is $861,000 in 2007 dollars.

706 "Simpson To Face Stern Test In City Golf Tournament," *The Morning Examiner*, 31 August 1950, p.6.

707 "Dinner Party At Hillcrest Is A Courtesy For Visitors," *The Morning Examiner*, 8 October 1950, p.16.

708 "State Agents Buy Drinks, Eat Steaks And Raid Marie's," *The Morning Examiner*, 2 December 1950 (sic. It should be 2 November), p.6

709 "Old Bartles Store, Destroyed By Fire, Was Filled With Historic Memories of Locality," *The Morning Examiner*, 10 December 1950, p.8.

710 IBID.

711 Miner, p.75.

712 "Complete Plans For Military Ball This Week," *The Morning Examiner*, 3 December 1950, p.19; "Hillcrest Has Dancing Party, 5 December 1950, p.20; "Dinner-Dance Club To Open New Season," 17 December 1950, p.20; "New Years Eve Ball Planned At Hillcrest," 24 December 1950, p.17.

713 State of Oklahoma, Secretary of State, Articles of Revival and Extension of Oklahoma Corporation, 16 February 1951.

There were 158 of the 250 shareholders at the meeting. At the time, shares were valued at $250.00.

714 IBID.

715 At the time that Gordon High was hired in 1948, it was reported that there were 350 Hillcrest members. In view of the inattention to the Articles of Incorporation at the time, it is possible that the stockholding membership exceeded the by-laws limitation by 100 members. If that is the case, they were bringing membership limitations in line with practice at the time, as well as allowing for recruitment of new members to help the budget.

706 "Medical Society Installation Is Held At Hillcrest," *The Morning Examiner*, 13 January 1951, p.3.

717 The Inflation Calculator, http://www. westegg.com/inflation/infl.cgi. $.70 in 1951 would be equal to $2302 in 2007 dollars, about the cost of a 48" high definition TV today.

718 "Dinner-Dance Club To Meet," *The Morning Examiner*, 14 January 1951, p.12; "Dinner-Dance Club Has Party," 25 February 1951, p.17; "Dinner-Dance Club Has March Party," 11 March 1951, p.15; Dinner-Dance Club Plans Final Dance For Year," 20 May 1951, p.15; "Hillcrest Club To Hold Dance On Saturday," 24 February 1951, p.5.

719 "Hillcrest Plans Programs For Coming Year," The Morning Examiner, 2 March 1951, p.20; "Egg Hunt Planned At Hillcrest," 22 March 1951, p.5; "Teenagers To Dance At Hillcrest," 24 March 1951, p.5; "Beaux Arts Ball A Big Attraction," 31 March 1951, p.4; "Costume Dance Is A Social Highlight," 1 April 1951, p.19; "Western Dance Set For Saturday," 22 April 1951, p.15; "Sat. Dance Will Close Season," 16 May 1951, p.4.

720 Don Wilkie, "Around the Fairways," *The Morning Examiner*, 11 February 1951, p.12; "Hillcrest Women To Open Season," 25 February 1952, p.13; Cold Weather Forces Golfers Into Clubhouse," 15 April 1951, p.10.

721 "Charles Selby Team Wins Hillcrest Stag," 22 April 1951, p.9; "Davis, Pettigrove Win 4-Ball Meet," 27 May 1951, p.11; "Millis Wins Reda Pump Golf Meet," 23 May 1951, p.9; "Burton Corn Cops Honors At Hillcrest," 20 May 1951, p.10.

722 Telephone conversation with Bill Yinger. There was not newspaper article about the accident or obituary in the Examiner.

723 "Mrs. Foster To Manage Hillcrest Temporarily," *The Morning Examiner*, 27 May 1951, p.14; "Hillcrest Dinner Dance Has Closing Party," 27 May 1951, p.15; "Hillcrest Plans Family Party," 27 May 1951, p.15; "Two Family Parties At Hillcrest," 17 June 1951, p.14; "Club Families To Celebrate 4th At Hillcrest," 1 July 1951, p.12.

724 "Tulsa Women's District Meet Is Held Friday," *The Morning Examiner*, 3 June 1951, p.11; "Hillcrest Turns In 1st Medal Cards," 5 June 1951, p.9; "Charles Selby Scores Top Upset In Amateur," 7 June 1951, p.7; "Selby Upsets Simpson In State Amateur," 8 June 1951, p.9; "5th Annual Golf Meet At Hillcrest," 19 June 1951, p.9; "Bill Simpson Wins Hillcrest Golf Championship," 10 June 1951, p.11; "Fames Trick-Shot Artist Will Be At H.C.C. Tuesday," 11 June 1 1951, p.7; "Anderson Wins DMF Golf Meet," 11 June 1951, p.7.

725 "Mike May Scores Repeat As Junior Golf Champion," *The Morning Examiner*, 16 June 1951, p.9; "Senior Chamber Wins Annual Golf From Jaycees," 28 June 1951, p.7; "FPMC Tee Play Ends Tomorrow," 6 July 1952, p.17; "Legion To Hold Golf Tournament," 15 July 1951, p.9; "City Golf Title Goes On The Line," 30 August 1951, p.7; "Captures Title With 6 and 4," 3 September 1951, p.7; "Al Roth Captures Tee Title," 25 September 1951, p.7; "Hillcrest CC Handicap Final Played," 5 October 1951, p.9.

726 "Country Club Closes For Summer," *The Morning Examiner*, 10 July 1951, p.4; "Miss Learned Becomes Bride of James L. Friday, Jr.," 26 August 1951, p.18.

727 "Bathing Beauty (?) Revue," 26 August 1951, p.17. Tyler's lay-out was conceptually like the old L.E. Phillips party house at Philson Farm. He built a flat-roof modern style party house, swimming pool, and tennis courts. It was not luxurious like the Foster Ranch.

728 Telephone conversation with Dorothy Glynn Adams, 2/21/04. "Hillcrest Reopening Announced," *The Morning Examiner*, 26 August 1951, p.23; "Open House At Country Club Set," 31 August 1952, p.15; "The New Hillcrest," 2 September 1951, p.13.

729 IBID, "The New Hillcrest."

730 "Hillcrest Reopening Announced," *The Morning Examiner*, 26 August 1951, p.23; "Two Groups Are Hosts To Visitors," 16 September 1951, p.16; "Style Show Is Held At Hillcrest Country Club," 23 September 1951, p.3; "Over 200 Are Expected For C. Of C. Fete," 13 September 1951, p.1; "Plan Buffet Supper," 20 October 1951, p.4; "Hillcrest Dance Club Opens Year," 21 October 1951, p.14; "Large Crowd Present For Dancing," 16 December 1951, p.16; "Announce Orchestra For Hillcrest Dance," 9 November 1951, p.4; "Thanksgiving," 18 November 1951, p.13; "Thanksgiving Dinner," 18 November 1951, p.18; "New Years Eve Ball Announced," 27 December 1951, p.2.

731 "Group Formed To Combat Fires In Hillcrest Area," *The Morning Examiner*, 1 November 1952, p.1.

732 "Hillcrest Women Kickoff 1952 Golf Campaign," *The Morning Examiner*, 2 March 1952, p.11; "Mrs. Wolters Captures Hillcrest Medal Tourney," 22 June 1952, p.11; "Mrs. Bill Hughes Wins HCC Title," 4 October 1952, p.7.

733 "Fire Destroys HCC workshop," *The Morning Examiner*, 5 April 1952, p.1. $55,000 in 2007 dollars.

734 "Gordons Cop HCC Stag Golf," *The Morning Examiner*, 20 April 1952, p2; "Match Cancelled," 16 April 1952, p.9; "Link Activities Start Saturday," 9 April 1952, p.9; "Dr. Davis, Pettigrove Win Hillcrest Four Ball Play," 25 May 1952, p.10.

735 "Booker's 78 Is Low Trial Run," *The Morning Examiner*, 15 June 1952, p.10; "Dick Brooks Fires 151 To Take FPMC Tee Title," 1 July 1952, p.3; "Bill Simpson Keeps HCC Golf Crown," 8 July 1952, p.2; "Simpson Nudges Vaughan For City Golf Crown," 2 September 1952, p.6; "C. C. Custer Wiins H'cap At Hillcrest," 30 September 1952, p.7.

736 "Folk Dance Is Planned At Hillcrest," *The Morning Examiner*, 20 January 1952, p.14; "Announces Dance For Saturday Night," 28 February 1952, p.4; "Another Dance Is Planned At Hillcrest," 2 April 1952, p.4; "Eighty Attend Initial Dinner-Bridge At Hillcrest," 30 March 1952, p.15; "Teeners Dance At Country Club," 7 May 1952, p.4; "Hillcrest Club Announces Its Closing Dance," 22 May 1952, p.3.

737 "Newcomers Honored," *The Morning Examiner*, 17 February 1952, p.11; Beaux-Arts Ball," 27 April 1952, p.13.

738 "Fireworks Are Planned Friday At Hillcrest," *The Morning Examiner*, 3 July 1952, p.4.

739 "Western Dance Is Announced For Saturday," *The Morning Examiner*, 1 October 1952, p.2; "Hillcrest Announces," 31 October 1952, p.8; "Hillcrest Dance Set For Oct. 23," 22 October 1952, p.4; "Party Planned For Friday At Hillcrest," 30 October 1952, p.4.

740 "Hillcrest November Activities," *The Morning Examiner*, 6 November 1952, p.4; "Doherty Girls Hold Annual Banquet," 21 November 1952, p.4.

741 "Plan Square Dancing At Hillcrest Saturday," *The Morning Examiner*, 5 December 1952, p.4; "Families To Share In Hillcrest Dinner," 10 December 1952, p.2; "Social Calendar," 19 December 1952, p.3; "Dinner-Dance." 25 December 1952, p.16.

742 "Ted Weems To Play For Dance At Hillcrest," *The Morning Examiner*, 28 August 1953, p.4.

743 "HCC Meeting," *The Morning Examiner*, 4 January 1953, p.9; "Square Dancing At Hillcrest Saturday," 7 January 1953, p.3.

744 "Doherty Club Holds Final Party," *The Morning Examiner*, 16 April 1953, p.4; "Hillcrest Benefit Draws One Hundred Guests," 18 April 1953, p.4; "Hillcrest Dinner Dance Club Has April Party," 19 April 1953, p.14; "Dinner-Dance At Hillcrest Is Farewell To R. L. Kidds," 31 May 1953, p.15.

745 "Growing Pains Explained For C. of C. Members," *The Morning Examiner*, 21 May 1953, p.1; advertisement, 28 March 1953, p.2.

746 "Divot Diggers Bury Sweet Swingers 47 1/2-39 1/2 At HCC," *The Morning Examiner*, 26 April 1953, p.10; "Holt Captures DMF Golf," 12 May 1953, p.7.

747 "Top Lady Golfers Gather At Hillcrest," *The Morning Examiner*, 5 June 1953, p.3; Hillcrest Women Golfers Hosts For State Tournament," 7 June 1953, p.13; "Social Affairs Arranged For Visiting Golfers," 10 June 1953, p.5.

748 "Seizes Early Advantage To Trounce Mrs. Horn," *The Morning Examiner*, 14 June 1953, p.10.

749 $618.500 in 2007 dollars.

750 Breakfast conversation with Peter Duncan, Oklahoma City businessman, Hotel Hassler, Rome, 17 March 2005. Duncan swam on the OU swim team with Dyason. Julian Dyason moved to Louisiana after graduation where he became very successful as an independent oilman. He died in 1979; Upchurch, Jay, "The South African Contingent," *Sooner Magazine*, fall 2005.

751 "HCC Finals Set Today," *The Morning Examiner*, 28 June 1953, p.11.

752 "Ketchum Captures Jaycee Tee Tourney," *The Morning Examiner*, 1 July 1953, p.7.

753 "Hillcrest To Have Usual Activities For Fourth Of July," *The Morning Examiner*, 2 July 1953, p.4; "Neumann's 76 Low At Hillcrest," 5 July 1953, p.9.

754 "Ware Takes FPMC Golf With A 133," *The Morning Examiner*, 28 July 1953, p.7; "Ketchum Cops Reda Golf," 9 August 1953, p.11; "Swatszel Wins HCC Tee Title," 26 September 1953, p.7; "Heller Low In Annual HCC Handicap Tourney," 4 October 1953, p.9; "HCC Annual Tournament Pairings," 16 September 1955, p.15.

755 "Ted Weems To Play For Dance At Hillcrest," *The Morning Examiner*, 28 August 1953, p.4.

756 IBID; "Football Buffet At Hillcrest," 24 September 1953, p.5; "Two Parties Planned At Hillcrest," 7 October 1953, p.3; "Dance Club To Open New Year," 11 October 1953, p.19; "Halloween Dance Planned At Hillcrest," 28 October 1953, p.4.

757 $2.25 for the dinner would be $17.50 in 2007 dollars. Notice of Annual Meeting, To All Stockholders of Hillcrest Country Club, 5 January 1954. The notice has pencil notes of the slate candidates elected at the meeting. Hillcrest Country Club, Balance Sheet, 31 December 1953. (Virginia Hubbell collection). This is the first annual meeting data to survive since the balance sheets included in the 1925 Engineer's Club report.

758 "Frank Lloyd Wright," *The Morning Examiner*, 8 January 1954, p.1.

759 Hillcrest Country Club letter to the members from C. T. Klein, President, 19 April 1954 (Virginia Hubbell Collection).

760 "Dunbar Golfer's Win Dinner In Annual Match," *The Morning Examiner*, 2 May 1954, p.14; "Jim Gullane Pro Golfer To Retirement," 4 May 1954, p.7.

761 Biographical information was variously gleaned: Personal interview with Charles Selby, 8/28/04; telephone interview with Harry Woods, 8/28/04; Interview with Duke Evans, 21 May 2004; telephone interview with Lee Phillips, Wichita, 7 September 2004; Interviews with Jerry Cozby, Art Gorman, B. J. LeFlore; U. S. Social Security Death Index, http://www.familysearch.org/Eng/Search/frameset_search.asp?PAGE=ssdi/search_ssdi.asp&clear_form=true, 30 September 2000; "Former Hillcrest Golf Course Pro Travis Dies," Tulsa World, 26 May 1986, Section 3B; "Tulsa Deaths," Tulsa World, 26 May 1986, Section B5; funeral record, Miller-Stahl Funeral Service, 200 S. Main, Newkirk, Ok.; *The Boots Adams Story*, p.96.

762 "Klein Wins CSOC Golf Tournament," *The Morning Examiner*, 25 May 1954, p.5; "Chuck Klein Wins Local CS Tourney," 15 June 1954, p.5; "Golfers' Wives Entertained At Hillcrest," 13 June 1954, p.14; "Selby & Tulloch Snatch Golf Win In 4-Ball Match," 1 June 1954, p.5; "George Mizee Second With Low Net Of 68," 6 June 1954, p.10.

763 "Jr. Golfers Told How To Do It," *The Morning Examiner*, 6 June 1954, p.10; "Mrs. Kenneth Grigsby Wins HCC Medal Title," 6 June 1954, p.11; "Mrs. Williford Wins Hillcrest Field Day," 12 June 1954, p.8; "Hillcrest Entries," 20 June 1954, p.14.

764 "Jack Baldwin Tops Junior A.A.U. Golf," *The Morning Examiner*, 25 June 1954, p.11.

765 "Bartlesville C of C To Hold Anniversary Ceremonies," *The Morning Examiner*, 29 June 1954, p.1; "C of C President Reaffirms Stand On Fair Grounds," 4 July 1954, p.1; "Civic Center Auditorium is Having A Face Lift," 7 July 1954, p.1.

766 "600 Served At July 4 Dinner," *Hillcrest Happenings*, August 1954, p.2.

767 "Bill Simpson Wins Golf Title," *Hillcrest Happenings*, August 1954, p.2; "Fifty-Four Enter For Flag Day At Hillcrest," *The Morning Examiner*, 7 July 1954,

p.5; "Bob McAfee Cops Honors In State JC Tourney Tuesday," 14 July 1954, p.5; "Old Pros Lose In Hot Match At Sunset CC," 13 July 1954, p.7. There was another tweak on 24 May 1955 when the sports page reported that Gullane entered the Oklahoma OPGA tournament at Indian Hills.); "Simpson Beats Lambdin At Hillcrest CC," 18 July 1954, p.11; "Simpson Edges Word For Title At Hillcrest CC," 20 July 1954, p.5; "Ken Pryor Wins Playoff To Take FPMC Tourney," 5 August 1954, p.7; "Kay Browning Wins H.C.C. Girls Gold Tile," 1 September 1954, p.7.

768 "Study Costs For Air Conditioning," *Hillcrest Happenings*, August 1954, p.1.

769 "Jean Ashley Is Victor In Tri-State Golf Meet; Virginia Hubbell Second," *The Morning Examiner*, 19 August 1954, p.9; "Selby Is Winner In City Tourney Qualifying Play," 19 August 1954, p.12; "Beats Hines For Third City Crown, " 8 September 1954, p.5

770 "Beaux Arts Ball," *The Morning Examiner*, 29 April 1954, p.6.

771 "Blachley Ignores Jinx To Win HCC Match," *The Morning Examiner*, 21 September 1954, p.7; "Mrs. Cook Cops HCC 9-Hole Flight Crown," 3 October 1954, p.10; :Sr. Chamber Triumphs Over JCC," 6 October 1954, p.13; "HCC Women's Golf Luncheon Set Wednesday," 31 October 1954, p.14; "Marilyn Smith To Hold Exhibition, Golf Clinic at HCC," 10 November 1954, p.7.

772 "Festive Affair For Doherty Club," *The Morning Examiner*, 21 November 1954, p.15; "The New Look," 23 September 1954; "Country Club Terrace," 14 November 1954, p.17; "New Church Work Start Announced," 23 December 1954, p.1.

773 Letters, telegrams, newspaper articles, press release, photographs in 2 scrapbooks of the 80th birthday party, belonging to Suzy Miller, Arlington, Texas, granddaughter of H. R. Straight.

774 "Celebrating Yuletide," *The Morning Examiner*, 19 December 1954, p.15; "Junior Dance At Hillcrest," 5 December 1954, p.22; "Holiday Dance For Youth At Hillcrest," 31 December 1954, p.3; "Phillips Annual Christmas Show Opens Before A Crowd Of 5,000 Persons," 16 December 1954, p.1; "Mr. And Mrs. K. S. Adams To Hold Open House," 25 December 1954, p.4.

775 Photograph, *Hillcrest Happenings*, March 1955, p.3; Notice of Annual Meeting, To All Stockholders of Hillcrest Country Club, P. S. Ambrose, Secretary, 31 December 1954 (Virginia Hibbell collection); Proxy Statement, Board of Directors, Hillcrest Country Club, C. T. Klein, president (Virginia Hubbell collection, this document has a penciled note "refered to committee"); Minutes of 2 February 1955 special committee meeting (Virginia Hubbell collection); "Special Stockholders' Meeting," March 1955, p.1; "Directors' Meeting," March 1955, p.3 (In possession of author): House Rules Golf Rules Swimming Pool Rules and By-Laws, Hillcrest Country Club, Bartlesville, Oklahoma, 27 July 1955 (Virginia Hubbell collection); "Western Night," October 1955 (Betty Pettigrove).

776 "Beaux Arts Ball Set For Saturday Night," *The Morning Examiner*, 2 February 1954, p.6; "Spring Tea At Hillcrest Closes Doherty Club Year," 29 April 1955, p.4; "Bar Association Plans Banquet," 25 May 1955, p.2; "Seniors Are Hosts For Dance," 26 May 1955, p.6.

777 "HCC Women's Gold Assn. Holds 1st Meet Of Year," *The Morning Examiner*, 6 February 1955, p.12; "Ladies Golf Notes," *Hillcrest Happenings*, March 1955 (HWGA #1 scrapbook); "Ladies Golf Lessons Popular," HWGA Scrapbook #1.

778 The initial live Salk vaccine was withdrawn because it was found to be contaminated with a green monkey virus. Recently a high incidence of Merckel cell carcinoma has been associated with recipients of this contaminated vaccine.

779 "Pairings Given For Today's HCC Golf Stag Event," *The Morning Examiner*, 30 April 1955, p.11; "Alf Hall Is CSOC Golf Meet Winner," 24 May 1955, p.7; "New Cities Service Golf Champ," 14 June 1955, p.7; 'Livingston Wins Reda Golf Tourney," 31 May 1955, p.7.

780 Regan Huffman, "Huffs and Puffs," *The Morning Examiner*, 7 June 1955, p.7; "Ketchum Captures Top Honors In Jaycee Golf Meet " 11 June 1955, p.8; Huffman, 7 June 1955, p.7; Huffman, 9 June 1955, p.11; "HCC's 1955 Tourney For Title Today," 18 June 1955, p.7; "Lambdin Scores Impressive Win In HCC Tourney," 21 June 1955, p.6; "Dinner Planned To Follow Golf," 24 June 1955, p.8.

781 "Reading The Greens," *The Morning Examiner*, 2 August 1955, p.5; "City Golf Championship," 4 September 1955, p.8.

782 "Dwight Travis Leads Bartians," *The Morning Examiner*, 29 September 1955, p.16; "C of C Golfers In 'Annual' Grudge Win Over Jaycees," 8 November 1955, p.6.

783 "New House Rules," *Hillcrest Happenings*, October 1955, p.2.

784 "Hillcrest Dinner-Dance Club Has Largest Party," *The Morning Examiner*, 18 December 1955, p.18; "A Christmas Party: Sorosis Club," 25 December 1955, p.11; "Juniors To Dance," 18 December 1955, p.18; "Social Calendar," 28 December 1955, p.2.

785 letter, G. R. Preston, chairman finance committee, to Stockholders, 15 January 1957. This includes the year-end balance sheet for 1956. (Virginia Hubbell collection);letter, Hillcrest Country Club, J. W. McColl, president to Fellow Member, 15 February 1957 (Virginia Hubbell collection).

786 "Bartlesville Course Ready For Amateur," *The Morning Enterprise*, n.d. probably spring of 1957. (Clipping from HWGA #1 scrapbook).

787 Letter, J. W. McColl to C. W. Hubbell, 28 June 1957; letter, Jim McColl to Fellow Members, Hillcrest Country Club, Bartlesville, Ok., 6 December 1957 (Virginia Hubbel collection).

788 "Simpson Wins Hillcrest CC Men's Golf Title," *Examiner-Enterprise*, 5 June 1956, p.7; "Junior Golf Meeting Set At Hillcrest," 27 May 1956, p.11; "Lynn Gray Wins Jaycee Tourney At Hillcrest CC," 13 June 1956, p.8; "Knight Wins Hillcrest CC Ladies Golf, 17 June 1956, p.10; "Pete Livingston Wins Reda Golf," 17 June 1956, p.10.

789 "First Birthday For Les Des," *The Morning Examiner*, 24 June 1956, p.13; "Pre-Nuptial Tea," 24 June 1956 p.19.

790 "Reese Tucker," *The Morning Examiner*, 31 July 1956, p.7; "Six Visiting Clubs Play At Hillcrest," 4 August 1956, p.9; "Davis Wins HCC Boys' Crown," 26 August 1956, p.11; "HCC Girls '56 Tourney Play Ends," 1 September 1956, p.11; "Bill Emerson Takes FPMC Golf Tourney," 11 September 1956, p.7; "Hillcrest Four-Ball Winners,"

18 September 1956, p.7; "Emerson Wins HCC Golf Play," 25 September 1956, p.7; "Mrs. Simpson Wins HCC Women's Play," 30 September 1956, p.15.

791 "Sunset Country Club To Erect New Clubhouse," *The Morning Examiner*, 3 August 1956, p.9.

792 "Gauntt Wins Tourney For 3rd Straight Year," *The Morning Examiner*, 5 October 1956, p.12; "42nd Oklahoma Open Invitational Golf Championship, October 2-3-4, 1956," Hillcrest Country Club, Bartlesville, Oklahoma (Jerry Cozby).

793 Kwitney, Jonathan, *The Mullendore Murder*, New York: Farrar, Straus and Giroux, 1974, p.132, 37,95.

794 "Bartlesville Course Ready For Amateur," *Examiner-Enterprise*, n.d. probably spring of 1957. (Clipping from HWGA #1 scrapbook.)

795 "Boys Club Hold Clinic for Caddies," *The Morning Examiner*, 15 May 1957, p.7; State Amateur Tourney Set Tuesday," 9 June 1957, p.13.

796 "State Amateur Semifinal Today," *The Morning Examiner*, 15 June 1957, p.10; "Goetz, Justice To Meet For Title," 16 June 1957, p. 10; "Goetz Wins State Golf Meet," 18 June 1957, p.7.

797 "Dance At Hillcrest," *The Morning Examiner*, 9 June 1957, p.22; "Jr. Golfers To Meet For Lessons," 15 June 1957, p.11; 37 Enter 18th Annual Tournament At Hillcrest," 21 June 1957, p.7.

798 "HCC Youths Hold Swim Exhibition," The Morning Examiner, 7 July 1957, p.10.

799 "Bill Simpson Wins HCC Golf Crown," *The Morning Examiner*, 16 July 1957, p.6; Phil Rippy Pads 1st Round Lead To Win Cities Service Golf Open," 23 July 1957, p.5; "Mayberry Wins Junior Crown," 24 August 1957, p.8; "Wins Crown After Four Extra Holes," 3 September 1957, p.7; "Blazing 127 Wins Crown Thill Second," 10 September 1957, p.7.

800 "October Calendar," *Hillcrest Happenings*, October 1957, p.2.

801 Notice of Annual Meeting To All Stockholders of Hillcrest Country Club, 31 December 1957, Bob Durand, Secretary

(Virginia Hubbell collection. This document has pencil notes of the election. Jack Straight replaced Reese Tucker, the slate candidate.); letter G. R. Preston, chairman finance committee, to Stockholders, Hillcrest Country Club, Bartlesville, Ok. 21 January 1958. (Virigina Hubbell collection).

802 *Hillcrest Happenings*, March 1958, p.1; April 1958, June 1958; July 1958; August 1958; November 1958, December 1958 (HWGA #1 scrapbook).

803 Leah, Harris, *Hillcrest Happenings*, March 1958, p.2; Bartlesville newspaper clipping, 25 May 1958; *Examiner-Enterprise*, "Simpson's 71 Leads Hillcrest 4-Ballers," 4 May 1958, p.12; "Maddux Wins Hillcrest Golf Meet," 9 June 1958; *Hillcrest Happenings*, June 1958; Examiner-Enterprise, "Hillcrest Swim Meet Scheduled For July 4th," 1 July 1958, p.11; "Hillcrest Swim Meet Is Termed Biggest Ever," 6 July 1958, p.10.

804 "Net Victor In Reda Pump Link Tourney," *Examiner-Enterprise*, 2 July 1958, p.11; "Shoots 138 Total To Win Over Wunsch By 2 Strokes," 22 July 1958, p.7; "Davis, McDonald Win Hillcrest Junior Championships," 16 August 1958, p.8; "Bob Crabtree Wins Cities Service Golf Meet," 26 August 1958, p.5; "Tops Field With 131 Net Total; Lehman Wins 2nd," 9 September 1958, p.5; "HCC Men's Golf Meet Ends In Tie," 23 September 1958, p.3; "Three Shoot Holes-In-One Over HCC," 31 December 1958, p.8.

805 Lee M. Haines and Paul William Thomas, *An Outline History of the Wesleyan Church*, Indianapolis, Indiana, Wesleyan Publishing House, 2000.

806 Telephone interview with Dorothy Glynn Adams, 1/28/2005. Charter members were: Mrs. K. S. Adams (Dorothy Glynn), Mrs. Scott Beesley (Helen Tyler), Mrs. Gerald Chaney (Virian), Mrs. John Cronin (Amelia), Mrs. Keiffer Davis (Keitha), Mrs. Paul Endacott (Lucille), Mrs. Carl Harbordt (Dorothy), Mrs. Frank Heller (Johnnie), Mrs. John Houchin (Louise), Mrs. Richard Kane (Mary), Mrs. Robert Kidd (Marjorie), Mrs. Stanley Learned (Mary), Mrs. Lloyd Lynd (Lois), Mrs. John Pettigrove (Betty), Mrs. Harold Price, Jr. (Carolyn), Mrs. Lloyd Rowland (Jane), Mrs. K. W. Rugh (Sue), Mrs. B. F. Stradley (Louise), Mrs. Rodd Thomas (Lorraine). (Bartlesville Service League, handbook)

807 *Hillcrest Happenings*, February 1959 (HWGA #1 scrapbook); Notice of Annual Meeting, To All Stockholders of Hillcrest Country Club, R. R. Durand, Secretary, 31 December 1958 (Virginia Hubbell collection).

808 Letter House Committee to Members, Hillcrest Country Club, Bartlesville, Ok., n.d. (Virginia Hubbell collection. There is an ink notation "Sent $10.00. check #140, 9/4/59, dating the letter.)

809 "Wets Win Hillcrest Meet Over Drys By Landslide," *Examiner-Enterprise*, 26 April 1959, p.10; "Lynn Leisure Wins Hillcrest Tourney," 4 June 1959, p.9; "Bill Simpson Wins Match Play At HCC," 15 June 1959, p.7.

810 "Klein Wins DMF Golf: Rain Stops "A" Flight," *Examiner-Enterprise*, 20 July 1959, p.6; "Klein Wins Cities Service Golf Meet," 24 August 1959, p.7; "Hank Mattix Repeats As City Golf Champion," 8 September 1959, p.8; "Patterson Wins FPMC Golf Championship," 14 September 1959, p.7; "Two Share HCC Men's Golf Title," 21 September 1959, p.9.

811 "Women's Golf News," *Hillcrest Happenings*, July 1959 (HWGA scrapbook);"Grigsby Is HCC Ladies Golf Champ," Examiner-Enterprise, 6 October 1959, p.9; "HCC Ladies Slate Tacky Day Outing," 25 October 1959, p.11.

812 "Johnsons Leaving," *Hillcrest Happenings*, September 1959, p.1 (HWGA scrapbook); Finance Committee Report to Stockholders, 12 January 1960 (Virginia Hubble collection).

813 Notice of Annual Meeting To All Sotckholders of Hillcrest Country Club, R. R. Durand, secretary, 31 December 1959 (Virginia Hubbell collection); "New Chairmen Appointed," *Hillcrest Happenings*, February 1960, p.1 (HWGA scrapbook).

814 Secretary's Minutes, Hillcrest Women's Golf Association, 1960-1961-1962-1963-1964.

815 "Porter and Engelbrecht Take 4-Ball," *Examiner-Enterprise*, 22 May 1960, p.13; "Maddox Rallies To Win Jaycee Junior Golf Cup," 5 June 1960, p. 11; "Maddux Toples Selby To Win Hillcrest Tourney," 20 June 1960, p.9; "Chaffin Is DMF Link Champion," 18 July 1960, p.7; "Reda Pump Company's 21st Golf Tourney Gets

Underway Saturday," 18 August 1960, p.9; "HCC Junior Champs" 4 August 1960, p.8; "McDonald Wins HCC Boys Meet," 12 August 1960, p.10; Betty Grover, "Women's Golf," *Hillcrest Happenings*, June 1960, p.1 (HWGA scrapbook); "WGA News,"*Hillcrest Happenings*, August 1960 (HWGA scrapbook); "Man Golfers Attention!" *Hillcrest Happenings*, September 1960, p.3 (Betty Pettigrove).

816 "E-E City Golf Tourney Ended," *Examiner-Enterprise*, 17 August 1960, p.11; "HCC Men's Golf-Fest Saturday," 29 July 1960, p.11; "HCC Festival Huge Success," 1 September 1960, p.7; "Tom Huffman Snares Cup In HCC Handicap Tourney," 19 September 1960, p.7; "Golfers Receive Awards At Luncheon." 6 November 1960, p.17.

817 "Club Modernization Program," *Hillcrest Happenings*, October 1960, p.1 (Betty Pettigrove) By June 1961, the committee had added Stanley Learned (Phillips engineer, VP), Gerald McGrew (slated to be 1962 president), and Budge Welty (former owner of the newspaper).

818 James E. Person, Jr., "Deadly Satire, Saving Grace," *Touchstone*, June 2005, p.34.

819 Lobsenz, p.80.

820 *Camelot* was a hit Broadway play, and later movie of the era, starring Richard Burton.

821 Telephone conversation with Glen Palmer. 7/15/2005. Palmer could not remember any of the names of the clubs. Some of the names are fairly easy to infer and names are suggested here; Manager John Sullivan and Golf Pro Jerry Cozby found the boxes of photographs in storage at Hillcrest in the 1970s. They have since been lost. Conversation, Jerry Cozby with Johnny Stinson (husband of Lisa Adams) 7/8/2005; Telephone conversations with George Downs, III, Anita Downs Hughes, and John Leisure, Jr., 7/8/2005.

822 "Stockholders To Meet," *Hillcrest Happenings*, January 1961, p.1, (Betty Pettigrove).

823 "Stockholders To Meet," *Hillcrest Happenings*, January 1961; "1961 A Good Year," January 1962 (HWGA scrapbook #2).

824 State of Oklahoma, Secretary of State, Amended Articles of Incorporation, 5526, Hillcrest Country Club; "Roster Changes," *Hillcrest Happenings*, July 1961, p.3; ;1961 A Good Year," January 1962 (HWGA scrapbook #2).

825 John Leisure, et. al, letter 8 June 1961, "Proposed Clubhouse, Hillcrest Country Club," 8 June 1961 (Hillcrest Country Club).

826 "New Year's Eve," *Hillcrest Happenings*, January 1961, p.1" "Calendar," January 1961, p.4. Hillcrest Women's Golf Association. Secretary's Minutes, 1960-1961-1962-1963-1964;

827 "Proposed Modernization Program," Hillcrest Country Club, 15 June 1961.

828 Washington County, Oklahoma, County Clerk, Warranty Deed, bk. 414, pg. 27.

829 Postcard in HCC files. This is a common practice of boards when opening a fund-raising campaign; Modernization Program 15 June 1961, Sec. VI. By the time the actual financing came about, the contribution had morphed into an assessment that could be paid over 3 years.

830 "1961 Good Year At The Club," *Hillcrest Happenings*, January 1962, p.4 (HWGA scrapbook #2).

831 "Stockholder's Meeting," *Hillcrest Happenings*, January 1962, p.1 (HWGA scrapbook #2). The charge for the stag stockholders dinner was $2.50. "Stockholder's Meeting," February 1962, p.1. A significant part of operating in the black in those days came from slot machine income.

832 "Roster Additions," *Hillcrest Happenings*, January 1962, p.1 (HWGA scrapbook #2); "Talent Party," February 1962, p.1 (Xerox copy).

833 "Clubhouse Progresses," *Hillcrest Happenings*, March 1962, p.1 (Betty Pettigrove); "New Clubhouse Progress," May 1962, p.1 (HWGA scrapbook #2); "Building Progress," June 1962, p.4 (Marie Freiberger)

834 Kwitny, p.42.

835 "Henry Manley Rites Planned Thursday P.M.," *Examiner-Enterprise*, 8 September 1970, p.6; "Golf Greens Are Problem," 30 July 1933, p.6; "Women To Meet," 16 April 1940, p.7.

836 "About GCSAA," *Golf Course Management Magazine*, The Golf Course Superintendent's Association of America, http://www.gcsaa.org/about/superhistory.asp, 1996-2004.

837 http://en.wikipedia.org/wiki/Standing_on_the_shoulders_of_giants.

INDEX

Index

Index

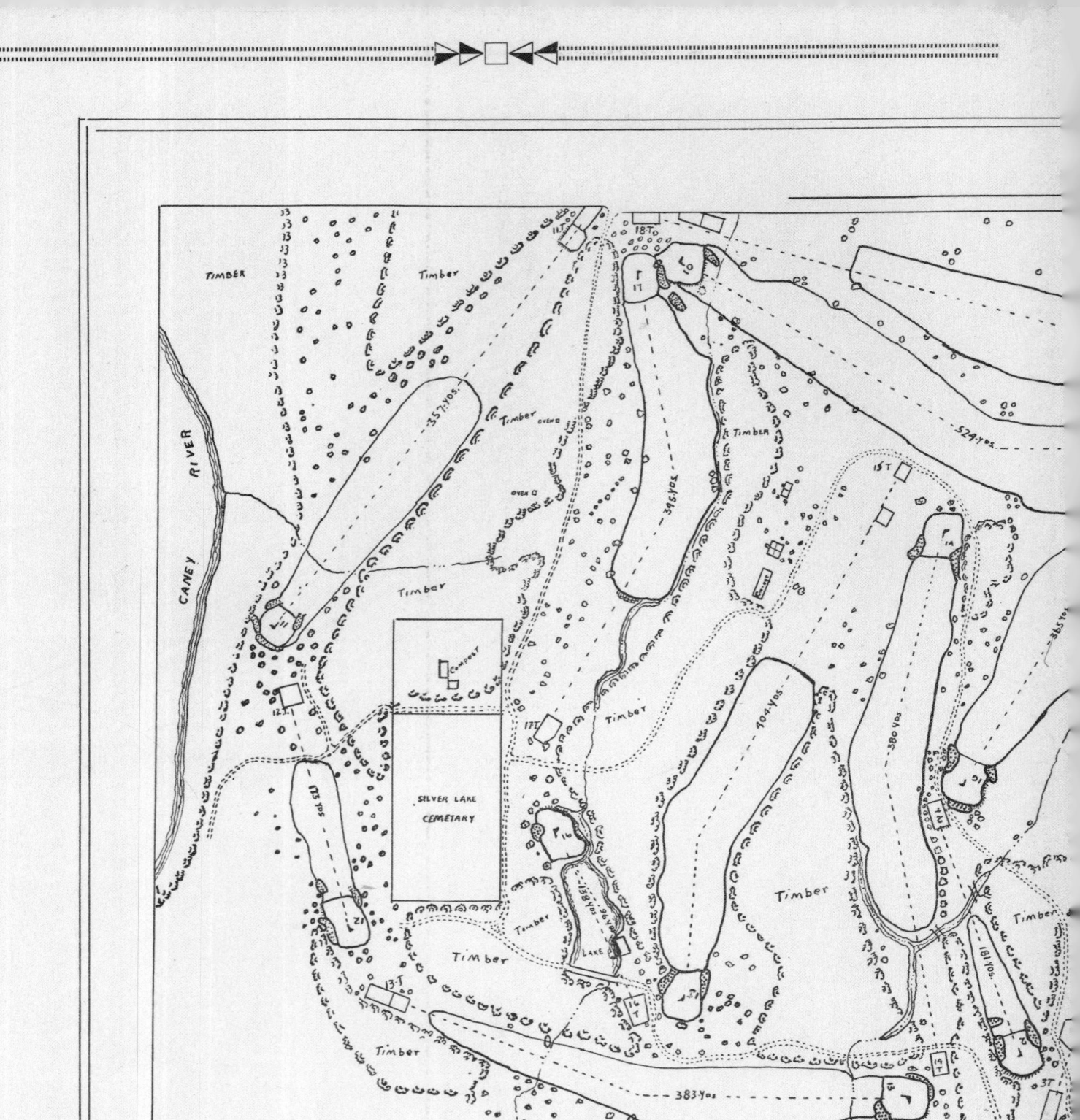